World Trade Organization and International Trade Law

Antidumping, Subsidies and Trade Agreements

World Scientific Studies in International Economics

(ISSN: 1793-3641)

Vol. 22 International Trade Policy Formation: Theory and Politics
by Wolfgang Mayer (University of Cincinnati, USA)

Vol. 23 Priorities and Pathways in Services Reform:
Part I — Quantitative Studies
edited by Philippa Dee (Australian National University, Australia)

Vol. 24 Globalizing Information: The Economics of International Technology Trade
by Keith E Maskus (University of Colorado at Boulder, USA)

Vol. 25 Priorities and Pathways in Services Reform: Part II — Political Economy Studies
edited by Christopher Findlay (University of Adelaide, Australia)

Vol. 26 World Trade Organization and International Trade Law: Antidumping, Subsidies and Trade Agreements
by Gary N Horlick (Law Offices of Gary N Horlick, USA & University of Bern, Switzerland)

Vol. 27 European Economic Integration and Fragmentation of Production
edited by Lucia Tajoli (Politecnico di Milano, Italy)

Vol. 28 Services Trade Reform: Making Sense of It
by Philippa Dee (Australian National University, Australia)

Vol. 29 The Social Value of the Financial Sector: Too Big to Fail or Just Too Big?
edited by Viral V Acharya (New York University, USA & Centre for Economic Policy (CEPR), UK), Thorsten Beck (Tilburg University, The Netherlands & Centre for Economic Policy (CEPR), UK), Douglas D Evanoff (Federal Reserve Bank of Chicago, USA), George G Kaufman (Loyola University Chicago, USA), & Richard Portes (London Business School, UK & Centre for Economic Policy (CEPR), UK)

Vol. 30 Economics and Politics of Trade Policy
by Douglas R Nelson (Tulane University, USA)

The complete list of the published volumes in the series can be found at
http://www.worldscientific.com/series/wssie.

26 World Scientific Studies in International Economics

World Trade Organization and International Trade Law

Antidumping, Subsidies and Trade Agreements

Gary N Horlick

Law Offices of Gary N. Horlick, Washington, DC
and University of Bern, Switzerland

World Scientific

NEW JERSEY • LONDON • SINGAPORE • BEIJING • SHANGHAI • HONG KONG • TAIPEI • CHENNAI

Published by

World Scientific Publishing Co. Pte. Ltd.

5 Toh Tuck Link, Singapore 596224

USA office: 27 Warren Street, Suite 401-402, Hackensack, NJ 07601

UK office: 57 Shelton Street, Covent Garden, London WC2H 9HE

Library of Congress Cataloging-in-Publication Data

Horlick, Gary N.

[Essays. Selections]

World Trade Organization and international trade law : antidumping, subsidies and trade agreements / Gary N Horlick, Law Offices of Gary N Horlick, USA & University of Bern, Switzerland.

pages cm. -- (World scientific studies in international economics ; vol. 26)

Includes bibliographical references and index.

ISBN 978-9814436984 (hardcover : alk. paper)

1. Foreign trade regulation. 2. Antidumping duties--Law and legislation. 3. Foreign trade regulation--United States. 4. World Trade Organization. I. Title.

K4600.H67 2013

382'.92--dc23

2013027574

British Library Cataloguing-in-Publication Data

A catalogue record for this book is available from the British Library.

In-house Editor: Lee Xin Ying

Typeset by Stallion Press

Email: enquiries@stallionpress.com

Printed in Singapore by World Scientific Printers.

Preface

This book brings together articles I have written (or co-authored) over the years focusing on three key topics in International World Trade Organization and international trade law.

Subsidies are a continuing important topic in international trade law discussions predating GATT/WTO, and a matter of high visibility now with the massive bailouts as part of the Global Financial Crisis (GFC) and arguments over "state capitalism." The article "WTO Subsidies Discipline During and After the Crisis" brings together and unites my current thinking on the subject.

Antidumping matters only because it is the most commonly used protectionist tool using WTO rules — more than 4,000 antidumping investigations were initiated by WTO members since January 1, 1995. If WTO members had raised tariffs above bound rates that many times, or even one-tenth as many times, there would be an uproar and scandal, but, as described in "Antidumping Policy as a System of Law," antidumping is just a way of raising tariffs, but the lack of transparency, and the lack of most favored nation treatment among countries, even among companies, importers and individual importers, is so grossly unfair and inefficient as to leave a wake of destruction benefiting only some protected special interest groups. The National Board of Trade of Sweden calculates a 4.5 Euro cost to local purchasers for every 1 Euro going to local producers protected by an antidumping duty.[1] These special interest groups are well aware that their gains are more than offset by the losses within their own countries, much less to the world economy, so they are willing to lobby more fiercely than are the more widely distributed losers. This classic description of political science is common enough, but does not justify the economic losses.

---

[1]Kommerkollegium, "Do European Producers and the EU Economy Really Benefit from Anti-Dumping Policy?", National Board of Trade: Stockholm, 2012.

The final section focuses on the issues which the success of the WTO has brought to the fore. *Preferential trade agreements* (PTAs) have become the exception in GATT 1994 Article XXVIII.8 (and GATS Article XIV), which swallowed many of the other GATT/WTO rules. As of this writing, imports from only nine countries pay the MFN rate to the European Union — all others of the more than 190 countries pay some non-uniform lower rate, and the EU is negotiating or contemplating PTAs with the larger of the nine. And that doesn't even begin to describe the chaos of differing rules of origin from different PTAs within the same trading country. After NAFTA went in effect, I chaired a public discussion for the US Customs and International Trade Bar Association where the leading customs lawyers and the US Customs Service (as it was then called before disappearing into the even more bureaucratic Department of Homeland Security, ICE) disagreed among themselves whether the US at that time applied 9, 19, or even more, different sets of rules of origin. Since then, the US has entered into 14 more regional trade agreements — each with slightly different rules of origin.

Trade and science is the area of greatest dispute within the WTO, as large members seek to use non-science based regulatory regulation to impose their wills on smaller, often more poor, countries. The WTO Appellate Body in US — Shrimp/Turtles supinely deferred to the unilateral action of the US, in one of its worst-crafted decisions (unless a footnote in the decision means the AB limited its decision to CITES Class 1 "endangered species" — but the AB did not say so expressly). The US and the EU are now pondering the consequences of having tried to construct a system based on deference to the unilateral power of the largest markets, while China now becomes the largest market for many products. The importance of this is amplified by the need to do something about climate change, as described briefly in "Climate Change Legislation in the United States and the WTO" (very brief, because it would be imprudent of me to write more on the subject while still in private practice!).

Gary N. Horlick
February 2013

Acknowledgements

Chapter 1
The World Trade Organization Antidumping Agreement
Reproduced with the permission of Wolters Kluwer Law & Business from Gary N. Horlick and Eleanor C. Shea, The World Trade Organization Antidumping Agreement, *Journal of World Trade*, 29(1), 5–32, 1995.

Chapter 2
How the GATT Became Protectionist — An Analysis of the Uruguay Round Draft Final Antidumping Code
Reproduced with the permission of Wolters Kluwer Law & Business from Gary N. Horlick, How the GATT Became Protectionist — An Analysis of the Uruguay Round Draft Final Antidumping Code, *Journal of World Trade*, 27(5), 5–17, 1993.

Chapter 3
Standards for Panels Reviewing Anti-dumping Determinations under the GATT and WTO
Reproduced with the permission of Wolters Kluwer Law & Business from Gary N. Horlick and Peggy A. Clarke, Standards for Panels Reviewing Anti-dumping Determinations under the GATT and WTO, *Volume 11: International Trade Law and the GATT/WTO Dispute Settlement System*, edited by Ernst-Ulrich Petersmann, pp. 315–324, 1997.

Chapter 4
A Personal History of Zeroing
Reproduced with the permission of Wolters Kluwer Law & Business from Gary N. Horlick, A Personal History of Zeroing, *Global Trade and Customs Journal*, 4(5), 161–163, 2009.

Chapter 5

Smoot-Hawley in Slow Motion

Reproduced with the permission of Wolters Kluwer Law & Business from Gary N. Horlick, Smoot-Hawley in Slow Motion, *Global Trade and Customs Journal*, 4(7/8): 271–272, 2009.

Chapter 6

Alternatives to National Antidumping and Countervailing Duty Laws: Are They Feasible or Appropriate in the Context of NAFTA?

Copyrighted by the National Planning Association, Gary N. Horlick and Eleanor C. Shea, Alternatives to National Antidumping and Countervailing Duty Laws: Are They Feasible or Appropriate in the Context of NAFTA?, *Trading Punches: Trade Remedy Law and Disputes Under NAFTA*, pp. 206–229, 1995.

Disclaimer: Repeated attempts to contact the original publisher were unsuccessful. Anyone claiming copyright can contact World Scientific Publishing Co.

Chapter 7

Nonmarket Economy Trade and U.S. Antidumping/Countervailing Duty Laws

Reproduced with the permission of American Bar Association from Gary N. Horlick and Shannon S. Shuman, Nonmarket Economy Trade and U.S. Antidumping/Countervailing Duty Laws, *The International Lawyer*, 18(4): 807–840, 1984.

Disclaimer: This information or any portion thereof may not be copied or disseminated in any form or by any means or downloaded or stored in an electronic database or retrieval system without the express written consent of the American Bar Association.

Chapter 8

Antidumping Policy as a System of Law

Reproduced with the permission of General Secretariat/Organization of American States and Brookings Institution Press from Gary N. Horlick and Steven A. Sugarman, Antidumping Policy as a System of Law, *Trade Rules in the Making: Challenges in Regional and Multilateral Negotiations*, pp. 341–364, 1999.

Chapter 9
Antidumping and Countervailing Duty Law Provisions of the Omnibus Trade and Competitiveness Act of 1988
Reproduced with the permission of Wolters Kluwer Law & Business from Gary N. Horlick and Geoffrey D. Oliver, Antidumping and Countervailing Duty Law Provisions of the Omnibus Trade and Competitiveness Act of 1988, *Journal of World Trade*, 23(3): 5–49, 1989.

Chapter 10
The 1994 WTO Subsidies Agreement
Reproduced with the permission of Wolters Kluwer Law & Business from Gary N. Horlick and Peggy A. Clarke, The 1994 WTO Subsidies Agreement, *World Competition, Law and Economics Review*, 17(4): 41–54, 1994.

Chapter 11
The Agreement on Subsidies and Countervailing Measures
Reproduced with the permission of Springer from Peggy A. Clarke and Gary N. Horlick, The Agreement on Subsidies and Countervailing Measures, *The World Trude Organization: Legal, Economic and Political Analysis: Volume I*, edited by Patrick F. J. Macrory, Arthur E. Appleton and Michael G. Plummer, pp. 679–734, 2005.

Chapter 12
Government Actions against Domestic Subsidies, an Analysis of the International Rules and an Introduction to United States' Practice
Reproduced with the permission of Wolters Kluwer Law & Business from Gary N. Horlick, Reinhard Quick and Edwin Vermulst, Government Actions against Domestic Subsidies, an Analysis of the International Rules and an Introduction to United States' Practice, *Legal Issues of European Integration*, 1: 1–51, 1986.

Chapter 13
Subsidies Discipline Under WTO and US Rules
Reproduced with the permission of Hart Publishing from Gary N. Horlick, Subsidies Discipline Under WTO and US Rules, *European Competition Law Annual 1999: Selected Issues in the Field of State Aids*, edited by Claus Dieter Ehlermann and Michelle Everson, pp. 593–603, 2001.

Chapter 14
United States: Court of Appeals for the Federal Circuit Opinion in PPG Industries, Inc. v. United States (U.S. Countervailing Duty Law)
Reproduced with the permission of The American Society of International Law from Gary N. Horlick, United States: Court of Appeals for the Federal Circuit Opinion in PPG Industries, Inc. v. United States (U.S. Countervailing Duty Law), *International Legal Materials*, XXX(5): 1179–1183, 1991. Permission conveyed through Copyright Clearance Center, Inc.

Chapter 15
WTO Subsidies Discipline During and After the Crisis
Reproduced with the permission of Oxford University Press from Gary N. Horlick and Peggy A. Clarke, WTO Subsidies Discipline During and After the Crisis, *Journal of International Economic Law*, 13(3): 859–874, 2010.

Chapter 16
WTO Dispute Settlement from the Perspective of Developing Countries
Reproduced with the permission of Cambridge University Press from Gary N. Horlick and Katherine Fennell, WTO Dispute Settlement from the Perspective of Developing Countries, *Law and Development Perspective on International Trade Law*, edited by Yong-Shik Lee, Gary N. Horlick, Won-Mog Choi and Tomer Broude, pp. 161–178, 2011.

Chapter 17
Problems with the Compliance Structure of the WTO Dispute Resolution Process
Reproduced with the permission of Cambridge University Press from Gary N. Horlick, Problems with the Compliance Structure of the WTO Dispute Resolution Process, *The Political Economy of International Trade Law*, edited by Daniel L. M. Kennedy and James D. Southwick, pp. 636–645, 2002.

Chapter 18
The Compliance Problems of the WTO
Reproduced with the permission of Arizona Journal of International and Comparative Law from Gary N. Horlick and Judith Coleman, The Compliance Problems of the WTO, *Arizona Journal of International and Comparative Law*, 24(1): 141–147, 2007.

Chapter 19
Political Questions in International Trade: Judicial Review of Section 301?
Reproduced with the permission of University of Michigan Law School from Erwin P. Eichmann and Gary N. Horlick, Political Questions in International Trade: Judicial Review of Section 301?, *Michigan Journal of International Law*, 10(3): 735–764, 1989.

Chapter 20
Mandatory Abolition of Anti-dumping, Countervailing Duties and Safeguards in Customs Unions and Free-Trade Areas Constituted between World Trade Organization Members: Revisiting a Long-standing Discussion in Light of the Appellate Body's *Turkey — Textiles* Ruling
Reproduced with the permission of Wolters Kluwer Law & Business from Angela T. Gobbi Estrella and Gary N. Horlick, Mandatory Abolition of Anti-dumping, Countervailing Duties and Safeguards in Customs Unions and Free-Trade Areas Constituted between World Trade Organization Members: Revisiting a Long-standing Discussion in Light of the Appellate Body's Turkey — Textiles Ruling, *Journal of World Trade*, 40(5): 909–944, 2006.

Chapter 21
NAFTA Chapter 11B: A Private Right of Action to Enforce Market Access through Investments
Reproduced with the permission of Wolters Kluwer Law & Business from Gary N. Horlick and Alicia L. Marti, NAFTA Chapter 11B: A Private Right of Action to Enforce Market Access through Investments, *Journal of International Arbitration*, 14(1): 43–54, 1997.

Chapter 22
Sovereignty, Trade and the Environment — A U.S. Perspective
Reproduced with the permission of Canada–United States Law Journal from Gary N. Horlick, Sovereignty, Trade and the Environment — A U.S. Perspective, *Canada–United States Law Journal*, 24, 177–182, 1998. Permission conveyed through Copyright Clearance Center, Inc.

Chapter 23
The World Trading System at the Crossroad of Science and Politics
Reproduced with the permission of Gary N. Horlick from his own work, The World Trading System at the Crossroad of Science and Politics, *The Next Trade Negotiating Round: Examining the Agenda for Seattle*, edited by Jagdish Bhagwati, pp. 257–260, 1999.

Chapter 24
Climate Change Legislation in the United States and the WTO
Reproduced with the permission of Wolters Kluwer Law & Business from Gary N. Horlick, Climate Change Legislation in the United States and the WTO, *Global Trade and Customs Journal*, 4(4): 125–127, 2009.

Chapter 25
Nonconclusions
Reproduced with the permission of Cambridge University Press from Gary N. Horlick, Nonconclusions, *Law and Development Perspective on International Trade Law*, edited by Yong-Shik Lee, Gary N. Horlick, Won-Mog Choi and Tomer Broude, pp. 395–402, 2011.

Chapter 26
Trade War or Growing Pains?
Reproduced with the permission of Law Business Research Ltd from Gary N. Horlick, Trade War or Growing Pains?, Who's Who Legal (www.whoswholegal.com), December 2010.

Chapter 27
China and the Future of Trade Law
Reproduced with the permission of Wolters Kluwer Law & Business from Gary N. Horlick, China and the Future of Trade Law, *Global Trade and Customs Journal*, 5(10): 421–422, 2010.

Contents

PART I

How Did Antidumping Get So Bad?

Part I. How Did Antidumping Get So Bad?

The rhetoric behind the first antidumping law, enacted by Canada in 1904 aimed at US steel imports, remains the rhetoric of antidumping today, even though whatever the justification the Canadian law might have had more than 100 years ago has long-since vanished.

The Canadian law was a very specific reaction to the formation in 1901 of the US steel "trust" — the United States Steel Corporation, sweeping up the J.P. Morgan steel holdings with the vast Carnegie Steel holdings and beginning the modern era of philanthropy (as Carnegie proceeded to give almost all his money away). In Canadian eyes (at least for the Canadian steel producers), US Steel effectively monopolized the US market, which was protected by high tariffs, and could produce at physically optimal rates, then price at monopoly prices, and sell any excess at whatever price it chose in Canada, destroying the Canadian producers and then raising its prices in Canada to monopoly levels. Whatever the truth of those allegations — which were never subjected to a court of law, even under the very primitive antitrust analysis of the day — they sounded plausible. They still sound great today, and are even less valid under current views of competition law.

The resulting law included exactly none of the elements described above. The Canadian antidumping law did not require any showing that the exporter had a home-market monopoly, market protection, home market subsidies, intent or ability to destroy the local industry, or ability to recoup any losses incurred while doing so. Enforcement was left to the tender mercies of local Canadian customs officials and whatever elected MP was sitting as finance minister, with no pretense of a neutral judge in sight. The Canadian approach was promptly picked up in numerous imperial British countries, including the UK itself, South Africa, New Zealand, and Australia.

The United States — by far the most sophisticated in competition law at the time — rejected the Canadian model. The United States passed the 1916 Antidumping Act, which required proof to a neutral federal district court judge appointed for life, of intent to destroy the local competitor — not ideal from a 2012 analysis of predatory pricing, but broad enough to include many of the elements. Within less than three years, the drumbeat began that a new US law "didn't work." It is unclear how anyone could have known the new law "didn't work" because no case could possibly have been litigated at that time. Perhaps more to the point, the party of free trade, the Democrats, was replaced in both houses of Congress and the White House and by 1921 the US passed an antidumping law modeled in large part on the Canadian law, with a slight protection of a requirement that the politician serving as Treasury Secretary also had to find injury in addition to price discrimination. The argument was that the German chemical industry — the first science research-based industry in history — would swamp the new US chemical industry, which had grown based on high prices for government purchases of explosives, and German patents appropriated during the war. The flood of German chemicals never occurred nor did the flood of antidumping cases, but the ironies abound. The US Steel Corporation became the largest single filer of antidumping cases in the world, and the German chemical industry filed numerous cases against US exports of chemicals to Europe. The leading scholar of antidumping, a Canadian trade economist named Jacob Viner, demonstrated how improbable was the type of predatory dumping on which the laws were based in 1923, and by 1950 finally gave up and publicly repented ever writing about the subject.

In 1947, when the US State Department drafted the GATT, it had clear marching orders: nothing can change US law. So, antidumping was included in GATT, in the form of the then-US law, including the injury test.[1]

While antidumping maintained a cult following among protected industries and bureaucratic collaborators after World War II, it did not become mass entertainment until the rise of competition from Japan (as the GATT drove down tariffs) required heroic measures. The Nixon Administration, in particular Secretary John Connolly's Treasury Department — a group not known for its timid deference to law — was ready to meet the challenge. A senior political appointee met with the Customs officers investigating alleged dumping of color televisions from Japan, and, after they told him they were finding no dumping, ordered them to find some. The Japanese companies and their lawyers knew their own numbers, and recognized

[1]Lebanon, at the time, a Francophone country (which then chose not to join the GATT), and Cuba — Spanish speaking — ganged up to insist on the addition of what is now the second line of Article VI, "dumping . . . is to be condemned if it causes or threatens to cause material injury." This has been claimed to show dumping is "unfair" but it says no such thing in any of the three languages and the WTO has been careful to avoid labeling "dumping" (selling at different prices) as "unfair" — since virtually all companies do so.

quickly that the calculation was inaccurate. While there was no explicit statutory provision for judicial review of antidumping decisions by the Treasury Department (where the responsibility for antidumping lay in the US until 1980), any customs duty could be "protested" and these were. As the facts became clear in the trial, the US Government was forced to embarrassingly settle the case with a face-saving payment of $66 million and the return of the $600 million in duties which had been illegally collected. It is worth noting that the same US television manufacturers sued the same television manufacturers for the same sales under US antitrust laws, including the 1916 Antidumping Act, and lost resoundingly up to and including the US Supreme Court, which dismissed the case, pointing out the improbability of predatory pricing (*Zenith vs. Mitsubishi*, 1985). It had not escaped anyone's notice that the antidumping duties on Japanese televisions had been in place for years before these errors were corrected and the duties dropped, and in the meantime it served as a very useful check on competition. More cases against many products were brought in the US and Europe in the 1970s, especially with the 1973–1975 recession, and also in Canada and Australia (the four countries collectively accounted for well over 95% of all dumping cases until 1987, when Mexico enacted an antidumping law and proceeded with considerable glee and velocity to apply its imports to the US). As a result, antidumping is by far the largest WTO-sponsored trade barrier, with more than 4,000 initiations since the WTO went into effect in 1995, compared to only several hundred countervailing duty and safeguards cases.[2] Developed countries no longer monopolize the weapon against imports — the leading user in the past five years is India, followed by Brazil and South Africa.

Why is Antidumping Bad?

1. As noted above, the laws still do not contain the elements which justified its passage; Antidumping laws are always justified with alleged examples of predation, but none of the elements of predatory pricing need to be proven, and certainly no neutral judge is involved.

[2]The WTO AD statistics permit only an analysis of only two categories — initiations and antidumping measures imposed. The latter category is quite suspect, as an unknown number of those cases reflect various sorts of "deals" over the years. In addition, since initiations have been shown to affect trade even if no measures are imposed, initiations are the relevant number for purposes of analysis.

2. The system is systematically rigged against imports.

    - The basic definition of dumping in Article VI is mathematically flawed. Alleged cross-subsidization of $1 from an allegedly protected small home market can lead to $19 of antidumping duties in a large market.
    - Developed country authorities continue to "tilt" the calculation by comparing individual apples to an average applesauce (also known as "zeroing" and continued in disguise in at least the US and EU).

3. The calculations are systematically "tilted" to discriminate against imports (through asymmetric adjustments — sales personnel salaries, level of trade adjustment, etc.).

    - Injury is found from the tiniest of import market shares, as little as 0.5% or less.
    - The WTO Appellate Body blesses abuses (e.g., a tie vote in US injury determinations is considered a reasoned decision to impose duties).
    - The higher the importing country's bound WTO tariff, the higher the dumping margin it can find (because tariffs are subtracted from export prices in the calculation)!

4. The politics of antidumping in WTO. Antidumping was not a major concern in the GATT, since there were not many cases and only one panel was brought (a particularly egregious antidumping duty imposed by Sweden on Italy in 1955) until 1985. But already by the early 1960s the British were irritated by the American habit of starting an investigation, imposing provisional duties, and then leaving the duty on for a year or more while leisurely determining that there was in fact no injury. As pressure mounted in the GATT to start including non-tariff barriers in GATT negotiations, it was decided to start with one such negotiation in the 1963–1967 Kennedy Round, and antidumping was the chosen subject. The result was the 1967 Antidumping Code — which did nothing to fix the problem identified by the United Kingdom (which continues today as an incentive for petitioners to file petitions just to disrupt trade, knowing full well that they were likely to lose a year later). The saving grace of the 1967 Code was the requirement that the dumping be the "primary cause" of injury. The US had entered the Kennedy Round antidumping negotiation suggesting that there be a fundamental reexamination of the logic of dumping to take into account competition law (GATT Doc. TN. 64/NTB/W.3, 10 January 1966), only to be stopped by the protectionist EEC (European Economic Communities) (Note of

the meeting of the Group on Antiduumping Policies held 25/26 January 1966 (Remarks of Mr. Klein (EEC))). But the US Congress fought the new Code and refused to make the necessary changes in US law. US was in a highly protectionist mood at the time. In the 1970s, as protection through VRAs for the steel industry came off, the steel industry went to President Carter in 1977 to ask for more relief. Prepared by his staff, Carter suggested that the steel industry instead try antidumping. The result was not only the first real "flood" of antidumping cases in the US, but also lead to a crucial strategic moment in GATT antidumping negotiations as the US steel industry decided to actively push for more protectionist rules in the Tokyo Round antidumping negotiations, and no other industry really opposed it. The result was the elimination of the "primary cause" requirement, and an informal agreement among the four big users (Australia, Canada, EC, US) that they would adopt a new US innovation: a finding of dumping *even if there was no dumping* ("*price discrimination*") as long as sales were "below cost." This had been added to US law in 1975 at the behest of one Louisiana senator trying to fix one case for one constituent (the Freeport Mining company). As long as Treasury administered the US antidumping law, it followed the stated congressional intent to use costs over a product lifecycle (the specific case cited by Congress was large commercial aircraft, which did not recover their costs for 20 or 30 years). But as soon as the US Commerce Department took over the responsibility in 1980, it switched to a measurement of cost for the last fiscal year. The result has been a spectacular increase in the protectionist nature of antidumping. For any industry with large fixed costs — traditional users of antidumping such as steel and chemicals — as demand goes down, unit prices go up, since fixed costs become a larger percentage of the total cost. The absurd result, "required" by current antidumping laws, is that imports should raise their prices as demand goes down while domestic producers quite logically lower their prices as demand goes down. The Commerce Department in 1985 and 1986 then took the next step of making the law "better" for protectionism by ignoring the product cycle and learning curve so that the first two years of an R&D intensive industry — such as semiconductors or large commercial aircraft — record very high costs and thus are always dumping (not based in any explicit language in the US legislative materials). The result is that antidumping law has completely escaped any link it might have had with business reality. As stated by the European Union in its regulations, the startup period of a business can never exceed six months — certainly news to companies which take two to three years to get a new factory up and running. The US chief negotiator explained to an astounded IBM marketing person that the startup of a new product does not include marketing. The European Union successfully inserted a rule in the Uruguay Round [WTO Antidumping Agreement (Article 2.2.2)] that a business calculates its profits by ignoring any sales at a loss — the exact rule followed most notoriously by Enron and Parmalat, but hardly a model for sound business practice.

None of this was an accident. The European Communities was ready to negotiate away some of the absurdities of antidumping practice in the Uruguay Round, but instead made a deal on November 1989 with the United States to seek as many protectionist devices as possible while fighting all attempts at positive reform. When it looked like that was not having enough effect, at the last minute, as GATT Director General Dunkel prepared his chairman's tax, the US had high level US political pressure put on Dunkel to instruct his staff that "nothing should be done that would help Japan" — and all other exporters. US exporters had mobilized in the Uruguay Round to seek less protection as dumping, as other countries followed Mexico's lead and began to apply antidumping to US exports. The US Government was completely captured, however, by protectionist elements. When US exporters such as IBM, Cargill, Catepillar, and Hewlett Packard suggested the need for certainly reforms, the head of the US delegation replied immediately "that's interesting, but [the] domestic industry won't like it" — the four companies, each of them considerably larger than any steel company in the US, were taken aback at this rather blunt statement of that they were no longer domestic industries if they didn't want protectionist dumping rules. They found out two years later when the Under Secretary of Commerce at the time literally would not speak with them while spending the last week of the Uruguay Round negotiations embedded with the US steel industry lobbyists.

The end result of the Uruguay Round negotiations was a standoff in trade negotiations that is called the balanced result, as somehow trade negotiators now like a result that increases protection in some areas while reducing it in others (a far cry from the first six GATT rounds, which, invariably reduced tariffs and, in the Kennedy Round Antiduumping Code, reduced antidumping protection through the short-lived "primary cause" requirement). There were distinct improvements, such as requirements of showing standing, requirements for sunset reviews, and the elimination of "averaging." In return, cost-of-production dumping was formally added to the agreement (but with the requirement that cost be measured over a reasonable period of time) and variety of idiotic positions were forced into the text by the US, such as the aforementioned definition of profit to be a fraudulent measure of profit, or an EU requirement of resale price maintenance by exporters (Article 9.3.3). The final fight, in the last days of the Round, was a US push to eviscerate dispute resolution in antidumping cases by stating that WTO panels and the Appellate Body should defer to national authorities' decisions in antidumping whenever those decisions were "reasonable." The danger of this language is revealed by the reaction when the US initially proposed that it apply to *all* WTO dispute resolution, in August 1993, and was promptly shouted down by its own very powerful intellectual property industries, which wanted no such deference to other countries' authorities. The US then tried to limit it to antidumping and countervailing duties, but that was rejected by the other members. This did not stop the US from a post-Round "charm offensive" claiming that in fact the language in the text said "reasonable" when it no longer did. This type of deference, described in some detail in my article with Peggy Clark, "Standards for Panels Reviewing Anti-dumping Determinations under the GATT and WTO," was rejected.

The US and EC, having lost half the battles in the antidumping negotiations, then tried to claw back victory by failing to implement the new rules. Both the US and EC 1994 implementing legislation are replete with examples of US or EU negotiating positions being put into national legislation in place of the finally agreed WTO text. This is described in part in "The World Trade Organization Antiduumping Agreement." This led to a long march of litigation, most notably the "zeroing" disputes as first the EU and then the US claimed that zeroing was somehow exempt from the "averaging" provisions, and of the "fair comparison requirement" of Article 2.4, despite the complete absence of textual support for that position. India won this point against the EU in an Appellate Body decision in 2000, relying in part on the "fair comparison" requirement which the US exporters' coalition helped to add (see "A Personal History of Zeroing"), and the US has spent 12 years refusing to comply.

By then, antidumping had been repurposed to keep out imports from China — not just in the US, but around the world. China was treated in some form or another as a "non-market economy" so that normal WTO rules do not apply (China had agreed to this travesty through 2016 as part of its WTO accession negotiations). This means that not only *none* of the rhetorical justifications for antidumping needed to apply, but none of the legal rules as well. To the contrary, the main charge against China was subsidies, but antidumping proved much more reliable as a generator of large protective tariffs. The US does not produce much of what China does, while medium-industrialized countries, such as Brazil and India, have many more sectors to protect (the largest China export categories to the US are footwear and wearing apparel, where the US industries have virtually disappeared). So antidumping remains stronger than ever, and is now entrenched worldwide — even China is a major user.

The World Trade Organization Antidumping Agreement

Gary N. HORLICK* and Eleanor C. SHEA**

I. INTRODUCTION

The Antidumping Agreement (Agreement) in the World Trade Organization (WTO) Agreements,[1] coupled with the WTO binding dispute resolution mechanism (DSM),[2] could be a revolution in world antidumping law. The Agreement's absolute requirement of a fair comparison, the improvement in language on causation of injury and the requirement of a sunset mechanism, along with numerous other improvements, marks the first world-wide agreement[3] on antidumping rules, and, more important, a reversal of a tendency to make the imposition of antidumping duties easier, even in the absence of a finding of predatory dumping causing injury.[4]

That said, one must emphasize the word "could". As with any set of rules, the effectiveness of the Antidumping Agreement will depend on the willingness of the governments that sign the Agreement to live up to the rules, and the willingness of WTO Members to challenge under the DSM other Members who do not live up to the rules.

This article provides a discussion of the negotiating history of the Antidumping Agreement and a review of the major provisions of that Agreement. It also discusses the relevant provisions of the DSM.

* O'Melveny & Myers, Washington, D.C., U.S.A. Formerly served as Deputy Assistant Secretary of Commerce for Import Administration and International Trade Counsel, U.S. Senate Committee on Finance.

**O'Melveny & Myers, Washington, D.C., U.S.A. Formerly served in the offices of Policy and Investigations, Import Administration, U.S. Department of Commerce.

[1] Agreement on Implementation of Article VI of the General Agreement on Tariffs and Trade 1994 (Antidumping Agreement), Final Act Embodying the Results of the Uruguay Round of Multilateral Trade Negotiations, at 145, GATT Doc. MTN/FA, 15 April 1994, (Final Act), reprinted in Message from the President of the United States Transmitting the Uruguay Round Trade Agreements, Texts of Agreements Implementing Bill, Statement of Administrative Action and Required Supporting Statements, H.R. Doc. No.316, 103d Cong., 2d Sess. 1453 (1994) (U.S. WTO Implementing Legislation).

[2] Understanding on Rules and Procedures Governing the Settlement of Disputes, Final Act at 353, U.S. WTO Implementing Legislation, at 1654.

[3] By 1993, forty-two countries were Members of the 1979 GATT Antidumping Code. By contrast, all WTO Members (currently numbering one hundred and twenty-five, and increasing rapidly) will be bound by the WTO Antidumping Agreement.

[4] For example, findings of "no dumping" by the U.S. Department of Commerce (Commerce) peaked at 16 percent in 1984, then dropped to zero in 1989 and 1990, two percent in 1991, and one percent in 1992. See I.M. Destler, *American Trade Politics*, 3d edition, forthcoming 1995, at Table 10.1.

II. Negotiating History

A. *Background*

The Ministerial Declaration that launched the GATT Uruguay Round in September 1986 did not mention antidumping law, or even dumping, as a topic for negotiation. The main reason for the omission is that the United States was the *demandeur*, both for having a new negotiating Round and for most of its agenda. At that time, the United States was at a high point of using its antidumping law, both as a tool of "back-door" industrial policy,[5] as well as an escape-valve for protectionist pressures arising from the sharp run-up of the U.S. dollar in the early 1980s and the consequent problems for U.S. import-competing and exporting industries. In effect, the U.S. Administration argued that higher duties against "unfair" imports were necessary in order to preserve free trade. There was also the possibility that some officials in the Administration actually believed the rather misinformed statements made on their behalf in connection with antidumping laws.[6]

More curious was the failure of other governments in 1986 to push for greater discipline on antidumping measures. As a factual matter, the use of antidumping law in the United States increased significantly in the 1980s, with U.S. cases totalling three hundred and forty-six from 1980 to 1986, compared with one hundred and thirty-five from 1970 to 1976.[7] More to the point, the governments of virtually every major U.S. trading partner had complained to the U.S. government, either bilaterally or in the GATT Anti-dumping Code Committee, in connection with one or more U.S. antidumping cases during the 1980s. Therefore, there clearly was some level of foreign government concern.

Yet, despite all the complaints by foreign governments to the United States, not one request for dispute resolution was filed in the GATT in connection with the U.S. administration of its antidumping laws. Indeed, as of 1986, there had been only two such complaints in the whole history of the GATT, one in 1955 by Italy against Sweden[8] and one in 1985 by Finland against New Zealand.[9] (It is noteworthy that both complaints were successful.) Simply put, senior officials in many foreign governments could not be bothered with antidumping cases, regardless of the trade volume involved, to the same degree as countervailing duty (i.e. anti-subsidy) cases, about which disputes could arise concerning the most minuscule of subsidy amounts or trade volume. In part, this was because government officials were trapped in an

[5] For example, the 1986 U.S.–Japan Semiconductor Agreements not only imposed high minimum prices on Japanese semiconductors involved in two antidumping cases, but also established a mechanism for a similar system for Japanese semiconductors for which no dumping or injury had ever been shown (or even investigated): *Arrangement Concerning Trade in Semiconductor Products*, 2 September 1986, U.S.–Japan, 25 I.L.M. 1409.

[6] See e.g. *Trade Is Everything But Unfair*, The Wall Street Journal, 22 June 1987, at 27: "the purpose of these laws is to defend American companies against loss of home market-share to predatory pricing . . . " There is no requirement in U.S. law that predation be shown before antidumping duties may be imposed, nor any requirement to show that predation is likely to succeed and losses be recouped, as U.S. courts would require: Organization for Economic Co-operation and Development, *Predatory Pricing*, 1989, 43–47.

[7] Based on calculations by the authors.

[8] *Swedish Antidumping Duties*, GATT BISD 3S/81, 26 February 1955.

[9] *New Zealand: Imports of Electrical Transformers from Finland*, GATT BISD 32S/55, 18 July 1985.

ingrained (and increasingly incorrect) belief that antidumping cases are private matters for private companies, while countervailing duty cases are between governments. This view ignores the fact that a government intervenes in a private firm's business by applying its antidumping laws. In addition, antidumping is an extremely arcane field, and cases could not readily be simplified so as to be explained to high levels of governments and companies. It was easier to take refuge in the idea that one should not want to appear to be a *demandeur* for antidumping reform in the Uruguay Round. Finally, the very term "dumping" had a pejorative ring to it,[10] and there was considerable ignorance about the exact content of the rules.[11]

By 1990, this attitude had changed substantially, as governments of most major trading entities[12] were formally on record as seeking antidumping rules based more on free market principles—a pressure resisted strongly by the trade negotiators for the United States and the European Community. Some of the reasons for this change in attitude by many governments, and for the opposition by the United States and the EC, can be inferred from the timing of the change.

The first country to press for inclusion of antidumping rules within the Uruguay Round was Korea, which filed a proposal on 21 May 1987. A Korean government official was the chairman of the negotiating group responsible for review of the Tokyo Round Codes (including antidumping), and Korean products had been increasingly subjected to antidumping cases brought by the EC, the United States, Canada, and Australia. In particular, a case had been filed in Canada against Hyundai motor cars, Korea's fastest growing export.[13] Other developing countries raised antidumping as an issue at the Montreal Mid-Term Review Meeting in late 1988.

Other proposals were filed in 1987 by the United States, India, Japan, and the Nordic countries. The U.S. proposal was based on the principle that dumping, as defined in U.S. law, was a practice to be deterred and remedied to a greater extent than under the existing GATT rules.[14] It is interesting to note that the GATT does not suggest any discipline on the practice of "dumping" and instead focuses solely on discipline on

[10] Kenneth W. Dam, *The GATT: Law and the International Economic Organization*, University of Chicago Press, Chicago, 1970, 168: "One coming to the dumping problem with a fresh eye, free of the traditional domestic industry perspective and alert to the pejorative radiations of the expressive term 'dumping' (which is so captivating that it has been absorbed without translation into the world's major commercial languages), may find antidumping duties a peculiar means for protecting domestic industry."

[11] As late as 1990, the Chief Executive Officer (CEO) of one of the companies seeking more trade-restrictive U.S. antidumping laws called up the CEO of a U.S. company seeking less trade-restrictive antidumping laws to ask why the CEO of the second company was seeking to protect the practice of sales below *marginal* cost. The CEO of the first company was apparently unaware that antidumping laws do not require sales below marginal cost, and in fact have no connection at all to the concept of marginal cost.

[12] Including three governments which were frequent users of antidumping laws in the 1980s: Australia, the largest user according to GATT statistics; Canada, the fourth largest user; and Mexico, the fifth largest user; see John H. Jackson, *Dumping in International Trade: Its Meaning and Context*, in *Antidumping Law and Practice: A Comparative Study*, John H. Jackson and Edwin A. Vermulst (eds.), University of Michigan Press, Ann Arbor, Michigan, 1989, 1, 15.

[13] The case was eventually rejected in the final injury determination, after a 35 percent dumping margin was found, primarily on the grounds that the petitioners did not produce competing small cars in significant volumes in Canada. The Canada Gazette, Part I, Vol. 122, No. 9, 27 February 1988, at 763; The Canada Gazette, Part I, Vol. 122, No. 14, 2 April 1988, at 1226.

[14] *Communication from the United States*, GATT Doc. MTN.GNG/NG8/W/22, 14 December 1987.

the use of antidumping rules. Although Article VI states that dumping is to be "condemned" if it causes injury (language not found in the initial U.S. draft for the GATT, but added later by Cuba and Lebanon[15]), a proposal by New Zealand[16] in 1955 that countries be made responsible for disciplining dumping by their exporters did not find acceptance.[17]

No serious examination has ever been undertaken in the GATT to determine exactly what a proper definition of dumping should be—in effect, what is a fair price in international trade? In 1966, at the beginning of the negotiations leading to the first GATT Antidumping Code in 1967, the United States posed all the right questions,[18] but the proposal was effectively blocked by the EC.[19]

The harshness of the 1987 U.S. position in part reflected a desire to pander to Congress during passage of what became the Omnibus Trade and Competitiveness Act of 1988 (1988 Act), and in part reflected heartfelt beliefs (whether well-founded or not) by some within the Administration that dumping was an unfair practice by foreigners intending to destroy fair-trading U.S. industries.

Attention in the United States to antidumping law in 1987–1988 was focused on proposed amendments to the 1988 Act. After major lobbying battles, the amendments to U.S. antidumping law in 1988 were fairly minor.[20] One Administration technique for fending off amendments was to promise that they would be taken up during the Uruguay Round.[21] At the same time, the 1987–1988

---

[15] W.A. Seavey, *Dumping Since the War: The GATT and National Laws*, Office Services Corp., Oakland, California, 1970, 20.

[16] In a report on a meeting of the Contracting Parties in 1955, it was reported that the New Zealand delegate had commented that: "[the New Zealand] delegation had come to the present Session [of the CONTRACTING PARTIES] convinced that the Agreement was heavily weighted against such countries as his own which were exporters of agricultural products, and in the hope of redressing the imbalance. They had found hostility to their efforts to protect themselves against dumping, and to the proposals which they had put forward with this in mind. Moreover, they had found that the country which was asking for an unfettered right to protect its own agriculture [the United States] had been against any strengthening of the provisions regarding dumping in the Agreement.": *Summary Record of the Forty-First Meeting of the Contracting Parties*, GATT Doc. SR.9/41, 15 March 1955, at 2.

[17] John H. Jackson, *World Trade and the Law of GATT*, Bobbs Merrill, Indianapolis, Indiana, 1969, 412. The United States was the leading target of the 1955 proposal and is currently the leading target of antidumping cases world-wide (based on GATT statistics from 1988–1993 for Members of the GATT Antidumping Code Committee).

[18] "Should antidumping measures be limited to prevention of market monopolization by foreign exporters? . . . Should antidumping measures permit alignment of exporters' prices to meet competitive prices in the export market? Should such provision be limited to meeting the prices of foreign but not domestic competitors in the export market? . . . Where a seller lowers his price to gain entry, i.e. consumer familiarity and acceptance, into an export market, should antidumping measures permit such price discrimination? . . . Where consumers' or competitors' information regarding changes in supply or demand varies in different markets, and the price moves up or down in response to those variances, should antidumping measures permit such geographic price discrimination?": *Note by the United States Delegation*, GATT Doc. TN.64/NTB/W/36, 10 January 1966.

[19] *Comments by the European Economic Community*, GATT Doc. TN.64/NTB/W/10/Add.1, 21 April 1966, at 2. Interestingly, by contrast, both the United States and the EC sought a fundamental re-examination of underlying principles in the WTO Subsidies Agreement negotiations.

[20] For a fuller description, see Gary N. Horlick and Geoffrey D. Oliver, *Antidumping and Countervailing Duty Law Provisions of the Omnibus Trade and Competitiveness Act of 1988*, 23 J.W.T. 3, June 1989, 5.

[21] The statute provided, in hortatory language: "The principal negotiating objectives of the United States with respect to unfair trade practices are: (a) to improve the provisions of the GATT and non-tariff measure agreements in order to define, deter, discourage the persistent use of, and otherwise discipline unfair trade practices having adverse trade effects, including forms of . . . dumping and other practices not adequately covered such as . . . diversionary dumping, [and] dumped . . . inputs; (b) to obtain the application of similar rules to the treatment of primary and non-primary products in the Agreement on the Interpretation and Application of Articles VI, XVI, and XXIII of the GATT.": Omnibus Trade and Competitiveness Act of 1988, § 1101(b)(8), 19 U.S.C. § 2901(b)(8) (1988).

legislative process saw the first ever involvement by major U.S. businesses—through a joint lobbying effort by the Emergency Committee for American Trade (ECAT) and the Business Round Table—to oppose trade-restrictive amendments to the antidumping rules at a technical level. In many respects, this was a useful experience for the companies involved, which gained further insights into the workings of antidumping law at a time when its potential impact on their business operations was dramatized by cases both in the United States[22] and overseas.[23] It also had an impact on perceptions of the antidumping issue within the United States, as the first time in memory that significant private sector interests in the United States had forcefully raised the exporters' point of view against the trade-restrictive use of U.S. antidumping laws.[24]

The U.S. Administration found itself caught between two forces. Many key Administration officials were well aware of the flaws in the world's antidumping rules, and the potential negative impact on U.S. competitiveness. At the same time, the Administration faced determined pressure from groups of import-competing industries which found some of those flaws useful as a way of restricting competition from imports within the United States. The Administration therefore seized on the areas where there was an agreement within all major groups in the United States—namely that antidumping rules should include provisions on due process and transparency, rules to prevent circumvention, and some measures to deter "multiple offenders".

The detailed U.S. proposal of 20 November 1989 comprised three tracks, which were directed primarily at addressing problems of circumvention and repeat offenders.[25] The first track of the proposal was a fairly straightforward anti-circumvention proposal, modelled on the best features of U.S. and EC anti-circumvention rules (Track I). The United States intended that Track I would address circumstances where changes in production of the product are so minor that, if circumvention were found, a new investigation of dumping and injury would not be necessary.[26]

[22] The imposition of antidumping duties on ball-bearing imports into the United States were opposed by several U.S. companies including Caterpillar, Rockwell, Xerox and 3M. See *Antifriction Bearings (Other Than Tapered Roller Bearings) and Parts Thereof from the Federal Republic of Germany, France, Italy, Japan, Romania, Singapore, Sweden, Thailand, and the United Kingdom*, USITC Publication 2185, Inv. Nos. 303–TA–19– 20 and 731–TA–391–399, Final, May 1989.

[23] For example, Mexico started an antidumping investigation of imports of personal computers made in the United States.

[24] Following the enactment of the 1988 Act, representatives of some of the U.S. exporters involved in the legislative effort (including IBM, Cargill, Caterpillar, and Hewlett-Packard) met to review the possible impact of the Uruguay Round on their businesses. Most of the companies were already involved in Uruguay Round efforts in connection with intellectual property, services and investments. The companies decided that, of the remaining issues, the one most likely to have an impact on their businesses world-wide over the next decade was antidumping, in view of the clear trend toward the increased use of the law within countries that already had antidumping laws, and a sharp increase in the number of developing countries enacting such laws and using them. In that regard, the Mexican example of the rapid use of a new antidumping law was viewed as a harbinger for future developments in other countries. In effect, antidumping laws had become opportunities for governments to impose price floors on these U.S. companies' products, and the Uruguay Round offered an opportunity to negotiate better rules for the imposition of such price controls.

[25] *Communication from the United States, Proposal for Improvements to the Antidumping Code*, GATT Doc. MTN.GNG/NG8/W/59, 20 December 1989.

[26] Id., at 4–5.

Track II of the U.S. proposal outlined a grab-bag of circumstances in which suspension of liquidation could also be imposed upon initiation of an investigation, reflecting the unsuccessful attempt in 1987–1988 of some congressmen and senators for amendments against "input dumping" and multinational corporations. The proposal was intended to counter "recurrent injurious dumping", which could occur through circumvention of an antidumping order where the changes in production of the product were more significant than under Track I, through "country hopping", or through the incorporation of a major input covered by a dumping order in an exported product (i.e. "input dumping").[27]

Track III was a "multiple offender" provision permitting immediate suspension of liquidation upon initiation of a case against a foreign producer that repeatedly dumps products within the same general category of merchandise as the products covered by the original antidumping order (also referred to as "recidivist dumping").[28]

In addition, the U.S. proposed amendments to set minimum standards of transparency and to permit labour unions and growers of agriculture products to have standing in antidumping proceedings. Most significantly, the United States took no position on most of the issues raised by the other delegations, thus leaving its negotiators with considerable bargaining flexibility to try to obtain their stated goals.

Needless to say, the U.S. proposal pleased neither side in the United States. Import-competing industries sought a punitive antidumping law, since the same rules would not be applied to their own sales within the United States, while exporters worried that such rules would be applied to their sales overseas.

Proposals were filed later that year by numerous countries. The Canadian proposal was fairly typical in advocating a wide range of reforms in antidumping rules.[29] The Canadian government had undertaken a detailed review in 1979 of GATT antidumping rules, spurred on in part by fears that the Mexican example would be imitated globally, and in part by complaints of Canadian exporters concerning U.S. antidumping rules. The Canadian proposal comprised two general parts. The first included proposals to achieve greater procedural uniformity and consistency in the application of antidumping measures, such as:

— the need to verify "standing of" before the initiation of an investigation and the need for an explicit definition of the term "major proportion" of the domestic industry;
— specific guidelines on the minimum information requirements for the initiation of an investigation;
— a minimum period after initiation of an investigation before provisional measures may be imposed; and

[27] Id., at 5–7.
[28] Id., at 7.
[29] *Amendments to the Antidumping Code, Submission by Canada*, GATT Doc. MTN.GNG/NG8/W/65, 22 December 1989.

— transparency of antidumping proceedings, particularly with respect to access to relevant information and the publication of a statement of reasons for each phase of the investigation.

The second part of the Canadian proposal contained recommendations to improve the standards for application of antidumping measures, including:

— more detailed guidance for determining when sales below cost may be disregarded and excluded from the calculation of normal value;
— an explicit *de minimis* margin standard;
— a more stringent test for demonstrating that dumped imports are causing injury;
— an automatic five-year sunset provision, unless a review establishes the need to maintain the measure for an additional three years; and
— a public interest test.

In addition, the Canadian proposal included a discussion of the need to develop rules on anti-circumvention to specify the conditions under which an order may be extended "*consistent with the Code*, to goods assembled domestically or in a third country from parts and components originating in a country subject to a finding." (emphasis added).[30]

Similar proposals were filed by Norway, Sweden, and Finland (the Nordic countries),[31] Singapore,[32] Hong Kong,[33] Japan[34] and, in shorter form, Australia.[35]

The EC filed a proposal[36] adopting some of the reforms proposed by Canada and the other delegations (e.g. the Nordic countries, Hong Kong and Singapore), but also proposing some changes of its own to make it easier to impose antidumping duties, especially against Japanese products, and particularly in situations in which low-priced imports were affecting one region of a customs union. The purpose of this aspect of the EC proposal was to take into account the side variations in pricing within the twelve different markets of the EC.

As a result, by January 1990, there were proposals from numerous countries,[37] which essentially overlapped, in addition to the very different U.S. proposal and an EC proposal that shared elements with several of the other proposals. In addition, on the "right wing" (i.e. free market) side, several participants (namely, Hong Kong, Singapore and the Nordic countries) had proposed a re-examination of the concept and definition of dumping, to see if the current GATT definition made sense from an

[30] Id., at 6.

[31] *Amendments to the Antidumping Code, Submission by the Nordic Countries*, GATT Doc. MTN.GNG/NG8/W/64, 22 December 1989.

[32] Proposed Elements for a Framework for Negotiations—Principles and Objectives for Antidumping Rules, Communication from the Delegation of Singapore, October 1989.

[33] *Amendments to the Antidumping Code, Communication from the Delegation of Hong Kong*, GATT Doc. MTN.GNG/NG8/W/51/Add.1, 22 December 1989.

[34] *Submission of Japan on the Amendments to the Antidumping Code*, GATT Doc. MTN.GNG/NG8/W/48, 3 August 1989.

[35] *Amendments to the Antidumping Code, Submission by Australia*, GATT Doc. MTN.GNG/NG8/W/66, 22 December 1989.

[36] *Communication from the European Communities to GATT Uruguay Round—Antidumping Code*, GATT Doc. MTN.GNG/NG8/W/63, 20 December 1989.

[37] Including the Nordic countries, Hong Kong, Singapore, Australia, Canada, Japan, Korea and India.

economic perspective.[38] On the "left wing" (i.e. pro-government regulation) side, some of the U.S. and EC negotiators' proposals were aimed at increasing the use of antidumping measures, either by relaxing the standards (in the EC proposal on regional industry, for example), or by giving litigation advantages to petitioners by allowing suspension of liquidation upon initiation (as proposed by the United States). Much of 1989 was spent in a series of philosophical discussions concerning the right-wing and left-wing proposals, with relatively little detailed work being done on the main body of overlapping proposals. To some extent, this was probably a matter of negotiating strategy; both sides knew that the deadline for concluding an agreement was not until late 1990, and therefore felt no need to get to work on the more practical issues. By the end of 1989, the discussion of basic principles had essentially been ended by U.S. and EC opposition to any reconsideration of the fundamental issues (the EC maintaining its position taken in 1966, and the United States switching positions to agree with the EC).

B. *Negotiations and Draft Agreements*

In November 1989, the United States and the EC had formed a "non-aggression pact" to resist all changes in antidumping rules that would make the system less trade-restrictive. On its face, this alliance seems a bit odd. U.S. exporters were the second leading victim of EC antidumping law in the years prior to the Uruguay Round, while EC exporters as a whole were far and away the leading target of U.S. antidumping cases in the same period.[39] Further, the United States had frequently used antidumping law to force the EC into grey area measures on steel, as the price for the withdrawal of antidumping petitions.[40]

Moreover, the main complaints about the two systems' practices were different. The EC faced more criticism for alleged manipulation of the price comparison, in particular by asymmetrical adjustments prejudicial to exporters, and for lack of transparency. The United States was criticized more for the use of an arbitrary eight percent profit margin; its application of the injury standard, in particular the inclusion of non-dumped imports as a cause of injury; and for the complexity and expense of some of its procedures (notably, the assessment of duties).

[38] In addition, there were similar proposals in 1989 within the EC, supported by several Member States, reportedly Germany, the United Kingdom, Denmark, the Netherlands, and Eire. However, the EC Commission was able to brush off all those Member States.

[39] United States General Accounting Office, *Use of the GATT Antidumping Code*, GAO/NSIAD–90–238FS, July 1990, at 19.

[40] See *Cold Rolled and Galvanized Carbon Steel Sheets from Belgium, France, the Federal Republic of Germany, Italy, the Netherlands, and the United Kingdom*, 43 Fed.Reg. 37,052, Treas. Dep't, 1978: termination of antidumping investigations; *Carbon Steel Cold Rolled Sheet, Hot Rolled Sheet, Galvanized Sheet, Plate and Structural Shapes from Belgium, the Federal Republic of Germany, France, Italy, Luxembourg, the Netherlands, and the United Kingdom*, 45 Fed.Reg. 66,833, Dep't Comm., 1980: termination of antidumping investigations.

The explanation for this alliance was that both the U.S. government and the EC Commission fundamentally still perceived themselves as users of antidumping laws, rather than as exporting countries. (This may seem odd, as the EC, as a whole, was by far the world's largest exporter, with the United States second.) In part, it is a reflection of trade politics in large countries, whose internal markets are so large that some politicians can still focus inward long after economic reality has forced middle-sized countries such as Canada and Australia to emphasize market access for its exporters over protection of the home market. It is also no accident that the United States and the EC are so vulnerable to special-interest lobbying, because neither has a government with a guaranteed parliamentary majority. The White House is always looking over its shoulder to count votes in Congress, which makes the Office of the United States Trade Representative (USTR) extremely sensitive to individual senators and representatives. The EC Commission is an executive body which is not controlled by any elected body, and thus interest-group politics play out within the complex internal politics of the Commission and the Council of Ministers. This opposition to reform by the United States and the EC was reinforced by, and perhaps reflected in, the choice of negotiators. The United States and EC maintained, as lead negotiators on antidumping matters, people whose primary job was enforcement of antidumping measures, while most other countries chose people whose main outlook was general trade policy.[41]

In view of the relatively slow progress on antidumping within GATT Negotiation Group 8 (which also included complex discussions on, *inter alia*, pre-shipment inspection and rules of origin), a special Informal Group on antidumping was set up under Charles Carlisle, the Deputy Director-General of the GATT. This group undertook detailed discussions in March, April, May and June of 1990. While little direct agreement was reached on issues in this Informal Group (in part because each party viewed every individual item as a bargaining chip), the process was quite useful in fleshing out most of the details under various options, and served as the basis for the subsequent discussion of the different issues.

In response to pressure for concrete progress in all areas by the end of July, on 6 July 1990, Carlisle released a discussion draft for a possible Antidumping Code (Carlisle I). Carlisle had rejected the claims of those who wanted no significant changes in the 1979 Code and instead attempted to make useful changes across a wide range of Code issues, without making radical changes in any one area. As a result, Carlisle I picked up perhaps three-quarters or more of the proposals made by the Nordic countries, Singapore, Hong Kong, and Canada, as well as certain private sector suggestions, while rejecting the requests by the Nordic countries, Hong Kong, and Singapore for a re-examination of the fundamental bases of antidumping rules.

[41] As the overall Uruguay Round negotiations became more and more intense in late 1990, the ability of general trade policy people to keep an eye on the antidumping negotiations diminished, and the influence of enforcers rose in a number of delegations.

In the last few days before releasing the draft, however, Chairman Carlisle, apparently, had become convinced that it was essential to accept almost all of the U.S. proposals to make the final package acceptable to the U.S. Congress.[42] As a result, a group of developing countries rejected the Carlisle I text as a basis for further negotiation, perhaps out of irritation that Carlisle had taken more of the U.S. proposals than of their proposals. The developing countries also rejected the text because of a deep-seated fear that the mere possibility of anticircumvention measures against "third-country assembly" would deter needed investment in manufacturing in their countries, which often must import components from other countries for viable, world-scale operations.

The discussions became quite bitter and personal, and stayed that way throughout the remainder of the negotiations. Chairman Carlisle reacted to the demands for revisions by pointing out that, if forced to revise his draft, he would be forced to include suggestions from all sides. In any event, the unhappy developing countries pressed ahead with their demands, and in a "Green Room" meeting in July 1990, Carlisle was asked to produce a second draft text on antidumping.

Carlisle II was released on 14 August 1990. As foreshadowed, Carlisle II was essentially Carlisle I on which was superimposed a wide range of proposals. Some of the proposals were rather extreme, such as a proposal that products subject to an Article XIX safeguard or textiles and wearing apparel products subject to a phase-out of the Multi-Fibre Arrangement be exempt from antidumping actions during the entire phase-out period, or the repeated attempts by the EC and United States to legitimize in a new Code practices that would likely be found by panels to violate the 1979 Code, such as "tilting" the "fair comparison" through misuse of adjustments and averaging.[43]

Virtually all of September and October 1990 was spent in a seemingly constant round of meetings in Chairman Carlisle's office among the representatives of the delegations with the most interest in the negotiations (i.e. Australia, Brazil, Canada, the EC, the Nordic countries, Hong Kong, Singapore, Mexico, Japan, Yugoslavia, Korea, New Zealand and the United States). Many of the delegations grew frustrated

---

[42] The authors thought at the time that inclusion of a large chunk of the U.S. proposal was necessary, but that Carlisle I included too much. This is a question on which reasonable people differed quite strongly during the last half of 1990. In the authors' view, the fear of protectionist elements in the U.S. Congress opposing the Code was well-founded, but those elements would have opposed Carlisle I in any event (and they did), whether or not it included the U.S. "anti-circumvention" proposals. They would oppose anything that made U.S. antidumping law a less useful tool against imports into the United States, without any particular concern for the effect of other countries' antidumping laws on U.S. exports.

[43] Carlisle II was followed very shortly by the release in August of the long-awaited Panel Report on Sweden's complaint against imposition by the United States of antidumping duties on stainless steel pipe. *Imposition of Antidumping Duties on Imports of Seamless Stainless Steel Hollow Products from Sweden*, GATT Doc. ADP/47, 20 August 1990 (Swedish Steel Panel Report). The Report condemned U.S. practices for checking standing (which were worse than those of the EC, Canada or Australia). The Panel used the insufficiency of U.S. practices for checking standing as a reason for not ruling on the more substantive aspects of the case, but it was rumoured that the Panel would have ruled against the United States on a number of aspects of the dumping calculation, which were similar to those followed by other major users of antidumping law (such as the misuse of averaging techniques).

with the apparent lack of progress, and an attempt was made to form an informal drafting group of eight delegations: Australia, Mexico, Canada, the Nordic countries, Hong Kong, the United States, the EC and Japan. The group would begin, on an informal, *ad referendum* basis, to move from the pre-existing negotiating positions from which the negotiation had started a year earlier.

Some of the members of the "group of eight" took the process seriously—e.g. the Nordic countries offered some flexibility on third-country circumvention—while other delegations evidently used the process as one more opportunity to show how "tough" they could be. To some extent, this reflected differing estimates of when the "end game" would begin for the entire Round, with some delegations—notably, the United States and Japan—feeling forced politically to appear "tough" until the last possible moment. The informal group was working against the deadline of mid-October 1990, when responsibility for all unfinished negotiations would move to senior negotiators.

GATT Director-General Arthur Dunkel had planned to have the entire Uruguay Round package wrapped up by mid-October 1990. While certain other negotiating groups (notably Agriculture and Services) were even further behind than Antidumping, antidumping had now become a major element in any Uruguay Round package for a number of developing countries and middle-sized exporting countries (such as the Nordic countries and Canada). The intransigence of U.S. and EC negotiators on antidumping was widely viewed as an attempt to retain their protectionist antidumping systems, while formally requesting market opening in the Round from others.

Two overlapping approaches were then attempted in rapid succession. A group of "neutral" countries (the Troika) was asked to prepare consensus drafts of the procedural aspects on antidumping, which had already been agreed to some extent. This process was completed by October 1990, but even by then, it had become clear that the group could not prepare a complete consensus text (although much of their work was ultimately incorporated into the final Agreement). In effect, the U.S. demands for limited transparency and judicial or administrative review would be conceded by developing countries, which would have to pay higher administrative costs, yet they would receive no commitments from the United States and the EC to the application of fair substantive standards.

Consequently, Director-General Dunkel requested that Hugh McPhail of the New Zealand Delegation serve as an "honest broker" and prepare a draft Code reflecting the best points from all of the proposals (and from a Canadian draft of October 1990). New Zealand I, as the first McPhail text came to be known, was made available to the negotiators on 6 November 1990, and was promptly rejected by the United States and the EC. After consultations with the United States and the EC, McPhail released New Zealand II on 15 November 1990. The U.S. and EC negotiators again rejected the draft, this time taking the unusual step of submitting a long list of objections formally signed on behalf of the European Communities and the United States[44] (although, at least in the case of the United States, the rest of the U.S. government had not been consulted).

The most remarkable aspect of this lengthy document was the degree to which it reflected the abandonment, by the United States, of long-held objections to protectionist aspects of the EC's antidumping law,[45] while the EC returned the favour by stifling such long-held objections as the twenty-plus years of attack on the U.S. use of a minimum 8 percent profit and minimum 10 percent general selling and administrative expenses in the calculation of constructed value. Both countries were also becoming quite emphatic about the need for provisions to overturn the GATT Panel Report which had found the application of the EC's anti-circumvention rules to be inconsistent with its obligations under Article VI.[46] The U.S. EC proposals included specific anti-circumvention rules or the authority (implicit or explicit) to use rules of origin to extend antidumping measures to products assembled in third countries in whole or in part from components and parts produced in the exporting country, as the EC had done in imposing an antidumping duty on copiers from Japan to those machines assembled in California.

McPhail subsequently prepared a third draft (New Zealand III), released on 23 November 1990, trying yet again to accommodate the U.S. and EC positions. This text served to alienate some of the exporting countries, because of the apparent willingness to adopt U.S. and EC proposals on third-country assembly and direct circumvention (including an explicit "local content" test). The U.S. and EC made one last attempt to salvage their position going into the Brussels Ministerial Meeting in December 1991, by trying to force an agreement through a Quad meeting of the United States, the EC, Canada and Japan (the Quadrilateral group), on the theory that it would be a more malleable forum. This limited group was no longer capable of writing an acceptable Antidumping Code single-handedly, as the United States and EC had done in 1978–1979. In the end, antidumping was one of only a few groups that went into the Brussels Ministerial with no agreed text, but rather with only a complex list of questions supposedly to be put to Ministers (some of whom would not have been amused that such technical and detailed issues had not been resolved by lower level negotiators).

In an attempt to streamline the negotiations in Brussels, the Contracting Parties included individual negotiating topics in larger groups. Antidumping was included within the "Rules Group", along with Subsidies and Safeguards. After some negotiation, Canadian trade minister John Crosbie was named Chairman of the Rules Group.

---

[44] Correspondence from the European Communities and the United States to Mr Arthur Dunkel, Director-General of the General Agreement on Tariffs and Trade, 19 November 1990.

[45] For example, the United States reversed the USTR's 1989 attack against the position taken by the EC in the case of the Ricoh copiers from California, and reversed a formal objection made by the USTR in 1986 to the EC practice of counting antidumping duties as a cost, thus "double-counting", in determining whether dumping had ceased. See *European Economic Community—Regulation on Imports of Parts and Components*, GATT BISD 37S/132, 16 May 1990.

[46] Id.

In the absence of an agreed-upon antidumping text,[47] on Tuesday, 10 December, Crosbie obtained general agreement to split antidumping into three slices (or *tranches*), with a first *tranche* to consist of relatively easy issues, the second *tranche* more difficult issues, and the third the most difficult. The Secretariat then hurriedly prepared lists of issues for the first two *tranches* (and, by implication, the third *tranche*) after consultations with several delegations and other individuals, and work began on the first *tranche*[48] on Wednesday afternoon, 11 December.[49]

Work on the first *tranche* went reasonably smoothly, since these issues had been pretty much agreed through the discussions in Carlisle's office in September and October 1990, the Troika draft, and New Zealand III. Within a few hours, the group produced an agreed text (subject to overall agreement on the Antidumping Code specifically and the Uruguay Round as a package) for parts of Articles 2, 5, 6, 7, 8, 9, 13, and 14. A text was produced and distributed to all the delegations. The group reconvened at ten o'clock that evening to begin work on the second *tranche* issues.[50]

Little agreement was reached on these issues, even though some of them were not that difficult or controversial. By this time, of course, it was well known to all the delegations that the U.S./Cairns Group–EC fight in the agricultural negotiations was reaching a breaking point, and it was quite clear that a number of delegations would reach no agreement on an overall package until the agricultural deadlock was broken. As a result, the meeting dragged on until four a.m., with no further progress achieved. At that point, the entire negotiation broke up, with delegations willing to begin work to reach agreement, only once the agricultural deadlock was broken.

The late spring of 1991 seemed the obvious time to complete the Uruguay Round, with politicians in the major developed countries enjoying good economic performances and without major electoral pressures. The opportunity was lost, however, but the U.S. Administration was able to obtain a two-year renewal of its "fast-track" negotiating authority. Antidumping negotiations resumed in a desultory fashion in the second half of 1991. There was no increase in concessions on any of the outstanding issues, and in late October 1991, the United States introduced new demands for anti-circumvention remedies covering parts from countries not previously the subject of an investigation (third-country parts). The United States also reiterated its insistence on special treatment of antidumping in the dispute settlement mechanism. It began to look as if the Secretariat would have to produce the

[47] The United States in particular could not agree to an antidumping text before Brussels (even if it might accept one at Brussels), so as to be in a position to say that it was forced to accept reforms as part of an overall package favourable to U.S. economic interests. Conversely, a number of the exporting countries were determined to hold out on "anti-circumvention" until the last possible moment. The EC would have welcomed any reason for the media to report that any issue other than agriculture was a roadblock.

[48] The first *tranche* issues included: standards for initiation, "all other rates", undertakings, transparency, judicial review, "best information", symmetry, exchange rates, and duty assessment procedures.

[49] The group included representatives of Switzerland, the United States, the EC, New Zealand, Canada, Japan, Singapore and Hong Kong, as well as the Secretariat.

[50] The second *tranche* issues included: conversion of currencies in related party transactions, averaging, standing, pre-initiation evidence, *de minimis* margins, negligible market share, maximum period of investigation, deadline for refunds, duty as a cost, sampling, new shippers rates, and circumvention by assembly in the importing country.

draft agreement. The United States and the EC tried again, unsuccessfully, to push a draft through the Quad. In November 1991, after consultations with a number of delegations, the Secretariat produced significant improvements in "non-papers" on cost of production issues and price averaging. At the request of the parties, a final attempt at consensus was made by Rudi Ramsauer, the Swiss negotiator, but it ended by 10 December, forcing the Secretariat to produce a final draft text by 20 December 1991.

C. *The Dunkel Text*[51]

In mid-December 1991, the United States and the EC stepped up their pressure on Director-General Dunkel for more trade-restrictive antidumping rules. The United States apparently orchestrated telephone calls from Senate Finance Committee Chairman Lloyd Bentsen and House Ways and Means Committee Chairman Dan Rostenkowski, telling Dunkel that Congress would not accept a less protectionist Antidumping Code. There was some element of bluff in these calls, as no one could predict what Congress would do until the shape of the agricultural and market access packages was clear.

Dunkel was in no position to ignore the two largest GATT members; thus, a number of U.S. and EC concerns had to be taken care of, and nothing could be done that would be portrayed as helping Japan. The U.S. and EC negotiators eventually presented a long list of demands. The result, with everyone tired and edgy, was an awkwardly constructed document (far less coherent than Carlisle I, for example) with at least one section dropped by accident and only restored at the end. The United States, which applied most of the political pressure, got very few of the changes it wanted. Most notably, the United States had placed its greatest emphasis on applying anti-circumvention measures to "third-country parts" (i.e. parts from countries not subject to the original antidumping order), but the draft did not include a concept so obviously violative of the GATT (since there would have been no dumping or injury investigation at all of parts and components from the third country).

The United States was also unsuccessful in obtaining special rules on dispute resolution for antidumping disputes, which would seek to ensure deference by GATT panels to U.S. antidumping authorities (as well as those of other countries, although that was not an overriding concern of the U.S. negotiators).

The main beneficiary of the political pressure was the EC, which obtained the inclusion of two very strangely worded provisions which had not appeared in that form in any previous draft. First, the Dunkel Text defined profit by accepting the rather bizarre EC rule of using actual profits, but only from sales "in the ordinary course of trade". In practice, this rule tends to exaggerate the profit level to be included in constructed value, as the EC simply excludes all individual sales below

[51] Draft Final Act Embodying the Results of the Uruguay Round of Multilateral Trade Negotiations, Agreement on Implementation of Article VI of the General Agreement on Tariffs and Trade, GATT Doc. MTN.TNC/W/FA, 20 December 1991 (Dunkel Text).

average cost, even though no business would be allowed to report its profits on such a selective basis to national securities regulators. At the same time, if a business made every single sale at a profit of 0.1 percent, the authorities would be required to accept that profit level, even if it were not "reasonable". As a result, protectionist industries in the United States could be forced to live with a 0.1 percent addition to cost in constructed value, rather than the minimum 8 percent provided in the existing U.S. statute. The problem with this rule can be seen in the following examples:

(1a) *Profits exaggerated by agreement*

Total revenue	=	\$8.00 for 4 units
Total cost	=	\$6.80 (average cost = \$1.70)
Total profit	=	\$1.20
Average profit as a percentage of cost		
	=	17.6% (\$1.20 ÷ \$6.80)

1 Sale at \$3.00	Profit = 76% (\$1.30 ÷ \$1.70)
1 Sale at \$2.00	Profit = 17.6% (\$0.30 ÷ \$1.70)
1 Sale at \$2.00	Profit = 17.6% (\$0.30 ÷ \$1.70)
1 Sale of a sample at \$1.00	Disregarded as "not in ordinary course of trade"
Total \$8.00	Average "profit" under new Antidumping Agreement = 37.3%
	(\$1.90 profit on sales "in the ordinary course of trade" ÷ \$5.10 cost of those goods sold)
	"Fair" export price = \$2.33 (\$1.70 + \$0.63)

(1b) *Same total profits accurately measured by agreement*

Total revenue	=	\$8.00 for 4 units
Total cost	=	\$6.80 (average cost = \$1.70)
Total profit	=	\$1.20
Average profit as a percentage of cost		
	=	17.6% (\$1.20 ÷ \$6.80)

4 Sales at \$2.00	Profit = 17.6% (\$0.30 ÷ \$1.70)
Total \$8.00	Average "profit" under new Antidumping Agreement = 17.6%
	"Fair" export price = \$2.00 (\$1.70 + \$0.30)

(2a) *Low profits accurately measured by agreement*

Total revenue	=	\$7.00 for 4 units
Total cost	=	\$6.80 (average cost = \$1.70)
Total profit	=	\$0.20

Average profit as a percentage of cost
= 2.9% ($0.20 ÷ $6.80)

4 Sales at $1.75	Profit = 2.9% ($0.05 ÷ $1.70)
Total $7.00	Average "profit" under new Antidumping Agreement = 2.9%
	"Fair" export price = $1.75 ($1.70 + $0.05)

(2b) *Same low profits exaggerated by agreement*

Total revenue = $7.00 for 4 units
Total cost = $6.80 (average cost = $1.70)
Total profit = $0.20
Average profit as a percentage of cost
= 2.9% ($0.20 ÷ $6.80)

1 Sale at $2.50	Profit = 47% ($0.80 ÷ $1.70)
1 Sale at $2.30	Profit = 35% ($0.60 ÷ $1.70)
1 Sale at $1.40	Disregarded as "not in ordinary course of trade"
1 Sale at $0.80	Disregarded as "not in ordinary course of trade"
Total $7.00	Average "profit" under new Antidumping Agreement = 41%
	"Fair" export price = $2.40 ($1.70 + $0.70)

Second, Article 9.3.3 of the Dunkel Text permits the EC to continue its practice of treating antidumping duties as a cost to be deducted from the export price, unless the exporter can "conclusively" prove that it has passed along any increase in price[52] in all "subsequent sales" (which, read literally, would include all sales by unrelated purchasers to subsequent unrelated purchasers).[53]

Probably just as unfortunate, from an exporter's point of view, is the watering down in the Dunkel Text, under U.S. and EC pressure, of many of the positive provisions of earlier drafts. For example, the negligible import share, instead of being 1 percent of market-share, was now defined as "normally" one percent of market-share,[54] thus eliminating the anti-harassment value of the "negligibility" concept.[55]

At the same time, the draft made certain that any post-1991 renegotiation of the Dunkel Text would involve some bargaining by the United States and the EC. In particular, the concept of "cumulation" for measuring injury was not included in the

[52] This is a much higher standard of proof than is applied to anyone else anywhere else in the Code, including for such fundamental findings as the determination of injury.

[53] In the extreme (and absurd) example, this could include sales by retailers to individual consumers. Even if it were possible for an exporter to check each such sale, it could require a degree of resale price maintenance, which could well be illegal under U.S. and EC antitrust law.

[54] Compare New Zealand III, Article 5.7, n. 11, with Dunkel Text, Article 5.8.

[55] The point of an absolute floor at some level of market-share was to protect small shippers from being forced out of the importing country market by the cost of defending a case (a not infrequent occurrence in the United States). The addition of "normally" could require mounting a defense in all cases.

Dunkel Text, undoubtedly as a "bargaining chip" for which the United States and the EC would have to pay in any renegotiation. In addition, the third-country anti-circumvention provisions (i.e. governing assembly in a third country of a product that had been subject to an antidumping order) were replaced by a much less intrusive third-country retroactivity provision (in Article 10.5), which required a new investigation for the imposition of duties on the assembled product from the third country, albeit with provisions for duties retroactive to initiation, rather than the usual duty retroactive only to the preliminary affirmative determination. Finally, the Dunkel Text's treatment of "start-up" costs—a footnote requiring the use of the cost at the end of the start-up period or later, rather than the average cost—while a bit unusual, reflected a position considerably more favourable to exporters than existing U.S. or EC practice.

D. *After the Dunkel Text*

The U.S. fast-track system for trade agreements legislation encourages interest groups that are not 100 percent satisfied to continue complaining until that legislation is finally passed. The release of the Dunkel Text without the package of tariff cuts meant that there was no constituency in the United States expressing full support for the Dunkel Text. Even the intellectual property groups in the United States, which had achieved incredible victories in the Round, were unhappy with the Dunkel Text. Far more important, of course, the EC would not accept the Dunkel Text on agriculture, although in the end that text did provide the basis for the negotiated solution.

A summer and autumn of sparring over the U.S./EC *Oilseeds* case,[56] and adoption in May 1992 by the EC of a reform of its Common Agricultural Policy, finally led to the Blair House agreement in November 1992. President Bush had already lost his re-election bid, and USTR Carla Hills, with Bush's backing, was determined to make one last push to obtain an agreement before the inauguration of Governor Clinton. That led to the submission by USTR of demands in three areas connected with antidumping: anti-circumvention, sunset, and panel reviews,[57] all of which were framed in such extreme form[58] that they were ridiculed when presented to the informal negotiating group of twenty senior representatives in Geneva on 14 December 1992.

USTR Hills took advantage of the arrival in January 1993 of a new EC chief negotiator, Sir Leon Brittan, to negotiate significant market access measures (essentially, promises of reciprocal sharp cuts in textiles and electronics tariffs).

[56] *European Economic Community: Follow-Up on the Panel Report, Payments and Subsidies Paid to Processors and Producers of Oilseeds and Related Animal-Feed Proteins*, GATT BISD 39S/91, 31 March 1992.
[57] *U.S. Requests Reopening of GATT Antidumping Text, Seeks Major Changes*, Inside U.S. Trade, 18 December 1992, at S-1.
[58] The U.S. proposal on sunset, for example, would have required Canada, Australia and the EC to postpone the sunset reviews of existing antidumping orders against U.S. exporters for five years: id.

However, Brittan was not yet in a position to deliver on them, and time ran out when Bill Clinton was inaugurated on 20 January.

The new Administration began with a clear and comprehensive statement in favour of freer trade, in a speech by the President on 26 February 1993, but also with some significant political debts. (For example, the steel workers union had been one of the largest contributors to the Clinton campaign.) It soon became clear from personnel moves at the working levels and from some decisions on specific cases, that the U.S. position on antidumping in the Uruguay Round would remain dominated by those at USTR, Commerce and in the Congress favouring a trade-restrictive approach.

Since no other country wanted to reopen the antidumping text (the EC was concerned that it might lose some of its gains in the areas of profit and duty-as-a-cost, but agreed to support the United States on antidumping as part of the deal on agriculture), the bruising fight in the United States over the North American Free Trade Agreement effectively postponed any discussion of antidumping until November 1993. Commerce had a long list of changes it wanted in the Dunkel Text on antidumping, primarily a result of pressure from some of the less successful U.S. steel companies. USTR was equally sensitive to the pressure from the domestic steel industry, but recognized the impossibility of getting all the desired changes.

Thus, the Administration had to balance the desire for antidumping changes against the need to get changes in other areas of the text, such as the trade-related aspects of intellectual property rights (TRIPS). In the end, a compromise was reached within the Administration, with USTR seeking four major changes on antidumping (deliberately worded to be within the bounds of acceptability) and Commerce seeking some highly unacceptable changes (such as changes in the measurement of profit and of start-up costs), worded in a way which would not be acceptable. Some technical changes to which no one would object were included, so that the United States could claim that it had achieved most of its changes. U.S. Ambassadors Mickey Kantor and Rufus Yerxa made antidumping the focus of their selling efforts, successfully convincing the EC, Japan and the Association of South East Asian Nations (ASEAN) negotiators that getting the antidumping changes was their number one priority.[59]

[59] In an interview on 17 December 1993, Director-General Peter Sutherland stated that "it had been made abundantly clear politically by Mickey Kantor from the very beginning that this was a crunch issue as far as the United States was concerned.": *Ending the Uruguay Round: An Interview with GATT Chief Sutherland*, Inside U.S. Trade, 24 December 1993, at 4. Japan's chief trade negotiator, Ambassador Nobutoshi Akao, also commented in an interview that "everyone knew that antidumping was critically important for the United States, and if all the U.S. proposals were rejected without any favourable consideration, then perhaps the Uruguay Round package would be dead-on-arrival in the U.S. Congress.": *Japan's Chief Negotiator, in Interview, Discusses GATT Round Endgame*, id., at 7. The Journal of Commerce reported on 22 December 1993: "Under pressure from Mr Gephardt and other Congressional leaders, the Clinton Administration made preserving the U.S. antidumping law its top priority in the last days of the negotiations and were able to line up support for that position by Canada and the European Union by backing off in all other areas.": John Maggs, *Gephardt Lends His Support to Uruguay Round Accord*, The Journal of Commerce, 22 December 1993, at 2A. EC and Canadian support on antidumping had been bought by the United States, with concessions on agriculture and subsidies, respectively. Indeed, the real "price" paid by the United States for its antidumping changes was in permitting those countries to infer that they could successfully ignore U.S. demands on audio-visual and financial services, since the United States (by its emphasis on antidumping) had made clear that success on its antidumping changes would be crucial to get U.S. agreement to the overall package.

It is significant that the changes from the Dunkel Text on antidumping to the Final Act on antidumping involved precisely the changes identified weeks in advance as being relatively saleable, with none of the radical changes accepted. Equally significant, no country made an effort to improve the antidumping rules in return for the U.S. changes. Consequently, all of the flaws in the Dunkel Text were carried through to the Final Act. In addition, exporters (including, of course, U.S. exporters) must now take into account a few new problems introduced by the U.S. proposals that were ultimately adopted.

III. Analysis of the Antidumping Agreement

A. *Procedures for Investigations*

The Antidumping Agreement includes new provisions concerning the initiation of an antidumping investigation which are intended to make the process more transparent and fair, and to protect against frivolous claims. Specifically, Article 5.2 of the Antidumping Agreement repeats the requirement from the prior Code that an application to initiate an investigation must include "sufficient evidence" of dumping, injury and the causal link between the two. It adds that "simple assertion, unsubstantiated by relevant evidence, cannot be considered sufficient to meet the requirements". In addition, Article 5.2 lists in detail the information that must be included in the application before an investigation may be initiated.

Article 5.3 of the Antidumping Agreement provides that "the authorities shall examine the accuracy and adequacy of the evidence provided in the application to determine whether there is sufficient evidence to justify the initiation." While this seems only logical, the 1979 Antidumping Code did not contain any such explicit requirement, and the degree of examination required has been an issue in three antidumping panels.[60]

Article 6 of the Antidumping Agreement requires that foreign producers or exporters receiving questionnaires in an antidumping investigation shall be granted at least thirty days for reply. Most antidumping authorities currently allow foreign producers and exporters at least thirty days to respond to questionnaires, although the 1979 Code does not specifically require it.[61] The explicit requirement in the new

[60] Swedish Steel Panel Report, *supra* footnote 43, at ¶¶ 3.13–3.36, 5.4–5.22: Article 5.1 requires administering authorities to take affirmative steps to assure themselves that the petition is supported by a major portion of the domestic industry; *United States: Antidumping Duties on Gray Portland Cement and Cement Clinker from Mexico*, at ¶¶ 3.3–3.3.31, 5.14–5.34, GATT Doc. ADP/82, 7 September 1992 (Mexican Cement Report): Article 5.1 requirement not met by relying on certification that petition is supported by major portion of domestic industry where standard is "all or almost all" of the domestic industry; *United States: Imposition of Antidumping Duties on Imports of Fresh and Chilled Atlantic Salmon from Norway*, GATT Doc. ADP/87, 30 November 1992 (Salmon Report): Article 5.1 requirement met by relying on certification that petition is supported by major portion of the domestic industry even in light of notice of withdrawal of support for petition and stated opposition by a member of the domestic industry .

[61] Although the 1979 Code does not specify thirty days, this time period was recommended as the minimum response time by the Antidumping Committee, in a recommendation adopted by the Contracting Parties in 1983: *Recommendation concerning the Time-Limits given to Respondents to Antidumping Questionnaires*, GATT BISD 30S/30, 15 November 1983.

Agreement should protect against unfairness and abuse by administering authorities. In addition, Article 7.3 of the Antidumping Agreement stipulates that provisional measures may not be applied less than sixty days after the initiation of the investigation.

B. *Standing*

The Antidumping Agreement incorporates a new provision on standing which requires a more active involvement of the administering authorities prior to the initiation of an investigation. Article 5.1 of the 1979 Code provides that an investigation "shall normally be initiated upon written request by or on behalf of the industry affected". However, the 1979 Code did not include an explicit standard for determining whether an application is filed "by or on behalf of the domestic industry".

Article 5.4 of the Antidumping Agreement provides that an antidumping investigation shall not be initiated:

> "... unless the authorities have determined, on the basis of an examination of the degree of support for, or opposition to, the application expressed by domestic producers of the like product, that the application has been made by or on behalf of the domestic industry."

Article 5.4 requires that an application be supported by producers accounting for at least 50 percent of the collective output of all producers expressing an opinion concerning the application. However, in no event may authorities initiate an investigation if the domestic producers supporting the petition account for less than 25 percent of total production of the domestic like product.[62]

C. *Calculation Methodology*

Article 2.6 of the 1979 Code refers to the need to effect a "fair comparison" in calculating dumping margins. Article 2.4 of the Antidumping Agreement requires that:

> "A fair comparison shall be made between the export price and the normal value. This comparison shall be made at the same level of trade, normally at the ex-factory level, and in respect of sales made at as nearly as possible the same time."

In contrast, the second sentence of Article 2.4 of the Dunkel Text read:

> "The two *prices* shall be compared at the same level of trade ... " (emphasis added).

The amendment to the language between the Dunkel Text and the final text shifted the focus from prices to a fair comparison. The change was made in the legal drafting group in 1992 to ensure a fair comparison regardless of whether the comparison is made between normal value and export price or constructed value and export price.

[62] The 25 percent level is used by Mexico and is the lowest level applied by any "major user" of antidumping measures. This percentage figure was drawn from a U.S. proposal tabled on 26 November 1993, just a few weeks before the conclusion of the Uruguay Round negotiations. The United States was concerned that a panel might establish a higher threshold for determining industry support for a petition.

Moreover, in recognition of the potential for abuse by administering authorities, the Antidumping Agreement sets forth in more detail an equitable methodology for calculating dumping margins (i.e. a comparison of individual prices to individual prices, or weighted average prices to weighted-average prices). At the same time, the Antidumping Agreement gives the administering authorities the express ability to address situations of "hidden dumping". That is, the Antidumping Agreement explicitly permits a comparison of individual prices in one market to weighted-average prices in the other if there is "a pattern of export prices which differ significantly among different purchasers, regions or time periods", and if the authorities provide an explanation as to why such differences would not be accounted for in a weighted-average to weighted-average or individual price to individual price analysis.[63] This strictly limits the current practice of several countries, which use a comparison of average normal values to individual export prices, to those situations where high-priced export sales are arranged to "mask" low-priced export sales to the same market and comparable low-priced sales are not made in the "normal value" market.

The Antidumping Agreement also addresses the issue of currency conversions and exchange rates in the calculation of dumping margins, which are areas for potential abuse by administering authorities. The Antidumping Agreement explicitly requires that, in converting currencies, the exchange rate in effect on the date of sale must be used. If a sale of foreign currency on forward markets is shown to be directly linked to the export sale being examined, the Antidumping Agreement requires that the exchange rate in the forward sale shall be used. In addition, the Antidumping Agreement protects against the situation in which exchange rate fluctuations yield or increase dumping margins. Article 2.4.1 of the Antidumping Agreement provides that exchange rate fluctuations are to be ignored and exporters are to be given sixty days in which to adjust their export prices in response to sustained currency movements.

D. *Sampling*

Whereas the 1979 Code is silent on the use of sampling to calculate dumping margins, Article 6.10 of the Antidumping Agreement provides that:

> ". . . where the number of exporters, producers, importers or types of products involved is so large as to make [a producer/exporter-specific or product-specific margin] determination impracticable, the authorities may limit their examination either to a reasonable number of interested parties or products by using samples which are statistically valid on the basis of information available to the authorities at the time of the selection . . . "[64]

Of particular significance in this provision is the requirement that the sampling

[63] See footnote 1, *supra*, Antidumping Agreement, Article 2.4.2; Final Act, at 147–48; U.S. WTO Implementing Legislation, at 1455–56.

[64] See footnote 1, *supra*: Antidumping Agreement, Article 6.10; Final Act, at 154–55; U.S. WTO Implementing Legislation, at 1462–63.

techniques must be "statistically valid".[65] The national laws or regulations of some of the major user-countries of antidumping remedies, such as the United States, currently permit the use of sampling in antidumping investigations. All too often, however, the sampling methodologies employed are not statistically valid and thus yield distorted results.[66]

E. *Sales Below Cost of Production*

The 1979 Code provides little guidance on the calculation of cost of production or when sales below cost should be ignored. The Antidumping Agreement provides considerable detail on the issue of sales below cost. Article 2.2.1 provides that sales below cost of production may be excluded from the calculation of dumping margins if 20 percent or more of total sales in the home market are below the fully allocated cost. Some U.S. steel industry lobbyists claim that the 20 percent threshold will reduce the likelihood of a finding of dumping and permit exporters to engage in significant sales below the cost at home. This concern is misplaced, however, because the Antidumping Agreement expressly provides that, if the weighted-average sales price is below the weighted-average cost, the administering authorities may disregard the below cost sales even if they account for less than 20 percent of total home market sales.[67]

Article 2.2.1.1 of the Antidumping Agreement also requires the administering authorities to adjust costs if a company subject to an antidumping investigation is in a start-up situation. This is a significant improvement over the existing Code to the extent that it protects exporters in a start-up situation from arbitrary findings of below cost sales before they have achieved adequate sales volumes to yield anticipated per unit costs. However, the Agreement fails to define explicitly the start-up period.

A significant flaw in the Antidumping Agreement concerns the definition of profit in the calculation of the cost of production. Article 2.2.2 of the Antidumping Agreement legitimizes the EC's much-criticized practice of using overstated profit figures to obtain highly inflated dumping margins. Specifically, under the Antidumping Agreement, administering authorities can calculate the profit margins based on selected sales, rather than following generally accepted accounting principles.

Another significant flaw in the Antidumping Agreement concerns the provision for treating dumping duties as a cost to be deducted from the export price. Article 9.3.3 made its way into the Antidumping Agreement as a result of aggressive negotiating by the EC. Under current EC practice, an exporter found to be dumping in the EC must raise its prices in the EC by double the amount of the dumping margin

---

[65] Id.

[66] For example, the Salmon Panel found that the United States, in selecting a sample of farms to determine the cost of producing salmon, had not ensured that the sample would be representative, in violation of the 1979 Code: *Salmon Report, supra*, footnote 60, at ¶ 426.

[67] See footnote 1, *supra*: Antidumping Agreement, Article 2.2.1, n. 5; Final Act, at 145–46; U.S. WTO Implementing Legislation, at 1453–54.

in order for the EC authorities to find no dumping. The EC essentially "double-counts" the duty in order to reduce competition. The Antidumping Agreement also requires that the second party in the sales chain (presumably excluding unrelated parties, so as to avoid infractions of competition rules against resale price maintenance) demonstrate that it, too, has raised its prices by the full amount of the dumping margin.

F. De Minimis *Dumping Margins*

The Antidumping Agreement includes a new *de minimis* dumping margin standard of 2 percent, below which antidumping duties shall not be imposed. This provision will require a change in U.S. law to raise the existing 0.5 percent *de minimis* standard to 2 percent. It is frequent practice in the EC and Canada to consider dumping margins of less than 1.5 percent to be *de minimis*. While Australia also does not have a formal *de minimis* rule, margins of 5 percent and 6.25 percent have been considered *de minimis*.

G. *Negligible Import Share*

The Antidumping Agreement includes a negligible import share provision whereby no injury would normally be found if imports from a single country accounted for less than 3 percent of imports of the like country, unless all *de minimis* exporters together equal more than 7 percent of imports.[68]

The inclusion of a negligibility provision recognizes the current practice of the major user countries, i.e. the United States, the EC, Canada and Australia. It has been the practice of these countries to consider imports to be "negligible" when they represent a limited share of the domestic market. For example, the United States and the EC generally dismiss cases on the basis of negligible market-share when imports account for less than 0.5 to 1 percent of the domestic market. Australia has dismissed cases when imports accounted for as much as 10 percent of the Australian market. It is more difficult to discern a clear rule used by Canada, though cases have been dismissed when imports accounted for as much as 4.6 percent of the Canadian market. The United States, with help from other administering authorities, was able to shift the basis for negligibility decisions in the final Agreement from market-share to share of total imports. The use of an import-share standard has quite odd results—the more effectively protected an industry is (as measured by low market-share), the easier it is to find that imports are not negligible. This was a gift from USTR and Commerce to the integrated steel mills[69] without any particular concern for, or even knowledge of, its effect on U.S. exports. For example, U.S. exporters had 0.5 percent of the EC wheat market, which would be negligible under the Dunkel Text's negligibility

[68] See footnote 1, *supra*: Antidumping Agreement, Article 5.8; Final Act, at 152; U.S. WTO Implementing Legislation, at 1460.

[69] Three percent of total finished steel imports is approximately 0.6 percent of the total U.S. market.

standard of 1 percent of market-share. However, U.S. wheat exports account for approximately 35 percent of total imports into the EC—well above the 3 percent negligibility standard in the final Antidumping Agreement. Even more puzzling was the EC willingness to sacrifice its small Member States (Belgium, Denmark, the Netherlands, Luxemburg, Eire, Portugal and Greece), which would have been better off with the Dunkel Text's market-share standard.[70]

H. *Anti-Circumvention Measures*

Although the Dunkel Text included substantial provisions concerning anti-circumvention measures, no final agreement could be reached among the delegations. Therefore, these provisions were dropped from the final text. Instead, the parties agreed to a Ministerial Declaration recognizing the problem of circumvention and referring the matter to the Committee for Antidumping Practices for resolution.[71] Although some U.S. officials have claimed that this permits the United States to continue to apply anti-circumvention measures, neither the Agreement nor the Declaration says this. Article 18.1 permits the imposition of antidumping duties only in accordance with the provisions of the Agreement, and there is no provision permitting anti-circumvention measures or the imposition of antidumping duties on products which have not been fully investigated and found to be dumped and causing injury.

I. *Best Information Available*

Article 6.8 of the Antidumping Agreement mirrors Article 6.8 of the 1979 Code and addresses the use of "best information available". Article 6.8 provides that:

> ". . . in cases in which an interested party refuses access to, or otherwise does not provide, necessary information within a reasonable period or significantly impedes the investigation, preliminary and final determinations, affirmative or negative, may be made on the basis of the facts available."

Unlike the 1979 Code, the Antidumping Agreement includes an Annex dedicated exclusively to the application of best information available. The circumstances under which the use of best information available is permitted are significantly

[70] For example, in the 1992–1993 U.S. antidumping investigations of flat-rolled steel products, the United States found that Belgian imports of cold-rolled steel products were negligible and thus not a cause of injury to the U.S. industry: *Certain Flat-Rolled Carbon Steel Products from Argentina, Australia, Austria, Belgium, Brazil, Canada, Finland, France, Germany, Italy, Japan, Korea, Mexico, the Netherlands, New Zealand, Poland, Romania, Spain, Sweden and the United Kingdom*, USITC Publication 2664, at 41, 111, Inv. Nos. 701–TA–319–332, 334, 336–342, 344, and 347–353 and 731–TA–573–579, 581–592, 594–597, 599–609, and 612–619 (Final) August 1993. Belgian imports of cold-rolled steel products accounted for 0.4 percent of the U.S. market in 1990 and 0.5 percent in 1991: id., at 111. In those same years, Belgian imports accounted for 5.2 percent and 6.9 percent of total imports: id., at I–137. Under the Dunkel Text's 1 percent market-share standard, Belgian imports of cold-rolled steel would be considered negligible. Under the final Agreement's 3 percent import-share standard, however, Belgian imports would not have been considered negligible and could have been found to cause injury.

[71] See Decision on Anti-Circumvention, Final Act, at 401; U.S. WTO Implementing Legislation, at 1694; *supra*, footnote 1.

circumscribed, and the information that administering authorities may rely on in making preliminary and final determinations is more tightly controlled than under the 1979 Code.

Specifically, Annex II of the Antidumping Agreement provides that:

— all information that is verifiable, appropriately submitted and supplied in a timely fashion should be taken into account by the authorities when making determinations;[72]
— the authorities may not disregard information submitted by interested parties, even though that information may not be ideal in all respects, provided that the interested party has acted to the best of its ability;[73]
— the authorities must notify a party if its information is not going to be accepted and must allow that party a reasonable opportunity to provide further explanation;[74] and
— if the authorities rely on information from a source other than the submitting party, they "should, where practicable, check the information from other independent sources at their disposal".[75]

J. *Sunset Provision*

The 1979 Code does not contain any specific limit on the duration of an antidumping duty order. Rather, it states that "an antidumping duty shall remain in force only as long as, and to the extent necessary to counteract dumping which is causing injury."[76] The historic major user-countries (Australia, Canada, the EC), with the exception of the United States, have a sunset provision in their domestic laws or regulations.

The Antidumping Agreement provides for the termination of antidumping orders after five years unless, in a review initiated prior to the five-year deadline, the administering authorities determine that the termination of the order would be likely to lead to the continuation or recurrence of dumping and injury.[77] The burden lies with the administering authorites—not the exporters—to determine whether it is necessary for the duty to remain in place beyond five years in order to prevent the continuation or recurrence of dumping and injury.

K. *Dispute Settlement*

The WTO Agreement contains an integrated dispute settlement mechanism

[72] See footnote 1, *supra*: Antidumping Agreement, Annex II, ¶ 3; Final Act, at 168; U.S. WTO Implementing Legislation, at 1476.

[73] See footnote 1, *supra*: id. at Annex II, ¶ 5; Final Act, at 168; U.S. WTO Implementing Legislation, at 1476.

[74] See footnote 1, *supra*: id., at Annex II, ¶ 6; Final Act, at 168; U.S. WTO Implementing legislation, at 1476.

[75] See footnote 1, *supra*: id., at Annex II, ¶ 7; Final Act, at 168–69; U.S. WTO Implementing Legislation, at 1476–77.

[76] 1979 Antidumping Code, Article 9, ¶ 1.

[77] See footnote 1, *supra*: Antidumping Agreement, Article 11.3; Final Act at 160–61; U.S. WTO Implementing Legislation at 1468–69.

which applies to all aspects of the WTO, including the Antidumping Agreement. It provides a timetable for various submissions so that panel reviews would be completed within nine months. It also sets out a procedure so that a losing party to a dispute would not be able to block a panel decision, as can be done under the 1979 Code. Finally, it provides a procedure to appeal a panel decision to an appellate tribunal on issues of law.

One of the changes to the final antidumping text insisted on by the United States concerned the standard of review to be applied in antidumping disputes. Article 17.6 of the Antidumping Agreement provides:

> "(i) in its assessment of the facts of the matter, the panel shall determine whether the authorities' establishment of the facts was proper and whether their evaluation of those facts was unbiased and objective. If the establishment of the facts was proper and the evaluation was unbiased and objective, even though the panel might have reached a different conclusion, the evaluation shall not be overturned;
>
> (ii) the panel shall interpret the relevant provisions of the Agreement in accordance with customary rules of interpretation of public international law. Where the panel finds that a relevant provision of the Agreement admits of more than one permissible interpretation, the panel shall find the authorities' measure to be in conformity with the Agreement if it rests upon one of those permissible interpretations."

The Antidumping Agreement's standard of review for questions of law (as opposed to questions of fact) requires an interpretation in accordance with the Vienna Convention on the Law of Treaties.[78] Commerce and USTR officials claim that the language of the Agreement recognizes that there may be multiple "permissible" interpretations of the language. This claim would be assessed in light of the rules of the Convention. Article 31 of the Vienna Convention provides that a treaty is to be interpreted in accordance with the ordinary meaning of the terms of the treaty, in context and in terms of the treaty's object and purpose.

Subsequent rules in the Convention address situations where the language is ambiguous or where the official texts in different languages give rise to different meanings. Article 31, paragraph 3 states that:

> ". . . there shall be taken into account together with the context . . . (b) any subsequent practice in the application of the treaty which *establishes the agreement of the parties regarding its interpretation*" (emphasis added).

Article 32 provides for recourse to the drafting history if the meaning of the terms is ambiguous or obscure, rather than permitting individual signatories to adopt their own interpretations of such ambiguous or obscure language. Article 33 provides that if the different official languages of the text disclose different meanings:

> ". . . *the meaning* which best reconciles the texts, having regard to the object and purpose of the treaty, *shall be adopted*" (emphasis added).

Thus, a position that envisions multiple "permissible" interpretations[79] may conflict with the normal standards of treaty interpretation.

[78] Vienna Convention on the Law of Treaties, 23 May 1969, 8 I.L.M. 679 (Vienna Convention).

[79] It should be noted that, although the United States is not a signatory to the Vienna Convention, it acknowledges the Convention as authoritative. See S. Exec. Doc. L., 92d Cong., 1st Sess. (1971): "although not yet in force, the Convention is already generally recognized as the authoritative guide to current treaty law and practice".

At one point in 1993, USTR proposed that a single (deferential) standard of review be applied by WTO panels reviewing all administrative decisions (apparently after being told in Geneva that a special standard just for antidumping would not be acceptable).[80] This proposal was greeted with fury by U.S. intellectual property interests, which did not wish to give to other countries' patent and copyright authorities the deference which USTR sought for Commerce and International Trade Commission antidumping decisions. The proposal was abandoned, and USTR was able to convince Director-General Sutherland and the negotiating parties that an explicit standard should be added for antidumping.[81]

[80] See *U.S. Moves to Limit Dispute Settlement Panels' Scope of Review*, Inside U.S. Trade, 5 November 1993, at 1.

[81] And possibly, to a vaguely defined degree, countervailing duties. See Declaration on Dispute Settlement Pursuant to the Agreement on Implementation of Article VI of the General Agreement on Tariffs and Trade 194 or Part V of the Agreement on Subsidies and Countervailing Measures, Final Act, at 403, U.S. WTO Implementing Legislation, at 1696, *supra*, footnote 1.

How the GATT Became Protectionist

An Analysis of the Uruguay Round Draft Final Antidumping Code

Gary N. Horlick*

"Just before Christmas, if all goes well, bleary-eyed officials will scramble out of a marathon negotiating session to claim triumphant success in the world's biggest ever round of trade talks—the Uruguay Round . . . Unfortunately, however, the big industrial countries that dominate the trading system will almost certainly have left themselves a wide protectionist loophole—which may make it even easier for high-cost producers to shut out more efficient foreign rivals."

International Herald Tribune, 15 June 1993.

That loophole of course, is the trade-restrictive GATT Antidumping Code devised by the United States, the European Communities and the GATT in late December 1991. The creation of a more restrictive dumping code was not some inadvertent occurrence or mistake. The two great powers were both well aware of the protectionist nature of the antidumping changes they were seeking. However, neither was able to withstand the pressure of protectionist lobbies at home. Indeed, both the United States and the EC were quite aware that they were sacrificing their own exporters, who are subject to other countries' antidumping laws, in order to protect certain industries.[1]

Introduction

Article VI of the General Agreement on Tariffs and Trade (GATT) contains the provisions regulating the use of antidumping laws.[2] In 1966–1967, the contracting

* O'Melveny & Myers, Washington, D.C., U.S.A.

Mr Horlick served as Deputy Assistant Secretary of Commerce for Import Administration and International Trade Counsel, U.S. Senate Finance Committee.

[1] Perhaps the strangest aspect of the negotiations was the "1989 Non-Aggression Pact" between the United States and the EC in the antidumping negotiations, with each of the two trading blocs committing itself to support the other's positions—even if it means a complete reversal of prior positions taken by one of the blocs against the other's practices. Thus for example, the United States in the antidumping negotiations has supported the EC in: (i) permitting the EC to extend antidumping orders to products assembled in third countries—completely undercutting the position taken by U.S. Trade Representative Carla Hills against that practice (the California *Ricoh copier* case); (ii) supporting the EC position that antidumping duties should be counted as a cost in determining whether dumping is continuing (which creates a vicious circle in which it is necessary for exporters to the EC to raise their prices by double the amount of dumping—an EC rule against which the United States formally complained in 1986); (iii) supporting the EC rule that "normal" profit levels be calculated by only looking at the profits on sales above average fully allocated cost (no business in the United States is allowed to report its profits that way, and the United States in its antidumping investigations does not measure the profit level that way); (iv) most damaging, ensuring that judicial review requirements in the new Code will not change current European Court of Justice practice, which is to give virtually *carte blanche* authority to the antidumping administrators; and (v) joining with the EC to attempt to limit GATT review of antidumping decisions (a perfect example of the U.S. and EC's attempt to insulate their own antidumping decisions from review, even if it means that their exporters can get no effective review of other countries' dumping decisions).

[2] General Agreement on Tariffs and Trade, GATT, B.I.S.D. Vol. I, 13 (1947).

parties negotiated the first Antidumping Code (AD Code) which provided more specific guidelines by which antidumping duties could be imposed under Article VI.[3] The AD Code was renegotiated during the Tokyo Round of multilateral negotiations which ended in 1979.[4] The 1979 Code is currently in force and is the subject of the revisions being proposed during the Uruguay Round of multilateral trade negotiations.

The use of antidumping laws to restrict competition from imports has increased significantly. During the 1980s, at least 1,456 new antidumping investigations were initiated by the signatories of the AD Code.[5] Of that number, 421 cases were initiated by Australia, 395 by the United States, 294 by Canada, and 271 by the European Communities.[6] Over 30 countries now have antidumping laws (counting the EC as one country), and 12 more are reportedly preparing them. To cite just one example, Argentina has promised "tough" antidumping legislation as part of its tariff reduction package.[7]

Exporters from around the globe have taken a strong interest in the Uruguay Round reform of the AD Code precisely because of their dependence on world markets and their concern over the growing impact of antidumping decisions on their competitiveness world-wide. Exporting companies realize that the antidumping rules that emerge from the Uruguay Round will regulate prices into the next century.

U.S. exporters, for example, have become more vocal proponents of dumping law reform as they have become more frequent targets of foreign antidumping investigations. A 1987 U.S. Trade Representative study indicates that at least 457 U.S. companies—many of them large ones—had been subject to foreign antidumping cases.[8] During the period 1980–1989, there were at least 144 antidumping cases initiated in U.S. export markets against U.S. companies' exports—more than the number brought in those countries against exporters from any other single country.[9] Of the 59 cases initiated by Mexico since the implementation of its dumping law in 1987, nearly 50 per cent have been against U.S. exporters.[10]

The Draft Final Act Embodying the Results of the Uruguay Round of Multilateral Trade Negotiations[11] contains the first attempt to reform antidumping practices since the signing of the 1979 AD Code.[12] The Dunkel Text has met with

[3] Agreement on Implementation of Article VI of the General Agreement on Tariffs and Trade, GATT, B.I.S.D. 15th Supp., 24 (1968).

[4] Agreement on Implementation of Article VI of the General Agreement on Tariffs and Trade, GATT, B.I.S.D. 26th Supp., 171 (1980).

[5] U.S. General Accounting Office, *Use of the GATT Antidumping Code*, NSIAD-90-238FS, at 4 (1990) (hereinafter *GAO Study*). This number is understated because several countries (including Brazil, India and the EC) did not report cases initiated against nonsignatory countries. Id. at note (a).

[6] Id.

[7] *Argentina to Extend Free Trade Policy Through Tariff Reforms*, Financial Times, 5 March 1991, Section I at 4.

[8] Office of the U.S. Trade Representative, *Antidumping Duty Cases Against U.S. Companies*, 7 August 1987.

[9] *GAO Study*, at 19.

[10] Information gathered through conversations with Mexican government officials.

[11] MTN.TNC/W/FA, 20 December 1991.

[12] Id. at Section F.

mixed reactions from all perspectives. The following sections of this article attempt to highlight the strengths and weaknesses of the antidumping provisions of the Dunkel Text.

I. Protectionist Features of the Dunkel Text Antidumping Code

The Dunkel Text on dumping is a great disappointment to exporters in the United States, and elsewhere. It incorporates far too few of the proposals that would have brought greater fairness and common sense to the application of dumping rules around the world. However, the Text does improve on the 1979 Code by providing greater specificity to some existing rules. The Text makes a few positive steps toward protecting exporters from unfair practices, but it also adds more openly protectionist provisions that make it easier for countries to use AD laws as barriers to trade.

Some U.S. critics have contended that, if adopted, the Dunkel Text would require major changes to the U.S. antidumping law. This view is false. The Dunkel Text provides more detail and clarity to the rules and principles set forth in the current Code, but introduces very few new concepts. Even the U.S. Administration has noted that the new text would require fairly limited changes to U.S. law. Anticircumvention is the major new concept in the Dunkel Text—a concept that the U.S. government fought hard to have included in the new Code.

On several key issues, the Dunkel Text is seriously flawed. It fails to include the safeguards against abuse which would protect exporters from the misuse of antidumping duty rules in their export markets.

A. *Profit*

The Dunkel Text's definition of profit[13] in the calculation of cost of production adopts the EC's current practice, which apparently allows the EC to "pick and choose" whatever profit figure it wants. The Dunkel Text gives the EC (as well as those developing countries which follow the EC lead on antidumping) the protection it needs to continue a practice that can result in highly inflated dumping margins. For example, the Dunkel Text would require antidumping authorities to calculate the profit margin based only on those individual sales above the average fully allocated cost. If a U.S. company used this method in its reporting to the Securities and Exchange Commission, it would be accused of fraud. The new Code should have required that profit be calculated in a manner consistent with current U.S. practice—i.e. by comparing the costs and revenues of all sales—to protect exporters from arbitrary profit calculations with no basis in normal business practices.[14] It is noteworthy that Mexico has begun using the EC approach.

[13] Dunkel Text, Section F, Article 2.2.2.

[14] With respect to the U.S. statutory requirement of applying a minimum 8 per cent profit margin, Professor John Jackson has stated, "... in times of slack demand, imposing an 8 per cent profit requirement for the computation of price can be quite unrealistic, when profit margins may only be 1 or 2 per cent. Indeed, this provision of the U.S. statute is very likely inconsistent with U.S. international obligations . . ." John H. Jackson, *The World Trading System*, 235 (1989).

B. *Start-up Costs*[15]

Because production volume is typically low for a start-up operation, the per unit costs will appear to be high until normal production levels can be achieved. That the Dunkel Text fails to include a minimum period for the allocation of costs is a cause of great concern and disappointment. By choosing to calculate unit costs for a new product or operation in the first year, national authorities can force imports to price at levels far above domestic producers in identical circumstances.

U.S. critics contend that the Dunkel Text would require the United States to change its practice with respect to the determination of whether prices are sufficiently high to recover costs over a reasonable period of time when the company subject to the dumping investigation is in a start-up situation. As one opposition group puts it, "the Department would have to ignore high costs during the period of investigation if lower costs were later achieved."[16]

The current U.S. antidumping statute provides that sales will be considered above cost if they are at prices which are sufficient to recover all costs "within a reasonable period of time."[17] The Dunkel Text requires the authorities to adjust costs if a company subject to investigation is in a start-up situation.[18] A change to U.S. law would not be required, however, since a "reasonable period of time" is not defined in the statute. If adopted, Commerce would have to change some of its protectionist practices with respect to start-up operations, but a 1987 Court of International Trade decision has already ruled that current Commerce practice on start-up operations violates explicit Congressional guidance to recognize the normal business practice of measuring cost recovery over a product's life cycle.[19]

C. *Duty as a Cost*

Another flaw in the Dunkel Text concerns the concept of duty as a cost.[20] Under current EC practice, an exporter found to be dumping in the EC must raise its prices by double the amount of the dumping margin in order to be found not to be dumping. The EC essentially "double-counts" the duty in order to reduce competition. In 1986, then-General Counsel of U.S. Trade Representative Alan Holmer sent a letter to Hans Beseler, the head administrator of the EC's antidumping law, objecting to this EC practice.[21]

The Dunkel Text contains a modified version of this "tilted" EC practice and goes one step further to require that the next parties in the sales chain—including

[15] Dunkel Text, Section F, Article 2.2.1.1.

[16] Letter from Labor Industry Coalition for International Trade (LICIT) to Senator Lloyd Bentsen of 8 January 1992, reprinted in Inside U.S. Trade, 10 January 1992, S-12, 13 (hereinafter *LICIT Letter*).

[17] 19 U.S.C. § 1677b(b) (2) (1988).

[18] Dunkel Text, Section F, Article 2.2.1.1.

[19] See *Toho Titanium v. United States*, 670 F. Supp. 1019 (Ct. Int'l Trade 1987).

[20] Dunkel Text, Section F, Article 9.3.3.

[21] See Letter from Alan F. Holmer, General Counsel, Office of the U.S. Trade Representative, to Hans Beseler, Director, Trade Policy Instruments, Directorate General for External Relations, Commission of the European Communities, of 31 March 1986.

unrelated retailers—demonstrate that they, too, have raised their prices by the full amount of the dumping margin. The way the provision would work is as follows: suppose Philip Morris is selling Kraft cheese to Safeway in the United Kingdom at 90 pence per kilo; it charges 100 pence per kilo in the U.S. market and, therefore, is found to be dumping by 10 pence. If Philip Morris raises its price to 100 pence in the United Kingdom, it is still dumping by 10 pence under the EC rule (and, thus, under the rule proposed in the Dunkel Text) unless Safeway in the United Kingdom raises its price of Kraft cheese to its customers by 10 pence. If Safeway runs a "loss leader" using Kraft cheese, Philip Morris would still be found to be dumping. Under the Dunkel Text, it is irrelevant that Philip Morris has no control over the prices charged by Safeway. In fact, Philip Morris would be required to provide proof of the price charged for every single individual retail sale of its product or be assessed dumping duties.

This provision, which codifies the EC's inappropriate use of dumping duties as a penalty, is not used by the United States. The provision as stated in the Dunkel Text is an overt retail price maintenance scheme which defies business logic.

D. *Short Supply*

A major deficiency in the Dunkel Text is the absence of a common-sense provision to remedy situations where domestic supply is non-existent or insufficient to satisfy demand for merchandise subject to antidumping duties. The result is a gain for the foreign producer being forced to charge a higher price to industrial users while domestic suppliers cannot benefit by expanding production. The higher costs resulting from antidumping duties on products that cannot be obtained from domestic sources have a serious adverse effect on the ability of industrial users to compete in world markets and may ultimately translate into a loss of jobs.

In one recent example, the United States imposed antidumping duties on certain flat panel display imports, even though the U.S. producer does not have sufficient production capacity to meet demand.[22] There have been public reports that Apple and Compaq were forced to move their lap-top computer operations off-shore because of the prohibitively high antidumping duties imposed on flat panel display imports of which there is insufficient supply in the United States. If there had been a time- and quantity-limited short supply provision requirement in the Code, U.S. computer manufacturers would have been able to import the needed components until there was sufficient U.S. production capacity to meet the demand. Instead, the result has been a loss of U.S. manufacturing jobs.

The EC and Canada have provisions in their laws that can be used to solve this problem (although they are rarely so used).[23] The only similar provision in U.S. law was the short supply provision for the steel voluntary restraint arrangements, which

[22] High Information Content Flat Panel Displays and Display Glass Therefor from Japan, 56 Fed. Reg. 43,741 (Dep't Comm. 1991).

[23] See Special Import Measures Act, S.C. 1984, c. 25, subsection 45 (1) (Canada); and Articles 11.1, 12.1 and 13.3, Council Regulation 2423/88, OJ (1988) L209/1 (EC).

permitted limited exemptions from import protection, but only when adequate domestic supply is not available.[24] The failure of the Dunkel Text to include a short-supply provision makes clear that the petitioner-focused nature of the GATT AD Code can be carried to absurd lengths.

E. *Premium Pricing*

Manufacturers have been charged with dumping and causing injury under several antidumping laws when their prices were substantially higher than the local industry's prices (e.g. for consumer goods). The new Code should require the authorities, in making their injury determination, to consider whether an exporter's pricing behaviour is a response to the prices of other competitioners—either domestic or foreign. One U.S. producer, for example, prices above local producers, but nevertheless has been subjected to antidumping actions in Israel, Korea and Taiwan, and has recently faced threats in Thailand and Nigeria. The Dunkel Text merely provides that such price competition be one of several "factors which may be relevant".[25]

F. *Sunset Provision*[26]

The Dunkel Text rejects the notion of an automatic termination clause, and instead adopts the current EC, Australian and Canadian procedure for reviewing antidumping orders after five years. Although U.S. law does not have a "sunset" provision, U.S. manufacturers of such important products as paper, chemicals, textiles, steel and medical equipment have benefitted from the sunset provisions under EC, Australian and Canadian antidumping laws.[27]

Contrary to statements made by some critics, the burden falls squarely on the authorities—not on petitioners or respondents—to determine whether the duty should remain in place beyond five years.[28] As one group opposed to the new sunset provision conceded, "the dumping text does, however, make clear that one year without dumping does not necessarily preclude a finding that the order should continue in effect."[29]

A potentially serious loophole in the sunset provision is the absence of an absolute

[24] 19 C.F.R. § 357 (1991).

[25] Dunkel Text, Section F, Article 3.4.

[26] Dunkel Text, Section F, Article 11.3.

[27] One of the first companies to be relieved of antidumping duties under Australia's new sunset provision was Becton Dickinson & Co., a U.S. manufacturer of medical products. In the past five years, the EC, under its sunset provision, terminated antidumping duties on U.S. exports of dense sodium carbonate, polyester yarn, acrylic fibres, lithium hydroxide, bisphenol, cellulose ester resins, paraxylene, orthoxylene, kraftliner paper, polyester fabrics, trichloroethylene, decabromodiphenylether and perchlorethylene. During the same period, Canada terminated antidumping duty orders against U.S. exports of steel pipe, artificial graphite electrodes, bottoming materials, charcoal briquets, cutting and creasing steel rules, saw blades, nickel and nickel alloy pipe, organic peroxide, photo albums and self-adhesive leaves, plate coils, porcelain insulators, soda ash, stainless steel pipe, surgical gloves, chain saws, yellow onions and vehicle washing equipment.

[28] Dunkel Text, Section F, Article 11.3.

[29] *LICIT Letter*, *op. cit.*, *supra*, footnote 16, at S-14.

deadline for the completion of sunset reviews. Without such a deadline, the sunset provision could prove ineffective, and antidumping orders could remain in place long after dumping and injury have ceased.

G. *Anticircumvention*

Under the anticircumvention provision in the Dunkel Text, authorities may apply duties to parts and components exported from a country subject to the antidumping duty order for assembly without conducting a new investigation to determine whether such parts and components are dumped or causing injury.[30] The Dunkel Text also permits the retroactive application of duties to parts and components exported for assembly in a third country, but only after a full investigation of dumping and injury.[31] "Country hopping"—i.e. the shifting of sources by a multinational company from one country to another after an antidumping investigation is initiated—is subject to similar rules.[32] The addition of anticircumvention provisions, including country hopping (which is not in current U.S. law), is a significant change to the current Code.

A 1989 GATT panel ruling against the EC (which the EC accepted) casts considerable doubt as to whether the extension of duties to parts imported for assembly in the importing country is consistent with the GATT or the current AD Code.[33] In that case, the EC did not even argue the legality under Article VI of the GATT of imposing duties on parts used in assembly in the EC without an investigation.

H. *Refunds of Duty Deposits*

Article 9.3.1 of the Dunkel Text provides that duties collected in excess of the actual amount of dumping should normally be refunded within 90 days.[34] However, the text does not set 90 days as a firm deadline. The United States, Canada and Germany are apparently the only countries that currently pay interest on excessive duty payments, but the new text does not make the payment of interest a requirement. There are two dangers with this provision. First, the lack of a stated deadline may result in continued delays by foreign authorities in refunding excessive duty payments; and second, the countries that currently pay interest on overpayments may cease doing so.

II. INDUSTRIAL USERS

Under Article 6.12 of the Dunkel Text, industrial users (and consumer groups, where the imported product is sold to the final consumer) are not only limited to

[30] Dunkel Text, Section F, Article 12.1.
[31] Dunkel Text, Section F, Article 10.4.
[32] Dunkel Text, Section F, Article 10.5.
[33] EEC "Screwdriver" Regulation, GATT, MIS20.DOC (26 March 1990).
[34] Dunkel Text, Section F, Article 9.3.1.

expressing an opinion on a case (i.e. authorities need not take users' views into account), but are limited to expressing it only on three issues: dumping, injury and causality.[35] This raises the interesting possibility that the EC and Canada could prohibit industrial users or consumers from commenting on the public interest proceedings in EC or Canadian antidumping investigations.

III. Criticism of the Dunkel Text—It's Not Protectionist Enough

Numerous criticisms have been made of the Dunkel Text by U.S. industries which have benefitted from existing antidumping laws.

A. *Dispute Resolution*

A fast, effective and binding dispute settlement provision, such as that contained in the Dunkel Text,[36] is essential, particularly in the areas of services, subsidies, antidumping and intellectual property rights. For example, software companies need a mechanism that will permit a challenge, not only to an administrative decision of a national copyright office not to issue a copyright for software, but also to the use of prosecutorial discretion by the local authorities to seek only meaningless small fines for illegal copying. Without the ability to challenge both the form and the substance of such administrative decisions, the Trips (Trade-Related Aspects of Intellectual Property Protection) agreement would be ineffective.

A fast, effective and binding dispute settlement provision in the AD Code is equally important to exporters. Some foreign courts grant substantially more deference to administrative agency decisions than do other countries. While U.S. decisions are frequently overturned, Canadian and EC antidumping decisions, for example, are rarely overturned by reviewing courts. The result is that foreign exporters to the United States have access to a fairly thorough judicial review process, while U.S. exporters have virtually no recourse against antidumping decisions abroad (except under Chapter 19 of the U.S.–Canada Free Trade Agreement). The new dispute settlement provision in the Dunkel Text alleviates this inequity by providing U.S. exporters with the same degree of review in the Gatt as foreign exports to the United States will receive.

According to statements made by some U.S. industry critics, the feared scenario is as follows:

> "A U.S. industry is found to be injured by subsidized imports of a product, and a countervailing duty is imposed. The decision is appealed to the Court of International Trade and then to the Federal Circuit, and both courts hold that [Commerce and the ITC] acted in accordance with U.S. law. A Gatt panel reviews the facts and . . . finds that the duty is inconsistent with the Gatt. The subsidizing country is authorized to retaliate against the U.S. unless and until the United States revokes the countervailing duty."[37]

---

[35] Dunkel Text, Section F, Article 6.12.
[36] Dunkel Text, Section F, Article 18.
[37] *Licit Letter, op. cit., supra* footnote 16, at S-12.

This is an interesting scenario because it is precisely what happened to U.S. exporters of corn to Canada. In 1987, Canada found that U.S. exports of corn were subsidized and caused injury to the Canadian corn industry. A countervailing duty was therefore imposed. The U.S. farmers appealed the decision to the Canadian Federal Court of Appeals and lost. The U.S. corn farmers then appealed the lower court's decision to the Supreme Court of Canada. Again, the U.S. farmers lost. The U.S. Trade Representative appealed the Canadian decision in the GATT. The GATT issued its decision in favour of U.S. corn farmers.[38] Exporters need that kind of dispute resolution.

B. *Calculation Methodology*

Some critics of the Dunkel Text point to the provisions on methodology for calculating dumping margins[39] as an example of the "weakening" of the trade laws.[40] The current AD Code requires a "fair comparison", as does the Dunkel Text. Some critics object to the provision requiring a comparison of individual transactions in the importing country to individual transactions in the home country or, alternatively, a comparison of weighted average prices to weighted average prices (the method used by Mexico).

Unlike the current Code (which requires a "fair comparison"), the Dunkel Text explicitly permits a comparison of individual prices to weighted average prices.[41] The Dunkel Text provides an equitable methodology for calculating dumping margins, while at the same time giving the authorities the express ability to address situations of "hidden dumping".

C. *Sales Below Cost*

The sales-below-cost provision in the Dunkel Text[42] has been the target of criticism by U.S. groups claiming that the text is less favourable to petitioners than current U.S. law, even though the text includes almost verbatim the U.S. statute on sales below cost.[43] By contrast, the existing Code nowhere expressly permits the current U.S. (and EC) practice of requiring sales to be above fully allocated cost. Critics object to the provision that sales below cost of production may be excluded from dumping margin calculations only if 20 per cent or more of total sales in the home market are below the fully allocated cost. Some claim that the 20 per cent threshold will "reduce the likelihood of a finding of dumping" and permit exporters to engage in significant sales below cost at home.[44] This concern is misplaced because

[38] See *Canadian Countervailing Duties on Grain Corn from the United States*, GATT, GC/R2 (January 1992).
[39] Dunkel Text, Section F, Article 2.4.
[40] See, e.g.*LICIT Letter, op. cit., supra* footnote 16, at S-13.
[41] Dunkel Text, Section F, Article 2.4.2.
[42] Dunkel Text, Section F, Article 2.2.1.
[43] Compare id. with 19 U.S.C. § 1677b (b) (1988).
[44] *LICIT Letter, op. cit., supra* footnote 16, at S-13.

the Dunkel Text expressly provides that, if total cost exceeds total revenue (a logical measure of cost recovery), the authorities can disregard the below cost sales even if below cost sales account for less than 20 per cent of total home market sales. In fact, the adoption of this provision as drafted would not require any change in the U.S. antidumping law.[45]

D. *Cumulation*

The Dunkel Text, like the current Code, has no explicit provision on cumulation. The United States, Mexico, the EC, Canada, Australia and other countries have applied cumulation rules despite the absence of any Code provision.

Some have criticized the Dunkel Text's failure to include an explicit provision authorizing cumulation of dumped imports from multiple countries when making an injury determination. In fact, one U.S. group has used an erroneous hypothetical example to demonstrate what it perceives as one of the major flaws in the Dunkel Text:

> "A GATT panel finds that cumulation of injury caused by dumped imports from more than one country is not authorized by the Antidumping Code. Twenty countries, all of them dumping, each take 2 per cent of the U.S. market for a textile product. Although dumped imports hold 40 per cent of the U.S. market, no single country is a cause of injury and no dumping case is possible."[46]

The conclusion that no single country with a 2 per cent market share could be found to cause injury is inaccurate. Nothing in the text would preclude a country from finding injury caused by imports from one country with 2 per cent of the market.

E. De Minimis *Market Share*

The inclusion of a *de minimis* market share provision[47] will not result in a great departure from current practice. It has been normal practice in the United States, the EC, Canada and Australia to consider imports to be "negligible" when they represent a limited share of the domestic market.

The United States and the EC generally dismiss cases on the basis of *de minimis* market share when imports account for less than 1 per cent of the domestic market. The Australian antidumping authorities have dismissed cases when imports accounted for as much as 10 per cent of the Australian market, stating that "the Authority has difficulty in accepting that import penetration of such a magnitude was sufficient to cause material injury." It is more difficult to discern a clear rule used by Canada, although cases have been dismissed when imports accounted for as much as 4.6 per cent of the Canadian market.

---

[45] Similarly, some critics claim that the Dunkel Text requires use of the exporting country's accounting standards to calculate cost, even if those standards are unreasonable. In fact, Article 2.2.1.1 of the Dunkel Text expressly requires that an exporters' records "reasonably reflect" its costs.

[46] *LICIT Letter, op. cit., supra* footnote 16, at S-13.

[47] Dunkel Text, Section F, Article 5.8.

F. De Minimis *Dumping Margins*

The Dunkel Text includes a new *de minimis* dumping margin standard[48] of 2 per cent below which antidumping duties shall not be imposed. This will require a change in U.S. practice to raise the existing 0.5 per cent *de minimis* standard to 2 per cent. In practical terms, however, this will have no impact on the vast majority of U.S. cases. Moreover, it is established practice in the EC and Canada to consider dumping margins of less than 1.5 per cent to be *de minimis*. While Australia does not have a formal *de minimis* margin rule, in one case the Australian authorities referred to 5 per cent margins as "quite insignificant". In another case, they referred to a 6.25 per cent margin as "so small". Duties were not imposed in either case.

G. *Standing*

Contrary to claims made by certain critics, the Dunkel Text on standing[49] does not represent any departure from the existing Code. Under current rules, petitioners are required to demonstrate, and the authorities are required to determine, prior to initiation, whether "a major proportion" of the domestic industry supports the case. A 1990 GATT panel decision explicitly affirmed this requirement.[50] In the United States, before filing a case, U.S. petitioners currently have to obtain industry support, because the Commerce Department regulations require a statement attesting to the fact that the case is filed "on behalf of" the U.S. industry.[51] Finally, fears of U.S. authorities that a required determination of standing will increase the administrative burden are misplaced. As a matter of course, the ITC currently collects information regarding whether individual producers support the case. Thus, the information to make such a determination is readily available for the Commerce Department to make this determination.

It is important to point out that the Dunkel Text does not require that 50 per cent of the domestic industry support the petition. It is highly unlikely that a GATT panel would ever interpret the term "a major proportion" to require 50 per cent support from the national industry.

H. *Labour Unions*

The Dunkel Text is silent on the issue of whether labour unions have standing to bring a case, but it expressly allows countries to permit anyone to be an interested party.[52] Although the current Code is also silent on labour unions, it is clear from the drafting history that it was contemplated that labour unions would indeed have standing to bring cases.[53]

---

[48] Id.

[49] Dunkel Text, Section F, Article 5.2.

[50] *United States—Antidumping Duties on Imports of Stainless Steel Pipes and Tubes From Sweden*, GATT, ADP/47 (August 1990).

[51] 19 C.F.R. § 353.12 (1991).

[52] Dunkel Text, Section F, Article 6.11.

[53] See *Priority Issues in the Antidumping Field*, GATT, COM.AD/W/83, 17 November 1978, at 10.

I. *Rules of Origin*

One U.S. industry association has complained that its manufacturers might not be considered a U.S. domestic producer in antidumping investigations since they often send their inputs abroad for assembly.[54] Under the Rules of Origin Code, the country of origin is the country where substantial transformation has occurred.[55] However, footnote 2 of the Rules of Origin Code expressly exempts origin determinations made for purposes of defining "domestic industry" or "like products of domestic industry" (terms most commonly used in antidumping investigations).[56] The exemption of these terms from the Rules of Origin Code would allow a country to determine freely which products have its origin in antidumping domestic like product determinations, notwithstanding the Rules of Origin Code's substantial transformation principle.

Conclusion

In the last stages of the drafting of the Dunkel Text (the week of 15 December 1991) the GATT yielded to intense political pressure by the EC and the United States, and substantially revised the draft AD Code, watering down reforms that would limit the ability of antidumping authorities to impose duties when there was no dumping or injury (as permitted under the current 1979 Code). The result is a draft even more favourable toward import protection than the 1979 Tokyo Round Antidumping Code, which does not expressly permit such "tilts" in favour of petitioners as requiring sales to be above fully allocated cost, allowing a selective calculation of profits, requiring resale price maintenance, and so on (although, admittedly, the United States, the EC and other countries have been ignoring the rules and following those practices anyhow).

An economist would find it surprising that the EC and the United States—the world's two largest exporters and the leading targets of other countries' antidumping cases—would have exerted such enormous pressure for an antidumping code which would harm its own exporters and their own economies by supplying import protection in excess of the amount of any "unfair" trade practice. Political scientists (and political economists) accustomed to the power of special interest groups would be less surprised and possibly more amused. Defenders of the GATT would probably not be surprised (the GATT in practice is not constructed to stand up to insistent demands from its two largest members, and reaching a "deal" in international trade negotiations is frequently more important to the governments involved than the content of the deal) but at least some of them would be saddened if distorted antidumping rules are planted so firmly into the GATT, authorizing any member to

[54] See *SIA Letter*, reprinted in Inside U.S. Trade, 10 January 1992, at S-11.
[55] Dunkel Text, Section D.
[56] Id. at note 2.

ignore at its discretion the basic GATT rules of tariff binding, most-favoured-nation and national treatment.

There are some signs that this danger is being recognized. The new U.S. Trade Representative, Michael Kantor (an able lawyer from Southern California, an area whose economy is based on an open trading system), has been careful to balance the imperative of preserving "our antidumping and countervailing duty laws as effective remedies against unfair trade practice" with the need "to prevent misuse of other countries' antidumping laws against U.S. exporters."[57] It will be interesting to see if the new EC GATT negotiator, Sir Leon Brittan, and the new GATT Director-General, Peter Sutherland—both former EC Commissioners for Competition (DG IV)—can also ensure that antidumping laws cannot be used to restrict competition and to close markets which the ongoing Uruguay Round (and prior Rounds) have opened.

[57] Letter from U.S. Trade Representative Michael Kantor to Senator Ernest F. Hollings, 29 June 1993, reprinted in Inside U.S. Trade, 2 July 1993, at 15.

8

Standards for Panels Reviewing Anti-dumping Determinations under the GATT and WTO

*Gary N. Horlick and Peggy A. Clarke**

I. INTRODUCTION

WTO dispute resolution concerning anti-dumping measures promises to be an active field. This is true in view of the relatively high frequency of such disputes in the recent past (24% of the GATT panels in the years 1990–1994 involved anti-dumping measures) and the fact that some exporters in the United States (the WTO member whose exporters have been subject to the largest number of anti-dumping charges in the last five years) perceive the judicial and/or administrative review systems of other countries as being more deferential to local authorities than the US courts are to US authorities. This perception increases the likelihood that US exporters will need WTO dispute resolution rather than rely solely on local courts or administrative tribunals. In addition, the failure of GATT members to implement panel reports adverse to their positions – even adopted ones – invites relitigation of many of the same issues which appeared in GATT panels under the new binding WTO dispute resolution system which the US and the EU had sought in the Uruguay Round.

The most obvious problem with dispute resolution in the anti-dumping area under the GATT was that very few of the panel reports had been adopted and implemented. Of seven panels brought under the Anti-dumping Code, only three have been adopted, and of those only two have actually been implemented (*Electrical Transformers* and *Polyacetal Resin*[1]). There was an early tendency of panels to relitigate cases (*Electrical Transformers*, where the panel effectively "reweighed" the facts) and a subsequent diffidence by panels that has been reflected in procedural problems including lack of full access by the panel to confidential information and burden of proof. In the most important area of anti-dumping practice, causation of injury,[2] the recent GATT anti-dumping panel reports reflect complete confusion which WTO panels will have to resolve.

* Both authors work for O'Melveny & Myers LLP, Washington, D.C.

[1] *New Zealand – Imports of Electrical Transformers from Finland* ("*Electrical Transformers*"), GATT BISD 32S/55 (adopted 18 July 1985); *Korea – Anti-dumping Duties on Imports of Polyacetal Resins from the United States* ("*Polyacetal Resin*"), GATT doc. ADP/92 (adopted 27 April 1993).

[2] This is the most important area because national authorities, with the exception of Mexico, routinely manage to find dumping in over 90% of all cases, meaning that the injury determination, and in particular causation, is decisive.

CHAPTER 8

The general principles for WTO dispute resolution review (i.e., by panels and the appellate tribunal) of anti-dumping determinations by administering authorities are fairly commonsensical. Panels are not themselves investigating whether dumping, injury, and causation have occurred, but rather whether the relevant authorities have complied with the international obligations contained in the WTO agreements. Thus, panels should not be seeking new information, but rather relying on information that was available. That presumes, of course, that the authorities have conducted a "fair and unbiased" investigation/evaluation pursuant to the new obligation added by Article 17.6 of the Anti-dumping Agreement. Equally important, authorities will have to document their investigation. Two GATT panels in the countervailing duty context have already expressed their doubts about the sufficiency of the evidence in the record, concerning determinations.[3] The US authorities should have some advantage here of already being accustomed to the fairly rigorous demands of the US Court of International Trade and Chapter 19 panels under the US–Canada Free Trade Agreement. Mexico and Canada are undergoing similar experiences with Chapter 19 (extended to Mexico through NAFTA), and possibly the EU by the transfer of initial review of the anti-dumping determinations to the Court of First Instance.

In addition, no authority seems safe from the rather sweeping use of the requirement of an "adequate explanation" *in the written determination* (i.e., notwithstanding whether adequate support can be found in the record), as evidenced by the US use of this weapon against Korea in the panel on *Polyacetal Resin*, followed by the successful use of the doctrine by the EU against the US in *Bismuth Steel* and against Brazil in *Milk Powder*.

A panel should not substitute its judgment in factual matters for that of the authorities. This degree of deference in factual matters of course requires that the authorities conducted a fair and thorough investigation (e.g., by not imposing different burdens on domestic producers and foreign exporters), and a fair evaluation of the facts (e.g., by not creating effectively irrebuttable presumptions). The panel requested by the US against Korea apparently did not believe that the Korean authorities had done so.[4] Similarly, the panel requested by Finland against New Zealand evidently did not feel that the injury/causation determination by New Zealand represented a fair evaluation of the facts – as far as can be ascertained, the panel (which included government representatives from the United States, Poland, and the Netherlands) found the New Zealand determination not credible, in view of the extremely low market share of the imports.[5]

The situation of panels reviewing national authorities' interpretations of international agreements is a curious one. As Croley and Jackson point out, a dispute resolution system reviewing 129 countries' decisions is in a rather different position than a national court reviewing that one country's administrative agency's decisions.[6]

[3] *Brazil – Imposition of Provisional and Definitive Countervailing Duties on Milk Powder from the European Economic Community* ("*Milk Powder*") GATT doc. SCM/179 (adopted 28 April 1994) and *US Imposition of Countervailing Duties on Certain Hot-Rolled Lead and Bismuth Carbon Steel Products Originating in France, Germany and the United Kingdom* ("*Bismuth Steel*"), GATT doc. DRS/1a (submitted to parties 14 October 1994).

[4] *Polyacetal Resin*, at para. 300.

[5] *Electrical Transformers*, at para. 4:7.

[6] See, Steven P. Croley and John H. Jackson in their contribution to this book.

STANDARDS FOR PANELS REVIEWING ANTI-DUMPING DETERMINATIONS

In almost all countries, except the US, Argentina and Canada, the entire anti-dumping determination is made by bodies reporting to a political head, and GATT panels in the past have shown some suspicion that national authorities, whether administrative or legislative, may tend to favour national producers.[7]

II. STANDARD OF REVIEW

The WTO anti-dumping dispute resolution provisions attempt to address some of the concerns raised by previous panels or to codify past panel practice. During the later stages of the Uruguay Round negotiations, the United States made several efforts to significantly narrow the scope of review by a dispute settlement panel with respect to disputes involving the imposition of anti-dumping duties.[8] The US proposals were strenuously resisted by most other countries, and received only tepid support, at best, from the European Union (the other major supporter of anti-dumping laws). Thus, over the course of the negotiations the US had to relax its position significantly, and in the end, achieved agreement on language that essentially codified existing panel practice concerning the standard of review. The following section compares the US proposals from November 1992 and November 1993 with the standard ultimately included in the final agreement.

In November 1992, the US proposed a narrow standard of review to be included in the Anti-dumping Agreement.[9] That proposal had three main restrictive elements:

(a) There could be no violation of the Agreement as long as the investigating authority's actions were consistent with any reasonable interpretation of the Agreement.
(b) The only review of factual issues to be permitted was whether there was no interpretation of the factual information before the investigating authority that could support its findings, and the burden of persuasion was on the complaining party to so demonstrate.
(c) The panel could not consider arguments that were inconsistent with those raised by that party's nationals to the investigating authority or that had not been raised by that party's nationals.[10]

[7] See, e.g., *Polyacetal Resin* at paras. 242, 276; this suspicion may well have been one of the underlying bases for the *Tuna/Dolphin I* Panel Report. See *United States – Restrictions on Imports on Tuna*, GATT doc. DS21/R (unadopted, 3 September 1991).

[8] The US also intended that the same standard should apply to disputes involving the imposition of countervailing duties, however, the negotiations on this issue occurred in the context of the Anti-dumping Agreement.

[9] For a complete text of the November 1992 US proposals for changes to the Anti-dumping Agreement, *see* "US Proposals for Changes to GATT AD Text", *Inside US Trade*, Washington Publishers, Special Report, 18 December 1992, at S–3. See also "Draft US Proposal on Scope of Review of", *Inside US Trade*, inside Washington Publishers, Special Report, 5 November 1993, at 7.

[10] This was an attempt to overturn several panel reports that rejected such an approach. See, e.g., *United States – Anti-Dumping Duties on Gray Portland Cement and Cement Clinker From Mexico* ("*Cement Clinker*"), GATT doc. ADP/82 (unadopted 7 September 1992); *United States – Imposition of Anti-dumping Duties on Imports of Fresh and Chilled Atlantic Salmon from Norway* ("*Salmon*"), GATT doc. ADP/87 (adopted 27 April 1994), para. 347. Jacques Bourgeois discusses the panels' reasoning on this issue in his chapter of this book.

In addition, the US sought to restrict the review to the record developed by the investigating authority during the investigation.[11] These proposals were rejected by the other negotiating countries.

In October 1993, the United States tried a slightly different approach – a restrictive standard of review to be applied to all WTO dispute resolution, rather than only anti-dumping and countervailing duties.[12] Although this had to be withdrawn (because US intellectual property groups wanted broad grounds to overturn other countries' authorities' intellectual property decisions), the final text of the WTO Agreement included a Ministerial Declaration providing for a review of the standard included in the Anti-dumping Agreement in three years with a view towards applying that standard to all disputes.[13]

In November of 1993, the United States put forward a new proposal for the standard of review. To achieve acceptance, this proposal was significantly more relaxed than the November 1992 proposal.[14] Rather than prohibiting the review of the facts unless no interpretation of the facts would support the investigating authority's determination, the November 1993 proposal called for an "objective assessment" of the facts and stated that the standard was whether the investigating authority's evaluation of those facts was "reasonable".[15]

[11] This issue has been raised in several cases. In general, the panels have restricted the factual record to that which was before the administering authorities. E.g., *United States – Anti-dumping Duties on Imports of Stainless Steel Plate from Sweden* ("*Swedish Steel Plate*"), GATT doc. ADP/117 (unadopted 24 February 1994), para. 26; *Cement Clinker*, at para. 3.1.5. But see *United States – Imposition of Anti-Dumping Duties on Imports of Seamless Stainless Steel Hollow Products From Sweden*, ADP/47 (unadopted 20 August 1990) ("*Swedish Seamless Steel*"). In *Swedish Seamless Steel*, the panel refused to make a general ruling and ruled on an item-by-item basis as it came up. This issue has also arisen in other contexts. See, *United States – Countervailing on Fresh, Chilled and Frozen Pork from Canada* ("*Chilled Pork*"), USA-89-1904-06 (US–Canada Free Trade Agreement Binational Panel Review ("CFTA") (28 September 1990)), which was decided under the dispute settlement provisions of the United States–Canada Free Trade Agreement. In that case, the panel considered information submitted by the Government of Alberta after the Commerce Department's final determination to correct a typographical error in an Alberta publication on which the Commerce Department had relied.

[12] The United States proposed notes to Article 11.1 of the draft DSU. Proposed Note 1 stated: "Where a measure adopted or enforced by a Member was based on the evaluation of particular facts, the panel's objective assessment of the facts shall be to determine whether the Member's evaluation was consistent with a reasonable interpretation of those facts, recognizing that reasonable minds could differ as to the significance to be attached to certain facts."

[13] Ministerial Decision on Review of Article 17.6 of the Agreement on Implementation of Article VI of the General Agreement on Tariffs and Trade 1994. Final Act Embodying the Results of the Uruguay Round of Multilateral Trade Negotiations (15 April 1994), GATT doc. MTN/FA at 145 ("Final Act"), at 402, reprinted in Message from the President of the United States Transmitting the Uruguay Round Trade Agreements, Texts of Agreements, Implementing Bill, Statement of Administrative Action and Required Supporting Statements, H.R. doc. No. 316, 103d Cong., 2d Sess. & 818 1695 (1994) ("House doc.").

[14] In addition to changing its proposal, the United States made clear to the other negotiators that having explicit language on the "standard of review" was a very high priority in the December 1993 finale of the Round – apparently higher than reaching a financial services agreement or a strengthening of the TRIPS Agreement. See "Ending the Uruguay Round: An Interview With GATT Chief Sutherland", *Inside US Trade*, Inside Washington Publishers, Special Report, 24 December 1993, at 4–6; "Japan's Chief Negotiator, In Interview, Discusses GATT Round Endgame", *Inside US Trade*, inside Washington Publishers, Special Report, 24 December 1993, at 6–10; John Maggs, "Services Battle Overshadows Anti-Dumping Fracas at GATT", *Journal of Commerce*, 1993, December, at 8A.

[15] In the recent countervailing duties panel on the United States' imposition of countervailing duties on lead and bismuth carbon steel from the EU, the panel noted that reviewing facts for consistency with the Agreement required "meaningful" but not *de novo* review and rejected the US standard, termed the "deference model". *Bismuth Steel*, at para. 369 (the panel rejected the EU argument that the standard of review for facts should be "reasonableness" although it noted that prior panels had frequently used the term "reasonable" in describing their view of the facts).

STANDARDS FOR PANELS REVIEWING ANTI-DUMPING DETERMINATIONS

The standard on legal issues also called for an objective assessment of the applicability of the Agreement to the measure. However, where the relevant provision of the Agreement was either ambiguous or did not specify how the obligation was to be performed, the panel was to determine whether the authority's action was "outside the range of actions consistent with that obligation". This proposal was rejected. On the last night of the negotiations the final language of Article 17.6 was adopted.[16] Rather than applying a test of reasonableness, the panel shall determine whether the authority's establishment of the facts was proper and if so, whether their evaluation was unbiased and objective.[17]

Thus, the panel will examine two aspects of the factual analysis by importing countries' authorities. If the authorities' procedure had been faulty in either respect, then the panel shall find that the country failed in its imposition of anti-dumping duties. This essentially codifies panel practice in recent dispute panels for both anti-dumping and countervailing duty cases.[18] Moreover, Article 11 of the Understanding on Rules and Procedures Governing the Settlement of Disputes (DSU) indicates that in any WTO panel, the panelists must make an objective assessment of the facts of the case.

With respect to legal analysis, Article 17.6(ii) provides first that the relevant provisions shall be interpreted in accordance with the customary rules of interpretation of public international law. Article 17.6(ii) then provides that if the panel finds that the relevant provision admits of more than one permissible interpretation, the authority's actions must rest upon one of the permissible interpretations to be in conformity.

The DSU also provides a similar standard for review of the legal issues. Article 11 requires that the panel make an objective assessment of the matter before the panel and the matter's applicability of and conformity with, the relevant covered agreements. In analysing conformity with the GATT, panels have typically applied the generally recognized rules of interpretation of public international law (normally as codified in the Vienna Convention on the Law of Treaties, Articles 31 and 32). Unlike the standard proposed in November 1993 for legal issues, the final language

[16] E. U. Petersmann, "The Dispute Settlement System of the World Trade Organization and the Evolution of the GATT Dispute Settlement System Since 1948", *Common Market Law Review* 1157, 1204 (1994).

[17] Anti-dumping Agreement, Art. 17.6(i), Final Act at 165, House doc. at 1473. Exactly what these terms mean will be established through subsequent panel decisions, however, the language necessarily implies several requirements. In determining whether the establishment of the facts was proper, the panel will have to determine whether the parties to the investigation had the opportunity to provide all relevant facts and to rebut or correct the "facts" upon which the authorities based their determination prior to that determination. In other words, the panel will consider whether the authorities used fair procedures to obtain evidence in accordance with Article 6 of the Anti-dumping Agreement. See e.g., Article 6.9 which requires that authorities inform all interested parties of the essential facts which will form the basis of the determination in sufficient time to permit the parties to defend their interests. This issue has arisen in other contexts. See *Chilled Pork*, at note 11 above (panel considered information submitted after the final determination to correct a typographical error on which the US Department of Commerce had relied because the exporters were unaware of the reliance on this error prior to the final determination). Moreover, the phrase "unbiased and objective" requires analysis free of political or economic bias and the weighing of evidence objectively. This raises a question of which parties have the burden of persuasion before the authorities and would argue against application of a rebuttable presumption of "guilt" (i.e., the assumption that the goods are dumped or causing injury unless the exporters demonstrate otherwise).

[18] *Swedish Steel Plate*, at para. 284.

CHAPTER 8

specifically imposes the discipline of customary public international law on questions of interpretation. Therefore, while the proposed language would have permitted unilateral and changing interpretations by each different national authority, the final language should lead to a consistent interpretation that is based upon a multilateral understanding of the provisions at issue.[19]

The US has stated that the final language creates a standard "similar to that used by US courts in reviewing anti-dumping determinations ...".[20] If such is the case, decisions will be subject to close scrutiny. The US court standard for review of an anti-dumping determination is whether the determination is supported by substantial evidence on the record or otherwise not in accordance with law.[21] As applied by the US courts it has not resulted in overwhelming deference to the authorities.

In determining whether a US decision is supported by substantial evidence, the court examines not only the evidence supporting the agency's determination but also any record evidence from which conflicting inferences can be drawn or that fairly detracts from the weight of the supporting evidence to determine whether the evidence is such "as a reasonable mind might accept as adequate to support a conclusion".[22] The courts have also overturned decisions by the Department of Commerce and International Trade Commission because they found the decisions to be "otherwise not in accordance with law".[23]

Since the standards laid out in the Anti-dumping Agreement (and the DSU) essentially codify recent panel review standards, the remainder of this commentary will examine recent panel implementation of those standards with respect to two

[19] As Croley and Jackson discuss in another chapter of this book, a single, consistent interpretation of the legal issues is not only in accordance with general public law regarding treaty interpretation, but also is consistent with the underlying purpose of the WTO. That purpose is to overcome problems concerning the coordination of international trade for the collective benefit of all members.

[20] US Department of Commerce, *Anti-dumping: Results of the Agreement*, 1 (undated fact sheet issued by USDOC Trade Information Center).

[21] 19 USC, Section 1516a(b)(1)(B) (1988).

[22] *Suramerica de Aleaciones Laminadas, C.A v. United States*, Slip Op., Ct. No. 93-1579 and 94–1021 (Fed. Cir. 30 December 1994) at 12, citing *Consolidated Edison Co. v. NCRB*, 305 US 197, 229 (1938) as quoted in *Matsushita Elec. Indus. Co. v. United States*, 750 F.2d 927, 933 (Fed. Cir. 1984), *Universal Camera Corp. v. NCRB*, 340 US 474, 487 (1951), and *Atlantic Sugar, Ltd. v. United States*, 744 F.2d 1556, 1562 (Fed. Cir. 1984). In *Suramerica*, the Court of Appeals for the Federal Circuit upheld a finding by the Court of International Trade that the ITC's finding of threat of material injury was unsupported by substantial evidence on the record. *Suramerica*, Slip Op. at 19 ("The lack of significant support for the petitions and the equivocal evidence as to the factors listed in the statute are not substantial evidence that the domestic EC rod industry faces a real threat of imminent material injury"). See also, *Micron Technology, Inc. v. United States*, No. 95–107 at Slip Op. 8 (Ct. Int'l Trade, 12 June 1995) (DOC's determination that R&D related to non-subject merchandise provided an intrinsic benefit to subject merchandise not supported by substantial evidence).

[23] E.g., *The Ad Hoc Committee of AZ-NM-TX-FL Producers of Gray Portland Cement v. United States*, 13 F.3d 398 (Fed. Cir. 1994) (DOC's deduction of pre-sale home market transportation expenses not in accordance with law); *Melex USA. Inc. v. United States*, No. 95–152 (Ct. Int'l Trade, 25 August 1995) (DOC's retroactive application of statute not in accordance with law); *Hosiden Corp. v. United States*, 810 F. Supp. 322 (Ct. Int'l Trade, 1992) (ITC's single injury determination for two classes or kinds of merchandise not in accordance with law.)

contentious issues, noting where language of the Anti-dumping Agreement would change that finding.[24]

III. RECENT PANEL DECISIONS ON SELECTED ISSUES

1. Burden of Proof

Burden of proof is a crucial issue with respect to reaching conclusions of law and fact. The question of whether a country acted in accordance with the agreement will frequently hinge on whether that country must demonstrate compliance or the complainant must demonstrate a lack of compliance.

Outside of the anti-dumping/countervailing duty context GATT practice has generally been to put the burden on the complaining party to demonstrate either violation or infringement. However, if the accused party claims reliance upon one of the exceptions to the GATT (for example, Article XX), then the party claiming the exception has the burden of demonstrating that its actions are consistent with that exception.[25]

In the anti-dumping and countervailing duty context the United States has routinely argued in the cases in which it is the defending party that Articles VI and XVI of the GATT are not exceptions. Given that the imposition of either anti-dumping or countervailing duties are contrary to the concepts of both tariff bindings (by raising import duties above the bound rates) and most-favoured-nation (by applying different tariff rates to different GATT members), Articles VI and XVI are considered by most scholars as permitted exceptions to these basic GATT principles.[26] Thus, in the anti-dumping and countervailing duty context the burden of proof would lay with the accused party.

However, in certain recent cases, not only have the panels refused to rule on whether Article VI is an exception, but they have placed a burden of proof on the

[24] A third highly contentious issue was the standing requirement. In *Swedish Seamless Steel*, the panel found that US authorities' reliance on a statement in the petition that the standing requirement was met was inconsistent with Code obligations. Rather the panel found that the language of the Anti-dumping Code required the authorities to take affirmative steps to satisfy themselves that the standing requirement had been met (*Swedish Seamless Steel*, at para. 5.19). In *Cement Clinker* the panel essentially concurred with the *Swedish Seamless Steel* opinion, finding that the authorities' reliance on a certified statement in the petition was inadequate (in part because of the wording of that certified statement). *Cement Clinker* at para. 5.34. In contrast the *Salmon* panel found that the authorities had acted consistently with their Code obligations in relying on a statement in the petition that petitioners had standing. *Salmon* at para. 362. The standing issue is resolved in the Anti-dumping Agreement by requiring that the authorities ascertain the "adequacy and accuracy" of the facts in the petition, Art. 5.3, including those required for meeting the new explicit standing requirements.

[25] E.g., *Canada – Import, Distribution and Sale of Alcoholic Drinks by Canadian Provincial Marketing Agencies*, GATT BISD 35S/37 (adopted 22 March 1988); *Canada – Administration of the Foreign Investment Review Act*, BISD 30S/140 (adopted 7 February 1984).

[26] See Jackson, *World Trade and the Law of the GATT*, 1969, 422; Petersmann, 45 *Aussenwirtenshaft*, at 187 ("Article VI was originally conceived as a narrow exception to the fundamental GATT principle of trade protection through non-discriminatory tariffs only"); Bierwagen, *GATT Article VI and the Protectionist Bias in Anti-Dumping Law*, 1990, vol. 7, at 21 and 50 (referring to Article VI as an "exception" to the basic principles of the General Agreement). See, e.g., *United States – Countervailing Duties on Fresh, Chilled and Frozen Pork from Canada*, DS7/R (adopted 11 July 1991), para. 4.4; *EEC – Regulation on Imports of Parts and Components*, GATT BISD 37S/132 (adopted 16 May 1990); *Swedish Anti-Dumping Duties*, GATT BISD 3S/81 (26 February 1955), para. 15.

complaining party that cannot be met. In both the *Salmon* panel and the *Audio cassettes* panel, the complaining party (Norway and Japan, respectively) has been required to demonstrate that United States and EU actions, respectively, have resulted in the imposition of duties in excess of the level of dumping. In both cases, it was not Norway or Japan (the parties which ultimately were assigned the burden) that had access to the facts, but rather the United States and the EU that had the facts to demonstrate that they did not impose excessive duties.

Both cases focused on a similar practice by the authorities in the United States and in the EU. In calculating a dumping margin, both authorities calculated a weighted average foreign market, or normal, value. To this they compared the individual prices of the imports to determine whether dumping existed.

In *Salmon*, Norway argued that in most, if not all, cases where prices fluctuate such a comparison will result in a finding of dumping greater than that which would result if a comparison of like-to-like (e.g., average-to-average) were made. Norway argued that since it had demonstrated that there was a likelihood that the US methodology would result in overstating the margins, the burden should be on the United States to demonstrate that it had not, in fact, overstated the margins. Moreover, the United States had the necessary confidential information to so demonstrate, whereas Norway did not have access to that information to demonstrate its position. Nevertheless, the panel rejected Norway's argument, finding that while Norway had presented a hypothetical example demonstrating that the margin could be overstated using the US methodology, there was no evidence before the panel demonstrating that the United States had *in fact* overstated the margins.[27]

In *Audio cassettes*,[28] Japan argued that the EU's practice of comparing an average normal value to individual transactions when combined with the practice of zeroing out above normal value sales, overstated the margin of dumping. Similar to the *Salmon* finding, this panel rejected Japan's argument on the grounds that Japan had not demonstrated that there would have been *no* dumping but for the average normal value to individual transaction and zeroing.[29] The language of the panel report implies that the panel would have found no violation had Japan demonstrated that the EU imposed a duty of, hypothetically, 20% when the actual margin of dumping was 10%. Thus, here not only did the panel put the burden on Japan to demonstrate violation when it was the EU that had the evidence, not Japan, but also interpreted the Code to state that no violation would occur if the EU had imposed duties higher than the actual level of dumping as long as *any* level of dumping existed.

2. Injury (Causation)

Another contentious issue in both the anti-dumping and countervailing duty context is the determination of causation, i.e., whether the injury found was caused by the

[27] *Salmon*, at para. 483.

[28] *EC – Anti-Dumping Duties on Audio Tapes in Cassettes Originating in Japan* ("*Audio cassettes*") GATT doc. (unadopted).

[29] *Audio cassettes*, at para. 358. The panel also said that the EU *could* have legitimately used a transaction-to-transaction comparison, and the Japanese had failed to demonstrate that such an analysis would not show dumping – even though the EU had not done a transaction-to-transaction analysis, and Japan could not conceivably have divined exactly how the EU would have done so (e.g., which time periods, product groups, etc.). *Audio cassettes* at para. 355.

dumped or subsidized imports.[30] Under the GATT, the requirement was interpreted differently from panel to panel, and, indeed, in the case of the *Salmon* panel several different interpretations were enunciated in the same report.

In both the Tokyo Round Anti-dumping and Subsidies Codes, in order to impose duties the authorities were required to demonstrate "that the dumped [subsidized] imports are, through the effects of the subsidy, causing injury within the meaning of this Agreement. There may be other factors which at the same time are injuring the domestic industry, and the injuries caused by other factors must not be attributed to the dumped [subsidized] imports".[31] Most scholars and many GATT parties have interpreted this language to require that the authorities separate the injury caused by the imports (or the dumping or subsidization) in question from injury caused by other factors and then determine whether the effect of those imports was such as to constitute injury within the meaning of the Code.[32] The US (when acting as defendant) does not support this interpretation.

Panels that have examined the issue have been contradictory. In the US complaint against Canadian countervailing duties on US grain corn,[33] the panel found that Canada acted inconsistently with this requirement in imposing duties because, although the CIT acknowledged the existence of other factors, it "made no effort to ensure that the injuries caused by other factors were not attributed to the subsidized imports... [and] attributed the injury only to subsidization of United States grain corn, and thus did not meet the express requirements of Article 6:4".[34] Thus, the panel

[30] Under the GATT, the standard was considered to be the same for anti-dumping and countervailing duty cases. Therefore, this section will consider previous interpretations in both anti-dumping and countervailing duty disputes. Under the WTO, the standard may no longer be the same. In the Agreement on Subsidies and Countervailing Measures there is no language equivalent to Art. 17.6 of the Anti-dumping Agreement. Accompanying the final WTO Agreement is a Ministerial Declaration noting the need for the consistent resolution of disputes arising from anti-dumping and countervailing duty measures. Declaration on Dispute Settlement Pursuant to the Agreement on Implementation of Art. VI of the General Agreement on Tariffs and Trade 1994 or Part V of the Agreement on Subsidies and Countervailing Measures. The United States takes the position that this applies the same standards to both Agreements. Agreement on Implementation of Art. VI of the General Agreement on Tariffs and Trade 1994 ("WTO Anti-dumping Agreement"), Final Act at 148, House doc. at 1453. Other drafters of the Declaration reject this position and consider that the declaration may only apply to parallel injury and procedural provisions.

[31] Anti-dumping Agreement, Art. 3.4, Final Act at 149, House doc. at 1457; Anti-dumping Code, Art. 3:4; Subsidies Code, Art. 6:4.

[32] E.g., Hans Beseler stated: "Following the negotiations, the need to demonstrate that the dumped imports were the principal cause of the injury suffered was abandoned, as was the requirement to weigh the effect of the dumping against the effect of all other factors adversely affecting the industry. Instead a new approach was adopted which consisted of *isolating* the injuries caused by each of the factors, including the dumping, and to treat each as a separate injury. It had then to be shown that the effect of the dumped imports was such as to cause injury within the meaning of the Code. This concept of differentiation between the injuries resulting from several factors was also included in the subsidy sector and was introduced into Community legislation following the negotiations". Beseler and Williams, *Anti-Dumping and Anti-Subsidy Law*, Sweet & Maxwell, London, 1986, 167 (discussing the Codes and the EC's implementation of those Codes) (emphasis added). See, also, *ICI Australia Operation Pty Ltd. v. Fraser*, 106 ALR 257 (discussing Australian anti-dumping law): "Where the Australian industry has suffered detriment from a number of probable causes the section [of 5.269TG] requires a determination of whether there was separate material injury, or any material incremental injury ... caused by the dumping *over and above detriment caused by other factors*" (emphasis added).

[33] *Canadian Countervailing Duties on Grain Corn from the United States* ("*Grain Corn*"), GATT BISD 39S/411 (adopted 26 March 1992).

[34] *Grain Corn* at para. 5.2.8.

required that the authorities take affirmative steps to avoid attributing injury from other factors to the imports.

In *Milk Powder*, the panel found Brazil's determination to impose duties to be inconsistent with its Code obligations, in part because Brazil apparently failed to consider the role of other factors.[35] Thus, this panel found that there was at least a requirement that other factors be considered.

In *Salmon*, it is unclear what the panel's standard was because in its report the panel stated several inconsistent formulations of the analysis required. In paragraph 551 of the anti-dumping report, the panel referred to an implicit requirement only to *consider* other factors. In paragraphs 555 and 560, the panel indicated that the required analysis was to examine other factors sufficiently "to ensure that it did not find that material injury was caused by imports from Norway when material injury to the domestic industry allegedly caused by imports from Norway was in fact caused by factors other than these imports". Finally, in paragraph 557, the panel implied that the analysis was whether injury was caused *entirely* by other factors.[36]

This language has been changed in the WTO Agreement. The Anti-dumping Agreement specifically requires that the authorities examine "any known factors other than the dumped imports which at the same time are injuring the domestic industry" and that the injuries caused by these factors "must not be attributed to the dumped imports".[37] This clarifies the previous language and supports the scholars' and many countries' interpretations of this provision as requiring a segregation of the injury caused by the imports from the injury caused by other factors. This reflects statements at the Committee meeting expressing a reservation concerning, *inter alia*, the treatment of causation in the *Salmon* panel report.

IV. CONCLUSION

While the standards of review of anti-dumping disputes found in the Anti-dumping Agreement, Article 17.6 are not radical departures from prior panel practice, they should offer support for the panelists' imposition of these standards and, when combined with the appellate procedure, lead to greater consistency between panel findings.

[35] *Milk Powder* at para. 346.

[36] The *Salmon* Panel Report was adopted subject to express reservations on several issues, among them, injury/causation (e.g. by Canada). As part of the adopted report there is a note from the Committee Chairman stating: "... However, I wish to stress that the purpose of a panel report is to resolve a specific dispute between the parties to the dispute. It does not create obligations on parties other than the parties to the specific dispute addressed by the panel report, nor does it represent binding legal precedent applicable to other disputes" Chairman, Committee on Anti-dumping Practices (27 April 1994).

[37] Anti-dumping Agreement, Art. 3.5, Final Act at 149, House doc. at 1457.

ARTICLE

A Personal History of Zeroing

Gary N. Horlick*

The author describes the origin of the 'fair comparison' language of Article 2.4 of the WTO Antidumping Agreement, and its impact on the 'Zeroing' disputes in the WTO.

Legally speaking, there is no agreed 'drafting' history for the Uruguay Round agreements. This is particularly true for the Antidumping Agreement, wherein most of the work was not done in the formal negotiating group and, indeed, a lot of it was done outside of even informal groups. Consequently, no single person really knows the entire history of the negotiation. Indeed, anyone claiming to know what happened by definition does not. So this brief contribution records my slice of the history without purporting to be comprehensive.

I first encountered the practice of 'zeroing' in late 1976 to early 1977. I was a young lawyer working on my first antidumping case in a period when the Treasury Department handled antidumping determinations in the Executive Branch. Quaint though it might sound, there was no *Antidumping Manual*, no *Federal Register* notices other than a bland paragraph or two saying dumping had been found, and no computer tapes and programs to explain what the Department had done to calculate margins (in fact, the Department did not use computers, although law firms and businesses in antidumping cases did – something which I changed as soon as I was put in charge of Import Administration at Commerce, with mandatory computer responses and, consequently, mandatory computer processing). Antidumping in 1977 was done by people at Customs on hand calculators. An official at Customs kindly agreed to explain the calculations to me in a series of conversations and telephone calls.

Zeroing was – and is – another form for 'averaging': the practice used by the Treasury Department and later by Commerce of comparing each individual export sale to the United States with a weighted average whole market price for that model. After he explained that aspect of the calculation to me, by telephone, I blurted out: 'but that doesn't make sense'. He agreed but said that is the way the calculation was done. This was not a moral issue – my firm did both petitions and responses – but even my moderate knowledge of statistics suggested to me that this would almost invariably 'tilt' the calculation in favour of a finding of dumping. After I finished the telephone conversation (which included such arcane matters as the 'rule of 100' used to settle by Treasury cases, even though it is nowhere written down except by implication in a footnote to a proposed rule that was never adapted), I called people with a better grasp of statistics and confirmed that, in fact, comparing a weighted average to individual export sales was indeed misleading. Since there was no effective judicial review of the antidumping calculations at the time, I noted this – one of many 'tilts' along with asymmetric adjustments for expenses, biased adjustments for differences in merchandise, and so on – and moved on.

By 1981, when I was appointed to head Import Administration at Commerce, there was a new law and, more important, full judicial review. As a result, I used our cases to do a 'roundup' review of the calculation methodology, to identify areas where we might be vulnerable in litigation. There was certainly no explicit authorization in the statute or regulation for averaging (including zeroing) although there was a very tenuous claim that one could torture the language of the 1921 Antidumping Act to permit a comparison of each sale to a single average 'fair value'.

Perhaps a judge without any other basis for ruling might accept that argument if he or she was being highly deferential – but it became clear by the end of 1981 that the new US Court of International Trade, despite formal obedience to concepts of deference, was in practice being completely undeferential in reviewing our decisions. In addition, computerization, combined with full access to our calculations by both sides, made it dramatically easier for anyone

Note

* Gary N. Horlick, Attorney at Law, <www.ghorlick.com>, Washington, DC.

Global Trade and Customs Journal, Volume 4, Issue 5

challenging our decisions to show the very high degree to which averaging (including zeroing) 'tilted' the calculations. Of course, averaging was far from being the only area where our practices lacked a firm ground in statute or regulation. That meant that I could have ended averaging/zeroing by fiat (and in retrospect, perhaps I should have done so) but I thought that these decisions should be made through legislation. Consequently, averaging became one of the more than fifty topics identified in a package we had assembled by early 1983 for legislative change. My able successor, Alan Holmer, managed to steer twenty of those changes through Congress in 1984, including explicit authorization for Commerce to compare averages to averages.

By the time these changes were enacted and filtered down, the Reagan Administration had gone into its highly protectionist mode continued throughout its second term, and Alan's successor unabashedly advocated for petitioners rather than act as a neutral arbiter and never used that authority.

The comparison of a weighted average to individual export sales was so demonstrably tilted that it became an easy example of the tilts in the antidumping calculation.

As a result, averaging was prominent on the list of topics for negotiation in the Uruguay Round, including the list drawn up by the member companies of my client, Emergency Committee for American Trade (ECAT – the companies working on the initial list were Cargill, Caterpillar, IBM, Hewlett-Packard, 3M, and Phillip Morris). Importantly, no differentiation was made between averaging and zeroing – they were viewed as the same phenomenon. As part of this effort, we suggested that, in addition to language prohibiting averaging, the text should also include a 'catch-all' language requiring a 'fair comparison'. This could be accomplished by changing the 1979 Tokyo Round Antidumping Code language in Article 2.6, which had provided that 'in order to effect fair comparison, ... [certain types of adjustments to be made]' to a stand-alone requirement that 'a fair comparison shall be made'.

6. ~~In order to effect~~ A fair comparison shall be made between the export price and the domestic price in the exporting country (or the country of origin) or, if applicable, the price established pursuant to the provisions of Article VI.1 *b*. of the General Agreement. The prices shall be compared at the same level of trade, normally at the ex-factory level, and in respect of sales made at as nearly as possible the same time.

Our suggestion was accepted and appears as the first line of Article 2.4 of the first draft made of the new agreement 'Carlisle I', as well as the final World Trade Organization (WTO) Antidumping Agreement, and as a stand-alone requirement of the US legislation.

What was I thinking when I wrote these words? I was well aware of all possible forms of averaging, including comparing the weighted average of 'normal value/fair value' of individual models against each sale of that model and then averaging the antidumping margins found on those models without including negative margins (i.e., zeroing). The goal was not just to ban zeroing or all averaging but rather to ban *all* tilts. The danger of listing each individual tilt, such as zeroing, was that national authorities might find new ones.

Conclusion

We all know the rest of the story – although we still do not know the ending! After the entry into force of the WTO Agreements, enforcement authorities around the world somehow decided that zeroing somehow was different than the averaging referred to in Article 2.4.2 of the Anti-Dumping Agreement (ADA) (this was hardly the only such obvious inconsistency of national practice with the new agreement – see Horlick and Shea[1] and Horlick and Vermulst[2]). Finally, India decided to point out that the Emperor's new clothes were imaginary and brought the *Bed Linens* case (*European Communities – Anti-Dumping Duties on Imports of Cotton-Type Bed Linen from India*) to the WTO. The panel and Appellate Body, aided by good advocacy by India, agreed on two grounds:

- The drafting of the ADA referred to a single 'product' so the authorities could not slice and dice the one product into different sub-products [model zeroing] in order to evade the clear requirements of Article 2.4.2. This had a certain irony, as the European Union and United States had strenuously resisted any attempt in the Uruguay Round to clean up the drafting of the ADA (which is composed of inconsistent layers resembling the archaeology of Troy, starting with prehistoric 1966 and 1979 language drafted with no thought that it would be subject to binding judicial parsing).
- The authorities had decided that it was more convenient to just ignore the requirement of a fair comparison in Article 2.4 – not just in zeroing but also in continuing inconsistencies in adjustments, product comparisons, and other parts of

Notes

1 Gary N. Horlick & Eleanor C. Shea, 'The 1994 WTO Antidumping Agreement', *Journal of World Trade Law* 29 (1995): 5.

2 Gary N. Horlick & Edwin Vermulst, 'The 10 Major Problems with the Anti-Dumping Instrument: An Attempt at Synthesis', *Journal of World Trade* 39, no. 1 (2005): 67-74.

the comparison. They said that they had asserted during the negotiations their intention to continue to zero. The panel and Appellate Body preferred to follow the text.

The European Union eventually complied – at least in part – with the ruling. And once the European Union took the public position that it was no longer zeroing – despite nasty rumours of unacknowledged routine abuse of the exception to Article 2.4.2 – it could hardly allow the United States to continue to do so. Many cases later and notwithstanding panels made up of current and former antidumping enforcers, the Appellate Body continues to rule that zeroing violates, inter alia, the fair comparison requirement. And the United States as of this writing awaits the EU retaliation that will eventually lead to US compliance, just in time for the likely upsurge of AD cases caused by the current economic debacle – and the consequent pressures to resume zeroing in disguise as targeted dumping! But that is another article!

As a paper from the US Department of Justice put it, '[Z]eroing appears to be a classic case of protectionism being created by the subtle use of the administrative processes of the United State Government.' Retaliation would add to the extra duties levied on US consumers' additional duties on European consumers, which cannot be what the drafters of the GATT sought. The Justice Department paper sensibly suggests that the United States should trade off zeroing for reduction in foreign agricultural barriers.[3]

Note

3 W.W. Nye, 'Competitive Advocacy Opportunity: Zeroing in U.S. Antidumping Enforcement', EAG 08-13 [Dec. 2008].

ARTICLE

Smoot-Hawley in Slow Motion

Gary N. Horlick

The G-20 leaders, meeting in Washington in November 2008, pledged not to impose new import barriers in light of the financial crisis and the memories of the worldwide increases in tariffs following the US Smoot-Hawley tariffs in 1930. They repeated the exercise in London at the beginning of April 2009. Both times they carefully allowed continued imposition of antidumping tariffs. However, antidumping tariffs – which can greatly exceed the 55% average Smoot-Hawley tariff – have special 'viral' qualities during a worldwide economic recession that could undermine the pledge in ways not foreseen when those laws were passed.

Originally, antidumping required a showing that sales in the export market were priced lower than sales in the home market. For goods produced by industries with high fixed costs where price is set mainly by reasonably competitive markets, this meant, for example, that if prices were higher in the US market than the Canadian market, Canada could find dumping by US exporters, but the United States could not find dumping by Canadian exporters. This all began to change in 1975, when the US law was 'reformed'(at the behest of the Chairman of the Senate Finance Committee, to fix one case for one constituent (on elemental sulfur)). This was not a global problem during the 1974 to 1975 recession because (1) the change in law was limited to the United States, and did not take effect until the near the end of the recession, and (2) the US Treasury (which ran the US antidumping law at the time) followed the explicit Congressional intent and measured 'cost' over the business cycle – and very few industries sell below full cost over a business or product cycle (the example given by the US Congress was large commercial aircraft, which do not recover their cost for decades). However, in 1978, antidumping enforcers from the United States, Europe, Australia, and Canada (the four countries responsible for 99% of antidumping activity at the time) met on the margins of the GATT Tokyo Round negotiations and agreed that applying the new 'cost test' was permitted under GATT rules (a good example of the dangers of non-transparent international negotiations by regulators not particularly concerned about long-term effects outside their own immediate purview), and all four of those countries began applying the new rule shortly thereafter. The US Congress transferred responsibility for antidumping enforcement from the US Treasury to the US Department of Commerce effective 1980 and the Commerce Department in steel cases in 1980 promptly began measuring costs on the basis of the most recent fiscal year, rather than a business cycle or product cycle. Everyone else followed suit, including countries just beginning to use antidumping.

By 1993, Canada and the United States found each other's exporters dumping steel products, which in theory would not have been possible under the original antidumping test (there is another trick to antidumping, which increases antidumping duties by the amount that the *importing* country provides tariff protection, but that was irrelevant by 1993 between the United States and Canada because the FTA between the two had eliminated tariffs between the two – and thus, in theory, the possibility of dumping). Even better, the United States and Mexico found each other dumping steel products, thus demonstrating that the 'new users' of antidumping were fully in the game.

Antidumping duties are, by definition, protectionist, because they apply less favourable rules to imported goods than domestic ones. Specifically, WTO rules permit countries to impose antidumping duties when 'dumping' is found to cause injury to the domestic industry. The definition of 'dumping' includes sales below 'fully allocated costs', while most countries' rules for internal trade (usually found in their competition laws) effectively allow prices down to 'marginal costs'. Thus, imported goods must recover their full fixed costs, while domestically produced goods need only recover their marginal costs. In the case of capital-intensive industries such as steel, cement, chemicals, and even R&D-intensive high technology industries, the gap between the fully allocated costs and marginal costs can be huge. Further, the definition of 'injury' used in antidumping cases, and blessed by the Appellate Body of the WTO, allows a very unrigorous 'qualitative' analysis that essentially focuses on whether any domestic competitor lost sales or could not raise its prices when faced with competition from imports. By contrast, most countries' competition laws require far graver damage, while

Global Trade and Customs Journal, Volume 4, Issue 7/8

damage to competitors (of the kind 'condemned' by antidumping laws) is usually ignored.

Antidumping duties are often quite high. The average US antidumping duty, for example – the simple average, because it is impossible to calculate weighted averages because of the lack of transparency of WTO Members' antidumping system – runs around 40% to 45%, more than ten times the WTO-permitted 'bound' US tariff. Antidumping has been pushed aggressively by the United States and European Union (EU), and then welcomed by countries around the world as a legitimated form of protection which can be applied when necessary politically. However, in a deep recession, the results could be far worse. With a severe decline in demand, producers of capital-intensive goods in all countries can be dumping at the same time, since all are selling below the somewhat distorted definition of 'cost'. Additionally, it is easy enough to find 'injury' to domestic industries that are bleeding red ink from the decline in demand, so any imports can be found to cause the very low standard of 'injury' applied by most countries. In short, just like the 1930s, countries around the world can raise tariffs, because almost all traded goods can be found dumped and causing injury (especially when one takes into account the manipulation of calculations routinely practiced by antidumping administratives around the world, and not effectively policed by a WTO system which relies on complaints by the same countries).[1]

Indeed, unlike the 1930s, there is no need for any one country to lead the way and cause retaliation – all countries can do it at the same time. In fact, as the ministers in Washington were issuing their proclamation, the EU was applying antidumping duties on Chinese candles and steel wire rod, while the United States was imposing duties on German and Chinese paper (ironically, the type of paper used in credit card receipts, for which demand is rapidly falling), and a junior Indian industry minister proclaimed that India – the world's largest user of antidumping in recent years – must strengthen its antidumping system!

Note

1 The definition of 'cost' is not even as distorted as the definition of 'profit' used in antidumping cases: profit is measured by only looking at the profit on profitable sales, ignoring any sales at a loss – exactly what Enron and Parmalat did to cook their books a few years ago.

PART V
POLICY ISSUES AND CONCLUSIONS

8. Alternatives to National Antidumping and Countervailing Duty Laws: Are They Feasible or Appropriate in the Context of NAFTA?

by Gary N. Horlick and Eleanor C. Shea

INTRODUCTION

The United States, Canada, and Mexico are gearing up for discussions on the possible elimination of antidumping (AD) and countervailing duty (CVD) laws within the North American free trade area. One of the most frequently discussed alternatives, at least with respect to antidumping law, is the adoption of competition laws to address cross-border price discrimination. In light of these upcoming discussions, it is timely to consider whether alternatives to the application of national AD and CVD laws are feasible or appropriate in the context of the North American Free Trade Agreement (NAFTA).

BACKGROUND

The Canada-U.S. Free Trade Negotiations

During the negotiations on the Canada-U.S. Free Trade Agreement (CUSFTA) in 1987-88, Canada proposed a new system to replace the bilateral application of antidumping and countervailing duty laws. This substitute system would have dealt with cross-border price discrimination by private companies in a manner consistent with competition law principles. Specifically, Canada proposed that, at the end of the transition period for eliminating tariffs, cross-border anticompetitive pricing practices by private firms would be handled under each country's existing domestic antitrust laws.

Although much political posturing occurred over subsidies and countervailing duties (some politicians on both sides of the border enjoyed claiming that the Canadian federal and provincial governments were more solicitous of their businesses and citizens than were the U.S. federal and state governments), both the U.S. and the Canadian negotiators set to work to define lists of acceptable and unacceptable practices. However, this effort was fruitless. The U.S. working-level negotiators eventually recognized that the United States could not negotiate only with Canada to increase discipline on U.S. domestic subsidies without similar discipline being negotiated with, for example, the European Union (EU), Japan, and Latin America, which could be done only through the General Agreement on Tariffs and Trade (GATT).[1]

Although somewhat attracted to the notion of eliminating antidumping laws between the two countries, the United States maintained that it would be virtually impossible for it to agree to Canada's proposal because of the strong political support in Washington for the U.S. antidumping law.[2] Certainly, some agencies and special interests were opposed to any liberalization of the antidumping law (notwithstanding that U.S. exporters consistently face more antidumping cases in Canada than Canadian exporters face in the United States).[3] But in fact, the real obstacle to a substitute system was probably the impossibility of reaching an agreement bilaterally to discipline subsidies, which permitted the blocking of the antidumping proposal as well.

In the end, the United States and Canada agreed to form a working group whose goal was to develop more effective rules and increased discipline on the use of government subsidies and to devise a substitute system to deal with "unfair pricing" (i.e., dumping) no later than seven years from the effective date of the agreement (CUSFTA, Articles 1906 and 1907). Meanwhile, the two countries agreed to the special binational dispute-settlement procedures set out in Chapter 19 of CUSFTA to handle antidumping and countervailing duty disputes.[4]

In the years following CUSFTA's entry into force, the United States and Canada never seriously discussed a substitute system, in part because both countries' focus in the late 1980s and early 1990s had shifted away from bilateral trade issues and toward the Uruguay Round multilateral trade negotiations in Geneva. In addition, the United States in particular knew that certain special interests would strongly oppose the elimination of antidumping or countervailing duty laws vis-à-vis Canada. Therefore, no progress was made under CUSFTA, and the seven-year deadline for devising a bilateral system to replace the application of national AD and CVD laws was overtaken by events—namely, the NAFTA negotiations.

The North American Free Trade Negotiations

Primarily because of pressure by both Canada and Mexico, Article 1504 of NAFTA established a trilateral working group that, within five years of enactment of the agreement (i.e., by January 1, 1999), is to report to the three NAFTA governments on issues concerning the relationship between competition laws and policies and trade in the free trade area. In addition, in exchange for the new Canadian government's December 1993 commitment to proclaim NAFTA in effect, the United States agreed to "seek solutions that reduce the possibility of disputes concerning the issues of subsidies, dumping and the operation of the trade remedy laws regarding such practices" and to set up a working group to complete this work by December 31, 1995.[5] The discussions of this trilateral working group are to focus largely on developing a replacement system for national antidumping and countervailing duty laws. As the U.S., Canadian, and Mexican economies become more economically integrated through NAFTA and the World Trade Organization (WTO), the rationale for reliance on antidumping and countervailing duty laws should decrease. Thus, alternatives to the continued application of antidumping and countervailing duty laws could be considered.

ALTERNATIVES TO THE APPLICATION OF ANTIDUMPING LAWS[6]

Replace Antidumping Laws with Competition Laws

One of the most frequently discussed alternatives to antidumping law is competition or antitrust law. Antidumping laws punish differential cross-border pricing regardless of whether such pricing is predatory and impedes competition or is nonpredatory and, in fact, promotes competition.[7] Dumping is remedied through the imposition of duties if the dumping has a material, injurious effect on the importing country's industry. However, antidumping laws do not examine or consider the effect on competition within the importing country of dumping or the imposition of antidumping duties. Competition law, in contrast, focuses on the activities that undermine the competitive process.[8] Typically, predatory pricing is associated with firms with market power. For example, price cutting by a firm with market power, the aim of which is to harm or seriously weaken smaller competitors or to obstruct entry into a market by potential competitors, would be considered predatory.[9] By contrast, Canadian, Mexican, and U.S. antidumping laws do not require that an exporter subject to an allegation of dumping have market power. Indeed, all three countries' antidumping laws routinely attack conduct that is permitted of domestic companies (for example, sales at prices above variable cost but below fully allocated cost for each separate fiscal year).

Antidumping laws often hinder free market competition and therefore frustrate one of the primary objectives of the North American free trade area: to improve the economic efficiency and competitiveness of North American firms and industries within a demanding global market. The 1994 [U.S.] *Economic Report of the President* noted that antidumping laws are overly restrictive and sometimes reduce competition and raise prices, unlike antitrust laws, which generally increase competition and lower prices.[10] The report also noted that "antidumping laws go beyond preventing anti-competitive practices—which *should* be their rationale—and often have the effect of protecting domestic industries from foreign competition."[11]

The problem with retaining and using antidumping laws within NAFTA is that this can defeat healthy and intense nonpredatory price competition. The application of antidumping laws can also lead to the protection of inefficient industries, thereby distorting the efficient allocation of resources within the three countries.[12] In addition, the mere possibility or threat of antidumping actions may be sufficient to impede the economic rationalization of enterprises operating in more than one of the three NAFTA countries. All of these factors run counter to the goal of improving the global competitiveness of North America's industrial base.

Replacing antidumping laws with competition laws is not as dramatic a change as might appear at first glance.[13] One of the most frequently stated rationales for antidumping laws is that protected home markets enable foreign producers to dump in export markets without fear of retaliation or the re-exportation of the dumped goods to their own markets. Whether or not that rationale is true,[14] the elimination of tariffs and other border measures under NAFTA will, over time, reduce and ultimately eliminate the rationale for antidumping laws.[15,16]

Is the Australian-New Zealand Approach a Viable Model for NAFTA?

In March 1983, Australia and New Zealand entered into the Closer Economic Relations (CER) pact, whose intent was to more closely integrate the two economies. In the first five years of the agreement, considerable progress was made toward reducing barriers to trade and investment between the two countries, including the elimination of nearly all tariffs and all direct export subsidies. As trade barriers were reduced and eliminated, bilateral trade increased significantly, and in 1988, the two countries agreed to take further steps to accelerate progress toward a single market.[17] By mid 1990, all bilateral tariffs as well as import and export barriers were eliminated. In addition, each country agreed to treat the other's producers as they treated their own—that is, antidumping laws were replaced by each country's competition laws (which penalize predatory pricing by competitors, domestic or foreign).[18]

In deciding whether to eliminate their antidumping laws, the two countries concluded that maintaining those laws would be contrary to the goal of achieving a single integrated market:

> In an open trans-Tasman market, the different thresholds for antidumping and competition laws would have led to the protection of relatively inefficient industries in the trans-Tasman context and hence would have hampered the efficient allocation of resources between the two countries. Moreover, it was felt that the removal of trade barriers would make dumping increasingly redundant as the scope for price discrimination between the domestic and export markets was reduced, and the risk of retaliation by competitors increased. Continuation of the antidumping remedy would also have enhanced the possibilities for prolonged disputation at an official level to the detriment of a beneficial commercial relationship.[19]

Several procedural changes were also made to the Australian and New Zealand competition laws to enable them to operate effectively. For example, both countries agreed that authorities in one country would have investigatory powers to obtain evidence in the other country for the purpose of enforcing the bans on the anticompetitive use of market power. Thus, New Zealand can issue a notice requiring an Australian company to supply information and documents needed in the investigation of a complaint. Failure to comply with such a notice is an offense under Australian law. In addition, the relevant courts in each country are able to sit in the other country or take evidence and submissions. Judgments and orders, including injunctions, are made by each court and are enforceable in the corresponding court in the other country.[20]

Are Competition Laws Feasible Within NAFTA?

In a fully integrated economy where barriers to the free flow of goods and services have been eliminated, replacing AD and CVD laws with competition laws makes good economic and political sense. Thus, both the United States and the EU rely on competition law rather than AD or CVD actions among their member states.

There are relatively few significant differences between the U.S. and Canadian competition laws.[21] Mexico enacted a new competition law in 1992, effective in July 1993, that replaces the antimonopoly law that had been on the books but was virtually never enforced since 1934.[22] The new Mexican law contains a comprehensive body of substantive antitrust provisions as well as an enforcement structure under the administration of a newly created Federal Competition Commission.[23] Despite the apparent comprehensiveness of the new competition law, some in the United States and Canada may be skeptical because of Mexico's lack of experience in applying and enforcing antitrust rules. At least in the short term, these differences will make it more difficult for all three countries to reach agreement on a single, unified approach to competition law.

However, mutual recognition and legal assistance, similar to that in the Australia-New Zealand CER pact, may be a more feasible approach for the NAFTA countries. The United States and Canada have had an antitrust cooperation agreement (Memorandum of Understanding between the Government of the United States of America and the Government of Canada as to Notification, Consultation, and Cooperation with Respect to the Application of National Antitrust Laws) since 1984, and an agreement on mutual legal assistance in criminal matters (Treaty on Mutual Legal Assistance in Criminal Matters, MLACM) since 1985. These agreements have facilitated the coordination and enforcement of antitrust laws between the United States and Canada, and in several cases U.S. and Canadian authorities have been able to obtain evidence on each other's behalf.[24,25] Indeed, the non-binding 1984 cooperation agreement on antitrust matters has been so effective that the U.S. and Canada recently entered into a binding agreement to further enhance the coordination of antitrust enforcement investigations.[26] The expansion of these mutual assistance agreements to include Mexico would greatly increase the ability of antitrust authorities in the NAFTA countries to conduct effective cross-border investigations of predatory pricing practices and could reduce and ultimately eliminate the need for national antidumping laws in NAFTA.

Create a Customs Union

Unlike a free trade area, where each member country maintains its own system to deal with third-party trade, a customs union is a more fully integrated market.[27] The NAFTA countries might consider creating a customs union or common market along the lines of the EU, Mercosur, or the Andean Pact. In a customs union, the member countries agree to eliminate tariff and nontariff trade barriers within the customs union and establish a common external tariff and coordinated economic strategy to deal with third-party trade.

Although it is politically unlikely that NAFTA will become a customs union in the reasonably near future, the NAFTA countries could consider establishing a single antidumping system to address price discrimination by non-NAFTA countries. That is, a supranational body could be established to consider allegations of dumped (or subsidized) imports into the region, to conduct investigations, and to decide what measures, if any, should be taken.

The absence of such a framework was noticeable in the 1987 Canadian antidumping case brought by Ford Canada and General Motors (GM) Canada against Hyundai of Korea.[28] In that case, it was determined that there was no material injury to the Canadian small-car industry, mainly because the petitioners' production of small autos was concentrated in the United States. Approximately 80 percent of the Canadian companies' sales in Canada consisted of autos produced in the United States. Like the Canadian-produced autos, the U.S.-produced autos sold in Canada experienced price suppression and market erosion as a result of Hyundai's dumped imports in the Canadian market. Nevertheless, the Canadian Import Tribunal did not include the U.S.-produced imports of Ford and GM in its injury analysis.[29] In a customs union, the U.S.- produced autos would be treated as part of the "domestic" industry of the customs union for purposes of the injury analysis. The situation would be even more complex if a labor union, protecting the interests of its members, filed a similar case.

In the EU, all antidumping cases are handled by a supranational commission and are viewed from the perspective of the customs union as a whole. For example, in 1994, the European Commission conducted an antidumping case that concerned gum rosin imports from China. For purposes of the antidumping investigation, the Portuguese gum rosin industry was considered the "EU industry."[30] In that case, the authorities determined that the EU industry was not injured. Whether the treatment of the customs union as a single market for purposes of injury analysis would increase the likelihood of an affirmative injury finding would depend on the facts in the case.

Mercosur, the South American common market comprising Argentina, Brazil, Paraguay, and Uruguay, is moving toward becoming a fully integrated customs union and is considering establishing a commission or investigative authority that would be responsible for investigating allegations of injury to the Mercosur industry resulting from dumped or subsidized imports from non-Mercosur countries.[31] It is envisioned that during the transition period, Mercosur member countries will continue to investigate allegations of dumped or subsidized imports from other Mercosur countries on a national basis. However, provisions (still in draft form) have been specifically designed to encourage the resolution of issues through consultation.

The Andean Pact, another regionally integrated market in South America that comprises Ecuador, Bolivia, Colombia, Peru, and Venezuela, is also moving toward the establishment of a customs union. In 1987, the Andean Pact countries established a mechanism to prevent or correct unfair trade practices that distort competition in the region. A central authority, La Junta del Acuerdo de Cartagena, was instructed to investigate allegations of unfairly traded imports and to encourage resolution of the issues through consultation. Under the provisions of the agreement, an Andean Pact member country may seek authorization from the Junta to impose duties if (1) dumped or subsidized imports from a member country cause or threaten to cause injury to the industry in an importing member country; (2) the dumped or subsidized imports cause or threaten to cause injury to exports of the petitioning industry in a third-country member market; (3) dumped or subsidized imports from a nonmember country cause or threaten to cause injury to an industry of a member country; or (4) dumped or subsidized imports from nonmember countries affect the national production of a member country and, to correct the problem, a modification to the agreement (e.g., the common external tariff) is required.[32]

Although the NAFTA countries could consider an approach to antidumping and countervailing duty rules based on the EU, Mercosur, or Andean Pact models, it might be politically difficult to do so at this time because it would require some form of supranational decisionmaking.

Include Antitrust Analysis in Antidumping Law

A July 1994 report of the Task Force of the Antitrust Section of the American Bar Association suggests that, as an intermediate step toward a harmonized competition policy, each NAFTA country could maintain its national antidumping and competition laws while agreeing to apply the definition of market, the predation standard, and injury analysis in competition law to antidumping analysis.[33] Although this approach has the political advantage of maintaining the primary objective of the antidumping law—protection for the domestic industry without considering the impact on consumers and industrial users—it reduces the types of commercially sound pricing practices currently subject to antidumping actions. In addition, under an antitrust or competition policy standard, injury would not be found unless the dumped imports were determined to be *the* cause, and not just *a* cause, of the injury to the domestic industry. (Under AD and CVD laws, the dumped or subsidized imports need only be *a* cause—not *the* cause or the *primary* cause of injury—for duties to be imposed.)

The NAFTA countries could also agree to adopt a "meeting-competition" defense, whereby injury would not be found if a foreign producer was setting its prices in an export market at the same level as the producers in that market. Under current antidumping rules, dumping duties may be imposed on imports even if a foreign producer is simply meeting the competition in the foreign market. Imports that are priced to meet the competition should not cause injury to a domestic producer.[34]

Another Task Force suggestion is that the NAFTA countries could adopt the average variable or marginal cost method of calculating production costs used in antitrust law, which would reduce the number of dumping findings and lower the level of protection currently afforded domestic industries.[35] Under current antidumping rules, the cost of production refers to the fully allocated cost of production. If a foreign producer is selling in its own market at prices that are lower than the fully allocated cost of production, the "constructed value" method of measuring dumping is used.[36] In this method, the fully allocated cost of production, plus an amount for profit and operating expenses, is compared with the foreign producer's export prices. This methodology results in the imposition of antidumping duties even when foreign producers are acting in a commercially rational manner—just like their domestic competitors—in pricing above their average variable or marginal costs.[37]

ALTERNATIVES TO THE APPLICATION OF NATIONAL COUNTERVAILING DUTY LAWS

Although AD and CVD laws are often discussed together as a single body of law (the "unfair trade laws"), and the same material injury standard applies to both, some significant differences exist between dumping and subsidies that may make it more appropriate to consider separately a substitute system for national countervailing duty laws within NAFTA. Most notably, antidumping laws address the pricing behavior of private companies, while countervailing duty laws address the unfair trade advantage that results from government-provided subsidies. The adoption of special rules on dumping within NAFTA is workable because the effect of such an arrangement does not automatically extend to non-NAFTA countries. However, the adoption of special rules to increase discipline on subsidies only within NAFTA would create a "free rider" problem: benefits from any increased subsidies discipline agreed upon by the three NAFTA countries would automatically extend to non-NAFTA countries without exacting any similar discipline from these free riders.[38]

National countervailing duties provide a remedy for subsidized goods in the importing country, but they do nothing to reduce the harmful effects of subsidies in third-country markets or in the subsidizing country's market. For example, U.S. imposition of a countervailing duty on imports of a subsidized product from Mexico will not necessarily lead to the elimination of the subsidy practice in Mexico; nor will it remedy the injury to U.S.

exports in third-country markets caused by competing Mexican exports. This is the primary difference between a countervailing duty system and a true discipline on subsidies.

Government-provided subsidies have long been viewed as distorting competition and international trade. As a result, establishing discipline on subsidies has been the subject of intense discussion since the creation of the GATT in 1947. With the exception of the significant, though limited, prohibition on export subsidies by developed countries included in the 1979 Tokyo Round Subsidies Code, not much real progress in disciplining government subsidies occurred during the first 40 years of the GATT's existence. However, as a result of the Uruguay Round of multilateral trade negotiations, a new Subsidies Agreement was negotiated, marking a dramatic step forward in establishing meaningful multilateral discipline on trade-distorting subsidies.[39]

Article 3.1 of the WTO Agreement on Subsidies and Countervailing Measures prohibits export subsidies and subsidies that are contingent upon the use of domestic over imported goods, regardless of whether those goods are exported. The new agreement specifies that subsidies provided to specific enterprises or industries within national borders are actionable (i.e., subject to countervailing duties or countermeasures) by affected parties, unless such subsidies meet the limited criteria for exemption from actionability.[40] The agreement also provides for binding determinations by the WTO Subsidies Committee to remove the effect of subsidies in any market, including third-country markets, if the subsidies cause "serious prejudice" to the interests of another country.[41] Thus, the new WTO Subsidies Agreement takes care of most or all of the free rider problem through increased multilateral discipline on subsidies agreed to by all member countries of the WTO, including the NAFTA countries. Consequently, most of the problems facing U.S. and Canadian negotiators in 1986-87 have been resolved, leaving a more focused menu of opportunities for improving the WTO agreement.

For example, the NAFTA members could agree to mutual disarmament in the subsidies race by limiting or eliminating the use of subsidies otherwise permitted by the WTO, including "green light" subsidies, in competition to attract new investments. Costly incentives are commonly offered by local, state, and provincial governments to lure new plants (often built by a foreign manufacturer) to particular locales. If a plant is definitely going to be established in one of the NAFTA countries, there is no net gain to the free trade area as a whole, except to the factory owner, from an internal bidding war by individual NAFTA governments to offer the greatest subsidies. Indeed, such bidding wars ultimately result in a net loss for taxpayers. Thus, the NAFTA member countries' federal and state or provincial governments could agree to eliminate these costly plant-snatching subsidies.

NEGOTIATE LESS TRADE-RESTRICTIVE ANTIDUMPING[42] AND COUNTERVAILING DUTY RULES TO BE APPLIED WITHIN NAFTA

Another, less ambitious, alternative is to negotiate less trade-restrictive AD and CVD rules that would be applied only to trade among the NAFTA countries. Each country would maintain its current AD and CVD rules applicable to third-party trade. Article XXIV of the GATT 1994, which governs free trade agreements, recognizes the desirability of encouraging free trade areas and customs unions, provided that the integration serves to promote trade among the participants but does not increase barriers to trade between FTA participants and nonparticipants. Thus, the negotiation of some less trade-restrictive rules in the context of NAFTA need not violate the GATT's most-favored-nation (MFN) principle.[43]

The following are some rules in national AD and CVD laws that could be amended and applied to trade in goods within NAFTA.

Preinitiation Consultations. The NAFTA countries could permit or require consultations among the governments and the private industries of the countries involved before the formal initiation of an investigation, with the appropriate safeguards to protect against antitrust problems. These consultations could help defuse tensions, provide a better understanding of the facts, and encourage an early resolution of the problem, without requiring a formal proceeding. In addition, several alternative dispute-settlement methods (e.g., arbitration or minitrials) could be explored.

Higher Standards for Initiating Cases. The NAFTA member countries could negotiate stricter standards for initiating AD and CVD investigations. For example, petitioning industries could be required to provide greater support for their allegations of dumping and/or subsidization, and the authorities could be required to corroborate the information's accuracy. Although the WTO Antidumping Agreement and the Agreement on Subsidies and Countervailing Measures require that the authorities examine the accuracy and adequacy of the evidence in the petition to determine whether the evidence is sufficient to justify initiating an investigation, the NAFTA countries could agree to strengthen this requirement by requiring actual corroboration of that information.[44] In addition, if the alleged margin of dumping or rate of subsidization was less than, for example, twice the minimum threshold percentage required by the WTO agreements, an investigation would not be initiated.

Higher Material Injury Standard. The NAFTA countries could establish a higher standard for an affirmative finding of material injury, particularly at the preliminary stage. The current U.S. standard—the existence of a "reasonable indication" that a domestic industry is materially injured or threatened with material injury—is very low. Under the Canadian system, the Canadian International Trade Tribunal (CITT) does not make a preliminary injury determination unless specifically requested, and the investigation continues unless, after a very limited inquiry, Revenue Canada fails to disclose any evidence of injury. As a result, most preliminary injury determinations in both the United States and Canada are affirmative. Adoption of a more rigorous standard for determining injury at the preliminary phase (e.g., less benefit of the doubt given to the petitioner in the United States, and less reliance on the petitioner's data only in Canada) could help to eliminate unwarranted cases.

Public Interest Test. The NAFTA member countries could agree to apply a public interest test that would determine whether the imposition of an AD or CV duty was in the overall economic interest of the importing country. Current U.S. law does not permit such an analysis. Although Canada's AD and CVD law contains a public interest provision, it is rarely used. (A notable exception was in 1987, when Canada relied on the provision to lower the amount of countervailing duties imposed on U.S. corn exports to Canada, from CAN $1.10 per bushel to CAN $0.46 per bushel.[45]) Mexico's AD and CVD law is less explicit, but recent Mexican decisions providing softer than necessary treatment for U.S. steel exports suggest that the Mexican authorities do consider public interest.[46]

Lesser Duty Rule. The NAFTA member countries could agree to impose a duty in an amount less the full margin of dumping or subsidization, if the lesser duty was sufficient to offset the injury to the domestic industry in the importing country. This approach is normally followed in proceedings conducted by the European Commission and is codified in the Commission's regulations (Council Regulation 3283/94, Article 9(4)).[47] In theory, the imposition of the lesser duty may exclude the exporter from the market anyway, but in practice, it is less preclusive than the higher duties that would otherwise be imposed.

Meeting Competition Defense. The NAFTA countries could adopt in their national antidumping laws the "meeting competition" doctrines found in U.S. antitrust law,[48] whereby dumped imports would not be found to cause injury if they are priced at the same level as domestic producers charge in the importing country. With such a provision, antidumping laws would better meet the objective of ensuring fair competition without discriminating against imports.

Temporary Suspension of Duties. The NAFTA member countries could agree to suspend antidumping and countervailing duties if the domestic industry in the importing country was not able to satisfy demand for the product subject to such duties within a reasonable period of time and at a nonaberrant price.[49]

Standard of Review. The NAFTA member countries could agree to develop a common standard of review for antidumping and countervailing duty disputes instead of applying the standard of review of each country. Absent a common standard of review, a U.S. exporter to both Mexico and Canada could win a dispute-settlement panel challenging the imposition of an antidumping duty in Mexico, while losing a panel challenging the imposition of an antidumping duty in Canada based on the same facts. A common standard of review would eliminate that possibility.

Further, as Daniel Schwanen notes in Chapter 6 here, the existing Chapter 19 dispute-settlement mechanism would be more binding if the three countries agreed to give dispute-settlement panel decisions precedential authority. However, that suggestion is likely to attract opposition from any industry that has lost a Chapter 19 panel.

Settlements. The member countries could agree that, wherever practicable, exporters found to be dumping or selling subsidized merchandise in a NAFTA importing market could enter into a suspension agreement or other legally permissible settlement, rather than being subject to antidumping or countervailing duties. In theory, the exporter that raises its prices to eliminate dumping pays no duties, whether under a dumping order or a settlement agreement, but the settlement agreement has the advantage of creating more commercial certainty.

Under U.S. law, settlement (or suspension) agreements may take two forms: the complete elimination of dumping or the complete elimination of injury. In practice, the United States enters only rarely into suspension agreements, in part because of the claimed administrative burden of monitoring such agreements, and in part because of a perception that suspension agreements somehow favor foreign producers and exporters.

Under the Canadian system, settlements are not as necessary as under the U.S. system. Exporters found to be selling dumped or subsidized merchandise in the Canadian market have the option of increasing their prices to a level equal to or above the "normal value" established by Revenue Canada to avoid paying any dumping duties. Under the U.S. system, however, exporters are caught in the lengthy and costly cycle of annual administrative reviews of the dumping margin, even if they cease dumping in the U.S. market.

***De Minimis* Margins and Market Share**. The GATT 1994 antidumping and subsidies agreements establish *de minimis* thresholds for dumping margins (2 percent), subsidy rates (1 percent), and import share (3 percent, though less stringent rules apply to developing countries). That is, an investigation must be terminated if the dumping margin is less than 2 percent, the subsidy rate is less than 1 percent, or the import share is less than 3 percent. The NAFTA member countries could negotiate higher *de minimis* standards to reduce or eliminate unwarranted cases. At some point, if the market share is small, the cost of defending a case can become an absolute embargo.

In addition, a minimum market share percentage could be adopted whereby imports from a NAFTA country would be considered *de minimis,* and an investigation would therefore be terminated if the imports accounted for less than a certain percentage of the market of the importing NAFTA country.[50] The presumption behind such a provision is that imports accounting for less than a certain minimum percentage of the importing country's market would not cause injury to the domestic industry. Such a provision would help protect small exporters from unwarranted cases.[51]

Prohibition Against Cumulating Imports from NAFTA Countries. Under current U.S. practice, the International Trade Commission normally cumulates the imports from all countries subject to an investigation to determine whether the dumped or subsidized imports caused injury to the domestic industry. An exception exists if the imports from a country are "negligible." The NAFTA member countries can negotiate a special rule prohibiting the cumulation of imports from another NAFTA member. This ensures that a determination will be made as to whether the imports from the NAFTA exporting country are, by themselves, causing injury to the NAFTA importing country.[52]

Price Comparisons in Antidumping Cases. Under Article 2.4 of the new WTO Antidumping Agreement, all parties are required to calculate the dumping margin based on a "fair comparison." As a matter of course, Mexico already compares average prices in each market to determine the margin of dumping,[53] and the United States[54] and Canada[55] typically compare individual export prices to a weighted average of prices in the exporting country. The United States has announced its intention to limit the application of the new fair comparison requirement to investigations, and does not intend to apply it in administrative reviews.[56] The NAFTA countries could agree that the margin of dumping in all phases of a proceeding would be based on a fair comparison—either a comparison of average prices in the exporting market to average prices in the importing country or a comparison of an individual transaction in the exporting country to an individual transaction in the importing country. This methodology for calculating the margin of dumping should yield less-distortive results.

Calculation of Cost of Production. The WTO Antidumping Agreement provides that sales at prices below the cost of production may be disregarded in calculating dumping margins only if such below-cost sales occur "within an *extended period of time* in substantial quantities and at prices which do not provide for the recovery of all costs within a *reasonable period of time*[57] (emphasis added). While the Agreement defines the "extended period of time" for measuring production costs as normally one year, but never less than six months,[58] it expressly leaves unlimited and undefined the "reasonable period of time" for cost recovery.[59] Therefore, the NAFTA countries could adopt a production cost calculation methodology based on normal business practices, taking into account business cycles and product life cycles as appropriate for different industries, and allowing a truly reasonable period of time to recover costs. The inclusion of such a provision in national antidumping laws would permit the NAFTA countries to take action against unfairly traded imports without interfering with the normal operations of free markets.

CONCLUSION

The continued application of antidumping laws (and perhaps to a lesser extent, countervailing duty laws) within NAFTA could interfere with the economic integration of the free trade area. Antidumping laws punish competitive cross-border pricing, regardless of whether such pricing is predatory and impedes competition. Competition laws, on the other hand, prohibit cross-border price discrimination only if it adversely affects competition. The replacement of antidumping law with competition law to be applied among the NAFTA countries (or among those countries that choose to agree to do so on a bilateral basis) is undoubtedly the most ambitious approach, but it is also the most consistent with the principle of a free market for North American business and consumers.

Notes

1. A great deal of the work done in the Canada-U.S. Free Trade Agreement (CUSFTA) negotiations later served as the basis for much of the World Trade Organization (WTO) Agreement on Subsidies and Countervailing Measures.

2. In 1985, when asked if a U.S.-Canada negotiation on AD and CVD laws was possible, both the majority and minority trade staffs of the Senate Finance Committee and the House Ways and Means Committee said, "Let's talk about it." The U.S. Trade Representative's office, however, claimed that Congress would not even discuss the issue.

3. According to data on antidumping actions compiled from the U.S. and Canadian semiannual reports to the GATT Anti-Dumping Code Committee, during the

period from 1989 to 1993 Canada initiated 26 antidumping investigations against U.S. exports, compared with 12 initiated by the United States against Canadian exports. The U.S. cases against Canada probably cover a larger absolute value of imports because the U.S. market is so much larger than the Canadian market. However, it is difficult to determine this with certainty because the statistics in the semiannual reports are not reported on a consistent value or volume basis.

4. See G. Bruce Doern and Brian W. Tomlin, *Faith and Fear: The Free Trade Story* (1991), pp. 195-199.

5. "Statement by the Governments of Canada, Mexico and the United States, Future Work on Antidumping Duties, Subsidies and Countervail," Reprinted in *Inside U.S. Trade*, December 3, 1993, p. 18.

6. Antidumping laws are designed to remedy material injury to domestic producers resulting from international price discrimination or below-cost sales; countervailing duty laws are designed to remedy material injury to domestic producers resulting from government-provided subsidies. Although the same injury analysis applies to both dumped and subsidized imports, the analysis pertaining to the underlying unfair trade practice is very different.

7. Price discrimination is the pricing of a good or service at different levels in different markets. Predation generally is regarded as the pricing of a good or service below marginal (or variable) cost with the intent of driving competitors out of the market. Antidumping laws address price discrimination by foreign producers that causes injury to the domestic industry in the importing country. Competition laws, as currently applied, address price discrimination within a market by producers—domestic or foreign—with a predatory intent. Organization for Economic Cooperation and Development (OECD), *Competition and Trade Policies: Their Interaction* (1984), p. 114.

8. Ravi P. Kewalram, "The Australia-New Zealand Closer Economic Relations Trade Agreement," *Journal of World Trade*, Vol. 27 (1993), pp. 111, 122.

9. Ibid. p. 123.

10. Council of Economic Advisors, *Economic Report of the President*, Washington, D.C., 1994, p. 239.

11. Ibid.

12. For an initial study of the trade-restrictive effects of the antidumping investigative process, even if no duties are imposed, see Robert W. Staiger and Frank A. Wolak, "Measuring Industry-Specific Protection: Antidumping in the United States," Working Paper 4696, National Bureau of Economic Research, April 1994.

13. Indeed, the first piece of U.S. antidumping legislation—the Antidumping Act of 1916—closely resembled antitrust law in that it contained a prohibition on predatory pricing of imports. At the time, the Supreme Court was perceived as having ruled that predatory behavior by firms exporting to the United States was not subject to U.S. antitrust laws (see *American Banana Co.* v. *United Fruit Co.*, 213 U.S. 347 (1909)), and therefore a special law was needed to fill the gap in U.S. antitrust law coverage. However, the predation standard was removed by Congress in 1921, partly in reaction to the absence of a predatory-intent standard in Canada's

antidumping law and partly in response to industry demands for increased protection against competitively priced imports. See J. Michael Finger, "The Origins and Evolution of Antidumping Regulation," in J. Michael Finger (ed.), *Antidumping: How It Works and Who Gets Hurt* (1993), pp. 13, 14-20.

The basic premise of the 1921 act has been carried through every subsequent piece of U.S. antidumping legislation—that is, it must be established only that a U.S. industry is suffering or is likely to suffer material injury as a result of dumped imports. The intent to harm competition or create a monopoly is not relevant. Over the years, the U.S. antidumping and antitrust laws have evolved in different directions, so that now the United States treats similar pricing practices quite differently, depending on whether the product being sold is produced and sold domestically or is produced in a foreign country and sold in the U.S. market.

14. Hong Kong, a country that has no border protection, has been the target of 28 dumping cases since 1980, which suggests that dumping cases are possible without the necessary conditions for dumping. Although final duties were not imposed in all cases, the commercial uncertainty caused by the initiation of an investigation has been substantial.

15. Article 91 of the 1957 Treaty Establishing the European Economic Community (Treaty of Rome) abolishes national antidumping laws within the European Union by member states, but permits the application of antidumping measures during the transition period granted to each new member state upon accession to the treaty. This reflects the view that once tariffs and quantitative restrictions are eliminated, antidumping issues are more appropriately handled by competition laws and authorities.

16. As Daniel Schwanen suggests in Chapter 6 here, the NAFTA countries could agree to identify sectors that would be free from the imposition of antidumping or countervailing duties, as tariffs and other border measures are eliminated in those sectors. In fact, some sectors, such as computers, might volunteer to eliminate AD and CVD laws. The U.S. computer industry, for example, has proposed to eliminate tariffs worldwide on computers, computer parts, semiconductors, and software by the year 2000 (see "Computer Industry Proposing Sweeping Tariff Elimination by 2000," *Inside U.S. Trade*, February 17, 1995, p. 1). If this proposal is carried out, the elimination of antidumping and countervailing duty laws in the computer industry would be a logical next step.

In addition, nothing would prevent any two of the NAFTA countries from agreeing to eliminate the application of antidumping and countervailing duty laws between them, either completely or as sectors are freed of tariffs.

17. Graeme Thomson and Christopher Langman, "The Removal of Trade Remedy Law in Trans-Tasman Commerce," *Canada-U.S. Law Journal*, Vol. 17 (1991), p. 203.

18. New Zealand's competition law prohibits any persons with a dominant position in a market in Australia and/or New Zealand from using that position to restrict entry into, to deter competition in, or to eliminate a person from a market in New Zealand. The Australian law provides that a corporation with "a substantial degree of market power in a trans-Tasman market" must not seek to eliminate or substantially damage a competitor, to prevent the entry of a person, or to deter competition in a market in Australia. The only exception to these laws is when the market in Australia or New Zealand is exclusively for services. Ibid., pp. 205-206.

19. Ibid., p. 204.

20. Ibid., p. 206.

21. The competition laws of the United States and Canada address predatory pricing in a substantially similar way. Prices that are unreasonably low with the effect of, or designed to have the effect of, substantially lessening competition or eliminating a competitor are illegal under both bodies of law and may be subject to criminal prosecution or actions for compensation. Potential problems may arise, however, concerning discovery of information, official cooperation, treatment of confidential information, venue, personal jurisdiction, subject matter jurisdiction, remedies (e.g., enforcement of orders for compensation, penalties and injunctions), etc. Ivan R. Feltman et al., "Competition (Antitrust) and Antidumping Laws in the Context of the Canada-United States Free Trade Agreement," *Canada-U.S. Law Journal*, Vol. 17 (1991), pp. 67-68.

22. Joshua A. Newberg, "Mexico's New Economic Competition Law: Toward the Development of a Mexican Law of Antitrust," *Journal of Transnational Law*, Vol. 33 (1994), p. 587.

23. Ibid.

24. See Geoffrey D. Oliver and David G. Litt, "Cooperation or Confrontation? The Clinton Administration's Enforcement of U.S. Antitrust Law," *Corporate Counsel's International Adviser*, Jan. 10, 1994, pp. 2, 6.

25. The Treaty on Mutual Legal Assistance in Criminal Matters does not limit the exchange of confidential information between U.S. and Canadian authorities. In fact, Article XIII states that the requested authority "may provide copies of any document, record or information in the possession of a government department or agency, but not publicly available, to the same extent and under the same conditions as would be available to its own law enforcement and judicial authorities." This provision also permits the authority providing the information to specify that the information be accorded confidential treatment. The treaty applies only in criminal antitrust prosecution cases and is regarded as a powerful tool in antitrust enforcement efforts. See Nina Hachigian, "Essential Mutual Assistance in International Antitrust Enforcement," *International Law*, Vol. 29 (Spring 1995), pp. 117, 140.

26. Agreement Between the Government of the United States of America and the Government of Canada Regarding the Application of Their Competition and Deceptive Marketing Practices Laws, reprinted in 69 Antitrust & Trade Reg. Rep. (BNA) 177 (August 10, 1995).

27. Michael Hart, "Dumping and Free Trade Areas," in John H. Jackson and Edwin A. Vermulst (eds.), *Antidumping Law and Practice: A Comparative Study* (1989), p. 326.

28. Cars Produced by or on Behalf of Hyundai Motor Co., Seoul, Rep. of Korea and Originating in or Exported from the Rep. of Korea [1988] C.I.T. No. 15, Inquiry No. CIT-13-87 (Mar. 23, 1988).

29. Ibid.

30. The European Community industry consisted of medium-sized firms located solely in Portugal (Folkert Graafsma and Bart Driessen, "Commerce Defense Actions and Other International Trade Developments in the European Communities VIII: 1 January 1994-30 June 1994," EJIL, Vol. 5 (1994) p. 9).

31. Mercosur has already reached an agreement on the allocation of jurisdiction over contractual disputes among the member countries. See *Protocol de Buenos Aires Sobre Jurisdiccion Internacional en Materia Contractual* [Buenos Aires Protocol on International Jurisdiction of Contractual Matters], Mercosur Doc. CMC-Dec. No. 1/94 (Aug. 5, 1994), in *XIV Reunion del Grupo Mercado Comun, VI Reunion del Consejo Mercado Comun, Encuentro Presidencial* (Aug. 5, 1994).

32. Decision 230 of the Cartagena Agreement, "Normas Para Prevenir o Corregir las Practicas que Puedan Distorcionar la Competencia Dentro de la Subregion" [Rules to Prevent or Correct Practices that May Distort Competition within the Subregion] (Dec. 11, 1987), in INCOMEX, *Normas Sobre Practicas Comerciales* [Rules on Trade Practices], 65 (1987).

33. Task Force of the Antitrust Section, American Bar Association, *The Competition Dimension of the North American Free Trade Agreement* (1994), p. 145.

34. Ibid.

35. Ibid.

36. *Agreement on Implementation of Article VI of the General Agreement on Tariffs and Trade 1994*, Article 2.2.1 (WTO Antidumping Agreement), "Final Act Embodying the Results of the Uruguay Round of Multilateral Trade Negotiations," April 15, 1994, Annex IA, GATT Doc. MTN/FA 145, 145 (Final Act), Reprinted in *Message from the President of the United States Transmitting the Uruguay Round Trade Agreements, Texts of Agreements, Implementing Bill, Statement of Administrative Action and Required Supporting Statements*, H.R. Doc. No. 316, 103d Cong., 2d Sess. 1453 (1994) (House Doc.).

37. Under existing antidumping rules and practice, once an antidumping duty order is in place, duties will continue to be imposed on imports even if there is a downturn in the business cycle and domestic producers lower their prices in response to a slump in demand.

38. One of the main objectives of the Canadian government in requesting the free trade negotiations with the United States in 1985 was to curtail the U.S. imposition of countervailing duties on Canadian goods. However, Canadian negotiators realized that any negotiation with the United States on the issue of countervailing duties could not move forward without also negotiating increased discipline on subsidies. This presented a problem at that time for Canada: first, because the elimination of many subsidy programs in Canada was not politically feasible; and second, because a bilateral agreement to increase subsidies discipline carried with it the free rider problem, which was intolerable to both Canada and the United States.

39. For an analysis of the new WTO Subsidies Agreement, see Gary N. Horlick and Peggy A. Clarke, "The 1994 WTO Subsidies Agreement," *Journal of World Trade*, Vol. 17 (June 1994), p. 41.

40. Articles 1.2, 7. Article 8 contains limited exceptions to the general prohibition on specific subsidies (the so-called green light subsidies) for certain kinds of research and development, regional development, and environmental assistance.

41. Articles 6.1, 6.3.

42. For detailed discussions and analyses of the WTO Antidumping Agreement, see Gary N. Horlick and Eleanor C. Shea, "The World Trade Organization Antidumping Agreement," *Journal of World Trade*, Vol. 29. (Feb. 1995), p. 5; and Mark Koulen, "The Uruguay Round Agreement on Anti-Dumping" (unpublished paper, College of Europe, Bruges, Belgium), Dec. 15, 1994. For a detailed analysis of the more controversial aspects of the U.S. legislation implementing the WTO Antidumping Agreement, see Alan F. Holmer, Gary N. Horlick, and Terence P. Stewart, "Enacted and Rejected Amendments to the Antidumping Law: In Implementation or Contravention of the Antidumping Agreement?" *International Law*, Vol. 29 (Summer 1995).

43. NAFTA, Chapter 8, for example, leaves the United States with three different sets of safeguard rules applicable to Canada, Mexico, and the rest of the world. The GATT may, in fact, require the elimination of antidumping (as well as countervailing duty) laws in a free trade area. Article XXIV(8)(b) of the GATT 1994 states, "A free-trade area shall be understood to mean a group of two or more customs territories in which the duties and other restrictive regulations of commerce (except, where necessary, those permitted under Articles XI, XII, XIII, XIV, XV, and XX) are eliminated on substantially all the trade between the constituent territories in products originating in such territories" (GATT Secretariat, *The Results of the Uruguay Round of the Multilateral Trade Negotiations: The Legal Texts* (1994), p. 524).

Because the exception to the general requirement to eliminate trade-restrictive regulations does not mention Article VI, which deals with AD and CVD measures, it can be inferred that such measures must be eliminated within a free trade area. For a comprehensive examination of this issue, see Michael M. Hart, "GATT Article XXIV and Canada-United States Free Trade Negotiations," *Review of International Business Law*, Vol. 1 (1987), pp. 317-355.

44. The new WTO Antidumping Agreement requires authorities to examine the "accuracy and adequacy of the evidence provided in the application to determine whether there is sufficient evidence to justify the initiation of an investigation" (WTO Antidumping Agreement, Article 5.3). See also WTO Subsidies Agreement, Article 11.3. The U.S. implementing legislation adopts a much lower initiation standard than that set forth in the agreement. Under U.S. law, the authorities need examine only the accuracy and adequacy of the evidence in the petition "on the basis of sources readily available" and determine whether the petition "alleges the elements necessary for the imposition of a duty" and "contains information reasonably available to the petitioner supporting the allegations." Tariff Act of 1930, § 702(c), amended by The Uruguay Round Agreements Act, Pub. L. No. 103-465, § 212, 1995 U.S.C.C.A.N. (108 Stat.) 4809, 4843 (to be codified at 19 U.S.C. 1671a(c)): Tariff Act of 1930, § 732(c), amended by The Uruguay Round Agreements Act, Pub. L. No. 103-465, § 212, 1995, U.S.C.C.A.N. (108 Stat.) 4809, 4845 (to be codified at 19 U.S.C. 1673a(c)).

45. The final report of the Canadian Import Tribunal (CIT) on the public interest issue noted that a countervailing duty above a price premium that the market was prepared to sustain would not enhance the long-term average price that Canadian corn producers could expect to receive for their product. Thus, the CIT recommended, and the government agreed, that the countervailing duty to be imposed on corn imports from the United States should be less than the full amount of the subsidy found. See Grain Corn Countervailing Duty Remission Order, 121 C. Gaz. Part II 2801 (July 22, 1987); Canadian Import Tribunal Information: Countervailing Duty on Grain Corn from the United States, C. Gaz. Part I 4190 (Oct. 31, 1987); Grain Corn Countervailing Duty Remission Order (Number 2), 122 C. Gaz. Part II 1183 (Feb. 4, 1988); Grain Corn Countervailing Duty Remission Order (Number 3), 122 C. Gaz. Part II 4848 (Nov. 1, 1988).

46. See, for example, Resolucion Definitiva de la Investigacion Antisubvencion Sobre las Importaciones de Productos Aceros Planos Recubiertos Originarias y Procedentes de los Estados Unidos de America [Final Determination in the Countervailing Duty Investigation of Imports of Flat-Rolled Coated Steel Products from the United States], *Diario Oficial* 32 (Nov. 11, 1994).

47. It is the Commission's standard practice to compare the prices at which the products under investigation are sold in the Community with either the actual prices of domestic products or, if actual prices are depressed, with "target prices" for domestic products computed on the basis of full cost of production plus a "reasonable" profit. If this margin of undercutting—the "injury margin"—is lower than the dumping margin, the antidumping duty is set at the level of the injury margin (Jean-Francois Bellis, "The EEC Antidumping System," in John H. Jackson and Edwin A. Vermulst (eds.), *Antidumping Law and Practice: A Comparative Study* (1992), pp. 41, 56-57).

48. For example, "upon proof being made, at any hearing on a complaint under this section, that there has been discrimination in price or services or facilities furnished, the burden of rebutting the *prima facie* case thus made by showing justification shall be upon the person charged with a [price discrimination] violation of this section . . . : Provided, however, that nothing herein contained shall prevent a seller rebutting the *prima facia* case thus made by showing that his lower price or the furnishing of services or facilities to any purchaser or purchasers was made in good faith to meet an equally low price of a competitor, or the services or facilities furnished by a competitor." 15 U.S.C. § 13(b).

49. The new EU antidumping regulations adopt a similar approach. See Council Regulation 3283/94, Article 14(4), 1994 O.J. (L349) 1, 17.

50. Although not required by the new GATT 1994 antidumping and subsidies agreements, the EU has a provision in its regulations that prohibits the initiation of an antidumping or countervailing duty investigation against imports from countries whose imports represent less than 1 percent of the Community's market share, unless such countries collectively account for 3 percent or more of consumption in the Community (Council Regulation 3283/94, Article 5(7), 1994 O.J. (L349) 1, 10; Council Regulation 3284/94, Article 7(11), 1994 O.J. (L349) 22, 31).

51. For example, in 1986, U.S. flower growers filed antidumping and countervailing duty cases against imports of cut flowers from nine countries, including Canada. Imports from Canada accounted for between 0.05 percent and 0.2 percent of the

U.S. market. However, because Canadian imports were cumulated with the imports from all the other countries for purposes of the injury analysis, AD and CV duties were imposed on Canadian imports, even though these imports accounted for only a tiny portion of the U.S. market. *Certain Fresh Cut Flowers from Canada, Chile, Colombia, Costa Rica, Ecuador, Israel, and the Netherlands,* USITC Pub. 1956 at A-112, A-113 n.2, Inv. Nos. 701-TA-275-278 (Final) (March 1987).

52. Under U.S. law, for countries with free trade agreements in effect with the United States prior to January 1, 1987 (e.g., Israel), such imports would not be cumulated with imports from other countries for purposes of the injury analysis, unless the U.S. International Trade Commission finds that the U.S. industry is materially injured or threatened with material injury by reason of imports from that one country. The Uruguay Round Agreements Act, Pub. L. No. 103-465, § 222(e)(2), 1995 U.S.C.C.A.N. (108 Stat.) 4809, 4873 (to be codified at 19 U.S.C. § 1677(7)(G)(iv)).

53. Reglamento de la Ley de Comercio Exterior, titulo IV, art. 40, Diario Oficial 73, Primera Seccion (Dec. 30, 1993).

54. U.S. Department of Commerce, Import Administration, International Trade Administration., *Antidumping Manual,* Chap. 6, Para. IV (1993).

55. See Special Import Measures Act, R.S.C. c. S-15, §§ 17, 55-56 (1985) (Can.) (amended 1989).

56. The Uruguay Round Agreements Act Statement of Administrative Action 173, Reprinted in House Doc. 656, 843. Under the U.S. methodology, a Canadian exporter selling identical products in the United States and Canada at identical but rising prices would always be found to be dumping in the U.S. market. For example, suppose a Canadian exporter had three sales of identical merchandise in the U.S. and Canadian markets at $1.00, $2.00, and $3.00. The U.S. Department of Commerce would compare the prices of each sale in the U.S. market to the average price of the identical sales in the Canadian market (i.e., $2.00). Thus, the $1.00 sale in the United States would be considered "dumped" because it was below the $2.00 average price in Canada, even though the prices in the two markets were identical.

57. WTO Antidumping Agreement, Article 2.2.1.

58. Ibid., fn. 4.

59. See Mark Koulen, "The Uruguay Round Agreement on Anti-Dumping" (Dec. 15, 1995) (unpublished manuscript presented at a conference organized by the College of Europe on "The Uruguay Round Results: A European Lawyer's Perspective," Bruges, Belgium, Nov. 18-19, 1994).

GARY N. HORLICK* AND SHANNON S. SHUMAN†

Nonmarket Economy Trade and U.S. Antidumping/Countervailing Duty Laws

While the period between World War I and World War II was marked by an upsurge of concern about the dumping of merchandise from the Soviet Union, especially timber and timber products,[1] no evidence has been found of how such practices would have been treated under the 1921 U.S. antidumping law. During the 1950s and 1960s, trade began to increase between the West and Comecon countries upon which Stalinist Soviet-style economic models had been imposed following World War II (Poland, Hungary, Czechoslovakia, German Democratic Republic, Romania, and Bulgaria). These changing trade patterns at times adversely affected U.S. industries, giving rise to concerns as to whether these new sources of competition were trading fairly. Thus, the U.S. was forced to develop a method of handling allegations of dumping by such countries as the traditional methods were considered unsuitable for the task of measuring price discrimination when these prices were set by a centralized public authority.

This article chronicles the search for an appropriate method of measuring fair value, and assesses the legal and economic justifications for such a

---

*O'Melveny & Myers, Washington, D.C. Formerly Deputy Assistant Secretary of Commerce for Import Administration.

†Coopers & Lybrand, Washington, D.C. Formerly Economist, Import Administration, U.S. Department of Commerce.

1. In 1930 and 1931, Soviet products were found to be dumped and restrictions were imposed in France, Belgium, Hungary, Romania, Yugoslavia and Canada. At this time, the United States imposed a prohibitively high tariff on Soviet match imports and mandated that all imports of Soviet timber be accompanied by certificates which stated that the products had not been processed by forced labor. The Soviets responded quickly to the imposition of these trade restrictions, cutting off all trade with France, Canada and several other countries. This action drew its desired response—France retracted her restrictions in July, 1931 and Canada lifted hers in February, 1935. Wilczynski, *Dumping and Central Planning*, 74 J. POL. ECON. 250 (1966).

method. It also reviews approaches used by the EEC and other countries. The article then extensively analyzes the problems with the U.S. law, and proposes solutions.

I. Background

A. U.S. Law Before 1979

1. *Treasury Decisions—Development of the Rationale*

The fair value calculation in the Antidumping Act of 1921[2] was adopted without specific regard for the special problems of determining the foreign market value of merchandise in nonmarket economy (NME) countries. This shortcoming in the original Act was recognized by the Treasury Department as early as 1960.[3] In *Bicycles from Czechoslovakia*,[4] the first NME dumping case to result in a determination of sales at less than fair value, the Treasury Department adopted the practice of referring to the domestic or export prices of similar articles manufactured in non-Communist market countries as the best evidence available of fair value. In *Jalousie-Louvre-Sized Sheet-glass from Czechoslovakia*,[5] the Treasury Department reaffirmed this practice by refusing to rely on the price of NME exports to other countries. A year later, in *Portland Cement from Poland*,[6] Treasury concluded that home market sales of NME imports did not qualify as sales "in the ordinary course of trade," as required by section 205(a) of the Antidumping Act of 1921. Indeed, in this cement case, Treasury relied upon the prices of West European cement *exported to the U.S.* as the basis for fair value. Since cement is usually priced uniformly within any single market, it is not surprising that Treasury found no dumping when comparing one export price to the U.S. with another.

This practice of using market-economy prices as a surrogate foreign-market value was formally adopted as Customs Regulation section 153.5 (b)[7] which stated:

> Merchandise from controlled-economy country: Ordinarily, if the information available indicates that the economy of the country from which the merchandise is exported is controlled to an extent that sales or offers of sales of such or similar merchandise in that country or countries other than the United States does not permit a determination of fair value under section 153.3 or section 153.4, the Secretary will determine fair value on the basis of the constructed value of the

2. 19 U.S.C. §§ 160 *et seq.* (1976).
3. The authors have been unable to ascertain how fair value was measured in a 1953–54 case involving East German potash in which no injury was found. 19 Fed. Reg. 8,020 (1954).
4. 25 Fed. Reg. 5,657 (1960).
5. 27 Fed. Reg. 8,457 (1962).
6. 28 Fed. Reg. 6,660 (1963).
7. 19 C.F.R. § 153.5(b) (1973).

merchandise determined under normal costs, expenses, and profits as reflected by the prices at which such or similar merchandise is sold by a non-state-controlled-economy country either (1) for consumption in its own markets; or (2) to other countries, including the United States.

A special problem was presented by cases involving imports from Yugoslavia—a country which claimed to have worker control rather than state control of individual enterprises, and (perhaps more importantly) with which the U.S. had maintained friendly ties since Tito's break with Stalin. Throughout the 1960s, Treasury generally relied upon Yugoslav home market prices to calculate foreign-market value. That treatment of Yugoslavia as a market economy was made more explicit in the case of *Animal Glue and Inedible Gelatin from Yugoslavia*.[8] The Treasury Department determined that Yugoslavia was *not* a state-controlled-economy country because (1) there was an established buying rate for Yugoslav currency; (2) the Customs Service could verify all information submitted by the Yugoslav government and manufacturer; and (3) at least for this product, the Yugoslav home market prices reflected the economic forces of supply and demand.

It is interesting to note that in coming to this conclusion, Treasury looked to both the market characteristics of the economy as a whole as well as of the particular commercial situation of the product under investigation. By examining the issues of currency convertibility and verifiability of information, Treasury was scrutinizing the country's monetary policies and its commercial sector's methods of recordkeeping in the ordinary course of business. By looking at the underlying supply and demand relationships, Treasury appeared to be viewing both country-wide factor and demand conditions as well as sector-specific determinants of prices for animal glue. Yugoslavia was ruled not to be an NME because it possessed a satisfactory amount of "market" characteristics at both the country *and* industry levels.

2. *1974 Trade Act*

While the technical problem of measuring alleged dumping from nonmarket economies was raised in numerous cases since 1954, the issue itself was not significant in terms of overall trade policy. Total volume of trade from these countries remained low as only Poland and Yugoslavia had most-favored-nation (MFN) trading status.[9] The remaining NMEs were subject to prohibitive Column 2 tariffs which were often 200–300% higher than their Column 1 equivalents. Total exports to the U.S. from the Soviet Union in 1972, for example, were only $95.5 million, of which the largest single item was platinum (approximately 47% of imports).

8. 42 Fed. Reg. 34,288 (Aug. 3, 1977).

9. Trade Expansion Act of 1962, Pub. L. No. 87–794, § 251, 76 Stat. 879 (1962) (codified at 19 U.S.C. § 1887 (1982)).

The Nixon Administration's policy of detente, and negotiations in 1972 towards an MFN agreement with the Soviet Union (which was never ratified), raised Congressional concerns that import relief for American industries would be sacrificed to foreign policy considerations. Consequently, the 1974 Trade Act, which sets out the provisions under which MFN treatment can be granted to Communist countries, also included two provisions dealing specifically with relief for domestic industries from imports from NMEs. These were section 205(c) of the Antidumping Act[10] and section 406 of the Trade Act of 1974.[11]

a. Section 205(b)—A response to Congressional fear of executive branch discretion

In section 321(d) of the 1974 Trade Act, Congress incorporated Customs Regulation section 153.5(b) into the Antidumping Act, using substantially identical language. Congress thus transformed into a statutory requirement that which had been an interpretive regulation issued as an act of administrative discretion. Apparently, Chairman Wilbur Mills of the Ways and Means Committee feared possible abuse of Executive Branch discretion in the then-current atmosphere of detente. The House Report explained the purpose of the amendment as follows:

> A new subsection (c) to section 205 is also added to adopt in the law the substance of the existing Treasury Department practice, as reflected in section 153.5(b) of the Treasury's antidumping regulations (19 C.F.R. 153.5(b)) . . . The amendment would confirm the Treasury practice under which the Secretary makes the necessary dumping determinations with respect to state-controlled-economy countries based on prices at which such or similar merchandise of a non-state-controlled-economy country is sold either for consumption in its home market or to other countries, or based on the constructive value of such or similar merchandise in a non-state-controlled-economy country.[12]

Congress, by placing the language of section 153.5(b) into the statute, ratified the Treasury practice which had developed during the previous fifteen years and significantly diminished the possibility of the adoption of an alternative methodology to solve this conceptually difficult issue.

b. Section 406—An alternate remedy

At the same time, the Congress added section 406 of the 1974 Trade Act, a separate safeguard provision aimed only at nonmarket Communist countries. Section 406 provided for relief from rapidly increasing imports from a

10. Trade Act of 1974, Pub. L. No. 93–618, § 321, 88 Stat. 2043 (1978) (codified at 19 U.S.C. § 160 (1976)).
11. Trade Act of 1974, Pub. L. No. 93–618, § 406, 88 Stat. 2062 (1978) (codified at 19 U.S.C. § 2436 (1976)).
12. H. Rep. No. 571, 93d Cong., 1st Sess. 72 (1973).

Communist country or countries, without regard to the fairness/unfairness of that trade. This approach had been foreshadowed by a "market-disruption" clause in the 1972 proposed U.S.-U.S.S.R. trade agreement.[13] Relief under this section was made subject to Presidential discretion and Congressional review. One stated purpose of section 406 was to provide a remedy for nonmarket economy imports in view of Congressional recognition that the antidumping laws could not be effectively applied to these imports.[14]

c. The *Polish Golf Car* Case

The next major development in the evolution of the U.S. antidumping law as it was applied to NME products came from the case brought against golf cars from Poland. Golf cars were produced in Poland solely for export to the U.S. There was no domestic market nor sales to other countries.

Initially, Treasury relied upon the home-market prices of a Canadian producer to establish foreign-market value.[15] When the Canadian producer went out of business in 1975, Treasury suddenly had to find a new standard for fair value upon which to base assessment of duties under the continuing order.[16] Although there was production of golf cars in Mexico, Italy, Japan and other countries, the only other large-scale producers were in the U.S.

In late 1977, in order to avoid using U.S. prices or costs for fair value, Treasury developed a method for determining "constructed value" based upon the Polish state-owned company's physical inputs (verified by Treasury at the Polish factory) valued at prices prevailing in Spain—a country determined by Treasury to be at a comparable level of economic development to Poland. The choice of Spain as the home-market surrogate arose from a study of Spain's economy prepared for Treasury by the Polish state trading company which was the respondent in the case. Based upon the public record, it is unclear what charges were made for capital costs and other indirect costs in the calculation.

The proposed use of this novel definition of fair value was discussed with the Poles during the visit of President Jimmy Carter to Warsaw in late 1977.[17] This approach was formally proposed as a Treasury regulation in January, 1978.[18]

---

13. Agreement between the Government of the United States of America and the Government of the Union of Soviet Socialist Republics Regarding Trade, May 29, 1972, Art. 3.

14. Trade Act of 1974, S. Rep. No. 1298, 93d Cong., 2d Sess. 210 (1974).

15. *Electric Golf Cars from Poland; Antidumping*, 40 Fed. Reg. 25,497 (1975).

16. U.S. International Trade Commission Publication 1069, *Electric Golf Cars from Poland* at A-4 (June 1980).

17. *See* Note, *Dumping from "Controlled Economy" Countries: The Polish Golf Cart Case*, 11 Law & Pol. in Int'l Bus. 777 (1979).

18. *Antidumping: Proposed Amendments Pertaining to Merchandise from State-Controlled-Economy Countries*, 43 Fed. Reg. 1,356 (1978).

d. 1978 Treasury Regulations

When proposed, these regulations generated an unusually large volume of critical comment both from Capitol Hill and from interested parties outside the government. Commentators representing domestic producers were critical of the "comparable economy" concept, the "factors of production" approach, and the resort to contructed value when there existed an actual sales price for such or similar merchandise (albeit sales by U.S. producers in the U.S. market). They argued that Congressional ratification of the longstanding Treasury Department practice of disregarding prices and costs in state-controlled-economy countries implied a Congressional judgment that price and cost relationships as expressed in the particular combination of factors of production in state-controlled-economy countries should not be considered comparable to those in market economies.

Despite the expression of strong disagreement from a variety of interests, on August 9, 1978 the Treasury Department adopted its new approach essentially as proposed.[19] The new regulation amended Section 153.7 of the Customs Regulations to provide for a new way to calculate the constructed value of merchandise produced in a state-controlled-economy country where such or similar merchandise is not produced in a market economy other than in the U.S. This type of constructed value calculation reflects the hypothetical market-economy cost of production of the merchandise under investigation if produced by the exact methods and processes used in the NME country.

The market economy used as the surrogate is that which is deemed to be at a comparable level of economic development as the nonmarket country. In other words, the actual input units needed to make a unit of merchandise are measured in the NME country (hours of labor, kilowatts of electricity, tons of each input of raw materials, etc.). These are then "priced" in a market-economy country deemed to be comparable in developmental terms. The sum of these hypothetical costs plus a mark-up for overhead and profit becomes the fair value. Because this exercise involves data from two foreign countries, verification of data must occur in both the NME country and in the market-economy country chosen as the surrogate.

e. Disposition of the *Polish Golf Car* Case

Oddly enough, the new 1978 dumping regulations fashioned to alleviate the "Polish problem" were never directly applied in the golf car case. In spring 1980, the Commerce Department wrote a letter to the International

19. *Antidumping Investigation Procedures Under Antidumping Act, 1921* 43 Fed. Reg. 35, 262, 35,265 (1978). An antidumping petition on lightbulbs from Hungary had been filed on June 21, 1978. *Lightbulbs from Hungary*, 43 Fed. Reg. 34,851 (1978).

Trade Commission implying that this new regulation would be applied to golf car imports after August 9, 1978 (U.S. prices would be used for 1976–78 entries) and furthermore, that under this approach no dumping margins would be found. The ITC subsequently issued a "no injury" finding terminating the order.[20] These speculations were conveyed to the ITC without the formalities of an investigation, verification, hearing or any meaningful participation of the domestic parties.

B. The 1979 Act

In the process of adopting the 1978 regulations, the Treasury Department had gone as far as possible in interpreting section 205(c) of the Antidumping Act. Influential members of Congress and interested parties in the domestic private sector remained highly critical of the Treasury approach which they considered potentially vulnerable to abuse of discretion for foreign policy motives.

Congressional skepticism of the Treasury Department's 1978 regulations is evident in the legislative history of the Trade Agreements Act of 1979.[21] This statute reenacted in substance section 205(c) of the Antidumping Act of 1921 as section 773(c) of the Tariff Act of 1930, as amended. The initial inclination of the House Ways and Means Committee was to include language in its Report disapproving the Customs regulations on NME dumping, but Treasury Department officials prevailed on the Committee to adopt a more neutral "wait-and-see" approach. Thus, the Report of the Committee on Ways and Means comments on section 773(c) were as follows:

> Although this report contains the general caveat that this bill is intended to implement only those changes in domestic law which are considered necessary or appropriate to make U.S. law consistent with the international agreements and is not intended as a general expression of approval of current regulations or administrative practice, the Committee believes it is necessary to emphasize the specific application of that caveat to the current law on dumping from non-market economy countries. The reenactment of current statutory provisions on this subject is not an expression of congressional approval *or disapproval* of the regulations promulgated by the Secretary of the Treasury on August 9, 1978 (43 Fed. Reg. 35, 262).[22]

The same language was placed in the Senate Finance Committee report.[23]

20. U.S. International Trade Commission Publication 1069, *Electric Golf Cars from Poland* at A-51 (June 1980).

21. *See* The Trade Agreements Act of 1979, S. Rep. No. 249, 96th Cong., 1st Sess. *reprinted in* 1979 U.S. Code Cong. & Ad. News 381 *et seq.*

22. H. Rep. No. 96–317, 96th Cong., 1st Sess. at 76–77 (1979) The underscored language was added following Treasury intervention.

23. The Trade Agreements Act of 1979, S. Rep. No. 249, 96th Cong., 1st Sess. 96, *reprinted in* 1979 U.S. Code Cong. & Ad. News 381 482.

C. European Communities' And Other Countries' Practices

The European Communities (EC) handle the problem of NME dumping under Article 2 of their Antidumping Regulations.[24] Under EC antidumping procedures, the imports' value is compared to the so-called "normal value" to see if there is dumping. For NME imports, the normal value of the product is based on:

(a) the price at which the like product of a market economy third country is actually sold:
 (i) for consumption on the domestic market of that country, or
 (ii) to other countries, including the Community; or
(b) the constructed value of the like product in a market economy third country; or
(c) if neither price nor constructed value as established under (a) or (b) above provides an adequate basis, the price actually paid or payable in the Community for the like product, duly adjusted, if necessary, to include a reasonable profit margin.

If the imports are from non-GATT countries, the EC has the ability to employ "special measures" under Article 16 of the same Regulation in order to determine the appropriate normal value.

Because of the proximity of Eastern and Western Europe and their historical trading relationship, NME trade is more substantial with Western Europe than with the U.S. These same historical relationships also lead to some unusual applications of the law. For example, since trade between East Germany and West Germany is considered "internal", no antidumping actions can be brought against East German products which are sold in the West German market. Still, in order to prevent West Germany from acting as a transition point for East German goods en route to other EC countries, any other member state can bring an antidumping action against East German goods.

1. *Review of EC Experience*

The EC practice in this area has been summarized recently by H.-F. Beseler and N. Williams (the administrators of the EC antidumping law):

> The Commission's practice, therefore, is to consider any substitute third country which may be suggested in the initial stage of the investigation, thereby ensuring that no possible analogue is excluded from examination. Thus, the Community industry is free to base the allegation of dumping in the complaint on any third market economy price or cost to which it has access. Providing the comparision is considered reasonable enough to justify the opening of an investigation, the analogue suggested is published in the notice of opening of the investigation. This gives other interested parties the opportunity to make any representations they wish on the proposed analogue and to suggest a more appropriate choice if one is known. If alternative analogues are proposed then these are considered by the

24. Council Regulation (EEC) No. 3017/79, 20.12.79., Art. 2.

Commission and may be accepted as being more reasonable or appropriate. In any event, whatever analogue is finally accepted the Commission publishes notice of the fact together with the reasons for the choice.

This pragmatic approach results in the consideration of a far wider range of alternatives than would otherwise have been the case. Thus, for the 23 products originating in state trading countries in which the investigation was terminated in the years 1980 to 1982, the normal value was based on prices or costs in 12 countries at all stages of economic development from India and Yugoslavia to Sweden and the United States. An idea of the Commission's open-minded approach in this matter may be demonstrated from the fact that only 11 of the 23 analogues finally chosen were those contained in the complaint, 10 being changed as a result of representations by other interested parties and 2 by the Commission in the light of evidence which came to light during the investigation. The reasons given for the choice of the analogue finally selected include, similarity of the scale of production and production techniques; similarity of access to raw materials; price controls ensured that prices in the substitute country were not unreasonably high; the low level of protection afforded to the domestic industry in the country chosen; insuffiency of data available on the country originally suggested and the fact that the additional administrative burden of carrying out an investigation in a further country was not justified.[25]

2. *Reliance on Price Undertakings to Offset Injury*

Between 1968 and 1982, the EC completed two hundred thirty-three antidumping investigations of which eighty-two involved products from Comecon (other than Yugoslavia). Of these, sixty were ended after "undertakings or similar solutions". The remaining twenty-two were ended before completion. Price undertakings are confidential agreements between the Commission and the foreign exporter to raise their prices to the EC to a degree determined sufficient by the Commission to offset injury.

Authority to put into effect safeguard provisions with regard to imports from NME countries was embedded in two recent EC Agreements. The 1974 draft Agreements between the EC and Comecon countries (which were never implemented) stated that safeguard provisions would be triggered when imported products from these countries were sold at prices lower than those which would prevail under competitive market conditions (termed the "actual value"). The 1978 Trade Agreement between the EC and the People's Republic of China (PRC) states that "trade in goods and the provision of services . . . shall be effected at market-related prices and rates."[26]

3. *Reliance on Other Trade Measures*

The EC on the whole is more aggressive than the U.S. in protecting its industry from injury caused by "unfairly" traded goods with respect to NME

25. H.-F. Beseler & N. Williams, from an unpublished manuscript at 18, 19 (Footnotes omitted).

26. Trade Agreement Between the European Economic Community and the People's Republic of China, Art. 7.

imports. For example, as described above, in its only trade agreement with a NME country (China), the EC has obtained a specific commitment that Chinese exports to the EC will be at market-related prices. This is a much stronger commitment to domestic industry protection than the weak exhortation in the U.S.-PRC Trade Agreement to "consult" if there is market disruption. The main mechanism for indigenous industry protection within the EC is still protective quotas. The current booklet of quotas lists more than 1,500 separate quotas applicable to NME exports to the EC. Beyond that, the EC antidumping regulations permit the administrative authority to use essentially any price as the standard for dumping by NMEs without agonizing over the level of economic development in a surrogate country or hypothetical factors of production. As a last resort, the EC regulations permit the use of the internal EC price—after it has been adjusted upwards to eliminate any price supressive influence of the NME imports. This adjustment, consequently, can ensure that the EC producer earns a reasonable profit.

4. *Canada and Other Countries*

The Canadian law, like that of the EC, adopts a much more flexible approach to dealing with alleged dumped imports from NMEs than that under U.S. law. Section 7 of the Canadian Antidumping Act merely states that if the country of export has a government which monopolizes its export trade or substantially distorts domestic prices, the "normal value" ". . . shall be determined in such manner as the Minister (of Finance) prescribes." Since Canadian dumping decisions generally say little about the underlying methodology employed in reaching the decision, little is publicly known as to how this Ministerial discretion has been employed. In at least one case, *Electrical Generating Machinery from the USSR*, the Canadians calculated fair value by simply assuming the Soviet price to Canada to be a certain (high) percentage less than fair value.[27]

The Canadians have proposed new legislation and regulations to implement the 1979 GATT Antidumping Code and incorporate it into domestic Canadian Law. In the proposed package of laws and regulations, their approach to NME dumping essentially parallels that of the EC.[28]

The Australian approach to NME dumping is contained in Article 5 of the Australian Antidumping Act (1975). In this Article, Australian authoritites are given great latitude in setting the normal value. The only constraint is that the Minister of Finance must try to use prices of like goods sold in a market country where the other country's costs of production are similar to

27. K. Stegemann, *The Net National Burden of Canadian Antidumping Policy*, 15 CORNELL INT'L L. J. 301 (1982).
28. Dept. of Finance, Canada, Proposals on Import Policy (July 1980).

those in the NME. Here, like in the U.S. regulations, some attention is paid to gross economic characteristics of the surrogate for the NME, although there is nothing here approaching the baroque hierarchy of choices found in the U.S. regulations.

II. Problems With Current U.S. Law

A. General

1. *Results Are Unpredictable*

The current procedures contain a high degree of uncertainty and possibility for abuse. Importers cannot predict which country will be chosen as a surrogate for the nonmarket economy, and thus cannot possibly set their prices to assure compliance with the dumping laws. At the same time, domestic producers, who usually rely on the dumping law because it contains no provision for political input, instead find that the determination of their cases can rest solely on the administering authority's choice of a "comparable country" or constructed value—a choice which could well be made on the basis of foreign policy considerations extraneous to the merits of the case. (Under the standard of judicial review requiring substantial evidence in the record, the administering authority could make almost any choice of surrogate country stand up in court.)

2. *Time Deadlines Too Short*

One practical problem which has become apparent in nonmarket-economy cases is that such cases are subject to the same deadlines as market-economy antidumping cases. In the nonmarket-economy country case, however, in addition to all the other steps required in any antidumping investigation, there are several preliminary phases which must be completed. First, a decision must be made and evidence placed on the record to show that the product involved is from a country which is determined to be state-controlled to an extent that sales do not permit the calculation of fair value. Second, the decision must be made as to the identification of the appropriate surrogate countries (again, always mindful to generate sufficient evidence to support the choice on the record). This decision involves an often complex analysis of the exporting country and the role and importance of the particular producing sector to the economy as a whole. Similar analyses are performed on an array of potential surrogate candidates. Third, once a surrogate country is identified, the administering authority must try to obtain the agreement of the government and of a producer or producers in that surrogate country to answer the antidumping price and/or cost questionnaires. Only after those lengthy procedures have been completed can the "normal" part of an antidumping investigation (sending the questionnaire, obtaining a reply, analyzing the results, calculating a margin) be completed.

3. *Unfair to Other Trading Partners?*

The alleged failure to adequately control NME dumping in this country is also a source of potential friction with our traditional trading partners. Permitting nonmarket importers to compete by means of artificially low prices, while free market nations are subjected to our dumping and countervailing duty laws, is inconsistent with this country's commitment to nondiscriminatory trade policies and unfair to those of our trading partners who have agreed to play by the free-market rules. Thus, for example, producers of Indian castings (which are subject to a countervailing duty order)[29] have complained that the People's Republic of China (PRC) can sell castings in the U.S. at prices far below those of Indian castings without suffering a similar penalty, while a case brought in 1982 against mushrooms from the PRC (which led to a finding of no dumping),[30] would have provided more benefit to Taiwanese exporters than to U.S. producers if it had resulted in an affirmative finding.

B. Use of Nonmarket Economy's Home Market Prices and Costs

1. *Unreliability of NME Prices and Costs*

With respect to NMEs, it is generally conceded that home-market prices and costs are meaningless as a source of "fair value."[31] The heavy intervention of the government in the setting of relative prices means that the ultimate prices and costs in NMEs reflect political, economic, or bureaucratic factors rather than local supply and demand. World-market prices are not decisive factors in a typical NME production function as the internal economy enjoys sufficient isolation from the world economy to effectively insulate its producers from these economic forces.

A legitimate question can be raised as to how reliable home-market prices and costs are in some sectors of market economies—especially when dealing with sectors (e.g., steel, agriculture) where there is heavy government influence. So far, Treasury and Commerce have taken the position that the overall market orientation of those economies provides sufficient commer-

29. *Certain Iron-Metal Castings from India*, 46 Fed. Reg. 3,302 (1981).

30. *Final Determination of Sales at Less Than Fair Value; Canned Mushrooms from the People's Republic of China*, 48 Fed. Reg. 45,445 (1983).

31. *See* Soltysinski, *The Application of U.S. Antidumping and Other Foreign Trade Competition Laws to the So-Called State-Controlled Economy Enterprises* in Interface Two: Conference Proceedings on the Legal Framework of East-West Trade 169 (Wallace and Flores eds. 1982).

cial yardsticks to permit a valid measurement for use in antidumping or countervailing duty cases. No further analysis of this issue has been undertaken.

2. *Currency Convertibility*

Indeed, even if Commerce could measure a "real" home-market price or cost in a nonmarket economy, they would have to find a way around the inconvertibility of all NME currencies (except perhaps the Hungarian *forint*). While various methods have been suggested for calculating "shadow" exchange rates for these currencies, those methods appear to be best suited for academic discussion of their economies. There is nowhere near sufficient consensus to permit the use of any one method for the decision of actual cases. Without an accurate notion of the exchange rate which would be applied in a case, neither domestic producers nor NME producers can know what import price would be considered "fair" under these statutes.

C. Use of Nonmarket Economy's Export Prices

The fact that NME producers face a nonconvertible currency can be a primary incentive to dump (to the extent that the notion of "dumping" is truly meaningful in a NME context). For example, earning precious hard currency to pay for imports, meet scheduled debt payments or to gain access to locally produced goods allocated by quotas elevates the importance of gaining sales in hard currency countries. Thus the need for hard currency which may cause dumping in the U.S. market is also likely to create the incentive to export at artificially low prices to other countries.

As noted above, Treasury rejected the use of NME export prices for establishing fair value in the 1950s. Commerce, most recently, rejected this approach in the case involving Romanian carbon steel plate in 1982.[32] The EC has also refused to use the nonmarket economy export prices to other markets as a measure for normal value presumably for the same reasons as the U.S.

D. Use of a Surrogate Country's Home Market Prices or Costs

1. *Overview and Theory*

The first choice for the determination of fair value in an NME antidumping case is the prices or costs of similar merchandise produced in a market

32. *Preliminary Determination of Sales at Less Than Fair Value: Carbon Steel Plate from Romania*, 47 Fed. Reg. 35,666 (1982); *Carbon Steel Plate from Romania; Suspension of Investigation*, 48 Fed. Reg. 317 (1983).

country deemed to be at a comparable level of economic development. Current Commerce Department regulations give little guidance as to how this comparability actually is to be determined. The regulations simply instruct the administering authority to find a market-economy country with approximately the same level GNP per capita and similar overall economic structure.[33]

The underlying theoretical basis for this quest for economic comparability rests in the belief that, but for the nonmarket character of the economy, the NME producer would have the same costs and sell at the same prices as producers in market countries with the same level of GNP per capita. Thus, these surrogate producers' prices and costs are the fair value for the NME producers' exports to the U.S.

Although this approach is a good attempt at addressing a nearly impossible problem, it falls short of its goal of mirroring what the fair value in the NME might be if it were measureable. This approach is weakened both by the way it defines comparability and by the implicit assumptions as to the role of the particular export industry in the economy as a whole.

On the first issue, the determination of overall comparability based on GNP per capita is particularly inappropriate when comparing a market economy with a NME. The biggest difficulty is in arriving at reliable measurements of macroeconomic values.[34] There is no indication that somehow the shakiness of NME prices and costs at the microeconomic level disappear through aggregation. Indeed heavily used statistical sources such as the World Bank explicitly caution against this type of cross-national comparisons.[35]

The second problem reflects the relationship of the producer to the country as a whole. Even if the perfect market-economy substitute at the macroeconomic level were to be found, the surrogate producer analysis would still be flawed. This is because the exporting industry is frequently an exceptional industry even within its own country. Often it has been nurtured in its development and "force-fed" capital in order to maximize its ability to generate hard currency.

Thus, the nonmarket industry will frequently be as large and technically sophisticated as those in far more developed countries—precisely because the state in NMEs will support capacity expansion and technological investment concentrated in this particular sector far in excess of what private investors would be expected to underwrite. For example, in the *Polish Golf Car* case, the Polish state aviation enterprise in the early 1970's developed a golf car facility oriented toward large volume production with the sole aim of

33. 19 C.F.R. § 353.8 (1983).
34. *See supra* notes 2–5 and accompanying text.
35. The World Bank, 1980 World Bank Atlas 16 (1980).

exporting golf cars to the United States. It would be highly unusual for a similar investment pattern to develop in a market economy at a similar level of development.

2. *Administrability*

Once a comparable country which produces such or similar merchandise to that under investigation is identified the job is far from over. Numerous practical difficulties evolve from Commerce's need to seek confidential business data from producers in countries not directly involved in these cases. Procedurally, a two-step process is followed. First, the government of the country chosen as surrogate must give permission to the U.S. government to approach that country's producers. Second, the producers themselves must be willing to cooperate. In the case involving Romanian carbon steel plate in 1982, for example, several countries refused to allow the U.S. Government such access to their producers. This is understandable especially if there is a chance the U.S. industry might file a case against the surrogate producers at a future time.[36]

Even when the host government is agreeable, Commerce must still find producers willing to open their books to U.S. government investigators. In most cases, from the surrogate producer's perspective, there is not much commercial benefit associated with cooperation while the risk and expenses to the producer of cooperation can be high. In the extreme case, such surrogate producer reluctance can become the dominant factor in the investiation. Thus, for example, in the 1982–83 case involving Chinese shop towels, Commerce pursued leads throughout numerous countries (Pakistan, Malaysia, Hong Kong, Dominican Republic and Colombia) to no avail. With two days left before the statutory deadline for the preliminary determination, Commerce was forced to rely on the average price of all imports into the U.S. (based on Census data) as the basis for fair value for lack of better information.[37] Similarly, in a recent preliminary determination concerning chloropicrin from the People's Republic of China, Commerce was forced to use Japanese data from the petition as the best information available even though it was explicitly noted that such information was inappropriate as a basis for fair value.[38]

Another technical problem has arisen because of the lack of "fit" of NME cases into the regulations governing access to confidential information under administrative protective order. In a normal (i.e., market economy)

36. *See Shop Towels of Cotton from The People's Republic of China*, 48 Fed. Reg. 37,055 (1983) and *Cotton Shop Towels from Pakistan*, 48 Fed. Reg. 43,187 (1983).

37. *Preliminary Determination of Sales at Less Than Fair Value: Shop Towels of Cotton from The People's Republic of China*, 48 Fed. Reg. 12,764 (1983).

38. *Chloropicrin from The People's Republic of China*, 48 Fed. Reg. 24,798 (1983).

antidumping case, the refusal of a respondent to supply data which is releaseable under an administrative protective order would lead to the possible return of its submission and the use of best information available—usually the petitioner's information. In NME cases, a producer in a surrogate country supplies the relevant foreign-market value data. The refusal of the surrogate producers to permit access of the petitioning and NME parties to the confidential data could never lead to any sanctions against those surrogate producers since they are only participating in the matter *ex gratia*. Nor can Commerce afford to force the issue, since if the surrogate producer withdrew his data in the course of their investigation, Commerce would once again find itself on "square one" with no useful information to analyze and little time left before a statutorily mandated decision. For example, in the 1982–83 case concerning Chinese print cloth, the possibility was raised that a dumping margin could be calculated based upon surrogate producers' data without being able to show either party how the margin was calculated.[39]

Another oddity in these cases was revealed by the "twin" cases of Potassium Permanganate from China and Spain.[40] Technically, the two investigations were separate, and the home-market data furnished by the Spanish respondents for use in the Spanish case could not be used as a surrogate for Chinese foreign-market value without the express permission of the Spanish respondents even though dependence upon this data made the most sense from an administrative as well as a commercial point of view.

3. *Adjustments for Non-Comparable Surrogate*

When Commerce is unable to find a country with a "comparable" market economy which produces the merchandise under investigation, prices or costs in a non-comparable market economy can be used (assuming Commerce can locate a producer willing to cooperate with the U.S. government) after adjustment for known differences in prices and costs.[41] While this exercise has never been done, its administration poses a bit of a mystery. If prices and costs inside the NME are unreliable by definition (which is why they are unusable to begin with), how can there be known differences in these costs for which allowance can be made? The concept of a "difference" implies both values are measurable. Since the non-measurability of NME prices and costs are precisely the cause of the original methodological difficulty, it is absurd to assume that some measurement of difference can be derived with a greater amount of accuracy.

39. *Griege Polyester/Cotton Printcloth from The People's Republic of China*, 48 Fed. Reg. 41,249 (1983).

40. *See Potassium Permanganate from Spain; Initiation of Antidumping Investigation*, 48 Fed. Reg. 11,481 (1983) and *Potassium Permanganate from the People's Republic of China; Initiation of Antidumping Investigation*, 48 Fed. Reg. 11,482 (1983).

41. 19 C.F.R. § 353.8 (1983).

E. Use of U.S. Price

1. *Price of Other Country Exports to U.S.*

While the regulations explicitly authorize the Commerce Department to use a U.S. market-based price when other actual price and cost data are unavailable, Commerce and its predecessor, Treasury, have generally been reluctant to do so. This, in part, reflects the fear that direct reliance upon a competitor's U.S. pricing might encourage that competitor to alter its commercial behavior in order to sustain or increase a dumping margin on NME exports to the U.S. after the imposition of an order. It also reflects, in part, the belief at the investigations phase that competing market-economy sales in the U.S. might be priced lower than they otherwise would be as the result of NME dumping. In the case of menthol from the PRC, for example, Commerce used the Paraguayan export price to the U.S. only after Commerce was satisfied that the New York and London menthol markets moved in unison (presumably limiting the effect of possible Chinese dumping in the U.S. though not world wide).[42]

The use of third-country imports to the U.S. does have a distinct advantage over the use of U.S. producers' data (as described below) for there must be significant U.S. industry (or else there is no investigation, since injury to a U.S. industry must be shown) which will moderate the foreign market-economy producer's market power in the U.S. In many respects, the surrogate foreign producer is in much the same position as the NME producer trying to stay competitive with the U.S. industry while overcoming transportation costs and tariff barriers which add to the minimum acceptable price.

Indeed, in situations where there is significant import competition in the U.S. market, the imported price (adjusted back to the ex-factory level) is probably one of the best measures of fair value as it generally allows continued NME access to the U.S. market while disallowing price undercutting. Like other surrogate-based measures of fair value, it ignores any 'true' comparative advantage which might be held by NME producers as well as their penchant for pursuing a low-price entry strategy in order to secure an initial market position. (The need to pursue that strategy is not, by any means, solely an NME approach to U.S. marketing, however).

2. *Price of U.S. Produced Goods Sold in U.S.*

The degree to which use of U.S. producers' prices as fair value encourages anticompetitive results depends in large part on the amount of competition experienced among U.S. producers and the market share held by the NME producer. Should fair value be pegged to an individual producer's U.S.

---

42. *Antidumping, Natural Menthol from the People's Republic of China; Final Determination of Sales at Less Than Fair Value*, 46 Fed. Reg. 24,614 (1981).

prices in a very competitive market, this would minimize the danger that the NME producer would be foreclosed from the market by U.S. industry price rises aimed at creating large dumping margins. No U.S. producer would be likely to raise their price to an uncompetitive level in order to force out NME competition for they would risk losing their market share as well (unless the price was pegged to the industry price leader). If, on the other hand, U.S. producers were few in number and there was no significant third-country import competition, the antidumping law could be used by the petitioners as a way to eliminate competition from NME sources. This problem is exacerbated by the way in which an NME dumping margin is calculated under current law. That is, the ex-factory price of the imported NME merchandise is compared to the ex-factory price of the U.S.-made goods. If the NME producer adopted a policy of strictly matching the prevailing U.S. price, it would always be dumping by the excess of its costs of transport, handling and duty on the sale to the U.S. over those of the domestic producer.[43]

The other instance where the anticompetitive aspects of use of a U.S. producers' price would be a concern is the situation where the NME had captured a significant portion of the U.S. market. By forcing the NME producer to parallel its pricing to a U.S. producer, the number of independent competitors has been diminished, for the NME producer has lost his pricing autonomy. This is anticompetitive to the extent that the NME was a significant factor in the U.S. market prior to the antidumping case.

A U.S. based price has a significant advantage over other current surrogate-based methods in one respect—it is a price with which the NME producer can be expected to have reasonable familiarity. In commercial terms, this is very important. Many NME producers claim they could be very competitive in the U.S. market without violating the antidumping laws if only they could know what would be considered a "fair" price. It is not "fair", nor is it commercially reasonable, to expect an NME producer to be familiar with the home-market price of a similar product in Finland or Paraguay or some other country which Commerce may decide *ex post facto* is the appropriate surrogate. It is even less reasonable to expect him to know the cost of production of a similar product in some unidentified third country. In effect, the U.S. is expecting the NME producer not only to know his product's price around the world but also to keep track of all of the prices of the inputs in the production function around the world. This uncertainty of methodology is a trade barrier in and of itself.

43. I.e., if those costs were $10, and the U.S. producer's ex-factory price were $30 and its transport/handling costs in the U.S. were $5, and both producers sold in the U.S. market at $35, the "foreign market value" for the NME producer's would be $30 (the U.S. producer's ex-factory price), and the NME producers' "U.S. price" would be $25, for a $5 dumping margin.

F. Use of a Hypothetical Constructed Value in a Surrogate Country

1. *Overview of Theory*

As described in Section I (A), above, Treasury in the *Polish Golf Car* case was anxious to avoid the use of the U.S. producer's price and cost experience as the basis for fair value. In its place, Treasury created a new methodology for determining the constructed value by valuing the physical inputs plus general expenses, labor and profit (but *not* capital) actually employed in the production of the product in the NME at prices in a "comparable" market economy. It is an approach which has some positive aspects, the most notable of which is ease of administration (since it does not require the giving of confidential data to the Commerce Department by anybody except the NME respondent). But, contrary to statements of its proponents, such a hypothetical exercise does *not* capture the comparative advantage of the NME through the use of its productive function. Any comparative advantage is obscured when the NME's production function is superimposed upon the array of prices from another country.

2. *Problems in Approach*

a. Difficulties in Choosing the "Right" Surrogate

The most obvious difficulty involves selecting the "right" surrogate. Indeed, for this exercise, a truly correct surrogate is not likely to exist. The macroeconomic comparability implied by the current selection process (which relies on per capita GNP, relative distribution of economic activity among sectors, and so on) does not mean that countries which look the same on the "macro" level will have the same set of relative prices. Relative prices are critical in determining the input mix in a production process. Comparative advantage reflects unique physical endowments as well as developed expertise, *not* macroeconomic sameness. These endowments and expertises are reflected in relative price arrays. Indeed, the bulk of our trade in manufactured goods is with other developed countries. Most of this trade would not exist if prices in countries of the same level of development were the same.

This simulation does not capture comparative advantage. Comparative advantage is reflected in the NME's production function which would emphasize those production characteristics in which the NME has an advantage. If, for example, energy is exceptionally plentiful and therefore relatively cheap compared to other inputs, the producer would be likely to produce his product in a way which minimizes total cost by maximizing energy use and reducing other inputs accordingly. This "comparative advantage" of cheap, abundant energy would only be captured in a hypothetical constructed value analysis if the chosen surrogate had the exact same relative prices. That is, if the relative values of the inputs were the same in both countries. Furthermore, there are some who feel that the search for a methodology which preserves "comparative advantage" is particularly misguided as applied to East-West trade.[44]

b. No Adjustment for Differences in Prices

As suggested earlier, when one takes a production function actually employed in a certain country and associates prices from another country with this production function, one is left with a result which is neither fish nor fowl. The resulting value is not an approximation of the cost of producing the NME article in the chosen surrogate (for if this item were to be actually produced in the surrogate, it would reflect the unique use of technology, expertise and resource endowment of the surrogate, not that of the NME), nor is it a hard currency approximation of the actual cost of production in the NME. The latter would be the case only if the relative prices of all inputs used in the NME's production function were identically arrayed in the surrogate and in the NME.

If only the Commerce Department could adjust for differences in the relative prices between the NME and the surrogate, the hypothetical constructed value of the product would be an accurate measure of the fair value of the merchandise under investigation. In order to make the adjustment correctly, Commerce would have to index the input prices in the NME and use this index to rearrange the relative prices in the surrogate. Using these derived surrogate prices, Commerce could then perform a constructed value calculation. The strength in this exercise is that it fits a production function to a set of relative prices which resembles the price array of the NME. The negative aspect of this price ordering is that it picks up relative prices which reflect not only natural abundances (usually the basis for comparative advantage) but also the price structure contrived by the NME central authority. The latter is most unlikely to reflect purely economic considerations.

c. Open to Abuse of Discretion

Finally, the use of the "Polish Golf Car" hypothetical constructed value is even more filled than other approaches with opportunities for a politicized administrator to exercise discretion in favor of one side or another. The choice of a surrogate country in a "normal" NME antidumping proceeding

44. As one recent student of antidumping theory has put it:

> Recent attempts by the United States authorities to apply a comparative advantage test in these cases make sense only if centrally-planned economies seek in the longer run to approximate a pattern of trade based on comparative advantage as understood by market-economy countries—a proposition that no student of East-West trade would surely accept.

R. Dale, Anti-Dumping Law in a Liberal Trade Order 194 (1980).

(i.e., one where an actual market economy producer's prices or cost will be used) is limited to a finite range of countries (those with actual producers), while the Polish Golf Car calculation opens up the entire set of market-economy countries as a source of possible surrogates. Further, in a normal market-economy constructed value case, the petitioner has some access to the country of the surrogate respondent, and can make his own inquiries as to the reasonableness of the production process described in a response. This is not generally the situation in an NME hypothetical constructed-value case where the inputs are being measured in the nonmarket economy. Finally, only the wealthiest petitioners can afford the expense of investigating both the exporter's actual operation (in order to estimate the production function), and the theoretical costs of that operation in a variety of countries (since the final choice of a surrogate is not known until well into the petitioning process).

As a side note, the deficiencies of the *Polish Golf Car* approach, while manifest, should not cloud the entire approach to NME import relief. In most cases, there should be actual surrogate producers available from whom the information can eventually be obtained. Thus far, the hypothetical constructed value has been rarely used, forming the basis for fair value only in the cases of montan wax from East Germany (where the market economy was West Germany)[45] and shop towels from China (where the market economy was Indonesia).[46]

G. Section 406

Section 406, introduced in 1974 as the solution to market disruption caused by NME economy imports, has not proven to be very useful to U.S. industry. Quite simply, no U.S. petitioner has ever received relief under section 406. The main problem for U.S. industry appears to be the availability of Presidential discretion; in every case where the ITC has made the requisite finding of injury, the President has refused relief. In the most notoriously politicized case, that involving Russian ammonia, the ITC found injury as required by statute in 1979. The President then refused to grant relief because the U.S. was seeking detente with the Soviet Union. Shortly thereafter, the Soviets invaded Afghanistan, at which time the President reinstituted the investigation on essentially the same facts as those upon which he had denied relief a few months earlier.[47] To his probable

45. *See Antidumping; Unrefined Montan Wax from the German Democratic Republic; Final Determinations of Sales at Less Than Fair Value*, 46 Fed. Reg. 38,555 (1981) as amended by 46 Fed. Reg. 43,727 (1981); *Unrefined Montan Wax from the German Democratic Republic; Early Determination of Antidumping Duty*, 47 Fed. Reg. 3579 (1982).

46. *Shop Towels of Cotton from The People's Republic of China*, 48 Fed. Reg. 37,055 (1983).

47. Presidential Proclamation 4714, *Temporary Duty Increase on the Importation into the United States of Certain Anhydrous Ammonia from the Union of Soviet Socialist Republics*, 45 Fed. Reg. 3,875 (1980).

surprise the ITC (whose membership had changed in the meantime) then denied relief in the case by finding no injury to the U.S. industry.[48]

The few cases brought since the Russian ammonia case apparently were filed because of the perception that section 406 cases are less costly for a U.S. industry to pursue than the extremely expensive proceedings required for an NME antidumping case. None of the cases filed in 1981–82 (Chinese dinnerware, Chinese mushrooms, East German montan wax)[49] were successful and the filings once again ceased.

One interesting legal issue is presented by section 406 which requires a finding, *inter alia*, of "material injury." When section 406 was enacted in 1974, "material injury" represented a degree of injury greater than the "injury" required by the antidumping laws, and less than the "serious injury" required for escape clause actions. When the antidumping laws were revised in 1979 to require a showing of "material injury," Congress made it clear that the new "material injury" standard for antidumping cases in the 1979 Trade Agreements Act was identical to the "injury" standard for antidumping under the 1974 Trade Act. In consequence, a good argument can be made that the antidumping "material injury" standard under the 1979 Act is a lesser degree of injury than the section 406 "material injury" standard under the 1974 Act.

In fact, this distinction was made in part in cases involving canned mushrooms from the People's Republic of China. As previously noted, the filing under section 406 was unsuccessful. A subsequent filing under the antidumping law[50] passed the injury hurdle with the commission noting in its preliminary finding, "Section 406 is a fair trade provision which requires the Commission to weigh various causes of material injury. The significant cause standard has been interpreted to require a more direct causal connection than the contributing cause standard applied in antidumping."

H. Nonmarket Economy Subsidization

1. *Problems in Applicability of Countervailing Duty Law*

For years, the applicability of the countervailing duty law to products from NME countries was an issue debated in the abstract among academi-

48. *Anhydrous Ammonia from the U.S.S.R.; Report to the President*, 45 Fed. Reg. 27,570 (1980). *Anhydrous Ammonia from the U.S.S.R.; Discontinuation of Temporary Restraints on Imports*, 45 Fed. Reg. 28,847 (1980).

49. *Certain Ceramic Kitchenware and Tableware from The People's Republic of China*, 47 Fed. Reg. 38,220 (1982); *Canned Mushrooms from The People's Republic of China*, 47 Fed. Reg. 45,981 (1982); *Unrefined Montan Wax from East Germany*, 47 Fed. Reg. 2,957 (1982). An investigation of ferrochromium from the Soviet Union was initiated at the request of the U.S. Trade Representative (and not the domestic industry) in late 1983, but was also unsuccessful. 49 Fed. Reg. 4,857 (1984).

50. *Canned Mushrooms from the People's Republic of China*, 47 Fed. Reg. 55,336 (1982).

cians and practitioners in the trade bar. With the filing and initiation of countervailing duty cases against all textile and apparel products from the People's Republic of China[51] and steel wire rod from Czechoslovakia[52] and Poland,[53] this academic issue has become a commercial reality.

There appear to be two schools of thought as to whether a countervailable subsidy can be found within an NME (leaving aside the technical, legal questions as to whether NME government actions are covered under the current U.S countervailing duty statutory language). These opposing views reflect how each group defines the essence of what makes an action a subsidy.

The first group would say that no countervailable subsidy can exist within an NME because the entire economy in an NME is driven through government intervention. In this mix of positive and negative subsidies touching every product, it is pointless to try to isolate any one of those "subsidies" for scrutiny under our countervailing duty law. Trying to correct the distortion caused by government intervention in the commercial marketplace has no meaning when the public sector and private sector are essentially one.

Attempting to apply a countervailing duty law to NME's could bring administrative problems as well. The U.S. countervailing duty law relies on the existence of commercial benchmarks to determine when a subsidy exists (i.e., a countervailed subsidy occurs when a government behaves in a way that is more beneficial to the recipient than the same commercial action based upon unrestrained market forces). Where, as in an NME, there are no significant commercial benchmarks, there is no commercial standard against which to compare the government intervention. Therefore, lacking a market-based norm, it is impossible to determine if a producer or exporter is receiving a subsidy and, if so, how to measure it.

The second school of thought defines a subsidy in a slightly different way and in so doing opens the door to countervailing NME products. This definition of subsidy hinges on the concept of preferentiality: if the government treats a group specially—to that group's benefit—a subsidy is conveyed. The approach could be characterized as follows: If a subsidy is thought of in economic terms as a governmental action such that one group benefits relatively more than others in a country, a countervailable subsidy exists to the extent that the level of benefit to the targeted recipient exceeds the normal or average level of benefit. This can be done in a market as well as nonmarket context as long as the average is measurable.

---

51. *Initiation of Countervailing Duty Investigations; Textiles, Apparel and Related Products from The People's Republic of China*, 48 Fed. Reg. 46,600 (1983).

52. *Carbon Steel Wire Rod from Czechoslovakia; Initiation of Countervailing Duty Investigation*, 48 Fed. Reg. 56,419 (1983).

53. *Carbon Steel Wire Rod from Poland; Initiation of Countervailing Duty Investigation*, 48 Fed. Reg. 56,419 (1983).

All economies in the world are mixed. Recognizing this, this approach advocates relying on benchmarks reflecting the normal or average commercial situation as faced by business in that country. In determining this benchmark in "market economy" causes, no attempt is made to strip out the influence of government in the investigated activity, only to establish the norm (for example, a government's monetary, fiscal and regulatory policy exerts heavy direct and indirect influence on a country's interest rate structure, but when evaluating the subsidy of a low-interest loan, the standard or benchmark loan rate is that to which the average borrower of similar commercial status has access, *not* the market-clearing interest rate which would prevail in an unregulated capital market).

All of these arguments were made in the context of a heated debate over the Chinese textile countervailing duty petition filed in September 1983. Although the Chinese case was withdrawn prior to a preliminary determination,[54] it had already been followed by countervailing duty petitions on steel wire rod from Poland and Czechoslovakia, thus forcing Commerce to decide the issue.

In the final determination in the Polish and Czech cases, Commerce came to a more conclusive result, determining that, while the statute by its terms does not exclude nonmarket economies, no subsidy could be found within an economy determined to be nonmarket. The essence of Commerce's analysis was that subsidies are distortions to the free market, and the concept made no sense in nonmarket economies.[55] Consequently, no countervailing duty could be imposed in a nonmarket economy case. Commerce reaffirmed this decision shortly thereafter, in refusing to investigate allegations of subsidization of potash from several Eastern European countries.[56]

III. Proposed Solutions

While there is quite a bit of debate as to how trade with NMEs should be handled under the U.S. unfair import laws, almost nobody claims the current cumbersome, arbitrary and costly procedure under the antidumping law, which yields unpredictable results, or the ambiguity of action taken under the countervailing duty law, is optimal. Acknowledging the need for change alters the debate from a question of "whether?" to one of "in what way?" The following are some of the proposals.

---

54. *Textile, apparel, and related products from The Peoples' Republic of China: Termination of Countervailing Duty Investigation*. 48 Fed. Reg. 55,492 (Dec. 13, 1983).

55. *Carbon Steel Wire Rod from Czechoslovakia; Final Negative Countervailing Duty Determination*. 49 Fed. Reg. 19,370 (May 7, 1984). *Carbon Steel Wire Rod from Poland; Final Negative Countervailing Duty Determination*. 49 Fed. Reg. 19,474 (June 7, 1984).

56. *Potassium Chloride from the German Democratic Republic; Rescission of Initiation of Countervailing Duty Investigation and Dismissal of Petition*. 49 Fed. Reg. 23,428 (June 6, 1984). *Potassium Chloride from the Soviet Union; Rescission of Initiation of Countervailing Duty Investigation and Dismissal of Petition*. 49 Fed. Reg. 23,428 (June 6, 1984).

A. Use of a "True" Exchange Rate

One method of overcoming the problems of measuring dumping from NMEs would be to base the concept of NME dumping on a sales-below-cost approach. Under this methodology, one would sidestep the problem of government allocation of goods, price setting and nonconvertible currencies through the use of a constructed exchange rate. There are numerous "constructions" of exchange rates available from a variety of sources—various agencies of the U.S. Government, certain money center banks and multilateral lending institutions to name a few. If the administering authority were to choose one source and make that choice publicly available, producers in NMEs could apply that rate to their costs of production and be able to ascertain their minimum "fair" price for U.S. sales. Similarly, U.S. producers could estimate the NME producer's cost of production (as they do at present with market economy producers) and by applying this constructed exchange rate, ascertain the fairness of the NME sales with which they are competing in the U.S. market. Uncertainty would be minimized.

One major technical difficulty would be the need to sufficiently lag the reference period for the cost of production calculation behind the sale in order for all components of the calculation to be known. Specifically, if an NME producer were trying to price its third quarter sales, it would have to use as a reference point its costs from a prior period as the basis for this calculation (generally one or two quarters depending upon how long items remain in inventory). This amount of time, between production and sales which Commerce would apply, should be generally known so that all parties could make their calculations on the same basis.

The attraction of the above method is that it is of relatively low cost to petitioners and respondents and is much more administrable than the present approach. Once an exchange rate basis is decided upon and applied to the values of inputs reported by the NME, analysis of the appropriateness of these inputs to the cost of production calculation and verification of these inputs would proceed as in a normal case.

The serious flaw in this approach appears to be that it accepts the NME's production function as "valid." That is, this methodology does not deal with the subsidies embedded in the price structure and quota allocations in the economy that the NME government provides to the producer. For example, if the NME government gives the producer oil for power generation at a very cheap rate (both in comparison to world prices for oil and the internal price for oil to other NME producers), this is likely to appear in the production function as a relatively high use of oil in relation to other inputs, and at a relatively low price. By pricing oil "low" and making it abundantly available to the exporting producer, the NME has artifically reduced the product's cost of production. Thus, in comparison a low export price to the U.S. would be found to be acceptable.

If the U.S. industry, in addition to a dumping case brought in the above fashion, has full and meaningful access to the countervailing duty law, this would not be a problem. In that case, a cost-of-production based dumping action would be brought and a tariff administered equal to any difference between the U.S. price and the actual cost of production (calculated as described above) of the goods. The additional benefit of the cheap oil would be reachable as a subsidy (which it would be) under the countervailing duty law.

However, constructed exchange rates are generally not considered for analysis at anything but the most aggregate macroeconomic level. These rates reflect very gross economic characteristics and trends. They lose much of their meaningfulness when applied to particular products such as shoes or wax or mushrooms which are quite small in comparison to the total economy.

B. "The Heinz Bill"

1. *Description*

First proposed as S. 1966 in 1979 and subsequently revised and resubmitted as S. 958 in 1981 and S. 1351 in 1983, the Heinz bill (as it is called after its chief sponsor) has gone the farthest in developing an alternative approach to handling NME import problems under the unfair trade laws (the Heinz bill was dropped in Conference at the end of the 1984 Small Fee Congressional Session). Under this legislative proposal the Commerce Department would not even seek to measure fair value in NMEs, but would simply look at other producers' prices within the U.S. market. To avoid comparing NME exporters with high-cost producers, the reference price would be the *lowest* average price in the U.S. charged by exporters from *any* free market country, including the U.S. (or any significant individual firm, foreign or domestic). Since NME producers are unlikely, in most cases, to be more efficient than the most efficient free-market producer, the difference between the NME producer's price and the lowest free-market price would measure the "dumping" by a nonmarket producer.

Under the Heinz bill, NME industries would not be compared to free-market producers that are subsidized or engaged in dumping. With this exception, nonmarket exporters who meet the lowest average prices charged by any single free-market seller in the U.S. would be considered to be trading fairly. In this way, importers of NME products would be able to match, and even undercut, the prices of their U.S. competitors in the U.S. market as long as they were matching other "fair" prices.

At the beginning of the investigation, the Commerce Department would consult with the nonmarket economy's government, soliciting from it information (if available) that would enable the Department to determine dumping or the presence of a subsidy subject to the standards used for "normal" market economy cases. Such information may or may not be available, depending on both the nature of the economy and the particular industry in question. If, in the Department's judgment, sufficient, verifiable information was provided to permit the case to be treated as a normal antidumping or countervailing duty case, then the Department would do so, moving the investigation to the appropriate "normal" track. The Department would also, from that point on, treat the case in accordance with the deadlines for "normal" cases.

In the typical case, where the nonmarket economy will not or cannot provide the necessary information which would allow the complaint to be handled in a "normal" way, the lowest-average-price standard of fairness would be employed. In the "1981" version of S. 958, the relief procedures under section 406 would have been abolished. Market disruption by NMEs would be handled through existing escape clause procedures under section 201 of the Trade Act of 1974. Although this approach is more consistent with the division in current law between fair and unfair trade practice relief provisions, the drafters of S. 1351 abandoned this approach leaving the current section 406 intact. The antidumping law is modified instead.

2. *Problems in Proposed Legislation*

a. Who Is a Nonmarket Economy Producer or Exporter?

Attaching a simplistic label such as "market" or "nonmarket" to something as complex as a national economy is inaccurate, but a necessity no matter which approach to import relief is chosen. Experience thus far shows that each case is unique and reflects the country and particular economic sector under investigation. It is likely that any statutory criteria defining "market" or "nonmarket" would be too brief to be truly meaningful. Yet as many investigators say, "you know it if you see it." The problem is more in the description of the criteria than in the ability to recognize the existence of market versus nonmarket economic behavior.

The European Communities antidumping regulations[57] and section 406 rely on legislated lists of countries. At first this approach appears desirable because it would greatly reduce the waste of time and resources involved in arguments over whether or not a given case should be treated as an NME case (most of them will be). However, the use of a fixed list, and the difficulty of changing the content of that list once one has been legislated, would make it politically and practically difficult in the U.S. to give recognition to the efforts which several NMEs are making to liberalize their economies. Given the overall U.S. interest in such liberalization, any regulatory system for dealing with NME dumping should be flexible enough to take

57. Council Regulation (EEC) No. 3017/79, 20.12.79, Art. 2.5.

account of those countries which make significant gains in such liberalization efforts.

b. Sole U.S. Producer Situation

When the NME import is the only competition for a product produced by only one U.S. company, there is a problem using the sole U.S. producer's price as the floor for both the U.S. industry and its foreign competition. If the U.S. industry is the sole producer of the product in this country or the industry is highly concentrated (not unlikely with narrow product definitions such as unrefined montan wax) and there is no other real source of import competition, the U.S. producer can continually raise its price and let the U.S. government force its competition, the NME import, to meet it. The presence of other imports could keep downward pressure on price to the extent that the foreign (free market) producer chooses not to raise his own prices to the U.S. In many circumstances, though, it is conceivable that both the U.S. producer and market economy importer could use a dumping complaint as a vehicle to enforce price rises to the detriment of national welfare.

In the above situation, if the fair import price were tied not to the NME importer's sole competitor's price but rather to the U.S. producers' verified production costs plus a mark-up for profit, the acceptable price of NME merchandise would be based upon cost, a factor which businesses attempt to minimize, rather than on prices, an item which businesses try to sustain at the highest level. This is especially important in the occasional case (such as with montan wax) when the U.S. industry is highly concentrated and able to restrict supply so that prices far exceed cost. In that instance, the nonmarket producer may be the only source of competition, and its market presence should be encouraged, not eliminated.

c. GATT Consistency

The GATT Working Party, considering Poland's accession to the GATT, explicitly declared its understanding that the nonmarket exception to the antidumping normal value test would apply to Poland.[58] This is interesting in two respects. It suggests that in the eyes of the GATT one need not take at face value the apparently strict GATT requirement for application of the NME exception that a country have "a complete or substantially complete monopoly of its trade" and that "all domestic prices [be] fixed by the State." Even in 1967, Poland probably did not fit this test if it were rigorously applied.

Second and more important, the Working Party explicitly recognized,

58. GATT, Working Party on Poland's Accession to the GATT in 15 BISD 111 (GATT 1968).

"that a contracting party may use as the normal value (e.g., "fair value") for a product imported from Poland the prices which prevail generally in its markets for the same or like products." This, of course, is precisely what is proposed by S. 1351. The EC applies its antidumping regulations governing NMEs (presumably, in compliance with the GATT), including the use of a methodology based on prices within the EC,[59] to countries which are GATT members.

Both the Polish and Hungarian GATT accession agreements attempted to directly address the low-priced import issue. Initially the Polish Protocol of Accession included promises by Poland that its exports would be priced at levels prevailing in the Western importing markets. Imports at lower prices would be potentially subject to duties to bring them up to this level. This proposal was never accepted but it is important in that it expressed the ideas of many of the contracting parties as to what constituted a fair import price for NME goods.[60]

The Working Party on the accession of Hungary addressed this issue in its 1973 report. In this report, the parties indicated that Hungary would be considered to be trading fairly if Hungarian exports were traded at world prices. In the absence of world prices, the prevailing prices in the countries of importation were to be taken into consideration.[61]

d. U.S. Industry Criticism—S. 1351 Legitimizes Nonmarket Dumping

Many U.S. industries are opposed to any system which would use the lowest average free-market price as the standard. They usually cite the following objections: (i) such a standard would assume, for fair value assessment purposes, that NMEs are *generally* as efficient as the most efficient free-market producer; (ii) it would permit a "safe harbor" for imports of injuriously dumped or subsidized NME products in the U.S. market; (iii) it could lead to a "meeting competition" injury defense for market economy producers selling dumped or subsidized imports in the U.S. market in competition with U.S. producers and NME imports; (iv) it could grant NMEs a lower pricing standard than that afforded to certain market suppliers whose costs or prices for a particular item are those of the

59. *See* Commission Decision 81/406/EEC:4.06.81., accepting undertakings in connection with the antidumping proceeding concerning imports of ball and tapered roller bearings, originating in Japan, Poland, Romania and the Soviet Union and terminating that proceeding; Commission Decision 82/220/EEC:14.04.82 terminating an antidumping proceeding in respect of imports of upright pianos originating in Czechoslovakia, the German Democratic Republic and Poland; Commission Regulation (EEC) No. 1958/82, 16.06.82. imposing a provisional anti-dumping duty on imports of photographic enlargers originating in Poland and the U.S.S.R., accepting an undertaking and terminating the proceeding in respect of imports of photographic enlargers originating in Czechoslovakia.

60. Dale, Anti-Dumping Law in a Liberal Trade Order 182 (1980).

61. *Id.* at 182.

lowest free market producer; and (v) there is disagreement as to how the Commerce Department could determine with any degree of accuracy the "lowest average free-market price."

e. Nonmarket Economy Countries' Criticism—
S. 1351 Denies Comparative Advantage

As a Joint Economic Committee study pointed out in 1979, the present system deprives NME producers of any "comparative" advantage unless by chance the "comparable" country chosen by the administrative authority under section 773(c) has the identical comparative advantage as the NME, which is most unlikely. This has been the theme of the most common criticism of section 1351 from NMEs. Indeed, *any* system of measuring the supposed home-market value of a NME product will inevitably deprive that economy of the certainty of receiving credit for its true comparative advantage, since that concept cannot be measured in a NME. Section 1351 would not attempt to measure comparative advantage (*or* home-market value) in an NME. Instead, it would allow an NME to sell in the U.S. as low as *anyone else* in the U.S. marketplace, thus implicitly assuring NME producers are as advantaged as the lowest priced U.S. market participant (some market economy exporters to the U.S. might well wish for the same treatment).

f. Technical Problems

There are a number of technical problems with the Heinz bill requiring attention. Suggestions are made below concerning these.

"Most suitable"—The bill provides as a yardstick the lesser of the lowest average price of "the most suitable" U.S. or foreign producer selling in the U.S. The reference to "the most suitable" producer should be changed to "any significant" U.S. or foreign producer selling in the U.S., to avoid a misunderstanding of the intent of the bill to use the lowest average price (except for prices of minor unrepresentative sales) as the benchmark for NME imports.

Time limits—The bill provides for preliminary Commerce determination by day 85, or if complicated by day 150; final Commerce determination by day 160, or if complicated by day 225. The time limits for an artificial pricing investigation, however, are appropriate for only those cases initiated and remaining on the NME track.

Timelimits for switching—Time limits of investigating cases are "switched" from "artificial pricing" to normal antidumping/countervailing duty procedures, or *vice versa*. Section 748 would permit Commerce an extra 30 days if a "switch" were made (i.e., if no preliminary determination had been made, the investigation would be placed at the same spot on the timetable of the new procedure as it was on the original procedure, with an additional 30 days allowed, while if a preliminary determination had been made, Commerce would have to issue a new one under the standards of the new procedures within 30 days).

The 30-day grace period may be sufficient for a "switch" from antidumping/countervailing to artificial pricing, since 30 days should be enough time to gather the minimally sufficient data to support a preliminary determination. A "switch" from artificial pricing to antidumping/countervailing, however, would require considerably more extra time (probably at least 60 days), since only a little (if any) of the information needed for an antidumping or countervailing duty determination would have been gathered for the decision to make the "switch."

GATT—Under the bill, artificial pricing investigations get the injury test if the exporting country is a GATT member. All other artificial pricing investigations get no injury test. A review should be made to determine if there are countries which are not GATT members to which the U.S. owes the injury test (such as the seven non-GATT members to which the U.S. extends an injury test in countervailing duty cases pursuant to pre-1979 bilateral agreements). If so, those countries must be given the injury test in artificial pricing cases. If an artificial pricing case is viewed, in essence, as a dumping case, an argument can be made that all petitions should be subjected to the injury test (although the lack of the injury test for cases against non-GATT members may be viewed as an incentive to non-GATT member NMEs to liberalize their economies enough to join the GATT).

Extension of time—Under the bill, extensions of time limits are permitted for number and complexity of transactions, novelty of issues, or number of firms to be investigated (tracking the similar provision of the AD law).

The following should be added to the reasons for extending the timetable for a case where an NME exporter is involved: the complexity of the economy being studied; and the difficulty of finding a market-economy producer that will provide the necessary data for calculation of the lowest average price in the U.S.

C. Section 406 Revision

Even though the elimination of section 406 has been dropped in the newest version of the Heinz bill, it would be preferable if section 406 were eliminated and a single, non-discretionary provision for cases involving unfair NME imports were created. This would leave cases of injury caused by NME imports not alleged to be unfair to section 201 (as is the case with imports from market economies). The fear underlying section 406 of a Communist country storing up goods and suddenly flooding the U.S. market with them in order to cause commercial havoc could be handled by adding the "emergency" provisions of section 406[62] to section 201.

1. *Minimize/Eliminate Discretion*

If section 406 is retained and no attempt is made to change the current potentially discretionary methodology of measuring antidumping from NMEs, then the Presidential discretion in section 406 should be eliminated, or at least severely restricted. At present, the U.S. industry has a non-discretionary remedy against imports from market economies (the anti-dumping/countervailing laws), as well as discretionary remedies (sections 201/301). Domestic industry should have the same access to a non-discretionary remedy against imports from nonmarket economics. If section 406 is the only practical remedy against imports from NMEs, then it should be non-discretionary, or, at least, the President's exercise of discretionary vetos should require Congressional concurrence (to the extent constitutionally feasible).

2. *Technical Changes*

A major flaw in section 406 is the burden it imposes on industries seeking relief. In an ordinary escape clause proceeding, the petitioner must show that imports are increasing, but section 406 adds a requirement that imports be increasing "rapidly." There is no clear reason for imposing a greater burden on industries faced with competition from NMEs than those facing world-wide competition.

3. *GATT Consistency*

Relief under section 406 is easier (at least on paper) than that outlined in the Polish, Romanian and Hungarian Protocols of Accession to the GATT. The possibility of conflict between the GATT rules and interpretations and section 406 has been recognized. For example, the 1975 U.S.-Romanian bilateral trade agreement recognizes that either party may apply its own import control laws (e.g., section 406).[63] The standards in section 406 should be conformed to the Protocols of Accession. If that is done, there should not be major GATT problems with reliance on section 406.

An additional inconsistency occurs in that the Polish, Romanian and Hungarian Protocols each include escape clause provisions which are more easily accessible than Article XIX. Of major importance in this area is the fact that action under these protocols does not run afoul of the GATT's most-favored-nation requirements. Arguably, section 406 would have to be

62. The Trade Act of 1974, Pub. L. No. 93–618.§ 406(c), 88 Stat. 2062 (1978) (codified at 19 U.S.C. § 2436(c) (1982)).

63. Agreement on Trade Relations between the United States of America and the Socialist Republic of Romania, April 2, 1975, 26 U.S.T. 2305, T.I.A.S. 8159, Annex 1.

conformed to the standards of the Protocols of Accession to escape the MFN requirements.

IV. Conclusion

The Heinz bill should be enacted after the appropriate changes (outlined above) are made. The use of antidumping laws is an accepted phenomenon around the world, whatever their economic rationale (or lack thereof). Similarly, their use against NME imports has become an accepted practice (including by the nonmarket economy exporters, who are the frequent target of EC antidumping cases), notwithstanding the lack of economic foundation for the surrogate-country procedure for calculating normal value. S. 1351 would make the procedure completely routine, to be handled at a technical level (which is where disputes over such items as golf carts and mushrooms should be).

The basic concept of the Heinz approach is fair—even if not perfect. Some more efficient NME producers will be penalized, and some inefficient NME producers will be spared antidumping duties, but in general the standard will provide access to the U.S. market for NME producers/countries to which the U.S. exports quite a bit, while mitigating the disruption caused by extremely low pricing. The best proof of the fairness of the Heinz bill can be seen in the equal opposition to it from both ends of the spectrum.

If the opposition to the Heinz proposal from both U.S. industry and NME producers means that there is insufficient support in the middle for the measure, the next best solution would simply be to exclude NME imports from the antidumping/countervailing duty laws. In its place should be provided a single, non-discretionary remedy—most likely a revised version of section 406 without presidential review.

If the President were totally excluded from the process, the ITC would simply vote on the existence of the requisite injury and causation and on the remedy to be applied (much as it does with the recommended remedies now under section 406 and section 201). This injury-only solution need not be overly harsh. The current ITC procedure of recommending relief could be amended to carry with it an opportunity for the President to negotiate relief other than that recommended by the ITC, but with the proviso that the petitioning domestic industry could challenge the President's alternative before the ITC. If the ITC agreed with the petitioner then it could substitute on a mandatory basis its own preferred form of relief.

Neither a modified version of S. 1351 nor an amended procedure under section 406 will create unusual problems within the trading community. Still, the problem of fitting NME imports into the context of "fair" trade as defined by the antidumping and countervailing duty laws is probably unsolvable as long as the standards of fairness reflect market rules of commercial behavior. Recognizing that this ideological difference in economic philosophy is likely to remain, the most appropriate approach to unfair trade relief from NMEs is to concentrate on rectifying the *symptoms* and *effects* of the import problems and sidestep the intellectual problem itself. S. 1351 (as modified) does this best. A new section 406 procedure with lowered discretion does this less well but still better than the current approach—the cumbersome, chaotic, and unpredictable methods under the antidumping and countervailing duty laws or the heavily politicized results under the current section 406.

CHAPTER FOURTEEN

Antidumping Policy as a System of Law

Gary N. Horlick and Steven A. Sugarman

Numerous articles, papers, and books have been written that offer rationales for the existence of antidumping laws.[1] They argue that imperfect trade conditions create dumping by foreigners, which harms domestic producers and consumers. At least in the United States, proponents work with their allies in Congress and the executive branch to preserve and expand laws that prevent such harms.[2] However, the product of their efforts, antidumping law, lacks a correlation to the rationales that serve as their justification. Thomas Howell, a leading proponent, states that "if certain defined trade-distorting practices that cause economic harm

1. Garten (1994), Labor/Industry Coalition for International Trade (LICIT) (1995), Howell (1998), and Mastel (1998). The last item is a "party line" U.S. Department of Commerce speech by the individual who was then undersecretary, who, aside from his stance on antidumping policy, was one of the best to occupy that position.

2. A public example of the imbalance of lobbying efforts in the United States between proponents and opponents can be seen in the response to a request for comments by the U.S. trade representative on the seemingly unrelated topic of the 1998 World Trade Organization (WTO) review of the Dispute Settlement Understanding, in *Federal Register* 63, no. 100 (May 26, 1998). Of the nineteen comments filed, twelve were by proponents of antidumping law (apparently concerned at the prospect that WTO panels would find the portions of U.S. antidumping law that they wrote inconsistent with the WTO rules) and none by opponents (the other seven focused on nondumping issues).

exist," antidumping laws are important, since they allow "the importing country [to] employ offsetting duties."[3]

Yet there are no WTO requirements or national antidumping laws to ensure that antidumping measures are applied only when "trade-distorting practices" are found to exist; further, no burdens are placed on petitioners or national authorities before raising WTO-bound tariffs on a non–most favored nation basis to show that the alleged dumping will produce a net economic harm to the domestic economy.[4] To the extent that antidumping laws impose sanctions absent a showing of trade barriers or unfair market conditions, they can be considered traditional protectionism rather than a proportional response to an identified problem.

This chapter reviews the underlying rationales offered as explanations of the phenomena of dumping and antidumping laws and explains the extent to which antidumping rules are tailored to achieve only those goals that justify their existence. Finally, it concludes with a modest proposal to change current antidumping laws in order to better link them to their rationales.

Dumping and Antidumping Rationales

Even proponents admit that antidumping laws are a system of second best. Greg Mastel states that if "evaluated from the perspective of perfectly competitive conditions, antidumping laws and all other government efforts to influence the market are difficult to justify because they necessarily alter the optimal market outcome."[5] The stated purpose of antidumping laws is to protect domestic producers and consumers from "mercantilistic commercial strategies pursued by foreign companies from behind their home governments' trade barriers."[6] Proponents assert that protected markets and other forms of trade

3. Howell (1998, p. 299).

4. The European Union (EU), for example, in its analysis of "Community interest," contradictorily finds that antidumping duties should be imposed because in the absence of antidumping duties EU consumers would suffer since EU suppliers would disappear, but that the antidumping duties will not harm consumers because they have many other non-Community sources that are not subject to the antidumping duties. See, for example, the EU's statement on the "consequences for users and consumers" of the antidumping duty on microdisks, *Official Journal* L 63/9, paras. 47–48.

5. Mastel (1998, p. 67).

6. LICIT (1995, p. 21).

barriers in foreign countries make antidumping laws necessary. For this reason it is interesting that no antidumping law of which the authors are aware requires the plaintiffs or the national authorities to prove that any substantial trade barriers or unfair practices exist before measures can be imposed to remedy conduct deemed to be dumping.

In *Keeping Trade Free and Fair: A Rational Defense,* LICIT states that "the *only* instances in which dumping can be pursued as a long-term strategy involve government activity (or inactivity) through one of the following channels: (1) government subsidies, (2) a protected home market, or (3) government toleration of cartels."[7] Yet neither the WTO nor antidumping laws require any showing of government support of any of these to impose a duty—often quite high—based on a claim alleging a long-term dumping strategy.[8] In order for a dumping claim to be substantiated and a measure imposed, none of the conditions that are rationales in support of antidumping laws need even be alleged to exist. Economically, domestic consumers are advantaged in the short term by dumping, and they are harmed only if foreign companies are able to win monopoly profits from them in the long term. Hence, only if those conditions are met can domestic consumers be harmed. It is inexplicable why there is not a requirement of, at a minimum, showing that at least one of these conditions exists. In this section each rationale that has been offered in support of antidumping laws is examined and its relevance to real-life antidumping law is reviewed.

Closed Home Markets

According to Greg Mastel, director of studies and vice president of the Economic Strategy Institute and a leading advocate of antidumping laws, "A closed or restricted home market is . . . a virtual precondition to a successful dumping strategy."[9] Other proponents have pointed to closed or noncompetitive foreign markets as a rationale for antidumping laws. These problem markets take two forms: sanctuary home markets and government-supported cartels.

7. LICIT (1995, p. 17). Emphasis added.

8. In 1993–95 the mean antidumping duty in the United States was 60.6 percent. See Congressional Budget Office (1998). The average U.S. tariff on manufactured goods was only 3 percent. See "Clinton Says World Should Start New Talks to Cut Trade Barriers," *The Investors' Business Daily* (May 19, 1998, p. A6).

9. Mastel (1998, p. 43).

A government may provide a sanctuary home market for its domestic producers. This type of market is a protectionist strategy that forbids the importation of a product into the country, thereby restricting market access to domestic producers. A sanctuary market could allow producers to earn monopoly profits domestically. Even if sanctuary markets are internally competitive, however, their domestic producers are afforded protection against foreign competitors. Therefore, if a company with a sanctuary home market chooses to dump products abroad, it need not fear reciprocation. Reciprocal dumping has been demonstrated to make an otherwise successful dumping campaign a losing strategy for foreign producers.[10] Therefore, eliminating the fear of reciprocal dumping could cause foreign producers to institute an otherwise unwise dumping campaign.

Foreign markets are also deemed restricted if domestic cartels, oligopolies, or monopolies are permitted to form and dominate the market. Foreign competitors theoretically would be permitted to export products into the market, but practically they could not compete with domestic producers because of the government's sponsorship or toleration of a cartel. Hence, domestic firms would be able to capture supercompetitive profits and use the profits to offset losses incurred by dumping products abroad.

Both forms of restricted or closed markets could exist in unison, providing domestic producers a competition-free home market. Proponents of antidumping laws point to closed home markets as a root cause of dumping. They claim that foreign companies that gain monopoly profits at home have the ability to subsidize predatory dumping abroad. Recognizing this as a threat to domestic producers in the short term and to consumers in the long term, they state that they fashion antidumping laws to prevent this practice.

Interestingly, neither the WTO's Agreement on Implementation of Article VI of the General Agreement on Tariffs and Trade (GATT) 1994 (WTO Antidumping Agreement or Antidumping Agreement) or any nation's antidumping laws require domestic industries to show that the foreign companies they accuse of dumping have closed or restricted home markets in any relevant sense. It is not

10. This is best exemplified by the Michelin-Goodyear case study by Mastel (1998, p. 43). Michelin allegedly began to dump tires in the United States, thereby decreasing Goodyear's market share. However, Goodyear simply began to dump in the EU to counter Michelin. Almost immediately Michelin stopped its dumping in the United States without the use or involvement of any antidumping laws.

necessary to even allege that a competitor has a home market.[11] The administrators of the EU's antidumping rules point out the following:

> If sales on the domestic market are not representative, for instance because they have only been made in small quantities, the normal value may be established on another basis, such as the prices of other sellers on the domestic market. Subsidies consist of a financial contribution from a Government, which confers a benefit to producers or exporters (e.g., grants, tax and duty exemptions, preferential loans at below commercial rates). In the majority of cases where dumping occurs on a more than incidental basis, a certain market segregation exists where that segregation may be due to government regulation, but also to other circumstances, including consumer preferences.[12]

This seems odd given Mastel's comments with regard to the Michelin-Goodyear case. Citing Goodyear's ability to effectively counter Michelin's dumping in the U.S. market by reciprocal dumping in Michelin's home market of Europe, he admits that "dumping strategies are difficult to pursue from an open market." Mastel further notes that "if markets are open, dumping often can be countered without resorting to an antidumping complaint."[13] In open markets antidumping laws interfere with and preclude the optimal result.

The WTO not only does not require any showing of a closed home market or any home market at all, but it permits a finding of dumping based on a product's price in a third country or its constructed value. These legal dispositions are inconsistent with the closed or restricted markets rationale. When the price of a product in a third market is used, there is no requirement to show that the third market is somehow protected for the alleged nonlocal dumper. Nor does it seem sensible to assume that an unaffiliated country would give one foreign company exclusive reign over its market without any evidence to support such an assumption. Given the potential differences in demand curves, export costs, and consumer preferences, absent proof that a third market (or even a home market, for that matter) is closed, price differentials between markets are of little to no probative value in a dumping inquiry. (Of course in

11. WTO (1994, Article 2.1). See also "Notice of Final Determination of Sales at Less Than Fair Value: Fresh Atlantic Salmon from Chile," *Federal Register* 63, no. 110 (June 9, 1998): 31411 for a finding that salmon from Chile is being sold or is likely to be sold in the United States at less than fair value, although there was no finding of a home market for the salmon.

12. Commission of the European Communities (1996, p. 2).

13. Mastel (1998, p. 43).

open or closed markets price differences between markets could arise as a result of market-driven forces unrelated to dumping.)

Imposing antidumping measures based on the use of a constructed value is also inconsistent with the requirement of a closed home market. Constructed values are used when there is no home market and there are no third-country sales. Under these circumstances dumping can occur only if it is cross-subsidized by another product.[14] However, no proof of cross-subsidization by another product is required in order to prove dumping under WTO rules, as we discuss a bit later.

Finally, the "sulfur amendment" added to U.S. laws in 1974 and then to the WTO Agreement in 1994 lends further credence to the finding that the restricted home market rationale for antidumping laws is not aligned with real-life antidumping laws. This amendment greatly expanded the concept of dumping to include a situation in which the price of a product sold in the exporting country is below its production "cost."[15] This exemption allows dumping to be found when it is shown that the price of an exported good is below "cost," even when the price of the exported good is above the price of the same good in the producer's home market. Because Article VI of the GATT does not permit the export price to be compared to constructed value except when there is no home market, the 1974 U.S. amendment defined *sales below cost* as being "not in the ordinary course of trade," and thus disregardable as home market sales under GATT Article VI and Article 2.4 of the 1967 GATT Antidumping Code. Once the prices in the home market are deemed below cost and therefore disregarded as not in the ordinary course of trade, a constructed value is compared to the exported product's price. This makes clear the lack of any requirement of a sanctuary home market (and the fact that the sulfur amendment eliminated the ability to use the absence of a sanctuary market as an affirmative defense) since a company can be sanctioned for dumping even when its products are priced lower in the home (or third-country) market than in the export market.

14. Dumping could also be found artificially by relying on private cross-subsidization by the same product from a different time period, and indeed both the United States and the EU do so, but it is unclear why this is "unfair." Yet it is certainly not uncommon in U.S. and EU business practices or business school teaching.

15. Further, Article 2.2.7 of WTO (1994) requires a definition of the profit to be imputed to cost that would constitute criminal securities fraud in the United States and many other countries.

It seems plausible to require that over some reasonable period of time a business recover all its costs for each separate product. Unfortunately, in practice this logic is flawed. For a business is able to project its revenues only over the course of time, and it cannot know until the end of the "reasonable period" whether it has made money on a product (as no business can predict recessions or changes in demand that will affect a product's profitability). But only foreign producers are punished with antidumping duties (or similar penalties) for retrospective failure to meet projections.

Further, the sulfur amendment has made real-life antidumping law even more distant from normal business practice, since the 1994 WTO Antidumping Agreement has been used by antidumping enthusiasts as a pretext to require that all costs be recovered within one year preceding the investigation rather than spread out over the product's life cycle or the business cycle.[16] This requirement appears to be contrary both to the intent of the legislature and to economic reasoning in general. The Senate committee that wrote the 1974 sulfur amendment offered as an example of a business that does not recover all its costs within a year or two a large commercial aircraft company. American businesses note that for some products it can take as long as thirty years to recover all costs. When large up-front fixed costs and small marginal costs are coupled with a sharp learning curve, this effect is especially noticeable. Further, start-up companies typically must make substantial investments in plants and equipment that can be recovered only over time. However, several national antidumping laws do not provide exemptions from the one-year requirement.[17]

16. The WTO Antidumping Agreement does not limit the reasonable period to one year. Compare Commission of the European Communities (1998) ("Account has to be taken of the fact that the Agreement states that the normal period for cost recovery for a product is 12 months") and U.S. House of Representatives (1994) ("Under current law, there is no clear definition of cost recovery—the measure of cost recovery could have been based on speculative estimates of future production costs. Under the amended law, if prices which are below cost at the time of sale are above weighted-average costs for the period of investigation or review (one year), such prices shall be considered to provide for recovery of costs within a reasonable period of time") with Koulen (1994, p. 205) ("Article 2.2.1 does not specifically define the 'reasonable period of time' for recovery of costs").

17. The WTO Antidumping Agreement expressly requires allowance for start-up costs. The EU has limited start-up by defining the period of start-up as irrebuttably less than one year, on the unsupported assertion that "a start-up phase can only constitute a

Nonetheless, Mastel attempts to defend the requirement by indicating that for the long term "all costs can be said to be variable."[18] However, all costs can be said to be variable only when a company can terminate all production without suffering any financial loss. Therefore, for a one-year time horizon to be considered the long term a company would need to have the ability to stop production at the beginning of any given year and not face losses from interest, rent, equipment, employment contracts, and so on. It is difficult to see how the proponents of antidumping laws can argue in any credible way that the one-year time horizon used by the EU and the United States constitutes the long term.

In sum, not only is showing a closed or restricted home market not required, but numerous provisions of the WTO Antidumping Agreement and national antidumping law indicate that this need not even be a consideration relevant to a finding of dumping.

Government Subsidies

A second rationale for antidumping laws is based on the existence of government subsidies. Proponents argue that "dumping and subsidization are . . . closely related. By lowering the cost of production or the cost of export sale, subsidies result in commercial behavior that can be characterized as dumping—selling below price in commercial home market or below production cost. . . . [Hence] government subsidies are a major underlying cause of dumping."[19] Since foreign companies must have the financial strength or resources to offset short-term losses in order to pursue dumping, dumping requires "the help of subsidies" or a closed home market.[20]

---

part of that period of cost recovery, and this is made clear in the proposed text" (Commission of the European Communities [1998, p. 3]), although the United States has irrebuttably presumed that start-up costs could never include marketing or other nonproduction costs, withstanding the plain language of Article 2.2.1.1 of the WTO Antidumping Agreement ("cost of production *and sale*") (emphasis added). See U.S. House of Representatives (1994, p. 837) ("However, sales expenses, such as advertising costs, or other non-production costs, will not be considered startup costs because they are not directly tied to the manufacturing of the product").

18. Mastel (1998, p. 107).
19. Mastel (1998, p. 51).
20. LICIT (1995, p. 17).

Again, this rationale may or may not lend support to antidumping laws, but antidumping laws in no way require that government subsidies be shown for dumping to be found. To the contrary, Article VI and the WTO Agreement do not even permit subsidies to be considered as dumping per se. Instead, Article VI and the WTO Agreement on Subsidies and Countervailing Measures separately provide for countervailing duties to offset subsidies and preclude "double counting." Therefore, although government subsidies are alleged to give foreign companies a trade advantage over domestic producers and thereby to harm consumers, this possibility is already offset by countervailing duties. Hence this rationale for antidumping laws is often just a red herring, but in any case antidumping laws do not require any showing of subsidies to support a dumping claim based on government subsidies.

Nonmarket Economies

According to this rationale, when the state owns or operates a business it may make non-market-based decisions. To the extent that decisions are made to sacrifice profits in order to attain some nonpecuniary benefit (for example, to maintain high levels of employment or increase foreign market share), they have much the same effect as a government's subsidizing a private company's implementation of a certain policy. Therefore, the effect on dumping would be identical to that in the discussion earlier. Again, there is no requirement (outside of cases aimed at current and former communist countries) to show either that a firm is government owned or controlled or even that its decisions are based on nonpecuniary factors in order to win a dumping case.[21] For that reason, the nonmarket economy rationale cannot support most dumping cases.

21. The "nonmarket economy" area is one area in which the WTO explicitly requires proof of the stated rationale. Application of the nonmarket economy methodology (that is, application of something other than an exporter's own prices and costs) is permitted only when "*all* prices" (emphasis added) are controlled by the state. See "Ad Note" to GATT (1994), Article VI. Most WTO users of antidumping laws—certainly including Australia, Canada, the EU, Mexico, and the United States—flout this requirement either all the time or virtually all the time. Indeed, it is hard to identify any WTO member that meets the criterion, which the Ad Note requires to be proved. Instead, the EU and the United States have offered to provide the normal treatment (which is legally required already unless all prices are controlled) only to those nonmarket economy companies that can prove that all of their costs are unaffected by state action. Certainly many European countries would have a very difficult

Cross-Subsidization of Dumping

The cross-subsidization of a dumped product is yet another rationale offered to justify the need for antidumping laws to level the playing field for domestic producers. In theory, if a company earns super-competitive profits from one product, it can utilize its excess profit pool to subsidize the dumping of another product. This rationale is based on the same assumption as the government subsidies rationale. Proponents argue that regardless of the source of funds, all that is needed for dumping is access to capital to finance short-term losses. The profits from one product are used as a private system of subsidies to finance unfair trade practices. Therefore, it is argued, antidumping laws are necessary.

Just as they can be cross-subsidized by sales of other products, dumped goods can be subsidized by profits from the same product that have been accumulated over time. By aggregating "excess" profits gained during times of prosperity a company can subsidize dumping during a recession to keep plants and equipment operating. This practice is referred to as cross-subsidization over time. Once again, there is no need to allege any form of cross-subsidization in order to "prove" dumping. It would seem logical to require a dumping action based on a claim of subsidization to prove the existence of a system of

time meeting that standard with respect to, for example, energy, other utilities, and much transportation.

Even if the major users could successfully delete the inconvenient words from the agreement (as they are attempting to do with China and Russia in accession talks), it would still be illogical to apply antidumping laws to nonmarket economies. If by definition the prices and costs of a nonmarket economy producer are not reliable, antidumping law cannot logically be applied. Safeguards would be better. The opponents of such proposals claim that the use of safeguards would be a "license to dump" for nonmarket economies, but it is impossible to know if a nonmarket economy exporter is dumping or not if its prices and costs are not reliable, so it is impossible for a logical person to claim that the use of safeguards would be a license to dump. By the same token, advocates for nonmarket economies claim that safeguards deprive nonmarket economy exporters of their competitive advantages. However, if the prices and costs are unreliable—and especially if exchange rates are fixed—how can one know where the nonmarket economy has true comparative advantage? In the end, the application of antidumping laws in a nonmarket economy is an application not of "interface," but of raw power. Small nonmarket economies take what they can get, and big nonmarket economies use their power where they choose to resolve cases outside of the WTO antidumping rules (for instance, those involving cartels, whether legal or not, on aluminum and steel).

subsidization, whether public or private, in order to be successful (even assuming that such ubiquitous private cross-subsidization should be attacked). However, the WTO does not make any attempt to distinguish dumping from "fair" competitive reasons for differential (including domestic) pricing.

Exporting Unemployment

Proponents of antidumping laws argue that dumping can be used to export unemployment during a recession. Again, no country's antidumping laws require any showing of such an intent or effect, and EU and U.S. antidumping laws expressly protect their local industries from imports by finding dumping when an exporter fails to raise its prices as demand drops (and unit costs rise).[22] Therefore, in a global recession all countries could raise their barriers to imports through findings of dumping based on the failure of prices to increase as demand decreases—a recipe for disaster from the 1930s.

A more sophisticated variation of the "exporting unemployment" argument is that antidumping rules serve as an "interface" between structurally different economies. The argument is that if Country A has a higher ratio of debt to equity than Country B, in a recession exporters in Country A will have to continue or increase production (because they must continue to meet their interest payments). Meanwhile producers in Country B, with low interest expenses, will cut production and dividends. The result will be a flow of exports from Country A to Country B that antidumping rules could prevent.[23]

22. Compare this antidumping policy to the laws of supply and demand as stated in any basic economics textbook, such as Samuelson and Nordhaus (1985).

23. Although the objective of this chapter is to illustrate the disjunction between antidumping law and its rationales, it is worth noting the basic flaws in this "interface" theory of exporting unemployment. It is true that Company A will need to increase its production or risk going bankrupt due to its high leverage; however, it is equally true that it would be in the financial interest of Company B to increase its production until the marginal costs of production are greater than marginal revenue. Hence, although it could be more important to the future viability of Company A to increase production (whereas Company B could choose to simply cut production and dividends and wait until the recession ends), it is in both companies' best interest to increase production as long as marginal revenue remains above variable costs. Further, it is in the interest of neither to produce when marginal revenue falls below variable costs. Simply put, assuming that other things are equal, a company's ratio of debt to equity should not affect its optimal production during a recession (or at any other time, for that matter). Therefore, it appears

However, no antidumping laws require that there be any showing (much less legally sufficient proof) that an exporting company in Country A has a higher ratio of debt to equity than its allegedly injured competitor in Country B.[24] In practice, dumping can be found where an exporter in Country A actually has a lower ratio of debt to equity than its competitor in Country B.

The rationales concerning the export of unemployment are in effect dependent on recessionary conditions, or at least a worldwide decline in demand for a product. However, there is no requirement to allege or prove that such a decline in demand exists. A finding of dumping to export unemployment does not need to be substantiated by evidence that there is a recession, that the price of a competitor's exported product is cheaper than the price charged in its home market, or that prices are below cost as a normal business would define it. Instead, if local producers can show that their market share decreased and foreign exports were somehow a factor in causing such decrease (that is, if they can show "material injury"), antidumping sanctions can almost always be imposed (the United States finds dumping in 95 to 99 percent of all cases). This can be extremely easy in recessionary conditions, since a recession can cause both domestic and foreign producers to lose money in the short term, as falling demand causes unit costs to rise while depressing price.

National Defense

Proponents sometimes point to national defense as a rationale for antidumping laws. In the context of technologically advanced products and other "defense"-related industries, it is argued that if foreign competitors were able to drive domestic companies out of business they could cause serious harm to a country's long-term national defense capabilities. This argument is difficult to respond to in the abstract; however, it should be noted that again there is no requirement that a relationship between a specific product and national defense be shown in order for antidumping laws to be used to call for sanctions. Although there is little debate that when national defense is truly an issue domestic production of necessary items can be protected, antidumping laws are

that this theory has mistaken the different levels of importance Company A and Company B give to the need to increase production with differing optimal levels of production. See Samuelson and Nordhaus (1985).

24. To the extent that the issue is differing ratios of fixed to variable costs, those ratios are more likely to vary by industry than by country.

so far removed from national defense policy that it seems unlikely that a country would tie its security to them, especially in light of the fact that these laws make no special exceptions or accommodations for petitioners alleging that national security issues are involved.[25]

Overproduction and Opportunistic Dumping

The EU has articulated a rationale for antidumping laws based on the competitive advantages a foreign company can reap from strategic dumping (the EU does not explain why the same rationale does not apply to domestic firms). This rationale is encapsulated in table 14-1.[26] The table illustrates how a foreign company can use dumping to reduce overall losses and loss margins, maintain employment, gain market share, and reduce marginal costs. In the example a company is able to successfully increase its profit margin from –34 percent to 0 percent by overproducing its demand. This table is used as evidence of the unfair nature of dumping, thereby providing a rationale for antidumping laws.

It is important to understand the unstated assumptions made by the EU in creating this table. First, the benefits realized by the imaginary producer are due to dumping only if the prices in the export market are below their "fair" value. If a foreign company is making a profit, dumping is predicated on a finding that export prices are below domestic prices for a specific product. No stated rationale for resort to antidumping law supports a finding of dumping, however, solely because a company is able to charge higher prices (8.75 in our example) in the domestic market and lower prices (6.00) in export markets. However, current antidumping law often bases the success of a dumping complaint solely on the price of a product in the company's domestic market. For example, if the company represented in the table sold its product for 4.00 in the home market and 6.00 in an export market, it would not be dumping. If that company sold its product for 6.00 in the home market and 6.00 in an export market, it would not be dumping.[27] However, if the company sold its product

25. To the contrary, the only exemptions from U.S. antidumping duties are military items, which is directly contrary to the national defense rationale. See 19 U.S.C. 1677(20).

26. Adapted from an EU handout, "Synthesis (figures)," given at a seminar in Moscow in September 1997.

27. For simplicity's sake we assume that there are no tariffs or transportation costs.

Table 14-1. Synthesis (figures)

Parameter	*Example*	*Dumping 1*	*Dumping 2*	*Dumping 3*
Domestic market				
Quantity sold	800	800	800	800
Unit price	8.75	8.75	8.75	8.75
Turnover	7,000	7,000	7,000	7,000
Export market				
Quantity sold	0	200	200	800
Unit price	0	3	6	6
Turnover	0	600	1,200	4,800
Profitability				
Fixed costs	7,000	7,000	7,000	7,000
Variable costs	2,400	3,000	3,000	4,800
Profit/loss amount	–2,400	–2,400	–1,800	0
Profit margin	–34%	–32%	–22%	0%

Source: European DG I/C3, PL/CS.

for 8.00 in the home market and 6.00 in an export market, it would be dumping.[28]

This example illustrates that current antidumping laws that categorically define *dumping* as "export price below domestic price" are often not punishing firms for dumping at all. In the example dumping would be found if prices in the home market were more than 6.00; however, no dumping would be found if they were less than or equal to 6.00. Therefore, in the EU's example it is not the price in the export market for which a foreign firm is necessarily punished; a firm is punished because it is able to charge higher prices for any reason in the home (or a third-country) market. This situation by itself has no recognizable relationship to the situations of importing (EU or U.S.) consumers or producers.

In order for this scheme to work as portrayed by the EU, the company would need to actually have a sanctuary home market (as opposed to assuming one). If the home market were open to international competition, by definition 8.75 would be the competitive price per unit on that market. In that case there would be nothing to prevent the company from selling 800 units at 8.75 in the export market and 800 units at 6.00 in the domestic market. This would benefit domestic consumers at the expense of foreign consumers, with no harm done to

28. For this example we assume that the company is able to make an overall profit under each scenario, and therefore the "sulfur amendment" does not apply.

the company (and little basis in the rationales for antidumping laws for an antidumping complaint). This scenario would be unrealistic only if 8.75 were a supercompetitive price. That, in turn, could occur only if the home market were closed or restricted.[29] Therefore, in order for the EU's example to have the harmful effects alleged to be caused by dumping, it would have to be based on an unproven assumption that the company in the example enjoyed a closed home market.

If the company's home market was not restricted or closed to imports, producers in the export market could employ the same dumping strategy as their foreign competitor. This reciprocal dumping would cause the firm depicted in the table to lose market share in the domestic market and no longer be able to sell 800 units of its product for 8.75 each. Therefore, such a strategy would backfire and cause the company to suffer greater losses than it would have experienced if it had not entered into dumping. To protect against opportunistic dumping, antidumping laws need to require a petitioner to prove a closed or restricted home market. As discussed earlier, they do not.

In the example there could be a finding of dumping even if the company charged 8.75 per unit for its goods in the export market. This is because antidumping laws calculate costs to include fixed expenditures during the past year. In this example the price would be 7,000 in fixed costs plus 3,000 in variable costs for each unit produced. If the company produced 1,000 units (as in examples 1 and 2) and charged 8.75 for all units (800 sold in the domestic market and 200 in the foreign market), it would not break even for the year. Therefore, a competitor from the export market could allege that, under the "sulfur amendment" described earlier, the price was less than the "cost." Actually the company could charge up to 15.00 per unit for 200 units in the export market (while maintaining the 8.75 per-unit price in the import market) and still not break even.[30] Therefore, dumping could be found even if prices in the export market were substantially above those in the "domestic

29. Or the product enjoys some degree of market power at home for reasons unrelated to the anticompetitive practices claimed as the rationale for antidumping.

30. The situation is even worse if one considers the requirement that export costs and tariffs be added to the price in the export market in order to avoid a finding of dumping. Garten (1994, p. 148) concedes that a finding of dumping based on an importing country's tariff is unjustifiable, but that dumping findings based on freight from a foreign producer to the customer are justifiable—even if the domestic competitor's freight cost to the customer is higher, which can easily occur (for example, if the product were shipped from Windsor, Ontario, north one mile to Detroit as opposed to a domestic competitor's shipping from Mackinac, Michigan, several hundred miles farther north of Detroit).

market."[31] All that would be required for the requisite showing of harm would be for the price in the export market to be slightly below that of an inefficient, uncompetitive producer whose domestic production was in the export market.

It should be mentioned that the EU table does not depict a case of predatory pricing (assuming that the EU industry is as efficient as the foreign one). In order to drive competition from a particular industry, as is the objective of predatory pricing, a foreign company must sell its products at prices below variable costs. Otherwise, it would be in its competitors' best interest to continue production. When sales are above variable cost but below total cost, as in the export market of the EU example, it is more profitable for the local industry to continue producing at "losses" than to discontinue production altogether and lose all sunk costs. Since there is no evidence that the objective of the company depicted in the table is predatory in nature, there is little evidence that there would be any net economic harm to the export market in the long term. Antidumping laws do not currently require a petitioner or authorities to provide any explanation as to how the alleged dumping harms the economy or consumers in general. They must show only that the local industry (in many U.S. cases, often just one or two companies) is harmed in some way. This is even true if domestic companies that use the imported product as inputs and domestic consumers who purchase the product are benefited in a more substantial way.

The EU table purports to be a numeric depiction of how opportunistic dumping could benefit foreign corporations. However, such opportunities are available only under specific conditions and assumptions.[32] Mastel articulates the importance of maintaining the proper perspective (which is counter to that of the table) by quoting William Culbertson: "The intent of foreign competitors is of secondary importance so far as national policy is concerned. The result is the thing that is to be prevented."[33] The LICIT seconds this idea, saying, "Merely because a practice might be rational for a business to undertake under

31. As long as the industry in the export market could show harm.

32. For the sake of argument, we accept the EU's definition of dumping in this case. But note that the price charged for exports may be above the product's variable cost. Some would argue that this would be dumping only if the price was below variable cost because any price over variable cost allows a company to be more profitable having made the sale than if it had not produced the unit at all.

33. Mastel (1998, p. 19).

some circumstances . . . does not mean a government should not act to counter the practice if it harms the larger national interest."[34]

In sum, assuming that the EU table accurately depicts a real-life firm, antidumping laws should not be used to sanction that firm unless harm to the domestic economy is also proven. Further, if the existence of at least one rationale was required in order to prove dumping, not only would there be protection against the EU's concern depicted in the table, but sanctions would be imposed only against firms engaging in practices that could arguably have a harmful effect on a country as a whole.

Discussion and Proposal of a New Antidumping Policy

The gap between antidumping laws and their rationales portends increasing problems for the future of international trade. If open competition between companies based in different countries is the optimal system of trade, antidumping laws must be tailored directly to their purposes such that they do not become so broad as to deter acts of beneficial competition. Current laws fail to achieve this objective. Garten states that dumping is often found when no "closed home markets, anti-competitive practices or predatory intentions" are found.[35] He further notes that "neither U.S. law nor our international obligations require a finding of any particular market conditions—like anti-competitive practices—in order to impose a dumping duty."[36] Only by limiting the application of antidumping laws to dumping that has been shown to be caused by one of the stated rationales for using antidumping laws—and that has the potential to cause a net economic harm to domestic markets—can it be ensured that such laws will not be used to inhibit fair trade.

Proponents have articulated numerous rationales detailing the need for antidumping laws, and without dismissing the strong and passionate positions on each side of the debate over antidumping laws, all should agree with the basic premise that antidumping laws should not exceed the scope of their rationales.[37] Without exposing domestic producers or consumers to the risks and dangers proponents allege can result from foreign dumping, the current system

34. LICIT (1995, p. 6).
35. Garten (1994, pp. 138–39).
36. Garten (1994, p. 139).
37. If more rationales are agreed to in the future, they could be added to this list.

of antidumping laws could be replaced with one correlated to the rationales justifying its existence. This would ensure that antidumping laws are not abused.

Currently antidumping laws are susceptible to protectionist misuse. They require a petitioner to show only that dumping occurred (within the statute's expansive—and expanding—definition of dumping) and that harm resulted for the petitioners. Although the WTO requires a causal link between these two factors, national authorities frequently rely on mere coincidence of the two factors. An inefficient company that is unable to compete in a free market can easily prove that it has been harmed by a foreign competitor's prices. Therefore, dumping should be appropriately defined such that no firms whose lower prices reflect only their competitive advantages are found to be dumping. Howell has stated: "From a policy perspective, the shape of a country's economy should be determined by the competitiveness of its industries, not maneuvering of anti-competitive business groups," and antidumping laws should seek to protect only this interest.[38] The rationales discussed earlier outline those conditions proponents have deemed necessary for a successful strategy of dumping to be undertaken. If antidumping laws can be invoked only upon showing that sufficient conditions exist for rational dumping, they may fulfill their stated purpose. Hence, we would like to propose a requirement that antidumping laws mandate such a showing.

In order to achieve consensus, our recommendation accepts the proponents' rationales for antidumping laws at face value and does not question their economic basis. With that in mind, we propose to amend current antidumping rules to require each petitioner who claims to have been harmed by dumping to (1) assert a rationale upon which to base the dumping claim that is sufficient to justify such a claim and (2) prove, or depend on the authorities to prove, the existence of such a rationale.[39] For example, if a petitioner alleged that a foreign competitor was receiving government funds to finance its dumping,

38. Howell (1998, p. 305).

39. Garten (1994, p. 138) asserts that antidumping laws should be designed to preserve the "natural competitive advantage" of a domestic company, and not to give it an advantage. Therefore, a company that would not be competitive in a system of perfect competition should not be allowed to use antidumping laws to become competitive. Such a company would not be allowed to file an antidumping petition unless it first showed that it was competitive with the foreign company alleged to be dumping and the authorities so proved.

this proposal would require the petitioner to prove its competitor is indeed receiving government funds and that they resulted in lower export prices than home market prices. If a petitioner alleged cross-subsidization from a closed home market, the case would require proof that those conditions that comprise a closed home market in theory in fact exist and that they result in the alleged amount of cross-subsidization.[40]

Garten uses three industry-specific examples—bearings, semiconductors, and steel—to illustrate what he depicts as the need for antidumping laws.[41] Our proposal would not compromise any of the examples he puts forward defending the use of antidumping sanctions to protect the domestic producers in these industries.

The Proposal Applied to Bearings

The U.S. antidumping investigations of antifriction bearings from numerous European and Asian countries are given as examples of antidumping complaints based on closed or sanctuary home markets. Accepting Garten's factual account of the complaints, closed home markets allowed foreign producers to earn protected monopoly profits at home and use such profits to dump excess production in U.S. markets. These claims by Garten may indeed be supported by factual evidence; however, neither the U.S. bearing manufacturers nor the authorities were required to either allege that closed markets existed or prove that the competitors were earning monopoly profits at home.

Under our proposal, antidumping procedures would be safeguarded against abuses. The U.S. bearing manufacturers would have been required to prove that its competitors benefited by sanctuary home markets where they reaped monopoly profits. Such proof would not have been difficult according to Garten's recounting of the investigations. Further, it would have been necessary to show

40. Under current antidumping rules a Monegasque company could sell one casino chip for U.S.$10.00 in Monte Carlo and each of twenty identical chips for U.S.$9.00 in the United States, thus earning an "unfair" profit of $1.00 that could be used to cross-subsidize the sales in the United States. The United States would then charge a total duty of U.S.$20.00 (20 × U.S.$1.00) to offset the total "cross-subsidization" of U.S.$1.00.

41. For a discussion of the role antidumping law played in "saving" these three industries, see Garten (1994, pp. 141–43). If the allegations were not provable, this could illustrate how enforcement of antidumping laws without having to prove the underlying rationale creates "client" pressure groups that will strongly support a continuation and extension of the existing system.

that such excess profits were being used to subsidize losses resulting from dumping. Again, Garten alleges as fact that their insulation from foreign competition in their home markets allowed foreign competitors to "afford to dump their excess production at low prices in the United States rather than disrupt the artificially high prices in their own markets."[42] Therefore, the bearing industry, after proving those allegations, would have remained protected under our proposal.

The Proposal Applied to Semiconductors

Garten alleges that "the experience of the U.S. semiconductor industry in the 1980s shows the pernicious effects of anti-competitive practices which can allow selling below the manufacturer's cost of production. A combination of a protected home market, a cartelized home market, substantial financial resources, and aggressive dumping, including selling below the cost of production, allowed Japanese companies to nearly decimate the U.S. semiconductor industry."[43] The first part of our proposed procedure (assert a rationale sufficient to justify an antidumping claim) should not have been difficult for the U.S. semiconductor industry to fulfill. The second part (prove facts sufficient to support such an assertion) would require only legally sufficient proof to support Garten's allegations. Either the petitioning company or the national authorities would need to prove that there actually was a "protected home market, a cartelized home market, substantial financial resources, and aggressive dumping." Once proven, the requirements of our proposal would be met, and the semiconductor industry would be protected. Our proposal would reject the petition only if the facts asserted by Garten were not proven facts, but unproven conjecture.

The Proposal Applied to Steel

Finally, Garten asserts that the steel industry provides a classic example of "sustained government intervention that led to excess production and dumping." He claims that European steel manufacturers have benefited from "substantial subsidies and other structural support from their government" that caused them to dump their overproduction in the United States.[44] Under our

42. Garten (1994, p. 141).
43. Garten (1994, p. 141).
44. Garten (1994, p. 143).

proposal U.S. steel manufacturers would first need to assert a rationale that would justify an antidumping claim. To do this they would need to assert that government subsidies in Europe not subject to countervailing duties and other specifically identified types of "structural support" have made it in the best interest of each of the separate European steel manufacturers to overproduce their demand and that these incentives have resulted in their dumping of excess production into U.S. markets. It would be necessary to prove such allegations, again, for each individual specified European producer (including some that received fewer subsidies than their U.S. counterparts). Assuming that Garten's discussion of the steel industry has a strong factual basis, such proof hardly would seem difficult.

Current antidumping laws, however, do not require even this minimum showing of proof. Therefore, a petitioner would need to show only that the prices of European steel companies in U.S. markets were below either the prices in European markets or the "cost" as defined in antidumping laws and below the price of U.S. steel in U.S. markets. This does not sufficiently protect U.S. consumers from findings of dumping unconnected to the rationales for antidumping law.

Antidumping rules have been incorporated into the WTO system. Therefore, all U.S. companies that export to other countries would be subjected to the same forms of treatment the United States is able to level against its importers. LICIT's paper argues that open, transparent adjudication of dumping complaints protects the interests of U.S. producers abroad.[45] However, even the most transparent and perfectly administered implementation of bad law can produce bad results.

As an example of how our proposal would eliminate some of the duties resulting from antidumping hearings, we look at the case of "Sweaters Wholly or in Chief Weight of Man-Made Fibers from Hong Kong."[46] Antidumping cases against companies based in Hong Kong provide a unique glimpse of the flaws in current law. Hong Kong is unique in its practice of free trade. It has no tariffs, no government subsidies to industry, and a general customs duty of only one-twentieth of 1 percent in most instances. Yet even a company in this haven of free trade is not safe from antidumping law. As demonstrated by the "Man-Made Sweaters" case and the twenty-seven others filed against companies

45. LICIT (1995, pp. 23–24).

46. See "Sweaters Wholly or in Chief Weight of Man-Made Fibers from Hong Kong," *Federal Register* 59, no. 35750 (July 13, 1994).

based in Hong Kong, antidumping law does not require proof of a closed or restricted home market or government subsidies. Further, in this case there was no showing of cross-subsidization of goods and, in the context of sweater making, national defense was presumably not an issue. However, even with the absence of each of these factors, authorities in the United States actually found that dumping existed and that such dumping had caused harm to domestic producers.[47] This result is not supported by any of the rationales for antidumping laws offered by proponents.

Our proposal would eliminate this undesirable result, since a rationale does not exist that can be substantiated and that would justify the imposition of duties in this case. Although the petitioner, National Knitwear and Sportswear Association, could have satisfied the first part of our proposal by showing a rationale other than a desire for protection to support its complaint, given Hong Kong's open markets and laissez-faire government policies it would be extremely difficult to substantiate such allegations.

Conclusion

The use of antidumping laws is likely to substantially increase in the future as nonmarket economies transition to capitalism.[48] Therefore, it is important to ensure that antidumping laws indeed promote the development of these nonmarket economies. In 1994 the Clinton administration proposed to change the application of antidumping laws to nonmarket economies currently transitioning to market-based economies. This implies that the current laws are providing disincentives for such countries and are not adequately promoting an international system of free and fair trade. Further evidence that implies that current antidumping law is being misused as a protectionist weapon comes from empirical research into the use of antidumping laws abroad. Currently companies from the United States and the EU, two self-declared open markets that according to their own statements do not enjoy sanctuary markets or lax antitrust policies, are among the most frequent subjects of antidumping cases. Further, Hong Kong's choice to open its markets to all trade has not prevented twenty-eight antidumping

47. See *Federal Register* 54, no. 47585 (November 15, 1989) and *Federal Register* 55, no. 20733 (July 27, 1990).

48. LICIT (1995, p. 20).

actions against its domestic firms. Finally, as barriers have disappeared under the North American Free Trade Agreement (NAFTA), antidumping actions between Canada, Mexico, and the United States should have become a thing of the past, yet such actions still exist. These facts indicate that current law is not serving the stated purposes of its designers and is unfairly restricting trade in free trade areas.

Our proposal seeks to reverse this trend. By requiring petitioners to allege with particularity a rationale justifying the need for antidumping sanctions in a particular situation, foreign firms will be protected from arbitrary duties. By requiring legally sufficient proof of such allegations, only the guilty will be punished. Our modest proposal will allow antidumping laws to maintain all the benefits proclaimed by their proponents while minimizing the possibility that they can be misused by domestic producers intent on constructing barriers to trade. At the same time the debate can continue regarding the fundamental desirability of antidumping laws themselves.

References

Commission of the European Communities. 1996. "Fifteenth Annual Report from the Commission to the Parliament on the Commission's Anti-dumping and Anti-subsidy Activities."

———. 1998. "Uruguay Round Implementing Legislation."

Congressional Budget Office. 1998. "Antidumping Action in the United States and Around the World: An Analysis of International Data." Congressional Budget Office Papers (June).

Garten, J. E. 1994. "New Challenges in the World Economy: The Antidumping Law and U.S. Trade Policy." Remarks made before the U.S. Chamber of Commerce. Washington, D.C. (April 7).

General Agreement on Tariffs and Trade. 1994.

Howell, T. R. 1998. "The Trade Remedies: A U.S. Perspective." In *Trade Strategies for a New Era: Ensuring U.S. Leadership in a Global Economy*. New York: Council on Foreign Relations.

Koulen, M. 1994. *The New Antidumping Code Through Its Negotiating History*. Bruges, Belgium: College of Europe.

Labor/Industry Coalition for International Trade. 1995. *Keeping Trade Free and Fair: A Rational Defense*. Washington, D.C. (June).

Mastel, G. 1998. *Antidumping Laws and the U.S. Economy*. Washington, D.C.: Economic Strategy Institute.

Samuelson, P. A., and W. D. Nordhaus. 1985. *Economics,* 12th ed. New York: McGraw-Hill.

U.S. House of Representatives. 1994. "Uruguay Round Agreement, Texts of Agreements, Implementing Bills, Statement of Administrative Action, and Required Supporting Statements, September 27, 1994."

World Trade Organization. 1994. "Agreement on the Application of Article VI of the General Agreement on Tariffs and Trade 1994" (Antidumping Agreement).

Antidumping and Countervailing Duty Law Provisions of the Omnibus Trade and Competitiveness Act of 1988

Gary N. Horlick* and Geoffrey D. Oliver**

Introduction

This article describes the amendments to the U.S. antidumping ("AD") and countervailing ("CVD") laws[1] included in the Omnibus Trade and Competitiveness Act of 1988[2] (the "1988 Act") as well as some of the amendments which were rejected. Those amendments comprise only 28 of the 467 pages of the 1988 Act, yet they occasioned some of the fiercest lobbying efforts of the entire bill, lasting literally until the very end of the House-Senate Conference Committee. That lobbying reflected the degree to which the U.S. AD/CVD laws have become the usual first choice for industries seeking protection from imports into the U.S.[3]

The 1988 Act is the fourth major revision to U.S. trade law in the last fifteen years. None of the revisions, however, has involved a comprehensive review of U.S. trade policy or AD/CVD laws. Rather, the revisions have been an *ad hoc* series of amendments derived from specific proposals from domestic companies involved in recent or anticipated cases. As a result, each major revision in U.S. trade laws, beginning in 1974, has seen AD/CVD amendments added to make it easier for domestic industry to obtain relief from imports. In some sense, that process became self-perpetuating; the easier it became to get relief, the more cases were brought, generating more interest in the use of these laws. Indeed, many of the proposals that led to amendments in the Trade and Tariff Act of 1984 and the 1988 Act originated in specific AD or CVD investigations, in which certain domestic industries were

*Partner in the Washington, D. C. office of O'Melveny & Myers; formerly Deputy Assistant Secretary for Import Administration, U.S. Department of Commerce from 1981 to 1983, and International Trade Counsel for the U.S. Senate Committee on Finance in 1981.

**Associate in the Washington, D. C. office of O'Melveny & Myers; a Robert Bosch Foundation Fellow in the Federal Republic of Germany in 1986-87.

[1] The U.S. AD/CVD laws are summarized in Horlick, *Summary of Procedures Under the Antidumping and Countervailing Duty Laws*, 58 St. John's L. Rev. 828 (1984).

[2] *Omnibus Trade and Competitiveness Act of 1988, Conference Report to Accompany H.R.3*, H.R. Rep. No. 576, 100th Cong., 2nd Sess. at 83-112 (20 April 1988) ("Conference Report").

[3] In fiscal year 1988 (1 October 1987-30 September 1988), there were 75 antidumping and 27 countervailing duty cases begun in the United States. More important, AD/CVD laws have become the means by which imports are controlled of such significant items of trade as steel, semiconductors, fertilizer, lumber, orange juice, ball bearings, and forklift trucks. The attraction of the U.S. AD/CVD laws for an import competing industry is that they are non-discretionary—that is, AD/CVD cases are to be decided based on statutory, non-political criteria, without interference for political motives, and fully subject to judicial review.

frustrated by their failure to obtain relief from imports. The legislative process leading up to the 1988 Act included a full share of such proposals. In the end, most of those proposals were left out of the 1988 Act, or were diluted to a point where they could not have much trade restrictive effect.

The Omnibus Trade and Competitiveness Act of 1988 was introduced in the House of Representatives as H.R. 3 on 6 January 1987[4]. The portion containing the AD/CVD amendments was reported out of the Committee on Ways and Means on 25 March 1987[5], and contained several amendments sought by coalitions of import-competing U.S. industry seeking more restrictive AD/CVD laws. A bill was passed by the House of Representatives on 30 April 1987[6], with no changes in the AD/CVD amendments, and sent to the Senate.

A substantially revised package was reported out of the Senate Finance Committee on 21 July 1987[7]. The AD/CVD amendments were greatly changed, following sustained lobbying by the Administration and by export-oriented large U.S. businesses. Several more restrictive AD/CVD amendments were added, none of which were in the House bill. The sheer complexity of the overall "Omnibus" bill made for an unprecedentedly complex conference committee including 199 congressmen and senators, seventy-six different configurations of House conferees, and eleven different configurations of Senate conferees.[8]

The difficulty of organizing such a complex conference meant that the first meeting of the sub-conference committee dealing with the AD/CVD amendments could not be scheduled until 24 October 1987.

Five days before the scheduled meeting, stock markets "crashed" all over the world. The conferees become cautious about agreeing to anything which could be painted as "protectionist" and action on the hotly contested AD/CVD amendments was put off until 1988. When the sub-conferees resumed work on the AD/CVD amendments in early 1988, the perception of an "export boom" from the U.S., fueled by the lower value of the dollar against several major trading currencies, coupled with intensive lobbying by the Administration and coalitions of export-oriented large U.S. businesses, and a thoughtful approach by the conferees and their staff, led to the rejection or dilution of nearly all the "restrictive" AD/CVD amendments.

As part of this process, the Congress engaged in a serious debate about what should be considered a countervailable subsidy, began to contemplate the effect of "globalization" of production on antidumping law (although without seriously reviewing the fundamental assumptions of antidumping law), and significantly improved procedural protection for parties in AD/CVD investigations. In the end, many of the substantive amendments only confirmed or clarified existing Commerce

---

4 4 Int'l Trade Rep. (BNA) 20, 7 January 1987).

5 *Id.* at 429 (1 April 1987).

6 *Id.* at 600 (6 May 1987).

7 *Id.* at 920 (22 July 1987).

8 See Conf. Rep. No. 576, 100th Cong., 2d Sess. at 497-514 (1988).

Department and International Trade Commission authority, especially to prevent circumvention of antidumping decisions, but several of the amendments, and the proposals which were not adopted, point the direction for the future fights over AD/CVD law.

I. COUNTERVAILING DUTY PROVISIONS

(a) *Definition of Countervailable Subsidy (Section 1312)*

Section 1312 of the Trade Act provides a list of factors for Commerce to examine in determining whether a particular benefit or program is an "actionable domestic subsidy" under the Trade Act of 1930. This section is a codification of current Commerce practice, and probably will not involve any major change in Commerce practice. It will, however, clarify a confusing situation caused by conflicting Court of International Trade ("CIT") decisions. The U.S. Commerce Department considers a foreign government program is not a countervailable subsidy unless it is specific to an industry or group of industries within the country. Under this general rule, for example, Commerce has consistently held that low-priced natural gas in fact sold by the government in Mexico at the same rates to all purchasers within Mexico is not a countervailable subsidy.[9] This should not be surprising since the United States in 1979-80 rejected claims by the European Economic Community ("EEC") that price-controlled U.S. natural gas sold to industrial users was a subsidy on U.S. exports to Europe of synthetic fibers and textiles made therefrom.[10]

This practice was complicated by three CIT opinions, one holding that non-industry specific government programs were not countervailable subsidies, one stating that such programs would be countervailable (unless they were tax programs), and one attempting to bridge the gap by creating a "competitive benefit" test.[11]

---

[9] *Anhydrous Ammonia from Mexico*, 48 Fed. Reg. 14,729 (Affirm. prelim.) (1983); 48 Fed. Reg. 28, 522 (Neg. final) (1983).

[10] Horlick, Bello & Levine, *The Countervailability of Subsidies: Specificity*, in Practicing Law Institute, *U.S. Import Relief Laws: Current Developments in Law and Policy* 35, 39 (1985). In 1979-80, the EEC threatened to impose countervailing duties on U.S. petrochemical products because of "unfair cost advantages" enjoyed by U.S. producers as a result of oil and natural gas price regulation in the United States. *Imports of Synthetic Fibers from U.S. Create Problems for the EEC*, Information memo from the Commission of the European Communities, Common Market Reporter (CCH) at ¶ 10,232 (1980); see also *Petrochemical Disputes Erupt*, Business Week (29 October 1979); *U.S. Petrochemicals Under Foreign Fire*, Chemical Week (10 October 1979). The EEC refrained from actually attempting to impose countervailing duties.

[11] *Carlisle Tire & Rubbeer Co. v. United States*, 564 F. Supp. 834 (Ct. Int'l Trade 1983) (generally available subsidies are not countervailable); *Bethlehem Steel Corp. v. United States*, 590 f. Supp. 1237 (Ct. Int'l Trade 1984) (generally available subsidies are countervailable, except for tax deductions); *Cabot Corp. v. United States*, 620 F. Supp. 722 (Ct. Int'l Trade 1985) (generally available subsidies are not countervailable unless they are in fact used by limited, specific industries or groups of industries). The Cabot case was further complicated by the unusual underlying facts, as the alleged subsidy—cheap access to carbon black feed stock—could only be used by the two companies in the one industry at issue. In its initial *Carbon Black* decision in 1983, Commerce held that those facts by themselves made the access to the input "generally available" (because equally available to all who could use carbon black feedstock). The error was cleared up in the first administrative review, which looked at whether, in fact as well as nominally, the carbon black industry got a better break on its inputs than other petrochemical producers in Mexico. Commerce found a subsidy to the extent that carbon black producers in fact received lower input prices than other Mexican producers. *Carbon Black from Mexico*, 51 Fed. Reg. 30,385 (Admin. Rev. final) (1986). This followed Commerce precedent established in and followed since 1982.

Furthermore, the third of these three cases, *Cabot Corp. v. United States,* was open to various interpretations.[12]

Certain domestic industries which had lost or anticipated losing such countervailing duty cases began a major lobbying effort to overturn the Commerce specificity test by means of a statutory amendment as early as 1983. The intent of this provision, known as the natural resources provision, was to designate as countervailable low-priced natural resources made available by a foreign government to producers in that country, even if the benefits of these low prices were available and were in fact used throughout the economy.[13] The U.S. ammonia industry, supported in 1984 by Senator Long and Congressman Moore of Louisiana and Congressman Gibbons of Florida, and by Senator Baucus of Montana in 1987–88, was the staunchest supporter of the provision; the U.S. cement and lumber industries also lobbied on behalf of the amendment. Senators Packwood, Bentsen and Bradley led the opposition, in part out of concern for the effect of potential mirror legislation by foreign countries on U.S. industry. For example, U.S. agriculture would be a prime target if cheap water were found to be a subsidy of agriculture and therefore countervailable.[14] The lobbying on both sides of the issue was intense from 1983. The proposed statutory change[15] lost by one vote in the conference on the 1984 Trade Act.

Both the House and Senate bills were drafted to codify the *de facto* test—that Commerce must look beyond the legal description of a benefit to determine whether it is in fact widely used. There were serious differences in the House Ways and Means and Senate Finance committee report language, however. The Ways and Means report adopted the full reasoning of the *Cabot* opinion. The resulting language was unclear but could be interpreted as stating that an input price for domestic sale that

---

[12] In *Cabot Corp. v. United States,* 620 F. Supp. 722 (ct. Int'l Trade 1985) a CIT judge rejected the established specificity test of the Commerce Department, which was used to differentiate countervailable subsidies from "generally available," non-countervailable government assistance. At issue was a Commerce Department ruling that the Mexican government's two-tier pricing scheme for petroleum products (one set price for all domestic consumers and a second, higher price for foreign consumers) was not a countervailable subsidy. The opinion stated that the programs at issue "are apparently available to all Mexican enterprises, but in their actual implementation may result in special bestowals upon specific enterprises." *Id.* at 732.

The language of *Cabot* was subject to three possible interpretations. First, if individual recipients of a government program could be identified, any benefits they received would be countervailable. Second, even if the individual recipients could be identified, the Commerce Department would have to analyze the operation of the program to determine whether certain recipients benefited more than others. Finally, Commerce merely had to confirm that, in addition to being generally available, the program was also widely used. See Hunter and Kubach, *Subsidies and Countervailing Duties: Highlights Since 1984* in D. Riggs (Chairman), *The Commerce Department Speaks 1987,* 491 at 514–15 (1987).

The issue remained unresolved for two years. In 1987 three judges of the CIT issued three parallel opinions adopting the third approach. In *PPG Industries, Inc. v. United States,* 662 F. Supp. 258 (Ct. Int'l Trade 1987), the court upheld a Commerce Department determination that the Mexican government's pricing system for natural gas was non-countervailable because it was generally available and in fact widely used, even though the export price was much higher than the home market price. In two subsequent cases, two other CIT judges adopted the same standard. See *Al Tech Specialty Steep Corp. v. United States,* 661 F. Supp. 1206 (Ct. Int'l Trade 1987); *Can-Am Corp. v. United States,* 664 F. Supp. 1444 (Ct. Int'l Trade 1987). The *PPG* case has been argued on appeal to the Court of Appeals to the Federal Circuit, but no decision has been issued as of this writing.

[13] See H.R. 4784, 98th Cong, 2d Sess. (1984); S. 1292, 99th Cong., 1st Sess. (1985).

[14] See e.g., *Fresh Asparagus from Mexico,* 48 Fed. Reg. 8830 (Neg. prelim.) (1983); 48 Fed. Reg. 21,618 (neg. final) (1983).

[15] See H. Rep. No. 1156, 98th Cong., 1st Sess. 170 (1984).

was lower than the export price for the same input would constitute a subsidy[16] (the opposite, curiously, would be dumping), and "generally *available* [subsidies], when actually bestowed, may constitute specific grants conferred upon specific identifiable entities, which would be subject to countervailing duties."[17] The Senate Finance report, by contrast, very carefully limited the reach of the *Cabot* case by adopting only "*the* holding in *Cabot* that in order to determine whether a domestic subsidy is countervailable, the Commerce Department must examine on a case-by-case basis whether the benefits provided by a program are bestowed upon a specific enterprise or industry, or a group of enterprises or industries (emphasis supplied)," thus discarding for the new statute all the other language in the *Cabot* opinion.[18]

The Administration strongly opposed the House version, on the grounds that it would ignore comparative advantage and expose U.S. industries to mirror legislation. The Administration mentioned irrigation water and small business loans as examples of U.S. programs that could be subjected to countervailing duties under the standard contained in the House bill.[19] The Conference Committee adopted the Senate version and Finance Committee report language.[20] This was directly confirmed in a floor statement by Senator Bentsen,[21] the Finance Committee chairman and floor manager of the bill (whose statement on the floor would be given much greater weight by a judge than those of other senators).[22]

Thus, Congress was finally able to resolve the question of how to define subsidies for U.S. countervailing duty law in a way which should prevent unfair trade which injures U.S. companies here without penalizing our exporters. The conference agreed that, in the future, the Commerce Department in determining whether a government program is provided to a specific industry or group of industries must

---

[16] H. Rep. No. 40, 100th Cong., 1st Sess. 123 (1987).

[17] *Id.* at 124 (referring to the CIT decision in *Cabot*). The House bill also contained a related amendment governing the proposed measurement of benefits bestowed. Commerce's position had been to compare the price of a government-provided resource to the industry under investigation with the price of that resource to other industries in the country with the difference being the amount of the countervailability subsidy. Preferentially Appendix, *Carbon Black from Mexico,* 51 Fed. Reg. 13,269, 13,272 (Admin. Rev. prelim.) (1986). (The price of the resource to other industries in the country is presumably the cost of the resource on a "generally-available" basis.)

The House provision would have required Commerce to compare the cost to the industry under investigation with "market value" in evaluating a subsidy. H.R. 3, Sec. 133, 100th Cong., 1st Sess. (1987). This would have ignored any cost advantages enjoyed by the input producers (and passed on in the form of lower prices to other industries) in that country.

[18] S. Rep. No. 71, 100th Cong., 1st Sess. 122 (1987).

[19] Letter from the United States Trade Representative ("USTR") to the Honorable Dan Rostenkowski, Chairman, Committee on Ways and Means, pp. 14-15, 30 October 1987 (the "30 October 1987 Letter"). Opponents of the House provisions included the Business Coalition on Trade (the Emergency Committee for American Trade, the Business Roundtable, the U.S. Chamber of Commerce, the National Association of Manufacturers, the U.S. Council for International Business, and the National Foreign Trade Council), the Pro Trade Group, and the Coalition to Promote American Trade.

[20] Conf. Rep. No. 576, 100th Cong., 2d Sess. 587 (1988). The Conference Committee instructed USTR to request a study by the ITC into foreign investment restrictions that prevent U.S. industries from establishing plants abroad to take advantage of lower priced natural resources. See Explanatory Statement of the Committee of Conference, 133 Cong. Rec. H2013, H2031 (daily ed. 20 April 1988) (hereinafter "Explanatory Statement".).

[21] 134 Cong. Rec. S10571, S10576 (daily ed. 2 August 1988).

[22] *Mills v. U.S.*, 713 F.2d 1249 (7th Cir. 1983).

look not only to its *de jure* availability, but also to its *de facto* availability within the country at issue.

Thus, Section 1312, which applies to future CVD investigations and administration reviews of past cases, will help to clarify the confusion over this issue created earlier by the conflicting CIT decisions. Presumably, the approach established by the CIT in *PPG Industries, Al Tech,* and *Can-Am,* i.e., testing *de facto* specificity by confirming that a particular subsidy is widely used, will continue to be followed by Commerce.[23]

Finally, a proposal by Congressman Gibbons was accepted for an ITC study of whether other governments deny foreign (i.e., U.S.) investors in their countries access to those governments non-industry specific programs, with USTR to initiate Section 301 cases against "egregious" examples.[24]

(b) *Calculation of Subsidies on Processed Agricultural Products (Upstream Subsidy) (Section 1313)*

In 1984, an amendment was added to the U.S. CVD law to set out how Commerce must calculate the degree to which subsidies on inputs affect downstream exported products exported to the United States (the "upstream subsidy" amendment).[25]

In a 1985 countervailing duty case involving imports of pork products from Canada, Commerce refused to apply the upstream subsidy amendment in calculating how subsidies on pig production should be allocated to pork exported to the United States, claiming that pigs and pork are really the same product, rather than pigs being an input into pork. Therefore, Commerce allocated the entire amount of the Canadian subsidies on pig production to pork exported to the United States.[26] The decision was challenged in the courts, and a CIT judge ruled in April 1987 that Commerce had violated the law by ignoring the 1984 amendment.[27] The Senate (with the Commerce Department's agreement) promptly passed an amendment overruling

---

[23] But note that the CIT recently revisited *Cabot,* ruling that Commerce should have followed the first *Cabot* ruling in determining in the administrative review whether carbon black producers received subsidies by reason of cheaply priced natural gas. *Cabot Corp. v. United States,* Slip Op. 88-96 (ct. Int'l Trade 21 July 1988).

[24] To the extent that foreign governments make incentives available to U.S. investors, they tend to provide incentives for U.S. investors to put their capital in facilities outside the U.S.

[25] This amendment was codified at 19 U.S.C. 1677-1 (Supp. IV 1986). It provided that in cases involving downstream products, Commerce should treat subsidies to producers of the input as being bestowed on the downstream product, under certain circumstances. Commerce should decide that a subsidy has been bestowed when the price for the input product "is lower than the price that the manufacturer or producers of merchandise which is the subject of a countervailing duty proceeding would otherwise pay for the product in obtaining it from another seller in an arm's-length transaction.".

[26] *Live Swine and Fresh, Chilled and Frozen Pork from Canada,* 50 Fed. Reg. 25,097 (Affirm, final) (1985). (As a matter of economics, the amount of the subsidy pass through will generally depend on market factors, such as the availability of unsubsidized competitors and other market factors. Rarely (if ever) will all of a subsidy be passed through between unrelated parties in the absence of a monopsonistic situation.).

[27] *Canadian Meat Council v. United States,* 661 F. Supp. 622 (Ct, Int'l Trade 1987).

the CIT decision, and effectively overruling the 1984 amendment in so far as it applied to agricultural products, contributing to the understandable incorrect impression by foreigners that the U.S. countervailing duty law can be manipulated politically with the open cooperation of the Administration. The Senate amendment, contained at Section 1313 of the Trade Act, requires that the entire subsidy on agricultural inputs be considered to flow through to processed agricultural products if the demand for the raw product is substantially dependent on the demand for the processed product (i.e., if the input is used almost entirely for the product exported to the U.S.) and there is relatively low value added to the raw agricultural product in the processing operation.[28]

This provision was pushed by Senator Baucus with Senators Grassley and Pryor also lending their support. There was no real opposition to the provision in the House, and the Administration never really took a stand.

This provision has potential to cause a great deal of trouble. A panel formed pursuant to the General Agreement on Tariffs and Trade has already ruled, in response to an EEC complaint about Canadian countervailing duty law, that a raw agricultural product is not a " like product" to boneless beef, then pigs are not "like product" to the processed agricultural product, albeit in the context of determining which industry is injured (as described below). The General Agreement on Tariffs and Trade ("GATT"),[29] the GATT Antidumping Code[30] and the GATT Subsidies Code,[31] require that any AD/CVD duties be applied only to a product like that which is dumped or subsidized. If, as the GATT panel has ruled, cattle are not a "like" pork, and a subsidy on pigs or cows cannot be assumed to flow through entirely to the processed product.[32] Further, the GATT Beef panel pointed out that there is no logical reason to limit this principle to agricultural products. Many final products reflect a relatively small degree of elaboration of inputs. Finally, the EEC is strongly opposed to complete flow-through of subsidies in agriculture in order to protect its exports of processed agricultural products. A similar EEC complaint before a GATT panel against U.S. AD/CVD cases involving wine was successful (although left in limbo by the EEC success in having the U.S. AD/CVD case dropped in the preliminary phase for lack of injury in 1984 and again in 1985).[33]

[28] Conf. Rep. No. 576, 100th Cong., 2d Sess. 588 (1988) (referring to § 338 of S. 1420).

[29] *General Agreement on Tariffs and Trade,* GATT, 1st Supp. BISD 11 (1953) (hereinafter "GATT").

[30] *Agreement on Implementation of Article VI of the General Agreement on Tariffs and Trade,* GATT 26th Supp. BISD 171 (1980) (hereinafter "GATT Antidumping Code").

[31] *Agreement on Interpretation and Application of Articles VI, XVI and XXII of the General Agreement on Tariffs and Trade,* GATT, 26th Supp. BISD 56 (1980) (hereinafter, "GATT Subsidies Code").

[32] GATT Panel Report, *Canada—Imposition of Countervailing Duties on Imports of Manufactured Beef from the EEC* (October 13, 1987) (blocked by the Government of Canada).

[33] See also *Table Wine from France and Italy,* 49 Fed. Reg. 10,587 (Neg. prelim.) (1984); *Table Wine from the Federal Republic of Germany, France, and Italy,* 50 Fed. Reg. 45,174 (Neg. prelim.) (1985). Note the possible contradiction between the EEC position opposing the 100 per cent flow-through of subsidies from inputs to processed agricultural products and the position taken by the EEC, described in Section III. A. below, imposing antidumping duties on inputs to prevent circumvention when the inputs are imported into the EEC and assembled there into a product that would be subject to an antidumping duty if imported into the EEC in its completed state.

(c) *Revocation of Status as Country Under the Agreement (Section 1314)*

In 1979, the United States agreed to conform its countervailing duty law to the GATT requirement that injury, as well as countervailable subsidization, be shown, but limited that concession to those countries which signed the GATT Subsidies Code,[34] and thereby accepted a strict discipline on export subsidies.[35] Certain conciliatory, although non-binding, language about the development needs of LDC's was included in Article 14. In the practice, this restriction of application of the injury test has worked mainly against LDC's, which feel the need to grant export subsidies to overcome the internal disincentives to exports of many developing countries, especially those whose import substitution policies have made sales in the home market considerably more attractive than competition in export markets.

The United States Trade Representative's office ("USTR") has always assumed that the injury test could be withdrawn if a country failed to live up to its commitments to impose discipline on export subsidies. While the U.S. has threatened Brazil with this withdrawal several times, in practice the "injury test" has been withdrawn only from New Zealand, as much a result of pique at New Zealand's nuclear policy as a result of its failure to live up to its obligations.

Section 1314 of the Trade Act confirms USTR's authority to withdraw the injury test.

This provision originated from a tougher proposal from the Trade Reform Action Committee, a coalition of import-competing companies ("TRAC"), following textile countervailing duty cases in 1984. The proposal was pushed primarily by Senator Heinz. The final provision is a watered-down version of the original proposal, and essentially corresponds to USTR's understanding of its existing power to withdraw the injury test under prior law. Section 1314 of the Act also requires a study of this policy in view of continuing compliance problems, with particular reference to Brazil and India.[36] (When a country's internal economic situation stagnates or declines, it sometimes feels the need to step up exports, no matter what commitments it might have made previously to reduce or eliminate the use of export subsidies.)[37] The commitments policy has always contained potential for a major commercial disaster, such as would result from imposition of countervailing duties on all Brazilian exports to the U.S. without an injury test, or on all Chinese exports to the U.S. if a

---

[34] See GATT Subsidies Code, Part I.

[35] India (properly) challenged this policy in the GATT as a violation of the Most-Favored-Nation obligations of the United States, and undoubtedly would have won, which led the United States to reach a "soft deal" with India to give it the injury test in return for relatively soft discipline on Indian export subsidies.

[36] "In particular, the Committee expects the USTR to review the Brazilian and Indian commitments in light of this provision, and to determine whether either country should no longer be considered a "country under the agreement" if the USTR concludes that it has not honored its obligations under the agreement." S. Rep. No. 71, 100th Cong., 1st Sess. 124 (1987).

[37] Sometimes the pressure to increase exports comes at the behest of foreign (including U.S.) creditors and development finance agencies.

CIT ruling in 1985 that the countervailing duty law was applicable to non-market economies had not been reversed by the Court of Appeals for the Federal Circuit.[38]

(d) *Cumulative Calculation of Subsidies Provided to Members of an International Consortium (Section 1315)*

A countervailable subsidy is defined as one given by the "government"[39] of the exporting country.[40] This definition is necessary in order to preclude the United States from countervailing overseas development assistance, such as World Bank loans below market rates or even U.S. Marshall Plan aid, both of which have been attacked as subsidies in U.S. countervailing duty cases. This statutory definition does not reach the situation—admittedly, an unusual one—where an *ad hoc* group of countries which does not qualify as a customs union agreed to subsidize a product that technically is a product of only one of those countries. This amendment would apply to the Airbus, which is allegedly the beneficiary of subsidies by France, Spain, Germany and the United Kingdom, although the aeroplane itself is technically a product of France.

Section 1315 of the Trade Act will permit Commerce to add up subsidies contributed by each of the countries directly to the consortium, as well as subsidies paid by each of the countries to the individual members of the consortium.[41] Boeing and McDonnell Douglas were the main companies lobbying in support of this provision to allow the cumulation of subsidies provided to consortia (Airbus was the specific target).

While the Airbus example is the best known of these consortia, it should be borne in mind that there are other projects which arguably could fall under the same definition,[42] including the European COGEMA project to construct a uranium

[38] *Georgetown Steel Corp. v. United States*, 801 F. 2d 1308 (Fed. Cir. 1986).

[39] The definition of subsidy under the Trade Agreements Act of 1979, Section 771, is not limited to government subsidies. Theoretically, the 1979 Act requires the application of countervailing duties to "private subsidies", although no hint is given as to how they would be defined or measured.

A private subsidy has been countervailed only once under the 1979 Act, and in extremely disguised fashion. See *Prestressed Concrete Steel Wire Strand from South Africa*, 47 Fed Reg. 33,310 (Affirm. final) (1982) (finding an export scheme for steel products administered by the South African Iron and Steel Industrial Corporation to be countervailable). Commerce refuses to treat the intercorporate transfer of funds as subsidies, leaving as the classic "private" subsidy a cartel of producers of a given input (e.g., steel) providing export rebates to exporters of steel-intensive finished products containing that input.

[40] A government subsidy would also include subsidies given by customs unions—i.e., the EEC—to exporters from member countries.

[41] In the case of Airbus, this would allow Commerce to total all subsidies paid by Britain, France, Germany and Spain to Airbus, as well as subsidies paid by Britain to British Aerospace, by France to Aérospatiale, by Germany to Deutsche Airbus or Messerschmitt-Bolkow-Blohm (or even to Daimler-Benz, as part of a deal for Daimler-Benz to take over MBB), and by Spain to CASA. Depending on how broadly the term "other participating entities" is interpreted, Commerce might try to include any subsidies paid by countries to suppliers of Airbus, such as Fokker of Holland and Belairbus of Belgium. Query whether alleged U.S. subsidies to General Electric and Pratt & Whitney, which makes engines for Airbus, should be counted (although not under Section 1315 of the Trade Act, as the United States is not part of the Airbus consortium)?.

[42] Although the Conference Committee was primarily concerned with Airbus, the provision is equally applicable to other transnational production projects that receive support from more than one government. See Explanatory Statement at H2031.

processor, the French-Italian ATR 42 commuter plane (already the subject of a countervailing duty case in 1982, although thrown out at the preliminary phase for lack of evidence of injury before any decision was necessary on the extent of subsidization),[43] the EEC's Esprit and Race high technology projects—and the Boeing 767 (if the Japanese participation includes any element of government subsidy). Interestingly, the language of Section 1315 does not appear to include money given by a country to a member of the consortium from a different country.

II. ANTIDUMPING PROVISIONS

(a) *Non-Market Economy Dumping (Section 1316)*

In dumping cases against non-market economy countries, previous law (a combination of statutory law[44] and regulations[45]) required the Commerce Department to look first to the price of the like product in a market economy.[46] (Commerce attempted to use a "comparable" economy, typically based on *per capita* GNP levels, as the basis for its comparison.)[47] This could lead to varied results, especially when the two products being compared were of different quality or attractiveness to consumers. This also required the cooperation of producers in those market economy countries, and that cooperation dried up substantially in the 1980's, especially after a dumping case was brought against the Finnish steel producer which had made its information available as a surrogate for a case on Romanian steel.[48]

In the absence of a third country producer's sales information, Commerce normally used the "factors of production" approach, calculating the actual constructed value by taking the volume of inputs in the imported product and finding their value in a market economy.[49] This had the advantage of avoiding the quality adjustment problem, but was based on the assumption that the unit volume of inputs used by the NME producer would be the same if the costs of those inputs were market-driven—an unlikely occurrence in state-controlled economy countries where energy, labor or capital are often made available at prices lower than world prices.

As a last resort, Commerce would use the prices in the United States of imports from market economy countries, although Commerce was inconsistent in adjusting

[43] *Certain Commuter Airplanes from France and Italy*, 47 Fed. Reg. 31,632 (Neg. prelim.) (1982).

[44] Section 773 of the Tariff Act of 1930, as amended, 19 U.S.C. § 1677b(c) (1982).

[45] 19 C.F.R. § 353.8.

[46] See e.g. *Chemical Products Corp. v. United States*, 650 F. supp. 178 (Ct. Int'l Trade 1986); *Potassium Chloride from the German Democratic Republic*, 50 Feb. Reg. 4559 (Neg. final) (1985).

[47] See *Natural Bristle Paint Brushes and Brush Heads from the People's Republic of China*, 50 Fed. Reg. 52,812 (Affirm. final) (1985); *Steel Wire Nails from the People's Republic of China*, 51 Fed. Reg. 10,247 (Affirm. final) (1986); *Shop Towels of Cotton from the People's Republic of China*, 48 Fed. Reg. 41,614 (Affirm, final) (1983).

[48] *Carbon Steel Plate from Romania*, 47 Fed. Reg. 35,666 (Affirm. prelim.) (1982); *Carbon Steel Plate from Finland*, 49 Fed. Reg. 8973 (Init.) (1984).

[49] 19 C.F.R. § 353.8.

or rejecting prices of dumped or subsidized market economy imports.[50] Under prior law, countervailing duty law did not apply to non-market economy countries.[51]

The results of U.S. non-market economy antidumping cases were perceived as so random by Congress, the Administration, and private parties that a consensus was reached that a change was necessary in the application of U.S. trade law remedies to imports from "non-market economy" imports. The specific form of the change to be implemented, however, was the subject of much discussion. Numerous proposals had been made in recent years:

1. The House bill included a proposal to apply U.S. countervailing duty law to imports from "non-market economy" countries "to the extent that the administering authority can reasonably identify, and determine the amount of, a subsidy provided by that country."[52] As introduced in the House, the proposal would have required application of U.S. countervailing duty law to non-market economy countries. Since none of the subject countries have joined the GATT Subsidies Code[53] or signed equivalent agreements, none of them receives the "injury test" (i.e., if subsidies were found, there was no need to show injury on any specific import). The practical effect would be that if, for example, the Chinese exchange rate system were found to be a subsidy of approximately forty per cent,[54] then any import from the PRC could have been automatically subjected to the same forty per cent duty upon filing of a very simple petition. This would have been most welcome to U.S. industries competing with imports from China, but the obvious problems this would have caused in U.S.-China trade were probably one of the reasons why the proposal was dropped in conference. This proposal was opposed by the administration on the ground that a subsidy is only one of many types of distortions present in a non-market economy, and it makes little sense to attempt to target one particular distortion for application of countervailing duty.[55]
2. The U.S. Chamber of Commerce had released a proposal that, instead of attempting to measure dumping margins or subsidies on imports from non-market economies (which by definition do not have market-based economies which would enable such measurement to be made), the U.S. should simply ascertain whether the NME imports caused enough injury to trigger the "market

[50] *Cf. Candles from the People's Republic of China*, 51 Fed. Reg. 25,085 (Affirm. final) (1986) (slightly subsidized prices from market economy surrogate rejected completely); *Welded Carbon Steel Pipes and Tubes from the People's Republic of China*, 51 Fed. Reg. 25,078 (Affirm, final) (1986) (subsidized prices from market economy surrogate adjusted to offset subsidies).

[51] *Georgetown Steel Corp. v. United States*, 801 F.2d 1308 (fed. Cir. 1986).

[52] H.R. 3, Sec. 157, 100th Cong., 1st Sess. (1987).

[53] *Agreement on Interpretation and Application of Articles VI, XVI, and XXIII of the General Agreement on Tariffs and Trade*, GATT, 26th Supp. BISD 56 (1980). Although Cuba is a signatory of the agreement, it has been subject to a U.S. trade embargo since 1964. The material injury test is, therefore, not an issue.

[54] See Pre-conference Brief on Behalf of American Textile Manufacturers Institute *et al.* in *Textiles, Apparel and Related Products from the People's Republic of China* (Inv. No. C-570-005) (Preliminary) (28 October 1983).

[55] See the "30 October 1987 Letter" at 15.

disruption" clauses in the various U.S. bilateral agreements with NME's,[56] and negotiate whatever import relief is necessary. This was already permitted under Section 406, although only one petitioner had ever received relief under that statute.[57] The Chamber proposal would have made a revised Section 406 (to permit less Presidential discretion) the sole remedy against imports from non-market economy countries (except, of course, to the extent that the more general Section 201 or Section 301 remedies might be applicable), thus eliminating the complex NME antidumping rules and precluding application of countervailing duty rules. As adopted by the House, Section 406 was revised in numerous technical ways, but as a supplement to the antidumping and countervailing duty rules, not as a substitute for them with respect to NME imports. The Conference made certain technical changes to Section 406,[58] but none of great significance, and it remains as a supplement to the AD laws as they apply to NMEs.

3. Numerous proposals were made to amend the antidumping laws as they apply to NME's. The Senate bill contained such a provision and, in the end, the Conference opted to rely heavily on the antidumping rules as a remedy to the NME imports, discarding entirely countervailing duty law (on the grounds that measuring subsidies made no sense in a non-market economy) and ignoring the opportunity to get rid of the dumping issues by relying on Section 406. This general approach was supported by the Administration.[59]

The decision to rely on the antidumping laws did not solve the question of how to measure dumping (a market-based concept) from NME's—a problem that experts had long considered a puzzle.[60] Beginning in 1981, the Administration sought to escape from the increasingly obvious practical and theoretical flaws of the surrogate country methodology in NME cases by proposing to use as a "benchmark" for the fair value at which NME imports could be sold in the U.S. the lowest average price of sales of comparable merchandise[61] from any significant source, whether import or domestic.[62] The underlying theory was that, if U.S. producers already had to compete with fairly traded competition from a market source at a given price level, competition at the same price level from NME imports was not likely to be injurious.

This proposal, which was introduced by Senator Heinz in 1979, in 1981, and

[56] See Conf. Report No. 576, 100th Cong., 2d Sess. 143 (1988).

[57] *Implementation of an Orderly Marketing Agreement on Ammonium Paratungstate and Tungstic Acid,* Proclamation 5718 of 2 Oct. 1987, 52 Fed. Reg. 37,275 (Pres. Doc.) (1987).

[58] See Conf. Rep. No. 576, 100th Cong., 2d Sess. 689-693 (1988).

[59] See 30 October 1987 Letter at 15.

[60] See e.g. *Current Perceptions of the U.S. Congress About U.S. Trade Relations with Nonmarket-Economy Countries.* F. David Foster in *Interface One,* George C. Spira, ed., (G'town Law Ctr. 1980); Horlick and Shuman, *Nonmarket Economy Trade and U.S. Antidumping/Countervailing Duty Law,* 18 Int'l Law, 807 (1984).

[61] The term "comparable merchandise" is broader than the "such or similar merchandise" normally used by Commerce to define like products. The Finance Committee wished to give Commerce greater flexibility, given the anticipated difficulties of finding merchandise from a market economy to serve as the basis of comparison. S. Rep. No. 71, 100th cong., 1st Sess. 106 (1987). Commerce was expected to make adjustments as necessary, however, to reflect differences in quality. *Id.*.

[62] S. 539, Sec. 5008, 100th Cong., 1st Sess. (1987).

again in 1983, was attacked by both sides: import-competing domestic producers claimed that it gave a "license to dump" to non-market economy exporters, who could not be the most efficient producers in the world, while non-market economy exporters claimed that it discriminated against them by preventing them from showing their comparative advantage over other producers. Neither side could explain how one could determine if a non-market economy producer was relatively more or less efficient than market economy producers in the absence, by definition, in the non-market economy of meaningful cost data and free-market exchange rate.

Senator Heinz modified this proposal in 1987 to set as the benchmark the price of the largest volume import. A number of domestic industries, including ammonia and steel, supported this approach, as it would essentially attribute world prices to NME exports. This proposal was widely attacked, however, for its likely results on imports from China (which would have to be priced at the same level as Japan for automobiles or steel, France for perfume, and so on).

The eventual prevailing proposal was introduced in the Senate as a "backup" to the Heinz proposal in 1987, apparently at the behest of certain domestic fertilizer producers. As passed, the provision changed previous law to make the "factors of production" approach the preferred method, with Commerce authorized to use import prices from comparable economies where the information necessary for the factors of production approach was not available. The Administration supported this approach, and Senator Heinz found the compromise acceptable.

This amendment assumes the validity of past Commerce practice of locating a "surrogate" market economy country for purposes of measuring home market prices or cost of production. The amendment does facilitate current practice by making it easier to locate a surrogate country.[63]

Some experts believe that basing the NME third-country comparison on factors of production is more likely to result in a finding of dumping margins than a comparison based on price. A number of NME's might be in for an unpleasant surprise when Commerce begins to apply this new section, if Commerce values energy or labour at relatively high "world market" rates.[64]

In addition to amending the method of calculating antidumping duties for NME imports, this section also provides Commerce with authority to enter into an agreement to suspend an NME antidumping investigation based on quotas (which are not permitted for suspension of other antidumping cases), provided that the agreement is in the public interest, effective monitoring is practicable and suppression or undercutting of domestic price levels would be prevented.[65] For purposes of the section, an

[63] Only one company is necessary to provide an acceptable "surrogate" under the current amendment.

[64] Interwoven throughout the Congressional discussion of trade remedies for NME imports was an energetic effort to achieve recognition for China's special status as an NME actively liberalizing its economy toward a more market-based model. A proposal by Senator Hecht would have relied on the factors approach, but taking the value in the NME of those factors determined by Commerce to be market driven (e.g., products of the decontrolled portion of the Chinese economy), while using third country or world prices for inputs the NME still determined to be non-market driven. The Administration opposed this strongly, and finally settled for a study of the issue. See amendment 452, 133 Cong. Rec. S9540 (daily ed., 9 July 1987).

[65] *Omnibus Trade and Competitiveness Act of 1988*, Pub. L. No. 100-418, 102 Stat. 1186 (1988).

NME is any country determined by Commerce not to operate on "market principles of cost or pricing structures."[66]

(b) *Third Country Dumping (Section 1317)*

U.S. antidumping law applies only to imports in the United States, yet industries operating on a basis of world scale production can be injured equally by sales of "unfair" sales of competing goods in third country markets (or, for that matter, in a competitor's home market, although Congress has not yet tried to extend the reach of U.S. law to that situation). The GATT Antidumping Code permits such third countries to conduct antidumping investigations of imports into their countries at the request of another country which exports to them.[67]

Section 1317 of the Act provides a procedure for the USTR to request a third country to conduct such an investigation. This provision, together with the provision regarding constructed value among related parties,[68] resulted from a compromise regarding the issue of diversionary input dumping. Domestic products claimed that foreign producers of downstream products would have access to "unfairly" priced inputs (either in the country of origin or in third countries), which in turn would give them a price advantage in selling the downstream products in the United States. Both input producers and producers of downstream products in the United States could be affected. The original diversionary input dumping proposal contained in the House bill was strongly opposed, however.[69] This compromise regarding third country dumping was intended to solve half of the potential problem—access by foreign producers of downstream products to dumped inputs in third countries.

As long as compliance by the third country is more or less voluntary, this provision should not produce a problem, although the new statutory language suggests that USTR should threaten the third country if it does not comply.[70] Curiously, there is no U.S. statutory framework for the U.S. to comply with a request under Article 12 from another country. In practice, it is unclear why the third country would seek to eliminate the import of low-priced goods just because the U.S. asked it to penalize those imports, absent some pressure from the United States. Consequently, these provisions could well lead simply to claims that "the law doesn't work" and drives by more industries for agreements such as the semiconductor

---

[66] Conf. Rep. No. 576, 100th Cong., 2d Sess. 59 (1988). It is worth noting that the Commerce determination of whether a country is to be classified an an NME is not subject to judicial review. *Id.*.

[67] See Article 12, GATT Antidumping Code.

[68] See *infra* Section II.C.

[69] *Id.*.

[70] The Trade Act states that, "If the appropriate authority of the [foreign] country refuses to undertake antidumping measures . . . [USTR] shall promptly consult with the domestic industry on whether action under any other law of the United States is appropriate." *Omnibus Trade and Competitiveness Act of 1988*, Pub. L. No. 100-418, 102 Stat. 1188 (1988). The legislative history does not shed any light on what actions, if any, USTR is expected to take against a foreign country that refuses to initiate an antidumping investigation following a U.S. request.

agreement[71] (the implementation of which as to the third countries was found illegal by a GATT panel)[72] or claims for relief by domestic industry under other provisions, such as Section 301.[73]

(c) *Constructed Value Between Related Parties (formerly "Diversionary Input Dumping") (Section 1318)*

Under previous U.S. law, dumping could be investigated based on one of two methods. Either the price at which the imported good was sold in the United States (after adjustment) was compared to the (similarly adjusted) home market or third-country market price was "unreliable," to the "constructed value" (fully allocated cost of production plus a statutory minimum of ten per cent for general selling and administrative expenses and a statutory minimum eight per cent profit).[74] In calculating the "constructed value", the statute allowed Commerce to ignore transfer prices between related parties, and substitute for them prices between unrelated parties in the market place.[75] The amendment, Section 1318 of the Conference bill, permits Commerce to substitute for the transfer prices not the "market prices", but rather the cost of production of the input to the subsidiaries (without any double counting of corporate overhead or profit). In practice, this could make Commerce's investigations a bit simpler, as research for the "market price" of the input was often abstract and more difficult to confirm than the actual costs of the company under investigation.

This amendment reflects an earlier proposal in Section 156 of the House bill, which was originally labeled as the "diversionary input dumping" amendment.[76] That amendment would have required Commerce, in cases involving both related and unrelated parties, to substitute for the cost of the input the "fair value" of any input found to be dumped. The concept of diversionary input dumping was originally contained in both the House and Senate versions of the 1984 Trade and Tariff Act, but was dropped in conference because of opposition by the Administration. Some members of Congress were concerned that this issue was a genuine problem (probably because of the inevitably "ripple" effects on downstream products of the

[71] Arrangement concerning trade in semiconductor products, with related letters. Exchange of letters at Washington 2 September 1986, entered into force 2 September 1986. The U.S.-Japanese semiconductor agreement contains agreements under Section 301 requested by the U.S. industry requiring the Japanese to sell above a calculated "fair market value" in third countries, as well as the United States.

Section 1314(e) would leave the door open for such agreements; it provides that, if the country in which alleged dumping is occurring refuses to initiate an antidumping investigation pursuant to the U.S. request, USTR "shall promptly consult with the domestic industry on whether action under any other law of the United States is appropriate.".

[72] 5 Int'l Trade Rep. (BNA) at 452 (March 30, 1988).

[73] 19 U.S.C. §§ 2411-2415 (1982 & Supp. IV 1986).

[74] 19 U.S.C. § 1677b(b) (1982).

[75] 19 U.S.C. § 1677b(e)(2), (e)(3) (1982).

[76] For a description of the issue involved in the diversionary input dumping proposal, see *supra* Section II.B.

protection granted the domestic steel industry beginning in 1968), even if a diversionary input dumping provision was not the ideal solution.

In 1987, the diversionary input dumping provision was resurrected under pressure from TRAC. The domestic steel industry was the main supporter of the provision, and Congressman Russo of Illinois was one of the most active proponents in the House.

The diversionary input dumping proposal would have caused enormous problems for companies anywhere using components produced in other countries,[77] would have raised serious questions of GATT violations[78] and led to some ludicrous results.[79] Very few U.S. companies are able to sell all of their products everywhere they sell them at fully allocated cost plus ten per cent for expenses and eight per cent profit. For these reasons, the opposition to this provision was extensive. Wholesalers, retailers, and a number of domestic manufacturer groups including the Emergency Committee for American Trade ("ECAT") and the Business Roundtable strongly opposed the provision, as did a number of foreign countries. The Administration was strongly opposed to the diversionary dumping provision on the grounds that it would violate GATT[80] and that "the United States is particularly vulnerable to mirror diversionary dumping legislation."[81] The Administration went so far as to label the provision "veto bait."

The Senate opposed the "diversionary input dumping" amendment, and the house then came up with a compromise limiting the reach of the amendment to transactions between affiliated companies. The Administration then caved in and accepted that proposal. After considerable discussion with the business community (i.e., ECAT and the Business Roundtable), the conferees and the Administration agreed to a proposal to permit (but not require) Commerce to disregard transfer prices for inputs between related parties and to use instead the actual cost of production of

[77] Even if a U.S. company in Korea knew, for example, that a Japanese component had been found dumped in the U.S., it would not be likely to know the unrelated Japanese producer's prices in its home market, and it could not possibly know the unrelated Japanese producer's fully allocated cost.

[78] Briefly, the argument is as follows: The GATT Antidumping Code provides that a country may impose an antidumping duty "only under the circumstances provided for" in Article VI of GATT and in the GATT Antidumping Code. Article 1, GATT Antidumping Code. The GATT Antidumping Code provides that an antidumping duty must be assessed based on a comparison of the export price with the home market price, third-country price, or constructed value of the "like product." Article 2.1, 2.4, GATT Antidumping Code. "Like product" is defined as a product that is "identical i.e. alike in all respects" to, or having "characteristics closely resembling those" of, the product under consideration. Article 2.2, GATT Antidumping Code. The proposed diversionary input dumping amendment would have allowed antidumping duties to be placed on a final product based on an investigation of the input, even if the final product was not being dumped. If the input being investigated and the final product subject to the antidumping order are not like products, the duty would violate the terms of the GATT Antidumping Code.

[79] In effect, companies are already found dumping in the United States if they sell below their fully allocated cost of production plus the statutory minimum of ten per cent for expenses and eight per cent profit. The effect of this amendment would force companies whose products are used as components of other products to sell not only in the United States, but also at home and at third countries at that same fully allocated cost plus eighteen per cent standard or have their customers outside the U.S. run the risk of the customers' products containing those components being found to be dumped under the diversionary input dumping approach.

[80] See *infra* footnote 72.

[81] 30 October 1987 Letter at 14.

the input. After the Conference, Committee staff tried to rewrite the agreement to ensure that the cost of production used be higher than the "market value", although Senator Danforth (in the only floor statement on the amendment) pointed out that the intent of the conferees was "to permit Commerce to use either the producer's cost of production or an arm's-length price."[82]

(d) *Fictitious Foreign Market Price (Section 1319)*

When dumping is measured by comparing the price in the U.S. market with the price in the home market or a third country market, Commerce will use the price of the home market if sales in that market are at least five per cent of total sales in the U.S. for the same period. Failing that, Commerce will use the exporter's sales to third country markets if they meet the "five per cent" test; this reflects a preference for comparing actual foreign market prices to the price in the U.S. rather than using "constructed value".[83]

In some circumstances, it would be worthwhile for a foreign respondent to establish a "fictitious" foreign market price with sales reaching five per cent of total U.S. sales (as long as that price exceeded the cost of production), in order to avoid, or reduce the amount of, U.S. antidumping duties.[84] Prior U.S. antidumping law provided that, for purposes of ascertaining foreign market value against which the U.S. selling price would be measured, Commerce should ignore sales or offers in the foreign market that are intended to establish a fictitious market price.[85] However, the statute did not provide any further explanation and Commerce has rarely investigated whether home market sales are fictitious.[86] (Some experts have speculated that Commerce has been reluctant to invoke its power to ignore fictitious market prices out of fear of reversal by the CIT on review.)

Section 1319 of the Trade Act amends the Tariff Act of 1930 by adding a new paragraph providing that Commerce should consider contrasting movements in prices of different forms of a product as evidence of a fictitious market if such price movements appear to reduce the amount by which the foreign market value exceeds the U.S. price.

This amendment confirms that Commerce has the authority to ignore such prices if it deems them "fictitious". The Senate Report makes it clear that Congress's main concern was with foreign manufacturers of a product that is produced and sold

---

82 134 Cong. Rec. S4912 (daily ed. 27 April 1988).

83 Constructed value is described *supra* in Section II.C.

84 Another alternative would be for the foreign producers to sell the products sold in the United States in small quantities at relatively low prices in the United States while selling most of the product in the foreign market in a slightly different form than sold in the United States so that its higher prices in the foreign market are not compared to the prices of the U.S. product.

85 19 U.S.C. § 1677b(a)(1) (1982 & Supp. IV 1986); 19 C.F.R. § 353.18.

86 See e.g. *Nylon Impression Fabric from Japan*, 51 Fed. Reg. 15,816 (Affirm. final) (1986) (rejecting allegation of fictitious home market sales); *Certain Carbon Steel Products from Brazil*, 49 Fed. Reg. 28,298 (Affirm, final) (1984) (same); *Bicycle Tires and Tubes from Taiwan*, 48 Fed. Reg. 19,437 (Neg. final) (1983) (same).

in multiple forms, only one form of which is exported to the United States or subject to an antidumping investigation.[87] It is possible that the producer could artificially set the home market prices of the various forms of the product in order to reduce the foreign market value of the form of the product identical to that which is exported to the United States to the lowest possible level.

(e) *Limiting Expedited Reviews (Section 1325)*

Under the 1979 Act, upon completing an antidumping investigation, Commerce could immediately perform an expedited review if the foreign exporter could produce the information necessary for one in a sufficiently short period of time.[88] The underlying purpose was to allow a foreign exporter inadvertently caught in dumping cases (either because of ignorance of the dumping law or because of changes in the exchange rates) to raise its prices to cease dumping. Since the stated purpose of the U.S. antidumping law is to force foreign producers to cease dumping, rather than to punish them for past dumping,[89] this expedited review under Section 736(c) reflected the GATT Anti-dumping Code.[90]

Such expedited reviews could only "favor" a foreign producer, however, since a foreign producer would never provide the information for a quick review unless it would benefit from the review. Consequently, granting a Section 736(c) review was viewed as a "favor" to foreigners and opposed by those bringing antidumping cases, who wanted to force the foreigner to experience at lease a full year of uncertainty after the final determination before a regular administrative review would occur. As a result, Commerce has not granted a request for such a review since 1984. Some import-competing companies nevertheless felt the need to have the provision eliminated.[91] A provision limiting expedited reviews was not included in the 1984 Trade Act, despite the support of some members of Congress.

Consequently, the Trade Reform Action Committee pushed for Section 1325 of the trade act, which prohibits such reviews in all cases that have been designated as extraordinarily complicated or in which the final Commerce determination was postponed (which has occurred in the majority of such cases, since most reviews are requested when the case has been so fouled up, for any number of possible reasons, that extensions are usually granted). The effect is to prohibit expedited reviews in the

[87] S. Rep. No. 71, 100th Cong., 1st Sess. 126 (1987).

[88] 19 U.S.C. § 1673e(c)(1) (1982).

[89] "Dumping duties are not penal in nature, but are additional duties to equalize the competitive conditions between exporter and American industries affected." *Imbert Imports v. United States*, 331 F. Supp. 1400, 1406 n.10 (Cust. Ct. 1971), aff'd 475 F.2d 1189 (C.C.P.A. 1973).

[90] "An antidumping duty shall remain in force only so long as . . . necessary to counteract dumping which is causing injury." Article 9.1, GATT Antidumping Code at 183.

[91] Petitioners complained to Congress about two early determinations in particular: *Carbon Steel Wire Rod from Brazil*, 49 Fed. Reg. 14,156 (1984) (reducing antidumping duties for Belga Mineira from seventy-six per cent to zero), and for COSIGUA from fourty-nine per cent to seven per cent); *Portable Electric Typewriters from Japan*, 45 Fed. Reg. 53,853 (1980).

vast majority of cases in which they were formerly theoretically available (although they have not been available in the past five years, as a practical matter). The main effect of the provision is to eliminate the ability of Commerce to correct quickly major mistakes in antidumping investigations.

The Administration failed to oppose this provision, claiming instead that this loss of flexibility to use Section 736(c) when necessary did not matter, because a review could be conducted any time after the initial investigation through the general administrative review provisions of Section 751.[92]

(f) *"Multiple Offender" Provisions for Short Life Cycle Products (Section 1323)*

Under the GATT, under current U.S. law, and under other countries' antidumping statutes, dumping is not considered to be criminal or immoral, but rather a business practice; the remedy, which is only necessary if injury is caused to a domestic industry, is to force the companies engaged in dumping to raise their prices, usually a net negative effect on the country imposing the duty.[93] Consequently, all companies are treated the same, no matter how many dumping cases are brought against any one company.

This approach was dramatically challenged during the course of 1987, as a number of interests pushed for changes that essentially treated companies engaged in dumping as wrong-doers. Two examples were the related provisions for a private right of action (which was not included in the final version of the Trade Act)[94] and for special provisions regarding multiple offenders.

Both the House and Senate versions of the Trade Act contained special provisions regarding multiple offenders. The Semiconductor Industry Association ("SIA") and the domestic steel industry were apparently the main supporters of this concept. The Senate version provided that, upon filing of a petition by an interested party, Commerce would have to monitor imports by a second "offender" if there was a reasonable likelihood of repeat dumping, and Commerce would have to monitor imports by a multiple "offender" regardless of likelihood of future dumping.[95] The House bill was similar, but even stricter; it required monitoring of first "offenders" if there was a likelihood of future dumping and of second "offenders" without such a likelihood.[96] Both bills required Commerce to initiate an expedited investigation of any dumping

[92] 19 U.S.C. § 1675 (1982 & Supp. IV 1986). Commerce has proposed regulations which would prevent this. See proposed regulation 19 C.F.R. § 353.22(f), 51 Fed. Reg. 29,046, 29,065 (1986).

[93] See *supra* note 84. The normal dumping scenario must be distinguished from "predatory" dumping or dumping with the intent to injure an industry in another country. This is subject to criminal penalties as well as treble damages, under the Antidumping Act of 1916. See *infra,* Section V. C.

[94] See *infra,* Section V. c.

[95] S. 1420 and. 324. 100th Cong., 1st Sess. (1987).

[96] H.R. 3, Sec. 165, 100th Cong., 1st Sess. (1987).

discovered by the monitoring, and the House bill stated that critical circumstances would be presumed.[97]

These provisions were supported most strongly by Congressman Matsui and Congressman Guarini. The Administration was opposed to the monitoring provisions,[98] and Congressman Frenzel joined the Administration position. These provisions were somewhat tarnished by their close association with the private right of action, which was actively opposed by a number of business groups.

Section 1323 was the result of a compromise, in which the private right of action and the monitoring provisions were dropped[99] in return for providing expedited procedures for "short life cycle" products. The compromise was proposed by industry, with some Administration support, although the Administration later backed off.

Section 1323 of the Trade Act provides that foreign exporters subject to two or more dumping orders (or suspension agreements) with dumping margins in excess of fifteen per cent within an eight-year period shall be considered second "offenders". Foreign producers subject to three or more dumping orders (or suspension agreements) in excess of fifteen per cent dumping duties within the prior eight years are considered multiple "offenders". Investigations involving a significant proportion of merchandise from second or multiple "offenders" are subject to expedited procedures if they involve a "short life cycle" product (i.e., one which "the [ITC] determines is likely to become outmoded within four years, by reason of technological advances, after the product is commercially available").[100] The expedited procedure would require a preliminary determination from Commerce within 100–120 days, rather than the 160–210 day period permitted under current law.

It is unclear what, if any, impact this amendment will have. If the goal is to give antidumping relief more quickly in cases involving these multiple offenders in short life cycle products, this provision might be partially successful, although typically more time is wasted preparing and deciding to file an antidumping case by a petitioner than by Commerce actually investigating one. In any event, Commerce can apply the duties retroactively to imports arriving within seventy days of the filing of the petition in a normal case if there is a "history of dumping."[101] The shorter time period will give the foreign exporter less time to deal with the case, and thus may lead to higher margins because of imperfect data. If this is a goal of the provision, it may well backfire in practice; the shorter deadline also means less time for petitioner's counsel

[97] *Id.*.

[98] See 30 October 1987 Letter at 16. The Administration did not discuss the multiple offender provisions in detail, but only stated its opposition to the monitoring that would have been required by various provisions in the House and Senate bills. The Administration termed the various monitoring provisions "unnecessary" and "almost useless" and stated that they would divert scarce resources from actual investigation. The Administration was also strongly opposed to the private right of action. *Id.* at 14.

[99] See *infra* Section V. C.

[100] *Omnibus Trade and Competitiveness Act of 1988*, Pub. L. No. 100–418, § 1323(a), 102 Stat. 1198 (1988).

[101] 19 U.S.C. § 1673d(a)(3) (1982 & Supp. IV 1986).

to analyze the exporter's data and point out any tricks being played. Dumping margins calculated on this expedited basis cannot be used against other shippers.[102]

It should be noted that there are numerous anti-dumping cases in Europe against U.S. textiles and chemicals, and probably numerous U.S. companies which thus fit this "multiple offender" label with respect to EEC cases. Presumably the "short life cycle" label is meant to preclude widespread use of this new wrinkle in dumping law by the EEC against U.S. companies.

III. Provisions applicable to antidumping and countervailing duty law

(a) *Anticircumvention Provisions (Section 1321)*

The existence of an antidumping or countervailing duty order on a product creates an economic incentive to change that product slightly (either directly or by minor assembly operations) into a different product outside the scope of antidumping or countervailing duty order. Under previous law, Commerce felt constrained from extending the order to cover such a product, as exhibited in its ruling that portable electric typewriters with calculators built in (at relatively low cost) would no longer be subject to an antidumping order on portable electric typewriters.[103]

As a result, a number of proposals for tightening anticircumvention measures surfaced. The administration drafted a proposal, in part as a compromise to defeat a proposed diversionary dumping measure. The steel industry, and the American Iron and Steel Institute in particular, emerged as the strongest supporters of the Administration proposal, and Congressman Pease of Ohio pushed the proposal strongly. As a result, the measure sailed through the House easily. The Senate followed a different tack, examining an EEC anticircumvention regulation closely, but finally drafted a proposal very similar to the House measure. The Senate version prevailed in conference, subject to a couple of minor amendments.

The new amendment (Section 1321) gives Commerce the authority to prevent this so-called "circumvention" by extending a prior antidumping or countervailing duty order on a product to include later-developed versions of that product,[104] products that are altered in only minor respects from the product originally investigated, and parts of the product that are imported from the country under investigation and assembled or finished in the United States. In addition, Commerce can extend prior antidumping orders to include products assembled in third countries from parts or components from the original country under investigation, in an

[102] *Omnibus Trade and Competitiveness Act of 1988*, Pub. L. No. 100-418, § 1323(b)(3), 102 Stat. 1199 (1988).

[103] *Portable Typewriters from Japan*, 52 Fed. Reg. 1504, 1505-06 (Admin, Rev. final) (1967), remanded on appeal sub nom, *Smith Corona Corp. v. United States*, 678 F. Supp. 285 (Ct. Int'l Trade 1987).

[104] Commerce's authority to include later-developed versions of a product had been recognized previously by the CIT. *Diversified Products Corp. v. United States*, 572 F. Supp. 883, 889 (Ct. Int'l Trade 1983). Nevertheless, clarification of this authority and the appropriate standard to be used were thought necessary.

attempt to change the country of origin to avoid the antidumping or countervailing duty.

With regard to parts assembled or finished in the United States or abroad, the only major limitation on Commerce is a requirement in the statute that the difference between the value of the finished product subject to the dumping order and the value of the imported parts be "small". This term is not defined in the statute or the legislative history, and will undoubtedly create major disputes of interpretation.[105] A somewhat similar regulation put into effect by the EEC in 1987 permits extension of the antidumping order to parts of products already subject to antidumping duty if more than sixty per cent of the parts by value come from the country subject to the original antidumping order and the parts are assembled or further manufactured by a person related to the party subject to the prior antidumping order.[106] This "sixty per cent" test was rejected in the Senate Finance Committee mark up in favor of a requirement that any change be "small",[107] so one can argue that the change must involve less than fourty per cent of the total value of the components (which could be a much lower percentage of total value) to permit extension of the antidumping order of the new product.[108]

Anticircumvention measures are necessary to any antidumping system. Although Commerce formerly had certain powers to prevent circumvention, these powers were perhaps too limited, especially in light of the CIT's decision in *Typewriters*. Section 1321 should prevent circumvention of antidumping and countervailing duty orders.

---

[105] The House Report, the Senate Report and the Conference Report all avoided attempting to define "small". The Senate Report was the only report to discuss the crucial term:

> The Committee has not attempted to develop a precise meaning for the term "small" as used in these sections, principally in recognition that different cases present different factual situations. The Committee does not, however, intend that the term "small" be interpreted as insignificant. While these subsections grant the Commerce Department substantial discretion in interpreting these terms, and invoking these measures, so as to allow it the flexibility to apply the provisions in an appropriate manner, the Committee expects the Commerce Department to use this authority to the fullest extent possible to combat diversion and circumvention of the antidumping and countervailing duty laws.

S. Rep. No. 71, 100th Cong., 1st Sess. 100 (1987).

[106] Council Regulation No. 171/87, 30 O.J. Eur. Com. (No. L 167) 9 (1987); *Electronic Scales (Japan)*, Council Regulation 1021/88, 31 O.J. Eur. Comm. (No. L 101) 1 (1988) (applying dumping duty to imported parts assembled in the EEC); *Electronic Typewriters (Japan)*, Council Regulation 1022/88, 31 O.J. Eur. Comm. (No. L 101) 4 (1988) (same). The trade bill might be narrower than the EEC regulation to the extent that a smaller degree of change or value added might escape the scope of an antidumping order under Section 1321, but it is broader in that Section 1321 does not require the U.S. importer or assembler to be related to the manufacturer subject to the prior dumping order. Furthermore, Section 1321 applies to assembly in third countries. The EEC regulation, by its terms, does not, and the EC Commission is currently grappling with the issue of how to treat assembly in third countries in connection with its ongoing investigation, *Plain Paper Photocopiers (Japan)* Council Regulation No. 2176/84, 31 O.J. Eur. Comm. (No. C 44) 3 (1988).

[107] The Senate Finance Committee examined the EEC "screwdriver plant" regulation very closely, and ultimately rejected it in favor of the current Section 1321. The Committee in mark-up expressly rejected the EC's sixty per cent test. [Hans Beseler (Director of Directorate—General IV, EC Commission) and supervisor of all EEC antidumping and countervailing duty actions, reportedly preferred Section 1321 to the EEC regulation.].

[108] S. Rep. No. 71, 100th Cong., 1st Sess. 100 (1987).

It is arguable, however, that Section 1321 goes too far;[109] it could allow Commerce to extend an existing antidumping or countervailing duty order to non-"like" products in contravention of the GATT Subsidies Code and GATT Antidumping Code.[110] For example, it is easy to imagine a situation in which components subject to an antidumping order (e.g., Japanese computer circuit boards) are assembled in the United States from quite distinct (i.e., not "like") parts, such as semiconductors, such that the total value of the Japanese components remains sizeable in comparison with the value of components originating in other countries. When imported into the United States, the parts imported from Japan, such as semiconductors, could be hit with the dumping duties on Japanese computer circuit boards if Commerce[111] determined that the difference between the value of the imported components and the value of the circuit board was small. Japan has already challenged the EEC regulation in the GATT; it remains to be seen if the U.S. applies its new rules in a manner which avoids GATT condemnation.

(b) *Downstream Product Monitoring (Section 1320)*

Present antidumping and countervailing duty law in the United States, like the GATT Antidumping Code, does not contain any provision for monitoring imports of "downstream" products (products made from or containing dumped or subsidized goods). Representatives of certain domestic industries argued that the lack of any monitoring system allowed foreign producers of dumped or subsidized goods to avoid antidumping or countervailing duties by selling the product at less than fair

---

[109] Section 1321 is also noticeably lacking in the procedural protections provided elsewhere in the AD/CVD statutes; presumably, Commerce will apply the necessary measures (notice, preliminary and final determinations, the opportunity to become a "party to the proceeding" for purposes of judicial review).

[110] See *supra* note 74.

[111] Debate arose during the Conference concerning the proper roles of Commerce and the ITC in determining the scope of an antidumping or countervailing duty order. If Commerce expands the scope of an investigation after the ITC has reached an injury determination, the United States would be in breach of its obligations under the GATT Antidumping Code and GATT Subsidies Code in that it failed to provide an injury determination for those products later included in the scope of the determination. This is not a new issue—see *Certain In-Shell Pistachios from Iran*, 51 Fed. Reg. 17,220 (1986) (Commerce clarification of scope of investigation to include roasted in-shell pistachios); 51 Fed. Reg. 23,254 (1986) (subsequent exclusion of roasted in-shell pistachios by Commerce because they were excluded from ITC investigation).

Commerce emerged victorious in the Trade Act from the long-standing turf battle concerning which agency has primary responsibility for determining the scope of an investigation. The Conference Committee, under strong pressure from Commerce, limited the role of the ITC to offering advice, which Commerce can ignore, even though the effect of the amendment is to impose antidumping duties on products which were not subject to injury investigations. See Conf. Rep. No. 576, 100th Cong., 2d Sess. 602-604 (1988).

Furthermore, the Conference Report states that the ITC should not analyze whether the parts and components imported into the United States (and upon which the antidumping or countervailing duty would be applied) are within its earlier injury determination, but rather whether the assembled or finished product sold in the United States is within its earlier injury determination. *Id.* at 603. As a result, the Conference Committee expects an ITC finding that proposed anticircumvention action is inconsistent with an earlier injury determination to be "relatively unusual." *Id.* at 602.

market value to customers abroad, who further process or manufacture the product and then export the new product to the United States.[112]

The Trade Act contains a provision, Section 1320, providing for monitoring imports of downstream products in order to identify potential diversionary practices. The provision applies only if a monitoring program already exists under the bilateral arrangements on steel imports, there is a large number of cases on related products from the same country, or there are two or more cases against one company on related products. The initial dumping margin must be at least fifteen per cent. Thereafter, "any imported manufactured article which incorporates" the product formerly found to be dumped can be subjected to monitoring by the ITC upon petition by domestic manufacturers of the dumped product or the downstream product.[113] Commerce is required to review the ITC reports to determine whether it should initiate an antidumping or countervailing duty investigation.

The result of the monitoring program is that Commerce could initiate an antidumping or countervailing duty investigation of a product, not based on any allegations of dumping or subsidization of that product, but rather based on foreign dumping of a component part and an increase in the volume of imports of the product. For example, a foreign producer of brass could be found to be dumping in the United States by a margin of fifteen per cent. Thereafter, imported lamps made of brass could be subjected to monitoring, and if imports of lamps increase, to an antidumping investigation. It is not necessary that the lamp producer be dumping—the producer could be selling at more than 100 per cent of fully-allocated costs. Nor is it necessary that the lamp producer was somehow the beneficiary of "dumped" brass.

This provision alters only the standards for initiation of an investigation, not for reaching an antidumping or countervailing duty determination. Ultimately, no duty could be imposed on the imported lamps without showing dumping of lamps—not dumping of brass—and injury to the U.S. lamp, not brass, industry. If the lamp industry were being injured by dumped imports it could file an AD petition under normal procedures, without all the buildup envisioned under Section 1320; therefore one can only surmise that some proponents of the amendment hope that the monitoring itself will have a trade-chilling effect, a consequence arguably precluded by Article 16.1 of the GATT Antidumping Code.[114]

The effect of this provision will depend in large part upon how it is implemented

[112] This is similar to the problem addressed by the anticircumvention provision, *supra* Section III.A., with the difference that the party using the product for further processing or manufacture need not be related to the party against which the antidumping or countervailing duty order was levied, and the product need not even be close to being a "like product" to the product originally found dumped. Indeed, because the dumped product is sold at an arm's-length transaction, the producer performing the further production or manufacture might not even realize that the input is sold at a dumped price.

[113] The determination of whether to initiate monitoring of a downstream product is not subject to judicial review.

[114] Article 16.1, *Agreement on Implementation of Article VI of the General Agreement on Tariffs and Trade*, GATT, 26th Supp. BISD 171, 186 (1980). One strong indicator of this motive is the inclusion of steel VRA products—most of which were never subject to dumping orders.

by the ITC and Commerce. It does have the potential of significantly increasing and complicating their workloads.

(c) *Agricultural Input Producers as Members of Domestic Agricultural Industry. (Section 1326)*

The International Trade Commission ("ITC") has a mixed record of counting producers of raw agricultural inputs as members of the industry producing the processed product in antidumping and countervailing duty cases against foreign exporters of the processed product.[115] This caution is well merited—as noted in Section I.B., above, a GATT panel has ruled that input producers cannot be included in the industry whose injury is being measured.[116] The EEC has also objected to U.S. attempts to include producers of raw agricultural inputs within the processed product industry.[117]

Section 1326 expands the definitions of domestic industry and interested parties who have standing to file a petition in cases involving processed agricultural products to include producers or growers of the raw agricultural product, if the raw product is introduced into a processed agricultural product through a single continuous line of production and there is a substantial coincidence of economic interest between the growers and the processors. This provision began as an amendment pushed by Representative Gephardt and Senator Moynihan.[118]

[115] *Table Wine from the Federal Republic of Germany, France and Italy*, Inv. No. 701-TA-258-260 (Neg. prelim.) USITC Pub. 1771 (1985) (including grape growers in the table wine industry); *Live Swine and Pork from Canada*, Inv. No. 701-TA-224 (Neg. final) USIC Pub. 1733 (1985) (excluding swine producers from pork industry) aff'd *sub nom. National Pork Producers Council v. United States*, 661 F. Supp. 633 (Ct. Int'l Trade 1987); *Frozen Concentrated Orange Juice from Brazil*, Inv No. 701-TA-184 (Affirm, final) USITC Pub. 1406 (1983) (including orange growers in the orange juice industry); *Lamb Meat from New Zealand*, Inv. No. 701-TA-80 (Affirm, prelim.) USITC Pub. 1191 (1981) (including lamb growers in U.S. lamb meat industry); *Certain Table Wine from France and Italy*, Inv. No. 701-TA-210-211, 731-TA-167-168 (Neg. prelim.) USITC Pub. 1502 (1984) (grape growers not included in U.S. wine industry). The ITC based its determinations on whether the raw agricultural product was part of a single line of production resulting in the processed product or whether there were other end uses for the raw agricultural product, and the degree of economic integration between producers of the raw agricultural product and producers of the processed product.

[116] The GATT Antidumping Code accords standing to the domestic producers of "like products." Article 4.1, GATT Antidumping code. "Like products" are products that are "identical" or "alike in all respects" or that have "characteristics closely resembling those" of the product under consideration. Article 2.2 GATT Antidumping Code. A GATT panel has ruled that this definition does not allow producers of raw agricultural products to have standing in an investigation of the processed product. GATT Panel Report, *Canada—Imposition of Countervailing Duties on Imports of Manufactured Beef from the EEC* (13 October 1987) (Canadian cattle raisers lacked standing to challenge imports of boneless beef). The panel report was blocked by the Government of Canada, and has not yet been published.

[117] See *Certain Table Wine from France and Italy*, Inv. Nos. 701-TA-210-211, 731-TA-167-168 (Neg. prelim.) USITC Pub. 1502 (1984) (objecting to U.S. grape growers acting on behalf of the U.S. wine industry).

[118] Although the text of the House and Senate provisions was virtually identical, the reports contained an important difference. Section 1326 in its final form states that a raw agricultural product is processed into a processed agricultural product through a single continuous line of production if (i) the raw agricultural product is "substantially or completely" devoted to production of the processed product, and (ii) the processed product is produced "substantially or completely" from the raw product. The House Report states that "substantially or completely" means "all or almost all." H. Rep. No. 40, Pt. 1, 100th Cong. 1st Sess. 121 (1987). The Senate Report indicates only that the term does not mean any fixed percentage, but should be interpreted "consistently with [certain] prior Commission determinations and the circumstances of the individual investigations." S. Rep. No. 71, 100th Cong., 1st Sess. 109 (1987). Clearly, the House language would narrow considerably the scope of growers of raw agricultural products that would have standing in an investigation of a processed agricultural product. The Conference Committee Report does not indicate that one prevails over the other, so both must be accepted as legislative history, and the two interpretations somehow reconciled.

There was not so much opposition to this proposal as concern that it might be GATT-illegal. Consequently, the Conference Committee included a provision stating that, if the USTR certifies that its application is inconsistent with the international obligations of the United States, the amendment shall cease to have effect.[119] The finding of inconsistency with the international obligations of the United States must be based on a final ruling of a GATT panel that is accepted by the United States[120] or of "an international tribunal authorized by the United States."[121] This could cause problems, as USTR has had to defend the U.S. position by arguing that the proposed ITC practice of including the input producer is GATT-legal, and thus would not want to undercut that argument, yet at the same time must recognize that the only two GATT panels that have dealt with this issue have said that the practice is not GATT-legal. This is one of several issues that must be dealt with by international consensus during the Uruguay Round.

(d) *Application of AD/CVD Laws to "Leases equivalent to Sales" (Section 1327)*

The U.S. AD/CVD laws, and the GATT Antidumping and Subsidies Codes, apply to "sales".[122] The U.S. Commerce Department has made clear since at least 1982 that it would consider leases which are the equivalent of sales to fall within the scope of the AD/CVD laws.[123] So far, the situation has not arisen in any case, but became a real possibility with the increasing degree of controversy over sales by Airbus Industry, and the threat of U.S. AD and/or CVD cases, since large commercial aircraft are typically leased, rather than purchased outright by the airlines (because of the huge capital requirements of airlines).[124]

[119] The Conference Report states that "the conferees are confident that [Section 1326 is] in full conformity with the international obligations of the United States under GATT, the Antidumping code, and the Subsidies Code." Conf. Rep. No 576, 100th Cong., 2d Sess. 624 (1988).

[120] The Conference Report states that Congress expects the United States to continue its policy of refusing to accept panel reports favorable to another Contracting Party if that Contracting Party has blocked panel reports favorable to the United States. (The United States blocked the GATT panel report on its *Wine* AD/CVD cases, which was adverse to the United States, after the EEC blocked an adverse panel report resulting from a U.S. complaint about *pasta*,). See *GATT Panel Report presented to the Contracting Parties at their Fortieth Session*, GATT, 31st Supp., BISD 259, 263 (1985).

[121] The term "international tribunal authorized by the United States" would presumably include bilateral dispute resolution panels formed under Chapter XIX of the Canada-U.S. Free Trade Agreement. Pursuant to Article 1902.2(d) (i) of the FTA, these panels have authority to test U.S. practices for conformity with GATT, the GATT Subsidies Code, and the GATT Antidumping Code. It is also worth noting that, although Congress' main concern was with conformity to GATT, the statute provides that the amendment will cease to be effective if found inconsistent with "the international obligations of the United States." This raises the possibility of Section 1326 being nullified by an FTA panel ruling that the amendment is contrary to the terms of the FTA (even though the FTA would presumably be satisfied if the United States merely ceased applying the provision in investigations involving Canada).

[122] Tariff Act of 1930, §§ 701 and 731; *Agreement on Implementation of Article VI of the General Agreements on Tariffs and Trade*, GATT, 26th Supp. BISD 171 (1980).

[123] In 1984, the AD/CVD statutes were amended to reflect this practice by including, in addition to sales, leasing arrangements "equivalent to the sale" of the product under consideration. 19 U.S.C. § 1671 (Supp. IV 1986).

[124] Leasing also arises frequently in other "big ticket" capital goods such as heavy electrical equipment, machine tools, and construction equipment. See Conf. Rep. No. 576, 100th Cong., 2d Sess, at 615 (1988).

Boeing and McDonnell Douglas lobbied for a more explicit provision in the Trade Act. The House bill was silent on the subject, but the two U.S. companies managed to have included in conference a Senate bill provision covering "all leasing arrangements". Staff on both sides were persuaded of the need to draft the language a little more exactly to prevent unintended consequences (e.g., an automobile rented in Canada and driven across the border for temporary use) while still applying to the aircraft example mentioned above. Thus, the statutory language of Section 1327, in applying the AD/CVD laws to leases that are equivalent to sales, provides a list of factors for Commerce to consider in determining whether a lease is equivalent to a sale.[125]

(e) *ITC Provisions*

1. *Material Injury (Section 1328)*

Section 1328 requires that the ITC state its reasoning for each investigation, and explain the analysis for each factor that arises in the investigation. It also "clarifies" that the ITC must consider price underselling, but not require that the imported pricing be "predatory".

The requirement that the ITC explain its consideration of each factor in an investigation was most strongly supported by the domestic cement industry in response to the ITC negative preliminary determination in *Portland Cement*.[126] This

[125] Section 1327 states that commerce shall consider the following factors:
"(A) the terms of the lease,
(B) commercial practice within the industry,
(C) the circumstances of the transaction,
(D) whether the product subject to the lease is integrated into the operations of the lessee or importer,
(E) whether in practice there is a likelihood that the lease will be continued or renewed for a significant period of time, and
(F) other relevant factors, including whether the lease transactions would permit avoidance of antidumping or countervailing duties."

The Conference Report indicated that Congress intends commerce to apply the AD/CVD laws to long-term leases, and to short-term leases if the product is integrated into the operations of the lessee or if a likelihood exists that the lease will be renewed for a significant period of time. Conf. Rep. No. 576, 100th Cong., 2d Sess. at 616 (1988). The Conference Report does not define "long-term lease" or "significant period of time".

[126] *Portland Hydraulic Cement and Cement Clinker from Columbia, France, Greece, Japan, Mexico, the Republic of Korea, Spain and Venezuela*, Inv. No. 731-TA-356-363 (neg. prelim.) USITC Pub. 1925 (1986). Four of the five ITC commissioners voted negative on the basis of almost universal indicia of health in the domestic industry: increases in consumption, increases in domestic production, increases in production capacity, increases in capacity utilization, increases in volume and value of domestic shipments, low levels of inventory, increases in labor productivity, and operating income of over 11 per cent (apparently higher than at any time since 1979). Only employment and number of hours worked declined during the period of investigation, and the majority attributed this mainly to increases in productivity. *Id.* at 13. Because the majority found no material injury to the domestic industry, only Commissioner Rohr, writing separately, went on to discuss the issue of causation (whether injury, if any, was caused by the imports under consideration). Commissioner Eckes wrote a dissenting view, in which he strongly criticized the majority for failing to consider the impact of imports on prices and domestic producers in its report. *Id.* at 36–37, 36 n.1. Commissioner Eckes argued that the subject imports undercut prices in certain geographic areas and that, absent the imports, domestic producers' profits might have been still greater. *Id.* at 46–47. This criticism of the ITC majority was apparently a catalyst in generating Congressional support for House and Senate amendments to the ITC's material injury analysis. At least one Congressional staffer stated, however, that the ITC decided *Portland Cement* correctly, and is concerned that Section 1328 would pressure the ITC to reach an affirmative determination (at least in the preliminary stage) in similar investigations in the future.

section evolved, however, into an attack on one of the ITC Commissioners by import-competing domestic industries which claimed that she voted against them based on an abstract five-factor analysis, without explaining her analysis of each case on an item-by-item basis. That group of companies also claimed that she would not find dumping in the absence of predatory pricing (which the Supreme Court in 1986 found to being probable in most cases, in the context of antitrust laws).[127]

The requirement of an ITC explanation of the consideration of each factor in a case is desirable, if taken seriously and performed routinely in antidumping and countervailing duty decisions. At least one Congressional staffer stated, however, that the ITC decided *Portland Cement* correctly, and is concerned that Section 1328 would pressure the ITC to reach an affirmative determination (at least at the preliminary stage) in similar investigations in the future. It will not serve much use, however, if it is merely transformed into a "checklist" of factors to be considered and a "boiler plate" explanation of the result for each factor.

Far more important to future ITC practice than this requirement that these factors be considered and explained is how the factors will be analyzed. Certain Commissioners, most notably Commissioner Cass, have recently begun to use a "but for" method of analysis that is heavily dependent on the measurement and application of certain elasticities.[128] The factors required to be considered in Section 1328 arguably are integral parts of this methodology.[129] Other Commissioners reject this approach, however, and it is not clear what method of analysis the majority of ITC Commissioners will ultimately adopt. It will be one or two years before it is possible to determine how, and how effectively, the ITC analyses the factors required to be explained in Section 1328.

The issue of "underselling" is rather more serious. A mechanical analysis of "price underselling" can often lead to a finding that imports have undersold domestic products 100 per cent of the time if at least one importer from a country undersold one of several domestic producers at least once in each quarter. In addition, the ITC sometimes is accused of ignoring differences in quality, servicing, and so on. As the ITC's chief economist has pointed out,[130] if an import over a long period of time consistently undersells a domestic product (or another import) by a consistent difference, it must reflect a difference in customer perception of quality (whether customer quantity, servicing backup or merchandise), and thus is not a true difference in price in

[127] *Matsushita Electric Industrial Co. v. Zenith Radio Corp.*, 475 U.S. 574 (1986).

[128] Commissioner Cass quoted the CIT's opinion in *USX Corp. v. United States*, 682 F. Supp. 60, 69 (Ct. Int'l Trade 1988) in asserting that "the use of elasticities in 'causation analysis has the potential for explaining, within the confines of the statutory framework and in an improved manner, how less than fair value imports affected the domestic industry . . . '"' R. Cass, "Responses to Questions from Senator Heinz," reprinted in "Finance Approves Cass and Newquist for ITC; Clears Way for Senate Approval," *Inside U.S. Trade* (BNA) at 6, 7 (12 August 1988).

[129] Commissioner Cass has summarized the purpose of the "but for" approach he uses as "[t]o understand what effect the less than fair value imports in fact had on the domestic industry's prices, sales, profits, employment, and so on . . . " R. Cass, "Responses to Questions from Senator Heinz," reprinted in "Finance Approves Cass and Newquist for ITC; Clears Way for Senate Approval," *Inside U.S. Trade* (BNA) at 6, 7 (12 August 1988).

[130] See Suomela, *Title VII Lost Sales, Underselling, and Causation and Injury*, Memorandum to the Vice Chairman, ITC, from the Director, Office of Economics, at 11–14 (3 January 1986).

the economic sense. ITC consideration of "underselling," as required by Section 1328, should be accompanied by systematic consideration of differences in customer perception of quality in order to avoid an unfair application of this provision.

Finally, Section 1328 directs the ITC to consider, as an indication of injury to the domestic industry, negative effects caused by dumped or subsidized imports to efforts to develop a new industry in the United States. Prior law provided that the ITC must consider all relevant factors, including (but not limited to) actual or potential decline in output, sales, profits, market share, return on investment, and capacity utilization, domestic price levels, and negative effects on cash flow, inventories, employment, wages, growth, investment, and ability to raise capital.[131] These factors are only directly relevant for an established industry. They do not measure injury to a start-up industry that might be growing, but at a far slower rate than it would absent dumped or subsidized imports. Certain consumer electronics industries are most likely to benefit from this provision if Japanese or other foreign competition begin exporting to the United States before an industry is fully established here.[132] This provision will make clear that the ITC must examine negative effects on the growth of the new industry as a part of its test of injury.

2. *Threat of Material Injury (Section 1329)*

Section 1329 directs the ITC to consider, as part of its test of threat of material injury, dumping by the same party of the same class or kind of merchandise in other GATT member markets. In addition to this provision, Congress expressed its concern with "past history of injurious dumping" and "worldwide dumping."[133] This provision is in part a response to U.S. producers of outboard motors, after Japanese producers had already been subjected to dumping remedies in the EEC and Australia, with margins of up to fifty per cent.[134] The Senate Report expresses the position that past dumping in other countries indicates "likely" behavior on the part of the foreign producer, which could be relevant to how a foreign producer might use existing excess capacity or large inventories.[135]

The Trade Act states that the ITC should consider dumping in the markets of foreign countries "as evidenced by dumping findings or antidumping remedies in other GATT member markets." This suggests that mere allegations by a U.S.

---

[131] 19 U.S.C. § 1677(7) (1982 & Supp. IV 1986).

[132] Congress expressed particular concern for the development of a new generation of products in "big ticket" industries, such as aircraft and heavy electrical equipment, where the loss of a few sales can have a major impact on future research and development. S. Rep. No. 71, 100th Cong., 1st Sess. 117 (1987). Nevertheless, this provision could prove even more important in the area of consumer electronics, where development and application of new technologies is equally important and fast-paced.

[133] S. Rep. No. 71, 100th Cong., 1st Sess. 119 (1987); H.R. Rep. No. 40, 100th cong., 1st Sess. 133 (1987).

[134] See 30 O.J. Eur. Comm. (no. L 82) 36 (1987); 30 O.J. Eur. Comm. (no. L 124) 1 (1987). (Section 1329 provides that, for purposes of this section, the European Communities shall be treated as a GATT member market.).

[135] S. Rep. No. 71, 100th Cong., 1st Sess. 119 (1987).

petitioner that a respondent is dumping in other GATT countries, and even ongoing proceedings in other GATT countries, should not be considered by the ITC.[136]

Finally, it should be noted that the Trade Act refers to dumping in "markets" of "foreign countries", as evidenced by dumping "findings" or other "remedies". The House Report speaks of "worldwide" dumping and a "pattern" of export practices,[137] and the Senate Report mentions "multiple dumping findings"[138]. This implies that the ITC should not consider a single, isolated dumping finding in one other country. It also implies that two or more dumping findings, to be considered, should be relatively concurrent, both among themselves and with the U.S. petition.[139] The use of the *Outboard Motors* example in the Senate Report implies that dumping findings in two foreign markets would be enough to warrant ITC consideration if they were within a sufficiently short time period and involved sizable margins.

Section 1329 further instructs the ITC to consider the effects of dumped or subsidized imports on "existing development and production efforts" of the domestic industry, including "efforts to develop a derivation or more advanced version" of the product. Apparently, Boeing was the company most responsible for initiating and pushing through this provision. The concern behind this provision is very similar to that behind Section 1328—that an industry can be threatened with material injury by virtue of its inability to develop to the extent necessary to fully take advantage of future markets.[140] Section 1329 focuses on "efforts" of research and development, rather than plans, in order to insure that the threat of material injury is real and imminent.[141] The dividing line between efforts and plans is not clear, but Sections 1328 and 1329 would seem to require that a petitioning U.S. company has spent money on a research and development program in order to have advanced beyond the planning stage.

---

[136] It should be noted that Section 1329 defines other "GATT member" markets as markets of signatories of the GATT Antidumping code. *Agreement on Implementation of Article VI of the General Agreements on Tariff and Trade*, 26th Supp. BISD 171 (1980). Thus, the ITC will not be required to base its threat of injury finding on previous dumping findings by non-code countries which might not provide an injury analysis as part of their determinations. Nevertheless, a serious concern remains: the ITC could be basing future threat of injury determinations in part upon results of investigations following somewhat varying standards and considerably different procedures in foreign countries.

[137] H. R. Rep No. 40, 100th cong., 1st Sess. 133 (1987).

[138] S. Rep. No. 71, 100th cong., 1st Sess. 119 (1987).

[139] The ITC currently faces the issue of whether dumping investigations are concurrent in determining when to cumulate imports for the injury proceeding. The ITC has not adopted any set rule, but had generally considered antidumping or countervailing duty determinations within the previous six–eight month period within which it will consider dumping investigations or findings concurrent and cumulate the imports to be sufficiently concurrent to warrant cumulation. See *infra* note 152. A longer period might be appropriate for this provision, because the issue is likely future behavior of the foreign company, rather than cause of current injury in the domestic industry.

[140] The Senate expressed particular concern with two industries—commercial aircraft and heavy electrical equipment. S. Rep. no. 71, 100th Cong., 1st Sess. 117 (1987). More specifically, Congress has been concerned about Britain, France, West Germany and Spain subsidizing Airbus. The requirement of an injury finding would have been a major obstacle to a countervailing duty suit by the domestic industry under the former practice—Boeing apparently remains a very profitable company. This provision would allow Boeing to allege injury, despite its continued profitability, if it could show that subsidized Airbus sales had forced Boeing to cut back its research and development programs, thus affecting its efforts to develop a new generation of planes.

[141] S. Rep. No. 71, 100th Cong., 1st Sess. 118 (1987).

3. Cumulation (Section 1330)

Prior to the Tariff and Trade Act of 1984, the ITC had discretion to cumulate imports from various countries subject to antidumping or countervailing duty investigations in appropriate cases, for purposes of determining whether the domestic industry was materially injured "by reason of" such imports. The Trade and Tariff Act of 1984, at the behest of domestic textile and steel companies, made cumulation of like and competing products mandatory.[142] As the ITC began to implement this provision, three main issues arose.

First was the question of potential exceptions to mandatory cumulation. Certain respondents argued that their imports should not be cumulated with others under investigation because they were of different quality, the volume of their imports was declining while the volume of other subject imports was rising, or the volume of their imports was *de minimis*. The 1984 Act left very little room for flexibility; unless the imports were of such different quality that they were not a "like product" or did not "compete with" other subject imports, cumulation was mandated.[143]

The most extreme result was reached in *Fresh Cut Flowers*.[144] In that investigation, involving imports from ten countries, imports from Columbia accounted for over eighty-five per cent of total subject imports in 1985; imports from Canada, Kenya and Chile accounted for 0.26 per cent, 0.36 per cent and 0.54 per cent of total subject imports respectively.[145] Although troubled by the result, four of the (then) five Commissioners decided that they could not exempt subject imports from cumulation because the volumes involved were *de minimis*.[146] The result was burdensome not only for the countries with small amounts of imports that were cumulated, but also for Commerce, which had to conduct a full investigation of minuscule values of imports from countries that otherwise would have been eliminated from the investigation at the ITC preliminary stage.

---

[142] The Trade and Tariff Act of 1984 amended the Tariff Act of 1930 by adding a new section:

> (iv) Cumulation. For purposes of [the material injury test], the Commission shall cumulatively assess the volume and effect of imports from two or more countries of like products subject to investigation if such imports compete with one another and with like products of the domestic industry in the United States market.

19 U.S.C. § 1677(7) (c) (iv) (Supp. IV 1986).

[143] Thus, one of the only investigations under the 1984 Act in which simultaneously investigated products were not cumulated involved pipe and tube from China. The ITC found that the Chinese pipe and tube was "grossly substandard"; most of it did not conform to ASTM standards, some was badly rusted and had to be sold for scrap, and the galvanized pipe had to be stripped and regalvanized. As a result, the ITC found that the Chinese pipe and tube did not "compete" with other imported pipe and tube under investigation. *Welded Carbon Steel Pipes and Tubes from the People's Republic of China*, Inv. No. 731-TA-292, (Neg. final), USITC Pub. 1885 (1986) at A-9 and A-3.

[144] *Certain Fresh Cut Flowers from Canada, Chile, Columbia, Costa Rica, Ecuador, Israel and the Netherlands*, Inv. Nos. 701-TA-275 to 275 (Affirm. final), USITC Pub. 1956 (1987) ("Fresh Cut Flowers").

[145] *Fresh Cut Flowers* at A-104. The ITC found seven different like products in the investigation, so these figures varied slightly from like product to like product. In only one like product did any of these countries account for more than one per cent of subject imports: imports of miniature carnations from Kenya accounted for three per cent of subjects imports in 1985. *Id.* at A-102.

[146] Commissioner Brunsdale noted that "there is a serious question . . . whether cumulation of all imports is appropriate where the overwhelming majority of subject imports comes from a single country . . . " *Id.* at 94 n.33.

The second issue concerned "cross-cumulation," or whether imports alleged to be sold at less than fair value should be cumulated with imports alleged to be subsidized for purposes of testing whether a domestic industry is materially injured by reason of such imports. Initially, the majority of ITC Commissioners did not cross-cumulate, on grounds of statutory construction.[147] The CIT ruled, however, that cross-cumulation was appropriate, and indeed mandated by the 1984 Act.[148] Thereafter, a reluctant majority of the ITC Commissioners cross-cumulated imports.[149]

The third issue was whether imports of a like product that were investigated at different times should be cumulated for purposes of testing material injury. It appears logical that imports from two countries that were subsidized or sold at less than fair value simultaneously in the United States should not escape cumulation merely because the investigations of the two countries happened not to be simultaneous. On the other hand, the longer the time period between the investigations, the more likely that the subsidies or sales at less than fair value were not simultaneous. The 1984 Act provided only indirect guidance on the issue, mandating cumulation of imports that "compete with each other."[150]

The Trade Act resolves the first of these issues. Section 1330(b), described by some as the only AD/CVD provision in the Act furthering free trade, establishes a *de*

[147] 19 U.S.C. § 1671(a) (1982 & Supp. IV 1986) provides for the imposition of a countervailing duty if Commerce determines that imports are being subsidized and if the ITC determines that a domestic industry is being materially injured "by reason of imports of that merchandise." 19 U.S.C. § 1673 provides for the imposition of an antidumping duty if Commerce determines that imports are being sold at less than fair value and the ITC determines that a domestic industry is being materially injured "by reason of imports of that merchandise." Nowhere does the statute refer to subsidized imports and imports at less than fair value together or to "unfairly traded imports." See *Certain Fresh Cut flowers from Canada, Chile, Colombia, Costa Rica, Ecuador, Israel, and the Netherlands* Invs. Nos. 701-TA-275 to 278 and 731-TA-327 to 331 (Affirm. final), USITC Pub. 1956 (1987) at 68–69 (additional views of Commissioner Rohr).

[148] *Bingham & Taylor Division, Virginia Industries, Inc. v. United States*, 627 F. Supp. 793 (Ct. Int'l Trade 1986), *aff'd*, 815 F.2d 1482 (Fed. Cir. 1987). The CIT noted that a separate section of the statute . . . 19 U.S.C. § 1677(7)—set forth the injury test for both antidumping and countervailing duty investigations, and the statute required cumulation of imports "subject to investigation." 626 F. Supp. at 797. The CIT also looked to the legislative history of the 1984 Act, and determined that Congress intended to prevent material injury "which comes about by virtue of several simultaneous unfair acts of practices." H.R. Rep. No. 725, 98th Cong., 2d Sess. 37 (1984), quoted in *Bingham & Taylor*, 627 F. Supp. at 796.

[149] Chairman Liebeler refused to cross-cumulate in the *Fresh Cut Flowers* preliminary, stating that the *Bingham & Taylor* decision was on appeal to the Federal Circuit and, because she believed the decision was wrong, she would not follow it until the Federal Circuit ruled on the issue. *Certain Fresh Cut Flowers from Canada, Chile, Columbia, Costa Rica, Ecuador, Israel, Kenya, Mexico, the Netherlands, and Peru*, Inv. No. 303-TA-17 to 18 and 701-TA-275 to 278 (Affirm. prelim.), USITC Pub. 1877 (1986) at 25–28. In the *Fresh Cut Flowers* final determination, Vice-Chairman Brunsdale declined to cross-cumulate, although she did not explain why; Commissioners Lodwick, Eckes and Rohr did cross-cumulate, although Commissioner Rohr explained in his additional views that he believed he was compelled to cross-cumulate by *Bingham & Taylor*, although he disagreed with that opinion. See *Certain Fresh Cut Flowers from Canada, Chile, Colombia, Costa Rica, Ecuador, Israel, and the Netherlands* Invs. Nos. 701-TA-275 to 278 and 731-TA-327 to 331 (Affirm. final), USITC Pub. 1956 (1987) at 68–69 (additional views of Commissioner Rohr).

[150] 19 U.S.C. § 1677(7) (c) (iv) (Supp. IV 1986).

minimis exception to mandatory cumulation. Apparently, Professor Jackson of Michigan was among those who supported the idea.[151] The administration supported the proposal,[152] as it allows the possibility of eliminating countries with minimal amounts of imports at the preliminary stage, thus avoiding the expense of the Commerce investigation (and the embarrassment of *Fresh Cut Flowers).* The Israeli lobby also managed to obtain a potential exemption for Israeli from cumulation unless the Israeli imports alone are first found to be causing injury to the domestic industry.

The impact of Section 1330(b) on ITC practice will depend on how the term *"de minimis"* is interpreted and applied by the ITC. The legislative history makes clear that Congress intends that "the ITC apply the exception narrowly", so as not to "subvert the purpose and general application of the requirement" of cumulation.[153]

Section 1330(a) provides the ITC with discretionary authority to cumulate imports in assessing threat of injury. This provision is extremely vague, as the legislative history gives no explanation of when the ITC should exercise this discretion.

Provisions affecting the issues of cross-cumulation and the relevant time period for cumulation were originally included in the House bill, but dropped during conference because it was felt that they were no longer necessary. The House bill stated explicitly that the ITC shall cumulate imports involved in antidumping and countervailing duty investigations. This provision originated from a TRAC proposal designed to further tighten the cumulation provision. The *Bingham & Taylor* decision really eliminated the need for this provision and ITC practice since that decision would not have been affected by the House proposal. The House bill also stated that imports currently under investigation shall be cumulated with any imports subject to

[151] Some experts believed that, because petitioners can launch investigations in the United States on the basis of a much less detailed and complete record than in other countries, such as the EEC or Canada, and because investigations tend to be much more expensive in the United States, a *de minimis* exception to cumulation is necessary to allow truly minor exporters to the United States the chance to obtain an ITC negative determination at the preliminary stage, thus avoiding the substantial costs of the full investigation.

[152] See 30 October 1987 Letter at 13.

[153] Conf. Rep. No. 576, 100th Cong., 2d Sess. 621 (1988); see also H.R. Rep. No. 40, 100th Cong., 1st Sess. 130-131 (1987). The Ways and Means Committee of the House of Representatives stated in its Report:

> "While this amendment gives some limited discretion to the ITC to refrain from cumulative injury assessment with respect to imports from a particular source, the Commission shall apply this exception narrowly and only in circumstances where it is clear that imports from that source are so small and so isolated that they could not possibly be having any injurious impact on the U.S. industry. The ITC shall apply this exception with particular care in situations involving fungible products where a small quantity of low-priced imports can have a very real effect on the market.
>
> . . . The Committee expects the ITC to apply the exception narrowly and only when the facts clearly justify its application. The Committee does not intend for this narrow, limited exception to subvert the purpose and general application of the cumulation requirement.
>
> The Committee does not provide in the legislation a specific numerical standard for what constitutes "negligible" in recognition that what may be "negligible" imports in volume or market share for one industry may be different than for another industry. For an industry which is already suffering considerable injury and has long been battered by unfair import competition, very small additional quantities of unfair imports may be more than negligible. For another industry, not so deeply injured, small additional quantities of unfair imports may have no discernible effect at all. The Committee intends that "negligible" be interpreted in light of industry conditions, and in a manner that makes sense given the realities of the marketplace."

H.R. Rep. No. 40, 100th Cong., 1st Sess. 130-131 (1987).

investigation in the previous twelve months "which resulted in a final order, suspension agreement, or termination based on a quantitative restraint agreement."[154] This would have modified current ITC practice[155] only slightly.[156]

4. Information Provisions (Section 1332)

Under prior law, Commerce and the ITC were permitted, but not required, to release confidential information (other than business proprietary information) to representatives of the Parties to the proceedings. Commerce routinely follows a procedure allowing for release of business proprietary information to attorneys and other representatives of a party upon the signing of an administrative protective order ("APO") under which the attorney or other representative promises not to release the information to any other person. Certain information not needed by the attorneys in a Commerce investigation (including customer names and trade secrets) is not released. A party submitting information to Commerce is required to certify that it has provided a copy of all releasable information to all attorneys or other representatives of opposing parties that have signed an APO.[157]

Prior to the Trade Act, the ITC, by contrast, did not release confidential information to attorneys or other representatives of the parties, other than very limited information concerning domestic prices or cost of production of like products. All other information was made available to attorneys and other party representatives only in the same form in which it is released publicly. Thus, on issues such as market share, capacity, use of capacity, sales, and employment rates, figures were available only for the industry as a whole (if there were more than four firms), and not for specific firms. This made it virtually impossible for attorneys representing the parties to determine, for example, whether all domestic firms within an industry were showing signs of injury (which would support an argument that injury was being caused by dumping) or whether some firms were suffering a great deal of injury while

[154] Conf. Rep. No. 576, 100th Cong., 2d Sess. 620 (1988).

[155] The ITC generally does not cumulate imports subject to investigation with imports subject to previously issued orders; it does, however, apply an exception providing for cumulation in the case of "recently issued orders." *Cold-Rolled Carbon Steel Plates and Sheets from Argentina,* Inv. No. 731-TA-175 (Final), USITC Pub,. 1967 at 60 (1986). The ITC has been willing in certain investigations to cumulate imports subject to orders issued up to 6–8 months previously, but has considered an order issued eight months earlier to be too removed in time. Compare *Certain Welded Carbon Steel Pipes and Tubes from the Philippines and Singapore,* Invs. Nos. 731-TA-293, 294, 296 (Final), USITC Pub. 1907 at 10-11, n.37 (1986) with *Certain Welded Carbon Steel Pipes and Tubes from Taiwan,* Inv. No. 731-TA-349 (Final), USITC Pub. 1944 at 19-20 (1987).

[156] Presumably, the term "final order" meant a final order by Commerce imposing an antidumping or countervailing duty. This would have prevented the ITC from resurrecting and possibly reconsidering previous negative final determinations.

[157] 19 C.F.R. § 355.20.

others remained healthy (a possible indication that any injury was caused by factors other than dumping).[158]

The provision in the final Trade Act, Section 1332, will essentially require Commerce and the ITC to release all business proprietary information in its AD and CVD cases, with limited exceptions for privileged or classified information. The bill further provides that the parties to such a case must serve such information (under APO) upon all other parties at the time it is filed with Commerce or the ITC.

These provisions should not affect current Commerce procedure. They will have a dramatic effect on ITC procedure, however, essentially forcing the ITC to adopt the method currently followed by Commerce.[159]

(f) *Critical Circumstances (Section 1324)*

Section 1324 explicitly authorizes Commerce to make a preliminary finding as to critical circumstances prior to the time of its preliminary determination at any time after the initiation of the investigation.[160] Although Commerce arguably had authority to issue such findings prior to a preliminary determination under prior law,[161] Commerce has been reluctant to do so in the past, in view of the GATT Antidumping Code requirement that no provisional measures be imposed without a preliminary affirmative finding of dumping.[162] Congress stated that this amendment is consistent with U.S. obligations under GATT because suspension of liquidation will not occur prior to the Commerce preliminary determination.[163] This section also authorizes Commerce to request the Customs Service to monitor trade information if there is a reasonable basis to suspect critical circumstances. Neither of these changes is likely to significantly alter current practice.

158 Thus, for example, an attorney representing a client for the ITC might only have learned that the five largest domestic companies in an industry controlled 75 per cent of the market. The attorney would not have been able to determine, based on the information released by the ITC, whether the market was made up of five roughly equal size competitors, one market dominant firm with four very minor competitors, or two or three moderate size competitors and a couple of smaller firms. An attorney representing one of those five firms had some advantage, based on his or her knowledge of that firm's market share, but such an attorney also lacked full information. Furthermore, if one firm accounted for 75 per cent or more of the sales included in the information compiled by the ITC, or two firms accounted for 90 per cent or more of such information, the ITC also refused to release the aggregate data on the ground that it might have been possible for one of the parties, after subtracting out its own data, to derive information about it competitors. This left attorneys with virtually no information on which to base their arguments.

159 The ITC has adopted interim rules to implement this new requirement. See 19 C.F.R. § 207.7, as amended, 53 Fed. Reg. 33,039, 33,041–42 (1988).

160 Section 1324(a) (2) and (b) (2) amend 19 U.S.C. §§ 1671b(e) (1) and 1673b (e) (1) to allow the administering authority to determine promptly "at any time after the initiation of the investigation" the existence of critical circumstances.

161 See S. Rep. No. 71, 100th Cong., 1st Sess. 92 (1987).

162 The GATT Antidumping Code provides "Provisional measures may be taken only after a preliminary affirmative finding has been made that there is dumping and that there is sufficient evidence of injury . . . " Article 10.1, *GATT Antidumping Code* at 181–82.

163 S. Rep. No. 71, 100th Cong., 1st Sess. 92 (1987).

The most important part of this section would clarify the standards used by the ITC in assessing critical circumstances in its final determination. The AD/CVD laws already specified that the ITC was to include a finding in its final determination as to whether massive imports caused material injury such that the antidumping (or countervailing) duty should be applied retroactively.[164] However, no further guidance was given to the ITC. The GATT Antidumping Code and GATT Subsidies Code are also not specific as to how it should make this finding. The ITC has very rarely made such a finding,[165] possibly in part because of lack of agreement on how the GATT Codes should be applied.[166]

The clarification of the test to be applied in determining critical circumstances began in 1985 with a TRAC proposal, which was introduced by Senator Heinz, to make critical circumstances determinations more likely.[167] TRAC resurrected the proposal in 1987, with support from the steel industry. The initial proposal was diluted somewhat by Senate Finance staff. Following the transformation of the proposal, apparently even the ITC (against which the original proposals were directed) did not oppose the amendment.

Section 1324 provides specific factors that the ITC must consider in reaching its critical circumstances finding.[168] The factors include the condition of the domestic industry, whether massive imports are evidence of efforts to avoid potential duties, whether foreign conditions led to massive imports, and whether massive imports are likely to continue. The original purpose—to encourage the ITC to levy a retroactive duty more frequently in cases involving surges of imports—will probably be realized by this amendment although the effects will depend on how it is implemented by the ITC.

(g) *Certification of Submissions (Section 1331)*

Section 1331 requires any person submitting factual information in an antidumping or countervailing duty investigation to certify that such information is accurate and complete to the best of that person's knowledge. The concern underlying the proposal was that certain persons submitting information (often small businesses,

[164] 19 U.S.C. §1671d(b) (4) (A) (1982); § 1673d(b) (4) (A) (1982).

[165] See *Potassium Permanganate from the People's Republic of China*, Inv. No. 731-TA-125 (Final), USITC Pub. 1480 (1984); *Oil Country Tubular Goods from Argentina and Spain*, Invs. Nos. 731-TA-191, 195 (Final), USITC Pub. 1694 (1985).

[166] Conf. Rep. No. 576, 100th Cong., 2d Sess. 611 (1988).

[167] See 131 Cong. Rec. S10079 (daily ed. 25 July 1985).

[168] Compare *Omnibus Trade and Competitiveness Act of 1988*, Pub. L. No. 100-418, § 1324, 102 Stat. 1199-2101 (1988) with 19 U.S.C. 1673d(b) (4) (A) (1982).

petitioners as well as respondents) have been suspected of submitting false information.[169] This proposal, with its overtones of "good government," appealed to both the House and the Senate.

The proposal appeared ready to sail through Conference without serious opposition when suddenly in the last couple of days of Conference, Commerce came out in opposition to it. Apparently, Commerce was concerned that certification of submissions would create problems for attorneys and other representatives, who would be unable to verify the contents of submissions. Commerce feared that the requirement of certification of the accuracy of "unknown" submissions could lead to threats and harassment by opposing counsel, and even to litigation.[170] However, the opposition was too late, and the provision passed Conference essentially unaltered.

Because of the limit contained in Section 1331, that the person making the submission certify its accuracy and completeness "to the best of that person's knowledge," it is unlikely to have a large effect on attorneys or other representatives of interested persons. The legislative history makes clear that "the submitter," as well as the submitter's legal representative, must review and certify the submission.[171] In other words, a party submitting information cannot shield itself by hiding behind its lawyer. Because the person or company supplying the information presumably has the requisite knowledge, these are the parties that will be affected by this provision in the future.

(h) *Correction of Ministerial Errors (Section 1333)*

Prior antidumping and countervailing duty law contained no specific provisions governing the correction of errors. In the early 1980's it was accepted that Commerce had the inherent authority to correct ministerial errors, and Commerce routinely made such corrections. Later, Commerce became reluctant to correct such mistakes. The only recourse available to the disadvantaged party was to appeal; as a result, the CIT was burdened with unnecessary appeals.

To correct this situation, the Trade Act provides that Commerce shall establish procedures for the correction of ministerial errors. This provision is not intended to

[169] For example, the petitioner in *Potassium Chloride from Canada*, Lundberg Industries, was accused of probable fraud by the presiding judge in a bankruptcy proceeding and had its sole financial report withdrawn by Ernst & Whinney because of "concealment of pertinent records and refusal to provide requested information." *In re Lundberg Industries, Ltd.*, No. 387-33269-RCM-11 (N.D. Tex. 4 Sept. 1987) (order appointing trustee); Emergency Motion to Appoint Trustee at 7, *In re Lundberg Industries Ltd.*, No. 387-33269-RCM-11 (N.D. Tex. 27 August 1987). Lundberg Industries was able to file a petition with Commerce and information regarding injury to it with the ITC on behalf of the domestic industry, without certifying that the information was accurate or otherwise taking measures to help ensure veracity, despite the probable fraud found in the federal bankruptcy court.

[170] Commerce apparently feared that certification of submissions would come to resemble SEC due diligence investigations. To this extent, the fears were misplaced; Section 1331 clearly limits the certification by a person making a submission "to the best of that person's knowledge." Thus, the main effect will be on persons and companies providing information.

[171] H.R. Rep. No. 40, 100th Cong., 1st Sess. 143 (1987); S. Rep. No. 71, 100th Cong., 1st Sess. 114 (1987).

allow commerce to alter substantive determinations after the final determination, but only to allow it to correct "mathematical or clerical errors or other unintentional errors."[172]

This provision was introduced in the House, although it is unclear where it originated. The Senate generally believed that the amendment was not necessary because Commerce already had the necessary powers, but gave in to the House.

This Section will not have a major impact on Commerce practice, however; it will simply restore the practice formerly followed by Commerce. This section might not even have been necessary; it appears that Commerce was taking steps to begin correcting errors again even without Congressional action.[173]

(i) *Duty Drawback (Section 1334)*

Under prior law, a U.S. manufacturer that imported and paid duty upon merchandise that was used to manufacture goods for export could apply for the refund of the duties paid on the imported merchandise at the time the completed goods were exported. The U.S. manufacturer was entitled to a refund in the amount of ninety-nine per cent of all duties paid, including antidumping and countervailing duties.

Section 1334 of the Trade Act amends prior duty drawback practice to exclude antidumping and countervailing duties from the duties eligible for drawback. The Congressional purpose is to eliminate any incentive for U.S. manufacturers to select foreign-origin dumped or subsidized products, despite an antidumping or countervailing duty, over a competing, more expensive U.S.-origin product for use in the manufacture of goods for export.

This provision was pushed by Senator Heinz, at the urging of TRAC and the domestic steel industry. ECAT and American Association of Exporters and Importers ("AAEI") opposed the measure, as did Congressman Gibbons, for fear that it would reduce U.S. exporters' competitiveness in foreign markets. The perceived "unfairness" of dumping and use of subsidies by foreign films, however, generated sufficient support for this measure to ensure its adoption.

[172] Conf. Rep. No. 576, 100th Cong., 2d Sess. 624 (1988). The trade bill defines ministerial errors as "errors in addition, subtraction, or other arithmetic function, clerical errors resulting from inaccurate copying, duplication, or the like, and any other type of unintentional error which the administering authority considers ministerial. *Omnibus Trade and Competitiveness Act of 1988,* Pub. L. No. 100-418, § 1333, 102 Stat. 1209 (1988).

[173] On 26 February 1988, Commerce published proposed regulations establishing procedures for the correction of errors. *Proposed Procedures for Review of Calculations and Correction of Clerical Errors,* 53 Fed. Reg. 5813 (1988). On 24 October 1988, Commerce published a notice renewing these procedures "until regulations under the 1988 Act are promulgated." 53 Fed. Reg. 41,617 (1988). Presumably, Commerce can satisfy its obligation under Section 1333 by adopting and implementing these same or similar regulations.

(j) *Government Importations (Section 1335)*

Prior law contained no provisions as to whether agencies of the U.S. government had to pay antidumping or countervailing duties upon importation of goods for use or consumption by the U.S. government agency. On a number of occasions, U.S. governments purchases of imported merchandise have been exempted from antidumping or countervailing duties that otherwise would have been applicable. In particular, complaints were made after the exemption from payment of antidumping duties on purchases by the General Services Administration for the national defense stockpile of imported titanium sponge that otherwise would have been subject to antidumping duties of between fourteen and fifty-six per cent.[174]

The House bill contained a provision subjecting all merchandise imported by or on behalf of the U.S. government to all applicable antidumping and countervailing duties. The Senate bill contained a similar provision, but with exceptions for certain Department of Defense purchases. The House amendment in particular aroused strong opposition from countries that have signed defense memoranda of understanding (which provide that no duties will be imposed on defense equipment), and also from U.S. defense equipment manufacturers (who correctly realized that the defense sector is not one that should want governments examining claims of subsidies or sales below fully allocated cost). The Administration was caught between crusaders against all "unfair" trade (including in defense products) and officials worried about violating our agreements with other countries.

Section 1335 of the Trade Act is a compromise[175] that provides that merchandise imported by the U.S. government is not exempt from countervailing or antidumping duties, unless the merchandise is acquired by, or for the use of, the Department of Defense in accordance with the terms of DOD memoranda of understanding in effect as of 1 January 1988, or the merchandise had no substantial non-military use.

IV. MISCELLANEOUS PROVISIONS

(a) *Steel Imports (Section 1322)*

Section 1322 of the Trade Act amends the Steel Import Stabilization Act of 1984 to include steel products made from steel that is melted and poured in a country subject to a voluntary restraint agreement ("VRA"), but that are manufactured in another country not subject to a steel VRA. The Steel Import Stabilization Act authorized USTR to enter into bilateral VRAs with major exporters of steel to the

[174] See *Titanium Sponge from Japan*, 49 Fed. Reg. 47,053, 47,054 (Affirm. final) (1984); 50 Fed. Reg. 32,459 (amend.) (1985).

[175] The General Service Administration was not a part of the final negotiations.

United States.[176] A number of countries were not included that are significant exporters of steel products, including, most notably, Canada. The possibility of claims of "circumvention" thus existed, as countries subject to VRAs could ship melted and poured steel to countries not covered by VRAs for further manufacture into products such as pipe and tube or steel wire. Because the further manufacture would usually result in a substantial transformation of the melted and poured steel,[177] the products would enter the United States as products of the country not subject to the VRA (and, therefore, they could enter the United States in potentially unlimited quantities).

The U.S. steel industry lobbied for this provision to end a perceived problem of circumvention by certain countries subject to VRAs. Steel products being completed in Thailand, Turkey and, to a lesser extent, Canada, were the chief causes of concern.[178] Their proposal, in the form it was adopted, would allow steel melted and poured in a country subject to a VRA, and further manufactured in a country not subject to a VRA, to be treated as a product of the first country and subject to the quantitative restrictions applicable to that country under its VRA. The issue was taken up by Senators Heinz and Pease against the opposition of the Administration, which viewed the problem of circumvention as less severe than the burden of administering the new provision.[179] The provision would require Commerce to trace the steel used in imported steel products back to the melted and poured stage to determine the country of origin.[180] Thailand opposed the measure, but simply lacked the political clout to counter the domestic interests.

---

[176] Pub. L. No. 98-573, Title VIII, 30 Oct. 1984 (codified in 19 U.S.C. § 2253). The countries that entered into VRAs of steel products with the United States are Austria, Australia, Brazil, Czechoslovakia, East Germany, Finland, Hungary, Japan, Mexico, Poland, Portugal, People's Republic of China, Romania, South Africa, South Korea, Spain, Trinidad and Tobago, Venezuela and Yugoslavia. The European Economic Company signed a separate agreement with the United States in 1982.

[177] United States law requires that every good imported into the United States be marked and labeled according to country of origin. Where a product is made in one country and then shipped to another country for further manufacture prior to export to the United States, the U.S. Customs Service applies a test of "substantial transformation" to determine country of origin. The product is deemed to continue to be a product of the first country of manufacture until it is subsequently "substantially transformed" in another country; it then becomes a product of the country in which it was substantially transformed. 19 C.F.R. § 134.1(b). The U.S. Customs Service interprets substantial transformation as a change in the "name, character or use" of the product. 28 U.S.C. § 2640(d). See, e.g, *Superior Wire v. United States*, 669 F. Supp. 472 (Ct. Int'l Trade 1987); *Ferrostaal Metals Corp. v. United States*, 664 F. Supp. 535 (Ct. Int'l Trade 1987); *National Juice Products Ass'n. v. United States*, 628 F. Supp. 978 (Ct. Int'l Trade 1986). Customs also considers factors such as the sophistication and know-how involved in the further manufacturing, the nature of the transformation involved, and the amount of value added in the further manufacture. See *Superior Wire*, 669 F. Supp. at 477; *Ferrostaal Metals*, 664 F. Supp. at 541; *National Juice Products*, 628 F. Supp. at 989. As a general rule, the greater the change in character or use of the product, the more sophisticated the further manufacturing process, and the greater the value added to the product, the more likely that Customs will find that a substantial transformation has occurred.

[178] Ironically, the Virgin Islands has supposedly succeeded in attracting investment to set up a steel pipe mill, to help diversify its economy. Section 1322 could be applied to steel pipe made in the Virgin Islands, and it is unclear whether the project will survive.

[179] The Administration stated that the provision is "impossible to enforce" and violates the existing VRAs. See 30 October 1987 Letter at 18.

[180] The Senate version of the amendment would have provided that the provision would be administered by the Treasury Department (which includes Customs). S. 1420, Sec. 323(b), 100th Cong., 1st Sess. (1987). The final version of the bill, however, provides for administration as directed by the President (which will mean using Commerce).

Senator Bentsen (the floor manager) and Senator Heinz agreed with Senator Packwood that the enforcement of the provision should alleviate the commercial uncertainty caused by the provision itself (importers could innocently purchase steel substantially transformed in a non-VRA country, and have that steel detained by Customs for lack of a VRA country export license). One method would be to publish advance notice in the Federal Register, following a determination of increased imports of steel products from a non-VRA country made from steel melted and poured in a VRA country, that Customs would require a VRA country export license for such imports beginning a certain number of days after publication of the notice.[181] It is not clear whether this provision will affect other countries' willingness to enter into renewed VRAs in 1989, when the current VRAs expire.[182]

(b) *Studies (Section 1336)*

Section 1336 of the Trade Act provides for two studies. The Secretary of Commerce is charged with investigating "the new market orientation of the People's Republic of China," and the possible need for changes in U.S. antidumping laws. USTR is instructed to review all bilateral subsidy commitments entered into by foreign governments with the United States and to provide recommendations as to how compliance by foreign governments might be improved.

The study on the People's Republic of China resulted from proposals by Senator Hecht and Congressman Downey. They were sympathetic to China, and believed that the United States should recognize and encourage its movement towards a market economy. Senator Adams of Washington was also a supporter of this measure.

The subsidies commitments study resulted mainly from dissatisfaction by textile companies. There was concern that a number of foreign countries entered into commitments with the United States to reduce subsidies to their textile industries to get the injury test in CVD cases, but then allegedly did not honor their commitments. Congressman Jenkins of Georgia was also a supporter of this provision.

The study on the People's Republic of China is likely to have only a limited effect

[181] Cong. Rec. S10370 (dailyed, 21 July 1987) (statement of Senator Packwood). Senator Heinz suggested requiring the export certificates to designate the "melted-and-poured" country for all steel sold to the U.S., but got no agreement.

[182] The relation of this provision with the Canada-United States Free Trade Agreement ("FTA") is unclear. The FTA provides specific rules of origin for purposes of according FTA benefits, and all products meeting these rules of origin are entitled to all the benefits of the FTA. Steel melted and poured in another country and further manufactured in Canada would qualify as a product of Canada under the FTA if it met the FTA rules of origin of goods. Article 301, FTA. Under the terms of the FTA, it could not be subjected to quotas, and would be eligible to enter the United States at rates of duty decreasing steadily until duty-free entry would be accorded in ten years. Article 401, FTA. If the United States attempted to enforce Section 1322 of the Trade Act against steel further manufactured in Canada, Canada could claim violation of the FTA.

The Administration has claimed that Section 1322 does not conflict with the FTA because Section 1322 is discretionary, and can be construed consistently with the FTA. *Statement of Administrative Action,* The United States-Canada Free Trade Agreement Implementation Act, reprinted in H.R. Doc. No. 216, 100th Cong., 2d Sess. 163 at 177. Such a construction could significantly limit the potential effects of Section 1322 regarding the importation of steel products manufactured in Canada from steel melted and poured in other countries.

on U.S. antidumping practice. It remains to be seen what effect the subsidies commitment study will have. This study might well be used by Congress or other or press for retaliation or sanctions against countries that are not in compliance with their commitments to the United States.[183]

V. MAIN PROVISIONS NOT ADOPTED

(a) *Sham Transactions*

Under current antidumping law, the importer of record is liable for payment of antidumping duties. A manufacturer, seller or exporter of merchandise can maintain lower prices in the United States than in the home market, despite the imposition of an antidumping duty, by paying the antidumping duties itself or refunding to the importer of record any duties paid by the importer. Under current practice, Commerce would account for this during the next administrative review by increasing the dumping margin by the amount of antidumping duties paid or refunded by the manufacturer, seller or exporter.[184] Certain parties argued that no relief from dumping was granted to domestic firms until such time as foreign producers actually passed the dumping duties on to the ultimate consumers, and that this might not occur until a number of years had passed, under current Commerce practice.

The Senate bill included a provision[185] that would have allowed Commerce to direct Customs to treat the United States end purchaser as the importer of record liable for the payment of antidumping duties, if Commerce found that the listed importer of record had engaged in a sham transaction with the manufacturer, producer, seller or exporter, thus allowing the manufacturer, producer, seller or exporter to absorb the antidumping duty. This provision was dropped in Conference in the final version of the bill.

(b) *Definition of Foreign Market Value*

Under current law, when a product subject to an antidumping investigation is imported into the United States by an importer related to the foreign producer, the U.S. price is calculated on the basis of the exporter's sales price ("ESP"). Direct and indirect expenses are deducted from the U.S. sales price. Direct expenses (such as shipment costs, packaging, insurance, etc.) are deducted from the foreign market price, but indirect expenses (overhead, advertising, salesmen's salaries, etc.) are

[183] Indeed, this study would appear to establish a basis for mandatory retaliation under the revised Section 301. Section 1301 of the Trade Act amends Section 301 of the Trade Act of 1974 by providing, subject to certain exceptions, for mandatory action by the USTR if he or she determines that an act, policy or practice of a foreign country violates, is inconsistent with, or otherwise denies benefits due the United States under a trade agreement.

[184] *Offshore Platform Jackets and Piles from Japan and Korea*, 52 Fed. Reg. 41,603, 41,604 (Order rvkd.) (1987).

[185] S. 1420 Sec. 332, 100th Cong., 1st Sess. (1987).

deducted only up to the amount of the indirect expenses deducted from the U.S. sales price.

The so-called "Hollings Amendment", contained in the Senate bill,[186] would have eliminated any deductions of indirect expenses from foreign market value. Furthermore, the provision would also have required Commerce to deduct a specific amount from the U.S. sales price for profit earned by the U.S. subsidiary. No such deduction would have been made from foreign market value. This measure would have had the effect of increasing dumping margins in all cases where the importer was related to the producer. The provision would have applied to imports from countries that are signatories to the GATT Antidumping Code.

Proponents of the provision included TRAC and the National Association of Manufacturers. They argued that the provision was necessary to match current EEC practice, which does not deduct any indirect expenses from foreign market value in its calculations.

Opponents of the provision were numerous; they included the National Foreign Trade Council, the Pro Trade Group, Consumers Union, and a group of large U.S. manufacturers. The Administration also strongly opposed the provision.[187] Opponents of the provision argued that the EEC classifies salesmen's salaries as direct, rather than indirect, expenses, and therefore deducts such expenses from both the EEC sales price and foreign market value. In most commerce determinations involving ESP calculations, salesmen's salaries make up the major portion of indirect expenses. By providing that the salesmen's salary would not be deducted from foreign market value, this provision went far beyond current EEC practice.[188]

The Hollings Amendment (after intense lobbying by both sides) was not included in the final version of the Trade Act.

(c) *Compensation/Recovery of Damages*

Under existing U.S. antidumping law, domestic firms injured by foreign firms' dumping practices are not entitled to any portion of any antidumping duties collected as a remedy. A private remedy does exist under the Revenue Act of 6 September 1916 ("Antidumping Act of 1916"), which makes it unlawful for any person systematically to import or sell articles in the United States at less than their actual market value with

[186] S. 1420 Sec. 339, 100th Cong., 1st Sess. (1987).

[187] See 30 October 1987 Letter at 15-16 (labelling the Hollings Amendment "an attempt to unfairly stack the deck against importers").

[188] Furthermore, the size of dumping margins determined in the EEC is often less important than in the United States because thhe EEC frequently imposes antidumping duties that are less than the actual dumping margin if such lesser antidumping duties are sufficient to prevent injury to EEC products. See Article 13(3), Council Regulation No. 2176/84, 27 O.J. Eur. Comm. (Nos. L 201/1, L227/35) (1984).

In practice, the amount of antidumping duties in the EEC are "mainly determined by the level of price undercutting . . . of the imports into the Community and by the level of resale prices that would be required to cover the costs of Community producers and provide a reasonable profit." I. Van Bael & J. Bellis. *International Trade Law and Practice of the European Community: EEC Anti-Dumping and Other Trade Protection Laws* 92-93 (1985).

the intent of injuring or destroying a U.S. industry. The act provides for the assessment of criminal penalties, and also allows an injured person to bring an action in federal district court for treble damages.[189]

These provisions have rarely been used by a U.S. industry, and no plaintiff has ever recovered damages under the 1916 act. Plaintiffs seeking recovery of treble damages face two main obstacles. First is the requirement of demonstrating intent, that the defendant "committed such acts with the intent of injury or destroying an industry." Even if a foreign producer's intent was to injure a U.S. industry—which is very rarely the case, as dumping is usually either unintentional or simply an attempt to maximize a firm's marginal returns—such intent on the part of a foreign producer is extremely difficult to prove. Second, pretrial discovery is limited because of the act's criminal penalties.[190] Thus, evidence of intent in the possession of the defendants often cannot be obtained.

The House introduced two provisions that would have allowed greater compensation to domestic firms injured by reason of dumping. The House bill provided for the establishment of a special compensation account, to be funded out of dumping duties, which would be available to compensate domestic producers injured by dumping. The ITC would be required to determine whether a particular domestic producer had been injured by reason of dumping, and in what amount, and would certify the producer's eligibility for compensation.[191] The House bill would also have revised the Antidumping Act of 1916 in order to make civil actions by domestic producers for recovery of damages more attractive.[192] The bill would have eliminated criminal penalties (thus allowing more open discovery) and limited recovery in a civil action to single rather than treble damages. More significant, however, was the provision establishing a rebuttable presumption of intent to injure a U.S. industry if the foreign manufacturer had been subject to three or more final determinations in dumping actions within a ten-year period.[193]

These provisions were similar to Congressional proposals made (and defeated) during the past nine years. The Administration was strongly opposed to these

[189] Revenue Act of 8 September 1916 (Title VIII, Sec. 801) 64th Cong., 1st Sess., Ch. 463 (1916), codified at 15 U.S.C. § 72 (1982).

[190] See *H. Wagner & Adler Co. v. Mali*, 74 F.2d 666 (2d Cir. 1935).

[191] H.R. 3, Sec. 167, 100th Cong., 1st Sess. (1987). Such findings would have required a substantial departure from current ITC procedure because the ITC does not estimate the dollar amount of injury suffered by U.S. industry, does not make specific injury findings for individual firms, and does not attempt to assess the percentage of injury caused by dumping as opposed to other factors (so long as dumping is a material cause of injury). Furthermore, the House provision did not explain how split votes would be treated (particularly if a majority found injury but estimates of damages for specific firms varied significantly).

[192] H.R. 3, Sec. 166, 100th Cong., 1st Sess. (1987).

[193] Neither the terms of the House bill or the House Report limited this to three or more final determinations regarding the same or related product. As a result, it would have been conceivable that a foreign manufacturer could have been subjected to three antidumping investigations in completely unrelated products within a period of ten years, and thereafter be subject to the presumption of intent to injure in any private action regarding any one of those products.

provisions on the grounds that they would violate GATT and the GATT Antidumping Code[194] and subject U.S. industry to retaliation by our trading partners.[195] The provisions were also opposed by a number of domestic business groups and industries, including the Business Coalition on Trade and the Retail Industry Trade Action Coalition. The final version of the Trade Act contains neither the provision for compensation awards by the ITC nor any amendments to the Antidumping Act of 1916.

[194] The GATT allows an antidumping duty "not greater in amount than the margin of dumping" as the sole remedy for dumping. Article VI.2, GATT. The GATT Antidumping Code provides that "no specific action against dumping of exports . . . can be taken except in accordance with the provisions of the General Agreement." Article 16.1, GATT Antidumping Code. The Antidumping Act of 1916 (in its present form) was allowed to remain in effect as grandfathered legislation at the time of entry into force of GATT (but not the GATT Antidumping Code). It is unclear, however, whether the legislation would continue to be regarded as grandfathered after such extensive admendments.

[195] See 30 October 1987 Letter at 14.

PART II
A Future of Subsidies Discipline

Part II. A Future of Subsidies Discipline

While antidumping thrives on its impenetrable complexity, so that even fair-minded policymakers don't want to take the time to figure out what their agencies are doing, subsidies thrive on transparency. Everyone loves "getting something for nothing" even though subsidies tend to redistribute income upwards from the average taxpayer to the (wealthier) average owner of company assets (and even with widespread shareownership by pension funds and the like, the vast majority of such assets, including non-traded companies, farms, and so on, are owned by people wealthier than the average taxpayer). But as the EC pointed out in the 1957 Treaty of Rome, subsidies can distort competition. The European Union has quite a strong subsidies discipline program run through DG Competition, but even that does not reach subsidies given by the EU itself. And no other country has any such formal discipline, relying instead on the weak feed of budgetary discipline to fend off politicians seeking to buy votes (frequently a losing battle). My article written for the European University Institute, "Subsidies Discipline Under WTO and US Rules," reviews some of those different attempts at discipline.[1]

Subsidies discipline in the GATT and the 1979 Subsidies Code was quite ineffective, most obviously because of the lack of binding dispute resolution, but more fundamentally, because of the lack of agreement to impose such discipline. The WTO Subsidies Agreement,[2] described in my article with Peggy Clarke, "The WTO Subsidies Agreement," seems to have been effective with respect to export subsidies and also import substitution subsidies, although they were on the decline in any event, probably because of their cost and relative lack of success. The Global Financial Crisis (GFC) in practice was a setback on that score, as many of the widely publicized industrial "bailouts" during the GFC contained prohibited import substitution

[1] Horlick, G., "Subsidies Discipline under the WTO and US Rules", *European Competition Law Annual 1999: Selected issues in the Field of State Aids*, Class-Dieter Ehlerman and Michelle Everson, Eds, 2001.
[2] Horlick, G. and Clarke, P., "The WTO Subsidies Agreement", 17(4), *World Competition, Law and Economics Review*, 41–54, 1994.

requirements which were not so widely publicized, and the only country to challenge those subsidies (China, through a countervailing duty case) did not pursue all aspects of the subsidies at issue.

Since all government give subsidies, they have been notably reluctant to challenge each other's gifts. Partly this is from the requirement to show adverse effects — only three such cases have been developed by the WTO Appellate Body, Brazil's challenge to the US cotton subsidies, and the US' and EU's mutual challenges to each other's subsidies to Boeing and Airbus — but several copies of Brazil's *Cotton* case, against similar US programs on rice and soybeans, have been put on hold by high prices for those commodities, and the consequent difficulty of showing damage (although it is worth noting that the price-related subsidies to those crops have virtually disappeared, so there are fewer subsidies to challenge). But a sense of embarrassment may also preclude bringing the cases — even the most hypocritical of the US steel companies condemns "subsidies," while excusing its own "tax breaks" to avoid the use of the "subsidy" word. The recent WTO Appellate Body decisions involving Boeing and Airbus may fill in some of the answers about subsidies and adverse effects in the WTO Subsidies Agreement, and possibly lead to more cases.

In the absence of much case law, one would have expected more proposals for reform in the WTO Doha negotiations but the proposals were very timid, again reflecting each country's defensive concerns.

The result is that one of the very best of the Uruguay Round WTO Agreements — the Subsidies Agreement — is starting to show its age. The Subsidies Agreement was the first serious attempt to get the rules right, so it is understandable that in hindsight some changes should be needed. There has to date been no serious discussion, just proposed tinkering around the edges. By contrast, the discussion of possible subsidies disciplines for services, in the General Agreement on Trade and Services (as required by Article 15 of that Agreement) led to some very interesting thinking, which can be found in the documents from that negotiation on the WTO website. But there is no sign of that negotiation going anywhere either.

The ideas listed below are far too radical to even be proposed within the closed WTO mechanism, but are worthy of mention, if only to provoke some thought:

- Some form of self-starting dispute mechanism or review mechanism, since it is now obvious that WTO member governments will not challenge each other in this area except on an extraordinary basis.

- A re-balancing between big countries and small countries. At present, big countries can use countervailing duties to protect the home markets of their industries, while small countries, whose industries depend on exports, can also use countervailing duties, but it doesn't protect a significant market ("The law in its majesty permits the rich and the poor alike to sleep under the bridges of Paris"),[3] so they are forced to rely on slower (and more neutral) WTO panels.
- A re-thinking of the dynamics of discipline. CVD is inherently subject to protectionist abuse, so the definition of subsidy subject to CVD should be strictly limited and protected from imaginative reinterpretation by unilateral-acting national authorities (who are subject only to ***very*** slow-acting WTO dispute resolution while the illegal duties remain in place). By contrast, the definition of "subsidy" for cases brought directly to the WTO should be made broader, and should include a wider range of types of assistance to be disciplined.

[3] Anatole France, *The Red Lily*.

The 1994 WTO Subsidies Agreement

Gary N. HORLICK* and Peggy A. CLARKE**

INTRODUCTION

The Subsidies Agreement in the 1994 World Trade Organization (WTO) Agreement (hereinafter Subsidies Agreement),[1] coupled with the enhanced, binding, general dispute resolution provisions that resulted from the Uruguay Round, will greatly expand international discipline on both subsidies and countervailing measures.

Unlike the existing 1979 Subsidies Code,[2] the Subsidies Agreement provides an internationally agreed-upon definition of subsidy for use both generally and in determining what specific practices are actionable (i.e. those practices against which either countervailing measures may be imposed or other remedies pursued). Moreover, it provides more specific standards for the conduct of a countervailing duty investigation—requiring transparency, some due process, and specific time-limits. Finally, it creates a detailed, enforceable, multinational subsidies dispute resolution system which could decrease the use of unilateral measures in addressing trade disputes.

If implemented faithfully by the WTO Members, the Subsidies Agreement should result in significant changes in their unilateral trade actions. Specifically, the United States would need to change its countervailing duty laws to bring them into conformity with the Subsidies Agreement. More important, the creation of an effective multilateral discipline and dispute resolution regime may lessen the pressure in the United States to take unilateral actions against perceived unfair trade practices by its trading partners by providing a more effective avenue of relief.

This article will describe the countervailing duty provisions of the Subsidies Agreement and how they differ from U.S. law and practice (the United States is by far the largest "user" of countervailing duty law). It will then discuss the multilateral discipline and dispute resolution regime of the Subsidies Agreement.

* O'Melveny & Myers, Washington, D.C.; formerly deputy Assistant Secretary of Commerce for Import Administration and International Trade Counsel, U.S. Senate Committee on Finance.

**O'Melveny & Myers; formerly Office of Policy, Import Administration, Department of Commerce.

[1] Final Act Embodying the Results of the Uruguay Round of Multilateral Trade Negotiations, 15 April 1994, Agreement on Subsidies and Countervailing Measures.

[2] Agreement on the Interpretation of and Application of Articles VI, XVI and XXII of the General Agreement on Tariffs and Trade.

I. Countervailing Duty Provisions

A. Subsidy definitions

The Subsidies Agreement provides a much more detailed definition of what constitutes a countervailable subsidy (these same definitions apply to subsidies for Agreement discipline purposes) than does the 1979 Code.[3] Many of the definitions—both as to what constitutes a countervailable subsidy and how to measure the benefit—follow U.S. law and practice.

1. *Article 1: Definition of a Subsidy*

Article 1 of the Subsidies Agreement defines the term subsidy (regardless of whether it is actionable) as applying to either of two situations.[4] The first is a financial contribution by a government or public body within the territory of a Member if:

(i) government practice involves a direct transfer of funds (e.g. grants, loans, and equity infusions) or potential direct transfers of liabilities (e.g. loan guarantees);

(ii) government revenue that is otherwise due is forgone or not collected (e.g. fiscal incentives such as tax credits);

(iii) the government provides goods or services other than general infrastructure, or purchases goods;

(iv) the government makes payments to a funding mechanism that carries out, or entrusts or directs a private body to carry out, one or more of the type of functions, illustrated in (i) to (iii) above, which would normally be vested in the government and the practice, in no real sense, differs from practices normally followed by governments.[5]

The second is any form of income or price support in the sense of Article XVI of the GATT.[6] For the practice to qualify as a subsidy in either situation, it must confer a benefit.[7]

Even if a practice meets this broad definition of a subsidy, it is not necessarily subject to either countervailing duty measures or Agreement discipline. Articles 2, 3, 8 and 14, discussed *infra*, identify when a subsidy may be countervailed.

2. *Article 2: Specificity*

To be found countervailable, a subsidy must be specific. Article 2 of the Subsidies Agreement provides that a subsidy is specific if it is explicitly limited to an enterprise

[3] Indeed, the 1979 Code does not provide any definition of subsidies in general. However, it does provide a list of prohibited export subsidies in an illustrative Annex to the Code.

[4] U.S. law provides no such general definition of a subsidy. U.S. law and practice are directed solely at identifying countervailable subsidies.

[5] Subsidies Agreement, Article 1.1(a)(1).

[6] Id., at 1.1(a)(2).

[7] The Subsidies Agreement does not define "benefit" but typically a subsidy confers a benefit when it puts the recipient in a better financial position than it would be, absent the government assistance.

or industry or group of enterprises or industries ("certain enterprises") within the jurisdiction of the granting authority.[8]

Article 2 states that if the legislation or the granting authority explicitly limits the subsidy to certain enterprises, the subsidy is specific.[9] This language tracks the *de jure* specificity analysis currently conducted by the U.S. Department of Commerce. However, Article 2 provides that if eligibility is limited, based on explicit, verifiable, objective criteria (i.e. criteria or conditions which are neutral, do not favour certain enterprises over others, are economic in nature, and are horizontal in application), the programme is not specific so long as eligibility is automatic and the criteria are strictly adhered to.[10] Department of Commerce (hereinafter Department) practice, although inconsistent, currently provides no exception to specificity for limitations based on objective criteria.[11]

Even if the programme appears to be non-specific, a Member may determine whether the programme is *de facto* specific if there is reason to believe the programme may, in fact, be specific.[12] In such an analysis, the investigating authority may consider the following factors:

— use by a limited number of certain enterprises;

— predominant use by certain enterprises;

— the grant of disproportionately large amounts of subsidy to certain enterprises; and

— the manner in which discretion is exercised by administering authorities.[13]

The *de facto* analysis is similar to current Department practice.[14] However, the Subsidies Agreement puts restrictions on the application of this analysis not found in U.S. law or practice. Specifically, the Agreement provides that, in determining *de facto* specificity, the investigating authorities should take account of the diversification of economic activities in the subsidizing country and the length of time the programme has been in operation.

Among the factors to consider in a *de facto* analysis is the discretionary nature of the programme. Department practice also considers this. However, the Subsidies Agreement specifies that when considering the discretionary application of a programme, the investigating authorities "shall" consider, in particular, information

[8] Subsidies Agreement, Article 2.1. Cf. the definition of specificity found in U.S. law, 19 U.S.C. § 1677(A) (ii) (1988).

[9] Id., at Article 2.1(a).

[10] Id., at Article 2.1(b).

[11] See *Certain Fresh Atlantic Groundfish from Canada*, 51 Fed. Reg. 10041, 10045 (Dept. Comm. 1986) (Industrial and Regional Development Program (IRDP) found to be a regional programme despite the fact that districts' assignment to a tier was based on neutral criteria); cf. *Certain Steel Products from Federal Republic of Germany*, 47 Fed. Reg. 39345, 39350 (Dept. Comm. 1982) (Labour assistance programmes found not to be targeted to specific regions where the aim was to relieve unemployment and eligibility was based on the unemployment level of the area).

[12] Subsidies Agreement, Article 2.1(c).

[13] Id.

[14] 19 U.S.C. § 1677 (5)(8) (1988). Department practice on specificity has been affirmed as consistent with U.S. law, *PPG Industries, Inc. v. United States*, 928 F 2d 1568, 1573 (Fed. Cir. 1991).

on the frequency with which applications for a subsidy are approved or refused and the reason for those decisions.[15]

Article 2.2 states that a programme available only to certain enterprises within a designated geographic region of the granting authority's jurisdiction is specific.[16] This represents a significant lessening of discipline from the Dunkel Draft,[17] which made all subsidies by sub-national governments, even if available to all enterprises within a certain area of the jurisdiction, specific.[18]

Article 2.3 states that any prohibited subsidy as defined in Article 3 (including low-cost loans contingent upon export performance, transportation rates more favourable for export shipments than for domestic shipments, and the excessive remission of taxes upon export) is specific.[19] This makes explicit an implicit assumption of the 1979 Code that the export subsidies enumerated in the illustrative list annexed to the Code are specific.

Finally, Article 2 requires that any determination of specificity must be "clearly substantiated" on the basis of positive evidence.[20] This final requirement of positive evidence is a significant departure from current U.S. practice. Currently, the Department presumes specificity unless positive evidence to the contrary is provided. The Subsidies Agreement changes this presumption to one of non-specificity.

3. *Article 3: Prohibited Subsidies*

In the 1979 Code, only export subsidies are prohibited.[21] The Subsidies Agreement expands this prohibition to include both export subsidies and subsidies, the receipt of which is, at least in part, contingent upon the use of domestic over imported goods.[22]

This latter category could significantly expand the definition of actionable subsidies (i.e. those subject to either Agreement discipline or countervailing duties). Under the 1979 Code, no Code discipline is explicitly available against import substitution subsidies because such subsidies are not prohibited. Moreover, at least under U.S. law, an import substitution subsidy would not be countervailable merely because it favoured domestic goods over imports. Under U.S. statute, the practice would have to provide a specific, non-commercial benefit to a certain enterprise or

[15] The refusal to disclose confidential information showing which applicants have been rejected has been a problem for some countries (e.g. *Fresh, Chilled, and Frozen Pork from Canada*, 54 Fed. Reg. 30774, 30779–80 (Dept. Comm. 1989), upheld by FTA Panel, *Fresh, Chilled, and Frozen Pork*, USA-89-1904-06 (28 September 1990).

[16] Subsidies Agreement, Article 2.2.

[17] Draft Final Act Embodying the Results of the Uruguay Round of Multilateral Trade Negotiations, MTN.TNC/W/FA, 20 December 1991.

[18] Dunkel Draft, Article 2.2. The change from the Dunkel Draft apparently was the result of a "deal" between the United States and Canada in late 1993 (which both countries will doubtless deny) in which the United States agreed to less discipline on subsidies in return for Canadian support for more trade-restrictive antidumping rules.

[19] Subsidies Agreement, Article 2.3.

[20] Id., at Article 2.4.

[21] 1979 Code, Article 9.

[22] Subsidies Agreement, Article 3.1 (". . . the following subsidies, within the meaning of Article 1 above, shall be prohibited . . . subsidies contingent, whether solely or as one of several other conditions, upon the use of domestic over imported goods.").

enterprises to be countervailable.[23] By contrast, the language of Article 3 of the Subsidies Agreement might allow an import substitution subsidy to be countervailed regardless of whether it was either *de jure* or *de facto* specific[24] or whether it provided a non-commercial benefit. This is unclear, because Article 4 of the Subsidies Agreement provides remedies for Members' use of prohibited subsidies other than the imposition of countervailing duties. Therefore, Article 3 may be interpreted as only providing a list of programmes that are always deemed specific, without otherwise addressing whether such programmes are countervailable.

4. *Article 8: Non-Actionable Subsidies*

Article 8 of the Subsidies Agreement is the counterpart to Article 3's "red light" prohibition against certain subsidies. Any subsidy falling within one of the three non-actionable categories of Article 8 cannot be subjected to countervailing duties or to Agreement discipline.

The first category covers subsidies that are not specific within the meaning of Article 2. U.S. law also limits the application of countervailing duties to "specific" subsidies.[25]

The second category of "green light" subsidies are subsidies for research and development (R&D) programmes. Assistance for R&D would not be actionable if provided to firms, higher education facilities, or research establishments acting under contract to firms if:

(i) the assistance covers not more than 75 percent of the costs of industrial research;[26] or
(ii) the assistance covers not more than 50 percent of the cost of pre-competitive development research.[27]

Additionally, the assistance must be limited exclusively to:

(i) personnel costs for staff employed exclusively in the R&D activity;
(ii) costs of buildings and equipment, including instruments, used exclusively and permanently for the R&D activity;
(iii) consultancy or equivalent services used exclusively for the R&D activity (this would include technical knowledge and patents), or
(iv) other overhead and running costs incurred directly as a result of the R&D activity.[28]

---

[23] 19 U.S.C. § 1677(5)(B) (1988).

[24] Subsidies Agreement, Article 2.3 ("Any subsidy falling under the provisions of Article 3 shall be deemed to be specific.").

[25] 19 U.S.C. § 1677(5) (1988).

[26] "Industrial research" is defined as: " . . . planned search or critical investigation aimed at discovery of new knowledge with the objective that such knowledge may be useful in developing new products, processes or services, or in bringing about a significant improvement to existing products, processes or services." Subsidies Agreement, Article 8.2(a) n. 25.

[27] "Pre-competitive development activity" is defined as: " . . . the translation of research findings into a plan, blueprint or design for new, modified or improved products, processes or services whether intended for sale or use, including the creation of a first prototype which would not be capable of competitive use." Subsidies Agreement, Article 8.2(a) n. 26.

[28] Id., at Article 8.2(a).

Both the numerical limits and the definitions are considerably broader than the R&D green light category in the Dunkel Draft (which allowed assistance only up to 25 and 50 percent, rather than 50 and 75 percent, and which stopped well short of allowing assistance for the creation of a prototype). This reflects the sudden and complete shift in the U.S. position in November/December 1993, from the Bush Administration's attempt to remove green light categories to the Clinton Administration's attempt to expand them.[29]

The Subsidies Agreement is quite different from U.S. practice regarding assistance for R&D. The United States currently will countervail assistance for R&D if it is specific and provides a non-commercial benefit (e.g. grants or low-interest loans) unless the results of the R&D are publicly available to all who choose to use those results.[30] Thus, there is a considerable tension between past U.S. practice and positions (which at times seemed to verge on the position that all subsidies, including those for R&D, are bad), and the Clinton Administration's view that the United States should be free to subsidize a wider range of activities, including R&D for the development of new technologies.

The third category of non-actionable subsidies concerns aid to disadvantaged regions within the territory of a Member given pursuant to a general framework of regional development.[31] For the subsidy to be non-actionable, each disadvantaged region must be a clearly designated, contiguous geographic area with a definable economic and administrative identity (e.g. a county or district) and must be determined to be disadvantaged based on explicit, verifiable, neutral and objective criteria.[32]

Current U.S. countervailing duty law does not provide any such safety net. Indeed, any subsidy that would be considered non-actionable under the Subsidies Agreement would be countervailable under U.S. law if it were specific and provided a non-commercial benefit. In particular, Department practice considers any regional programme to be specific regardless of how the region is determined (i.e. even if based on neutral and objective criteria).[33]

[29] One can easily imagine a meeting in which the EC negotiators, after seven years of being attacked by the United States for favouring subsidies, could watch their chief negotiator—a former EC Commissioner for Competition—lecture the United States on the need for tight discipline on subsidies.

[30] See *Certain Fresh Cut Flowers from Kenya*, 52 Fed. Reg. 9522, 9523 (Dept. Comm. 1987) (government funding of flower research was not countervailable because results of research published by government in a handbook were made available to the public for a fee upon request); *Pure Magnesium and Alloy Magnesium from Canada*, 57 Fed. Reg. 30946, 30950 (Dept. Comm. 1992) (research done by Institute of Magnesium Technology not countervailable because membership in institute is open to all parties and all parties obtain results on equal terms); *New Steel Rail, Except Light Rail, from Canada*, 54 Fed. Reg. 31991, 31997 (Dept. Comm. 1989) (research grant not countervailable because results of study were made public).

[31] Subsidies Agreement, Article 8.2(b).

[32] The term "neutral and objective" means criteria that do not favour certain regions beyond what is appropriate for the elimination or reduction of regional disparities within the framework of the regional development policy. The criteria must include a measurement of economic development based on either: (i) income per capita, household income, or GDP per capita, which must be at least 15 percent below the average for the territory concerned; or (ii) unemployment level, which must be at least 10 percent above the average for the territory concerned. Subsidies Agreement, Article 8.2(b)(ii) and (iii).

[33] See *Certain Fresh Atlantic Groundfish from Canada*, 51 Fed. Reg. at 10045 (IRDP found to be a regional programme despite fact that districts' assignment to a tier was based on neutral criteria).

Finally, Article 8.2(c) defines as non-actionable assistance to adapt to new environmental requirements (so long as the assistance is limited to 20 percent of the cost of the necessary adaptation and is given on a one-time only basis). This was the result of a last-minute Mexican proposal (drawn from a 1989 EC proposal) that the United States was unable to block (because U.S. credibility in opposing green light status had been shredded by its flip-flop on R&D subsidies).[34]

To be considered non-actionable, green light subsidies must be notified in advance to the Committee on Subsidies and Countervailing Measures.[35] The Committee, upon requests, will review the practice to determine if the requisite conditions have been met.[36] Even if the conditions of Article 8 have been met, if a Member has reason to believe that its domestic industry has suffered serious adverse effects from another Member's green light programmes, that Member may request consultations and review by the Committee. If the Committee's recommendations are not followed, the Committee would then authorize the injured Member to take countermeasures.[37]

5. *Article 14: Calculation of Subsidies*

While Article 14 is intended to provide standards for measuring the benefit conferred by certain types of actionable subsidies, it also implicitly amplifies the identification of those subsidy practices defined under Article 1 that are actionable if specific. Assuming specificity, the following subsidies are actionable under this Article:

— government provision of equity on terms inconsistent with the usual investment practices of private investor in that country;
— government loans at less than the cost of a comparable commercial loan to the receiving firm;
— government loan guarantees if the amount (including guarantee fee) the recipient pays for the guaranteed loan is less than the amount it would pay for a comparable commercial loan, including an adjustment for any differences in fees; and
— government provision of goods or services for less than adequate remuneration, or government purchase of goods for more than adequate remuneration.[38]

The treatment of government equity and loans under this Article is consistent with current Department practice. However, the government loan guarantee analysis

[34] By coincidence, the GATT Director-General, Peter Sutherland, had been the EC Competition Commissioner on whose "watch" were developed the EC State aids rules from which the Mexican proposal eventually derived.

[35] Subsidies Agreement, Article 24. This Article creates a Committee on Subsidies and Countervailing Measures composed of representatives of the signatory countries. Among its responsibilities is the establishment of a Permanent Group of Experts—a body of five, independent persons, qualified in the fields of subsidies and trade relations. The Group is to provide advice on the existence or nature of subsidies.

[36] Subsidies Agreement, Article 8.3 and 8.4. At U.S. insistence, subsidies may be found to be green light subsidies even if not notified to the Committee. Id., at Article 10, n. 35.

[37] Id., at Article 9.4.

[38] Adequacy of remuneration is to be determined based on the prevailing market conditions in the country of provision or purchase. Subsidies Agreement, Article 14(d).

is different. Department practice currently is to find a subsidy if the fee for the government guarantee is less than a comparable commercial guarantee fee.[39] The Department does not look at the interest differential unless it determines that a countervailable subsidy exists.

Finally, the analysis for the provision of goods or services or purchase of goods is different from Department practice.[40] U.S. law does not specifically identify[41] as a countervailable subsidy government procurement of a good, although the United States has indicated several times[42] that it would consider procurement countervailable. U.S. law provides that the government provision of goods or services is a countervailable subsidy if the good or service is provided to certain enterprises at a preferential rate, i.e. a rate that is lower for those enterprises than for other purchasers.[43] Thus, the United States does not consider the adequacy of the remuneration at all. In fact, if the good or service provided is usable by only a small number of enterprises or industries, the Department may find the price to be preferential even if there is no price discrimination. In such circumstances, the Department has a hierarchy of tests for preferentiality.[44] They are:

— the price the government charges for a similar good or service, adjusted for any cost differences;
— the price charged by other sellers within the government's jurisdiction for identical goods or services;
— the government's cost of providing the good or service; or
— the price paid for the identical good or service outside the government's jurisdiction.

6. *Measurement of Benefits*

Article 14 is the only Article to provide guidance on the measurement of the benefit conferred by actionable subsidies for countervailing duty purposes.[45] It

[39] *Fresh Cut Flowers from the Netherlands*, 52 Fed. Reg. 3301, 3306 (Dept. Comm. 1987) (full cost of loan examined as BIA); *Live Swine from Canada*, 50 Fed. Reg. 25097, 25105 (Dept. Comm. 1985); *New Steel Rail, Except Light Rail, from Canada*, 54 Fed. Reg. 31991, 31996–97 (Dept. Comm. 1989).

[40] At U.S. insistence, the government procurement of services was deleted as an actionable subsidy.

[41] 19 U.S.C. § 1677(5)(A)(ii)(II) (1988).

[42] *Industrial Nitrocellulose from France*, 48 Fed. Reg. 11971, 11972-73 (Dept. Comm. 1983); *Steel Rails from the Federal Republic of Germany*, 47 Fed. Reg. 42774, 42775 (1982) (notice of initiation).

[43] *Fresh Cut Flowers from the Netherlands*, 52 Fed. Reg. at 3303.

[44] See *Carbon Black from Mexico*, 51 Fed. Reg. 13269, 13272 (Dept. Comm. 1986) (prelim.) ("Preferentiality Appendix"); *Softwood Lumber from Canada*, 57 Fed. Reg. 8800, 8805 (Dept. Comm. 1992) (prelim.) (discussion of preferentiality practice of the Department); *Countervailing Duties—Notice of Proposed Rulemaking and Request for Public Comments*, 54 Fed. Reg. 23365, 23381–23382 (1989) (hereinafter Proposed Regulations).

[45] Annex IV to the Subsidies Agreement provides guidance on the measurement of the benefit for purposes of serious prejudice analysis, but specifies that this Annex applies only to that situation. For serious prejudice purposes, the Annex provides that the benefit shall be calculated as the cost to the government providing the subsidy. The U.S. approach in countervailing duty cases is to measure the benefit to the recipient. The split between Annex IV (to measure serious prejudice) and Article 14 (to measure countervailable subsidies) represents the denouement of the theological battle that the EC and the United States waged through the 1980s about whether subsidies should be measured by the "cost to the government" (the EC position, although the EC relied so frequently on "opportunity cost to government" as to blur any distinction) and "value to recipient" (the U.S. position, although Commerce refused to recognize that the value to a recipient could well be less than the face value (or cost to government) if the subsidy carried with it obligations, either explicitly—to keep an uneconomic plant open, or implicitly—to maintain a bloated work force).

requires that any calculation methodology employed by an investigating authority be provided for either in the national legislation or in the investigating authority's implementing regulations. The Department is slowly moving towards this, having published proposed countervailing duty regulations in 1989.[46] However, it has never published final regulations. Article 14 would require the Department to do so.

The measurement of the benefit under the Subsidies Agreement is based on the analysis for determining whether the subsidy is actionable. Article 14 does not specify how to measure the benefit from the government provision of equity capital. The benefit from a loan is the difference between what the recipient pays for the government loan and what it would pay for a comparable commercial loan. The benefit from a government loan guarantee is the difference between the amount the recipient pays for the guaranteed loan (including the guarantee fee) and the amount it would pay for a comparable commercial loan absent the government guarantee.

Article 14 does not specify how to measure the benefit from the government provision/purchase of a good or service. Presumably, the measure would be the difference between the actual remuneration and the "adequate" remuneration.

B. Procedures for conducting countervailing duty investigations

The Subsidies Agreement provides for a transparent investigative process that affords interested parties the opportunity to participate in the investigation. This article will highlight only those provisions that might affect U.S. practice (as the most elaborate).

Article 11 requires the administering authority, prior to initiating an investigation upon a petition, to determine on the basis of positive evidence that the petition is made "by or on behalf of" the domestic industry.[47] Specifically, for a petition to have been made "by or on behalf of" an industry, the domestic producers who support the petition must account for more than 50 percent of the total production of the like product of those producers that express either support for, or opposition to, the petition. No investigation may be initiated if the producers who support the petition account for less than 25 percent of the total production of the like product produced by the domestic industry.[48] Current Department practice is to accept at face value a petitioner's statement that the petitioner represents the domestic industry.[49] The Department will only question a petitioner's standing if a substantial proportion of the domestic industry writes to the Department to state specifically its opposition to the investigation.[50]

[46] Proposed Regulations, *supra*, footnote 44.

[47] This language clarifies the requirements for initiation. In one GATT panel, the panel found that the 1979 Anti-Dumping Code (and, presumably, the parallel 1979 Subsidies Code) required this determination. *United States—Imposition of Antidumping Duties on Swedish Stainless Steel Hollow Products*, Committee on Anti-Dumping Practices, No. 90-1160, GATT, 20 August 1990. This panel report has not been adopted by the Signatories because of the objections of the United States.

[48] Subsidies Agreement, Article 11.4.

[49] See *Pure Magnesium and Alloy Magnesium from Canada*, 57 Fed. Reg. at 30947.

[50] Typically, such a letter is only considered after the investigation has been initiated.

Article 15.3 states that when imports from more than one country are simultaneously the subject of countervailing duty investigations, the investigating authorities may cumulatively assess the effects of those imports as long as:

(i) the amount of subsidization of the imports from each country is more than *de minimis* and the volume of imports from each country is not negligible; and

(ii) cumulation is appropriate in light of the competition between the imported products and the domestic products.

Article 11.9 of the Subsidies Agreement states that the amount of a subsidy shall be considered *de minimis* if it is less than 1 percent *ad valorem*. (For developing countries, subsidies of less than 2 percent *ad valorem* will be considered *de minimis*.) Current U.S. practice is to consider a subsidy to be *de minimis* if it is less than 0.5 percent.

Article 15.5 clarifies that in determining whether the domestic industry is being injured by subsidized imports, the injury must come through the effects of the subsidized imports—the administering authority must not attribute injury caused by other factors to the subsidized imports. U.S. practice currently does not make fine distinctions between the sources of injury.

Article 19 permits the administering authority to suspend an investigation in the following two situations:

(i) the exporting government agrees to eliminate or limit the subsidy or to take other measures to limit its effects; or

(ii) the exporter agrees to revise its prices to eliminate the injurious effect of the subsidy.

U.S. regulations also permit the Department to suspend its investigation in certain circumstances.[51] The Department may suspend an investigation if:

— the exporting government or exporters accounting for substantially all the merchandise ("substantially all exporters") agree to eliminate or offset completely the net subsidy;
— the exporting government or substantially all exporters agree to cease exports;
— the exporting government or substantially all exporters agree to take measures to eliminate the injurious effect[52] of the subsidies; or
— the exporting government agrees to restrict the volume of exports to the United States.

Article 21 creates a sunset provision for countervailing duty orders. The duties shall remain in force only as long as necessary to counteract the injurious subsidization.[53] Such duties shall be terminated within five years except for good cause shown, which requires a review of the order. Such a review must determine "that the expiry of the duty would be likely to lead to continuation or recurrence of subsidization and injury" for the sunset provision to be overridden.[54] U.S. law and

[51] 19 C.F.R. § 355.18 (1991).

[52] Public interest restrictions are applied (in theory) to this type of suspension agreement. Moreover, the Department must find that the suspension agreement prevents the suppression or undercutting of prices of like products in the United States and eliminates at least 85 percent of the net subsidy.

[53] Subsidies Agreement, Article 20.1. This language is identical to language in the 1979 Code. 1979 Code, Article 4.9.

[54] Subsidies Agreement, Article 21.3.

practice do not have a specific sunset provision; however, Department regulations provide for the revocation of an order in special circumstances, i.e. when all subsidies have been eliminated or if the continuation of the order is no longer of interest to the domestic interested parties.[55]

A specific provision for preventing circumvention was added to U.S. law in 1988. Proposals for adding parallel provisions to the Agreement were included in the Dunkel Draft.[56] The Dunkel Draft differed from U.S. law in that it included a specific percentage for the requisite value-added, it covered only assembly in the importing country,[57] and it required that the exporter and assembler be related. This latter element is merely a factor to consider under U.S. law—it is not required to find circumvention.[58] At U.S. insistence, all provisions for anticircumvention measures were dropped from the Agreement. Thus, any application of countervailing duties to different like products, or the same like product from different countries, will be subject to the usual requirements of the Agreement.[59]

II. Agreement Discipline and Dispute Settlement on Subsidies

International control over the use of subsidies by Members is imposed via a two-track approach in the Subsidies Agreement.[60] One track is that of countervailing duty measures, which may be imposed by any Member experiencing injury to its domestic industry in its domestic market as an effect of the import of another Member's subsidized goods. The second track is that of Agreement discipline. Agreement discipline controls the use of subsidies both through provisions prohibiting certain practices and through provisions setting forth remedies to be pursued by any Member that believes it has been seriously prejudiced by another Member's subsidies, including situations in which a Member's domestic industries are being injured in any market by the sale of the subsidized goods of another Member.[61]

The 1979 Code has very limited disciplinary provisions. A signatory may request consultations:

(i) whenever it has reason to believe another signatory is providing an export subsidy inconsistent with the Code; or

(ii) if it has reason to believe that another signatory provides a subsidy that injures its domestic industry, nullifies or impairs its benefits under the GATT, or causes serious prejudice to its interests.

If consultations do not resolve the dispute, the parties can request a panel to review the facts and reach a conclusion. However, either party to the dispute can block adoption

---

[55] 19 C.F.R. § 355.25 (1993).

[56] Dunkel Draft at I.26-I.27 (Agreement on Subsidies and Countervailing Measures, Article 21).

[57] The U.S. statute applies in certain circumstances if assembly occurs in third countries. 19 U.S.C. § 1677j(b) (1988).

[58] 19 U.S.C. § 1677(a)(2)(B) and (b)(2)(B) (1988).

[59] Subsidies Agreement, Article 32.1.

[60] Id., at Article 10, n. 31.

[61] Id., at Article 6.3.

of the panel report. As a result, the existing Code discipline is widely perceived as ineffective.[62]

Section I of this article focused on the use of countervailing duty measures. This section will discuss the use of Agreement discipline in situations of serious prejudice.[63] It will also examine the use of disciplinary proceedings in situations of injury to a Member's domestic industry or nullification or impairment of its benefits under the WTO Agreement.

A. Serious prejudice

1. *The General Provision*[64]

A Member can initiate discipline proceedings if it believes it has been seriously prejudiced by another Member's subsidies. Serious prejudice will be presumed if:

— the total *ad valorem* subsidization[65] of a product exceeds 5 percent;[66]

— the subsidies are to cover operating losses sustained by a specific industry;

— the subsidies are to cover operating losses sustained by an enterprise and are not one-time measures, unrepeatable, given only to provide time to avoid social disruption and develop long-term solutions; or

— the subsidies are either forgiveness of government-held debt or grants to cover debt repayment.[67]

The presumption of serious prejudice can be rebutted only if the subsidizing Member demonstrates that none of the following effects resulted from the subsidies.[68] Moreover, other subsidies may be found to cause serious prejudice if at least one of the following effects exists:

— the subsidy displaces or impedes imports of a like product into the market of the subsidizing signatory;

— the subsidy displaces or impedes exports of another signatory to a third-country market;

[62] See Omnibus Trade and Competitiveness Act of 1988, Conf. Report 100–576, 100th Cong., 2d Sess, 20 April 1988, at 16–18. (. . . principal trade negotiating objective for dispute settlement in the Uruguay Round negotiations was " . . . to ensure that [dispute settlement] mechanisms within the GATT and GATT agreements provide for more effective and expeditious resolution of disputes and enable better enforcement of U.S. rights."; the principal trade negotiating objective for unfair trade practices was " . . . to improve the provisions of the GATT . . . in order to define, deter, discourage the persistant use of, and otherwise discipline unfair trade practices having adverse trade effects, including forms of subsidy . . . ").

[63] Challenges to countervailing duty issues will be handled through the normal WTO dispute settlement procedures (Subsidies Agreement, Article 30) although there is a Ministerial Declaration that: "Ministers recognize . . . the need for consistent resolution of disputes arising from antidumping and countervailing duty measures."

[64] Subsidies Agreement, Article 6.

[65] The *ad valorem* subsidization is to be calculated in accordance with the provisions of Annex IV to the Agreement, which requires that it be calculated in terms of the cost to the government. This differs from the calculation of benefits to be used for countervailing duty purposes. See *supra*, footnote 45. Moreover, non-actionable subsidies shall not be included in the calculation of the *ad valorem* subsidization. U.S. government officials have indicated that they interpret Annex IV to apply and require the cost to government measurement of the subsidy only in serious prejudice situations. For countervailing duty purposes and for all other areas of Agreement discipline, they would apply the provisions of Article 14.

[66] Annex IV also provides that in a "start-up" situation, serious prejudice can only be found if the *ad valorem* subsidization exceeds 15 percent of the total funds invested.

[67] Subsidies Agreement, Article 6.1.

[68] Id., at Article 6.2.

— the subsidy leads to price undercutting by the subsidized product as compared to the price of a like product in the same market;
— imports of the subsidized product result in price suppression or depression or lost sales in the same market; or
— the subsidy increases the world market share of the subsidizing signatory in a specific subsidized product as compared to its market share over the previous three years and this increasing trend has been consistent since the subsidy was granted.[69]

2. *The Process*

To initiate a serious prejudice challenge, a WTO Member would use the dispute settlement provisions of Article 7. The first step would be to submit a request for consultations. If consultations do not resolve the matter within sixty days, any Member involved in the dispute may refer the matter to the Dispute Settlement Body (DSB), established pursuant to the Agreement Establishing the World Trade Organization, for resolution. If a panel is established by the DSB, it must reach its conclusions within one hundred and twenty days.[70]

Annex V describes the procedures for gathering information concerning serious prejudice. It requires Members, including third-party Members, to co-operate in providing all relevant information. Annex V specifically states that, in making its determination, the Committee should draw adverse inferences from any non-co-operation by any party involved in the information gathering process.

Annex IV appears to indicate that to determine the *ad valorem* subsidization level for a serious prejudice challenge, subsidies should be measured for each company. The aggregate subsidies received by a firm in one year (the most recent twelve-month period for which sales data are available) would be divided by the recipient firm's sales of the product in the most recent twelve-month period for which sales data are provided, subject to the provisions of paragraphs 3 through 5.

How these firm-specific subsidization rates are to be aggregated to determine whether the country's *ad valorem* rate exceeds 5 percent is unclear. Equally unclear is how the requirement of paragraph 4 of Annex IV, that the threshold *ad valorem* rate for serious prejudice from firms in a start-up situation is 15 percent, ties in with the country-wide rate. Possibly, subsidies to a start-up firm would be excluded from the aggregate country calculation if they do not exceed 15 percent of the investment.

B. Other disciplinary proceedings

A Member can initiate a disciplinary proceeding not only in the case of serious prejudice, but also when it has reason to believe that another Member's subsidy practice as defined in Article 1[71]—i.e. not necessarily countervailable—is:

[69] Id., at Article 6.3.
[70] Id., at Article 7.5.
[71] Except for Annex IV purposes (i.e. the calculation of *ad valorem* subsidization for serious prejudice purposes), the Subsidies Agreement contemplates applying the same definitions of subsidies—actionable and non-actionable—to both countervailing duty proceedings and Agreement discipline proceedings.

(i) injuring the complaining party's industry; or
(ii) resulting in the nullification or impairment of its benefits under the WTO Agreement.[72]

Such proceedings also follow the provisions of Article 7.

To start the proceedings, the Member would request consultations with the subsidizing Member. Such consultations should begin as quickly as possible.

If no mutually acceptable solution has been agreed to within sixty days of this request, any party to the consultations may send the matter to the Committee. The Committee will review the matter referred to it and present its conclusions within one hundred and twenty days.

If the Committee finds that a Member's subsidy has adversely affected the interest of another Member, the subsidizing Member is required to either take steps to remove the adverse effect or agree to compensate the affected Member. If no such steps are taken within six months and if no agreement on compensation has been reached, the Committee shall authorize the affected Member to take countermeasures.

Article 7 should remedy many of the defects of the current discipline system. Currently, there are no time limitations and dispute settlement can drag on for years. The time-limits in Article 7 would complete the process within a year.

Under the current system, a signatory may block adoption of an adverse panel finding. In such situations there is no authorized action the affected signatory may take, nor is the subsidizing signatory obliged to take steps to remove the adverse effects. Under Article 7, the offending Member will no longer be able to block all action. At the very least, the affected Member will ultimately be able to take countermeasures without violating the WTO Agreement.

[72] Subsidies Agreement, Article 7.1.

CHAPTER 16

THE AGREEMENT ON SUBSIDIES AND COUNTERVAILING MEASURES

Peggy A. Clarke and Gary N. Horlick*

TABLE OF CONTENTS

* Ms. Clarke and Mr. Horlick are partners at Wilmer Cutler, Pickering, Hale and Dorr, LLP. Mr. Horlick was the first Chairman of the WTO's Permanent Group of Experts, established under Art. 25 of the ASCM. The authors wish to express their appreciation for the contributions of Kevin J. Cuddy, Andrea G. Staebler, and Sean McElduff, without whose assistance this chapter would not exist. The opinions expressed herein are solely those of the authors.

I. Introduction

The Agreement on Subsidies and Countervailing Measures ("ASCM" or "Agreement") interprets and expands on the subsidies and countervailing duty portions of Article VI and Article XVI of the General Agreement on Tariffs and Trade 1994 ("GATT 1994"). It provides disciplines both over the use of subsidies that may distort trade and over the application of countervailing duties by individual Members of the WTO designed to offset the effect of subsidies. This chapter provides a detailed overview of the rights and obligations established by the ASCM and its interaction with other portions of the WTO Agreement. It will briefly discuss the history of subsidies and countervailing measures since the initiation of the GATT in 1947 and will then discuss each provision of the ASCM in detail. A separate chapter in this book (Chapter 17) discusses injury determinations in anti-dumping and countervailing duty investigations, as governed by the ASCM and the Agreement on Implementation of Article VI of the General Agreement on Tariffs and Trade 1994, also known as the Anti-dumping Agreement or ADA.

II. Historical Perspective

A. GATT Subsidy Discipline

In 1947 when the General Agreement on Tariffs and Trade ("GATT 1947") was signed, the Contracting Parties recognized that countervailing duties could constitute non-tariff barriers to trade. Accordingly, Article VI of the GATT 1947 set out rules on the use of countervailing duties, as well as anti-dumping duties, to prevent such measures from becoming non-tariff barriers on their own. These rules included the following:

- The duty could not be in excess of the estimated bounty or subsidy determined to have been granted (Article VI:3);
- No countervailing duties could be imposed by reason of exemption from, or refund of, taxes paid when destined for consumption in the home market (Article VI:4);
- No product should be subject to both anti-dumping and countervailing duties for the same situation of dumping or export subsidization (Article VI:5);
- No duty could be imposed unless it was found that the effect of the subsidization is to cause or threaten to cause material injury to an established industry, or to materially retard the establishment of such industry, in the country of importation (Article VI:6).[1]

The GATT Contracting Parties also recognized that subsidies or dumping could cause distortions to trade and could nullify or impair benefits negotiated in the GATT 1947.[2] However, the GATT 1947 addressed only subsidies that operate "directly or indirectly to increase exports,"[3] and merely required contracting parties to notify the GATT of any such subsidies, and to discuss with other Contracting Parties the possibility of limiting them where they caused or threatened serious prejudice to the interests of those contracting

[1] This requirement was weakened by the fact that the Protocol of Provisional Application to the GATT 1947 allowed the grandfathering of pre-existing laws. Because the United States already had a countervailing duty law that did not require an injury finding, the United States took the position that Article VI:6 of the GATT 1947 did not require it to conduct an injury investigation before imposing countervailing duties.

[2] The very first GATT subsidies case so held. *See* Report of the GATT Working Party, *The Australian Subsidy on Ammonium Sulphate*, CP.4/39, BISD, Vol. II 188 (1950).

[3] *See* GATT 1947, Art. XVI:1.

parties (Article XVI:1). There was some effort to discipline the use of *export* subsidies (although unlike "dumping" the term, "export subsidy" is not defined).[4] Article XVI:4 of the GATT 1947 provided for a standstill, noting that no Contracting Party shall extend the scope of subsidization of any non-primary product beyond that existing as of January 1, 1955. Article XVI:4 also anticipated that an agreement to abolish all remaining subsidies by January 1, 1958 would be reached by the end of 1957, or if not, that the standstill should be extended until such time as an agreement was reached.[5] However, no such agreement was reached and the Contracting Parties adopted an annual standstill agreement only until 1962.[6]

Despite the goal of reaching agreement on the elimination of export subsidies by the end of 1957, subsidies and countervailing duties were not the subject of further extensive negotiation until the Tokyo Round, which concluded in 1979.[7]

B. The 1979 GATT Subsidies Code[8]

By the time of the Tokyo Round of tariff negotiations, the use of subsidies and countervailing duties had become a more contentious issue. In part as a result of the lowering of tariffs, the use of non-tariff barriers and the impact of subsidies raised the level of interest in developing discipline over the use of both subsidies and countervailing duty procedures.[9]

While countries such as the United States sought greater discipline on the use of subsidies, there was significant counter-pressure to apply greater discipline to the imposition of countervailing duties, in particular to require the application of an injury test to all imports.

[4] *Compare* GATT 1947, Art. VI:1 *with* GATT 1947 Art. XVI:1.

[5] GATT 1947, Ad Art. XVI:4. The standstill was periodically extended. *See, e.g.*, GATT Declaration, *Extension of the Standstill Provisions of Article XVI:4*, BISD, 9th Supp. 33 (1960).

[6] In 1962, a declaration applying the obligations of Article XVI:4 was opened for signatures. However, for numerous reasons, many Contracting Parties were unwilling to sign the declaration. Thus, until the WTO Agreement, Article XVI:4 commitments were only binding on the few Contracting Parties that had signed onto the 1962 declaration.

[7] An Experts Group was formed in 1959 to consider the use of anti-dumping and countervailing duties; however, due to time constraints, the Group limited itself to anti-dumping duties. *See* Report of the GATT Working Group, *Anti-Dumping and Countervailing Duties*, L/978, BISD, 8th Supp. 145 (1959). In 1960, a GATT Working Party established an illustrative (non-exhaustive) list of export subsidies. *See* Report of the GATT Working Party, Provision of Article XVI:4, BISD, 9th Supp. 185 (1960). In contrast, dumping and anti-dumping duties had been the subject of serious negotiations, and an agreement in the Kennedy Round. *See* Kenneth W. Dam, The GATT: Law and the International Economic Organization, pp. 174–177 (1970), and Chapter 11 of this book. After the Kennedy Round, the Contracting Parties again tried to address the subsidy issue. In December 1967, a GATT Working Party was formed. However, in large part due to a dispute between the United States and the European Communities, no agreement could be reached on the terms of reference and the Working Party never met. *See The Tokyo Round of Multilateral Trade Negotiations*, Report by the Director-General of the GATT at 55 (1979).

[8] *Agreement on Interpretation and Application of Articles VI, XVI and XXIII of the General Agreement on Tariffs and Trade*, BISD, 26th Supp. 56 (1980) ("*1979 Subsidies Code*").

[9] Additionally, in the early 1970s the United States expanded the coverage of its countervailing duty laws to include goods that entered the U.S. on a duty-free basis. Because these goods previously had not been subject to countervailing duties, the United States could not claim the protection of the Protocol of Provisional Application. In conformity with its GATT obligations, it therefore required an injury finding before duty-free goods could be subject to countervailing duties. As noted above, the United States, the main user of countervailing duty procedures, did not apply the injury test generally because it claimed the grandfathering of its existing laws under the Protocol of Provisional Application.

At the end of the Tokyo Round, the GATT Director General stated:

> The issue of government subsidies, and the countervailing duties that are applied to offset them, has been one of the most difficult, sensitive and important of the Tokyo Round negotiations. Production and export subsidies have had a growing and distorting influence on international trade, often protecting inefficient production at the expense of competitive industries. The use of countervailing duties has grown proportionately, and resort to both measures has been encouraged by increasing protectionist pressures over the past few years.[10]

The outcome was the 1979 Subsidies Code, which contained a "two-track" approach. The first track instituted disciplines for imposing countervailing duties, including detailed requirements for an injury finding,[11] while the second track contained disciplines on the use of subsidies. The discipline on the use of subsidies continued to reflect the considerable disagreement among the Contracting Parties regarding the benefits and costs of subsidies. The Code prohibited the use of export subsidies.[12] However, that prohibition did not apply to export subsidies for primary products (which, therefore, exempted agricultural products from any prohibition on the use of export subsidies) and developing countries were also exempted from the prohibition.[13]

Annex I to the Subsidies Code provided an "Illustrative List" of potential export subsidies. In addition, Article 11 contained the first statements on the use of domestic subsidies. This Article is notorious for its ambiguity, reflecting the division of views among the Contracting Parties. Article 11 noted that on the one hand there are many legitimate policy reasons for granting domestic subsidies, but that on the other hand there is recognition that such subsidies may nullify and impair benefits accruing to Contracting Parties under the GATT.

Article 11.3 contained the language that led to the practice of requiring a finding of specificity with respect to domestic subsidies before such subsidies could be countervailed.[14] It noted that the aims identified in paragraph 1 may be obtained by means of subsidies granted with the aim of giving advantages to "certain" enterprises, either by granting such subsidies regionally or by sector. It also contained an illustrative, but non-exhaustive, list of the forms such subsidies might take. This

[10] General Agreement on Tariffs and Trade, *Multilateral Negotiations, Statement by GATT Director-General on Tokyo Round, reprinted in* 18 I.L.M. 553, 569 (1979).

[11] The injury requirements were negotiated as part of the negotiations on the Anti-dumping Agreement and the language negotiated there was transferred into the Subsidies Code. The United States ultimately took the position in its national legislation implementing the Tokyo Round Agreements that it need only extend the injury test to products from countries that were signatories to the 1979 Subsidies Agreement, rather than to all Contracting Parties, or to countries that made similar commitments to the United States. This was challenged by India as a denial of Most Favored Nation ("MFN") treatment, but the dispute was settled without a ruling or change in practice. *See* ROBERT HUDEC, ENFORCING INTERNATIONAL TRADE LAW: THE EVOLUTION OF THE MODERN GATT LEGAL SYSTEM, (1993). *See also,* Report of the GATT Panel (adopted), *United States—Denial of Most-Favored-Nation Treatment as to Non-Rubber Footwear from Brazil*, DS18/R, BISD, 39th Supp. 128, 153–154 (1992) (finding no justification for retroactively applying an injury test to duty-free merchandise but not to dutiable merchandise, and, therefore finding a violation of GATT Article I:1 MFN requirements).

[12] 1979 Subsidies Code, Art. 9.

[13] Article 10 did however establish certain limits on the use of export subsidies with respect to primary products. Specifically, parties agreed not to grant export subsidies on primary products in a manner that resulted in that Contracting Party's primary product "having more than an equitable share of world export trade in such product." *Id.*, Art. 10.1. *See also, id.*, Art. 14.2.

[14] The specificity issue is discussed in detail in the commentary on Article 2 of the ASCM, *infra*.

provided substantial latitude to define what constituted a subsidy for countervailing duty purposes.

The 1979 Subsidies Code contained little effective discipline on subsidies. It provided for consultations[15] or resort to conciliation and general dispute settlement. In addition, any panel findings could be blocked by the losing party and frequently were (particularly in the later years prior to the entry into effect of the WTO Agreement).

Because subsidies were an area of considerable controversy, few countries ultimately signed onto the 1979 Subsidies Code, which only applied to those Contracting Parties to the GATT 1947 that specifically agreed to it.[16]

C. The Uruguay Round Negotiations

It soon became clear that the 1979 Subsidies Code had not resolved the problems of subsidies and countervailing measures. In 1985, the GATT Secretariat released a "Report of Eminent Persons on Problems Facing the International Trade System."[17] In this Report, the Eminent Persons stated that the increasing use of subsidies and the abuse of countervailing measures (as well as the growth in "voluntary export restraints") had resulted in the failure of the world economy to benefit from the promises of trade liberalization arising from the Tokyo Round. They also stated that the 1979 Subsidies Code had proven inadequate.[18] One particular need with respect to subsidies noted by the report was the need for a clear definition of what was included within the term "subsidy."[19]

As a result, the Uruguay Round of negotiations was launched with a mandate to improve "GATT disciplines relating to all subsidies and countervailing measures that affect international trade."[20] The main objective was "to restore the equilibrium of rights and obligations in terms of equivalent disciplines regarding subsidies on the one hand and countervailing measures on the other . . . "[21] The main concern was to improve disciplines in order to eliminate distortions to trade caused either by the use of subsidies or the unilateral application of countervailing measures. At the first meeting of the negotiating group, numerous concerns were identified. These were summarized in the minutes of that meeting, as follows:

> Several delegations considered that the international disciplines over the use of subsidies in world trade had faded and that there was little or no consensus over the meaning of vital provisions of the GATT and the Subsidies Code (hereinafter called "the Agreement"). Some rules were so vague as to invite differences of interpretation, some others were so

[15] *Id.*, Art. 12.

[16] The signatories to the 1979 Subsidies Code (both the original signatories and those who signed later) were: Argentina, Australia, Austria, Brazil, Canada, Chile, Colombia, Egypt, the European Economic Community, Finland, Hong Kong, India, Indonesia, Israel, Japan, Korea, New Zealand, Norway, Pakistan, Philippines, Sweden, Switzerland, Turkey, United States, and Uruguay.

[17] General Agreement on Tariffs and Trade: *Report of Eminent Persons on Problems Facing the International Trade System*, *reprinted in* 24 I.L.M. 716 (1985) ("*Leutwiler Report*").

[18] *Id.* at 735.

[19] *Id.*

[20] *GATT Ministerial Declaration on the Uruguay Round of Multilateral Trade Negotiations*, Doc. No. MIN.DEC. (September 20, 1986) *reprinted in* 25 I.L.M. 1623, 1626 (1986).

[21] *See* Negotiating Group on Subsidies and Countervailing Measures ("NGSCM"): *Checklist of Issues for Negotiations*, Note by the Secretariat, Doc. No. MTN. GNG/NG10/W/9, at ¶ I (September 7, 1987) ("*Checklist*").

> weak as to provide few constraints over subsidy practices that adversely affected the interests of other countries. Furthermore, the dispute settlement provisions had not been able to provide effective recourse against these practices. It was also said that in certain instances, the GATT and the Agreement drew distinctions between permitted and prohibited subsidy practices that appeared to have little basis in sound economic policy. Some delegations thought that the problem was not only one of inadequacies, because even those rules which were clear had not been observed by governments. Several delegations pointed out that a number of problems existed also in the area of countervailing measures where loopholes in the existing rules permitted unilateral practices and interpretations, resulting in considerable arbitrariness, uncertainty and harassment of exporters. These problems were particularly acute for those developing country participants which, despite continuing efforts, could not obtain the Agreement's treatment from one important signatory [*i.e.*, the United States, the most significant user of countervailing measures].[22]

Thus, negotiations occurred on a broad range of issues. Among the most contentious were the balance between subsidy disciplines versus disciplines over the use of countervailing measures, special treatment for and the graduation of developing countries, and the definition of subsidy (including whether some subsidies were acceptable and others not).[23] A series of draft texts were issued through 1990. In December 1990, the overall negotiations were suspended because of an inability to resolve an impasse on agriculture—including subsidies—at the Brussels Ministerial Meeting. Chairman Dunkel tried to revive the negotiations in 1991 and late in the year issued a document entitled "Draft Final Act Embodying the Results of the Uruguay Round of Multilateral Trade Negotiations."[24]

The final text of the Agreement on Subsidies and Countervailing Measures, ultimately agreed to in 1994, contains only a few changes from the language of the *Dunkel Text*.[25]

[22] *See* NGSCM: Meeting of 16–17 March 1987, Note by the Secretariat, MTN.GNG/NG10/1 at ¶ 5 (March 27, 1987).

[23] In 1988, the United States proposed eliminating the distinctions between primary and non-primary export subsidies. NGSCM: Communication from the United States, MTN.GNG/NG10/W/20 (June 15, 1988). Certain negotiators insisted that any discussions involving agricultural subsides could not be addressed until agreement was reached in the Negotiating Group on Agriculture, while other countries sought to limit the discussions concerning government practices regarding natural resources. *See, e.g.*, NGSCM: Meeting of 28–29 June 1988, Note by the Secretariat, MTN.GNG/NG10/8 (July 11, 1988); NGSCM: Meeting of 28–29 June 1989, Note by the Secretariat, MTN.GNG/NG10/12 (July 14, 1989); and Meeting of 30 November—1 December 1989, Note by the Secretariat, MTN.GNG/NG10/15 (January 10, 1990). As a result, there was no mention of primary products in the various draft texts, pending the outcome of the agriculture negotiations. Thus, the distinction between primary and non-primary product subsidies (other than agricultural subsidies) was eliminated in the final text.

[24] *GATT Draft Final Act Embodying the Results of the Uruguay Round of Multilateral Trade Negotiations*, Doc. No. MTN.TNC/W/FA (December 20, 1991) ("*Dunkel Text*").

[25] The purpose of this chapter is not to provide a detailed description of the history of the Agreement or of the negotiations leading to the final agreement. This history is discussed in a number of places. *See, e.g.*, JOHN JACKSON, THE WORLD TRADING SYSTEM (1997); Gary N. Horlick and Peggy A. Clarke, *The 1994 WTO Subsidies Agreement*, 17 J. WORLD COMPETITION 41 (1994); Terry Collins-Williams and Gerry Salembier, *International Discipline on Subsidies: The GATT, the WTO and the Future Agenda*, 30 J. WORLD TRADE 5 (1996); G. Depayre, *The Results of the Uruguay Round Negotiations in the Field of Subsidies and Countervailing Measures*, in THE URUGUAY ROUND RESULTS: A EUROPEAN LAWYERS' PERSPECTIVE, College of Europe, 18/19 (1994); and THE GATT URUGUAY ROUND: A NEGOTIATING HISTORY (1986–1992), (Terence P. Stewart ed. 1994).

III. The Agreement on Subsidies and Countervailing Measures

The Agreement on Subsidies and Countervailing Measures that grew out of the Uruguay Round negotiations greatly expanded international discipline on both subsidies and countervailing measures.

Unlike the 1979 Subsidies Code or the GATT 1947, the ASCM provides an internationally agreed-upon definition of the term subsidy for use both generally identifying subsidies (whether or not actionable) and in determining what specific practices are actionable (*i.e.*, those practices against which either countervailing measures may be imposed or multilateral remedies pursued). Moreover, it provides more specific standards for the conduct of a countervailing duty investigation—requiring transparency, some due process, and specific time limits.[26] In addition, it established special detailed, enforceable rules for disputes involving subsidies in the context of the WTO dispute resolution system.[27]

Finally, in a significant change from the 1979 Subsidies Code, the ASCM is an integral part of the WTO Agreement, which must be interpreted as a whole. Prior to 1995, signatories to the 1979 Subsidies Code had the choice of bringing a subsidy dispute under *either* Articles VI and XVI of the GATT 1947 *or* under the 1979 Subsidies Code, as long as the other party to the dispute was also a signatory to the 1979 Subsidies Code.[28] This enabled parties to "forum shop" for the result they wanted. The Philippines-Brazil dispute put an end to such forum shopping and confirmed the unified nature of the WTO Agreement.

The Philippines resorted to WTO dispute settlement in order to challenge Brazil's 1995 decision to impose countervailing duties on imports of desiccated coconut from the Philippines, based on an investigation initiated prior to entry into force of the WTO Agreement. Article 32.3 of the ASCM states that the ASCM applies only to investigations or reviews initiated pursuant to an application made *after* entry into force of the WTO Agreement. While agreeing that the ASCM did not apply, the Philippines argued that Article VI of the GATT 1994 established rights and obligations applicable to such transitional procedures. Therefore, according to the Philippines, it had the right to invoke Article VI of the GATT 1994.[29]

The Panel, affirmed by the Appellate Body, found that the WTO Agreement was a unified whole to be interpreted together.

> The SCM Agreements do not merely impose *additional* substantive and procedural obligations on a potential user of countervailing measures. Rather the SCM Agreements and Article VI together define, clarify and in some cases modify the whole package of rights and obligations of a potential user of countervailing measures.[30]

[26] These standards are very similar to those imposed by the Agreement on Implementation of Article VI of the General Agreement on Tariffs and Trade 1994 on anti-dumping investigations. *See* Chapter 11 of this book.

[27] The problem of enforcement remains an issue. While the adoption of Panel decisions effectively can no longer be blocked, countries have developed many techniques for delaying implementation as long as possible.

[28] *See, e.g.*, Report of the GATT Panel (adopted), *United States-Countervailing Duties on Fresh, Chilled and Frozen Pork, Complaint by Canada*, BISD, 38th Supp. 30 (1991); Report of the GATT Panel (adopted), *European Economic Community-Payments and Subsidies Paid to Processors and Producers of Oilseeds and Related Animal-Feed Proteins, Complaint by the United States*, BISD, 37th Supp. 86 (1990).

[29] *See* Report of the Appellate Body, *Brazil-Measures Affecting Desiccated Coconut*, WT/DS22/AB/R at 5 (1997). Ms. Clarke was counsel to Brazil in this dispute. It should be noted that the United States, as a third party intervener, supported this interpretation of the separability of the rights and obligations of the ASCM and the GATT 1994, Art. VI.

[30] *Id.* at 16 (emphasis in original).

Therefore, because ASCM Article 32.3 precluded the application of the ASCM to the dispute, it also precluded the application of the GATT 1994, since both are integral parts of a single treaty—the WTO Agreement.

Aside from the unified nature there are other substantive differences from the 1979 Subsidies Code. International discipline over the use of subsidies by Members of the WTO is imposed through a two-track approach in the ASCM.[31] One track, known as "Track One", is that of unilateral countervailing duty measures, which may be imposed by any Member experiencing injury to its domestic industry in its domestic market as an effect of the import of another Member's subsidized goods. The ASCM recognizes the right of Members to take unilateral action in this fashion, but regulates the way in which they do so in order to prevent countervailing duties being used in a protectionist manner. "Track Two" refers to the use of multilateral measures through the discipline of the Agreement.[32] The Agreement controls the use of subsidies both through provisions prohibiting certain practices and through provisions setting forth remedies to be pursued by any Member that believes it has been seriously prejudiced by another Member's subsidies, including situations in which a Member's domestic industries are being injured in *any* market by the sale of the subsidized goods of another member.[33]

The 1979 Subsidies Code had very limited disciplinary provisions. A signatory could request a panel,[34] however, either party to the dispute could block adoption of the panel report and, in the 1980s, parties frequently did.[35] In contrast, the ASCM provides specific procedures, definitions of subsidies and "serious prejudice," and binding dispute resolution. As such, it is likely to be used much more frequently than the previous system.[36]

The Agreement is divided into several parts, discussed in detail in the remainder of this Chapter. Part I of the Agreement provides a definition of the term "subsidy. Part II deals with prohibited subsidies, which may be challenged by a Member without any showing of harm to that Member. Part III covers actionable subsidies, which while not prohibited, may be challenged by another Member whose interests are harmed by such subsidies. Part IV defines three types of subsidy that are not actionable, although this part of the Agreement is now in abeyance. Part V sets forth detailed rules covering the imposition of countervailing measures. The remaining parts of the Agreement deal with various procedural issues, as well as providing special and differential treatment for developing countries.

PART I—General Provisions

Part I of the Agreement deems a subsidy to exist if there is a "financial contribution" and a "benefit" is thereby conferred. It also provides that to be actionable under the Agreement

[31] ASCM, Art. 10, n. 35.

[32] The Track One remedy is faster and more effective than Track Two, since it results in the imposition of countervailing duties, whereas Track Two merely produces a recommendation that the Member come into compliance with the ASCM, and implementation is often lengthy. However, Track Two is the only available remedy where subsidies hurt a Member's exports to a third country or to the subsidizing Member, since countervailing measures only address harmful imports into the complaining Member's domestic market.

[33] ASCM, Art. 6.3.

[34] *1979 Subsidies Code*, Art. 12.

[35] Of the fifteen GATT panel disputes brought under GATT Articles VI, XVI, or the 1979 Subsidies Code from 1980 on, adoption of eight was blocked at least temporarily. In 1994 and 1995, three of the decisions that had previously been blocked were adopted with the completion of the Uruguay Round negotiations.

[36] From 1947 through 1994, there are records of resort to dispute resolution proceedings 42 times on subsidy and countervailing measures issues (subsidy disputes under GATT Articles VI, XVI or the 1979 Subsidies Code). Between January 1, 1995 and June 14, 2002, there have been 28 requests for consultations and 15 requests for panels involving subsidy disputes.

or to be subject to countervailing measures, a subsidy must be "specific," as defined in Article 2.

Article 1: Definition of a Subsidy

One of the key concerns expressed as the negotiating countries began the subsidy negotiations in the Uruguay Round was that there was a lack of discipline on the use of subsidies because there was no consensus on the definition of what constituted a subsidy. The resulting agreement contained several definitional provisions.

Article 1 of the ASCM defines the term "subsidy" as applying to either of two situations. The first is a financial contribution by a government or public body within the territory of a Member. The second is any form of income or price support in the sense of Article XVI of the GATT.[37] For the practice to qualify as a subsidy in either situation, it must confer a benefit on the recipient.

The two-step definition: a financial contribution (or price or income support) and a benefit conferred thereby, makes clear that not all government actions constitute subsidies. It is possible for the government to make a financial contribution that does not confer a benefit. An example would be a government loan at market rates. In such case, the contribution would not be a subsidy. Similarly, and perhaps more controversially, it is possible for a government to provide a benefit but not a financial contribution. An example would be a government restraint on exports, which may benefit users of the product by lowering the price in the domestic market, but is not a financial contribution.[38] Again, no subsidy is provided in such a case.

This two-step definition reflected a compromise between two broad schools of thought on the definition of a subsidy. During the negotiations the controversy was summarized by the GATT Secretariat as follows:

> Some delegations proposed a number of criteria to define an actionable subsidy while some others considered that the category of actionable subsidies should rather be a residual category, i.e., comprising those subsidies not fulfilling the criteria for either prohibited or non-actionable subsidies. Criteria proposed under the first approach were that a subsidy (i) had to confer a quantifiable benefit to the recipient, (ii) be limited to actions which imply expenditure of public funds or otherwise cost to a government (including revenue foregone) and (iii) be specific to a firm or an industry (the concept of specificity covering de jure and de facto specificity). Other delegations said that although they were not objecting to those criteria, they did not consider them as covering all cases. In their view, a charge on the public account was not always a necessary criterion for a subsidy to be countervailable or otherwise actionable. Other measures which were dependent for their enforcement on government action should also be included, for example any government action which conferred a benefit to the recipient firm.[39]

The final language reflected a rejection of the second approach. The United States (the chief proponent of the second approach) had sought to include a provision in the definition

[37] ASCM, Art. 1.1(a)(1) and (2). A 1960 Panel report, considered what constituted an "income or price support" within the meaning of Article XVI of the GATT 1947. The panel generally agreed that a system "under which a government, by direct or indirect methods, maintains such a price by purchases and resale at a loss is a subsidy." Report of the Panel, *Review Pursuant to Article XVI:5*, (adopted May 24, 1960) BISD, 9th Supp. 188, 191. The Panel also considered that there could be methods by which a government maintained a fixed price above the world price without resort to a subsidy. *Id.*

[38] Report of the WTO Panel, *United States—Measures Treating Export Restraints as Subsidies*, WT/DS194/R (2001) at ¶ 8.73 ("*U.S. Export Restraints*").

[39] *See NGSCM: Meeting of 30 November—1 December 1989*, Note by the Secretariat, MTN.GNG/NG10/15 at ¶ 6, (January 10, 1990).

that would permit action to be taken against measures that it claimed were trade distorting such as targeting[40] and other industrial policy measures.[41] However, Article 1.1 reflects a balancing of the various definitions proposed for a subsidy, between the U.S. proposal of any government action that conferred a benefit and other proposals that the definition should include only those government actions which resulted in a charge on the public accounts or a cost to the government.[42] It is possible to have a financial contribution that does not involve a cost to the government; for example, if the government were to provide a loan to a company at below market interest rates but above the government's cost of borrowing and administration, such a loan would fall within the definition of a subsidy although there would ultimately be no charge on the public accounts.[43]

1. Financial Contribution. Article 1.1(a)(1) defines the term "financial contribution," which is the first prong of the definition of a subsidy. It requires a financial contribution by a government or any public body, including quasi-governmental entities. Financial contribution is defined more broadly than a charge on the public accounts. Article 1.1(a)(1) identifies four categories of financial contribution, and makes clear that the four categories are an exclusive list of financial contributions, not an illustrative one.

The first category is the least controversial and the least open to debate. It involves a *direct transfer of funds* (*e.g.*, grants, loans, and equity infusions) and any potential direct transfers of funds (*e.g.*, loan guarantees).[44]

The second category indicates that there is a financial contribution if the government or public body *foregoes revenue that is otherwise due*.[45] In the *FSC* case, the Appellate Body clarified that this does not mean entitlement to the funds in the abstract because in theory, the government could claim entitlement to tax all revenues.[46] Thus, to establish whether revenue has been foregone, it is necessary to determine whether the definitions and tax regime applied established an initial government entitlement to the general category of

[40] In an early communication from the United States to the NGSCM, the United States (the chief proponent of addressing targeting through the ASCM) defined "targeting" as "a government plan or scheme of coordinated measures to assist specific export-oriented industries," and noted that not all practices encompassed by this term were clearly covered by subsidy disciplines. NGSCM: Communication from the United States, MTN.GNG/NG10/W/1 at ¶ III.A (March 16, 1987).

[41] *See, e.g., id.* (seeking to "clarify what remedies are available for the trade distortions and economic damage associated with targeting and other industrial policy measures that affect trade"); NGSCM: *Elements of the Framework for Negotiations,* Submission by the United States, MTN.GNG/NG10/W/29 (November 22, 1989) (proposing the following definition of subsidy "A subsidy is any government action or combination of government actions which confers a benefit on the recipient firm(s)").

[42] *See, e.g., NGSCM: Communication from the EEC,* MTN.GNG/NG10/W/7 (June 11, 1987) ("subsidies in international trade exist only when a financial charge has been incurred by a government or administrative authority on behalf of a beneficiary").

[43] The loan would provide a benefit to the recipient (by enabling it to borrow at below-market rates) and would meet the definition of financial contribution found in ASCM, Article 1.1(a)(1)(i) without cost to the government, since the government would receive back more in interest than it cost it to borrow. Article 1.1(b) requires that a benefit be conferred thereby. In *Canadian Civilian Aircraft I* the Appellate Body clarified that this meant a benefit to a recipient. Report of the Appellate Body, *Canada—Measures Affecting the Export of Civilian Aircraft*, AB-1999–2, WT/DS70/AB/R (1999) at ¶ 154 ("*Canadian Civilian Aircraft I*").

[44] ASCM, Art. 1.1(a)(1)(i).

[45] *Id.*, Art. 1.1(a)(1)(ii).

[46] *See* Report of the Appellate Body, *United States—Tax Treatment For "Foreign Sales Corporations"*, AB-1999-9, WT/DS108/AB/R (2000) ("*FSC*") at ¶ 90 ("This cannot, however, be entitlement in the abstract, because governments, in theory, could tax *all* revenues. There must, therefore, be some defined, normative benchmark against which a comparison can be made between the revenue actually raised and the revenue that would have been raised 'otherwise'". (emphasis in original)).

revenue and then exempted the revenue at issue from that entitlement. Applying that reasoning, the Appellate Body found that U.S. law defined taxable income to include the revenue that was subsequently excluded through the Foreign Sales Corporations provisions of the Internal Revenue Code.[47] Similarly in *Canadian Autos*, the Appellate Body found that because the Canadian government had established a 6.1 percent MFN import duty on imports of automobiles and then exempted from payment of that duty automobiles that met the terms of the Motor Vehicles Tariff Order, that exemption constituted revenue foregone that was otherwise due.[48]

The third category addresses the government *provision of goods or services* (other than general infrastructure) or the *purchase of goods*.[49] This category has the potential for controversy regarding the question of what constitutes a good and what constitutes a service. The advent of electronic commerce has raised the question of whether there exists another category of "thing" that is neither a good nor a service (*e.g.*, in which category does intellectual property fall). If so, does the government provision or purchase of this third category ever constitute a financial contribution?

A recent dispute addresses this provision in some detail.[50] Canada argued that the United States' preliminary determination that Canada's stumpage programs provided a good for less than adequate remuneration were not in accordance with the WTO. First it argued that "stumpage" (which Canada stated is the right to harvest standing timber) is not a good. The Panel however, concluded that what Canada was providing was standing timber, the "stumpage" at issue was merely the means of providing the timber.[51] The Panel further found that "timber" was a good within the meaning of the ASCM, noting that the term "goods" in Art. 1.1(a)(1)(iii) referred to "tangible or movable personal property, other than money."[52] The Panel also rejected a Canadian argument that Article 1.1(a)(1)(iii) does not apply to rights to exploit natural resources *in situ*.[53] According to the Panel, the term "goods and services" covers "the full spectrum of in-kind transfers the government may undertake by providing resources to an enterprise," the only exception being the one explicitly mentioned in Article 1.1(a)(1)(iii), the provision of general infrastructure.[54]

The fourth category is perhaps the most controversial and contains several parts. First, it states that a financial contribution exists when a government (but not necessarily a public body) makes *payments to a funding mechanism*. Second, a financial contribution

[47] *Id.* at ¶ 95.

[48] Report of the Appellate Body, *Canada—Certain Measures Affecting the Automotive Industry*, AB-2002-2, WT/DS139 and 142/AB/R (2000) at ¶¶ 90–94 ("*Canadian Autos*").

[49] ASCM, Art. 1.1(a)(1)(iii).

[50] Report of the WTO Panel (not appealed), *United States—Preliminary Determinations with Respect to Certain Softwood Lumber from Canada*, WT/DS236/R (2002) ("*Softwood Lumber II*"). On May 3, 2002, Canada requested establishment of a Panel under the DSU with respect to the U.S. final determination to impose countervailing duties on imports of softwood lumber from Canada. The United States based its final subsidy analysis on the same basic methodology that it used for the challenged preliminary determination.

[51] *Id.* at ¶ 7.17 ("In our view the only way to supply *standing* timber to harvesting companies is by allowing them to harvest the timber. We consider that this is precisely what the stumpage agreements do. We therefore find that standing timber is provided to the tenure holders through the provincial stumpage programmes." (Emphasis in original)).

[52] *Id.* at ¶ 7.23. The Appellate Body subsequently adopted a somewhat broader definition of the term "goods," noting that the French and Spanish terms used included a wide range of property. *See United States—Final Countervailing Duty Determination with Respect to Certain Softwood Lumber from Canada*, AB-2003-6, WT/DS257/AB/R (2004) at ¶ 59 ("*Softwood Lumber III Appellate Body Report*").

[53] *Softwood Lumber II*, *supra* note 50, at ¶ 7.26.

[54] *Id.* at ¶ 7.28. This does not mean that the government provision of a good or service necessarily provides a subsidy, it must still be specific and provide a benefit to the recipient.

exists if a government *"entrusts or directs" a private body* to carry out one or more of the type of functions described in the first three categories, "which would normally be vested in the government and the practice, in no real sense, differs from practices normally followed by governments."[55]

Only one panel has addressed this category to date and there are no relevant Appellate Body discussions. In *U.S.—Export Restraints*, Canada claimed that U.S. law and practice established that the United States would find that restraints on exports of input products constituted a subsidy to the downstream product in violation of the ASCM.[56] Article 1.1(a)(1)(iv) provides that, in order for there to be a financial contribution, a government must entrust or direct a private body "to carry out one or more of the type of functions illustrated" in the first three categories; "which would normally be vested in the government," and that "the practice, in no real sense, differs from practices normally followed by governments."[57] The dispute decision hinged on the meaning of the term "entrusts or directs." The Panel found that the term encompassed three elements: (1) "an explicit and affirmative action, be it delegation or command;" (2) "addressed to a particular party;" and (3) "the object of which action is a particular task or duty."[58] In addition, the Panel found that the second two elements were aspects of the first element—an explicit and affirmative action of delegation or command.[59] It held that export restraints did not fall within this definition of financial contribution.[60]

In making this finding, the Panel rejected the argument of the United States that read this provision much more broadly to include actions, the effect of which was functionally equivalent to an affirmative action. According to the Panel,

> [g]overnment entrustment or direction is thus very different from the situation in which the government intervenes in the market in some way, which may or may not have a particular result simply based on the given factual circumstances and the exercise of free choice by the actors in that market.[61]

In making such a finding, the Panel reaffirmed that not all government actions that confer a benefit necessarily constitute a subsidy. Thus, the Panel reaffirmed the negotiated balance of the subsidy definition as discussed above.

[55] ASCM, Art. 1.1(a)(1)(iv). In *U.S. Export Restraints*, the Panel notes with approval the interpretation by the Group of Experts of a 1960's panel on subsidies "reference to 'practice . . . in no real sense different from that normally followed by governments' was a general reference that to the *delegation* to private parties of particular government functions of taxation and expenditure of revenue, and *not* a reference to government market interventions in the general sense." *U.S. Export Restraints*, *supra* note 39, at ¶ 8.72 (emphasis in original).

[56] *U.S. Export Restraints, supra* note 38. Prior to the completion of the Uruguay Round, the United States had countervailed against restraints on leather exports imposed by the Government of Argentina and restraints on exports of logs imposed by the Government of British Colombia. *See*, *Leather From Argentina*, 55 Fed. Reg. 40,212 (Dep't Comm. October 2, 1990) (final determ.); *Certain Softwood Lumber Products From Canada*, 57 Fed. Reg. 22,570 (Dep't Comm. May 28, 1992) (final determ.). In each case the United States reasoned that the export restraints resulted in domestic users of the restrained products obtaining inputs at lower prices than would have prevailed without the restraints. Canada argued that the legislative history of the Uruguay Round implementing legislation and regulations promulgated under that legislation indicated that the United States would continue to countervail export restraints. Canada's challenge was to the U.S. law and practice "as such", rather than to their application in a particular case.

[57] *U.S. Export Restraints*, *supra* note 38, at ¶ 8.25.

[58] *Id.* at ¶ 8.29. This was the position Canada had taken as to the meaning of the phrase.

[59] *Id.* at ¶ 8.29.

[60] However, the Panel also found that U.S. law did not, as Canada had argued, require that export restraints be countervailed, and it therefore made no recommendations.

[61] *U.S. Export Restraints*, *supra* note 38, at ¶ 8.31.

2. A Benefit is Conferred Thereby. As explained above, it is possible to provide a financial contribution without conferring a benefit on the recipient. However, to be considered a subsidy within the meaning of the ASCM, a financial contribution must also confer a benefit on the recipient. Whether it requires a benefit to the recipient or a benefit to the manufacture, production, or export of the good in question has been debated. In *Canadian Civilian Aircraft I*, the Appellate Body stated: "A 'benefit' does not exist in the abstract, but must be received and enjoyed by a beneficiary or a recipient. Logically, a 'benefit' can be said to arise only if a person, natural or legal, or a group of persons, has in fact received something."[62]

That the term "benefit" in Article 1.1(b) refers to a benefit to the recipient of the financial contribution, is supported by the language in the chapeau of ASCM Article 14 which provides guidance in calculating "the benefit to the recipient conferred pursuant to paragraph 1 of Article 1."[63] In finding that the term refers to a "benefit to the recipient" of the financial contribution, the Appellate Body has specifically rejected the notion that the "benefit" in Article 1.1(b) can be calculated in terms of the cost to the government of the financial contribution.[64]

Although the term "benefit" is not explicitly defined in the ASCM, panels have clarified that a benefit occurs when a company is placed in a better position financially than it otherwise would be absent the financial contribution or price support. In *Lead Bar*, the Appellate Body stated: "[t]he question whether a 'financial contribution' confers a 'benefit' depends, therefore, on whether the recipient has received a 'financial contribution' on terms more favourable than those available to the recipient in the market."[65] This is consistent with the previous findings on this issue. In *Canadian Civilian Aircraft I,* the Appellate Body articulated the requirement as follows:

> We also believe that the word 'benefit', as used in Article 1.1(b), implies some kind of comparison. This must be so, for there can be no 'benefit' to the recipient unless the 'financial contribution' makes the recipient 'better off' than it would otherwise have been, absent that contribution. In our view, the marketplace provides an appropriate basis for comparison in determining whether a 'benefit' has been 'conferred', because the trade-distorting potential of a 'financial contribution' can be identified by determining whether the recipient has received a 'financial contribution' on terms more favourable than those available to the recipient in the market.[66]

In addition to this question of what is meant by the term "benefit," the question of identifying the recipient has also proven controversial, with most countries objecting to the U.S. practice with respect to subsidies to privatized companies. Certain types of subsidies are considered to confer a benefit over several years.[67] However, with the waive of privatizations of formerly state-owned firms in the late 1980s and early 1990s, the question arose as to whether the newly private firm continued to benefit from such

[62] *Canadian Civilian Aircraft* I, *supra* note 43, at ¶ 154. This language was reiterated in the subsequent Report of the Appellate Body, *United States—Imposition of Countervailing Duties on Certain Hot-Rolled Lead and Bismuth Carbon Steel Products Originating in the United Kingdom*, AB-2001-1, WT/DS138/AB/R (2000) ("*Lead Bar*").

[63] ASCM, Art. 14.

[64] *See Canadian Civilian Aircraft I, supra* note 43, at ¶ 155.

[65] *Lead Bar, supra* note 62, at ¶ 68. This leaves open the question of how to determine if "strings" attached to a financial contribution (*e.g.*, to keep a facility open) mean that the recipient is *not* better off (or by how much) than without the financial contribution.

[66] *Canadian Civilian Aircraft I, supra* note 43, at ¶ 157.

[67] *See Report of the Informal Group of Experts to the Committee on Subsidies and Countervailing Measures*, G/SCM/W415/Rev.1 (March 4, 1998) ("*Report of the Informal Group of Experts*").

long-term subsidies bestowed on the state-owned entity. The United States considered that the benefit did pass through the privatization, regardless of whether the sale of the company was at arm's-length, for fair market value.[68] The Appellate Body affirmed the Panel's conclusion that, based on the facts of the case (*i.e.*, an arm's-length sale for fair market value) no benefit existed.[69]

The case law at the WTO has indicated that since a benefit is to a "person," not to the productive assets, there must be an analysis, if raised, of subsequent events to see if the producer exporting the good at the time the duties are imposed is benefiting. The main dispute with the United States, however, has been whether an arms-length transaction for fair market value eliminates any benefit to the subsequent company. In *Lead Bar*, the Panel found that the question was whether or not the company was indirectly benefited from the original subsidy. Specifically, the Panel noted:

> As noted above, we consider that an untied, non-recurring "financial contribution" bestowed on a prior company may constitute a "financial contribution" bestowed indirectly on a successor company. This is because the untied, non-recurring "financial contribution" will be deemed to have been invested in the productive assets etc. of that company. Thus, when those productive assets etc. are acquired by the successor company, the successor company indirectly acquires the "financial contribution" embodied in those productive assets etc. Assuming "financial contributions" bestowed directly on BSC could be deemed to have been bestowed indirectly on UES and BSplc/BSES, this fact alone could not mean that pre-1985/86, untied, non-recurring "financial contributions" bestowed on BSC necessarily confer any "benefit" on UES or BSplc/BSES. *This would only be the case if those "financial contributions" were found to have been bestowed indirectly (i.e., through the relevant change-in-ownership transactions) on UES and BSplc/BSES respectively on terms more favourable that UES and BSplc/BSES respectively could have obtained in the market. We consider that such a finding would only be possible if fair market value were not paid for all productive assets etc. acquired by UES and BSplc/BSES respectively from BSC.*[70]

The United States then changed its methodology, arguing that the *Lead Bar* decision indicated that if it concluded that the new entity was essentially the "same person" as the pre-privatized entity, then there was no need to reconsider whether the benefit incurred to the new entity. This too was addressed by a WTO panel, which found that the United States' distinction between a company and its shareholders (the essence of its "same person" test) was not appropriate in the context of the ASCM. According to the Panel,

[68] Over the years, the United States has employed several methods of determining the measure, the most recent has been the "gamma" methodology, which assumed the benefit passed through but that some portion of the purchase price went towards repaying a portion of the pre-existing subsidies. *See* Report of the WTO Panel, *United States—Imposition of Countervailing Duties on Certain Hot-Rolled Lead and Bismuth Carbon Steel Products Originating in the United Kingdom*, WT/DS138/R at ¶ 6.61–6.62 ("*Lead Bar Panel Report*"), *aff'd Lead Bar*, *supra* note 62. Subsequently, the United States (claiming it was implementing the *Lead Bar* decision and a decision of the U.S. courts which echoed the findings of *Lead Bar*) considered whether the newly privatized entity was the 'same person" as the entity prior to privatization. If it was then according to the United States, it continued to benefit from the pre-privatization subsidies. The United States virtually always found the entity to be the "same person" and this methodology has been rejected both by a WTO panel and the U.S. court. *See, e.g.*, Report of the WTO Panel, *United States—Countervailing Measures Concerning Certain Products from the European Communities*, WT/DS212/R, ("*Privatization Subsidies*"); *aff'd in part, rev'd in part*, Report of the Appellate Body, *United States—Countervailing Measures Concerning Certain Products from the European Communities*, AB-2002-5, DS212/AB/R (2002) ("*Privatization Subsidies Appellate Body Report"); Allegheny Ludlum Corp. et al. v. United States*, 182 F. Supp. 2d 1357 (Ct. Int'l Trade 2002); *Acciai Speciali Terni S.p.A v. United States*, No. 99-06-00364, 2002 WL 342659 (CIT), 2002 Ct. Int'l Trade LEXIS 25, 24 ITRD 1108 (Ct. Int'l Trade Feb. 1, 2002).

[69] *Lead Bar*, *supra* note 62, at ¶ 68.

[70] *Lead Bar Panel Report*, *supra* note 68, at ¶ 6.81 (footnotes deleted, emphasis added).

the "concept of benefit is independent of the legal business structure established pursuant to national corporate law."[71] Thus, when confronted with information that a company has changed ownership since receipt of a subsidy, the authorities must examine the evidence to determine whether the company with new ownership still benefits from the prior subsidy—it may not "presume" such continued benefit.[72]

Another dispute on this issue also involved the United States. In *Softwood Lumber II*, the Panel found that the United States had incorrectly assumed that producers of the downstream product, lumber, benefited from subsidies to the upstream product provided by the licensing of the right to harvest timber (the input). The United States had before it evidence that there were producers of the downstream product who were not affiliated with the holder of the harvest rights (the alleged subsidy) and that a sizeable number of producers purchased log and lumber inputs from unrelated suppliers, allegedly at arm's length. Therefore, according to the Panel, the U.S. authorities should have determined whether and to what extent any benefit passed through to the lumber producers.[73]

Even if a practice does constitute a financial contribution and confers a benefit, it is not necessarily actionable, either multilaterally through the WTO dispute settlement mechanism, or unilaterally through the application of countervailing measures. Article 1.2 provides that a subsidy is actionable only if it is also specific[74] as defined in Article 2.

Article 2: Specificity

To be considered actionable or countervailable, a subsidy must be specific, as indicated in Article 1.2. Article 2 of the ASCM defines several situations in which a subsidy is deemed to be specific. The specificity requirement was a standard of U.S. countervailing duty law. The purpose of the requirement is to act as "an initial screening mechanism to winnow out only those foreign subsidies which truly are broadly available and widely used throughout an economy," since "all governments, including the United States, intervene in their economies to one extent or another, and to regard all such interventions as countervailable subsidies would produce absurd results."[75]

1. Subsidies Limited to Certain Enterprises. Article 2.1 provides that a subsidy is specific if it is limited to an enterprise or industry or group of enterprises or industries

[71] *Privatization Subsidies, supra* note 68, at ¶ 7.50, *aff'd, Privatization Subsidies Appellate Body Report, supra*, note 69 at ¶ 146.

[72] *See Privatization Subsidies Appellate Body Report, supra* note 68, at ¶ 147. The Appellate Body further noted that an arm's length privatization for fair market value presumptively extinguishes any benefit from prior subsidies. The effect of such privatization "is to shift to the investigating authority the burden of identifying evidence which establishes that the benefit from the previous financial contribution does indeed continue beyond privatization." *Id.* at ¶ 126.

[73] *See Softwood Lumber II, supra* note 50, at ¶ 7.78. In addition, the Panel noted that, at least in an investigation, the authorities must determine "whether and to what extent a subsidy has been granted to the producer of the subject merchandise." The authorities may not, as the United Sates did, simply assume the existence of a benefit. *Id.* at ¶ 7.75. This reasoning was later affirmed by the Appellate Body in a related case. *See Softwood Lumber Appellate Body Report, supra* note 52, at ¶¶ 146 and 158.

[74] ASCM, Art. 1.2.

[75] *See "Statement of Administrative Action"* in H.R. REP NO. 103–36, Vol. 1 at 929 (1995). It has been explained that "the purpose of the CVD law is to counteract government-induced distortions to the relative positions of firms within an economy." A. Holmer, S. Haggerty and W. Hunter, *Identifying and Measuring Subsidies under the Countervailing Duty Law: An Attempt at Synthesis*, in THE DEPARTMENT OF COMMERCE SPEAKS ON IMPORT ADMINISTRATION AND EXPORT ADMINISTRATION, 455 PLI/Corp. 301, (1984). Countervailing a subsidy that was generally available throughout the economy would not serve this purpose.

("certain enterprises") within the jurisdiction of the granting authority.[76] The subsidy is specific if the legislation or the granting authority explicitly limits the subsidy to certain enterprises ("*de jure*" specificity).[77] However, if eligibility is limited, based on explicit, verifiable, objective criteria (*i.e.*, criteria or conditions which are neutral, do not favor certain enterprises over others, are economic in nature, and are horizontal in application) the program is not specific, so long as eligibility is automatic and the criteria are strictly adhered to.[78]

Even if the program appears on its face to be non-specific, the program may be found to be *de facto* specific, based on the following factors:[79]

- Use by a limited number of enterprises;
- Predominant use by certain enterprises;
- The grant of disproportionately large amounts of subsidies to certain enterprises; and
- The manner in which discretion is exercised by administering authorities.

While this *de facto* specificity analysis was, again, similar to the test applied by the United States, the ASCM places restrictions on the analysis that were not found in U.S. practice and that reflect many countries' concerns regarding the U.S. practice in this area. In particular, in determining *de facto* specificity, the investigating authorities should take account of the diversification of economic activities in the subsidizing country and the length of time the program has been in operation. This first item would appear to be helpful to many smaller, or developing economies, which may have a limited range of economic activity in the country.

Moreover, the ASCM provides that in considering the discretionary application of a program, the investigating authorities "shall" consider, in particular, information on the frequency with which applications for a subsidy are approved or refused and the reasons for those decisions.[80]

2. Regional Subsidies. Article 2.2 states that a program available only to certain enterprises within a designated geographic region of the granting authority's jurisdiction is specific. This represents a significant decrease in the discipline from that proposed in the *Dunkel Text*,[81] which made all subsidies by sub-national governments, even if available to all enterprises within that sub-national government's jurisdiction, specific.[82]

[76] To a large extent, the language of this article tracks the definition of specificity that was applied by the United States, the largest user of countervailing duty laws at the time. There are, however, some differences from the U.S. approach.

[77] ASCM, Art. 2.1(a).

[78] *Id.*, Art. 2.1(b). This is one of the differences from the U.S. approach, which did not provide exceptions for limitations based on objective criteria.

[79] ASCM, Art. 2.1(c).

[80] This item can be problematic for the government of an exporting country defending a program. The authorities administering the subsidy program often do not maintain statistics of this type, or if they do, confidentiality rules within the country may prevent the disclosure of such information to the investigating authorities of the importing country. Failure to provide the information might then be used to justify a finding of specificity of a discretionary program.

[81] *See Dunkel Text*, *supra* note 24, at Art. 2.2.

[82] *Compare* ASCM, Art. 2.2 *with Dunkel Text*, Art. 2.2. The change from the *Dunkel Text* apparently was the result of a "deal" between the United States and Canada in late 1993 (which both countries will doubtless deny) in which the United States agreed to less discipline on subsidies in return for Canadian support for more trade-restrictive anti-dumping rules.

Export and Import Substitution Subsidies. Article 2.3 states that all prohibited subsidies as defined in Article 3, *i.e.*, export subsidies and import substitution subsidies, are specific.

Article 2.4 requires that any determination of specificity must "be clearly substantiated on the basis of positive evidence."[83] This requirement arguably places the burden of proof on the investigating authorities (or the complaining Member) to demonstrate specificity. Prior to this, at least in the United States, the practice was to presume a program was specific, unless positive evidence to the contrary was provided. Because the defending exporting Member is the entity most likely to have access to the information regarding specificity or the lack thereof, this has the potential for creating a significant hurdle to taking action.

PART II: Prohibited Subsidies

Part II of the Agreement covers prohibited subsidies, which consist of export subsidies and import-substitution subsidies. Members are required to eliminate such subsidies, which may be challenged by another member without a showing of harm to the interests of that member. Article 3 defines prohibited subsidies, while Article 4 provides for an expedited dispute resolution procedure in cases involving prohibited subsidies.

Article 3: Prohibition

In the 1979 Subsidies Code, only export subsidies were prohibited.[84] The ASCM expands that prohibition to include both export subsidies and import substitution subsidies, *i.e.*, subsidies the receipt of which is, at least in part, contingent upon the use of domestic over imported goods. A prohibited subsidy is by definition specific and therefore actionable.

The definition of an export subsidy appears to be more restrictive than the broad definition assumed prior to the ASCM. The 1979 Subsidies Code included a blanket prohibition on the granting of "export subsidies on products other than certain primary products."[85] The ASCM, however, provides a more limited prohibition by stating that only those "subsidies *contingent*, in law or in fact, ... upon *export performance*" are prohibited.[86] This limitation is further clarified by a footnote which notes that to be contingent in fact, the subsidy must be tied to actual or anticipated exports or export earnings.[87] Finally, that footnote clarifies that the mere fact that the enterprise granted the subsidy is an exporter is not sufficient to make a subsidy contingent in law or in fact upon exportation.[88] Thus, the use of the term "contingent" arguably narrows the definition of what constitutes a prohibited subsidy.

[83] ASCM, Art. 2.4.

[84] *1979 Subsidies Code*, Art. 9.

[85] *Id.*

[86] ASCM, Art. 3.1(a) (emphasis added). It should be noted that until the ASCM, the term "export subsidy" was not defined, leaving it open to a broad range of interpretations. There was considerable discussion concerning how to define subsidies for purposes of prohibition. *E.g.*, *NGSCM, Submission by Japan*, MTV.GNG/NG10/W/27 (October 6, 1989) (suggesting that the Illustrative List of Export Subsidies in the Annex to the 1979 Subsidies Code be converted to an exhaustive, definitive list, with some modifications); NGSCM, Submission by the United States, MTV.GNG/NG10/W/29 (November 22, 1989) (suggesting that the prohibition be expanded to include all subsidies provided to firms predominantly engaged in export trade, as being in effect as trade distortive as a more traditional export subsidy).

[87] *Id.*, Art. 3.1(a) n.4.

[88] *Id.*

There have been several panel and Appellate Body reports addressing what constitutes a subsidy "contingent" upon exportation. The Appellate Body has indicated that in order to determine whether a subsidy is contingent upon export performance in law, one should consider whether the "condition can be demonstrated on the basis of the very words of the relevant legislation, regulation or other legal instrument constituting the measure."[89] A condition to export can exist in law if it is implicitly in the instrument deriving the measure, *i.e.*, that such conditionality can be derived by necessary implication from the words actually used in the measure.[90] In the *Canadian Autos* case, the Appellate body found that the ratio requirements in the law required the company receiving the subsidy to export in order to maintain the ratios. The Appellate Body therefore found that the measure was contingent in law upon export performance.[91]

In *Canadian Civilian Aircraft I*, which involved an issue of whether the measure was contingent in fact upon export performance, the Appellate Body noted that it was not enough that a government granting the subsidy *anticipated* that exports would result. The prohibition requires that the granting of the subsidy be *contingent* upon export performance.[92] Moreover, the Appellate Body noted that the phrase "tied to" in the footnote indicated that this required that the export performance or earnings be a limit or restriction as to conditions.[93] In making such a decision, a panel must consider the structure and design of the measure as well as the specific facts of the case. In that case, the Appellate Body affirmed the Panel decision that the measure was contingent in fact upon export performance, based on the Panel's consideration of numerous factors.[94]

In another case involving the question of whether certain measures were contingent in fact upon export performance, a Panel ruled differently on two measures, in a manner that provides guidance on the meaning of the term "contingent in fact."[95] In *Australian Leather*, the Panel considered two subsidies, a grant and a loan, provided to a single company, Howe. In both cases, the Panel noted that the grant and the loan were part of a package of assistance that would not have been granted but for the removal of leather from eligibility for certain export subsidies. Similarly, it noted that Howe, in fact, exported a significant percentage of its production and that its continued economic viability was dependent on exporting some portion of its production. However, the two subsidies differed in certain respects. The contract providing for the grant established certain specific sales performance targets (overall sales, not export sales explicitly) and obligated Howe to make best efforts to meet those sales performance targets. The loan contract did not address Howe's sales performance at all and was secured by a lien on the assets and undertakings of Howe's parent company, ALH (which had other interests besides Howe).

After reviewing the facts, the Panel found that given the totality of the evidence and because the grant was specifically conditioned upon sales performance targets that could not be met without exporting, the grant constituted a prohibited export subsidy.[96] The Panel found that the loan, however, was not a subsidy that was contingent in fact upon

[89] *Canadian Autos*, *supra* note 48, at ¶ 100.
[90] *Id.* at ¶ 100.
[91] *Id.* at ¶ 104.
[92] *Canadian Civilian Aircraft I*, *supra* note 43, at ¶ 171.
[93] *Id.*
[94] *Id.* at ¶ 179.
[95] *See* Report of the WTO Panel, *Australia—Subsidies Provided to Producers and Exporters of Automotive Leather*, WT/DS126/R (1999) ("*Australian Leather*").
[96] *Id.* at ¶¶ 9.71–9.72.

export performance because there was nothing in "the terms of the loan contract itself which suggests a specific link to actual or anticipated exportation or export earnings."[97]

Thus, the cases indicate this provision requires that there be some explicit or implicit linkage in order for a subsidy to be considered contingent in law or fact upon export performance.

Annex I of the ASCM provides further guidance in determining whether a subsidy is a prohibited export subsidy by providing an Illustrative List of Export Subsidies. If a measure is defined in Annex I as not constituting an export subsidy (such as the non-excessive remission of import charges on imported inputs consumed in the production of the exported product), it does not fall within the scope of the prohibited subsidies of Article 3.1(a). It may, however, still be an actionable subsidy if it is otherwise specific.[98]

Panels and the Appellate Body have found that portions of the Illustrative List may be raised as an affirmative defense to the charge of maintaining prohibited export subsidies. For example, Item (k) of the Illustrative List identifies the grant of export credits at below market rates as an example of an export subsidy, in so far as they are used to secure a material advantage in the field of export credits. However, the second paragraph indicates that if the credits are granted by a Member that is also a party to an international undertaking on official export credits (this refers to the OECD Export Credit Arrangement)[99] or if the Member acts in conformity with the interest rate provisions of such undertaking (and it in practice applies those provisions) then such export credits are not an export subsidy. Several panel and Appellate Body reports have indicated that this second paragraph may be raised as an affirmative defense, but then the Member raising the defense has the burden of proof, which the panels and Appellate Body have interpreted strictly.[100]

Similarly, in addressing whether the United States tax program implemented to comply with the original ruling on *FSC*,[101] the Appellate Body agreed that the fifth sentence of footnote 59, which permits measures taken by Members to avoid double taxation in certain circumstances, was an affirmative defense. However, the Appellate Body found that the United States had not met its burden of proof that its measure in fact conformed to the requirements of that affirmative defense.[102] It is not clear, however, that all portions of the Illustrative List can be raised as an affirmative defense.[103]

The Illustrative List is not new. There was an Illustrative List in the 1979 Subsidies Code that was quite similar to the one found in the ASCM. One significant change, however, addresses the non-excessive remission or exemption of prior-stage cumulative

[97] *Id.* at ¶ 9.75. It is worth noting that the Panel implicitly rejected the United States' proposed broad reading of Article 3.1(a) when it found that the loan was not a prohibited export subsidy. The United States had argued that "if the totality of the circumstances reveals that the subsidy in question is designed to promote exports, then that subsidy comes within the ambit of Article 3.1(a), and is prohibited." *Id.* at ¶ 9.52.

[98] *See FSC*, *supra* note 46, at ¶ 93.

[99] The OECD Export Credit Arrangement is available from OECD on its website: www.OECD.org.

[100] *See, e.g.*, Report of the WTO Panel, *Canada—Export Credit and Loan Guarantees for Regional Aircraft*, WT/DS222/R (2002) ("*Canadian Regional Aircraft*") at ¶¶ 7.161 and 7.180 (it is an affirmative defense, but to meet its burden of proof, Canada had to demonstrate that as a matter of law its actions fell within the meaning of this provision. The Panel found Canada had failed to meet that burden.)

[101] *FSC*, *supra* note 46.

[102] *See* Report of the Appellate Body, *United States—Tax Treatment for "Foreign Sales Corporations", Recourse to Article 21.5 of the DSU*, AB-2001-8, WT/DS108/AB/RW (2002) at ¶ 186.

[103] *See* Report of the WTO Panel, *Brazil-Export Financing Programme for Aircraft (Second Recourse to DSU, Article 21.5)*, WT/DS246/RW(2), (2001) at ¶¶ 5.274–5.775 (finding that the first paragraph of Annex I, Item (k), does not contain any affirmative statement that a measure is not an export subsidy nor that a measure not satisfying the conditions of the paragraph is not prohibited. Therefore, the Panel found the first paragraph of Item (k) cannot provide an affirmative defense to claims of a violation of ASCM, Article 3.1(a)).

indirect taxes on goods or services used in the production of exported products.[104] This provision is of particular importance to countries that do not have a value-added tax regime. Essentially, the Illustrative List would permit the non-excessive remission of such cumulative taxes if they were levied on inputs that are "consumed in the production of the exported product." In the 1979 Subsidies Code, they were permitted only if they were levied on inputs that were physically incorporated in the exported product.[105]

The reason for this change was that in certain countervailing duty cases the concept of what was physically incorporated in the exported product was heavily debated. There were questions such as whether a catalyst that was consumed in the production of a good was incorporated in that good or whether fertilizer was physically incorporated in the flower that was ultimately harvested. The other area that had generated controversy was the consumption of energy in the production process. Therefore, as a result of the negotiations, this provision was revised to permit the non-excessive remission of taxes as long as the taxes had been levied on products *consumed* in the production of the exported product.[106]

The ASCM's prohibition on the use of export subsidies is narrower than the more general prohibition found in the 1979 Subsidies Code. However, the prohibition covers a broader scope of products than previously. While the 1979 Subsidies Code did not prohibit export subsidies for "certain primary products," the current Agreement extends the prohibition to all products, except as provided in the WTO Agreement on Agriculture. The WTO Agreement on Agriculture places restrictions on the use of export subsidies, and applies to a narrower category of products than did the term "certain primary products."[107]

Article 3.2 provides that Members may not grant or maintain prohibited subsidies.

Article 4: Remedies for Prohibited Subsidies

This Article has been used to challenge various alleged export subsidies.[108] The Article provides that any Member that has reason to believe that another Member is using a prohibited subsidy may request consultations with the other Member. The consultation request must include a statement of the available evidence with regard to the existence and nature of the subsidy in question.[109]

If the consultations do not result in a mutually agreed solution within thirty days of the request for consultations, any Member party to those consultations may refer the matter to the Dispute Settlement Body ("DSB") for the immediate establishment of a panel, unless the DSB decides by consensus not to establish a panel.[110] This differs from requests under the Understanding on Rules and Procedures Governing the Settlement of

[104] ASCM, Annex I, Item (h).

[105] 1979 Subsidies Code, Annex I, Item (h).

[106] ASCM, Annex I, Item (h). Note, the ASCM also includes guidance for determining whether an input is consumed in the production process. *See* ASCM, Annex II. Nonetheless, this continues to be a controversial topic as an implementation issue.

[107] *See* Chapter 6 of this book.

[108] The following cases alleging the use of prohibited export subsidies have been through the dispute settlement process: *Australian Leather*, *supra* note 95; Report of the Appellate Body, *Brazil—Export Financing Programme for Civil Aircraft*, AB-1999-1, WT/DS46/AB/R (1999); *Canadian Civilian Aircraft I*, *supra* note 43; Report of the Appellate Body, *Canada—Measures Affecting the Importation of Milk and the Exportation of Dairy Products*, AB-1999-4, WT/DS103, 113/AB/R (1999); *FSC*, *supra* note 46; and *Canadian Autos*, *supra* note 48. It should be noted that implementation issues linger for at least four of these six cases.

[109] ASCM, Art. 4.1 and 2.

[110] ASCM, Art. 4.4.

Disputes ("DSU").[111] When a Member requests a panel under the DSU, Article 6, the panel will be established at the meeting of the DSB following the meeting at which the panel is originally requested.

Once established, the panel may request the assistance of the Permanent Group of Experts ("PGE") with regard to whether the measure at issue is a prohibited subsidy.[112] None of the panels established through this mechanism to date have requested the assistance of the PGE.

While the panel is established under the auspices of the DSB and the DSU, it is subject to certain special rules that differ from those found in the DSU in several significant respects, as long as the claims are limited to Article 3 subsidies. If other claims are included, then the dispute would be subject to the normal rules of the DSU.

Most importantly, Article 4 disputes are subject to much shorter time limits than normal disputes. A panel may be requested thirty days after making the request for consultations, compared to sixty days under the DSU.[113] Once a panel is formed, the panel is to submit its final report to the parties within ninety days of the establishment of the terms of reference,[114] compared with the normal six months under the DSU.[115]

Similarly, under Article 4, the report of the panel is to be adopted within thirty days of circulation of the report to all the Members, unless appealed[116] (the normal period under the DSU is sixty days).[117] If appealed, the Appellate Body is to issue its decision to the Parties within thirty days of the notice of appeal, extendable to sixty days[118] (the comparable periods under the DSU are sixty and ninety days).[119] It should be noted that the parties to the dispute may agree to a different timetable for any part of the proceeding.

The timing of the dispute settlement procedures is not the only significant difference between an ASCM Article 4 proceeding and a proceeding under the general DSU procedures. Article 4 provides that *if* a panel finds the existence of a prohibited subsidy, the panel shall recommend that the party *withdraw the subsidy* without delay and *shall* specify the time period within which the measure must be withdrawn.[120] In the *Australian—Leather* case, this was interpreted as requiring a complete repayment of the export subsidy, not just the benefit remaining at the time of the Panel ruling.[121] The *Canadian Regional Aircraft* Panel addressing an argument raised by Canada concerning the prospective nature of WTO remedies noted that it was not obvious that the WTO

[111] *Understanding on Rules and Procedures Governing the Settlement of Disputes* ("DSU").
[112] *Id.*, Art. 4.5. *See also*, the discussion of Article 24, *infra*, describing the PGE.
[113] *Compare* ASCM, Art. 4.4 *with* DSU, Art. 4.7.
[114] ASCM, Art. 4.6.
[115] DSU, Art. 12.8.
[116] ASCM, Art. 4.8.
[117] DSU, Art. 16.4.
[118] ASCM, Art. 4.9.
[119] DSU, Art. 17.5.
[120] ASCM, Art. 4.7.
[121] Report of the WTO Panel, *Australia—Subsidies Provided to Producers and Exporters of Automotive Leather, Recourse to Art. 21.5 of the DSU*, WT/DS126/RW (2000) ¶¶ 6.39–6.49. It should be noted that this decision by the Panel generated considerable surprise since it went beyond the remedy requested by either party. Rather, the parties had agreed to implementation in the form of repayment of the balance of the benefit remaining but sought arbitration to resolve the question of what that balance was. The Panel did not require repayment with interest, however—in effect blessing an interest-free loan contingent upon exportation, *i.e.*, a subsidy prohibited by Article 3. The parties settled based on partial repayment and some lowering of Australian duties on other products.

provided only for prospective remedies in the case of prohibited export subsidies; it may be that in certain instances the appropriate remedy is repayment of the subsidy.[122]

In contrast, under the DSU, if a panel finds that the measure in question is inconsistent with the Agreement, it shall recommend that it be *brought into conformity* and *may* suggest ways the Member could do so.[123] Thus, there is no requirement in the general DSU that a panel recommend the withdrawal of an inconsistent measure. Neither does the DSU direct the panel to establish the timetable for implementation.

PART III: Actionable Subsidies

Part III of the Agreement deals with subsidies which, while not prohibited, may be challenged through the multilateral dispute mechanism if they have "adverse effects" on the trade interests of another Member, or be subject to countervailing duty measures if they cause or threaten material injury to a domestic industry.[124] It defines the types of adverse effect that can give rise to an action and the remedies available. It also defines certain types of subsidy as "non-actionable," although this provision has lapsed.

Article 5: Adverse Effects

This Article begins the definition of what constitutes an actionable subsidy and what actions can be taken. The original basis for this provision is Article XVI of GATT 1947, which provided for consultations if the effect of a subsidy was to increase exports, directly or indirectly, such that it caused serious prejudice to another Contracting Party's interests.[125] The ASCM expands upon this, stating that no Member, through the use of a subsidy, shall cause adverse effects to the interests of another Member.[126]

Article 5 defines those adverse effects as taking any of three forms: (1) injury to the domestic industry of another Member in the sense that this term is used in Part V of the Agreement, dealing with countervailing duties; (2) nullification or impairment of benefits accruing directly or indirectly to other Members under GATT 1994;[127] or (3) serious prejudice to the interest of other Members.

It should be noted, however, that this article explicitly excludes from its reach subsidies on agricultural products, in conformity with Article 13 of the WTO Agreement on Agriculture.[128]

Article 6: Serious Prejudice

Article 6 defines the term "serious prejudice," one of the three types of "adverse effect" that form the basis of a challenge to an actionable subsidy. Paragraph 1 provides that serious prejudice will be presumed if any of four situations existed. In other words, if a

[122] *See Canadian Regional Aircraft, supra* note 100, at ¶ 7.170.

[123] DSU, Art. 19.1.

[124] ASCM, Art. 10, n.35 provides that while the provisions of Part II or III may be invoked in parallel with the provisions of Part V (countervailing measures), with respect to the effects of the subsidies in the domestic market of the complaining Member, only one form of relief shall be available (*i.e.*, relief through the imposition of countervailing measures *or* relief under the provisions of Parts II or III, not both).

[125] GATT 1947, Art. XVI:1.

[126] ASCM, Art. 5.1.

[127] The concept of "nullification and impairment" of benefits originated in Article XXIII of GATT 1947. *See* Chapter 5, Part V.B, of this book.

[128] Article 13, however, restricts the application of countervailing measures for agricultural subsidies only temporarily. It expired at the end of 2003. *See* Agreement on Agriculture, Articles 1(e) and 13, and Chapter 6 of this book.

complaining Member makes a *prima facie* showing that any of these situations exist, the burden of proof shifts to the responding Member to rebut the claim. The four situations are:

- A total *ad valorem* subsidization of a product exceeding five per cent;[129]
- Subsidies to cover operating losses sustained by an industry;
- Subsidies to cover operating losses sustained by a company other than one time, non-recurring and non-repeatable subsidies;
- Direct forgiveness of debt.

This paragraph had a five-year life before requiring renewal.[130] It lapsed in the aftermath of the Seattle WTO Ministerial Meeting in 1999, so that there is no longer any situation in which serious prejudice will be presumed.

Paragraph 3 indicates what must be demonstrated in order to make a *prima facie* case of serious prejudice in the absence of the paragraph 1 presumption. To make a *prima facie* case, the complaining Member must demonstrate with positive evidence that the effect of the subsidy is adverse to the complaining Member's trade interests through displacing or impeding its exports to the subsidizing Member's markets or to third country markets, price undercutting, price suppression or lost sales, or increasing the subsidizing Member country's share of world trade in a particular subsidized primary product or commodity.[131] This analysis must focus on the effects of the subsidy on the product "like" the subsidized product.[132]

Paragraph 4 provides that in order to demonstrate that the "effect of the subsidy is to displace or impede the exports of a like product of another Member from a third country market,"[133] a complaining Member may show a change in relative market shares over a representative period. This paragraph does not apply when the complaint alleges displacement or impedance of imports in the market of the subsidizing Member.[134]

Paragraph 5 provides that price undercutting may be shown by a comparison of prices of the subsidized product with prices of a non-subsidized like product supplied to the same market, although it does not preclude other means. Where possible, the comparison is to be made at the same level of trade and at comparable times, and account is to be taken of other factors affecting comparability. To make an affirmative finding of serious prejudice through price undercutting, the panel must find that the complaining Member has demonstrated that the price undercutting is significant and is a result of the effect of

[129] ASCM, Art. 6.1(a). It should be noted that in accordance with Annex IV of the ASCM, the percentage of subsidization is calculated in accordance with the cost to the government, unlike in a countervailing duty investigation in which the percentage of subsidization is calculated as the benefit to the recipient. Suggestions on how to measure the degree of subsidization in accordance with Annex IV can be found in the report of an informal group of experts formed to determine just that. *See Report of the Informal Group of Experts*, *supra* note 67. It should be noted that, since most of the "experts" in this group come from the Members' authorities charged with administering countervailing duties, the methods contained in this report provide significant guidance as to the methodology to be used for determining benefits for purposes of countervailing duty actions as well.

[130] ASCM, Art. 31. *See also*, the discussion in Article 27 of the implications for developing countries of the lapsing of this provisions.

[131] The increase must be as compared with the Member's average share during the previous three-year period, and it must follow a consistent trend over a period when subsidies have been granted. This provision does not apply when other multilaterally-agreed rules apply to trade in the product or commodity in question.

[132] *See* Report of the WTO Panel, *Indonesia—Certain Measures Affecting the Automobile Industry*, WT/DS54, 55, 59, 64/R (1999), at ¶ 14.164 ("*Indonesia—Automobile Industry*").

[133] ASCM, Art. 6.3(b).

[134] *See Indonesia—Automobile Industry*, *supra* note 132, at ¶ 14.208.

the subsidy.[135] The displacement or price undercutting, however, must be demonstrated with respect to product originating in the complaining Member's territory.[136]

One issue to be addressed in such cases is how to gather the necessary evidence to prove or rebut a claim of serious prejudice. The ASCM seeks to provide guidance in this regard. First, Paragraph 6 requires that the Member in whose market serious prejudice is alleged to have occurred shall make available to the panel *all relevant* information that can be obtained as to changes in market shares of the parties to the dispute and prices of the products involved. While the information to be provided by parties to a dispute is "all" relevant information, it is more limited if the serious prejudice is alleged to have occurred in a third country market.[137] Annex V to the ASCM prescribes procedures for collecting the necessary evidence. Paragraph 3 of that Annex, while acknowledging the right of the parties to seek information from the government of the third country Member where third country serious prejudice is alleged, places limits on the degree of cooperation required of the third country Member. A third country Member need only supply information that has already been gathered or that is readily available and need not provide information that is normally maintained as confidential by the government.[138] It is notable that there are no such limitations on the information to be provided by the parties to the dispute.

Among the procedures for collecting information is the designation by the DSB of a representative to facilitate the information-gathering process.[139] The information gathering should be completed within sixty days of the date on which the matter was referred to the DSB.

Annex V provides for the possibility of the failure of the subsidiary or a third-country Member to cooperate with the information-gathering process.[140] In such circumstances, the panel is to base its decision on the best information available to it and the complaining member may present its case based on the available information, which would include the fact that the subsidizing or third country Member had failed to cooperate.[141] Finally, the ASCM notes that in deciding to base its decision on the best information available, the panel should consider the advice of the DSB representative.[142] The panel is not obliged to follow that advice, however, only to consider it.

Article 7: Remedies

This Article provides for dispute settlement proceedings (1) in a case of serious prejudice, (2) when a Member has reason to believe that a subsidy as defined in Article 1 provided by another Member is injuring the complaining Member's industry, or (3) when the subsidy

135 *See id.* at ¶ 14.255 (It should be noted that this is the only serious prejudice case to date to go to a panel and that the Panel found that the European Communities, one of the complaining Members, had demonstrated serious prejudice through significant price undercutting).

136 *See id.* at ¶ 14.204. It is not sufficient that there be serious prejudice to a company of the complaining Member; the serious prejudice must be to a *product* of the complaining Member. *See id.* at ¶ 14.201 (finding that the United States could not establish serious prejudice on the basis of harm to the Indonesian subsidiaries of U.S. companies).

137 ASCM, Article 6.6 notes that the requirement to provide all relevant information, when applied to third country Members, is subject to the provisions of Annex V, paragraph 3.

138 ASCM, Annex V:3.

139 ASCM, Annex V:4. It should be noted, however, that the *Indonesia—Automobile Industry* case is the only serious prejudice dispute brought to date and serious prejudice was only one of the claims of violation of the WTO Agreement.

140 ASCM, Annex V:5.

141 ASCM, Annex V:6.

142 ASCM, Annex V:7.

results in nullification or impairment of the complaining Member's benefits under the WTO Agreement. Like the Article 4 remedy available in the case of prohibited subsidies, the procedures under Article 7 differ in a number of respects from the procedures in disputes covered by the Dispute Settlement Understanding.

To begin the proceedings, the Member requests consultations with the subsidizing Member. Such consultations should begin as quickly as possible. Under the DSU, a request for consultations must state the reasons for the request, including an "indication of the legal basis for the complaint."[143] Under ASCM, Art. 7.7, a request for consultations must also include a statement of the evidence with regard to the nature and existence of the subsidy in question and either the injury, serious prejudice, or nullification or impairment of benefits caused to the interests of the complaining Member.[144]

If no mutually acceptable solution has been agreed within sixty days of the request, any party to the consultations may refer the matter to the DSB for the establishment of a panel. The composition of the panel and the terms of reference are to be established within fifteen days of the request.[145] The panel is to review the matter and present its final report to the parties. That report is to be circulated to all Members within 120 days of the panel's establishment, in contrast to the six months provided under the DSU.[146] Within thirty days thereafter, the report is to be adopted, unless either appealed by one of the parties, or the DSB decides, by consensus, not to adopt the report. The normal DSU period is sixty days.[147] If appealed, the Appellate Body is to issue its report within sixty days, extendable by an additional thirty days. This is the same period as in regular DSU proceedings.

If a report is adopted in which it has been determined that a subsidy has resulted in an adverse effect to the interests of another party, then the subsidizing Member shall take appropriate steps to remove the adverse effects or to withdraw the subsidy. If such steps are not taken within six months from the date of the adoption of the report, the DSB may authorize countermeasures. Such countermeasures must be commensurate with the degree and nature of the adverse effects determined to exist.

PART IV: Non-Actionable Subsidies

Article 8: Identification of Non-Actionable Subsidies

Article 8 of the ASCM provides that non-specific subsidies are not actionable,[148] and it also defines three categories of "green light" subsidy that are not actionable even if they are specific.[149] For the first five years of the Agreement, green light subsidies could not be subjected to countervailing duties[150] or to discipline under the Agreement. However, Article 8 was a temporary provision subject to renewal.[151] In the aftermath of the 1999 Seattle Ministerial, this is one of the provisions that was allowed to lapse. All such "green

[143] DSU, Art. 4.4.

[144] ASCM, Art. 7.2.

[145] ASCM, Art. 7.4. This is a somewhat faster time frame than under the DSU. The DSU provides that a panel shall be established "at the latest at the DSB meeting following that at which the request first appears," in other words, approximately one month after the initial request for the panel is made. DSU, Art. 6.1. In addition, under the DSU, normally the panel composition and the terms of reference are determined within twenty days of the establishment of the panel. DSU, Art. 7.1.

[146] *Compare* ASCM, Art. 7.5 *with* DSU, Art. 6.8.

[147] DSU, Art. 16.4.

[148] ASCM, Art. 8.1.

[149] ASCM, Art. 8.2.

[150] *See ASCM,* Art. 10, n.35.

[151] ASCM, Art. 31.

light" programs are therefore currently actionable, and will remain so unless this Article is reinstated at some future date.

The first "green light" category consists of subsidies for research and development ("R&D") programs. Assistance for R&D would not be actionable if provided to firms, higher education facilities, or research establishments acting under contract to firms if:

i. The assistance covers not more than 75 percent of the costs of industrial research;[152] or
ii. The assistance covers not more than 50 percent of the cost of pre-competitive development research.[153]

Additionally, the assistance must be limited exclusively to:

i. Personnel costs for staff employed exclusively in the R&D activity;
ii. Costs of buildings and equipment, including instruments, used exclusively and permanently for the R&D activity;
iii. Consultancy or equivalent services used exclusively for the R&D activity (this would include technical knowledge and patents); or
iv. Other overhead and running costs incurred directly as a result of the R&D activity.[154]

Both the numerical limits and the definitions are considerably broader than the R&D green light category in the *Dunkel Text* (which allowed assistance only up to 25 and 50 percent, rather than 50 and 75 percent, and which stopped well short of allowing assistance for the creation of a prototype). This reflects the sudden and complete shift in U.S. position in November/December 1993, from the Bush Administration's attempt to remove green light categories to the Clinton Administration's attempt to expand them.[155]

The second category of green light subsidies concerns aid to disadvantaged regions within the territory of a Member given pursuant to a general framework of regional development.[156] For a subsidy to be non-actionable, each disadvantaged region must be a clearly designated, contiguous geographic area with a definable economic and administrative identity (*e.g.*, a county or district), and must be determined to be disadvantaged based on explicit, verifiable, neutral and objective criteria.[157] It is this requirement for

[152] "Industrial research" is defined as: ". . . planned search or critical investigation aimed at discovery of new knowledge with the objective that such knowledge may be useful in developing new products, processes or services, or in bringing about a significant improvement to existing products, processes or services." ASCM, Art. 8.2(a) n. 28.

[153] "Pre-competitive development activity" is defined as: ". . . the translation of industrial research findings into a plan, blueprint or design for new, modified or improved products, processes or services whether intended for sale or use, including the creation of a first prototype which would not be capable of commercial use." ASCM, Art. 8.2(a) n. 29.

[154] ASCM, Art. 8.2(a).

[155] *See* Hugo Paeman and Alexandra Bensch, From the GATT to the WTO: The European Community In The Uruguay Round 131 (1995). One of the Clinton Administration's goals was to protect its Partnership for a New Generation of Vehicles, a subsidy to U.S.-owned automobile companies, which expired after the payment of US $1.5 billion in grants.

[156] ASCM, Art. 8.2(b).

[157] The term "neutral and objective" means criteria that do not favor certain regions beyond what is appropriate for the elimination or reduction of regional disparities within the framework of the regional development policy. The criteria must include a measurement of economic development based on either: (i) income per capita, household income, or GDP per capita, which must be at least fifteen percent below the average for the territory concerned; or (ii) unemployment level, which must be at least ten percent above the average for the territory concerned. ASCM, Art. 8.2(b)(ii) and (iii).

explicit, verifiable, neutral and objective criteria that has been the most difficult for a defending country to demonstrate. Often, while regions identified as disadvantaged are, in fact, disadvantaged when examined under these criteria, the original decision to provide the assistance was based more on political considerations than on established explicit economic criteria.

The final category of green light subsidies is assistance to companies to help them adapt to new environmental requirements (as long as the assistance is limited to twenty percent of the cost of the necessary adaptation and is given on a one-time only basis). This was the result of a last-minute Mexican proposal (drawn from a 1989 EC proposal) that the United States was unable to block (because the U.S. credibility in opposing green light status had been compromised by its change in position on R&D subsidies).

Finally, Article 8 requires that, to be considered to be non-actionable, a green light subsidy must be notified in advance to the Committee on Subsidies and Countervailing Measures.[158] Nonetheless, language was added at U.S. (and possibly EC) insistence in late 1993 that subsidies may be found to be green light subsidies, even if not notified to the Committee in advance. If, in the course of a proceeding, it is determined that a subsidy meets the requirements, then that subsidy shall be treated as non-actionable.[159] The Committee, upon request, will review the practice to determine if the requisite conditions have been met.[160]

Article 9: Consultations and Authorized Remedies

Although green light subsidies as defined by Article 8.2 were considered non-actionable, Article 9 provided for some remedy when such a subsidy resulted in serious adverse effects to the domestic industry of another Member. Article 9 permitted the Member whose domestic industry was experiencing serious adverse effects to request consultations with the Member granting or maintaining the subsidy.[161] The purpose of such consultations was to clarify the facts and to arrive at a mutually acceptable solution.[162]

If no mutually acceptable solution had been reached within ninety days of the request for consultations, the requesting Member could refer the matter to the SCM Committee.[163] The Committee would then immediately review the effects and evidence of adverse effects. If the Committee determined that adverse effects existed, it could recommend that the granting Member modify the subsidy so as to eliminate the adverse effects. The Committee was to present its conclusions within 120 days of the matter being referred to it.[164]

If the granting Member had not followed the recommendation within six months, the SCM Committee could authorize the requesting Member to take appropriate countermeasures. Such countermeasures must be commensurate with the degree of adverse effects found to exist.[165] The Article 9 procedure was not used during the five years that Articles 8 and 9 were in effect.

158 ASCM, Art. 8.3.
159 *Id.*, Art. 10, n. 35.
160 *Id.*, Art. 8.3 and 4.
161 *Id.*, Art. 9.1.
162 ASCM, Art. 9.2.
163 *Id.*, Art. 9.3.
164 *Id.*, Art. 9.4.
165 *Id.*

PART V: Countervailing Measures

While the previous sections of the ASCM deal with rules governing the use of subsidies by WTO Members, as well as setting forth the procedures under which subsidies may be challenged within the WTO system, Part V of the Agreement outlines the rules and procedures that Members must follow when they take unilateral action against subsidies through the imposition of countervailing measures. The purpose of the Part V provisions is to limit the use of such measures in order to ensure that they are not used in a protectionist manner.[166]

Article 10: Application of Article VI of GATT 1994

Article 10 of the ASCM provides the foundation for the Agreement's provisions on the conduct of a countervailing duty investigation and requirements that must be met before countervailing duties can be imposed. Members are permitted to impose countervailing duties *only after* they have initiated and conducted an investigation in accordance with the provisions of Part V of the ASCM. A countervailing duty is defined in Article 10 as "a special duty levied for the purpose of offsetting any subsidy bestowed directly or indirectly upon the manufacture, production or export of any merchandise."[167] The remedy provisions of Parts II and III of the ASCM regarding prohibited and actionable subsidies may be invoked in tandem with the procedural provisions of Part V, however, only one form of remedy, a countervailing duty or a form of countermeasure (as outlined in Articles 4 and 7) may be imposed to offset the impact of a particular subsidy.[168]

Illustrating the integrated nature of all of the WTO Agreements, Members are also obliged by Article 10 to take account of Article 13 of the WTO Agreement on Agriculture. Article 13, the Due Restraint clause,[169] outlines exceptions to the provisions of Part V of the ASCM. For example, domestic agricultural support measures for which a Member had claimed an exemption from reduction commitments[170] shall be "non-actionable subsidies for purposes of countervailing duties," exempt from remedy action taken under Article XVI of GATT 1994 and Part III of the ASCM on actionable subsidies, and "exempt from actions based on non-violation nullification or impairment of the benefits of tariff concessions accruing to another Member."[171] Members are also required to use

[166] Countervailing measures are not applied as often or by as many countries as anti-dumping measures. Between 1995 and June 30, 2002, eleven WTO Members had imposed a total of 84 countervailing measures (fourteen Members had initiated a total of 147 investigations), compared with over eleven hundred anti-dumping measures imposed by 29 countries (and over 1900 investigations initiated). *See* statistics on the WTO Website (www.wto.org). The United States was by far the largest user, with 34 measures (and 59 initiations). It was followed by the EC with fifteen measures, and Mexico with seven.

[167] ASCM, Art. 10, n. 36.

[168] *Id.*, Art. 10, n. 35.

[169] Article 13 is also referred to as the Peace Clause. Given the contentious nature of agricultural trade in the multilateral trading system over the past fifty years, this "loophole" provision designed to prevent countervailing duty investigations against certain agricultural subsidies is aptly named. It will be interesting to see how the agriculture liberalization negotiations stemming from the Doha Round of multilateral trade negotiations will deal with countervailing duties on agricultural goods.

[170] *WTO Agreement on Agriculture* at Annex 2:1.

[171] *Id.*, Art. 13(a)(i), (ii), and (iii). In addition, this article provides that domestic agricultural support measures that conform with Article 6 of the WTO Agreement on Agriculture (which contains provisions regarding Member's domestic support commitments) shall be exempt from countervailing duties unless there has been a determination of injury or threat of injury to the domestic industry producing the like product in accordance with Article VI of GATT 1994 and Part V of the ASCM on countervailing measures. *Id.*, Art. 13(b)(i). Similarly Art. 13(c) provides that export subsidies conforming to Part V of the Agreement on Agriculture (*e.g.*, subject to reduction commitments), may only be countervailed upon a determination of injury or

"due restraint" with respect to the initiation of a countervailing duty investigation.[172] It should be noted that Article 13 exceptions applied only during the "implementation" period, which was defined as nine years beginning on January 1, 1995, *i.e.*, through December 31, 2003.[173] Arguments have already begun about the legal consequences of expiry—will all agricultural export subsidies be prohibited under Article 3 of the ASCM?

Article 11: Initiation and Subsequent Investigation

The ASCM requires a transparent investigative process that affords interested parties the opportunity to participate in the investigation prior to the imposition of countervailing duties.[174] The requirements outlined in the Agreement include: (1) standards that need to be met for the initiation of an investigation; (2) the determination of domestic industry support for the application for the imposition of countervailing duties; and (3) rules of evidence for access to, and ability to comment on, information submitted during an investigation.

Article 11.1 and 2: Application for Imposition of Countervailing Measures. Article 11.1 of the ASCM requires that a countervailing duty investigation be initiated after written application by or on behalf of the affected domestic industry that includes the following information: (1) the existence of a subsidy and its alleged amount, if possible; (2) the existence of injury to the domestic industry producing the like product; and (3) the existence of a causal link between the subsidized imports and the alleged injury to the domestic industry.[175] Applicants for the imposition of countervailing duties must go beyond a "[s]imple assertion, unsubstantiated by relevant evidence" in order to meet the requirements set forth for the initiation of a countervailing duty investigation.[176] In special circumstances, the authorities of an importing Member may self-initiate an investigation without receiving an application. In such circumstances, the authorities must meet the same evidentiary requirements as a written application.[177]

The application for the imposition of countervailing duties must contain the following information before it is considered sufficient for the administering authority to initiate an investigation: (1) the identity of the petitioning party and a description of the volume and value of domestic production of the like product by the petitioner;[178] (2) a "complete" description of the allegedly subsidized imported product, the country or countries of origin of that product, and the identity of each known exporter or foreign producer and

threat of injury to the domestic industry. Moreover, such export subsidies are not subject to actions based on ASCM, Art. 3, 5, or 6. However, since the ASCM already provides that no countervailing duty may be levied without a determination of injury or threat of injury to a domestic industry, the Article 13 limitation appears to have little practical effect for countervailing duty purposes, except for measures falling within Article 13(a) of the Agriculture Agreement. It has worked to prevent recourse to the multilateral disciplines of the ASCM.

172 It is not clear what "due restraint" means in this context, but it may require Members not to self-initiate investigations as opposed to initiating upon receipt of an application. Self-initiation of countervailing duty investigations is extremely rare.

173 *Id.*, Art. 1(f) and Art. 13.

174 These procedural rules are quite similar though not identical to the rules found in the ADA. *See* Chapter 11 of this book. Interpretations of ASCM obligations can be derived from panel and Appellate Body decisions of the comparable obligations found in the ADA.

175 ASCM, Art. 11.1 and 2.

176 *Id.*, Art. 11.2.

177 ASCM, Art. 11.6. As noted above, self-initiation by the Importing Member is extremely rare.

178 *Id.*, Art. 11.2(i).

any known domestic importers;[179] (3) evidence regarding the nature and amount of the alleged subsidy;[180] and (4) evidence that the domestic industry is being injured by the subsidized imports "through the effects of the subsidies."[181]

Article 11.3: Obligation to Review Evidence Prior to Initiation. Each Member's administering authority is charged with reviewing the evidence presented in each application for the imposition of countervailing duties "to determine whether the evidence is sufficient to justify the initiation of an investigation."[182] It should be noted that while an applicant need only provide such evidence that is reasonably available, the administering authorities have a separate obligation to determine that the evidence before them is sufficient to justify initiating an investigation. Thus, if the evidence "reasonably available" to the applicant is not sufficient to justify initiation, the administering authorities have two possible actions they can take. The administering authorities can either reject the application and refuse to initiate an investigation or they can seek "sufficient evidence" from other sources. According to the Panel report in *Guatemalan Cement II*, interpreting similar language in the Anti-dumping Agreement, "investigating authorities need not content themselves with the information provided in the application but may gather information on their own in order to meet the standard of sufficient evidence for initiation."[183]

It should also be noted that, in line with past GATT practice, while the evidence of the various elements (subsidies and injury or threat of injury thereby) must be sufficient, it need not reach the level necessary to sustain an affirmative preliminary or final determination. The *Guatemalan Cement II* Panel noted that the "type of evidence needed to justify initiation is *the same subject–matter or type of evidence* as that needed to make a preliminary or a final determination, although the quality and quantity needed for the initiation of an . . . investigation is less than for a preliminary or final determination."[184]

179 *Id.*, Art. 11.2(ii).
180 ASCM, Art. 11.2(iii).
181 *Id.*, Art. 11.2(iv).
182 *Id.*, Art. 11.3. In *Thailand Steel*, a WTO panel reviewing an anti-dumping measure imposed by Thailand, citing the Report of the WTO Panel, *Mexico-Anti-dumping Investigation of High Fructose Corn Syrup (HFCS) from the United States*, WT/DS132/R (2000) ("*HFCS*"), noted that the Anti-dumping Agreement (which contains comparable requirements for an application) "does not require an application to contain analysis, but rather to contain information, in the sense of evidence, in support of allegations." The panel went on to conclude that "the fact that the application contains data that is relevant . . . but does not contain explanation or analysis of much of this data does not, in and of itself, lead to a violation." *See* Report of the WTO Panel, *Thailand—Anti-dumping Duties on Angles, Shapes and Sections of Iron or Non-Alloy Steel and H-Beams from Poland*, WT/DS122/R (2001) at ¶¶ 7.75 and 7.76.

Similarly, in *EC Bed Linen*, a WTO panel concluded that the authorities must examine the evidence in the application to determine its sufficiency to warrant initiation, but the ADA (and also similar provisions in the ASCM) "says nothing regarding the nature of the examination to be carried out. Nor does it say anything requiring an explanation of how that examination was carried out." *See* Report of the WTO Panel, *European Communities—Anti-dumping Duties on Imports of Cotton-Type Bed Linen From India*, WT/DS141/R (2001) at ¶ 6.198.

In *Guatemalan Cement II*, the Panel said that an application must contain evidence of all the necessary elements—dumping, injury, and causation—and that the "evidence must be such that an unbiased and objective investigating authority could determine that there was sufficient evidence of dumping within the meaning of Article 2 to justify initiation of an investigation." Report of the WTO Panel, *Guatemala—Definitive Anti-dumping Measures on Grey Portland Cement from Mexico*, WT/DS156/R (2000) at ¶ 8.35 ("*Guatemalan Cement II*").

183 *Guatemalan Cement II*, *supra* note 182, at ¶ 8.62.
184 *Id.* at ¶ 6.57 (emphasis in original). *See also, HFCS, supra* note 182, at ¶ 7.74 .

Similarly, in the GATT dispute on *Softwood Lumber*, the panel stated that "in analyzing further what was meant by the term "sufficient evidence," the Panel noted that the quantum and quality of evidence to be

In interpreting similar obligations to be met prior to initiating an anti-dumping investigation, in *Guatemalan Cement II*, a WTO Panel found that the Guatemalan authorities had violated Article 5.3 of the ADA when they initiated an anti-dumping duty investigation of imports of cement from Mexico without sufficient information to justify initiation.[185] Mexico claimed that the original application for anti-dumping duties failed to provide sufficient information for the investigating authority to "have properly determined that there was sufficient evidence of dumping, still less of a threat of material injury, and of a causal link between the imports allegedly dumped and the alleged threat of material injury to the Guatemalan domestic industry, to justify initiation of an anti-dumping investigation."[186] For example, with respect to the existence of dumping, the application contained only two invoices as evidence of normal value in the Mexican market, and those invoices failed to identify the type of cement sold, the amount sold, and the source of the sale. In addition, the Panel concluded that, based on the evidence submitted in the application, normal value and export price sales were at a completely different level of trade. According to the Panel report, "{t}he existence of these stark differences in quantity and in level of trade, . . . should have triggered at a minimum some reflection on the part of the investigating authorities as to the possible non-comparability of the sales in question."[187] *Guatemalan Cement II* highlights the importance of the procedural rules established by the ADA and the ASCM. In order to be sufficient for initiation, an application for the imposition of anti-dumping or countervailing duties must provide positive evidence of dumping or subsidization that causes material injury to the domestic industry producing the like product that is not based merely on "[s]imple assertion."[188]

Article 11.4: Standing. The authorities are also charged with determining the degree of support for, and opposition to, the application for the imposition of duties and to examine whether the countervailing duty application is being made "by or on behalf of the domestic industry." Article 16 of the ASCM defines the domestic industry as the "domestic producers as a whole of the like products or . . . those of them whose collective output of the products constitute a major proportion of the total domestic production of those products."[189] Article 11.4 states that the application will be deemed to have been

required of an investigating authority prior to initiation of an investigation would necessarily have to be less than that required of that authority at the time of making a final determination." Report of the GATT Panel, *United States—Measures Affecting Imports of Softwood Lumber from Canada*, at ¶ 332, SCM/162 (adopted 27 October, 1993) BISD, 40th Supp., 358.

185 *Guatemalan Cement II*, *supra* note 182, at ¶ 8.39.

186 *Id.*, at ¶ 8.29.

187 *Id.* at ¶ 8.37.

188 ASCM, Art. 11.2. *See* Notice of Initiation of Countervailing Duty Investigation: *Certain Cold-Rolled Flat-Rolled Carbon Quality Steel Products from Brazil, Indonesia, Thailand, and Venezuela*, 64 Fed. Reg. 34,204, 34,207 (U.S. Dep't Comm. June 25, 1999) ("While Petitioners have documented the committed investment element of SIDOR's privatization, a simple assertion that the investment was a condition of SIDOR's sale is insufficient to demonstrate the existence of a direct or indirect financial contribution by the GOV to SIDOR. Thus, we are not investigating the investment commitments which were made a part of the privatization of SIDOR").

189 ASCM, Art. 16.1. The "standing" of the applicants to submit an application was one of the most controversial issues under the 1979 Subsidies and Anti-dumping Codes, giving rise to several dispute proceedings. Article 16.1 and the comparable provision in the ADA reflect the negotiators' efforts to resolve the controversy by establishing clearer rules.

See, e.g. Swedish Steel, where a GATT panel ruled that the U.S. Department of Commerce had not "taken steps which could reasonably be considered to be sufficient to ensure that the initiation of this investigation was based on an application filed on behalf of the domestic industry affected." Report of the GATT Panel,

made on behalf of the domestic industry if it is supported by domestic producers whose collective output is at least 25 percent of the total production of the like product.[190] In addition, the domestic producers expressing support for the petition must account for at least fifty percent of the domestic production expressing an opinion either in favor of or against the petition.[191]

In *HFCS*, a WTO panel, interpreting identical language in the Anti-dumping Agreement, found that Mexico had acted inconsistently with Articles 3.1, 3.2, 3.4, and 3.7 of that agreement when it conducted its standing analysis on only the market segment which sold sugar cane to industrial users, ignoring the segment of the industry that sold to households (which constituted 47 percent of the domestic industry).[192]

Article 11.5–11.11: Initiation and Subsequent Investigation. Article 11 also dictates timelines for the completion of an investigation and standards concerning when an administering authority is required to terminate an investigation. Under Article 11.11, countervailing duty investigations are to be concluded within one year of initiation and in no case shall they last longer than eighteen months. The administering authorities conducting an investigation are required to terminate the investigation "promptly" when they are satisfied that there is not sufficient evidence of subsidization or injury to the domestic industry.[193] For example, if the amount of a subsidy is determined to be

United States—Imposition of Anti-dumping Duties on Imports of Seamless Stainless Steel Hollow Products from Sweden, ADP/47 (1990) (unadopted) at ¶ 5.19 ("*Swedish Steel*").

In a case involving a regional market, a GATT panel in *Cement from Mexico* ruled that the United States had violated its GATT obligations "because the United States authorities did not satisfy themselves prior to initiation that the petition was *on behalf of producers of all or almost all of the production in the regional market.*" Report of the GATT Panel, *United States—Anti-dumping Duties on Gray Portland Cement and Cement Clinker from Mexico*, ADP/82 (1992) (unadopted) at ¶ 5.34 (emphasis added) ("*Cement from Mexico*").

See also, e.g., Salmon CVD, where a GATT panel determined that the U.S. Department of Commerce acted consistently with its obligations when it initiated anti-dumping and countervailing duty investigations against salmon imports from Norway based on a petition filed on behalf of the domestic salmon industry. Norway argued that the Department of Commerce failed to determine if the petitioning party actually represented the affected domestic industry. However, the Panel ruled that the Department of Commerce "could reasonably have relied on statements in the certified petition that these firms accounted for well over a majority of production. . . and that these firms supported" the petition (even though Commerce had received a letter from some of those domestic producers stating that they did not support the petition). Report of the GATT Panel, *United States—Imposition of Countervailing Duty on Imports of Fresh and Chilled Atlantic Salmon from Norway*, BISD, 41st Supp., Vol. II at 576 at ¶ 232 (1994) (adopted).

190 This means all production, including production by firms that may be excluded for purposes of the fifty percent test, *i.e.*, those that are themselves importers of the subject product or affiliated with the foreign producers of the subject product.

191 ASCM, Art. 11.4. In the United States, prior to the implementation of the ASCM and the Uruguay Round Agreements Act, the U.S. Department of Commerce practice was to accept at face value the petitioner's claim that it represented the domestic industry. The Department of Commerce would only question the petitioner's standing if another member of the domestic industry specifically expressed their opposition to the Department in writing. Even then, such a letter of opposition was only considered after an investigation had been initiated. In *Swedish Steel,* a GATT Panel rejected Department of Commerce practice concerning petitioner's standing. At the time, the United States blocked adoption of the decision of the Panel. *See Swedish Steel, supra* note 189.

During the Uruguay Round negotiations, the *Checklist* of issues specifically noted opposition to the U.S. approach of "assuming standing" unless a majority of the domestic industry actively opposed the petition, and noted that a petition or application should contain positive evidence that it is brought on behalf of the domestic industry. *Checklist, supra* note 21, at III.5.1.

192 *See HFCS, supra* note 182.

193 ASCM, Art. 11.9.

de minimis, *i.e.*, less than one percent *ad valorem*, or the volume of imports or material injury to the domestic industry are negligible, the administering authority must terminate the investigation.[194]

In *United States—CDSOA*, the Appellate Body reversed a panel finding that the U.S. Continued Dumping and Subsidy Offset Act (known as the "Byrd Amendment" after the Senator who introduced it), violated Article 11.4. The statute provides for the distribution of anti-dumping and countervailing duties collected by the U.S. Customs Service to the companies that supported the original petition resulting in the order under which the duties were collected. The Panel stated that the statute created:

> the spectre of an investigation being pursued where only a few domestic producers have been affected by the alleged dumping, but industry support is forthcoming because of the prospect of offset payments being distributed if dumping is found in consequence of the investigation and anti-dumping duties imposed. In consequence the CDSOA may be regarded as having undermined the value of AD Article 5.4/SCM Article 11.4 to the countries with whom the United States trades, and the United States may be regarded as not having acted in good faith in promoting this outcome.[195]

The Appellate Body disagreed. In its view Article 11.4 provided no basis for examining the motives of petitioners; "it is the "quantity", rather than the 'quality', of support that is the issue."[196] However, as noted below, the Appellate Body did uphold the Panel's finding that the statute violated Article 32.1 of the ASCM.

Article 12: Evidence

Article 12 establishes standards for rights of access to, and presentation of, data and information during an investigation. Interested parties[197] are to be given notice of the information that the administering authorities require to conduct the investigation[198] and they are to be given at least thirty days in which to respond to the questionnaires (requests for deadline extensions should be considered and granted where practicable).[199]

[194] *Id.*

[195] Report of the Panel, *United States—Continued Dumping and Subsidy Offset Act of 2000*, WT/DS217/, 234/R (2002), ¶ 7.63.

[196] Report of the Appellate Body, *United States—Continued Dumping and Subsidy Offset Act of 2000*, WT/DS217/, 234/AB/R (2003) (*United States—CDSOA"),* ¶ 283.

[197] *Id.* Art. 12.9 defines the term " interested parties" as including "(i) an exporter or foreign producer or the importer of a product subject to investigation, or a trade or business association a majority of the members of which are producers, exporters or importers of such product; and (ii) a producer of the like product in the importing Member or a trade and business association, a majority of the Members of which produce the like product in the territory of the importing Member." Interested Member governments are also allowed to present evidence during an investigation. In addition, Article 12.10 states that the administering authority shall also accept information from industrial users of the product under investigation, or from consumer groups if the product is commonly sold at the retail level. In practice, however, the effect or impact of user or consumer group input has been limited. For example, in the United States there is no evidence that authorities actually take account of the views of users or consumer groups. *See, e.g.*, Decision Memorandum accompanying the Notice of Final Determination of Sales at Less Than Fair Value: *Certain Softwood Lumber Products from Canada*, 67 Fed. Reg. 15,539 (U.S. Dep't Comm. April 2, 2002) (final determ.) (The Department of Commerce noted that it had received a case brief from a consumer group; however, none of the group's views were discussed in the Department's Decision Memorandum.)

[198] ASCM, Art. 12.1.

[199] *Id.*, Art. 12.1.1. This minimum time period was established by the negotiators to resolve controversies over what constituted a "reasonable opportunity" to respond.

The WTO panel in *Guatemalan Cement II* provided some clarification regarding the presentation of arguments and information. According to the Panel, Article 6.1 of the Anti-dumping Agreement (which corresponds to Article 12.1 of the ASCM) "does not require investigating authorities to set time-limits for the

The administering authority is required to provide a complete, full-text copy of the application for the imposition of countervailing duties to all interested parties as soon as an investigation has been initiated[200] and, in addition, the authorities are to ensure that all information presented by one interested party is made available to all other interested parties.[201] Confidential business information, the release of which could cause a "significantly adverse effect" upon the submitting party, shall be treated as confidential by the administering authorities.[202] Interested parties are required to provide non-confidential summaries that "provide a reasonable understanding of the information submitted in confidence" of any information for which confidential treatment had been requested.[203] Once the information has been submitted to the administering authorities by the interested parties, the authorities have the right under Article 12 to conduct on-site verification of any information submitted by any interested party during the course of the proceeding.[204]

If an interested party refuses access to, or otherwise does not provide the requested information within a reasonable time period, or significantly impedes the investigation (*e.g.*, the accuracy of the information presented is not verifiable), the administering authority may make its preliminary or final determinations on the basis of "facts

presentation of arguments and evidence during the final stage of the investigation." Article 6.1 only requires that investigating authorities provide respondents with "at least 30 days for replying to questionnaires" and that the authorities provide interested parties with 'ample' opportunity to present evidence and 'full' opportunity to defend their interests." *Guatemalan Cement II, supra* note 182, at ¶¶ 8.118 and 8.119.

200 ASCM, Art. 12.1.3. The Panel in *Guatemalan Cement II* clarified the meaning of "as soon as," stating that this phrase "conveys a sense of substantial urgency" and that "'immediately' and 'as soon as' are considered to be interchangeable." Thus, full copies of the application for the imposition of duties must be presented to interested parties immediately upon initiation and not several days later. *Guatemalan Cement II, supra* note 182, at ¶ 8.101.

201 ASCM, Art. 12.1.2. Similar provisions in the Anti-dumping Agreement have been reviewed by the Dispute Settlement Body. For example, in *Guatemalan Cement II,* the panel stated that Article 6.4 of the Anti-dumping Agreement "provides that an interested party shall have 'timely opportunities' to see all information that is relevant to the presentation of its case." However, if the authorities require parties to serve copies of all submissions on all other parties, access to the official file may not be necessary. In the event that the parties are not required to serve submissions, "access to the file may be the only practical means by which evidence presented by one interested party" may be "'made available promptly.'" *Guatemalan Cement II, supra* note 182, at ¶ 8.133.

202 ASCM, Art. 12.4. In the United States, confidential business information is submitted under an Administrative Protective Order, which binds the Order's signatories (usually the lawyers for the various parties) to not disclose any information marked as confidential. Mexico permits access to confidential business information only to Mexican lawyers and confidential information can only be reviewed at the offices of the administering authorities (after the parties have posted a large bond to ensure compliance with the protective order). The treatment of confidential information is extremely difficult for administering authorities. While interested parties need access to information in order to present arguments, companies, both applicants and exporters, are concerned that the application of rules such as those used by the United States in other countries, could lead to the inadvertent disclosure of their business and trade secrets.

In *Guatemalan Cement II*, the Panel ruled that an administering authority *cannot delay* making available evidence submitted by an interested party merely because the submitting party had requested confidential treatment for the information submitted. *Guatemalan Cement II, supra* note 182, at ¶ 8.143.

203 ASCM, Art. 12.4.1.

204 ASCM, Art. 12.5 states that the authorities shall "satisfy themselves as to the accuracy of the information supplied" by interested parties. Article 12.6 provides the authorities with the right to conduct on-site verification of information submitted by parties and governments in the territory of other Members so long as the companies involved agree and the Member's government is "notified and does not object." Further, Annex VI of the ASCM outlines the "Procedures for On-The-Spot Investigations Pursuant to Paragraph 6 of Article 12." Annex VI provides basic guidance with respect to the notification of parties of the need for on-the-spot investigations and the requirement that administering authorities notify interested parties in the exporting country of the nature of the information that they will be required to provide prior to the commencement of the on-the-spot investigation.

available."[205] However, "due account" is to be taken of any problems or difficulties experienced by interested parties, especially small companies, in providing the requested information in a complete and timely manner.[206] What constitutes appropriate "facts available," and when recourse to them is appropriate, is a matter of considerable controversy.

This issue of "facts available" is one area where the ASCM and the ADA rules differ.[207] The ADA contains an Annex providing guidance on the use of facts available. Paragraph 7 of the Annex notes that "if an interested party does not cooperate and thus relevant information is being withheld from the authorities, this situation could lead to a result which is less favourable to the party than if the party did cooperate."[208] This use of information leading to less favorable results is often used to justify the use of "adverse facts available" in the case of a non-cooperating respondent or a respondent that otherwise significantly impedes an investigation. Unlike the ADA, however, the ASCM contains no similar provision. Therefore, it is unclear that investigating authorities can ever justify the use of facts that systematically apply to the disadvantage of the responding party in a countervailing duty investigation or review.

Even if resort to adverse facts is permitted in countervailing duty cases, their use is highly controversial. U.S. practice with respect to the use of facts available, especially adverse facts available determinations, has come under attack in the WTO ADA. While the ADA provides more guidance than the ASCM on the use of facts available, a discussion of a key dispute on this issue may provide some guidance for ASCM purposes. In *Hot-Rolled Steel from Japan*, a WTO Panel ruled, and the Appellate Body affirmed, that the U.S. Department of Commerce had violated the relevant provisions in the ADA by unjustifiably assigning adverse facts available to three Japanese respondents during an anti-dumping duty investigation of hot-rolled steel imports from Japan.[209] Two of the respondent companies, NSC and NKK, received adverse facts available determinations because the Department of Commerce refused to accept requested information (in this case, a theoretical-to-actual weight conversion factor) on the grounds that the information was submitted after the pre-established deadlines outlined in the Department's regulations. The Panel ruled that, since the information was submitted before the start of verification, and was not information such as prices or costs that would impede the Department's ability to complete its investigation in a timely manner, "an objective and unbiased investigating authority could not... have reached the conclusion that NKK and NSC failed to provide necessary information within a reasonable period."[210] The inability of respondent companies to meet the often-tight deadlines established by administering authorities is a constant problem in both anti-dumping and countervailing duty proceedings. *Hot-Rolled Steel from Japan* provides guidance to the authorities as to what actually constitutes a "reasonable period" in which to expect respondents to provide requested information.

205 ASCM, Art. 12.7.

206 *Id.*, Art. 12.11.

207 *Compare* ASCM, Art. 12.7 and 11 *with* ADA, Art. 6.8 and Annex II.

208 ADA, Annex II.7.

209 Report of the WTO Panel, *United States—Anti-dumping Measures on Certain Hot-Rolled Steel Products from Japan*, WT/DS184/R (2001) ("*Hot-Rolled Steel from Japan*"), *aff'd* Report of the Appellate Body, *United States—Anti-dumping Measures on Certain Hot-Rolled Steel Products from Japan*, AB-2001-2, WT/DS184/AB/R (2001). It should be noted that the rules governing the use of facts available in the ADA are more detailed than those found in the ASCM. While the language in ASCM Art. 12.7 is identical to the first sentence of Article 6.8 of the ADA, the ADA also contains Annex II, which provides detailed guidance on the use of facts available. The ASCM does not contain similar guidance. Some Members have argued for inclusion in the ASCM of provisions similar to Annex II of the ADA.

210 *Hot-Rolled Steel from Japan*, *supra* note 209, at ¶ 7.60.

The issues surrounding the U.S. Department of Commerce's facts available determination for the third company in *Hot-Rolled Steel from Japan*, KSC, illustrates why the procedural rules established by the WTO Agreement were necessary to regulate the conduct of trade remedy cases among Member states. KSC was requested by the Department of Commerce to provide resale prices and further manufacturing costs for an affiliated purchaser in the United States, California Steel Industries ("CSI"), a normal request in many anti-dumping proceedings. However, while CSI was fifty percent owned by KSC, KSC had no direct control over the company, as evidenced by the fact that CSI was one of the applicants in the case. KSC had requested that the Department of Commerce not require it to provide data on sales to CSI because of the inherent conflict present in the case. KSC had also presented the Department of Commerce with the correspondence demonstrating its efforts to obtain the requisite information from CSI and CSI's refusal to cooperate with KSC. In its determination, the Department of Commerce ruled that KSC had not acted to the best of its ability to obtain the requested reseller data and assigned an adverse facts available product-specific margin to KSC. The Panel ruled that since there was no disputing the fact that KSC had not provided the requested information, the Department of Commerce was justified under Article 6.8 of the ADA in making a determination based on facts available because KSC had not provided the requested information. However, the facts in this case demonstrated that KSC could not have reasonably been expected to provide affiliated reseller data when it did not have direct control over the reseller and the reseller was an applicant in the case and had interests directly opposed to those of the respondent, KSC.[211] Therefore, the application of *adverse* facts available was not appropriate.

Article 13: Consultations

When a countervailing duty application is filed with a Member government, Article 13 of the ASCM requires that Member to provide the opportunity for consultations, prior to initiation, to any Member government whose products may be subject to the countervailing duty investigation.[212] The pre-initiation consultations have the "aim of clarifying" the information submitted in the application, including the nature and amount of the subsidy, injury to the domestic import competing industry, and a causal link between the subsidized imports and the alleged injury.[213] The goal of the consultations is to encourage the parties to arrive at a "mutually agreed solution" to resolve the dispute. In practice, however, while pre-initiation consultations have sometimes resulted in a few subsidy programs not being investigated by the investigating authority (which in practical terms is a worthwhile outcome for the responding Member), they do not appear ever to have led to a complete withdrawal of a case.

Consultations are to be permitted throughout the countervailing duty investigation and are not to be limited to just the pre-initiation stage.[214] Note 44 of Article 13.2 specifies that "no affirmative determination whether preliminary or final be made without reasonable opportunity for consultations having been given." The Member's investigating authority is also required to provide affected Members with access to all non-confidential evidence presented during the investigation.[215] However, Article 13 does not prevent a Member

[211] *Id.* at ¶ 7.73.
[212] ASCM, Art. 13.1
[213] *Id.*, Arts. 11.2 and 13.1.
[214] *Id.*, Art. 13.2.
[215] *Id.*, Art. 13.4.

from proceeding "expeditiously" with respect to initiation of an investigation or reaching a preliminary or final determination, as long as the Member has provided affected Member governments the "reasonable" opportunity for consultations.[216]

Article 14: Calculation of the Amount of a Subsidy
Article 14 provides guidelines for the measurement of four types of subsidy in countervailing duty investigations:

- Government provision of *equity capital* is not to be regarded as conferring a benefit unless the investment decision is inconsistent with the usual investment practices of private investors in the Member country.
- The benefit from a *loan* is the difference between what the recipient pays for the government loan and what the recipient would pay for a comparable commercial loan.
- The benefit from a government *loan guarantee* is the difference between the amount the recipient pays for the guaranteed loan (including the guarantee fee) and the amount it would pay for a comparable commercial loan absent the government guarantee.
- The government *provision of a good or service* or *purchase of a good* is only to be treated as a benefit if the provision is made for less than adequate remuneration or the purchase for more than adequate remuneration. Article 14 does not define "adequate remuneration," though it does require that the adequacy of remuneration be determined in relation to prevailing market conditions for the good or service in question in the country of provision or purchase.[217] It does not indicate how this is to be measured if the Government is the sole provider/purchaser of the good or provider of the service in the country in question; however, the language restricting the comparison to the market in the country of provision or purchase could be viewed as prohibiting cross-border comparisons.[218]

[216] *Id.*, Art. 13.3.

[217] ASCM, Art. 14(d).

[218] In *Softwood Lumber III*, however, the Appellate Body left the door open to the possibility of a cross-border comparison, although it stated that "the possibility under Article 14(d) for investigating authorities to consider a benchmark other than private prices in the country of provision is very limited." *Softwood Lumber III Appellate Body Report*, *supra* note 53, ¶ 102. The Appellate Body indicated that if the investigating authorities use an alternative benchmark, they have an "obligation to ensure that the resulting benchmark relates or refers to, or is connected with, prevailing market conditions in the country of provision. . . ." *Id.* at ¶ 106. While noting it might in certain instances be possible to use a benchmark from outside the country of provision, suitably adjusted, doing so would be extremely difficult. *See id.* at ¶¶ 108–109:

> . . . it seems to us that it would be difficult, from a practical point of view, for investigating authorities to replicate reliably market conditions prevailing in one country on the basis of market conditions prevailing in another country. First, there are numerous factors to be taken into account in making adjustments to market conditions prevailing in one country so as to replicate those prevailing in another country; secondly, it would be difficult to ensure that all necessary adjustments are made to prices in one country. . . . In any event, any comparative advantage would be reflected in the market conditions prevailing in the country of provision and, therefore, would have to be taken into account and reflected in the adjustments made to any method used for the determination of adequacy of remuneration, if it is to relate or refer to, or be connected with, prevailing market conditions in the market of provision.

In the view of the authors, it was not the intention of the drafter of the language to permit cross-border comparisions, nor was it of Mexico, the GATT Contracting Party which had pushed the language of Article 14 (d) to preclude the U.S. from substituting cross-border U.S. energy prices for Mexican ones.

Article 14 is the only Article to provide guidance on the measurement of the benefit conferred by actionable subsidies for countervailing duty purposes.[219] It provides for guidelines for measuring the benefit to the recipient for purposes of defining a subsidy under Article 1.1(b) of the ASCM (defining subsidy as a financial contribution or price or income support which confers a benefit on the recipient) for countervailing duty purposes.[220]

While the chapeau to Article 14 states that it provides guidance for countervailing measures purposes, it also indicates that it is to calculate the benefit to the recipient conferred pursuant to Article 1.1(b). Thus, this Article has been used by Panels to inform their determination of whether a subsidy existed under Article 1 for other purposes as well.[221]

Article 14 requires that any calculation methodology employed by an investigating authority be provided for either in the national legislation or in the investigating authority's implementing regulations.

Article 15: Determination of Injury

The provisions of the ASCM and of the Anti-dumping Agreement with regard to injury determinations are discussed in Chapter 17 of this book.

Article 16: Definition of Domestic Industry

Article 16 defines the term "domestic industry" for purposes of the ASCM. For countervailing duty purposes, the domestic industry must be identified both in order to determine if an application was submitted by or on its behalf (Article 11.1) and to assess whether the subsidized imports have caused or threaten to cause it material injury (Article 15). The definition is also important for multilateral action concerning the definition of adverse effects based on injury to a domestic industry (Article 5). Article 16.1 indicates that "domestic industry" can refer either to the producers as a whole *or* to those producers whose collective output constitutes a major proportion of the total domestic production of the like products. However, it explicitly permits the exclusion of those companies that are related to either the exporters or the importers of the allegedly subsidized products[222] or who are themselves importers of the allegedly subsidized products. This exception creates the potential to ignore a significant percentage of the domestic industry if an investigating authority so chooses. For example, the situation could arise in which there

[219] Annex IV to the ASCM provides guidance on the measurement of the benefit for purposes of serious prejudice analysis (Article 6.1(a) only, which has expired), but specifies that this Annex applies only to that situation. For Article 6.1(a) purposes, the Annex provides that the benefit shall be calculated as the cost to the government providing the subsidy. Article 14 provides means of calculating the benefit amount as the measure of the benefit to the recipient. This dichotomy of treatment represents the denouement of the theological battle that the European Communities and the United States waged throughout the 1980's about whether subsidies should be measured by the "cost to the Government" (the European Communities position, although the European Communities relied so frequently on "opportunity cost to the government" as to blur any distinction) and "value to the recipient" (the U.S. position, although the U.S. Department of Commerce refused to recognize that the value to the recipient could well be less than the face value if the subsidy carried with it obligations, either explicitly to keep an uneconomic plant open, or implicitly to maintain a bloated workforce).

[220] ASCM, Art. 14, chapeau. The Appellate Body has found that this textual reference to Article 1 in the chapeau of Article 14 indicates that benefit is used in the same sense in both Articles as referring to a benefit to the recipient. *See Canadian Civilian Aircraft I*, *supra* note 43, at ¶ 155; *Lead Bar*, *supra* note 62, at ¶ 57.

[221] *See, e.g.*, *Canadian Civilian Aircraft I*, *supra* note 43.

[222] ASCM, footnote 48 defines the situations in which a producer will be deemed to be related to an exporter or importer.

were four domestic producers, each accounting for twenty-five percent of the domestic production, however three of those producers fall within the exception. In that circumstance, this paragraph permits the Member to define the "domestic industry" as the single company, which in reality accounts for only twenty-five percent of the domestic production. Thus, if this was the only company of the four suffering injury, whereas the other three producers were unharmed, the investigating authorities could still be entitled to find injury to the "domestic industry," *i.e.*, the one company. Moreover, this company could be considered to file on behalf of the domestic industry, even if the remaining seventy-five percent of production opposed the application. Nevertheless, Members that apply countervailing duty laws desired this exception out of concern that the related companies or importers would be sheltered from the negative effects of the subsidized imports or would place the interests of the exporting companies above their own domestic interests.

Article 16.2 and 16.3 deal with the situation where the producers in a regional market can be treated as a separate industry. This has primary relevance in the context of injury, and is discussed in Chapter 17 of this book. However, it is also relevant in terms of standing to file an application for an investigation. In brief, the producers in a regional market may be treated as a separate industry for both standing and injury purposes if they sell all or almost all of their production in that market, the demand in that market is not supplied to any substantial degree by other domestic producers, and the subsidized imports are concentrated in that market and are causing injury to the producers of all or almost all of the production in that market.[223]

Article 16.4 notes that where two or more countries have entered into a customs union within the meaning of Paragraph 8(a) of GATT 1994, Article XXIV, and have reached such a level of integration that they have the characteristics of a single, unified market, the term "domestic industry" applies to the producers in the entire customs union. This paragraph would require that the European Community treat the entire territory of the European Community as a single market for purposes of defining the domestic industry. Again, this is relevant for both standing and injury purposes.

Article 17: Provisional Measures

This article addresses the use of provisional measures in the course of a countervailing duty investigation. Provisional measures are designed to provide a certain degree of protection to domestic industries from the harmful effects of subsidized imports at a fairly early stage in the investigation. Any imports to which provisional measures are applied will be assessed for countervailing duties if a definitive measure is imposed at the end of the investigation, so that exporters are likely to exercise a little more caution after they have been applied.

Provisional measures may only be imposed if the following criteria are met:

- An investigation must have been initiated in accordance with Article 11 of the ASCM;
- There must have been public notice of that initiation;
- Interested parties must have had an adequate opportunity to submit information and make comments;
- There must have been a preliminary determination that a subsidy exists and that the domestic industry is injured by reason of the subsidized imports; and

[223] *See, e.g., Cement from Mexico, supra* note 189, at ¶ 5.22–5.23.

- The authorities must determine that such measures are necessary to prevent injury being caused during the investigation.[224]

Once those criteria are met, provisional measures may be imposed. The ASCM specifies what measures are acceptable. The only provisional measures permitted are the use of provisional countervailing duties guaranteed by cash or bonds equal to the amount of the provisionally calculated subsidization. Moreover, the provisional measures must be refundable. It should be noted that in applying the provisional measures, a Member must also follow the relevant provisions of Article 19, relating to the application of countervailing duties (discussed, *infra.*).

Finally, there are time limits on the application of provisional measures. Such measures should be applied for as short a period as possible, may not be applied sooner than sixty days after the date of initiation of the investigation, and may not exceed four months.[225] The application of these requirements was addressed in *Softwood Lumber II.* Canada had challenged the manner in which the United States had imposed provisional measures under the "critical circumstances" provision of ASCM, Art. 20.6. The Panel found that Article 20 did not permit an exception to the requirements of 17.3 and 4. The U.S. had argued that the period of application of Article 17.4 applied only to the time frame during which the duty deposit or bond was collected, but did not address the date of entry of the imports on which that duty or bond was assessed. The Panel rejected this argument, stating that such an approach would render meaningless the disciplines imposed by Article 17.[226] If the Member country's final determination is issued more than four months after the imposition of provisional measures, the imports during that post-four month gap period are not subject to the provisional measures and must be permitted entry without hindrance.

Article 18: Undertakings

This article deals with undertakings that may be the basis for suspension or termination of an investigation without the imposition of provisional measures or countervailing duties. In order to accept such an undertaking, the following criteria must be met:

- The undertaking must be voluntary;[227] and
- The authorities of the importing Member must have made a preliminary affirmative determination of subsidization and injury to the domestic industry therefrom.[228]

Undertakings may take two different forms: (1) an agreement by the government of the exporting Member to eliminate or limit the subsidy or to take other measures concerning its effects[229] or (2) an agreement by the exporter(s) to revise prices so as to eliminate the injurious effect of the subsidies. There are several restrictions on such exporter-based

224 ASCM, Art. 17.1.

225 ASCM, Art. 17.4. *Compare* ADA, Art. 7.4, permitting a two-month extension if requested by any exporters representing a significant percentage of the trade involved. *See HFCS, supra* note 182, at ¶ 7.181 (finding ADA, Art. 7.4, which contains a similar limit on the length of time provisional measures could be imposed, was not ambiguous and provisional measures could not be imposed for more than six months).

226 *Softwood Lumber II, supra* note 50, at ¶ 7.102.

227 *ASCM,* Art. 18.1

228 *Id.*, Art. 18.2.

229 Frequently the Government of the exporting Member imposes an export tax, thus receiving the revenue generated by the measures itself rather than allowing the importing Member to collect them in the form of duties.

undertakings. First, the price increases must not be higher than necessary to eliminate the amount of the subsidy and preferably will be less than the amount of the subsidy, if that lesser amount would be sufficient to remove the injury to the domestic industry.[230] In addition, exporter-based undertakings cannot be sought or accepted by the importing Member unless it has obtained the consent of the exporting Member.[231]

The importing Member need not accept an undertaking if it determines that such undertaking is not practical. In such case, the importing Member, to the extent practicable, must provide the exporters with an explanation of the reasons for considering such an undertaking inappropriate and provide the exporter an opportunity to comment on those reasons.[232] Similarly, while the importing Member may suggest an undertaking, it cannot force an exporter to enter into such an undertaking. Moreover, the fact that either party did not offer or accept an undertaking may not prejudice the outcome of the investigation.[233] However, in a regional domestic industry case, the importing Member must offer the exporters an opportunity to enter into an undertaking if the countervailing measures would be imposed nation-wide.[234]

Once an undertaking is accepted, if either the exporting Member requests it or the importing Member so decides, the investigation may be continued and completed. If, as a result, there is a negative finding of either subsidization or injury caused by the subsidized imports, then the undertaking must lapse.[235] The only exception is if the negative determination is due, in large part, to the existence of the undertaking. If that is the case, then the importing Member may require that the undertaking be continued for a reasonable period. It should be noted that "reasonable period" is not defined and there have been no dispute challenges on this issue yet to interpret the meaning of "reasonable period." If an affirmative determination of subsidization and injury is made, then the undertaking may continue, consistent with the requirements of the ASCM.[236]

Finally, this Article permits the authorities of the importing Member to require any government or exporter that has entered into an undertaking to provide information periodically, and permit verification of that information, concerning its fulfillment of the provisions of the undertaking.[237] If there is a violation, the authorities of the importing Member may, in conformity with the ASCM, immediately impose provisional measures based on the best information available.[238] Definitive duties may be levied in accordance with the ASCM on products entered for consumption not more than ninety days prior to the imposition of provisional measures, but in no case may the retroactive assessment apply to entries prior to the date of the violation of the undertaking.[239]

Article 19: Imposition and Collection of Countervailing Duties

This article provides the rules for the imposition and collection of countervailing duties. Specifically, the first paragraph notes that, if after consultations a Member makes a final determination regarding the existence and amount of a subsidy and finds that the

[230] ASCM, Art. 18.1(b).
[231] *Id.*, Art. 18.2.
[232] *Id.*, Art. 18.3.
[233] ASCM, Art. 18.5.
[234] *Id.*, Art. 16.3.
[235] *Id.*, Art. 18.4.
[236] *Id.*
[237] ASCM, Art. 18.6.
[238] *Id.*
[239] *Id.*

subsidized imports are thereby causing injury, it may impose countervailing duties unless the subsidy or subsidies are withdrawn. One issue that has been raised repeatedly is whether or not a Member should impose duties only to the level necessary to eliminate the injury caused by the effects of the subsidy. This is known as the "lesser duty" rule. The second paragraph of this article makes clear that use of the lesser duty rule is not required and that the decision of whether to impose a duty less than the level of subsidization found is a decision to be made by the importing Member country alone. Nonetheless, the paragraph notes that use of the lesser duty is desirable.[240]

Paragraph 3 provides some procedural safeguards. It requires that the imposition of a countervailing duty be levied on a non-discriminatory basis from all sources found to be subsidized and causing injury. In other words, if a Member country finds that imports from countries A, B, and C are subsidized and causing injury, it cannot impose duties only on imports from countries A and B.[241]

This paragraph also provides that an exporter that was not individually investigated, other than because it failed to cooperate with an investigation, is entitled to an expedited review in order to determine its individual countervailing duty rate.[242]

Finally, paragraph 4 of this article provides that no duty shall be levied on an imported product in excess of the amount of the subsidy found to exist, calculated in terms of subsidization per unit of the exported product. This requires that the amount of subsidy must have been determined in a manner consistent with the Agreement, before a duty can be levied. In other words, even if a Member's authorities calculate a per unit subsidy of 25 percent and impose a duty of 19 percent, that is unacceptable if the subsidy that would have been determined in an ASCM consistent manner was less than 19 percent.

Article 20: Retroactivity

This article prevents the application of retroactive duties. Specifically, paragraph 1 provides that provisional measures and countervailing duties may only be applied to products entered for consumption *after* the date on which the authorities make either a preliminary or final determination of subsidization and injury from subsidized imports through the effects of the subsidies.

Paragraphs 2 and 4 provide that countervailing duties may not be levied retroactively for the period for which provisional measures were applied, if the authorities only found a threat of injury. This is logical since, if injury is only threatened, the duties during the provisional measure period are not necessary to offset or prevent injury—there was none. The only exception is if a final finding of present injury would have been reached but for the effect of the provisional measures.[243]

Paragraph 3 provides that if the definitive duty is higher than that imposed under the provisional measures, the importing Member may not collect the difference. If the

240 *Id.*, Art. 19.2. The United States does not apply the lesser duty rule. The European Union applies the rule and Canada may apply a lesser duty if it concludes such duty is in the public interest.

241 If, however, the authorities find all three are subsidized but only A and B are causing injury, then the Member must limit the imposition of duties only to imports from countries A and B.

242 In *Softwood Lumber II*, Canada raised a claim that U.S. law and regulation with respect to expedited reviews violated this provision in situations in which the United States made its initial subsidy determination on an aggregate basis. The Panel, however, found that U.S. law did not mandate action in violation of the ASCM, and that the expedited review process had not yet arisen in the underlying case (since there was not yet a final determination of subsidies at that point). It therefore rejected Canada's claims in this respect. *See Softwood Lumber II*, *supra* note 50, at ¶¶ 7.142 and 7.159.

243 ASCM, Art. 20.2.

definitive duty is lower, then the importing Member must reimburse the provisional measure or release the bond expeditiously. Similarly, if the final determination of injury or threat thereof is negative, then the importing Member must refund the provisional measures or release any bond posted.[244]

The language of paragraph 6 creates a very limited exception to the prohibition of retroactive assessment, referred to as "critical circumstances."[245] For critical circumstances to exist there must have been injury from massive imports of a product benefiting from subsidies paid or bestowed inconsistently with the provisions of GATT 1994 and the ASCM, *i.e.*, export and import-substitution subsidies. Thus, the only imports that should be included in the determination of massive imports (and injury therefrom) are those that actually benefited from the prohibited subsidies. In addition, the paragraph specifically provides only for the assessment of definitive countervailing duties on products entered not more than ninety days prior to the date of application of provisional measures. It does not create an exception to permit the application of provisional measures to those same entries prior to the application of definitive duties. Finally, the ninety-day period must be counterbalanced against the provision prohibiting the application of provisional measures not sooner than sixty days after the date of initiation of the investigation.[246]

Article 21: Duration and Review of Countervailing Duties and Undertakings

This article again reflects the Members' concerns about the trade restrictive effects of a countervailing duty. It begins by declaring that "a countervailing duty shall remain in force only as long as and to the extent necessary to counteract subsidization which is causing injury."[247] From there, it notes the procedures for the review of the imposition of duties.

In general, authorities are instructed to review the need for the continued imposition of duties on their own or upon request from any interested party, assuming a reasonable period of time has elapsed since the imposition of the definitive countervailing duty.[248] While the term "reasonable period" has not been interpreted through the dispute resolution process, many countries provide for an annual review of the imposition of definitive duties. The second paragraph provides that interested parties shall have the right to request the authorities to examine whether the continued imposition of definitive duties is necessary to offset subsidization, whether injury would be likely to continue or recur if the duty were changed or eliminated, or both. This, however, is not an absolute right and Members may require the requesting party to submit positive evidence substantiating the need for such a review.[249] If after review, the authorities determine that the imposition of definitive duties is no longer warranted, the duties must be terminated immediately.

In conducting a review under Article 21.2,[250] the investigating authority need not examine all issues anew, but is entitled to make certain presumptions based on its previous

[244] *Id.*, Art. 20.5.
[245] *Id.*, Art. 20.6.
[246] *Id.*, Art. 17.3.
[247] ASCM, Art. 21.1.
[248] *Id.*, Art. 21.2.
[249] *Id.*
[250] The *Lead Bar* Appellate Body Report indicated that the United States' administrative review procedure, whereby it determines the amount of duties to assess for prior entries, fell within the purview of Article 21. This position was also taken by the Appellate Body in the *Privatization Subsidies* dispute. *See Privatization Subsidies Appellate Body Report, supra* note 68, at ¶ 140. *But cf. Softwood Lumber II, supra* note 50, at ¶ 7.151 (stating that Article 21.2 is silent on the question of administrative reviews).

findings. However, any presumptions used must be rebuttable and the investigating authority is required to review those findings on the basis of any evidence before it at the time of review. The Appellate Body in *Lead Bar* found that the United States was not entitled to presume that a benefit continued to flow after a company had been privatized. Specifically, the Appellate Body stated:

> In an administrative review pursuant to Article 21.2, the investigating authority may be presented with "positive information" that the "financial contribution" has been repaid or withdrawn and/or that the "benefit" no longer accrues. On the basis of its assessment of the information presented to it by interested parties, as well as of other evidence before it relating to the period of review, the investigating authority must determine whether there is a continuing need for the application of countervailing duties.[251]

In *Korean DRAMS,*[252] a panel considered an identical provision of the ADA.[253] Korea challenged the U.S. application of the standard of review for continuing an anti-dumping duty in the context of ADA, Article 11.2 (comparable to ASCM, Article 21.2). Specifically, the provision provides:

> Interested parties shall have the right to request the authorities to examine whether the continued imposition of the duty is necessary to offset dumping, whether the injury would be likely to continue or recur if the duty were removed or varied, or both. If, as a result of the review under this paragraph, the authorities determine that the anti-dumping duty is no longer warranted, it shall be terminated immediately.

Korea challenged the U.S. regulations requiring the Department of Commerce to be satisfied that future dumping "is not likely" before it revokes an order.[254] The Panel determined that ADA 11.2 must be interpreted in light of Article 11.1: "an anti-dumping duty shall remain in force only as long as and to the extent necessary to counteract dumping which is causing injury."[255] The Panel found that this "necessity" requirement established that there must be positive evidence demonstrating that objective conditions existed to demonstrate that circumstances "demand" the continued imposition of duties.[256] Thus, to continue a duty, the administering authorities must have positive evidence that continued subsidization or injury is likely if the duty is removed. Similarly, the Panel found that the U.S. standard that it must be demonstrated that dumping or subsidization and injury were "not likely" to continue or recur before an order would be revoked was not equivalent to the requirement established by the ADA, that the continuation or recurrence must be demonstrated to be likely for continuation of an order.[257] Rather, the panel found that determining something is likely to occur carries the same meaning as determining that it is "probable" that something will occur.[258]

Regardless of whether reviews under paragraph 2 occur, paragraph 3 provides that no definitive duties shall last longer than five years unless specific findings are made. The paragraph provides for termination after five years, but permits continuation of the duties in certain circumstances. Such wording creates a presumption that most duties will be

[251] *Lead Bar, supra* note 62, at ¶ 61. *See also Privatization Subsidies Appellate Body Report, supra* note 68, at ¶ 141.

[252] Report of the WTO Panel, *United States—Anti-Dumping Duty on Dynamic Random Access Memory Semiconductors (DRAMS) of One Megabit or Above from Korea*, WT/DS99/R (1999) ("*Korean DRAMS*").

[253] *Compare* Anti-dumping Agreement, Art. 11.2 and 3 *with* ASCM, Art. 21.2 and 3.

[254] *Korean DRAMS, supra* note 252, at ¶¶ 6.35–6.54.

[255] *Compare* ADA, Art. 11.1 *with* ASCM, Art. 21.1.

[256] *Korean DRAMS, supra* note 252, at ¶ 6.42.

[257] *Id.* at ¶ 6.50.

[258] *Id.* at ¶ 6.48, n. 494.

terminated after five years and that the continued imposition of definitive countervailing duties will be the exception rather than the rule.[259] This provision was put in place to end the practice of keeping duties in place long after any economic rationale for the duties had ended. Prior to the establishment of the WTO, the United States was the only significant user of countervailing duty laws that had no such "sunset" provision. Subsequently, the United States put a provision in place, however, disputes have been raised as to the burden established by U.S. law.

Article 21.4 provides that the provisions of Article 12 regarding evidence and procedure apply to any review carried out under this Article and that any such review shall normally be concluded within twelve months of the date of initiation.[260] Finally, the Article provides that the review requirements apply equally to reviews of price undertakings entered into pursuant to Article 18.[261] Certain other provisions of the ASCM, such as Articles 15.3 and 19, also apply to review undertaken pursuant to Article 21.3.

Article 22: Public Notice and Explanation of Determinations

This is another article particularly concerned with procedural due process issues. Article 22 addresses the requirements of public notice and explanation of determinations. Paragraph 1 provides that if the authorities of an importing Member are satisfied that there is sufficient evidence to justify initiating a countervailing duty investigation pursuant to Article 11, they must provide public notice and, in addition, notify both the Member or Members whose products are subject to investigation and any other interested parties known to them.

Paragraph 2 identifies the minimum information required that must be included in the notice or in a separate report that is readily available to the public. To ensure that it is readily available, it is best to reference the existence of the report and whom to contact to obtain a copy in the public notice.[262] A separate report does not eliminate the requirement that there be public notice. Most countries fulfill the public notice requirement by publishing a notice in their official gazette or other legal publication. The minimum information that must be provided is: (1) the name of the exporting country(ies) and product(s) involved; (2) the date of the initiation of the investigation; (3) a description of the subsidy practices to be investigated; (4) a summary of the factors on which the allegation of injury is based;[263] (5) the address to which interested parties should send their information, statements, etc.; and (6) the time limits for interested parties to submit their views.

In addition to the public notice of initiation of a countervailing duty investigation, the importing Member must provide public notice of the following: any preliminary or final determination (whether affirmative or negative); any decision to accept an undertaking; the termination of an undertaking; and the termination of any definitive duty. Paragraph 3

[259] Several WTO Members have shorter time periods for the expiration of duties. For example, Chile provides for duties to last one year.

[260] ASCM, Art. 21.4.

[261] *Id.*, Art. 21.5.

[262] In *Guatemalan Cement II*, interpreting a similar provision in the ADA, the Panel found that failure to reference the separate report in Guatemala's public notice meant that the separate report was not "readily available." *See Guatemalan Cement II*, *supra* note 182, at ¶¶ 8.93 and 8.96.

[263] This requirement is only for a summary of the factors on which the allegation is based. Although it is desirable from a transparency standpoint, there is no obligation to include in a notice of initiation any *conclusions* that have been reached by the investigating authorities, such as which producers constitute the domestic industry. *See HFCS*, *supra* note 182, at ¶ 7.88.

requires that such public notices must set forth in "sufficient detail" the findings and conclusions reached on all issues of fact and law considered material by the investigating authorities. Finally, the importing Member is required to forward such notices and reports to the exporting Member or Members whose products are subject to the determination and to any other interested parties known to the importing Member. Thus, if the importing Member is aware of the specific exporters affected by the determination, this would require the importing Member to forward notice of the decision to those exporters.

Paragraph 4 sets forth specific notice requirements for the imposition of provisional measures. Specifically, the public notice or a publicly available separate report must contain a sufficiently detailed explanation of the preliminary determinations on the existence of a subsidy and injury and shall identify, or at least refer to, the matters of fact and law that lead to specific arguments being accepted or rejected. While recognizing the need to protect the confidentiality of information, the notice or report must contain: (1) the names of the suppliers—or if impracticable—the supplying countries; (2) a description of the product that is sufficient for customs purposes; (3) the amount of the subsidy established and the basis on which the existence of the subsidy has been determined; (4) considerations relating to injury as identified in Article 15; and (5) the main reasons leading to the determination.

Similar notice requirements exist for the notice of the decision to impose definitive duties, or the conclusion or suspension of an investigation pursuant to an undertaking. In addition to the information described above, the notice or report must address the reasons for acceptance or rejection of relevant arguments or claims by interested Members, the exporters, and the importers.[264] In addition, the public notice of the conclusion or suspension of an investigation pursuant to the acceptance of an undertaking must include or make available the non-confidential portion of the undertaking accepted.[265] These notice requirements also apply to any reviews undertaken pursuant to Article 21 and to any decisions pursuant to Article 20 to apply duties retroactively.[266]

Article 23: Judicial Review

This provides specific rules aimed at ensuring the rights of the various parties affected by a countervailing duty action. Article 23 requires that any Member whose national legislation provides for countervailing duty measures must maintain procedures for the prompt review of administrative actions relating to final determinations and reviews pursuant to Article 21. Those tribunals may be judicial, arbitral, or administrative in nature, but they must be independent of the authorities responsible for the determination in question. In addition, all parties that participated in the administrative proceeding and that are directly and individually affected by the administrative action must have access to such review.

PART VI: Institutions

Article 24: Committee on Subsidies and Countervailing Measures and Subsidiary Bodies

This article establishes the institutional provisions for the Agreement and the Committee on Subsidies and Countervailing Measures ("SCM Committee"). Each Member has a

264 ASCM, Art. 22.5.
265 *Id.*, Art. 22.6.
266 *Id.*, Art. 22.7.

representative on the Committee, which meets at least twice a year. Under the 1979 Subsidies Code, there was a similar Committee only for Code Signatories; however, the current SCM Committee includes all WTO Members.

In a departure from the institutions established under the 1979 Subsidies Code, Article 24 provides for the establishment of a Permanent Group of Experts ("PGE"). These experts are not representatives of the Member governments, rather they are five independent persons, highly qualified in the field of subsidies and trade relations. The experts serve for staggered five-year terms and are elected by the SCM Committee.

One responsibility of the PGE is to assist any panel established under Article 4 (remedies for the use of prohibited subsidies), if requested, by reviewing the evidence with regard to the nature and existence of the measure at issue and reporting its conclusions of whether or not the measure at issue is a prohibited subsidy to the panel, which must accept those conclusions without modification.[267] To date, none of the panels established pursuant to Article 4 have requested the assistance of the PGE. Outside of a panel, any Member may consult the PGE, which may issue advisory opinions as to the nature of any subsidy, proposed or currently maintained by that Member. Such advisory opinions will be confidential and may not be invoked in proceedings under Article 7. In the first five years of the PGE's existence, no such advisory opinions were requested.

The reasons for the lack of referral to the PGE are difficult to determine. The main reason appears to be the reluctance of panels to let the PGE do their work. The lack of requests for advisory opinions is more straightforward—governments do not want to ask for an opinion which may condemn one of their programs.

The SCM Committee is authorized to establish any other subsidiary bodies it deems appropriate.[268] In the course of carrying out their functions, the SCM Committee and any subsidiary bodies established may consult with and seek information from any source they deem appropriate.[269] This enables the SCM Committee and its subsidiary bodies to consult non-governmental organizations if they so choose. However, before the SCM Committee or subsidiary body seeks information from a source within the territory of a Member, it must inform the Member involved.[270] This final requirement respects the sovereignty of the individual Members and reflects the balance of interests between national sovereignty and a common international position.

PART VII: Notification and Surveillance

Article 25: Notifications

This Article reflects the desire of the negotiating countries to install some subsidy discipline through the use of transparency with respect to the granting of subsidies. Specifically, this Article provides that Members must notify any subsidy, within the definition of Article 1.1, granted or maintained within their territory that is specific within the meaning of Article 2.[271] Such notifications are to be submitted no later than June 30th of each year.[272]

Many of the Members do not submit the notifications provided for by this Article. There have been several discussions within the SCM Committee on ways to

[267] ASCM, Art. 4.5.
[268] *Id.*, Art. 24.2.
[269] *Id.*, Art. 24.5.
[270] *Id.*
[271] ASCM, Art. 25.2.
[272] *Id.*, Art. 25.1.

improve conformity. Most of the developed country Members conform to some extent. However, there can be a great degree of difficulty in notifying programs, particularly for programs provided by the sub-national governments. For example, the United States notifies over 200 programs, however, a search of the individual state websites indicates a wide range of state programs that have not been notified. Beyond that, there may also be subsidies provided at the municipal level that have never been notified.

In addition to the notification requirement, this Article permits Members to query other Members about the nature and extent of any subsidy granted or maintained by another Member, or the reasons why the maintaining Member does not consider such measure as subject to the notification requirement. Several Members are quite active in this regard.

In addition to the notification of subsidies, the Members are required to report expeditiously to the SCM Committee all preliminary or final actions taken with respect to countervailing duties.[273] The WTO issues a report every six months of any countervailing measures imposed within the preceding six months. It should be noted that these semi-annual reports are available on the WTO website (although some Members flout the requirement to report the value of subject imports, thus precluding the use of these data for sophisticated analysis).

Finally, Members are required to notify the SCM Committee of the competent authorities within the Members' governments designated to initiate and conduct investigations as well as the Members' domestic procedures governing the initiation and conduct of an investigation.[274] This information is also available on the WTO website.

Article 26: Surveillance

This Article operates in conjunction with Article 25 and provides for oversight by the SCM Committee of the notifications made pursuant to Article 25. Specifically, the SCM Committee is to examine new and full notifications of subsidies submitted at special sessions held every third year. The notifications in the interim period, which merely update the most recent full notification, are reviewed at each regular meeting of the SCM Committee.[275] Similarly, at each regular meeting, the SCM Committee examines the semi-annual reports of countervailing duty actions submitted pursuant to Article 25.11.[276]

PART VIII: Developing Country Members

Article 27: Special and Differential Treatment of Developing Country Members

This Article addresses the thorny issue of the proper role of subsidies in economic development. It begins by recognizing "that subsidies may play an important role in economic development programmes of developing country Members."[277] Nonetheless, while there are provisions for special and differential treatment with respect to the multilateral disciplines, the special and differential treatment to be accorded developing countries in the course of a countervailing duty proceeding is fairly minimal.

273 *Id.*, Art. 25.11.
274 *Id.*, Art. 25.12.
275 ASCM, Art. 26.1.
276 *Id.*, Art. 26.2.
277 *Id.*, Art. 27.1.

In particular, Article 27 grants a permanent exemption for the least developed Members from the prohibition on export subsidies,[278] while they are granted eight years to phase out import- substitution subsidies.Other developing country Members are exempted from the prohibition on export subsidies for eight years from the date of entry into force of the WTO Agreement and from the prohibition on import-substitution subsidies for five years. In the wake of the Doha Ministerial Conference in 2001, there is considerable debate about extension of these time periods.

There are however considerable restrictions on the eight-year grace period for the phase-out of export subsidies by developing country Members. The level of the export subsidies may not be increased in that period. Moreover, if the use of such subsidies is inconsistent with the Member's development needs, the Agreement requires them to eliminate such export subsidies in a shorter period.[279] In addition, a developing country Member must phase out its export subsidies for any product within two years of its reaching export competitiveness.[280]

Special rules also apply with respect to the serious prejudice provisions when applied to developing country Members. Specifically, there may be no presumption of serious prejudice under Article 6.1 (as noted above, though, Article 6.1 lapsed at the end of 1999). Serious prejudice must be demonstrated by positive evidence.[281] No action may be taken with respect to actionable subsidies granted or maintained by a developing country, other than those described in Article 6.1, unless nullification or impairment of tariff concessions or other obligations under the GATT 1994 are found to exist as a result of the subsidy and that nullification or impairment occurs in such a way as to displace or impede the imports of a like product of another Member into the market of the subsidizing developing country Member or injury occurs to a domestic industry in the complaining Member's market.[282] In other words, no action can be taken because of harm suffered as a result of such subsidies in third country markets.

The lapsing of Article 6.1 also raises other questions with respect to the application of the serious prejudice provisions with respect to developing country Members. ASCM Article 27.9 provides that developing country Members are not subject to claims that their actionable subsidies have caused serious prejudice *unless* those subsidies fall under the provisions of ASCM Article 6.1. It might, therefore, be possible to argue that, because Article 6.1 has lapsed, there is no longer any situation in which a developing country Member may be subject to a serious prejudice claim. On the other hand, since the presumption of serious prejudice arising in Article 6.1 never applied to developing country

[278] These Members are defined in the ASCM, Annex VII, to include any Member designated as Least Developed by the United Nations, and certain specified countries (Annex VII(b)) as long as their GNP per capita remains below $1,000 per annum.

[279] ASCM, Art. 27.4. This last stricture to eliminate export subsidies in less than eight years if the export subsidies are inconsistent with the country's development needs is a peculiar construct. If they are inconsistent with the development needs of the country, presumably the country would eliminate them in its effort to meet its development needs although there may be instances in which the recipient is sufficiently powerful to block their elimination.

[280] ASCM, Art. 27.5. "Export competitiveness" is reached when that Member's exports of that product account for at least 3.25 percent of the world trade in that product for two consecutive calendar years. For least developed countries that have reached export competitiveness in a particular product, the ASCM provides for phase-out over an eight-year period. There is current discussion in the SCM Committee about what should occur if the developing country later loses that export competitiveness.

[281] *Id.*, Art. 27.8.

[282] *Id.*, Art. 27.9. Note that this paragraph also permits the application of countervailing duties if injury to the domestic industry of the importing Member is found by reason of these actionable subsidies.

Members, it could be argued that the definitional aspect of Article 6.1 still applies, in order to raise a serious prejudice complaint against a developing country Member.

With respect to countervailing duties, the only special and differential rules for developing countries concern the definition of *de minimis* subsidies and "negligible" levels of imports. Specifically, the Article requires that a countervailing duty investigation against a developing country Member be terminated immediately if the investigating authorities determine that the overall level of subsidies is no greater than two percent[283] (the *de minimis* level applicable to developed countries is one percent), or that the volume of subsidized imports represents less than four percent of the total imports of the like product in the importing Member. This was intended as a "safe harbor" such that developing countries would not have to pay the (often large) costs of defense if their exports represent a small part of the market.

This four percent limit is subject to the exception that if imports are cumulated among countries for injury purposes, then the four percent limit does not apply if all the developing countries accounting individually for less than four percent of the total imports of the like product, collectively account for more than nine percent of the total imports—which effectively removes the safe harbor.[284] In other words, if there are countervailing duty investigations of the same like product from three developing countries simultaneously and each country accounts for 3.5 percent of total imports of the like product, then the four percent negligible import limit would not apply. This is the case even though none of the developing countries can control the exports of the others, and if total imports are small, four or nine percent of those imports may be truly negligible in terms of impact on the overall market.

A final provision indicates that the provisions of Part III of the ASCM, covering actionable subsidies, does not apply to certain types of subsidies for developing countries. Those are direct forgiveness of debt, and subsidies to cover social costs—in whatever form—when directly linked to a privatization program of a developing country. Therefore, those specific types of subsidies, in the very limited circumstances of this provision, do not constitute actionable subsidies within the meaning of the ASCM for purposes of the multilateral disciplines of Part III.[285] This would not appear to prevent authorities from imposing countervailing duties on the use of such subsidies, since the provisions regarding countervailing duties are found in Part V of the ASCM.

Part IX: Transitional Arrangements

Article 28: Existing Programmes

Article 28 provides for bringing existing arrangements into conformity with the WTO Agreement after the date of entry into force of the WTO Agreement for that particular Member. Any subsidy programs that were established prior to the date on which the Member signed the WTO Agreement and that are inconsistent with the provisions of the ASCM must be notified to the SCM Committee within ninety days after the date of entry into force of the WTO Agreement for that Member and must be brought into conformity within three years after the date of entry into force of the WTO Agreement.[286] In addition,

[283] Three percent in certain circumstances. *See* ASCM, Art. 27.10(a) and 11.

[284] *Id.*, Art. 27.10(b).

[285] *Id.*, Art. 27.13.

[286] ASCM, Art. 28.1.

a Member may not extend the scope of such a program or renew it upon its expiry, even if that occurs within the three-year transition period.

Article 29: Transformation into a Market Economy

Article 29 establishes special rules for countries in the process of transformation from a centrally-planned economy to a market-based, free enterprise economy. Paragraph 1 provides that such Members may apply programs and measures necessary for such transformation. It should be noted that while this paragraph eliminates any prohibition on the use of specific types of subsidies, it does not restrict the actionability of any subsidies employed.

Paragraph 2 provides more specific rules concerning the actionability of such subsidies. It provides a seven-year phase-out period for otherwise prohibited subsidies (within the meaning of Article 3) and prevents the resort to dispute settlement under Article 4 during that phase-out period. The seven-year phase out applied from the date of entry into force of the WTO Agreement.[287]

This paragraph not only exempts the transition Members from the Article 4 disciplines, it affords them the exemptions from the serious prejudice dispute settlement accorded to developing countries under Article 27.9. In addition, unlike developing countries, that exemption from serious prejudice applies even if the program used involves debt-forgiveness.[288]

Paragraph 3 nevertheless attempts to establish transparency by requiring the transitional Member to notify its subsidy programs on the first practical date after the date of entry into force of the WTO Agreement. Additional notifications may be made up to two years after the entry into force of the WTO Agreement.

Finally, this Article permits such Members to depart from their notified programs and measures and their time frame for phase-out, in exceptional circumstances, if the SCM Committee deems such departures necessary for the process of transformation.[289]

Part X: Dispute Settlement

Article 30: Dispute Settlement

This article provides that the provisions of Articles XXII and XXIII of GATT 1994 (nullification or impairment) as elaborated in the DSU shall apply to disputes concerning the ASCM. It is the general rules that apply, except to the extent specifically provided in the ASCM.

While general dispute settlement is discussed in other chapters of this book, certain aspects specific to the ASCM are discussed here. First, as discussed earlier in this chapter, there are certain additional rules beyond the DSU that are established in the ASCM.[290] These apply to disputes brought under the auspices of Article 4 of the ASCM with

[287] When China acceded to the WTO, it agreed to eliminate all prohibited subsidies upon accession. In addition, China will view subsidies provided to state-owned enterprises as specific if those state-owned enterprises are the "predominant recipients" of such subsidies. *See Accession of the People's Republic of China,* WT/L/432, Article 10 (November 23, 2001).

[288] ASCM, Art. 29.2(a). Debt forgiveness may prove to be the most used type of program for a transition economy as it prepares state-owned companies for privatization.

[289] ASCM, Art. 29.4

[290] For a complete list, *see* Annex 2 to the DSU.

respect to prohibited subsidies, and to disputes brought under the auspices of Article 7 with respect to serious prejudice cases.

The standard of review to be applied to a dispute is the same as that applying in all cases brought under the DSU. Unlike the ADA, there is no special standard of review established for disputes concerning the ASCM.[291] It should be noted that the United States has unsuccessfully argued that the standard of review established in the ADA, Article 17.6, applies to the ASCM.[292] This was rejected by the Appellate Body in *Lead Bar*.[293]

The Ministers issued a "Decision on the Application and Review of Article 17.6 of the Agreement on Implementation of Article VI of the General Agreement on Tariffs and Trade 1994" in which they indicated that ADA Article 17.6 was to be reviewed after three years, with a view to considering the question of whether it is capable of general application. However, there has been no subsequent decision of the Members to extend its application beyond the ADA. Therefore, it does not, at this time, apply to the ASCM. In addition, and of great importance, is that countervailing duty proceedings, unlike anti-dumping proceedings,[294] may be challenged as soon as the investigation is initiated.

Part XI: Final Provisions

Article 31: Provisional Application

This article indicates that Articles 6.1, 8, and 9 are to apply for a period of five years beginning with the entry into force of the WTO Agreement (*i.e.*, January 1, 1995). As discussed previously, Article 6.1 establishes a presumption of serious prejudice, and Articles 8 and 9 deal with non-actionable subsidies. Article 31 also provides for a review by the SCM Committee not later than 180 days before the end of this period (*i.e.*, December 31, 2000) to determine whether to continue the application of these provisions. In the aftermath of the 1999 Seattle Ministerial, however, no agreement could be reached on this issue. Therefore, as noted previously, Articles 6.1, 8, and 9 are no longer in effect.

Article 32: Other Final Provisions

Article 32.1 states that no specific action against a subsidy can be taken except in accordance with the provisions of GATT 1994, as interpreted by this Agreement. This is the heart of the dispute brought by several countries against the United States' Continued

[291] The ADA is the only one of the Uruguay Round Agreements to contain its own standard of review.

[292] The United States has cited the *Declaration on Dispute Settlement Pursuant to the Agreement on Implementation of Article VI of the General Agreement on Tariffs and Trade 1994 or Part V of the Agreement on Subsidies and Countervailing Measures* in support of its position. The Declaration states that the Ministers:

> "*Recognize*, with respect to dispute settlement pursuant to the Agreement on Implementation of Article VI of GATT 1994 or Part V of the Agreement on Subsidies and Countervailing Measures, the need for the consistent resolution of disputes arising from anti-dumping and countervailing duty measures."

[293] *See Lead Bar*, *supra* note 62, ¶¶ 44–51.

[294] See ADA, Art. 17.4, which provides that only decisions to impose definitive anti-dumping duties or to accept price undertakings, or the imposition of provisional measures having a significant impact, may be the subject of dispute settlement proceedings.

Dumping and Subsidy Offset Act of 2000, described in the discussion of Article 11.4 above. On 21 December 2000, Australia, Brazil, Chile, the European Communities, India, Indonesia, Japan, Korea, and Thailand, requested consultations with the United States concerning this law. The complaining Members alleged, among other things, that the distribution of antidumping and countervailing duties to domestic producers that had supported the petition constituted specific actions against dumping or subsidies not in accordance with the provisions of GATT 1994. Upholding the Panel's finding that the United States was in violation of Article 32.1, the Appellate Body found that:

> the CDSOA has an adverse bearing on the foreign producers/exporters in that the imports into the United States of the dumped or subsidized products (besides being subject to anti-dumping or countervailing duties) result in the financing of United States competitors—producers of like products—through the transfer to the latter of the duties collected on those exports. Thus, foreign producers/exporters have an incentive not to engage in the practice of exporting dumped or subsidized products or to terminate such practices. Because the CDSOA has an adverse bearing on, and, more specifically, is designed and structured so that it dissuades the practice of dumping or the practice of subsidization, and because it creates an incentive to terminate such practices, the CDSOA is undoubtedly an action "against" dumping or a subsidy, within the meaning of Article 18.1 of the *Anti-Dumping Agreement* and of Article 32.1 of the *SCM Agreement*.[295]

Paragraph 2 of Article 32 prevents Members from entering into reservations with respect to the ASCM unless all Members consent. Thus, this would prevent a Member from reserving application of the Agreement to some newly acceding Member unless that acceding Member takes certain actions.[296]

Paragraphs 3 and 4 address transitional issues concerning the application of this Agreement. Specifically, paragraph 3 notes that the provisions of the ASCM do not apply to investigations or reviews initiated before the entry into force of the WTO Agreement for that Member. This was the critical provision that prevented the Philippines from bringing its dispute against Brazil concerning the imposition of countervailing duties on desiccated coconut, discussed *supra*.

Paragraph 4 establishes a starting date for determining when five-year reviews or termination of a measure are required under Article 21.3. Specifically, all measures in effect prior to the date of entry into force of the WTO Agreement for the administering Member, shall be deemed to have entered into force on the date of entry into force of the WTO Agreement for that Member. Thus, for the original Members, all countervailing duty measures in effect prior to January 1, 1995 were to be deemed to have gone into effect on January 1, 1995 for purposes of Article 21.3. This permitted the United States to extend existing countervailing duty measures a full five years, even if they had been in place for years.

Paragraph 5 is also a transitional provision, which states that Members must take all necessary steps to ensure that their laws, regulations, and administrative procedures comply with the provisions of the ASCM no later than the date of entry into force of the WTO Agreement for that Member.

295 *United States—CDSOA, supra,* note 196, at ¶ 256. However, as explained above, the Appellate Body reversed the panel's finding that the U.S. statute violated Article 11.4 of the ASCM. It is worth noting that the question of whether the Byrd Amendment payments might be specific actionable subsidies to the industries receiving distributions has not be adjudicated.

296 Under the 1979 Subsidies Code, certain Signatories, notably the United States, would require bilateral agreements with new Code Signatories before applying the 1979 Subsidies Code obligations to that country.

Paragraphs 6 and 7 are transparency provisions. Paragraph 6 requires notification to the SCM Committee of any changes to the laws and regulations or their administration that are relevant to this Agreement. Paragraph 7 provides for annual review of the implementation and operation of the ASCM.

Finally, Paragraph 8 states that the Annexes to the ASCM constitute an integral part of the ASCM.

Annex I contains the Illustrative List of Export Subsidies and is discussed in more detail in the comments on Article 3 of the ASCM, *supra* of this Chapter. Annexes II and III provide guidance on certain issues that have been controversial in the past in determining whether certain practices fall within the Illustrative List of Export Subsidies contained in Annex I. Specifically, Annex II provides guidelines for determining when a product is consumed in the production process.[297] Similarly, Annex III provides guidelines for determining when duty drawbacks or refunds on inputs consumed in the production process are determined to be in excess, and therefore, an export subsidy in accordance with Annex I(i). As discussed previously, Annex IV provides guidance in determining the total ad valorem subsidization for purposes of ASCM, Article 6.1.[298] Annex V provides guidance for procedures for developing information concerning a claim of serious prejudice.[299]

Annex VI provides guidance for verifications of exporting firms' responses in a countervailing duty investigation. During the course of a countervailing duty investigation, the administering authorities of the importing Member, may decide to investigate the responses at the company or government submitting the response in order to verify the accuracy of the information submitted. Annex VI establishes procedures for such "on-the-spot investigations," otherwise known as "verifications." They require that the firm and the government of the exporting Member be notified in advance of the trip. The administering authorities should obtain the explicit agreement of the firms to be visited. There should be "sufficient" advance notice. What constitutes "sufficient advance notice" has not been specified, however. In addition, the authorities should advise the firms concerned of the general nature of the information to be verified, and any further information which needs to be provided.[300]

The final annex, Annex VII, identifies the developing country Members referenced in ASCM, Article 27.2(a). These are the developing country Members to which the prohibition on the provision of certain types of subsidies, found in ASCM, Article 3.1(a), does not apply. These include those countries designated as "least developed" by the United Nations, that are Members of the WTO. In addition, certain countries are included until their GNP per capita reaches $1,000 per annum, after which time they will be subject to the eight-year phase-out of prohibited subsidies found in ASCM, Article 27.2(b).[301]

297 *See* the discussion of rebate or remission of prior stage indirect taxes in text accompanying notes 104–106 *supra*.

298 *See* discussion of Article 6.1 *supra*. It should be noted that, because Article 6.1 was of temporary duration and has expired, the reason for this Annex IV has also expired.

299 *See* the discussion of Article 6, *supra*, for a description of the requirements of Annex V.

300 ASCM, Annex VI(7). Note that this does not preclude the visiting officials from requesting further details during the visit, in light of the information obtained.

301 ASCM, Annex VII(b). Those countries are: Bolivia, Cameroon, Congo, Côte d'Ivoire, Dominican Republic, Egypt, Ghana, Guatemala, Guyana, India, Indonesia, Kenya, Morocco, Nicaragua, Nigeria, Pakistan, Philippines, Senegal, Sri Lanka, and Zimbabwe.

IV. Conclusion

The ASCM is a comprehensive document that significantly expands on Articles VI, XIV, and XVI of the GATT, however, it remains a work in progress.

The mandate of the negotiations for the Uruguay Round included the mandate to improve "GATT disciplines relating to all subsidies and countervailing measures that affect international trade."[302] When negotiations began, the parties established that the main objective of the negotiations on subsidies and countervailing measures was to "restore the equilibrium of rights and obligations in terms of equivalent disciplines regarding subsidies on the one hand and countervailing measures on the other. . . . " While it is clear that the overall mandate has been met, in that there has been an improvement in GATT disciplines, there are still issues of concern regarding both the use of subsidies and the use of countervailing measures.

The extent to which the ASCM will be renegotiated in the Doha Round remains unclear. There are implementation issues, such as export competitiveness, that continue to be negotiated. Similarly, there remain issues concerning how parties implement the countervailing measures, including how they define subsidies, the use of adverse facts, the standing of parties to make an application, etc. The most important issue in terms of the success of the negotiations is the issue of incorporating agricultural subsidies into the overall subsidy discipline framework. This will likely drive much of the negotiations on this Agreement in the future. Beyond agriculture, however, looms the fact that, in practice, the current Agreement seems to provide at least some discipline on export subsidies and import substitution ("red light") subsidies, but little effective discipline on other ("amber") subsidies.[303]

[302] Ministerial Declaration on the Uruguay Round, GATT Doc. No. MIN.DEC (September 20, 1986) at 7.

[303] *See* Gary N. Horlick, *Subsidy Discipline Under WTO and US Rules*, in EUROPEAN COMPETITION LAW ANNUAL 1999: SELECTED ISSUES IN THE FIELD OF STATE AID, (Ehlermann and Everson, eds., 2001). The *Indonesia—Automobile Industry* dispute involved an allegation concerning an amber subsidy, among other non-ASCM issues. *See Indonesia—Automobile Industry, supra* note 132. This is the only dispute brought concerning an amber subsidy despite the numerous subsidies notified in accordance with ASCM, Art. 25.4.

GARY HORLICK,* REINHARD QUICK,† EDWIN VERMULST‡

GOVERNMENT ACTIONS AGAINST DOMESTIC SUBSIDIES, AN ANALYSIS OF THE INTERNATIONAL RULES AND AN INTRODUCTION TO UNITED STATES' PRACTICE

'The United States has become far and away the largest user of countervailing duty proceedings. All other nations combined have probably not used countervailing duties explicitly to offset subsidies more than about two dozen times. . . .
(T)he United States is blazing a trail.'§

I. INTRODUCTION

In the present world economic situation subsidies have become an important and actual issue. The industrialized countries, facing difficult structural changes in their economies, are subject to severe political pressure to use subsidies to aid the adjustment process (indeed, subsidies are sometimes used to slow down the adjustment process, although protectionist measures are used more frequently for that purpose). The heavily indebted developing countries, considering exports the only means of paying off their debts and so diminishing their burden, try to boost their export activities by granting subsidies to their producers. The effects of such government aids, however, go beyond the intentional goals of the subsidizing countries and can create serious distortions in other countries. For this reason, and because government intervention is growing almost worldwide, the need for abiding by international rules becomes more and more acute.

Difficulties in tackling the problem of government aids are encountered at the very beginning, when it comes to defining what is, and what is not, to be considered a subsidy. The difficulty is faced by government officials at the decision-making level, negotiators in international fora and economists. Even

* O'Melveny & Myers, Washington, DC, formerly Deputy Assistant Secretary of Commerce for Import Administration (1981-1983); International Trade Counsel to the Senate Finance Committee (1981); J.D. Yale 1973.

† Verband der Chemischen Industrie, e.V., Frankfurt, LL.M. Michigan 1984, Dr. Jur. Mannheim 1983.

‡ Van Bael & Bellis, Brussels; Foreign Associate O'Melveny & Myers, LL.M. Michigan 1984, J.D. Utrecht 1983.

§ Jackson, 'Import Practices: Are They Really Unfair?', 30 L. Quadrange Notes, 26, 30 (1986).

when a definition is found, difficulties remain in calculating the size and effects of subsidies. One of the most satisfactory broad definitions so far has been suggested by Malmgren: he considers a subsidy to be

> 'any government action which causes a firm's, or a particular industry's, total net private cost of production to be below the level of costs that would have been incurred in the course of producing the same level of output in the absence of the government action'.[1]

Presumably, this would include the subsidizing effect (*e.g.*, extra revenue for the firm) from measures not conventionally considered as subsidies, such as tariff protection.

There are two basic kinds of subsidies: domestic subsidies and export subsidies. Those which are not contingent on the export destination of the production can be termed domestic subsidies; those which are granted on condition that the product is exported are export subsidies. (Although import competing interests sometimes claim that domestic subsidies to goods in excess of domestic demand are export subsidies – a definition which could impact quite heavily on small countries minimum efficient-size exporting plants.)

The scope of the present article will be limited to an analysis of domestic subsidies.

Discussions and negotiations in international fora in recent years have focused mainly on export subsidies whose impact on international trade is self-evident. The result has been a certain degree of regulation. However, negotiators have been unable to reach satisfactory agreement on the way domestic subsidies should be treated, mainly because of divergent opinions among countries on what is to be considered an unacceptable domestic subsidy. Not only is governmental involvement in national economics increasing, government officials also find more and new ways of helping the economy of their countries, means which are often indirect, hidden and difficult to quantify.

Governments decide to grant subsidies because of various social and political reasons which are not always justified in economic terms. By providing financial support governments try to correct the distortions which are present in the economy of their countries and which are often a result of one or more of the following factors: infant-industry situations, ailing industries, dislocation costs, overvalued currencies and 'externalities'.

Infant-industry situations exist when a country has the potential to produce a given product but cannot afford it because the initial costs appear prohibitive.

In the case of an ailing industry, the government acts to save or adjust a specific industrial sector which it considers vital to the need of its country, *e.g.*, for strategic or political (employment) reasons.

1. Malmgren, *International Order for Public Subsidies*, at 22 (1977). *Cf.* Holmer, Haggerty, Hunter, 'Identifying and Measuring Subsidies Under the Countervailing Duty Law: An Attempt at Synthesis', in *The Commerce Department Speaks on Import Administration and Export Administration*, at 315 (1984): '. . . a subsidy exists where there is (1) selective government treatment . . . and (2) the selective government treatment is different from the treatment that the recipient otherwise would receive in the marketplace.'

Dislocation costs are expenses solely incurred by a producer when relocating to an economically disadvantaged area or region.

An 'externality' is present when there is a discrepancy between private and social costs or benefits of an enterprise.

The reason why domestic subsidies are so widely used is that they are considered more efficient in correcting distortions than either tariffs or quotas because the distortions are inherent in the domestic market. If quotas were used, in some situations the effects would be the same, but there would be a risk to create new distortions which might give rise to the adoption of corrective measures elsewhere and so start a chain reaction.

Domestic subsidies, however, may have adverse effects on other countries. They may increase the flow of imports into another country and thus injure its industry; also, they may reduce the exports of other countries to third countries, or to the subsidizing country itself. This 'beggar thy neighbour' effect of domestic subsidies is obviously unacceptable to other countries. Under GATT they may therefore levy countervailing duties against subsidized exports or start an international proceeding against those exports.

The present article focuses on domestic subsidies and countervailing duties. The first part deals with the international rules provided by GATT, particularly Articles VI and XVI[2] and the Subsidies Code.[3] The second part is devoted to the application of US countervailing duty laws against domestic subsidies and includes a brief analysis of the 1984 Trade and Tariff Act provisions on upstream subsidies.

II. THE INTERNATIONAL RULES ON SUBSIDIES AND COUNTERVAILING DUTIES

A. THE GATT PROVISIONS ON SUBSIDIES AND COUNTERVAILING DUTIES

1. GATT ARTICLE XVI

Although the GATT Preparatory Work[4] – and later the Havana Charter[5] –

2. In the following, Articles in roman numbers are those of GATT.
3. In the following, Articles in arabic numbers are those of the Subsidies Code.
4. See for example: US Suggested Charter, Dep't. State Pub. No. 2598, Art. 25, at 18-20 (1946); 'Report of the First Session of the Preparatory Committee, London Report', UN Doc. E/PC/T/33 (1946), Art. 30, at 32; Report of the Second Session of the Preparatory Committee, Geneva Report, UN Doc. E/PC/T/186 (1947), Arts. 25-29, at 26-28.
5. 'Havana Charter for an International Trade Organization, Contained in the Final Act of the United Nations Conference on Trade and Employment'. UN Doc. E/Conf. 2/78; UN Pub. Sales No. 1948 II.D.4; Arts. 25-28; for a discussion of the articles of the Havana Charter relating to subsidies see Wilcox, *A Charter For World Trade*, pp. 126 *et seq.* (1949).

contained rather detailed provisions on subsidies,[6] Article XVI originally only required the contracting parties to notify the GATT Secretariat of their subsidies and to consult with other contracting parties whenever their subsidies caused injurious effects.[7] The reluctance of the contracting parties to adopt the proposed rules on subsidies shows that the subject was controversial already in 1948: opinions differed on the different treatment accorded to domestic and export subsidies[8] and on the somewhat ambiguous distinction between export subsidies on manufactured and primary products.[9]

At the 1955 Review Session the CONTRACTING PARTIES amended Article XVI by adding a section B (Article XVI paragraphs 2-5), which dealt solely with export subsidies. Furthermore they added a series of Interpretative Notes to Annex I.[10] Recognizing the distortive effect of export subsidies and basically following the pattern of rules laid down in the Havana Charter,[11] they established limitations on the use of export subsidies both on primary[12] and non-primary products.[13] Thus, they incorporated into GATT not only the distinction between domestic and export subsidies but also the different treatment of export subsidies on primary and non-primary products. Many developing countries, however, objected to the latter;[14] indeed the amendment seemed to favour the subsidy programs of industrialized countries.[15]

6. The basic ideas regarding international rules on subsidies were the following: (1) prohibition of export subsidies on manufactured products, (2) more lenient rules on export subsidies on primary products and (3) the acceptance of domestic subsidies coupled with a notification and consultation requirement. For a discussion of the proposals see Jackson, *World Trade and the Law of GATT*, 376-371 (1969) (hereinafter cited Jackson, *World Trade*); Tarullo, The MTN Subsidies Code: Agreement without Consensus, pp. 6 *et seq.*, unpublished article, to be published in: *Interpretation and Implementation of International Economic Agreements, the American Society of International Law*; see also Phegan, 'GATT Article XVI:3 – *Export Subsidies and "Equitable Shares"* ', 16 J.W.T.L. 251, 252 (1982).
7. The original text of Art. XVI can be found in GATT, *Basic Instruments and Selected Documents* (hereinafter cited GATT, BISD), Vol. I, at 39, 40 (1952).
8. See Jackson, *World Trade*, at 369, particularly footnotes 8 and 10.
9. This distinction was proposed by the US during the negotiations in order to legitimize its price support and export subsidy programs for agricultural products and was objected to by less developed countries; see Jackson, *World Trade*, at 369; for a criticism of this approach see Brown, *The United States and the Restoration of World Trade*, at 115-119 (1950); Dam, *The GATT*, 132 (1970) (hereinafter cited Dam, *The GATT*).
10. The amendments came into effect in 1957 for those nations accepting them; 278 UNTS 168 (1957).
11. See generally Jackson, *World Trade*, at 371; for a discussion of the 1955 amendment in comparison with the subsidy provisions of the Havana Charter see Tarullo, *supra* n. 6, pp. 9 *et seq*.
12. Art. XVI para. 3 urges the contracting parties 'to seek to avoid the use of subsidies on the export of primary products' and contains the obligation not to grant export subsidies on primary products that would result in 'more than an equitable share of world export trade' for the subsidizing country.
13. Art. XVI para. 4 contains the obligation not to grant any export subsidy on non-primary products 'where the subsidy results in the sale of such product for export at a price lower than the comparable price charged for the like product to buyers in the domestic market.'
14. See Jackson, *World Trade*, at 372.
15. The more lenient treatment of export subsidies on primary products which are likely to be granted by developed countries and which seem to be directed against the competition of less developed countries conflicts with the prohibition of export subsidies on non-primary products which are likely to be granted by less developed countries in order to build up an industry.

Therefore it was not surprising that in 1960 only few developing countries accepted the 'Declaration Giving Effect to the Provisions of Article XVI Paragraph 4'[16] and thereby agreed to prohibit export subsidies on non-primary products.[17] The Declaration was prepared by a Working Party on Article XVI which included in its report a non-exhaustive list of eight practices which were regarded as export subsidies.[18]

In summary, until the end of the Tokyo Round, the GATT rules on subsidies were the following:

(1) the notification and consultation requirement of Article XVI paragraph 1, accepted by all contracting parties;

(2) the undertaking not to grant export subsidies on primary products that would result in more than an 'equitable share' of world export trade in that product, accepted by all contracting parties since 1969;[19]

(3) the prohibition of export subsidies on non-primary products which result in 'dual pricing', accepted only by seventeen developed countries.[20]

While the 1955 amendments and the above mentioned report of the Working Party were attempts to clarify the existing GATT provisions on subsidies, no agreement was reached on probably the most important issue, *definition* of the term subsidy.[21] Such definition 'might neither be necessary nor feasible' with regard to the operation of Article XVI,[22] but certainly would be useful with regard to Article VI.[23]

As far as domestic subsidies were concerned, the only applicable rule consisted of the notification and consultation requirement of Article XVI paragraph 1. Domestic subsidies were not forbidden as such.[24]

The phrase 'increased exports' was clarified by the CONTRACTING PARTIES in 1948 as follows:

> 'The phrase increased exports in line 3 of Article XVI of the General Agreement was intended to include the concept of maintaining exports at a level higher than would otherwise exist in the absence of the subsidy. . . .'[25]

In 1960 the CONTRACTING PARTIES elaborated the 1948 statement:

16. GATT, BISD, 9th Supp., p. 32, 33 (1961).
17. For a description of this confusing process of stand-still agreements, acceptance of the prohibition of Art. XVI para. 4, and nonacceptance thereof see Jackson, *World Trade*, pp. 371 *et seq.*; see furthermore Dam, The GATT, p. 144, 145; Butler, 'Countervailing Duties and Export Subsidization: a Re-emerging Issue in International Trade', 9 Va. J. Int'l. L. 82 90-93 (1968).
18. GATT, BISD, 9th Supp. 185-188 (1961).
19. Jackson, *World Trade*, 376; Tarullo, *supra* n. 6 at 11.
20. Jackson, *World Trade*, 374.
21. For criticism of this lack of definition see Pestieau, *'Subsidies and Countervailing Duties: The Negotiating Issues'*, Report to the Canadian Economic Policy Committee, at 6 (1976).
22. GATT Panel Report on the Operation of the Provisions of Art. XVI, GATT, BISD, 10th Supp., 201, para. 23 at 208 (1962).
23. See *infra* nn. 46 to 50 and accompanying text.
24. GATT, BISD, 9th Supp., 190 (1961).
25. GATT, BISD, Vol. II, p. 44 (1952).

> '*Mutatis mutandis* this interpretation must apply to the effect on imports. The criterion is therefore what would happen in the *absence* of a subsidy. While the Panel agreed that in most cases such a judgment cannot be reached only by reference to statistics, nevertheless, a statistical analysis helps to discern the trends of imports and exports and may assist in determining the effects of a subsidy. The Panel considers it fair to assume that a subsidy which provides an incentive to increased production will, in the absence of offsetting measures, *e.g.*, a consumption subsidy, either increase exports or reduce imports.'[26]

Furthermore, the CONTRACTING PARTIES laid down procedural rules to strengthen the effect of the notification requirement:[27] whenever a contracting party feels that serious prejudice is caused or threatened it can request consultations with the subsidizing country.[28] Of course, consultations can also be held under the general procedures of Articles XXII, XXIII. The term 'serious prejudice' is not defined in GATT. In the 'Report on the Operation of the Provisions of Article XVI' a panel stated that a complaining party could ask for consultations whenever it considered that serious prejudice was caused, without having to await a prior action by the CONTRACTING PARTIES.[29] Therefore, GATT leaves it up to the complaining country to determine what it considers to constitute 'serious prejudice'.

The discussion of Article XVI paragraph 1 reveals that this paragraph is not, and was not intended to be, an adequate device to stop contracting parties from granting domestic subsidies. At the time GATT was drafted domestic subsidies were not of great concern.[30] Nevertheless, Article XVI paragraph 1 has two important functions. First, the notification requirement increases transparency of subsidy programs. In the second place, the consultation requirement makes the contracting parties aware of the possible transnational effects of their subsidies.[31]

This last function, however, lost more and more of its meaning.[32] Not only did contracting parties resort to domestic subsidies more often,[33] thereby triggering reactions by other contracting parties,[34] but they also did not

26. GATT, BISD, 9th Supp., 191 (1961).
27. See GATT, BISD, Vol. II, 19 (1952); GATT, BISD, 3rd Supp., 224-225 (1955); GATT, BISD, 9th Supp., 193 (1961); GATT, BISD, 11th Supp., 58 (1963); for a detailed analysis of the notification requirement see Jackson, *World Trade*, pp. 387 *et seq.*
28. See generally, Jackson, *World Trade*, 391-392; Butler, *supra* n. 17, at 94-96.
29. See GATT, BISD, 10th Supp., 201, 207 (1962).
30. Tarullo, *supra* n. 6, at 7.
31. Jackson, *World Trade*, at 392.
32. Rivers, Greenwald, 'The Negotiation of a Code on Subsidies and Countervailing Measures: Bridging Fundamental Policy Differences', 11 Law & Pol'y Int'l Bus., 1447, 1459 (1979); Butler, *supra* n. 17, at 94; see also *Report of the Committee on Finance, United States Senate on H.R. 4537 to Approve and Implement the Trade Agreements Negotiated under the Trade Act of 1974*, and for other purposes, Report No. 249, 96th Cong., 1st Sess., 39 (1979) (hereinafter cited *Senate Report no. 249*).
33. Tarullo, *supra* n. 6, pp. 16 *et seq.*
34. In 1973, the US Treasury entered a countervailing duty order against '*radial tires from Canada*', 38 Fed. Reg. 1018 (1973); this was the first countervailing duty order in many years against a product that benefitted from a domestic subsidy; for an analysis of the case see Guido, Morrone, 'The Michelin Decision: A Possible New Direction for US Countervailing Duty Law', 6 Law & Pol'y Int'l. Bus., 237 (1974); Horlick, *Current Issues in Countervailing Duty Law,* in *The Trade Agreements Act of 1979 – Four Years Later*, 23 (1983).

comply with the obligations of Article XVI paragraph 1.[35] According to two authors 'there is no record of any country ever having limited a subsidizing practice as a result of consultations under Article XVI paragraph 1'.[36]

As a result, next to the controversial rules of Article XVI paragraphs 3 and 4[37] the limitation on the use of domestic subsidies was one of the major issues during the negotiations of the Subsidies Code.[38]

The fact that GATT allows domestic subsidies does not preclude contracting parties from availing themselves of GATT remedies against domestic subsidies. Already in 1955 a GATT Working Party stated:

> 'So far as domestic subsidies are concerned, it was agreed that a contracting party which has negotiated a concession under Article II may be assumed, for the purpose of Article XXIII, to have a reasonable expectation, failing evidence to the contrary, that the value of the concession will not be nullified or impaired by the contracting party which granted the concession by the subsequent introduction or increase of a domestic subsidy on the product concerned.'[39]

Therefore a contracting party can always invoke Article XXIII to demonstrate that an action of another contracting party – *e.g.* introduction of a subsidy after a tariff concession has been negotiated – nullifies and impairs its benefits under GATT, even if this action is normally allowed. The basis for the above

35. Butler, *supra* n. 17, at 94; Evans, 'Subsidies and Countervailing Duties in GATT: Present Law and Future Prospects', 3 Int'l. Trade L.J. 211, 230-231 (1977); Metzger, *Lowering Nontariff Barriers*, 121-122 (1974); Sabourin-Herbert, 'De la validité des subventions au regard de l'accord general sur les tarifs et le commerce: Une application Canadienne', 6 Rev. Gen. de Droit (Ottawa), 339, 348 (1975).
36. Rivers, Greenwald, *supra* n. 32, at 1459, 1460.
37. To deal with the interpretative problems of Art. XVI para. 3 and 4 goes beyond the scope of this paper.
    However, two weaknesses of these paragraphs deserve mentioning: First, para. 3 does not constitute a viable prohibition of the use of export subsidies on primary products since those subsidies are normally not as massive as to change world market shares; see Dam, *The GATT*, at 143; furthermore, the term 'equitable share' was not defined, nor did the case law give any guidance as to what constituted an 'equitable share'; see generally the first *French Wheat Case*, GATT, BISD, 7th Supp., pp. 46 *et seq.* (1959). The panel found that subsidized French wheat exports displaced Australian wheat exports from traditional Australian markets in South East Asia, but it did not provide any answer as to what constitutes an equitable share; see Ribers, Greenwald, *supra* n. 32, at 1461 n. 77; Jackson, World Trade, at 394-5; Phegan, *supra* n. 6, at 255. Second, the bi-level pricing element in para. 4 was very difficult to prove and therefore eased the prohibition of export subsidies on non primary products; see Rivers, Greenwald, *supra* n. 32, at 1461; Barcelo, 'Subsidies and Countervailing Duties – Analysis and a Proposal', 9 L. & Pol'y Int'l. Bus. 779, 783-4 (1977). Several panel decisions in the 70s tried to overcome this difficulty by adopting the rebuttable presumption of dual pricing once the existence of an export subsidy had been established; see *e.g.* The *DISC Case* and the *European Tax Cases*, GATT, BISD, 23rd Supp., pp. 98 *et seq.* (1976); see also GATT, BISD, 26th Supp., pp. 330 *et seq.* (1980); for a criticism of this presumption see Jackson, 'The Jurisprudence of International Trade: The DISC Case', 72 A.J.I.L., 747, 768-71 (1978).
38. Rivers, Greenwald, *supra* n. 32, 1469, 1470-1475.
39. GATT, BISD, 3rd Supp., 222, 224 (1955).

cited statement is the *Australian Ammonium Sulphate Case*,[40] one of the most important cases in GATT.[41]

Furthermore, a subsidy program can be attacked as a violation of other GATT-Articles. An example thereof is the *Italian Tractor Case*[42] in which Italy gave favourable loans to purchasers of tractors if the tractors were purchased from a domestic producer. A panel decided that this action violated the national treatment clause of Article III, paragraph 4. The exemption of Article III, paragraph 8 did not apply because the subsidy went to the buyer of the tractor, not the producer.

Finally, Article VI, to which we will turn next, allows unilateral imposition of countervailing duties to offset subsidies.

2. GATT Article VI

Article VI, paragraph 3 permits the unilateral imposition of countervailing duties[43] 'for the purpose of offsetting any bounty or subsidy bestowed, directly or indirectly, upon the manufacture, production or export of any merchandise'.

The text makes it clear that countervailing duties may be levied against any form of subsidy whether export or domestic, prohibited or allowed.[44] Therefore, Article VI could be seen as a sort of compensation for the rather lenient treatment of subsidies in Article XVI: countervailing duties are the accepted means for offsetting subsidies in the GATT framework.

Article VI paragraph 6(a) limits the use of countervailing duties insofar as it requires that the subsidized imported product must cause or threaten to cause 'material injury to an established domestic industry' in the importing country.[45] Article VI paragraph 3 limits the countervailing duty to the actual amount of the subsidy. A further restriction is contained in Article VI paragraph 4 which forbids imposition of countervailing duties on products exempted from indirect taxes in the country of exportation or origin.

Like Article XVI, Article VI does not define subsidies. Rather it incorporates a new notion, *i.e.*, the possibility of levying countervailing duties against both 'subsidies' and 'bounties'. One could therefore conclude that Article VI

40. GATT, BISD, Vol. II, pp. 158 *et seq.* (1952); partly reproduced in Jackson, *Legal Problems of International Economic Relations*, p. 426-8 (1977) (hereinafter cited as Jackson, *Legal Problems*).
41. For a recent overview of GATT cases and the effectiveness of the GATT dispute settlement process, see *Review of the Effectiveness of Trade Dispute Settlement Under the GATT and the Tokyo Round Agreements*, USITC Pub. 1793 (1985).
42. GATT, BISD, 7th Supp., pp. 50 *et seq.* (1959).
43. A countervailing duty is a special duty on subsidized imports, which is designed to offset the amount of subsidies paid on the imports and which is levied in addition to any regular duty.
44. Barcelo, *supra* n. 37, at 784; Pestieau, *supra* n. 21, at 6; Sabourin-Herbert, *supra* n. 35, at 351.
45. Until 1980 the US was the only major industrial nation which could impose countervailing duties without having to prove material injury. The US was exempted from Art. VI para. 6(a) under the so called 'grandfather clause' of the Protocol of Provisional Application of the GATT. This clause permits nations with legislation antedating GATT to continue to apply their domestic law if certain conditions are fulfilled; see Jackson, *World Trade*, at 425.

allows countervailing duties against actions which are not covered by the meaning of subsidies in Article XVI. On the other hand, one commentator has asserted that the drafters of Article VI considered 'subsidies' and 'bounties' to be identical in meaning.[46] A second question is whether the term subsidy has an identical meaning in both articles. In 1960 a Working Party on Subsidies stated:

> 'The GATT does not concern itself with such action [subsidies] by private persons acting independently of their governments except insofar as it allows importing countries to take actions under other provisions of the Agreement.'[47]

Such actions under other provisions of the agreement could be countervailing duties according to Article VI. A Working Party on Antidumping and Countervailing duties stated shortly thereafter:

> 'A large majority of the experts considered that it [the term subsidy] covered only subsidies granted by governments and semi-governmental bodies. Three experts considered that the word should be interpreted in a wider sense and felt that it covered all subsidies, whatever their character and whatever their origin, including also subsidies granted by private bodies.'[48]

Thus the concept of subsidies in Article VI does not seem to be the same as used in Article XVI.[49] Article VI seems broader in that it allows imposition of countervailing duties against actions which are not necessarily covered by Article XVI. Support for this thesis can be found in the GATT itself. If the concept of subsidy in both articles would have been the same, the explicit limitation of countervailing duties in Article VI paragraph 4 would have become superfluous after the 1955 amendments to Article XVI. A 1955 interpretative note to Article XVI states:

> 'The exemption of an exported product from duties or taxes borne by the like product when destined for domestic consumption, or the remission of such duties or taxes in amounts not in excess of those which have accrued, shall not be deemed to be a subsidy.'[50]

46. Evans, *supra* n. 35, at 218.
47. GATT, BISD, 9th Supp., para. 12 at 192 (1961).
48. Id., at 200, para. 34. In practice, private subsidies seldom occur. An exception might be export subsidies, given by a cartel of protected input producers to exporters of the finished product, see, *e.g.*, *Steel Wire Rope from South Africa*, 47 Fed. Reg. 40203 (1982) (prel. aff.). This possibility is discussed in Horlick, 'Current Issues in the Definition and Measurement of Subsidies under US Countervailing Duty Law', in *The Trade Agreement Act of 1979: Four Years Later* (1983).
49. McGovern, however, is of the opinion that the concept of subsidies in both Articles is the same; McGovern, *International Trade Regulation: GATT, the United States and the European Community*, at 263 (1982).
50. GATT, Annex I, Notes and Supplementary Provisions, Ad Art. XVI.

However, Article VI paragraph 4 was not deleted in the 1955 amendments.

The major drawback of Article VI, however, does not lie in its lack of clarity but in its unilateral character.[51] Since Article VI gives extremely vague guidelines on the use of countervailing duties against subsidized exports the contracting parties were quite free to adopt their own countervailing duty laws. This lack of precision gave them the possibility to apply their countervailing duty laws in a manner which could be, and was, regarded as a nontariff trade barrier itself.[52]

Another trend which strengthened the demands for more precise international rules on countervailing duties was the increasing resort to countervailing duty proceedings by some countries, particularly the United States.[53] This increasing resort was not only due to an increase of subsidization[54] but also to an increasing concern about the pervasiveness of governmental support of the private sector and the perceived unfairness thereof.[55] Given the potential negative effect of countervailing duty proceedings on the export trade of certain industries in certain countries it was not surprising that Article VI was put on the agenda of negotiations.[56] However, before the Tokyo Round began some states wanted the negotiations to focus only on countervailing duties whereas others insisted on the inclusion of subsidies (Article XVI) as well.[57]

51. Pestieau, *supra* n. 21, at 8.
52. Butler, *supra* n. 17, at 86; Evans, *supra* n. 35, at 233; see also Dam, *The GATT*, at 178; Dam also concedes that countervailing procedures might be abused for protectionist purposes but does not believe that this was done very often. One writer in 1966 characterized the old US countervailing duty statute as a 'sleeping giant' because of the lack of legislative guidelines and judicial control governing its applicability (Davis, 'The Regulation and Control of Foreign Trade', 66 Colum. L. Rev. 1428, 1446 (1966).
53. Butler, *supra* n. 17, at 85-86; Malmgren, *International Economic Peacekeeping in Phase II*, 105 (1972); Marks, Malmgren, 'Negotiating Nontariff Distortions to Trade', 7 Law & Pol'y Int'l. Bus. 327, 346, particularly n. 85 which contains a list of US countervailing duty cases (1975). Since the US did not have to comply with the injury requirement of Art. VI para. 6(a) – see *supra* n. 45 – it could resort to its countervailing duty law more easily, much to the concern of other countries.
54. The Common Agricultural Policy of the EEC, domestic susidies granted by Japan and several Western European nations to auto, computer and steel industries, and export promotion measures of less developed countries through subsidizations are three of many examples; for more details see Tarullo, *supra* n. 6, pp. 16 *et seq.*, particularly nn. 31-33; see also Baldwin, *Nontariff Distortions of International Trade*, pp. 113 *et seq.* (1970).
55. Due to a decline of tariffs subsidies had more visible effects. Since they were, and are, considered to be 'unfair' measures – no industry can effectively compete with foreign treasuries – contracting parties felt obliged to take actions against subsidized imports, not only export subsidies but also domestic subsidies.
56. Already during the Kennedy Round proposals for a Countervailing Duty Code were made; see Marks, Malmgren, *supra* n. 53, at 345.
57. Malmgren, *supra* n. 53, at 104.

GOVERNMENT ACTIONS AGAINST DOMESTIC SUBSIDIES 11

B. THE SUBSIDIES CODE[58]

1. Background

The Tokyo Round was the first GATT negotiating round to shift the focus from the reduction of tariffs[59] to the elimination of, or at least more effective international discipline with regard to, nontariff trade barriers.

As far as subsidies and countervailing duties were concerned, dissatisfaction with the existing GATT rules was voiced.[60] Although the need to improve international discipline in that field was generally acknowledged the negotiations were extremely difficult because of the opposing views of the negotiating parties as to what should be done with subsidies.

The United States was generally opposed to subsidies and therefore wanted to facilitate actions against subsidized imports.[61] Its main concern was the increased resort to subsidies by its trading partners, particularly the Common Agricultural Policy of the EEC.[62] Another controversy between the US and the EEC concerned the rebate of indirect taxes on exports.[63] According to the US this practice gave the EEC exports an unfair advantage[64] and should therefore be included in the discussions. In the course of the negotiations, however, this point was dropped as it did not seem to be negotiable.[65]

58. Agreement on Interpretation and Application of Articles VI, XVI, and XXIII of the General Agreement on Tariffs and Trade, done April 12, 1979; in force January 1, 1980; reprinted in GATT, BISD, 26th Supp., 56 (1980); EEC OJ L/71 p. 72 (1980); 18 ILM 5 (1979); TIAS 9619; Agreements Reached in the Tokyo Round of the Multilateral Trade Negotiations, H.R. Doc. No. 153, 96th Cong., 1st Sess., pt. 1 at 257 (1979).
59. See generally Jackson, 'The Birth of the GATT-MTN System: A Constitutional Appraisal', 12 L. & Pol'y. Int'l. Bus., pp. 21 *et seq.* (1980); see also McGovern, *supra* n. 49, at 7 and at 413 for a bibliography on the Tokyo Round.
60. See *supra* nn. 32 to 38 and nn. 51 to 57 and accompanying text.
61. Grey, 'Some Notes on Subsidies and the International Rules', in *Interface III* (1984).
62. See Tarullo, *supra* n. 6, at 18, 19; Rivers, Greenwald, *supra* n. 32, at 1452.
63. This problem arose out of a difference in treatment by the GATT of indirect and direct taxation. According to GATT rules rebates of indirect taxes on exports are neither subsidies in the sense of Art. XVI nor countervailable subsidies in the sense of Art. VI. A rebate on direct taxes on exports, however, is regarded as a subsidy and is countervailable. The reason for that difference in treatment can be found in classical economic theory which holds that indirect taxes have an effect on prices and, therefore, have to be borne by consumers. Direct taxes have no such effect and are borne entirely by the producer. Although this theory is nowadays questioned the GATT distinction between the effects of direct and indirect taxes still applies; see generally Steinaecker, *Domestic Taxation and Foreign Trade, The United States – European Border Tax Dispute*, pp. 20 *et seq.* (1973); see also McGovern, *supra* n. 49, at 256.
64. In connection with subsidies and countervailing duties this problem is intensively discussed by Marks, Malmgren, *supra* n. 53, at 351-355; Barcelo, *supra* n. 37, 808-816; Tarullo, *supra* n. 6, pp. 19 *et seq.*; see also Chambers, 'The Steel Products Decisions: An Inquiry into the Treatment of VAT under the Countervailing Duty Law', 9 Vand. J. Transnat'l L., pp. 819 *et seq.* (1976).
65. Rivers, Greenwald, *supra* n. 32, at 1458. It is interesting to note that the US Supreme Court in 1978 upheld the Treasury Department's decision that rebates of indirect taxes were no subsidies; *Zenith Radio Corp.* v. *United States*, 437 US 443 (1978); a lower court had found in favour of the plaintiff a year earlier; *Zenith Radio Corp.* v. *United States*, 430 F. Supp. 242 (Cust. Ct. 1977); for a discussion of the case see Schwartz, 'Zenith Radio Corp v. United States: Countervailing Duties and the Regulation of International Trade' (1978) Sup. Ct. Rev. 297; Arkin, 'The Countervailing Duty Law after Zenith', 18 Va. J. Int'l. L., 245 (1978). The decision of the Customs Court which clearly violated Art. VI para. 4 was a serious threat to the negotiations.

In general, most of the other parties held the view that, since practically all governments use subsidies in one way or another, actions against subsidies should only be allowed if the subsidized imports caused considerable damage in the importing country.[66] One of the main concerns of this group was to get the US to accept the injury standard in its countervailing duty law.[67]

Another important issue in the negotiations was determining which remedies should be available against those subsidies which resulted in damage to producers because of distorted competition in third markets or displacement of exports due to subsidization in the domestic market. This was an issue which neither Article VI paragraphs 6(b) and (c) nor Article XVI addressed to the satisfaction of the negotiating parties.[68]

Given this background we will now proceed to analyze how the Subsidies Code negotiators handled these controversial topics.[69] The Subsidies Code is divided into two parts, commonly referred to as Track I and Track II,[70] both of which lay down rules to control the trade effects of government subsidies. Track I[71] is related to Article VI and describes the situation in which a country may levy countervailing duties on subsidized imports. Track II[72] is related to Articles XVI and XXIII; basically, it contains rules on domestic and export subsidies and lays down the procedure for GATT complaints against these subsidies.

We will analyze Track II first so as to follow the same order as used above when describing the GATT rules.

2. Track II

The provisions of Track II can be divided into four categories:
(1) general rules on subsidies;
(2) specific rules on specific subsidies;
(3) preferential rules for less developed countries;[73] and

66. Grey, 'United States Trade Policy Legislation: A Canadian View', *The Institute For Research and Public Policy*, at 38 (1982).
67. See remarks of Bergsten, A.S.I.L. Proceedings of the 73rd Annual Meeting, at 66 (1979).
68. See n. 66 above.
69. For a detailed analysis of the negotiations see Rivers, Greenwald, *supra* n. 32, pp. 1465 *et seq*.
70. The terminology used by the negotiators became quickly accepted in the literature, see for example Bergsten, *supra* n. 67.
71. Track I consists of Arts. 1 to 6 of the Subsidies Code.
72. Track II consists of Arts. 7 to 19 of the Subsidies Code.
73. These rules will not be dealt with in this paper. For an analysis of Art. 14 of the Code and a discussion of the problems with the implementation of this Article, particularly the US commitments policy, see Haubauer, 'Subsidy Issues After the Tokyo Round', in: *Trade Policies in the 1980s*, p. 40-44. (Cline ed.), at 341 (1983); see also Tarullo, *supra* n. 6.
An analysis of Art. 14 is contained in *MTN Studies No. 6, Part 1, Agreements Being Negotiated at the Multilateral Trade Negotiations in Geneva – US International Trade Commission Investigation No. 332-101; Analysis of Nontariff Agreements, Introduction and Overview of Legal Issues, Subsidies/Countervailing Duty Measures Agreement, A Report Prepared at the Request of the Committee on Finance, Subcommittee on International Trade, United States Senate, 96th Cong., 1st Sess., at 196-200 (1979)* (hereinafter cited as *MTN Studies No. 6*).

(4) institutional or procedural rules.

a. General Provisions

The general provisions on subsidies are contained in Article 8 of the Code. Paragraph 1 of this Article reflects a compromise insofar as it recognizes the importance of governmental subsidization programs and simultaneously their possible adverse effects. Therefore, Article 8, paragraph 1 brings into the Code the point of view of both opponents and supporters of subsidies. The acceptance of both opinions is a '*Leitmotiv*' which recurs throughout the whole Code; a red line which reflects the same disagreement on the use and the propriety of subsidies which existed in 1948. However, the Code does not merely acknowledge this disagreement but elaborates on it and develops obligations of the signatories, thereby creating a stricter international discipline.

Article 8 paragraph 2 prohibits the use of export subsidies which are inconsistent with the provisions of the Code.

Article 8 paragraph 3 provides that signatories will seek to avoid 'damages' to other signatories through the use of subsidies. The expression 'seek to avoid' is the same as used in Article XVI paragraph 3 and, as in that case, implies that subsidies which have 'damaging effects' are not prohibited as such; rather, the signatories bind themselves to make an effort to refrain from using such injurious subsidies.

The word 'damage', as we use it, is an oversimplification of the provisions of paragraph 3 and actually stands for:
(a) injury to the domestic industry of another signatory,
(b) nullification and impairment of benefits under the GATT, or
(c) serious prejudice of the interests of another signatory.
These concepts are either drawn from GATT Articles VI and XVI or from the GATT subsidies case law.

'Injury' is explicitly related to Track I of the Code[74] and is therefore a reflection of the injury standard of the countervailing duty law; it is worth noting, however, that the term 'material' is omitted in paragraph 3(a). One could therefore conclude that even in the absence of material injury to a domestic producer, a signatory could start a Code procedure[75] against a subsidizing country. The differences in procedures and remedies in Track I and Track II[76] support this conclusion.

The term 'serious prejudice' is directly taken from Article XVI paragraph 1. A footnote[77] explains that it is used in the same sense. The term was not defined in GATT[78] and was even criticized as being of little use to the functioning of Article XVI paragraph 1.[79] Because of the institutional and

74. Subsidies Code, Art. 8 n. 23.
75. Subsidies Code, Art. 12 para. 3.
76. See nn. 106 to 122 *infra* and accompanying text.
77. Subsidies Code, Art. 8 n. 25.
78. See nn. 24, 25 *supra* and accompanying text.
79. Hudec, 'Regulations of Domestic Subsidies Under the MTN Subsidies Code', in *Interface III* at 71 (1984).

procedural provisions of the Subsidies Code, however, attempts to give it body might be more successful in the future. Therefore, we do not concur with the criticism[80] that 'there is little apparent reason why the serious prejudice standard should prompt any greater discipline than it did when embodied in GATT Article XVI paragraph 1'.

The inclusion of the 'nullification and impairment' notion into the Subsidies Code is a reflection of the above cited case law on subsidies.[81] It is particularly suitable to strengthen international discipline since it does not require breach of a legal obligation, as the *Australian Ammonium Sulphate Case* shows.

Article 8 paragraph 4 describes three situations in which subsidies might adversely effect the interests of another signatory and provides guidance as to when to take Track II action against subsidies:

(1) it refers to the effects that subsidized imports might have on the domestic market of the importing country through displacement of domestic production;
(2) it refers to the effects that subsidized imports might have on the market of the subsidizing country, thereby addressing the case of displacement of imports; and
(3) it refers to the effects subsidized exports might have on third markets, thereby addressing the problem of displacement of the exports of the complainant.

'Nullification or impairment' or 'serious prejudice' exist if one of the three situations leads to adverse effects for the complainant.

With regard to the first situation Track II and Track I overlap. Thus a signatory might decide to levy a countervailing duty against subsidized imports, provided that all conditions are fulfilled, or to bring a Track II action against these subsidies. The difference between the two actions lies in their aims. The former gives relief to the domestic industry by neutralizing the subsidy with a countervailing duty while the latter tries to abolish the subsidy as such.[82] In the other two situations complaining states have a cause of action which was not explicitly provided for in GATT but which might have been attacked under Article XXIII.[83]

Undeniably, the language of Article 8 paragraph 4 will create interpretative problems, particularly regarding the definition of 'adverse effects to the interests of another signatory'; these problems, however, should be overcome by the Subsidies Committee. Since Article 8 paragraph 4 not only refers to 'nullification or impairment' but also to 'serious prejudice' it seems clear that 'adverse effects to the interests' can be interpreted in a broader sense than the concept of 'nullification or impairment of benefits' in Article XXIII.[84]

80. Estabrook, European Community Resistance to the Enforcement of GATT Panel Decision on Sugar Export Subsidies', 15 Corn. Int'l. L. J. 397, 410 (1982).
81. See *supra* n. 41 and accompanying text.
82. See Hudec, *supra* n. 79, at 19, 20.
83. Hudec has concluded that with regard to import replacing subsidies the Subsidies Code 'will not add very much to the existing Article XXIII remedies' and that the remedy with regard to third market displacements 'could be explained under an extended version of conventional nullification and impairment theory'; Hudec, *supra* n. 79, at 16, 19.
84. For a discussion of the concept of nullification and impairment see generally Jackson, *World Trade*, pp. 178 *et seq*.

It is interesting to note that Article 8 footnote 4, read together with Articles 12 paragraph 1, 13 paragraph 4 and 14 paragraph 4, creates a presumption of adverse effects to the complainant whenever another signatory has used a prohibited export subsidy.[85] In the case of a complaint against a domestic subsidy, however, the complainant has to prove 'that the subsidy has either reduced its exports or damaged its domestic industry through increased imports';[86] in other words it has to prove, presumably with the use of statistical evidence of trade diversions, 'adverse effects.'

In summary, Article 8 gives signatories an indication as to when they can act, within the limits of Track II, against subsidies granted by other signatories.

b. Special Provisions

The special provisions on specific subsidies are contained in Articles 9, 10 and 11.

Article 9 paragraph 1 prohibits bestowal of export subsidies on industrial and mineral products. The Code does not define export subsidies but it contains a non-exhaustive illustrative list of export subsidies in Annex A, to which Article 9 paragraph 2 refers.[87]

Article 10, the provision on export subsidies on primary products, is an elaboration of Article XVI paragraph 3. In paragraph 1 it retains the criticized concept of 'more than an equitable share';[88] Paragraph 2 attempts to clarify that concept but does not improve the position of the complaining country, on the contrary it retains the strong position of the subsidizing country, as the *EEC Wheat Subsidy Case* shows.[89] Paragraph 3 prohibits export subsidies on

85. Barcelo, 'Subsidies, Countervailing Duties and Anti-dumping after the Tokyo Round', 13 Corn. Int'l, L. J. 257, 266 (1980).
86. Barcelo, 'The Two-Track Subsidies Code – Countervailing Duties and Trade Retaliation', in: *Non-Tariff Barriers after the Tokyo Round*, (Quinn, Slayton eds.), at 121, 137 (1982).
87. It goes beyond the scope of this paper to discuss the Code's provisions on export subsidies. In short it can be said that the bi-level pricing element of Art. XVI para. 4 is, in principle, omitted in the Code. Yet it is not absolutely clear whether this element will not again be discussed in the context of the Code. First, item (1) of the illustrative list refers to Art. XVI para. 4 and therefore to the bi-level pricing requirement. Second, since the list is not exhaustive any export subsidy not included in it could be argued to be prohibited only if it resulted in bi-level pricing; see Rivers, Greenwald, *supra* n. 32, at 1476. For an analysis of Art. 9 and the illustrative list, see generally McGovern, *supra* n. 49, pp. 253 *et seq.*; Tarullo, *supra* n. 6, 32-35; Hufbauer, *supra* n. 73, 342-350; Simon, 'Can GATT Export Subsidy Standards Be Ignored by the U.S. in Imposing Countervailing Duties', 5 Nw. J. of Int'l. & Bus., 183, pp. 187 *et seq.* (1983); Low, 'The Definition of "Export Subsidies" in GATT', 16 J.W.T.L., pp. 375 *et seq.* (1982); see also MTN-Studies No. 6, *supra* n. 73, pp. 175 *et seq.*
88. See *supra* n. 35.
89. The findings of the panel are partly reproduced in *18 U.S. Export Weekly* (hereinafter cited as *ITEX*), March 29, 1983 at 1047.

Although subsidized EEC wheat exports increased considerably during the time under consideration the panel did not consider them as resulting in more than an equitable share of world trade.

primary products which result in sales to particular markets at materially lower prices than those of other suppliers.[90]

Article 11 is the key provision of the Code for domestic subsidies. Like Article 8 it incorporates into the Code the two polar positions of supporters and opponents of subsidies but does not immediately point out the possible adverse effects of domestic subsidies. Rather it states that domestic subsidies 'are widely used as important instruments for the promotion of social and economic policy objectives' and that the signatories 'do not intend to restrict the right of signatories to use such subsidies'. Paragraph 1 furthermore contains a list of the social and economic policy objectives which can be achieved by assistance. The list includes, *inter alia*, regional development (*cf.* dislocation costs), restructuring and adjustment assistance programme (*cf.* ailing industries), research and development (*cf.* infant industries; externalities) and redeployment in order to avoid congestion and environmental problems (*cf.* externalities).

Paragraph 2 restates the three types of adverse consequences listed in Article 8 paragraph 3 and reaffirms the undertaking of the signatories to 'seek to avoid causing such effects through the use of subsidies'. Moreover, it obliges signatories to weigh national benefits against possible adverse effects on international trade of domestic subsidization programs they are about to establish.

Paragraph 3 contains illustrative examples of domestic subsidies such as government financing of commercial enterprises and subscription to their capital, including government grants, loans or guarantees, government performed services, fiscal incentives, and government financing of research and development.

Read together with Article 8, Article 11 provides a cause of action against domestic subsidies. Whenever such subsidies result in either injury or trade displacement which cause adverse effects to the interests of the complaining signatory they can be attacked under Track II.

As noted above though, the signatory attacking a domestic subsidy has the burden of proof to show the adverse effects; since it seems to be quite difficult to translate subsidies into statistical evidence of trade diversion[91] it is not surprising that domestic subsidies are normally not attacked under Track II but are neutralized with countervailing duties. The importance of Track II lies primarily in the trade displacement situations described in provisions (b) and (c) of Article 8 paragraph 4. In fact, since domestic subsidies may have effects which cannot be neutralized by countervailing duties, such as the decrease in exports of the complaining signatory to third countries or to the complaining country itself, Track II is the only remedy. But here also the complainant faces the difficult burden of proof and, to the knowledge of the

90. For an analysis of Art. 10 see generally McGovern, *supra* n. 49, 258-260; Tarullo, *supra* n. 6, 35-37; Rivers, Greenwald, *supra* n. 32, 1476-1479; Phegan, *supra* n. 6, pp. 251 *et seq.*; Estabrook, *supra* n. 80, pp. 406 *et seq.*; Hufbauer, *supra* n. 73, 339, 340; see also MTN-Studies No. 6, *supra* n. 73, pp. 187 *et seq.*

91. See MTN-Studies No. 6, *supra* n. 73, 191; Barcelo, *supra* n. 86, 140.

authors, no signatory has ever attacked a domestic subsidy with a Track II procedure.[92]

c. Procedural Provisions

Article 7 reflects an attempt to strengthen the much criticized notification obligation of Article XVI paragraph 1[93] by providing a mechanism to enforce the obligation. Paragraph 1 of Article 7 entitles signatories to request written information 'on the nature and extent of any subsidy granted or maintained by another signatory'. Thus, a signatory can request information on any practice which it deems to be a subsidy, even if the other signatory has not notified this practice according to Article XVI paragraph 1. Under paragraph 2 the signatories are obliged to respond to requests for information. Furthermore, the requesting signatory may bring the matter to the attention of the Subsidies Committee if it considers the information inadequate. Paragraph 3 provides that any signatory may ask another signatory to notify a practice which the former deems to be a subsidy and that, if the latter fails to do so, the former itself can notify the Subsidies Committee of the practice in question.

Compared to the notification requirement of Article XVI, Article 7 is a definite improvement and practice shows that it is quite extensively used by the signatories.[94] Thus, the Code makes subsidy programs more transparent and, therefore, at least in theory, easier to attack for other signatories.

It has already been noted that a signatory who wants to attack a domestic subsidy under Track II has to prove either injury, or nullification or impairment, or serious prejudice. If adverse effects are alleged the Code's elaborate dispute settlement procedure is initiated. Article 12 paragraph 3 provides for consultations between the complaining and the subsidizing countries and paragraph 4 requires the complainant to present evidence of the nature of the subsidy and its adverse effects. The purpose of this article is to give the signatories the opportunity to clarify the factual situations and to reach

92. If the government does not act on its own motion any interested party in the US might start an action under § 301 of the Trade Act of 1974 as amended by the Trade Agreements Act of 1979; Pub. L. 96-39; 19 U.S.C. §§ 2411-2416 (1982); or in the EEC under the New Commercial Policy Instruments, Reg. 2641/84, OJ L 252, (1984). For a detailed analysis of § 301 see Hudec, 'Retaliation Against Unreasonable Foreign Trade Practices', 59 Minn. L. Rev., pp. 461 *et seq.* (1975); Fisher, Bart S., Steinhart, 'Section 301 of the Trade Act of 1974: Protection for U.S. Exporters of Goods, Services and Capital', 14 L. & Pol'y. Int'l. Bus., pp. 569 *et seq.* (1982); Coffield, 'Using Section 301 of the Trade Act of 1974 as a Response to Foreign Trade Action: When, Why and How?', 6 N.C. J. Int'l. L. & Comm. Reg., pp. 381 *et seq.* (1981). For a detailed analysis of EEC Reg. 2641/84 see Bronckers, 'Private Response to Foreign Unfair Trade Practices – United States and EEC Complaint Procedures', 6 N.W. J. Int'l. L. & Bus. 651 (Fall 1984); Bourgeois, Laurent, 'Le "Nouvel Instrument de Politique Commerciale"; un pas en avant vers l'elimination des obstacles aux échanges internationaux' 21 RTDE 41 (1985); Steenbergen, 'The New Commercial Policy Instrument', 22 CMLR 421 (1985).
93. See nn. 25 to 31 *supra* and accompanying text.
94. For example, in 1982 Canada and the EEC accused the US in the Subsidies Committee of not having declared DISC a subsidy; see 406 *ITEX* 238, 239. May 18, 1982.

compromise through bilateral consultations without getting involved in the formal dispute settlement procedure of the Code.[95]

However, if the consultations do not lead to a mutually acceptable solution within sixty days of the request, any consulting signatory may refer the matter to the Subsidies Committee for conciliation. This deadline reflects an effort to speed up the conciliation and dispute settlement process and may even act as an incentive towards compromise during consultations. If conciliation is requested the Subsidies Committee has one month to help to arrive at a mutually acceptable solution; after that, any signatory involved may request the establishment of a panel.

Article 18 contains the core dispute settlement provision of the Code. The function of the panel is to review the facts and to present the Subsidies Committee its findings concerning the rights and obligations of the parties to the dispute. Paragraph 2 contains two deadlines in that it requires that a panel be established within thirty days of a request thereof and that it delivers its findings to the Subsidies Committee within sixty days of its establishment. Provisions on the establishment, the functioning, and the composition of the panel are also provided. Paragraph 6 provides for mediation by the panel. It requires that each panel informs the parties to the dispute of its report and conclusion before it circulates them to the Committee. Although one author asserts 'that the panel is generally limited to determining the facts and legal obligations of the disputants, rather than becoming involved in mediation efforts. . . .'[96] we tend to believe that paragraphs 6 and 7 recognize the mediation function of the panel. If no compromise is reached the panel has to submit a written report to the Subsidies Committee, covering the facts and findings of the case and the reasons and basis of its decision.

The Subsidies Committee then acts as conciliator a second time insofar as it gives the parties recommendations which should be based on the panel's report. If the recommendations are not followed it may authorize 'appropriate countermeasures'. Again the Committee has to act quickly as the recommendations have to be presented to the parties within thirty days of the Committee's receipt of the panel report.

The following chart shows the procedural steps and the Code's time-line of a Track II action against domestic subsidies.[97] It has to be noted that the Code provides for conciliation at each step in order to leave the possibility of agreement open.

Compared with GATT[98] and other MTN-agreements,[99] the dispute settlement procedure set out in the Subsidies Code is definitely an improvement.[100]

95. See MTN-Studies No. 6, *supra* n. 73, at 192, 193; Barcelo, *supra* n. 86, 139; Rivers, Greenwald, *supra* n. 32, 1487.
96. Tarullo, *supra* n. 6, 45.
97. For a more detailed description of the Code's dispute settlement procedure, see MTN Studies No. 6, *supra* n. 73, pp. 192-195 and 205-212.
98. For an analysis of the problems with the GATT dispute settlement see Jackson, *supra* n. 59, pp. 40-44; Jackson, 'Governmental Disputes in International Trade Relations: A Proposal in the Context of GATT', 13 J.W.T.L. 1, pp. 4 *et seq.* (1979); see also Hudec, 'GATT Dispute Settlement After the Tokyo Round: An Unfinished Business', 13 Corn. Int'. L.J. pp. 145 *et seq.* (1980); Meng, 'Streitbeilegung im GATT', 41 ZaoRV 69, pp. 78 *et seq.* (1981).
99. See Jackson, *supra* n. 59, pp. 44-47; Jackson, 'GATT Machinery and the Tokyo Round Agreements', in: *Trade Policies in the 1980s*, (Cline ed.), 159, pp. 185 *et seq.* (1983).
100. Tarullo, *supra* n. 6, at 45; Rivers, Greenwald, *supra* n. 32, at 1489.

Chart 1

	Articles	
(1)		Allegation of a domestic subsidy which causes injury, or nullification or impairment, or serious prejudice.
(2)	12:3	Consultations: 60 days
(3)	13:2, 17	Conciliation, Committee: 30 days
(4)	18:2	Establishment of a panel: 30 days after request thereof
(5)	18:6	Mediation
(6)	18:2	Panel report: 60 days after establishment
(7)	18:9	Recommendations of the Committee: 30 days after the receipt of the panel's report
(8)	18:9	Authorization of appropriate countermeasures by the Committee.

Extremely important informal ways of dispute settlement, such as consultation and conciliation, are woven into a formal and legalistic net of provisions which ultimately authorize countermeasures. Together with the time limits it seeks to guarantee that trade disputes concerning subsidies are expeditiously resolved, either by compromise or by a 'trial-like' decision of the Subsidies Committee.

3. Track I

Track I establishes elaborate procedural rules which the signatories have to follow in a countervailing duty investigation. The reason behind these detailed rules has already been mentioned: because of the great discretion Article VI accords to the contracting parties with regard to procedural rules, countervailing duty investigations themselves could be used as an instrument for keeping unwanted imports out of the country.[101] Since the provisions of Track I had to be incorporated into national laws we will refer to them later when discussing the corresponding provisions of the Trade Agreements Act of 1979[102] and at this point turn to five main features of Track I.

First, Track I does not define the term subsidy but only requires the acting signatory to show that a subsidy was granted. A description of the term, however, is provided by footnote 22 to Article 7 in Track II which reads:

> 'In this Agreement the term subsidies shall be deemed to include subsidies granted by any government or any public body within the territory of a signatory. . . .'

Thus one could argue that the Code narrows the meaning of the term subsidy as used in Article VI and gives it the meaning used in Article XVI. This argument is buttressed by the fact that the Code never refers to 'bounty' but

101. See *supra* n. 52.

102. For a detailed description of Arts. 1 to 6 of the Subsidies Code see MTN-Studies No. 6, *supra* n. 73, pp. 114 *et seq*.

only to 'subsidy', and by the wording of footnote 22 which seems to contradict the above mentioned broad interpretation of the term subsidy as including 'private subsidies'.[103]

On the other hand, one could assert that the use of 'subsidy' and not of 'bounty' is not indicative because the terms were originally considered identical[104] and particularly because Article I explicitly provides that signatories can only impose countervailing duties in accordance with Article VI, thereby allowing the assumption that 'bounty' is covered by the Code. Indeed, the Code in theory merely interprets Articles VI, XVI, and XXIII. (See the preamble.) Furthermore, the wording of footnote 22 is not exhaustive: the phrase 'shall be deemed to include' might allow private subsidies.

Therefore, the question of the meaning of 'subsidy' within the Subsidies Code remains open.

It is submitted, however, that the Code does not give the term subsidy a narrower meaning than Article VI but rather incorporates the broad meaning referred to above. Thus, like GATT, the Code maintains the different scope of the term subsidy depending on what type of action is taken.[104a]

The second feature of Track I is the 'injury-test', one of the most important issues during the negotiations.[105] A countervailing duty can be levied against subsidized imports only if the administering authority has found 'material injury' to a domestic industry. Article 2 furthermore requires the establishment of a causal link between subsidized imports and injury and Article 6 paragraph 4 explains this causal relation as follows: 'it must be demonstrated that the subsidized imports are, through the effect of the subsidy, causing injury. . . .'[106]

The third feature of Track I is the regulation of provisional measures against subsidized imports. The need for these regulations is beyond doubt because Article VI does not refer to provisional measures and so leaves it up to the discretion of the contracting parties.

The fourth feature of Track I is the extensive regulation of the countervailing duty proceedings. Its main characteristic is an expeditious investigation which offers both sides the possibility to state their case.

The fifth feature of Track I is conciliation. Articles 3 and 4 provide for consultations and negotiated settlements with either the subsidizing country or individual exporters. Thus, like Track II, Track I offers signatories the possibility to resolve subsidy disputes informally without having to resort to a more formal sanction mechanism which could have repercussions on the trade relations between the signatories. Since the acting signatory can impose countervailing duties unilaterally without having to await an authorization by the Subsidies Committee it is in a strong bargaining position. Nevertheless, as the 1982 *US-EEC Carbon Steel Cases* show[107] agreements between the

103. See *supra* nn. 47 to 50 and accompanying text.
104. See *supra* n. 46.
104a. For an opposing view see Benyon/Bourgeois, 'The European Community – United States Steel Arrangement', 21 CMLR 305, 327 (1984).
105. See *supra* n. 67; see also Rivers, Greenwald, *supra* n. 32, at 1483.
106. For a discussion of the drafting of this language see Grey, *supra* n. 61, at 9-10 and *supra* n. 66, at 46-47; see also Rivers, Greenwald, *supra* n. 32, at 1483, 1484.
107. See *7 U.S. Import Weekly* (hereinafter cited as *ITIM*) 99, Oct. 27, 1982.

signatories are possible – sometimes even outside the provisions of Article 6.[108]

C. FINAL REMARKS ABOUT THE INTERNATIONAL RULES

The entry into force of the Subsidies Code represents a considerable change in the application of the GATT provisions on subsidies and countervailing duties. Both substantive and procedural rules are elaborated with the objective to render them more meaningful than the GATT provisions and to exert control over the signatories in order to avoid abuses. The signatories now have two alternatives to attack subsidies: either they can unilaterally impose countervailing duties on subsidized imports which materially injure their domestic industry, or they can lodge a complaint according to Track II. This might give the impression that GATT now functions well with regard to subsidies. Practice, however, shows a different reality: Suffice it to say that many recent international trade disputes have to do with subsidies or countervailing duties.[109] The reason for that is the disagreement among the contracting parties and signatories on the appropriate use of subsidies, disagreement which extends to all three kinds of subsidies. Most developed countries agree on prohibition of export subsidies on industrial products but the less developed signatories can rely on the exception in Article 14. Another cause of difficulty is that many contracting parties are not signatories to the Code[110] and for them only the GATT rules apply.[111] With regard to export subsidies on primary products the Code does not seem to have achieved much. The prerequisite of 'more than an equitable share' is very difficult to prove and some signatories, particularly the EEC, seem to be quite confident in granting these subsidies.[112] The divergence of opinions among the signatories on the

108. See a discussion of the arrangement *infra*. See also Benyon, Bourgeois, 'The EC-U.S. Steel Arrangement', 21 CML Rev. 305 (1984).
109. See for example the above mentioned *Steel cases*, *supra* n. 107; the *EEC Wheat Subsidies case*, *supra* n. 89; the *Pasta case*, *infra*. n. 112 and the *Steel Subsidies cases of Argentina and Brazil*, 9 *ITIM* 916 (1984). See also the annual reports of the Subsidies Committee, published in the GATT BISD series.
110. As of June 1, 1983 20 states and the EEC were signatories of the Code; see GATT Doc. L/5517 p. 25.
111. As noted above this does not mean that those countries have accepted Art. XVI para. 4; see *supra* nn. 14 to 20 and accompanying text.
112. The EEC repeatedly stated that export subsidies on primary products are permissible as long as they do not lead to market disruption; see 20 *ITEX* 138, 139 1983/84; the difficulties in proving 'more than an equitable share of world export trade' favour this position; see the *EEC Wheat Subsidies Case*, *supra* n. 89, in which a GATT panel could not agree that the EEC's subsidization of wheat exports resulted in more than an equitable share of world trade. With regard to the quarrel between the U.S. and the EEC on the appropriateness of export subsidies on primary products another case deserves mentioning. On April 19, 1983 a GATT panel ruled that EEC subsidies on durum wheat flour used to produce pasta for export constituted an export subsidization of a non-primary product and thus violated Art. 9; see 8 *ITIM* 468, 1983; although the *Pasta Case* is not an Art. 10 case both cases have produced a considerable deadlock in the work of the Subsidies Committee; see 20 *ITEX* 138, 158, 313, 1983/84.

appropriateness or nonappropriateness of the use of subsidies is most apparent in the case of domestic subsidies.[113] On the one hand, Article 11 recognizes the use of domestic subsidies for the promotion of social and economic policy objectives and on the other hand it states that they may adversely affect the conditions of normal competition. Besides, to avoid discussions among the signatories on what constitutes a domestic subsidy,[114] the Code, oddly enough, does not give any guidelines on what it considers to be a domestic subsidy[115] but simply allows these practices unless they lead to 'injury', 'nullification or impairment', or 'serious prejudice'. However, the burden of proof in a Track II proceeding against a domestic subsidy constitutes an obstacle so difficult to overcome that, to the best of our knowledge no signatory has ever brought a Track II complaint against a domestic subsidy or against a unilateral definition of domestic subsidy in a Track I proceeding.[116] Thus, the Subsidies Committee has never had a chance to define the term 'domestic subsidy'. Furthermore, since signatories can unilaterally levy countervailing duties against subsidized imports, they do not see any need in having domestic subsidy problems discussed in the Subsidies Committee. Given the fact that the decision to levy countervailing duties is made by national authorities, the power to define domestic subsidies has been shifted from the international to the national level. No great imagination is needed to see that this practice leads to different interpretations and that those countries which are generally opposed to subsidies will be more active in levying countervailing duties than those who accept them. Thus, with regard to domestic subsidies Track I has replaced Track II[117] and the lack of consensus on how to deal with domestic subsidies all but confirms this. By opening the possibility to interpret the term 'subsidy' in Track I in a broad sense, the Subsidies Code enhances reactions against all kinds of assistance to industries, reactions which can be used as import barriers, particularly in times of high dollar-rates, economic recession or high trade deficits. It is clear that the lack of definition of the term subsidy in the Code and in GATT may have negative effects: signatories are free to extend their definitions of domestic subsidies to include any new practice which they find particularly disturbing.[118]

113. Rivers, Greenwald, *supra* n. 32, 1470; Tarullo, *supra* n. 6, 37; Marcuss, 'Understanding Direct and Indirect Subsidies: Are the Problems Negotiable or Incurable' in *Interface III*, 51, at 54 (1984).
114. See Rivers, Greenwald, *supra* n. 32, at 1473.
115. An attempt to include a nonexhaustive list of domestic subsidies into the Subsidies Code was rejected by most delegations. The list was only supposed to be a guideline and would not have been indicative as to which practices were prohibited. Still, many countries feared that such a list would over time lead to a distinction between acceptable and unacceptable practices and they could not accept such a distinction. The text of this list and an analysis thereof can be found in the article of Rivers and Greenwald, *supra* n. 32, pp. 1470 *et seq.*; see also Tarullo, *supra* n. 6, pp. 37 *et seq.*
116. Track II complaints have been brought mostly against export subsidies on industrial products, see for example the *Pasta Case*, *supra* n. 112, or against export subsidies on primary products, see for example the *EEC Wheat Subsidies Case*, *supra* n. 89, but *always* involving agricultural products.
117. See Marcuss, *supra* n. 113, at 12.
118. For example, equity and loans to state owned enterprises have been subject to countervailing duty investigation only in the last few years; see Hufbauer, *supra* n. 73, at 353. In a very recent case, the ITA seriously considered countervailing unemployment insurance for fishermen, see *Certain Fresh Atlantic Groundfish from Canada*, 51 Fed. Ref. 10041 (1986)

On the other hand, one could argue that the leading countervailing countries, particularly the US, could develop, through a coherent and non-arbitrary application of their countervailing duty laws, clearcut principles which could eventually lead to a catalogue of accepted and unaccepted practices.[119] The leading countervailing nation, through the use of its countervailing duty law, would set precedents for other nations to follow, and a consensus on the appropriateness of certain practices could be achieved through practice. At that point it would be easier to incorporate a catalogue of practices into the Code.

The negative aspects of such a development would be that consensus would be reached on protectionist grounds as it would be due to everybody accepting the practice of the country which makes most use of its countervailing duty laws. It is not very likely that the latter country would give up its well established practice only because other countries are more liberal in the application of their countervailing duty laws. Rather, these countries would follow the stricter rules either because they think they are right or because they would want to be able to retaliate. Thus, relying on national practices to develop international consensus might lead to protectionist application of countervailing duty laws. Recent practice already shows that domestic industries try to interpret the countervail laws to cover all sorts of practices.[120] The fact that they are able to do so under the GATT – Track I does not prescribe many limits – is one reason why the international procedure against domestic subsidies has never been set into motion.

The Subsidies Code creates an 'asymmetry'[121] in remedies which clearly favours unilaterally imposed countervailing duties over internationally agreed upon solutions or authorized countermeasures. The same asymmetry is carried on in the way countries are treated depending on their size and export activities. For example, if the firm which receives a domestic subsidy is situated in a small country which heavily relies on exportation its exports might easily be subjected to countervailing duties.[122] Some authors even go as far as to say that those subsidies are not domestic subsidies but hidden export subsidies.[123] There is no doubt that the importing country can levy countervailing duties against such subsidized exports; yet the question remains as to what a signatory

(footnote 118 cont.)
(fin. aff.), but see n. 169 *infra.* and accompanying text; for a different approach with regard to the meaning of subsidy in Track I and Track II see Benyon, Bourgeois, *supra* n. 104a at 327.

119. Marcuss, *supra* n. 113, at 17.

120. The Report of the House Ways and Means Committee on the Trade Agreements Act of 1979, for example, states:

    'In particular but not exclusively a subsidy includes those export subsidies enumerated in Annex A to the Agreement . . . and those practices as may be added by regulation by the Authority'.

    Trade Agreements Act of 1979, *Report of the Committee on Ways and Means, House of Representatives, to Accompany H.R. 4537*; House Report No. 96-317, 96th Cong., 1st Sess. (hereinafter cited as *House Report No. 96-317*), at 74 (1979).

121. For Grey this asymetry is 'a major failure of the Tokyo Round Agreement'; Grey, *supra* n. 61, at 3.

122. The above cited *Michelin Case* is a typical example: 75% of the output of that firm was shipped to the United States; see *supra* n. 34.

123. Marcuss, *supra* n. 113, at 3.

can do against a domestic subsidy of another signatory which either does not export at all or only exports to third countries. In both cases the complaining signatory can only use Track II and it will have to prove that the subsidy resulted in adverse effects to its interests. Taking the Chrysler loan as an example of the first situation, any complaining signatory would have had to show that because of the loan its car exports to the United States decreased so much as to cause serious prejudice. The same would apply to the second situation, *i.e.* that of export displacement.

The example confirms the asymmetry referred to above[124] in that it shows that in some cases countries can unilaterally use their national laws whereas in others they have to resort to the more complex international procedure. The prerequisites of Track II are more difficult to prove than those of Track I; and even assuming the opposite, still it must be borne in mind that Track II requires an international proceeding in which the complainant has to convince both the panel and the Subsidies Committee whereas Track I only requires a national investigation.

In short, the disagreement of the signatories on the use of domestic subsidies [their heavy reliance on Track I against them and the failure to define and provide rules for the calculation of these subsidies], are all factors which hamper the functioning of the Subsidies Code. In order to give signatories some guidelines it might therefore be necessary to define potentially troublesome domestic subsidies and to include an illustrative list of these practices in a new Annex B to the Code, as was indeed proposed by the United States in the Tokyo Round negotiations. Furthermore, signatories should be encouraged to use Track II against export displacing domestic subsidies to lessen the asymmetry between the remedies of Track I and Track II.[125]

III. UNITED STATES COUNTERVAILING DUTY LAWS AS WEAPONS AGAINST DOMESTIC SUBSIDIES

A. THE TRADE AGREEMENTS ACT OF 1979 – A SURVEY OF THE COUNTERVAILING DUTY LAW

1. BACKGROUND

The implementation of the Subsidies Code into US law[126] mandated major

124. For a detailed analysis of the asymmetry argument see Grey, *supra* n. 61, pp. 3 *et seq.*
125. Hufbauer, *supra* n. 73, at 358.
126. For a description of the way how the Tokyo Round Agreements were implemented see Jackson, Louis, Matsushita, 'Implementing the Tokyo Round: Legal Aspects of Changing International Economic Rules', 81 Mich. L.R. 267 (1982).

changes in the old countervailing duty law:[127] the Trade Agreements Act of 1979 (hereinafter, TAA) amended the Tariff Act of 1930 by adding title VI which contains the new countervailing duty and anti-dumping laws.[128]

Section 701(a)[129] lays down the general principles of the new law according to which a countervailing duty can be imposed if subsidized imports materially injure a domestic industry. The two main elements of the law are 'subsidy' and 'material injury'. The application of the new law is limited to 'countries under the agreement', meaning that only those countries which either accepted the Subsidies Code or equivalent obligations,[130] or which were granted unconditional most favoured nation treatment by the United States, are subject to the new law; for the other countries the old law still applies.[131] (No injury test for dutiable goods.)

127. The countervailing duty law applicable before January 1, 1980 was § 303 of the Tariff Act of 1930, as amended by the Trade Act of 1974, Pub. L. 93-615, tit. 3, § 331, 19 USC § 1303 (1976). However, the effectiveness of the 1974 amendments was hampered by the fact that the Secretary of the Treasury could waive the imposition of countervailing duties according to § 303(d), 19 USC § 1303(d) (1976), whenever he determined that such imposition would jeopardize the outcome of the Tokyo Round negotiations. For a discussion of this waiver see Jackson, *Legal Problems*, 816, 822-823; Jackson, *et al.*, *supra* n. 126, 356.

For an analysis of the 1974 amendments see O'Neill, *US Countervailing Duty Law: Renewed, Revamped, and Revisited – Trade Act of 1974*, 17 BC Indust. & Comm. L. Rev., 832, pp. 853 *et seq.* (1976). Before 1974 § 303 of the Tariff Act of 1930, ch. 497, tit. 3 § 303, 46 Stat. 687, governed the imposition of countervailing duties. For an analysis of § 303 see Ehrenhaft, 'Protection against International Price Discrimination: United States countervailing and anti-dumping duties', 58 Colum-L. Rev., 44 pp. 54 *et seq.* (1958); Butler, *supra* n. 17, pp. 96 *et seq.*; Feller, 'Mutiny against the Bounty: an Examination of Subsidies, Border Tax Adjustments, and the Resurgence of the Countervailing Duty Law', 1 Law & Pol'y Int'l. Bus., 17, pp. 19 *et seq.* (1969).

128. 'Trade Agreements Act of 1979), Pub. L. 96-39, tit. 7, 19 USCA §§ 1671-1677g (West Supp. 1984).

129. 19 USCA 1671(a) (West. Supp. 1984):
(§ 1671. Countervailing duties imposed
(a) General rule. – If –
(1) the administering authority determines that –
(A) a country under the Agreement, or
(B) a person who is a citizen or national of such a country, or a corporation, association, or other organization organized in such a country,
is providing, directly or indirectly, a subsidy with respect to the manufacture, production, or exportation of a class or kind of merchandise imported into the United States, and
(2) the Comission determines that –
(A) an industry in the United States –
(i) is materially injured, or
(ii) is threatened with material injury, or
(B) the establishment of an industry in the United States is materially retarded,
by reason of imports of the merchandise,
then there shall be imposed upon such merchandise a countervailing duty, in addition to any other duty imposed, equal to the amount of the net subsidy.)

130. For an explanation of § 701(b)(2) and (3) see Senate Report No. 249, *supra* n. 32, 44-45; Feller, *US Customs and International Trade*, Vol. 1, § 17.04(1) (1984).

131. Section 303 of the Tariff Act of 1930, as amended, 19 USC § 1303 (1976). It is interesting to note that under § 303 only non-dutiable goods from GATT members are subject to an injury test. Countervailing duties on dutiable goods can be levied without a finding of injury to domestic producers; see O'Neill, *supra* n. 127, 855-860. Two recent cases show the application of old and new law. On April 19, 1984 the ITA found that certain steel imports from Argentina and Brazil were subsidized, see 9 *ITIM* 916 (1984); in the case of Argentina which is not a country under the agreement § 303 of the Tariff Act of 1930 governed the

The major changes of the countervailing duty law were not only a result of the international negotiations but also of a growing dissatisfaction with the application of the old countervailing duty law.[132] The increasing resort of governments to subsidization obviously resulted in an increase of countervailing duty investigations[133] by the Department of the Treasury, which administered the old law, but nevertheless the Department came under criticism for not taking enough actions against this kind of unfair trade.[134] The Trade Act of 1974[135] had already addressed these problems insofar as it limited administrative discretion, imposed deadlines for the determinations by the Treasury Department and allowed judicial review,[136] but the Trade Agreements Act of 1979 provided for an even more expeditious procedure, abolished administrative discretion completely, and expanded judicial review.[137] Furthermore, the 1979 Act contained detailed rules for disclosure of confidential information[138] which are quite far-reaching if one takes into account that the respondent in a countervail case is usually a foreign government. The TAA rendered countervailing duty procedures more adversarial and less discretionary in order to guarantee a fair and equitable application of the law. This 'legalization' of the trade laws is a unique feature of the Act.[139]

B. SECTION 771(5) AND (6) – SUBSTANTIVE RULES ON SUBSIDIES

1. Background

Since the imposition of a countervailing duty requires, *inter alia*, the finding of a subsidy, the administering authority, since 1980 the International Trade

(footnote 131 contd.)
case whereas in the case of Brazil the TAA was applicable. In the Argentinian case the findings of the ITA immediately resulted in the imposition of countervailing duties whereas in the Brazilian case the ITC had to find material injury before a countervailing duty could be imposed. For a comparison between the old and new countervailing duty law see Feller, *supra* n. 130 § 17.07.

132. See Bryan, *Taxing Unfair International Trade Practices*, 252 (1980); Jackson *et al.*, *supra* n. 126, 356.
133. This trend started with the enactment of the Trade Act of 1974, see Jackson, *Legal Problems*, 822.
134. See O'Neill, *supra* n. 127, pp. 837 *et seq.* The discretionary power of the Secretary of the Treasury was supported by a decision of the Court of Customs and Patent Appeals which in *United States* v. *Hammond Lead Products, Inc.* ruled that the Secretary's action was not reviewable by the courts, 440 F. 2d 1024, 1031 (CCPA 1971); see also Murphy, 'Anti-Dumping and Countervailing Duties under the Trade Agreements Act of 1979: A Preliminary Analysis', 14 Int'l. Lawyer 203, 205 (1980).
135. Pub. L. 93-618. 19 USC. §§ 2101-2487 (1976).
136. Bryan, *supra* n. 132, 251-252; O'Neill, *supra* n. 127, 860-861.
137. Section 516A, 19 USCA § 1516a (West Supp. 1984).
138. Taylor, Vermulst, 'Disclosure of Confidential Information in Antidumping and Countervailing Duty Proceedings Under American Law: Lessons for the European Communities', 20 Int. Law. To be published in 1986.
139. Jackson *et al.*, *supra* n. 126, 383.

Administration (hereinafter, ITA) of the Department of Commerce, has had to have some guidelines on what constitutes a subsidy. These guidelines are contained in § 771(5).[140] The finding of subsidization, however, is not sufficient: in addition, the ITA has to *valuate* and *calculate* the subsidy for duty assessment since § 701(a)[141] limits the imposition of a countervailing duty to the amount of the 'net subsidy'. The TAA does not contain provisions on the valuation of a subsidy but in § 771(6) it provides the ITA with guidelines for the calculation of the net subsidy.[142]

Section 771(5) is threefold:

(1) it states that the term subsidy has the same meaning as the term 'bounty or grant' as used in § 303 of the Tariff Act of 1930.[143] Thus, it incorporates into the Act the definition of 'bounty or grant' as developed under the old countervailing duty laws. Since neither term was defined by statute the ITA may have recourse to the judicial and administrative practice developed under the old law.[144] This first part furthermore provides that the definitions which follow are not exhaustive but illustrative and in so doing makes another reference to the definitions under the old law.[145]

140. 19 USCA § 1677(5) (West Supp. 1984):
'(5) Subsidy. – The term 'subsidy' has the same meaning as the term 'bounty or grant' as that term is used in section 1303 of this title, and includes, but is not limited to, the following:
(A) Any export subsidy described in Annex A to the Agreement relating to an illustrative list of export subsidies.
(B)The following domestic subsidies, if provided or required by government action to a specific enterprise or industry, or group of enterprises or industries, whether publicly or privately owned, and whether paid or bestowed directly or indirectly on the manufacture, production, or export of any class or kind of merchandise:
(i) The provision of capital, loans, or loan guarantees on terms inconsistent with commercial considerations.
(ii) The provision of goods or services at preferential rates.
(iii) The grant of funds or forgiveness of debt to cover operating losses sustained by a specific industry.
(iv) The assumption of any costs or expenses of manufacture, production, or distribution.'

141. 19 USCA § 1671(a) (West Supp. 1984).

142. 19 USCA § 1677(6) (West Supp. 1984):
'(6) Net subsidy. – For the purpose of determining the net subsidy, the administering authority may subtract from the gross subsidy the amount of –
(A) any application fee, deposit, or similar payment paid in order to qualify for, or to receive, the benefit of the subsidy.
(B) any loss in the value of the subsidy resulting from its deferred receipt, if the deferral is mandated by Government order, and
(C) export taxes, duties, or other charges levied on the export of merchandise to the United States specifically intended to offset the subsidy received.'

143. 19 USC § 1404 (1976).

144. For an analysis of the administrative and judicial definitions of the term bounty or grant prior to the Trade Agreements Act of 1979 see Chambers, *supra* n. 64, pp. 830 *et seq.*; Berger, 'Judicial Review of Countervailing Duty Determinations', 19 Harv. Int'l, L.J. 593, pp. 604 *et seq.* (1978); O'Neill, *supra* n. 127, pp. 846 *et seq.*; Hummel, 'Customs Title I of the Trade Agreements Act of 1979 – An Improvement over the Present Countervailing Duty Law', 4 Suff. Transnat'l. L.J. 213, pp. 215 *et seq.* (1980); Marks, Malmgren, *supra* n. 53, pp. 348 *et seq.*; Guido, Morrone, *supra* n. 34, pp. 242 *et seq.*.

145. See Senate Report No. 249, *supra* n. 32, at 85.

(2) it states that the term subsidy includes the practices enumerated in the illustrative list of the Subsidies Code.[146] The examples in the list which practically correspond to the interpretation of 'bounty or grant' under prior practice[147] are *per se* countervailable assuming the existence of material injury.

(3) § 771(5)(B) includes examples of domestic subsidies.

The list of domestic subsidies in § 771(5) contains practices similar to the examples in Article 11 paragraph 3 of the Code. Thus, the incorporation of domestic subsidies in the TAA is nothing but a reflection of the provisions of the Subsidies Code. Yet it has been argued that '§ 771(5) promotes protectionist goals and counteracts the free trade ideal of the Subsidies Code'.[148] This contention deserves closer attention. The Subsidies Code allows international actions against domestic subsidies under Track II. As far as countervailing duties are concerned, the international rules do not even make a distinction between export and domestic subsidies. The Code allows the imposition of countervailing duties against subsidized imports when certain conditions are met,[149] no matter whether they have received domestic or export subsidies. Section 771(5), therefore, is in compliance with the Code. One could go even further and say that the conditions prescribed in § 771(5) are not necessary under the Subsidies Code. Since Track I allows a broad definition of the term subsidy[150] one could interpret the meaning of the Code as covering any subsidy.[151] No signatory is precluded from applying a more rigorous definition than the ones given in the examples of Track II. Track II provides international relief against subsidies, which must be distinguished from unilaterally imposed relief.

Section 771(6) provides specific guidelines for calculating offsets. It differs considerably from prior practice[152] under the old law in that it limits the discretion of the ITA to offset certain practices and allows offsets only for those few minor items which it specifically lists.

2. Section 771(5)(B) – Domestic Subsidies

The inclusion of domestic subsidies in the definition of subsidies in § 771(5) reflects the development of the application of the countervailing duty law against domestic subsidies. As noted above,[153] in 1973 the Treasury, in the

146. For reference see *supra* n. 87.
147. See Feller, 'Countervailing Duties', at 123-124, in: *1 Lawyers Guide to International Business Transactions*. Surrey, Wallace (2nd ed. 1977); see also Butler, *supra* n. 17, 96-124; Feller, *supra* n. 127, at 19-38.
148. MacDonnell, 'Offset Policy Under the New Countervailing Duty Law', 15 Corn. Int'l. L.J. 429, 439 (1982).
149. See *supra* nn. 101 to 108 and accompanying text.
150. See *supra* n. 103 and accompanying text.
151. See Section C.3.
152. See for example *Bromine From Israel*, 43 Fed. Reg. 56764 (1978); for a description of this practice see MacDonnell, *supra* n. 148, 440-442.
153. See n. 34 *supra*.

Michelin Case,[154] for the first time in years countervailed domestic subsidies, albeit by claiming it was really countervailing export subsidies. In analyzing the case under § 303 of the Tariff Act of 1930 the Treasury determined that a Canadian regional assistance program to a locally depressed area constituted a 'bounty or grant . . . paid or bestowed on exports'.[155] Since then the Treasury continued to impose countervailing duties against domestic subsidies;[156] however, it interpreted § 303 to be applicable only against domestic subsidies which were 'export oriented'.[157] Thus, the Treasury took into account the size of the subsidy, the volume of merchandise exported and the effects that the subsidy had on the exports.[158] If the domestic subsidy was not 'export oriented'. the Treasury did not find any bounty or grant in the sense of § 303.[159] The inclusion of the 'export orientation-test' in the definition of a countervailable subsidy was later rejected by the Court of Customs and Patent Appeals[160] which ruled that § 303 did not require such a test and that any subsidy found to be more than *de minimis* had to be interpreted as a bounty or grant under § 303.

The explicit inclusion of domestic subsidies in the definition of subsidies in § 771(5) can only be interpreted as meaning that the ITA has to levy countervailing duties against (domestically) subsidized imports, regardless of the export orientation of the output of the subsidized enterprise, provided that all other conditions of the statute are met. Section 771(5)(B), however, does not open the floodgates of countervailing duty actions against all domestic subsidies. The first paragraph of § 771(5)(B) contains certain conditions which have to be met before a practice can be characterized as a countervailable subsidy. Before turning to the examples given in § 771(5)(B)(i) to (iv) we will discuss these conditions and analyze the text of this first paragraph.

a. De Minimis Test

Although it is nowhere mentioned in § 771(5), the ITA applies a '*de minimis*

154. *X-rated Steel Belted Tires from Canada*, 38 Fed. Reg. 1018 (1973), 7 Cust. Bull. 24 (1973). See also Horlick *supra* n. 34.
155. For a critical analysis of this case see Guido, Morrone, *supra* n. 34, pp. 251 *et seq*.
156. See for example: *Carbon Steel Plate and High Strength Steel Plate From Mexico*, 41 Fed. Reg. 1273 (1976) (freight rate subsidy); *Float Glass From Italy*, 41 Fed. Reg. 1274 (1976) (regional subsidy); *Tomato Products From the European Community*, 44 Fed. Reg. 49248 (1979) (production subsidy to offset price supports on tomatoes); *Certain Optic Liquid Level Sensing Systems From Canada*, 44 Fed. Reg. 1728 (1979) (research and development grant); *Certain Fish From Canada*, 44 Fed. Reg. 1372 (1979) (regional grants).
157. See generally Bryan, *supra* n. 132, 296, 297; Barcelo, *supra* n. 86, at 126; Barcelo, *supra* n. 85, at 273; Verrill, 'State Owned Enterprises and the Countervailing Duty Law: Where, oh Where to Draw the Line', in *Interface III*, 35 (1984).
158. See *ASG Industries, Inc.* v. *United States*, 467 F. Supp. 1200, 1214 (Cust. Ct. 1979), rev'd on other grounds, 610 F. 2d 770 (CCPA 1979) in which the Court sanctioned this test for defining domestic subsidies as 'bounties or grants'.
159. See for example *Float Glass From Germany*, 41 Fed. Reg. 1300 (1976), in which a regional development grant was received by the firm which produced the allegedly subsidized items, however, 80 to 99 per cent of the output of the subsidized industries was sold in the domestic market; see also *Float Glass From France*, 40 Fed. Reg. 56697 (1975). For a criticism of this interpretation, see Verrill, *supra* n. 157.
160. *ASG Industries, Inc.* v. *United States*, 610 F.2d 770, 775-778 (CCPA 1979) reversing 467 F. Supp. 1187 (Cust. Ct. 1979).

test' when defining subsidies. This rule provides that total subsidies equal to or lower than 0.5 per cent of *ad valorem* value of the merchandise under investigation are considered to be *de minimis* and therefore noncountervailable.[161] The Court of International Trade has upheld the *de minimis* test.[162]

b. Specificity Test

Section 771(5)(B) limits the definition of domestic subsidies to those which are provided 'to a specific enterprise or industry, or group of enterprises or industries'. Thus, whenever a domestic subsidy program is available to move a few industries or group of industries within a country, the ITA will not hold such a program countervailable.[163] With this interpretation § 771(5) tries to distinguish between 'general domestic subsidies' (including but not limited to, public roads, irrigation projects, high quality transportation systems, police, fire protection and public health programs, national fiscal policy, and broad economic policies) which do not have trade distorting effects, and *de jure* or *de facto* selective domestic subsidies.[164] Because of this distinction, which has been upheld by the court,[165] the ITA does not have to evaluate the amount of a general domestic subsidy on a specific imported product, which, according to Barcelo, would be a task not only difficult but also arbitrary.[166]

The only reference to the specificity test in the Subsidies Code is contained in Article 11 paragraph 3 which reads:

> 'Signatories recognize that the objectives mentioned in paragraph 1 above may be achieved, *inter alia*, by means of subsidies granted with the aim of giving an advantage to *certain* enterprises' (emphasis added).

However, this sentence appears in Track II and not in Track I. Track I, setting the standards for national countervailing duty laws, does not contain any provision which could be interpreted as to require directly a specificity test.

161. See for example *Fireplace Mesh Panels from Taiwan*, 48 Fed. Reg. 11305 (1983); 5 ITRD 1124 (1984).
162. *Carlisle Tire and Rubber Company* v. *United States*, 517 F. Supp. 704 (US CIT 1981); 2 ITRD 1577 (1982).
163. In *Certain Steel Products From Belgium*, 47 Fed. Reg. 39304 (1982), 4 ITRD 1507, 1515 (1983) the ITA held that funding of certain environmental projects was generally available and thus the grants which Belgium steel companies received under these projects could not be regarded as countervailable subsidies; see also *Anhydrous and Aqua Ammonia From Mexico*, 48 Fed. Reg. 28522 (1983); 5 ITRD 1253 (1984) in which the ITA found that Mexican pricing policy for natural gas did not constitute a bounty or grant as long as the gas price within Mexico was the same for industrial users. For a detailed discussion of the specificity test see Horlick, Bello, Levine, 'The Countervailability of Subsidies: Specificity', in *US Import Relief Laws*, 35 (1985).
164. For a detailed analysis of and the differences between domestic subsidies see Barcelo, *supra* n. 37, pp. 836 *et seq*.
165. See *Carlisle Tire and Rubber Company* v. *United States*, 564 F. Supp. 834 (Ct. Int'l. Trade 1983). But see *Bethlehem Steel Corp.* v. *United States*, 5 ITRD 2337, slip op. 84-67 (1984), *Cabot Corp.* v. *United States*, slip. op 85-102 (1985).
166. Barcelo, *supra* n. 37, at 836.

It could be argued that such a test has crystallized through the practice of the signatories. Although general domestic subsidies might benefit companies by indirectly lowering their cost of production, the signatories have never taken countervailing duty actions against these subsidies;[167] such practice might indicate that the signatories do not consider non-specific domestic subsidies countervailable. This argument, however, does not take into account possible further developments in the application of the countervailing duty laws. Since Track I of the Subsidies Code, which is an interpretation of Article VI, does not give any definition of subsidies, the definition of a countervailable subsidy is left to the discretion of the signatories. Therefore, it could be argued that signatories are not bound to apply a specificity test, but are free to extend the meaning of countervailable subsidy to cover all kinds of general domestic subsidies without violating the Code.[168] However, that would present insurmountable practical problems and open the country itself to major retaliation.[169]

c. *The meaning of 'if provided or required by government action'*

Like § 303 of the Tariff Act of 1930, § 701(a)(1)(b) of the TAA authorizes the imposition of countervailing duties against private subsidies.[170] This conclusion is buttressed by the incorporation of § 303 in § 771(5) of the TAA.

In theory, the possibility to countervail private subsidies could have far-reaching implications. In practice, however, the American authorities have made a prudent use of this authorization and have only incidentally countervailed private subsidies. More specifically, all cases, in which countervailing duties were imposed on private subsidies concerned export subsidies given by a cartel of protected input producers to exporters of the finished product. In a 1926 case, countervailing duties were imposed on German steel products because the German steel cartel had entered into an agreement with the steel consuming industries under which the latter received certificates upon export

167. See Horlick *supra* n. 163. See also the Canadian case, *Beef from the European Communities*, (1986); Community law does not explicitly mention a specificity test. Article 3, 1 of Reg. 2176/84 (OJ L 201/1 (1984)) provides in general terms that a countervailing duty may be imposed for the purpose of offsetting any subsidy bestowed, directly or indirectly, in the country of origin or export, upon the manufacture, production, export or transport of any product whose release for free circulation in the Community causes injury. In practice, however, the Community has, until now, almost exclusively countervailed programs, which were specificially aimed at promoting exports. The only case in which a domestic subsidy program was countervailed was *Sheets and Plates of Iron or Steel from Brazil* (OJ L 45/11 (1983)) where the CDI investment program, under which duty-free treatment and exemptions from IPI taxes were granted to imported machinery, was considered to center a countervailable subsidy. See Van Bael, Bellis, *International Trade Law and Practice of the European Community*, at 145, 149 (1985). The same program was countervailed by the ITA. See *e.g. Iron One Pellets from Brazil*, 50 Fed. Reg. 2322 (1905) (fin. aff.).

168. The ITA addressed the differences between Track I and Track II and their relations to national countervailing duty laws in *Certain Steel Products From Belgium*, 4 ITRD, pp. 1546 *et seq.* (1983), particularly comment 9.

169. See Horlick *supra* n. 163. It raises the interesting possibility of a country countervailing a general US subsidy, such as investment tax credits and claiming Code consistency.

170. See Senate report No. 249, *supra* n. 32, at 85.

of the steel-input goods which could be used as credit on future orders of steel from members of the cartel (in an amount equal to the difference between the cartelized German price of the steel input and the world price).[171] In a more recent case,[172] the Commerce Department in somewhat ambiguous form countervailed rebates, given by the South African Iron and Steel Industrial Corporation (to which primary steel producers contributed funds) to secondary steel producers upon exportation of certain products containing rolled, drawn, or target steel.

The ITA has consistently declined to countervail intra-corporate transfers.

In between assistance provided by the government and subsidies by private companies one could locate subsidies, provided by private companies at the order of the government. It is this government-mandated type of assistance that the phrase 'required by government action' intends to cover. A good example of this practice can be found in the 1982 *Certain Steel Products from Spain Case*,[173] in which the ITA found that the Spanish government had directed banks to lend certain funds to exporting companies in Spain at preferential rates and found this to confer a countervailable subsidy.

d. 'Whether publicly or privately owned' – Non-Market Economies

This phrase indicates that the countervailing duty law covers domestic subsidies regardless of who receives them. It also reflects the intent of Congress to make the countervailing duty law fully applicable to government owned industries.[174]

Government-owned industries should not be confused with industries in non-market economies. The TAA does not contain any reference to subsidies in non-market economies. The Subsidies Code, on the other hand, provides for countervailing duty investigations against imports from non-market economies[175] and prescribes a test on how to measure such subsidies; the test is similar to the one laid down in the Anti-Dumping Code although there is a separate injury test.[176] Therefore, countervailing duty investigations against subsidized imports from state controlled economies are possible under the international rules, albeit using anti-dumping measurements.

The issue whether the US countervailing duty laws are applicable to subsidized imports from non-market economies, is unresolved at this time. In several decisions in 1984 the ITA ruled that 'bounties or grants' cannot be

171. See Horlick, *supra* n. 34, at 16.
172. *Steel Wire Rope from South Africa*, 47 Fed. Reg. 40203 (1982) (prel. aff.).
173. *Certain Steel Products from Spain*, 47 Fed. Reg. 51438 (1982) (fin. aff.).
174. Verrill, *supra* n. 157, at 23. In *Certain Steel Products From Belgium*, for example, the ITA found several practices of the Government of Belgium from which privately and publicly owned steel firms benefitted countervailable subsidies; 4 ITRD 1507 (1983).
175. Art. 15 para. 1 which refers to the Notes and Supplementary Provisions of GATT, Annex I, Ad Art. VI para. 1 point 2.
176. Agreement on the Implementation of Article VI of the General Agreement on Tariffs and Trade, Art. 2 paras. 4 and 5; GATT, BISD, 26th Supp. 171 (1980). Art. 15, para. 1 of the Subsidies Code contains a specific requirement of injury, in addition to the general GATT requirement of injury for antidumping or countervailing duties.

found in non-market economies, since in a 'non-market economy system the government does not interfere in the market process but supplants it'.[177] The US Court of International Trade overturned these decisions[178] and that decision is presently on appeal before the Court of Appeals for the Federal Circuit.

e. *'Whether paid or bestowed directly or indirectly'*

This phrase allows countervailing duties against practices which indirectly benefit the imported goods, and thus might be used against all kinds of selective domestic subsidies which do have such an effect; however, not every selective domestic subsidy which gives an indirect benefit is countervailable. As an example, Mundheim and Enhrenhaft[179] in a paper soon after the 1979 Act (and before many cases) mentioned 'benefits to the mining industry' which 'would arguably be too remote from fabricated products such as refrigerators made of steel produced from the assisted iron ore'. The 1984 amendment of the US countervailing duty law to include 'upstream subsidies' marks the present dividing line between countervailable and non-countervailable indirect benefits. (See G.2.)

f. *Section 771(5)(B) and Export Subsidies*

The phrase of § 771(5)(B) 'whether paid or bestowed . . . on the manufacture, production, or export of any class or kind of merchandise' appeared in a similar wording in the old countervailing duty law. Section 303 of the Tariff Act of 1930 read:

> 'Whenever any country . . . shall pay . . . any bounty or grant upon the manufacture, or production, or export of any article. . . .'[180]

177. See *Carbon Steel Wire Rod From Czechoslovakia*, 49 Fed. Reg. 19370 (1984); *Carbon Steel Wire Rod From Poland*, 49 Fed. Reg. 19374 (1984). The main arguments of the ITA were the following:

> 'In a market economy, scarce resources are channeled to their most profitable and efficient uses by the market forces of supply and demand. We believe a subsidy (or bounty or grant) is definitionally any action that distorts or subverts the market process and results in a misallocation of resources encouraging inefficient production and lessening world wealth.
>
> In NME's, resources are not allocated by a market. With varying degrees of control, allocation is achieved by central planning. Without a market, it is obviously meaningless to look for a misallocation of resources caused by subsidies. There is no market process to distort or subvert. Resources may appear to be misallocated in an NME when compared to the standard of a market economy, but the resource misallocation results from central planning, not subsidies.
>
> It is this fundamental distinction – that in an NME system the government does not interfere in the market process, but supplants it – that has led us to conclude that subsidies have no meaning outside the context of a market economy . . .'

49 Fed. Reg. 19370, 19371 (1984).

178. *Continental Steel Corp.* v. *United States*, Slip. Op. 85-87, 7 ITRD 1001 (CIT 1985).
179. Mundheim, Ehrenhaft, 'What is a "Subsidy"?', in *Interface III*, 95, at 96 (1984).
180. 19 USC § 1303(a)(1) (1976).

Whereas this paragraph covered both domestic and export subsidies, in the TAA export subsidies are accorded special treatment. Section 771(5)(A) comprehends in the definition of 'subsidy' the illustrative list of export subsidies in Annex A of the Subsidies Code. Thus, the TAA covers not only the export subsidies of the illustrative list but also the domestic subsidies which are directly or indirectly paid on the export. This combination of old and new law raises the question of the differences between § 771(5)(A) and § 771(5)(B). The requirements of (B) do not have to be met whenever a practice is considered to constitute an export subsidy, but must be fulfilled when the ITA finds domestic subsidies directly or indirectly paid on the exports.[181]

The question remains what the ITA will do if it finds a practice an export subsidy which is not covered in Annex A of the Subsidies Code. One could argue that, since the practice is not covered by the illustrative list, the ITA can only define it a countervailable subsidy under the provision of § 771(5)(B). The ITA, therefore, would have to meet the standards of § 771(5)(B). This argument, however, is not compatible with the wording of § 771(5)(B) which defines a subsidy as a bounty or grant as used under § 303 of the Tariff Act of 1930 and which includes the examples given in (A) and (B), but does not limit the definition to those examples. Since § 771(5) does not limit the definition of countervailable subsidies to the examples given in (A) and (B), the ITA is not required to apply the limitations of (B) to practices which it deems to be export subsidies, even if these export subsidies are not covered by the illustrative list of the Subsidies Code. Obviously, the question whether this interpretation of § 771(5) is compatible with the Subsidies Code remains open. The ITA has answered this question in its preliminary affirmative determination in *Rail Passenger Cars From Canada* in which it decided that export credit financing at preferential rates constituted a countervailable subsidy, regardless of whether it was prohibited by item (k) of the illustrative list or not:

> 'The MTA contends that only the difference between the EDC [Canadian government agency] rate and the rate specified in the [OECD] Arrangement constitutes a countervailable benefit because item (k) provides that government-funded export credit practices which conform to such international undertakings as the OECD Arrangement are not 'considered an export subsidy prohibited by this Agreement' [the Subsidies Code]. Thus, the MTA reasons that only benefits conferred at interest rates below the OECD Arrangement rate are countervailable. We reject this contention because it fails to distinguish between those unfair trade practices which are 'prohibited by the Agreement' and those practices which are countervailable under the United States countervailing duty law. If a country engages in 'prohibited' conduct, the affected country may pursue its dispute settlement rights under Part II of the Subsidies Code in addition to acting under its countervailing duty laws. By contrast,

181. See *Certain Steel Products From Belgium*, 4 ITRD 1507, 1546 (1983) in which the ITA clarifies this difference: 'This standard for domestic subsidies (the specificity test) is clearly distinguishable from that for export subsidies which are countervailable regardless of their availability in the country of exportation'.

if a country implements a nonprohibited subsidy practice, the Department may nevertheless be required to take the latter course. Therefore, we have concluded that our benchmark for export credits is not limited by the rate set in the Arrangement'.[182]

Here again the difference between Track I and Track II is crucial for the decision whether the practice of the ITA is compatible with the Code. The illustrative list of the Subsidies Code is part of Track II and not part of Track I, which does not contain any definition of the term subsidy. Thus a signatory is bound by the definitions of the list, not in the application of its countervailing duty law, but rather in Track II procedures against subsidies.

The criticism expressed in the literature[183] of this practice of the ITA is unjustified because it does not take into account the differences between Article VI and Article XVI.[184] One might argue that the lack of definition of subsidy in Track I is a major deficiency of the Code; however, one cannot turn this argument around and contend that the practice of the United States 'is flatly contrary to the language of the Code itself'.[185] There is no provision in Track I which obliges the US to apply the definitions of the illustrative list to its countervailing duty law, and the language of Track II has to be distinguished from national proceedings as the history of the Subsidies Code clearly shows.[185a] Indeed, the export credit subsidies referred to in item (k) are a good example of a classic subsidy (loans below rates available to the borrower absent government action) which should be countervailed even if there is no international agreement to prohibit them.

g. Section 771(5)(B)(i) to (iv)

In analyzing whether a certain practice is a countervailable domestic subsidy the ITA can resort to § 771(5)(B)(i) to (iv) which provides a list of certain practices covered by the definition of subsidies.

The first group of domestic subsidies is 'the provision of capital, loans or loan guarantees on terms inconsistent with commercial considerations'. In the 1982 *EEC Steel Cases*[186] the ITA found that certain EEC governments provided specific steel industries with capital grants,[187] loans[188] or loan

182. *Rail Passenger Cars From Canada*, 47 Fed. Reg. 53760 (1982), 4 ITRD 1340, 1343 (1984); in its final determination the ITA affirmed this argument, 48 Fed. Reg. 6569 (1983), 5 ITRD 1167, 1172 (1984).
183. Simon, *supra* n. 87, at 198
184. See *supra* Section B, 1 and 2.
185. Simon, *supra* n. 87, at 198.
185a. For an opposing view see Benyon/Bourgeois, *supra* n. 104a, at 327.
186. 47 FR 263, 9087, 39304, 49058 (1982). See also Barshefsky, Mattice, Martin, 'Government Equity Participation in State Owned Enterprises: An Analysis of the Carbon Steel Countervailing Duty Cases', 14 L & Pol'y Int'l Bus. 1101, pp. 1105 *et seq.* (1983).
187. See for example *Certain Steel Products From Belgium*, 4 ITRD 1507, 1511 (1983).
188. See for example *Certain Steel Products From France*, 47 Fed. Reg. 39332 (1982); 4 ITRD 1605, 1609 (1983); *Certain Steel Products from Italy*, 47 Fed. Reg. 39356 (1982); 4 ITRD 1677, 1679 (1983).

guarantees.[189] In these cases the ITA, for the first time, addressed the problem of government equity participation and concluded that such participation, whether in the form of true equity or stock ownership in a corporation, or in the form of outright grants to such firms, constituted a countervailable subsidy if the funds were provided on terms inconsistent with commercial considerations.[190]

The wording of subsection (i) makes it clear that those practices can only be regarded countervailable subsidies if they are provided on terms inconsistent with commercial considerations. The Act, however, does not define commercial considerations. Rather, it is the task of the ITA to decide on a case by case basis if a practice is inconsistent with commercial considerations. As one author has remarked,[191] this expression could be interpreted to mean 'terms more advantageous than those in the country of export that apply to non government capital contributions, loans or guarantees, to the same enterprise'. There is no doubt that this interpretation is the starting point of the inquiries of the ITA in which it not only considers the firm's profit and loss record but also assesses these elements from the perspective of a private investor.[192] This shows that one cannot formulate a generally applicable test of what commercial considerations are, since this depends much on the facts of the particular case. The fact that commercial considerations have to be assessed in a case by case analysis[193] becomes apparent in a fairly recent opinion of the Court of International Trade in which it stated:

> 'The Court therefore considered the evidence regarding equivalent financing from independent sources. It first had to pass on Amicus' assertion that the search for comparable financing had to be limited to Canada. Amicus argued that allowing reference to rates outside the country in which the dutiable goods were produced might allow cost of money to the lender. This possibility does exist, but it does not violate the Court's understanding of the countervailing duty statute. The law is not concerned with the sacrifice made by the party supplying a financial resource but rather with the benefit experienced by the recipient. The making of a loan at a rate of interest below the cost of money to the lender would not assure the existence of a bounty any more than the making of the loan above the cost of money to the lender would assure the absence of a bounty. For a company lacking creditworthiness in its national setting even a loan yielding profit to the lender could be a bounty. On the other hand, a company with the ability to obtain financing from international sources would not necessarily receive a bounty from

189. See for example *Certain Steel Products From Belgium*, 4 ITRD 1507, 1511 (1983).

190. *Certain Steel Products From Belgium*, 4 ITRD 1507, 1513 (1983); *Certain Steel Products From Italy*, 4 ITRD 1677, 1679 (1983); the principles applied by the ITA with regard to government equity participation are set forth in Appendix 2 to the Belgian determination, 4 ITRD 1507, pp. 1528 *et seq.* (1983); for an analysis of the principles see Barshefsky *et al.*, *supra* n. 186, pp. 1129 *et seq.*

191. Bryan, *supra* n. 132, at 297.

192. Barshefsky *et al.*, *supra* n. 186, 1130-1131.

193. Barshefsky *et al.*, point out the dangers inherent in such an approach; Barshefsky *et al.*, *supra* n. 186, 1131.

a loan which appeared preferential within a particular national financial market'.[194]

The second group of domestic subsidies is 'the provision of goods or services at preferential rates'. In *Certain Softwood Products from Canada*[195] the ITA found that Canadian Stumpage Programs[196] constituted a 'provision of goods' (albeit neither specific nor preferential) according to subsection (ii). In *Certain Steel From Italy*[197] the ITA, on the basis of the best information available, found volume rebates by the state-owned Italian railroad to Italian steel companies to be a 'provision of services' according to subsection (ii). Here again the provision of goods or services does not constitute a countervailable subsidy *per se*; in order to be covered by § 771(5) the goods or services must be provided at preferential rates. Basically, the ITA interprets preferential as 'more favourable to some within the relevant jurisdiction than to others';[198] however, it concedes that there might be cases of hidden preferentiality in which this definition might have to be expanded.[199]

It has to be emphasized that the concept of preferentiality in subsection (ii) requires a different test than the inquiry whether a practice is inconsistent with commercial considerations in subsection (i), although both tests rely on a comparison of the practice with other practices available in the same country.[200]

The third group of domestic subsidies is 'the grant of funds or forgiveness of debt to cover operating losses sustained by a specific firm'. These examples speak for themselves and need not be explained.[201]

The fourth group of subsidies is 'the assumption of any cost or expenses of manufacture, production or distribution'. In *Certain Steel Products From France*[202] the ITA gave as an example a subsidy to relieve debt expenses. The similarity of this example with the examples given in subsection (iii) raises two questions: the scope of subsection (iv) and the relationship among the subsections. In *Certain Softwood Products From Canada*[203] the ITA gave subsection (iv) a limited meaning: it stated that the most reasonable interpretation of 'assumption' is that 'it refers only to government activity which relieves an enterprise or industry of a pre-existing statutory or contractual obligation'.[204] The reason for this stringent interpretation is the relationship among the subsections. The ITA considers the subsections to be 'mutually

194. *Michelin Tire Corp.* v. *United States*, 3 ITRD 1177, 1183 (1983) (US CIT Slip. Op. 81-94, 1981).
195. *Certain Softwood Products From Canada*, 48 Fed. Reg. 24159 (1983); 5 ITRD 1471, 1486 (1984).
196. 'Stumpage Programs' are systems by which individuals and companies acquire rights to cut and remove standing timber from government forest lands; see 5 ITRD 1485.
197. 4 ITRD 1677, 1682 (1983).
198. *Carbon Black From Mexico*, 48 Fed. Reg. 29564 (1983); 5 ITRD 1514, 1522 (1984).
199. *Certain Softwood Products From Canada*, 5 ITRD, 1486 (1984).
200. Ibid.
201. *Certain Steel Products From Belgium*, 4 ITRD 1507, 1533 (1983).
202. *Certain Steel Products From France*, 4 ITRD 1605, 1627 (1983).
203. *Certain Softwood Products From Canada*, 5 ITRD 1471, 1486 (1984).
204. Ibid.

exclusive'.[205] This means that if one subsection covers a practice the ITA will not look further and inquire whether the same practice could also be covered by another subsection. However, since subsection (iv) could be interpreted as to cover all the other three subsections,[206] the concept of mutual exclusivity would be rendered void and the reference to other domestic subsidies than assumption of cost useless. Therefore, the ITA drew the conclusion[207] that:

> ''assumption', as used in subsection (iv) means something other than the universe of governmental activities which could have the effect of reducing or absorbing a cost of production. Rather it refers to a specific type of activity, . . . [*i.e.*], the relief from pre-existing or contractual obligations.'

A final word on the definition of domestic subsidies. § 771(5) does not limit the definition of countervailable subsidies to the examples given there; they are considered illustrative, not exhaustive.[208] Thus, the ITA is free to define other practices as countervailable subsidies. Indeed, the ITA seldom refers to one of the subsections of § 771(5)(B).

3. Valuation and Net Calculation of Domestic Subsidies

After the ITA has found a certain practice a countervailable domestic subsidy it has to value it and calculate its net amount for duty assessment. Valuation, as used here, means the process of translating a practice into a measurable subsidy. Taking for example a $100 million grant, inconsistent with commercial considerations, one would have to transform this subsidy into an *ad valorem* percentage of the benefit received through it on every produced and exported item. After valuation the process of net calculation translates the subsidy into a net amount which is the basis for duty assessment. This net calculation is used to offset certain payments and to crystallize the real benefit.

a. Valuation

The TAA contains no guidelines on the valuation of a subsidy. The general rule of § 701 only mentions that a countervailing duty must equal the amount of the net subsidy. The reliance of the Act on the notion of net subsidy is a reflection of Article 4 paragraph 2 which provides that

> 'no countervailing duty shall be levied on any imported product in excess

205. Ibid.
206. The practices 'described in subsections (i) to (iii) could be regarded as activities which all reduce or absorb – and thereby arguably assume – cost of production'. *Certain Softwood Products From Canada*, 5 ITRD 1471, 1486 (1984).
207. Ibid.
208. *Certain Softwood Products From Canada*, 5 ITRD 1471, 1486 (1984).

of the amount of the subsidy found to exist, calculated in terms of subsidization per unit of the subsidized and exported product.'

The Subsidies Code prohibits the imposition of a countervailing duty in excess of the amount of the subsidy but it does not provide the signatories with a test on how to value subsidies; a footnote merely remarks that

> 'an understanding among signatories should be developed setting out the criteria for the calculation of the amount of the subsidy.'[209]

The Subsidies Code Committee through a group of experts[210] has sought to develop such criteria which until now, though, has not resulted in adoption by the Committee.[211] Thus, until the Subsidies Code Committee adopts criteria on the calculation of the amount of the subsidy, the signatories are free to develop their own methodology on how to translate a subsidy in terms of percentage per unit of exports. The ITA has done so in the above mentioned 1982 *Steel* cases, as modified by the 1984 *Mexican and Argentinian Steel* cases. In Appendix 2 to the final determination in *Certain Steel Products From Belgium*[212] it enunciated its methodology for dealing with government assistance to firms in the form of grants, loans, equity infusion, loss coverage, research and development projects and labour programs.[213] This methodology was then clarified and partly revised in Appendix 2 of the preliminary determination *Certain Carbon Steel Products from Mexico*[214] and in the Subsidies Appendix to the final determination *Cold-Rolled Carbon Steel Flat-Rolled Products from Argentina*.[215]

It goes beyond the scope of this paper to deal with the questions, more economic than legal, of how to translate a subsidy into an *ad valorem* percentage per unit of exports; however, since the TAA obliges the ITA to calculate the net subsidy, we will discuss the basic principles of the concept.

The legislative history of the TAA provides little guidance. The Senate Report[216] states that the valuation of a subsidy must be based on the 'commercial and competitive benefit' to the recipients. The House Report[217] likewise focuses on the benefits to the recipient and furthermore addresses the valuation of certain domestic subsidies. With regard to subsidies which provide an enterprise with capital equipment or a plant it states:

209. Art. 4 para. 2 n. 15.
210. GATT Doc. L/4983 para. 7 (1980).
211. See GATT, BISD, 30th Supp. 46 (1984).
212. 47 Fed. Reg. 39304, 39316 (1982).
213. For a critical analysis of the methodology of equity infusions see Barshefsky *et al.*, *supra* n. 186, pp. 1141 *et seq.*
214. 49 Fed. Reg. 5142, 5149 (1984).
215. 49 Fed. Reg. 18006, 18018 (1984). For an excellent overview of the ITA's methodology in identifying, valuating and calculating subsidies, see Holmer, Haggerty, Hunter, 'Identifying and Measuring Subsidies Under the Countervailing Duty Law, An Attempt at Synthesis', in *The Commerce Department Speaks on Import Administration and Export Administration*, 301 (1984).
216. See Senate Report No. 249, *supra* n. 32, at 86.
217. See House Report No. 96-317, *supra* n. 120, at 74, 75.

> 'in such cases, the net amount of the subsidy should be amortized over a reasonable period, following the beginning of full scale commercial operation of the equipment or plant and assessed in relation to the products produced with such equipments or plants during such period.'

With regard to grants or loans the House report states:

> 'in calculating the *ad valorem* effect of non recurring subsidy grants or loans reasonable methods of allocating the value of such subsidies over the production or exportation of products benefitting from them will be used. Such method should include relating the benefits of the commercial advantage to the recipient, or relating the value of a subsidy for acquiring assets to their anticipated useful life, based on generally accepted accounting principles.'

The legislative history indicates that Congress intended to have the ITA examine the benefit received by the recipient rather than just look at the nominal value of the subsidy when making its valuation. To follow the guidelines of the reports the ITA allocates the benefit to the production or exportation of the products benefitting from the subsidy over time when calculating the *ad valorem* effect of one-time grants or loans. The most elaborate valuation concepts are contained in the above mentioned methodology.[218]

Since the final determinations of the ITA are subject to judicial review Courts can rule on the valuation of a subsidy and decide whether the *ad valorem* percentage per unit of export has been calculated in accordance with the law. Thus, the methodology becomes subject to judicial review. The scrutiny with which the Courts examine the ITA's methodology of translating a subsidy into a countervailable net subsidy is well shown in the recent decisions of the Court of International Trade in the *Michelin Tire Cases*.[219] All three decisions concerned the correct valuation of certain cash grants received by Michelin Canada. Relying on the concept of 'benefit' as the basic rule for the valuation of subsidies the Court held that the valuation of the ITA was not in accordance with the law and remanded the case three times.

One aspect of the last decision[220] deserves mentioning. Prior to the *Steel Cases* the ITA always allocated the face value of a grant in equal increments over the appropriate time period.[221] After the ITA recognized that this technique ignored the fact that 'money has a changing value as it moves through time'[222] it changed its methodology with regard to the allocation of benefits over time. The Court in upholding this technique stated:

218. See *supra* nn. 214, 215.
219. *Michaelin Tire Corp.* v. *United States:* 3 ITRD 1177, (US CIT, Slip. Op. 81-94. 1981); 4 ITRD 1450, (US CIT, Slip. Op. 82-115, 1982); 5 ITRD 1545, (US CIT, Slip. Op. 83-136, 1983).
220. 5 ITRD 1545 (1984).
221. See *Certain Steel Products From Belgium*, 4 ITRD 1507, 1528 (1983).
222. 'It has been argued that $100 million today is much more valuable to a grant recipient than $10 million per year for the next ten years since the present value of the series of payments is considerably less the amount if initially given as a lump sum' ibid.

> 'The Court does not read the language of the law or the international agreement as requiring that the valuation of subsidies be limited to their face value. On the contrary, the law and the international agreement obviously foresee a process of measurement.
>
> No authority has been cited for the proposition that a grant whose benefit is to be experienced over a term of years is permanently fixed in the exact form and amount in which it is initially bestowed. The reality of financial experience is that money is affected by time and those methods which reasonably adjust to this commercial reality do nothing more than preserve and express the full meaning of the original financial transaction. For this reason the Court finds that a method of providing for the time value of money is in harmony with the law and with the relevant international agreements.'

In the 1982 *Steel Cases*[223] the concept of 'benefit to the recipient' was criticized by the EEC as not being in conformity with GATT. The EEC contended that Article VI paragraph 3 provided that a countervailing duty may not exceed the amount of subsidy 'determined to have been granted'. According to the EEC, the word 'granted' meant that the countervailable amount was the financial contribution of the government rather than the benefit of the recipient. It furthermore contended that, had GATT relied on the benefit it would have used the word 'received' instead of 'granted'.[224]

In rejecting this argument the ITA held that the word 'granted' in Article VI paragraph 3 did not control the question of calculation of the amount of a subsidy but merely referred to the existence of a subsidy. To defend its position it relied on Article 4 paragraph 2, and particularly on footnote 15. Until the signatories reached consensus on the valuation of a subsidy the United States was free to use the concept of benefit received by the producer or exporter, as long as the valuation did not result in an excessive countervailing duty.[225] In underlining this position the ITA stated:

> 'However, the Code does not require inaction by signatories with regard to areas not clearly covered by the Code or by agreed interpretations of the Code. Such a requirement would be inconsistent with practice under the GATT as it has developed since its inception in 1947. The fact that the Code is silent with respect to whether a specific practice constitutes a subsidy does not mean that no signatory may make a determination with respect to that practice in the course of a proceeding. The fact that the signatories have not agreed on a methodology for the calculation of the amount of a subsidy does not mean that no signatory may adopt a methodology in the absence of such agreements, since the inability to calculate the amount of the subsidy found to exist would clearly frustrate the intent of the Code and the GATT.'[226]

223. See *supra* n. 186.
224. *Certain Steel Products From Belgium*, 4 ITRD 1507, 1528 (1983).
225. Ibid.
226. Ibid.

The absence of any language on valuation in the Code and the explicit reference of footnote 15 would seem to justify the position of the United States.

Another problem with the valuation of a subsidy occurs when the subsidy is indirectly bestowed on the exported product.[227] Here the ITA has the difficult task of translating this benefit into an *ad valorem* percentage for duty assessment. Since indirect benefits are sometimes quite remote from the production of the product in question it is very often impossible to measure them. Let us take the example of a research and development grant provided to the producer of military aircrafts, the results of which are then used in the construction of a superior commercial aircraft by the same firm.[228] Or let us consider a government procurement activity that gives the supporting firm a substantial commercial boost and enables it to drive competitors off the market.[229] All these are benefits indirectly bestowed which may theoretically be countervailable but may be too difficult to measure.

b. Net Calculation

The second step of the valuation of a subsidy for duty assessment is the calculation of the net subsidy which is achieved by deducting from the gross subsidy[230] those factors which reduce the real value of the subsidy.

Section 771(6)[231] furnishes guidelines on which factors the ITA is allowed to deduct. Under prior law the determination of the net subsidy was a matter of administrative practice in which the Department of the Treasury 'attempted to maintain flexibility and discretion, and to emphasize trade distortion effects rather than the mere conferral of a government benefit'.[232] Therefore, in its net subsidy calculation, it subtracted for example certain dislocation costs.[233] The TAA severely limits the discretion of the ITA as far as offsets are concerned. Section 771(6) contains a restrictive list of offsets and obliges the ITA to subtract only the specified factors. The relevant passage in the Senate Report states:

> 'The bill defines "net subsidy" to place clear limits on offsets from a gross subsidy. The gross subsidy is the value of the subsidy provided, or made available, and used. . . . For the purpose of determining the net subsidy there is subtracted from the gross subsidy only the items specified in § 771(6). This list is narrowly drawn and is all inclusive. For example,

227. See also Section C.
228. See *Certain Steel Products From Belgium*, 4 ITRD 1507, 1533 (1983).
229. For a discussion of these problems and for further examples see Mundheim, Ehrenhaft, *supra* n. 179, pp. 3 *et seq.*
230. A 'gross subsidy' can be defined as the value of the subsidy provided, or made available and used, regardless of the factors which reduce its value; see Senate Report No. 249, *supra* n. 32, at 85; MacDonnell, *supra* n. 148, at 431.
231. See n. 142 *supra*
232. Barcelo, *supra* n. 85, at 273.
233. 'Dislocation costs' are expenses solely incurred by a producer when relocating to an economically disadvantaged region; MacDonnell, *supra* n. 148, at 440.

offsets under present law which are permitted for indirect taxes paid but not actually rebated, or for increased costs as a result of locating in an underdeveloped area, are not now permitted as offsets.'[234]

Furthermore, § 771(6) is not mandatory but merely states that the ITA '*may*' subtract the factors listed in its calculation of the net subsidy. In order to have an item subtracted from the gross amount of a subsidy the burden of proof is on the respondent. Here again the Senate Report is very definite:

> 'in determining the amount of offsets which are permitted it is expected that the administering authority will offset amounts which are definitely established by reliable, verified evidence.'[235]

After the enactment of the TAA the ITA has not offset dislocation costs or unrebated taxes any longer but rather found the full amount of the grant or loan countervailable,[236] even if it exceeds the true economic value of the subsidy to the recipient.

Section 771(6) contains the following three groups of items which may be subtracted from the gross amount of the subsidy:

(1) application fees or deposits, or similar payments made to qualify for or to receive the benefit of the subsidy;[237]

(2) any loss in value of the subsidy due to its deferred receipt if the deferral is mandated by government order. This item was included since a government-required delay in payment of a subsidy may reduce its value, due to inflation or currency fluctuations, between the date of accrual of the benefit and the date of payment. Normal administrative delays, however, are not offset since they are not regarded as required by law;[238]

(3) 'export taxes, duties or other charges levied on the export of merchandise to the United States specifically intended to offset the subsidy received'.[239]

The narrow offset policy prescribed by the Act has been criticized as not being in comport with the theory of comparative advantage as far as dislocation costs are concerned.[240] Here again the possible broad interpretation of the term subsidy under Track I of the Subsidies Code allows both the argument

234. Senate Report No. 249, *supra* n. 32, at 85, 86.
235. Ibid., at 86.
236. See for example *Rail Passenger Cars From Canada*, 48 Fed. Reg. 6569 (1983); 5 ITRD 1167 (1984); and *Certain Softwood Products From Canada*, 48 Fed. Reg. 24159 (1983); 5 ITRD 1471 (1984).
237. For an example of an offset of this group see *Portland Hydraulic Cement and Cement Clinker From Mexico*, 48 Fed. Reg. 43063 (1983); 5 ITRD 1912, 1916 (1984) in which the ITA allowed to offset four percent supervision fee paid by recipients of tax rebates certificates.
238. See for example *Cotton Sheeting and Sateen From Peru*, 48 Fed. Reg. 4588 (1983); 5 ITRD 1029, 1039 (1984).
239. See *Certain Textiles and Textile Mill Products From Malaysia*, 44 Fed. Reg. 41001 (1979); 2 ITRD 5331, 5332 (1982).
240. MacDonnell, *supra* n. 148, pp. 442 *et seq.*

that the full amount of regional dislocation subsidies may be covered by national countervailing duty laws, and the rebuttal that only the actual subsidy component can be countervailable. So far, given the fact that the Code lacks any provision on the valuation and net calculation of a subsidy it is difficult to oblige the signatories to offset regional dislocation costs in their net calculations no matter how strong the economic arguments for those offsets might be.

C. THE TRADE AND TARIFF ACT OF 1984 (TTA)[241]

1. Background

Given the strength of the dollar in 1982 and 1983, the increasing US trade deficit and rising imports, together with the concerns these trends created in the US industry, the Subcommittee on Trade of the House Committee on Ways and Means in 1983 discussed whether the trade laws worked effectively against unfair trade practices. After extensive hearings[242] the Subcommittee made several proposals to amend the trade laws.[243]

Before these proposals had been drafted into a Bill a group of import competing industries, known as the Trade Reform Action Coalition, came up with a protectionist version of trade law reform which was then introduced in the House in October 1983.[244] Faced with this competition from the protectionist side, the Subcommittee, in February 1984, introduced the Trade Remedies Reform Act (H.R. 4784).[245] The enactment of the Bill would have changed § 771(5) significantly. Section 104 of the Bill added three types of subsidies to the existing examples of § 771(5)(A) and (B):

(1) export targeting subsidies,
(2) natural resource subsidies and
(3) upstream subsidies.

The proposals of the Bill reflected a growing dissatisfaction with certain negative countervailing duty investigations of the ITA[246] which led to considerable protest by certain domestic industries.[247]

241. *Trade and Tariff Act of 1984*, Pub. L. No. 92-573, 98 (Stat. 2948), 1904.
242. *Options to Improve the Trade Remedy Laws, Hearings Before the Subcommittee on Trade of the Committee on Ways and Means of the House of Representatives*, 98th Cong., 1st Sess., S 98-14, 98-15 (1983) (hereinafter cited as *Hearings*).
243. See 8 ITIM 1009 (1983).
244. HR 4124, *Trade Law Reform Bill*, 98th Cong., 1st Sess.; see 9 ITIM 92, 648 (1983/84).
245. HR 4784, *To Reform the Remedies Available to United States Producers Regarding Unfair Import Competition, and for other purposes*, 98th Cong. 2nd Sess., commonly referred to as the *Gibbons-Bill* or *The Trade Remedies Reform Act*.
246. The most criticized decisions were:
(1) *Certain Steel Products From West Germany*, 48 Fed. Reg. 39345 (1983), 4 ITRD 1659 (1983).
(2) *Anhydrous And Aqua Ammonia From Mexico*, 48 Fed. Reg. 28522 (1983), 5 ITRD 1253 (1984).
(3) *Certain Softwood Products From Canada*, 48 Fed. Reg. 24159 (1983), 5 ITRD 1471 (1984).
247. The dissatisfaction was expressed in the *Hearings*, *supra* n. 242; see for example Statement of Donald V. Borst, ibid., pp. 296 *et seq.*; statement of Terrence P. Stewart, ibid. 610, pp. 713 *et seq.*; statement of Richard O. Cunningham, ibid. 880, 884.

The bill was passed by the House in July 1984, but never made it into law because of heavy opposition of both the Reagan Administration and the Republican leadership in the Senate. Instead, the Senate basically used a much less controversial trade bill, which had been adopted by the House practically simultaneously,[248] as a vehicle for implementing its ideas about trade reform. The Bill was passed by the Senate and the House on September 20 and October 3, 1984, respectively.[249] After joint House and Senate mark-up sessions, Congress passed the bill on October 9th. President Reagan signed the bill into law on October 30th, 1984.

While the provisions on natural resource subsidies and targeting were deleted, a revised version of the original Ways and Means bill proposal on upstream subsidies had remained. However, the revised version

> 'clearly and unambiguously manifests our intent generally to codify current Commerce Department practice in the area,'[250]

as Senator Dole put it.

2. Upstream Subsidies

The TTA added a new Section 771A to the Tariff Act which contains the provisions on upstream subsidies. The Bill defines upstream subsidy as

> 'any subsidy described in section 771(5)(B)(i), (ii), or (iii) by the government of a country that
> (1) is paid or bestowed by that government with respect to a product (hereafter referred to as an 'input product') that is used in the manufacture or production in that country of merchandise which is the subject of a countervailing duty proceeding;
> (2) in the judgment of the administering authority bestows a competitive benefit on the merchandise; and
> (3) has a significant effect on the cost of manufacturing or producing the merchandise.'[251]

The TTA would seem to limit investigation to only one stage upstream.

The second prong of the test requires a decision by the ITA that the price for the input product for use in the product under investigation is lower than the price that the manufacturer or producer of the product under investigation would otherwise pay for the input product in obtaining it from another seller in an arms-length transaction.[252]

248. HR 3398, 130 Cong. Rec. H4516-24 (June 28, 1984).
249. For an overview of the passage and the background of the bill, see Holmer, Bello, 'The Trade and Tariff Act of 1984: The Road to Enactment', 19 Int'l Law 287 (1985).
250. 130 Cong. Rec. § 13,970 (Oct. 9, 1984).
251. TTA *supra* n. 241, § 771 A, codified at 19 USC § 1677-1 (1985). § 771(5)(B)(iv) was omitted by error.
252. Id.

Two authoritative authors have concluded that the upstream provision was 'narrowly and carefully drafted':[253]

'(1) it was made applicable only to CVD cases. . . .;
(2) it substituted for the generally available price determination a determination that the upstream subsidy bestows a competitive benefit on the downstream product;
(3) it provides for greater discretion in adjusting for artificial price depressions;
(4) it establishes a higher 'reasonable grounds to believe or suspect' standard before the Commerce Department investigates upstream subsidy allegations; and
(5) Commerce is permitted to extend specially the deadline for either its preliminary determination or the final determination, if reasonable grounds to believe an upstream subsidy is involved do not develop until after the preliminary determination.'[254]

The upstream subsidy provision and the cases (both prior to and after adoption of the TTA) in which upstream subsidies have been discussed, have been analyzed extensively in a recent article.[255] Therefore, we will focus on whether the provision is in conformity with GATT law.

3. Compatibility with GATT and the Subsidies Code

The question of the compatibility of the upstream subsidy provision with GATT and the Subsidies Code is linked with the scope of the definition of subsidy, the specificity test and the problem of indirect benefits.

Upstream subsidies raise the question whether GATT allows the levying of countervailing duties against imports which indirectly benefitted from a subsidy. Since both Article VI and XVI include indirect benefits without defining the term there can be no question that the concept is compatible with international rules. The argument that GATT 'indirect subsidies' are limited to subsidies granted to the producer of an input which the government requires to be passed through to the producer of the exported product and that upstream subsidies therefore are not covered by this interpretation does not find justification in GATT law or practice. Furthermore, the provision is a codification of consistent ITA practice since 1982.[256] While some form of upstream subsidies is thus in conformity with GATT, this does not necessarily mean that the specific provision adopted was GATT-legal, or wise from a policy point of view. The United States is already the most agressive enforcer and interpreter of the Subsidies Code and of its national countervailing duty

253. Bello, Holmer, 'The Trade and Tariff Act of 1984: Principal Antidumping and Countervailing Duty Provisions', 19 Int'l Law. 639, 645 (1985).
254. Ibid.
255. Giesen, 'Upstream Subsidies: Policy and Enforcement Questions After the Trade and Tariff Act of 1984', 17 L. & Pol'cy Int'l Bus., 241 (1985).
256. Id., at 324.

law and it should keep in mind that every move it makes to extend the scope of its countervailing duty law is followed with argus-eyes by the rest of the world. While a prudent application of the new provision by the ITA might prevent direct international confrontations, the United States should nevertheless be ready to expect (and accept) implementation of mirror legislation (or practice) by its trading partners. This could obviously include countervailability of downstream subsidies (subsidies to products in which the product under investigation has been used as an input).

IV. CONCLUSIONS

In recent years the countervailing duty laws have come under strong criticism from supporters of two extreme positions: a 'protectionist' and a 'liberal' one. The protectionist position, mostly argued by import competing industries, criticize the effectiveness of countervailing duty laws whereas the liberal trading position, mostly argued in academic literature, questions the economic efficiency or wisdom of those laws.

The criticism voiced by import competing industries is based on the argument that, despite the flood of countervailing duty petitions in recent years, imports continue to rise and damage domestic industries. Thus, it is argued that the countervailing duty law does not protect the domestic industries.[257] This criticism, however, reflects a wrong understanding of the countervailing duty law. The steel industries, for example, want protection from injurious imports, whether subsidized or not. To achieve this result they started countervailing and antidumping actions against various steel imports, many of which were indeed justified since the products were either dumped or subsidized. The antidumping and countervailing duty laws, however, do not protect ailing industries from imports as such; they only protect an industry from *unfair* trade. As a result of the complaints the major steel exporting countries limited their steel exports to the United States voluntarily. The result, however, was not a halt in the increase of imports, since less developed countries soon filled the gap[258] – a typical reaction in the case of a voluntary export agreement of a 'big' exporter.[259] Only after they had exhausted the unfair trade laws arsenal did the steel industries bring a complaint under § 201 of the Trade Act of 1974 to limit steel imports as such.[260] Section 201 provides protection for the domestic industry which is seriously injured by imports and is the appropriate means for protecting an ailing industry. The countervailing duty laws, on the other hand, are not equipped to deal with such far-reaching problems and therefore should not be used in cases in which the industry wants protection as such and not only protection from unfair imports.

257. See for example *New York Times*, May 25, 1984, at 28.
258. See *New York Times*, February 2, 1984, at 21.
259. For a more detailed discussion of the trade diversions as a result of voluntary export restraint agreements see Quick, *Exportselbstbeschraenkungen und Artikel XIX GATT*, pp. 59 *et seq.* (1983). See also Savage, Horlick, *Voluntary Restraint Agreements: Practical Considerations and Policy Recommendations*, (to be published).
260. See *New York Times*, January 25, 1984, at 23.

The criticism of the countervailing duty law expressed in the literature is not as easy to qualify as that of domestic industries. It ranges from the lack of discretion in applying the law up to the questioning of the necessity of the law.[261]

The 'legalization' or 'judicialization' of the countervailing duty law has not been praised uniformly. Some authors see in this judicialization a major deficiency of the TAA.[262] While they admit that the adjudicatory nature of the proceedings assures transparency and certainty[263] they are of the opinion that the automatic relief of the law is not appropriate since important issues of foreign countries are at stake, which might bring foreign policy consideration into play.[264] The US government, however, has no means to withdraw a case which it considers inappropriate from an economic or foreign policy point of view; it can only try to convince the petitioner to withdraw the petition and offer him instead a bilaterally negotiated settlement. The dilemma in which the US government can find itself is expressed very clearly in the *EEC Steel Cases* and in the *Chinese Textiles Case*.[265] In both cases the imposition of countervailing duties on the allegedly subsidized products would have deteriorated the relations between the United States and the countries in question so much that the government could not follow the legalistic concept of the TAA but had to operate behind the scenes and convince the petitioners to withdraw their petitions. Therefore, critics argue that if the important cases are solved outside the system and only the less important ones are decided within it, then the system requires too much man-power and cost for the result it achieves.[266] The deadlines of the proceedings and the limits on suspension agreements are put forward in support of their criticism. Since the ITA and the ITC have only limited time to investigate, the result of the investigations will never be precise but only approximate,[267] a result which conflicts with the idea of the legalistic approach to come to the right decision. Furthermore, the restrictions on the negotiations of suspension agreements necessarily propel solutions outside the proceedings.[268]

The criticism that the law does not work satisfactorily in the big political

261. For an extensive description of the different 'schools', see Hufbauer, Erb, *Subsidies in International Trade* (1984).
262. See Ehrenhaft, 'The "Judicialization" of Trade Law', 56 Notre Dame Lawyer 595, pp. 609 *et seq.*; see also statement of Noel Hemmendinger, *Hearings*, *supra* n. 242, at 448, 449 and statement of Peter Ehrenhaft, ibid. pp. 1055 *et seq.*
263. See Ehrenhaft, 'What the Anti-Dumping and Countervailing Duty Provisions of the Trade Agreements Act (Can) (Will) (Should) Mean for US Trade Policy', 11 Law & Pol'y Int'l. Bus. 1361, 1398 (1979).
264. Ibid. p. 1398.
265. In textiles from the PRC several US textile industry associations filed a countervailing duty petition against textile imports from the PRC which the ITA accepted for investigation, see 9 ITIM 52 (1983/84). The petitioners alleged that the PRC's dual exchange rate constituted a countervailable subsidy. The petition was ultimately withdrawn. See 9 ITIM 110, 226, 373, 428 (1983/84).
266. Jackson, 'Perspectives on the Jurisprudence of International Trade: Costs and Benefits of Legal Procedures in the United States', 82 Mich. L. Rev. 1570, 1580-1581 (1984); Ehrenhaft, *supra* n. 262, at 611.
267. See Hemmendinger, *supra* n. 262 at 449; Ehrenhaft, *supra* n. 263, at 1399.
268. See Barringer, Dunn, 'Antidumping and Countervailing Duty Investigations Under the Trade Agreements Act of 1979', 14 J. Int'l L. & Econ., I, 36 (1980).

cases cannot be denied. Yet it is open to question whether, as a consequence, the law should be revised and made more discretionary. The practice between 1974 and 1979 shows that the discretionary approach had many deficiencies as well. Thus, it might be better to stick to the adjudicative approach knowing that this approach will be effective in most cases and will be inadequate only in few. The system has the advantage that the parties have a chance to present their views, that the decision making is based on their contentions and that there are no 'back room deals' which might undermine the position of one party. In sum, it can give the parties the feeling of a fair process. Besides, the fact that a foreign government is involved should not be given too much weight. In fact the foreign government is offered a fair chance since it can actively participate in the decision making process and possibly avoid a final affirmative determination or reduce the percentage of the countervailing duty. The necessity of participation should be self-evident since all countries recognize the right to unilaterally levy countervailing duties. It is this recognition which necessarily leads to the situation in which the foreign government is the defending party and it should therefore guarantee that the parties take up their role in the proceedings. Even in big cases, trade relations do not necessarily have to suffer; if the foreign country is not satisfied with the implementation of United States countervailing duty law it can challenge the action in GATT or under the Subsidies Code.

Barcelo, the most outspoken critic of countervailing duty laws,[269] questions the propriety of the law altogether. With regard to domestic subsidies he doubts that the economic arguments advanced for justification of countervailing duties, *i.e.*, that subsidies are (1) distortive and (2) unfair, are economically sound and concludes that these arguments are either weak or unsupportable. Regarding the first argument he convincingly points out that domestic subsidies are not distortive for the subsidizing country and should not be countervailed against since, on balance, the importing country benefits from the cheap imports even if they materially injure its producers of like products. According to his theory, action is justified only if the imports cause serious injury, or what he calls 'first level injury'. With regard to the second argument Barcelo shows that the notion of fairness has inherent weaknesses too. He contends that only specific subsidies are considered to be unfair while there are other government actions, such as education, fiscal and monetary policy, or lack of environmental policies which might give certain industries competitive advantage just as well, even though they influence the economy as a whole. Since such a subsidy might have an unfair, beggar-thy-neighbour effect countries should be allowed to take actions against them whenever the subsidized imports result in first level injury. Therefore he suggests replacing the countervailing duty law with a modified escape clause or using Track II procedures against subsidized imports. A similar strategy has been proposed by Lowenfeld[270] who questions the distinction between fair and unfair trade and wonders whether a new Safeguards Code might not render the Subsidies Code unnecessary.

269. See Barcelo, *supra* n. 86, pp. 130 *et seq.* and *supra* n. 85, pp. 277 *et seq.*
270. Lowenfeld, 'Fair or Unfair Trade: Does It Matter', 13 Corn. Int'l. L.J. 205, 219 (1980).

The arguments put forward by both writers are convincing and might be taken into consideration in new GATT negotiations. Those negotiations could ultimately lead to a 'general agreement on import relief measures' which would render the Subsidies and Antidumping Codes and the import relief provisions of GATT superfluous. For the time being, however, the replacement of the countervailing duty laws with the escape clause not only seems unrealistic but also inappropriate. Since there is no consensus in GATT on how to deal with injurious fair trade – the contracting parties have been negotiating a Safeguards Code since 1973 without any success until now[271] – the use of the escape clause against unfair trade would certainly be very problematic as well. One would have to deal with the questions of selective application of safeguard measures,[272] the length of the application of those measures[273] and the definition of serious injury, all of which are not provided for in Article XIX GATT. Since it is furthermore not very likely that the contracting parties will replace the Anti-Dumping and Subsidies Code with a 'general agreement on import relief measures' in the short term the shortcomings of the Subsidies Code have to be eliminated by either amending it or giving it some meaningful interpretation in order to limit the application of national countervailing duty laws.

The Subsidies Code favours unilaterally imposed countervailing duties over internationally agreed upon solutions.[274] The fact that the signatories are reluctant to attack subsidies under Track II is due not only to their freedom to solve their problems with foreign subsidization subsidies through countervailing duties but also to deadlocks in the decision-making process of the Subsidies Committee. The Committee cannot agree on the outcome of two important cases[275] involving the United States and the EEC and thereby demonstrates that the dispute settlement procedure of Track II does not work as effectively as intended by the Code. The reason for this deadlock lies in the unanimity rule which *de facto* applies to the decisions of the Committee although the Code does not require it. Thus, if the defeated party does not agree with the panel report the Committee cannot recommend any actions. A way to overcome this deadlock would be a qualified unanimity rule according to which the two litigating parties would not have the right to vote. Of course, an alternative might be a majority vote, but since this seems to be unacceptable for most of the signatories we refrain from proposing an ideal solution which does not seem feasible in practice. The revitalization of Track II procedures would guarantee more international discipline with regard to subsidies.

271. For a description of these problems and a proposal for a new Safeguards Code see Quick, *supra* n. 259.
272. Art. XIX is generally understood to require *erga omnes* application of safeguard measures; see Quick, *supra* n. 259, pp. 128 *et seq.*; but see Bronckers, *Selective Safeguard Measures in Multilateral Trade Relations*, p. 12-110 (1985).
273. Although the escape grants only temporary relief statistics of Art. XIX actions show that the contracting parties tend to apply these actions permanently; see Quick, *supra* n. 259, pp. 125 *et seq.*
274. See § D.
275. See the *EEC Wheat Case*, *supra* n. 89 and the *Pasta Case*, *supra* n. 112.

The more important changes, however, must take place in Track I. Although Track I lays down procedural rules it does not contain any substantive rules and thus allows signatories to apply their countervailing duty laws practically without any substantive limitations. Since the Code does not provide an answer to the divergences between Articles VI and XVI but simply incorporates them, it is an 'Agreement without Consensus' as Tarullo[276] has rightly called it. Any improvement of the Code, therefore, has to start with consensus on substantive rules for Track I. These rules should not only address the definition of the term subsidy but also its valuation and calculation for countervailing duty assessment. The most necessary change of all, however, concerns the definition of subsidies. A first step would be an exhaustive list of practices which are understood to constitute countervailable subsidies. If a country used one of those practices they would be countervailable *per se*; provided that the other requirements such as material injury and causation were fulfilled. Practices, that are not included in the list, would be held countervailable only upon prior authorization by the Subsidies Committee. As a corollary, the Committee should obviously have the power to add practices to the list. Such a system would put a limit on unilateral, and possibly protectionist, national interpretation of countervailing duty laws. Countervailing duty laws have become major obstacles to free trade and countries that oppose more international control,[277] should keep in mind that broad unilateral interpretations will grow unfettered in the absence of such control.[278]

276. Tarullo, *supra* n. 6.
277. During the Tokyo Round, for example, the EEC opposed an illustrative list of domestic subsidies in Track II. See Rivers, Greenwald, *supra* n. 32, at 1473.
278. The natural resources provision of the Gibbons bill for example would have expanded the scope of the US countervailing duty law significantly. See Bello, Holmer, 'Subsidies and Natural Resources: Congress Rejects a Lateral Attack on the Specificity Test, 18 G.W.J. of Int'l L. & Econ. Pol'y, 501 (1984); see also Barshefsky, Diamond, Ellis, 'Foreign Government Regulation of Natural Resources: Problems and Remedies under United States International Trade Laws', 21 Stanford J. Int'l L. 29 (1985).

VII

*Gary N. Horlick**

Subsidies Discipline Under WTO and US Rules

I. Introduction

Subsidies appear to be all-pervasive, at least in developed countries.[1] The EU updates the WTO Protocol every year, pursuant to Article 25 of the WTO Subsidies Agreement,[2] with over 500 pages of subsidies given by the EU and the 15 Member States (the basic underlying notification was over 1000 pages).[3]

A recent study in the US for the Council on Foreign Relations estimates that four out of five large and medium-size companies receive state and local government incentives.[4] The US notification of subsidies to the WTO is only 71 pages long.[5] That may be because the US lists sub-federal subsidies, rather than describing them in detail as does the EU, and does not list the subsidy programmes described on individual state's websites, much less non-state sub-federal subsidies, even though city and county tax exemptions are probably the largest single type of US subsidy. Most US subsidies are off-budget (for example, tax holidays) and are less transparent to the federal government. Also, EU Member States are accustomed to a subsidy reporting system—US states are not. One extremely unscientific estimate of US federal and non-federal subsidies to business is $170 billion a year.[6]

This paper will assume that subsidies can distort international trade. Indeed, export subsidies in international trade are considered *per se* distortive—they

* O'Melveny & Myers LLP.

[1] Developing countries may have less money for subsidies, and the information about subsidies may be less available.

[2] Agreement on Subsidies and Countervailing Measures (SCM Agreement) at Art. 25, Final Act Embodying the Results of the Uruguay Round of Multi-lateral Trade Negotiations (Final Act) (April 15, 1994) at 297.

[3] *New and Full Notifications Pursuant to Article XVI:1 of the GATT 1994 and Article 25 of the SCM Agreement*, G/SCM/N/38/EEC/Add. 1–15 (Dec. 21, 1998).

[4] (Fry 1997:117).

[5] *Loc. cit.* n. 3.

[6] The Cato Institute, a free-market think-tank, estimates US federal subsidies at $65 billion a year (Moore & Stansted 1995). Some may argue that the $170 billion includes much broadly available assistance—but much of that is negotiated individually ('specific', in WTO terms). With all that, the US has been ranked, in 1997, only fourth in providing incentives sufficient to attract foreign investments, behind Ireland, Singapore, and Malaysia, and just ahead of the United Kingdom. Italy ranked 40th, just behind Germany and ahead of Poland, Korea and Japan. IMD (The World Competitiveness Yearbook 1998 (Lausanne) at page 235). The same source ranked the US as the 23rd least projectionist.

are prohibited[7] for all developed-country WTO members and on a creeping basis (ending in 2003, or even 2005) for all developing country WTO members thought likely to have any significant impact on international trade; the exception from the prohibition is for the very poorest of developing countries. The EU similarly prohibits export subsidies on trade among its Member States.[8] The WTO also prohibits import-substitution subsidies, although it is not clear to the author that import substitution subsidies are exactly identical in their effects on trade to export subsidies; or, indeed, that the effects of import substitution subsidies do not overlap at least to some degree with the effect of normal, WTO-permitted tariffs.

However, the WTO also recognises that subsidies are not always 'bad'—both the WTO and the EU state aid rules expressly permit certain subsidies either on an explicit basis (i.e., if they meet certain predefined conditions),[9] or on a variety of 'rule of reason' bases (for example, for the WTO, if they do not cause 'serious prejudice').

II. Sources

There is no comprehensive treatise on the WTO Subsidies Agreement. The obvious starting point is Terry Stewart's compilation of Uruguay Round documents,[10] but that is inevitably incomplete, especially as regards the Subsidies Agreement, which, more than some other negotiations, was based only in part on formal written proposals. The best analysis I have seen in English is by

[7] SCM Agreement, Art. 3 at 266.

[8] See, US Germany—Aircraft, SCM/142, 4 March 1992 (unadopted).

[9] For example, Art. 8 of the SCM Agreement permitted 'green-light' subsidies for research and development (R&D), regional development, and environmental improvements. *Cf.*, (Clarke & Horlick 1994:695–701). It is unclear how well crafted that Article was to meet its laudable goals. The R&D provision, for example, may instead encourage wasteful investment in commercial research that the company itself does not think is worth funding. In the steel area, for example, the energy-based projects are funded 70% by the Department of Energy and 30% by industry. This year, approximately 50 proposals were received by the AISI from national laboratories and universities. AISI recently signed a compact with the DOE securing $19 million in funding through to 2004, and Kavanagh estimated that between $3 million and $4 million would be available to fund six or seven of the projects submitted last month. The first cuts will be made by a review committee this month and then whittled down to the final candidates in June. The crucial factor in a proposal moving from paper to reality is matching an idea to a steel company willing to capitalise 30% of the project (emphasis added) (*American Metal Market*, 7 April, 1999, page 1). Ironically, one of the research programmes that Art. 8 was intended to protect, the US Partnership for a New Generation of Vehicles, may well be doomed by new air quality rules (*Automotive News*, 7 December, 1998, at 3). *Cf.*, also (Evans 1989:3)

[10] (Stewart 1993).

Dan Hunter.[11] I would note, in passing, that this is a problem for many of the Uruguay Round Agreements—the literature to date often only repeats the provisions of a given agreement without pointing out possible interpretations or lacunae. By contrast, there is a great deal of good published analysis of EU state aids law.

III. Discussion

This paper will explore a typology of subsidies disciplines, classed in one of three categories:

a) inherent (for example, constrained by lack of resources, or failure of a proposed subsidy to meet some perceived cost-benefit test);
b) self-imposed (for example, constitutional limits in some US states); and
c) externally imposed (for example, the EU state aids code, or the WTO Subsidies Agreement).

Through this typology, this paper will attempt to explore why the WTO Subsidies Agreement does not discipline subsidies as well as the EU system does, and why the US system does not effectively discipline subsidies. Some possible reforms are mentioned, but not with great hopes for their adoption.

A. Inherent Subsidy Disciplines (Type I)

The most obvious constraint on subsidies is a budgetary one. Subsidies normally represent a transfer from the average taxpayer to the average company owner(s). In the United States, for example, this means that most subsidies represent upward income redistribution.[12]

Few governments would admit to having unlimited resources. So, one would expect some popular resistance to subsidies; indeed, most requests to governments for money are turned down in the budgetary process. Connoisseurs of

[11] (Hunter 1994: 547). Note also my Article with Peggy Clarke, (Clarke & Horlick 1994).There are also some interesting comments in a Journal of World Trade article by Terry Collins-Williams and Gerry Salembier, two of Canada's negotiators of the Agreement, (Collins & Salembier 1996:5)

[12] Unsurprisingly, the distribution of subsidies is frequently a result of rent-seeking behaviour (and justifications) not unlike the distribution of trade protection. The US integrated steel mills, for example, were able to extract one half a billion dollars from Congress in 1982, at the same time as it got the first VRA, and then got another half a billion dollars in 1986, just after the second round of VRAs. The US lumber industry got a bailout of over 1 billion dollars in 1983 from Congress, just before it successfully obtained "grey area" protection by going a political route to reverse an earlier Commerce Department finding against imposing countervailing duties on lumber from Canada.

'public choice' theory will recognise that the constraint is not always effective. In practice, elected representatives and appointed officials may well maximise their own career goals precisely by handing out money to businesses in return for certain behaviour by the subsidised company.[13]

While there are often protests about 'giveaways' and 'corporate welfare,' more often the pattern is one of rent-seeking behaviour in the halls of government: a relatively small but determined group with a lot at stake will often triumph over the welfare of a larger group which has so little at stake individually as to not be worth organising an equally strong counter-lobbying effort. T.J. Rodgers, a leading critic of corporate subsidies in the US, and the CEO of a leading US semi-conductor company, explains the phenomenon well:

> Even though I have made seven trips to Congress to oppose corporate subsidies, I would without hesitation, pursue any important subsidies offered to my company, because it is my obligation to our shareholders to do my best for them, including obtaining any available low-cost funding. A company that failed to do so would be as foolish as an individual who refused to take income tax deductions because of a strong belief in a flat tax.[14]

This may explain the leading US critic of subsidised foreign steel, the CEO of Bethlehem Steel, taking a moment out from his attacks on 'unfair' foreign steel

---

[13] Countervailing duty administrators often avoid this issue, because the *quid pro quo* is often not spelled out explicitly. British Steel, twenty years ago, certainly understood that the very large subsidies it was receiving from a Labour government carried an obligation to employ twice as many people as was necessary and to use British coal and iron ore, even if that was not spelled out. This situation may be dramatic for some state-owned enterprises in 'transition' economies. In conceptual terms, this means that subsidy money is not fungible, unless it has been suitably discounted to reach the actual calculation of the true benefit to the recipient. For example, assume that a company agrees to keep open two plants, each of which can produce 100 widgets, in order to produce 50 widgets at each plant, rather than close one plant and produce the 100 widgets at one plant, but only if the government agrees to pay the added $100 cost of maintaining two plants, rather than one. The cost to the government is $100, but the benefit to the company is zero. Yet, the US Commerce Department and the EC Commission, under their new regulations, would find a benefit to the company of at least 100. Alternately, assume that a government gives a $3 billion subsidy to build a new steel mini-mill, and the result is a mill equivalent to one built elsewhere on a private sector basis for $500 million. The cost to government is $3 billion. What is the value to recipient? $3 billion?—what if $2 billion had been skimmed off in kickbacks to the ruling party? Or suppose the government grants transferable credits, which are resold at less than face value (i.e., the cost to the government exceeds the value to the recipient)—the EU has recently preliminarily countervailed the full face value as the 'benefit', *cf.*, Commission Regulation (EC) No. 618/1999 of 23 March 1999 (provisional countervailing duty on stainless steel wire from India). The (often unstated) *quid pro quo* makes the true value of a subsidy rather awkward to measure. In a system of pure subsidies discipline, this is not a problem (the remedy is prohibition) but it is a major problem if trying to offset the subsidy by countervailing duties or by requiring restitution.

[14] (Rogers 1998).

to thank 'federal, Maryland and Baltimore area officials for their help, resulting in assistance to help build this new mill and train its employees'.[15]

The results often seem random: a major US manufacturer gets a tax exemption in a New York suburb in the face of citizen complaints that the Japanese-owned company in town pays at least its full taxes, while the US-owned company does not (and thereby undermines the local school system, which is mainly funded locally). Similarly, numerous critical newspaper articles do not prevent a major US service provider from playing off Maryland against Virginia to see who will offer the best deal to build a new headquarters (the 'winner' promised $50 million).[16]

The mechanism is quite direct:

> The competition between South Carolina and Virginia for the steel mill was fierce. Politicians and businessmen involved in the campaign described F. Kenneth Iverson, chairman and chief executive officer, and John D. Correnti, president and chief operating officer, as relentless negotiators who 'play their cards to the hilt'. Indeed, a local newspaper reported Iverson saying, in January, that South Carolina might be losing its bid because it was not offering the power rates and tax incentives he wanted.
>
> The economic development incentives that South Carolina threw in its package were comparable with Virginia's offer as well as with what Nucor won when it built the Indiana and Arkansas mills, according to Jim Coblin, Nucor's personnel manager. Among the perks, was a fluctuating electric rate with discounts on the hourly rate, construction of a rail spur, off-site road improvements, job-creation tax benefits, pre-employment training and a fee-in-lieu property tax option whereby the Nucor property will be assessed at 'considerably less' than the 10.5% that other property is

---

[15] 'Bethlehem Steel to retain mill near Baltimore', *The Washington Post*, 30.10.1997, at E1. The steel industry may be getting sensitive. When it was criticised for adding a steel-only programme (with a Buy American provision) to the 1998 federal highway legislation, the steel industry joined with the lumber and concrete industries to cover all three industries—and raise the total to $100 million.

[16] Depending on future inflation, $49–73 billion. The Maryland deal led a junior Congressman, Rep. David Minge, to reintroduce an earlier unsuccessful legislative proposal which, in effect, would ban state subsidies whose interest or effect was to attract or retain business: 'I don't fault Maryland for providing whatever incentives they are providing,' said Rep. David Minge (D), author of the bill, which would impose special taxes on companies that receive public incentives. 'It can't disarm unilaterally. But, generally, states recognise these raids or defensive positions are not in their long-term best interest. They are shifting the costs to other taxpayers.' Maryland lawmakers continued to warn yesterday that the deal would set a precedent that other large Maryland companies may now consider their right. 'It's disgraceful for them to come looking for government subsidies of that magnitude when they are a profitable company—and not just profitable but making profits of hundreds of millions of dollars,' said Sen. Brian E. Frosh (D-Montgomery). 'It's a harmful precedent, and it's not the way the free market economy is supposed to work. But Montgomery County Council President Isiah Leggett (D-At Large) likened the decision to a professional basketball team paying Michael Jordan more than other players because 'he fills the arena.' *Washington Post*, 12.3.1999, at A1.

assessed at for a period of 20 years. The value of the incentives has not been determined.[17]

A consultant warns:

> Hoping to improve economic conditions, almost every state in the United States is attempting to increase business activity through the use of economic development incentives.
>
> Tax credits, exemptions, and abatements, as well as other financial incentives, are all available to companies that know how to take advantage of them.
>
> Business must actively seek out these opportunities as well as other tax minimisation techniques, or else their potential will be lost. Although some benefits may be easy to secure, many are not and many require leverage to negotiate.
>
> The most important incentive is the one that makes a project happen. It may be a building permit or a variance. It may be a clover-leaf on the highway. It may be just about anything. Unless programmes are investigated, the benefits can never be secured.
>
> And remember, although you may not make a priority of securing state and federal economic development incentives, your competition probably does.[18]

The empirical evidence for the conclusion that an inherent subsidies discipline is ineffective takes two forms: the repeated award of subsidies, and the numerous attempts to impose controls of the second or third type because Type I control does not work consistently.[19]

B. Self-Imposed Subsidies Discipline (Type II)

Self-imposed controls are those imposed by a polity on itself: i.e., to be applied by the polity to itself. In effect, they are *ex ante* attempts, or hopes, to eliminate, or at least reduce, the rent-seeking behaviour described in Type I. A good example of the Type II discipline are the provisions in the constitutions of some states in the United States prohibiting subsidies to business. These provisions, which were adopted to ensure equality of treatment among all taxpayers, appear to prohibit many subsidies which, in fact, are given. In theory, and in practice, a private citizen/taxpayer, or unhappy competitor, can challenge successful rent-seeking behaviour in the state courts, after all its costs have been incurred, and strip away the ill-gotten gains.

In practice, state courts facing the same pressures as legislators from competition from other states have interpreted their way around the constraints. This is typified by the decision of the Kentucky Supreme Court, albeit by only a 4–3

[17] *American Metal Market*, 13.3.1995 at 1. Nucor has accounted for over 6 million tons of added steel capacity in the US in the past 10 years.

[18] John Skowrowski, Grant Thorton LLP, 'Don't Miss Out on Incentives to Grow your Business', *Tax & Business Advisor*, January/February 1998, at 4–6.

[19] One of the ironies is that Type I discipline—public outrage or lack of money—may preclude subsidies to the 'second-comer,' thus creating 'more' distortion than subsidies to everyone!

vote, in effect to ignore the anti-subsidy provision of the Kentucky State constitution in order to enable Kentucky to outbid Kansas for a new Toyota plant, with a lavish assortment of subsidies, such as Kentucky paying to fly newly recruited local workers to Japan for training. The Court instead relied on a clause allowing the state to aid the 'general welfare'. At the other end of the investment cycle, the city of Ypsilanti, Michigan sued a major US manufacturer to prevent it from closing an existing plant in Ypsilanti rather than an existing plant in Texas (after Arlington, Texas offered a better deal to keep its plant open).

With new polities such as the EU and WTO, a question is raised as to whether the anti-subsidy provisions of the Treaty of Rome/Amsterdam, and the subsidy discipline provisions of the WTO Agreements, fit within this category. Probably not—these are better seen as externally imposed disciplines that will be explored under Type III. By contrast, an interesting example of self-imposed subsidies discipline would be the law passed by Congress to limit the issuance by municipalities and states of 'industrial development bonds' which were exempt from federal tax. This followed an explosion in the issuance of such bonds whose cost was effectively borne by the Federal Treasury through the exemption from federal personal income tax. Once municipalities figured out that if they could borrow on a tax-exempt basis at 6 percent, and the market rate was 10 percent, they could relend the money to companies at 7 percent and both the subsidised business and the municipality could make a profit (from the Federal Treasury), the activity became so intense that, for example, Fairfax County, Virginia had borrowed so much money to lend that it ran out of businesses to subsidise in Fairfax and wound up subsidising a new McDonald's in a neighbouring county, just to earn the profit. Congress did not abolish the tax exemption, but it limited the amount that could be issued within each state.[20] While this did not completely eliminate the rent-seeking behaviour, it limited the total amount of bonds available, which may have actually increased the rent-seeking behaviour, as groups competed for the benefit within each state.

It would appear that the less formal the self-imposed (Type II) restraint, the less durable it is. Thus, while the constitutional constraint has not been particularly binding, at least it permitted a challenge all the way to the Supreme Court of Kentucky, while a purely executive agreement among the governors of New York, New Jersey, and Connecticut not to engage in subsidies wars fell apart the very first time a footloose company sought bids from all three.

An interesting mix of Type II and Type III can be seen in the Commonwealth of Virginia's adventures with a large internet service provider in the United States. The Attorney General of the state issued a ruling that individual counties could not subsidise new businesses by buying the building materials for new factories, thus avoiding the sales tax that the company would have to pay, since the counties are tax-exempt. After the state government imposed this Type II

[20] Tax Reform Act of 1984, Pub. L. No. 98–369, 98 Stat. 494, 915 (1984).

(or maybe Type III) restraint on its counties, the state legislature promptly enacted legislation exempting the internet service provider from paying sales tax on the building materials for its new headquarters (a negative Type II, perhaps).[21]

C. Externally Imposed Subsidy Discipline (Type III)

The EU subsidies discipline system is a good example of a well-developed Type III restraint. While, at first glance, the EU system may look like a Type II restraint—a polity restraining itself—the EU system, in fact, constrains subsidisation by its sub-federal Member States, rather than by the EU itself. Further, while the rules are implemented primarily by the EU executive branch through the Competition Directorate whose decisions are subject to review by the Commission ('an essentially political body[22]) and the Council, which is made up of the very Member States whose actions are meant to be restrained, with consequent potential for 'log-rolling', the EU also provides for direct access to a supranational authority, the ECJ, which cannot be overridden easily by the Member States.

The US federal statute mentioned above that limits the use of tax-exempt bonds is arguably, in part, a Type III regime as well as a Type II regime. The actual subsidy came from the federal treasury, although it was given out by municipalities. Thus, the statute imposed an external limit on the sub-federal entities (Type III) in order to limit federal subsidies (Type II). Because of the nature of the subsidy, no elaborate enforcement or judicial review provisions were necessary—bonds issued outside the limit do not benefit from the tax exemption. Beyond that, the US federal government seems disinclined to intervene against federal[23] or state subsidies; understandably, as the federal legislators who would have to act are the ones who demand the federal subsidies, and most are former state or local officials. The US Supreme Court has made clear its willingness to allow distortive and discriminatory) state subsidies[24].

The WTO subsidy discipline system is a Type III system as well. Indeed, the SCM Agreement only covers subsidies by Member Governments. It excludes coverage of subsidies by other international organisations such as the UN and the various multi-lateral development banks.[25]

---

[21] *The Washington Post* 2.3.1999, at B1.

[22] (Ehlermann 1995).

[23] The Office of Management and Budget in the White House provides a 'watchdog' role (combining Types I, II and III) on Federal subsidies before the Congress takes over.

[24] *Hughes* v. *Alexandria Scrap Corp.*, 426 U.S. 794 (1976), and *New Energy Co.* v. *Limbach*, 486 US 269 (1988). For an excellent description of the impasse, *cf.*, Schaefer 1998.

[25] This is accomplished by limiting the coverage of the Agreement to governments, and defining governments as being national, rather than multi-national, SCM Agreement, Art. 1(a)(1), Final Act at 264.

IV. Conclusion?

Which type of subsidy system is most effective in disciplining subsidies? In a literal sense, probably Type I, since most raids on the public treasury are rejected. There are far too many exceptions to that rule, however, to consider Type I a successful or adequate means of disciplining subsidies so that they cannot distort competition. The exceptions are so visible and widespread that it is probably not just the perception of subsidisation which creates a demand for some discipline, but the reality visible in daily newspapers.

In a WTO sense, Type I is successful for the circular reason that the WTO Agreement is written to accommodate a great deal of subsidisation not caught by Type I self-discipline. Logically, in a democracy—or other types of government where there is a free-for-all among competing interest groups—the tendency is not to discipline all subsidies, but rather to subsidise everyone at a low level, so that everyone feels that they have 'got something.' If written properly, such subsidies would escape WTO discipline as being not 'specific.'[26]

Type II subsidies discipline systems would seem to have a better chance of effectiveness. The United States relies to a high degree, at least relative to other countries, on self-policing mechanisms. This is particularly true in the competition area, including the use of private antitrust suits and competitive policing of unfair advertising in labels.

The EU appears to have the most aggressive Type III subsidies discipline structure, including a private right of action for competitors to challenge a subsidy before a supra-national court, as well as an 'Attorney-General' (Competition Directorate) to challenge a subsidy even if no private entity does. All that is missing, apparently, is a right of action for the subsidising taxpayers to challenge the misuse of their money before European courts.

The WTO subsidy system lacks most of these features. The WTO has a relatively soft notification system. Moral persuasion has been sufficient to have most major trading countries notify at least some of their subsidies, even though the majority of WTO members have not done so.[27] No WTO member has enough dedicated resources to search out other members' subsidies aggressively, but the dynamic of reciprocal cross-notification—for example, the EU pointing out US subsidies which the US has not notified, and the US countering—has certainly increased the amount of such notifications.[28] WTO countervailing duty provisions, and their enforcement by WTO member states,

---

[26] The pattern of middle-class subsidisation in the United States and Western Europe and the reductions in welfare payments fit this model nicely, and is probably paralleled by the widespread programmes for small and medium enterprises.

[27] Apparently the workload is too intense, leading to recent proposals to change the annual updates to a biennial report.

[28] But not much—no WTO member has cross-notified even a significant fraction of the programmes found on the individual US states' websites.

provides an indirect incentive for exporters to eliminate subsidies programmes which are likely to lead to exclusion for their exports from major markets.

Finally, the WTO dispute settlement system is limited as a subsidy discipline system because cases can only brought by Members.[29] So far, all but one of the cases that have been brought have involved prohibited export or import substitution subsidies under SCM Article 3,[30] which may suggest that members may not wish to challenge each other's 'domestic' subsidies, on the traditional principle that governments which live in glass houses do not throw stones. Thus, the business competitors of the subsidised enterprise cannot challenge a subsidy on their own (they may prefer to get their own subsidies, rather than litigate), but only through a WTO member (which may have other factors which lead it not to file a challenge), nor can the subsidising taxpayers, and there is no 'Attorney-General' in the WTO to bring the case if a WTO member will not.

V. Possible Changes

It is difficult to imagine changes which would improve Type I discipline, i.e., beyond the usual 'good government' remedies for excessive play for rent-seeking behaviour, such as limitations on campaign finance and other forms of corruption, more transparency, and so on. One can imagine a requirement (WTO-based) that WTO members be forced to publicise the subsidies they notify to the WTO at home—the problem is not transparency in a literal sense, but rather the overload of information already available. For federal states, even this is not very realistic, since they are often not aware of the subsidies given by sub-federal units—perhaps one could require that they set up internal notification systems?[31]—and may not be politically able to control them in any event.

Type II offers more promise. As we have seen, existing restrictions have been essentially subverted, but this does not mean they could not work. Stronger prohibitions at a constitutional level, if accessible to competitors[32] and even taxpayers through the courts, could be the most effective form of subsidies discipline. The question is whether those changes are best generated internally, or

[29] In addition, it remains to be seen if Art. V of the SCM Agreement will be used to provide a 'discovery' mechanism sufficient to support the discipline subsidies promised by the Agreement.

[30] And the exception—Indonesia Autos (*Indonesia: Certain Measures Affecting the Automobile Industry*, WTO DOC. WT/DS54/R, 55/R, 59/R, 64/R (July 28, 1998)) was part of an import substitution scheme.

[31] Would the added bureaucracy discourage subsidies?

[32] Including workers? Four Alabama steelworkers union members sued the Tennessee Valley Authority—a Federally-owned electric power supplier—to block a favorable electricity contract given to a new non-union steel mill set up by British Steel, Sumitomo and LTV ('TVA sued over Trico Steel Deal', *American Metal Market*, 13.3.1997, at 2).

through international agreement to provide Type II remedies domestically (presumably backed up by Type III international disciplines).

A wide range of Type III remedies is easy to imagine, although the degree of difficulty of reaching agreement may be quite high. One does not expect to see the WTO open up its dispute resolution system for subsidies matters to enraged private competitors, much less to taxpayers, but perhaps the current WTO enthusiasm for placating environmental NGOs could be turned to good purpose here by requiring an environmental assessment of subsidies. This would create an additional constituency interested in ferreting out the details of a number of, although not all, subsidies, thus leading to better transparency and information, and possibly enforcement.

The most important problem in the WTO system with respect to subsidies discipline is eliminating the 'glass-house' problem'. It seems unlikely that the WTO Secretariat would be given any powers to initiate anti-subsidy moves and irritate its members! One possibility would be to build on a mechanism based on EU state aids rules which was dropped, under US pressure, at the very end of the Uruguay Round[33]—a condition that 'actionable' subsidies (i.e., not currently prohibited, but not permitted under Article 8) be prohibited, or at least suspended, prior to notification. This has the advantage of forcing the subsidising country to throw the first stone, or at least provide the rocks—and for that reason is unlikely to win acceptance easily.

One completely different approach would be to change the rules to make them easier to apply to subsidies. Thus, for example, Article 6.1 of the SCM Agreement creates a presumption that subsidies greater than 5% of the value of the product are creating the requisite serious prejudice to be disciplined.[34] The number could be lowered, or even made stricter by replacing the presumption of serious prejudice with a flat prohibition of these 'dark amber' subsidies or at least above a certain amount, on the principle that small subsides do not cause much harm, while large ones can.

---

[33] See n. 10, Art. 25 of SCM Agreement.

[34] But Art. 6.1 expires at the end of this year unless it is expressly renewed.

UNITED STATES: COURT OF APPEALS FOR THE FEDERAL CIRCUIT OPINION IN PPG INDUSTRIES, INC. v. UNITED STATES*
(U.S. Countervailing Duty Law)
[March 22, 1991]
+Cite as 30 I.L.M. 1179 (1991)+

Introductory Note
by
Gary N. Horlick

The much-awaited decision by the U.S. Court of Appeals for the Federal Circuit in PPG v. United States ("PPG")[1] may have finally resolved the core issue in the U.S. countervailing duty law and, in so doing, finally put an end to the myth that Cabot Corp. v. U.S., 620 F. Supp. 722 (Ct. Int'l Trade 1986), required that all government assistance to any identifiable beneficiary be considered a countervailable subsidy. PPG, together with the 1988 amendments to the U.S. countervailing duty law[2], may have ended one chapter in a debate that has raged since at least 1979. It is also likely to serve as the lodestone for the negotiators of a new Subsidies Code in the GATT Uruguay Round.

In PPG, the CAFC affirmed a CIT ruling[3] (by the same CIT judge who wrote the Cabot opinion) upholding a Commerce Department rule in effect since 1982 (although never promulgated as a regulation) that Commerce will determine that a foreign subsidy is countervailable if its availability is limited either in form (de jure) or in practice (de facto) to a "specific industry, or group of industries", 19 U.S.C. §1677(5) (1988). Commerce's

---

[1]PPG Indust., Inc., v. United States, 928 F.2d 1568 (Fed. Cir. 1991).

[2]Pub. L. No. 100-418, Title I, Subtitle C, part 2 §1312, 102 Stat. 1184. As the CAFC points out in PPG, the amendment "codified that portion of the decision in Cabot v. United States, 620 F. Supp. 722 (Ct. Int'l Trade 1986), which rejected nominal general availability as a test for countervailability". PPG, 928 F.2d 1571 n.3.

[3]PPG Indus., Inc. v. United States, 662 F. Supp. 258 (Ct. Int'l Trade 1987). The Office of Import Administration

*[Reproduced from 928 F.2d 1568-84 (Fed. Cir. 1991). The Introductory Note was prepared for International Legal Materials by Gary N. Horlick, O'Melveny & Myers, and member of the I.L.M. Editorial Advisory Committee. Mr. Horlick was formerly Deputy Assistant Secretary of Commerce for Import Administration.]

1180

interpretation of the "specificity" language in the statute is thus that a subsidy is countervailable only if it is limited to specific industries; conversely, if a subsidy is available to and actually used[4] by a wide variety of industries, it is not "specific", as required by the statute.[5]

---

of the International Trade Administration of the U.S. Department of Commerce ("Commerce") is responsible for determining whether foreign subsidies are countervailable, and the U.S. International Trade Commission ("ITC"), is responsible for determining whether the subsidization has caused material injury. If both findings are affirmative, Commerce issues an order imposing countervailing duties on the imported merchandise. Decisions by Commerce and the ITC are appealable in the first instance to the U.S. Court of International Trade ("CIT"), and then to the U.S. Court of Appeals for the Federal Circuit ("CAFC"). 19 U.S.C. §1516A (1988).

[4]Thus, the assertion in the PPG Dissent, 928 F.2d at 1581, that Commerce had never applied a de facto test prior to 1985 is incorrect. Certain politicians in the Administration and Congress found it convenient to so claim in 1985-86, as a pretext for the Commerce preliminary determination in October 1986, under enormous political pressure, to reverse its 1983 decision in Certain Softwood Products from Canada, 48 Fed. Reg. 24,159 (Dept't Comm. 1983) (Final Negative Countervailing Duty Determinations). Yet in that decision, which was upheld by the CIT, U.S. Coalition for Fair Canadian Lumber Imports v. United States, 563 F. Supp. 838 (Ct. Int'l Trade 1983), Commerce expressly relied upon actual (de facto) use by a wider group of, inter alia, roads (48 Fed. Reg. at 24,172) and stumpage rights (48 Fed. Reg. at 24,167). See also Oil Country Tubular Goods from Korea, 49 FR 46,776, 46,779 (Dep't Comm. 1984).

Commerce officials still feel the need to pay obeisance to the CIT by claiming that Commerce did not apply a de facto test before 1985, although they are well aware of the numerous cases expressly applying a de facto test from 1982 on. See Powell, Geisse, and Jackson, Current Administration of U.S. Antidumping and Countervailing Duty Laws: Implications for Prospective U.S.-Mexico Free Trade Talks, 11 N.W. J. Int. L. & Bus. 177, 237 (1990).

[5] The reasoning underlying this interpretation is that, if a subsidy is used by a wide variety of industries within a country, there will not be a distortion of comparative advantage within that country in favor of the industry whose product(s) is under investigation.

1181

Conclusion

The passage of the 1988 amendment (reflecting Senate view (and Senate Finance Committee report), and rejecting the House view and legislative history[6], together with the CAFC PPG case, means that the two highest domestic authorities (assuming no Supreme Court review) have finally ruled in favor of the practice followed (albeit not perfectly) by Commerce since 1982.

In addition, Commerce recognized that, in the absence of the specificity rule, all government intervention in the economy (including roads, schools, and so on, as well as such broadly spread programs as investment tax credits, all of which are common in the U.S.), could create benefits to their recipients, requiring countervailing duty investigations of all imports.

[6]Conf. Rep. No. 576, 100th Cong., 2d Sess. 587 (1988). See Horlick and Oliver, Antidumping and Countervailing Duty Law Provisions of the Omnibus Trade and Competitiveness Act of 1988, 23 J. World Trade L. 5,9 (1989).

I.L.M. Content Summary

TEXT OF OPINION - I.L.M. Page 1184

[Opinion delivered by Chief Judge Nies]

[Introduction] - I.L.M. Page 1184
[The International Trade Administration (ITA) determined that countervailing duties could not be applied to unprocessed float glass from Mexico, because the benefits derived by its Mexican producer from certain related Mexican programs did not constitute a "bounty or grant" under U.S. law. The Court of International Trade (CIT) upheld the ITA's decision. This is an appeal from the CIT's decision]

1182

I [Excerpts from applicable U.S. law (19 U.S.C. secs. 1303, 1677)] - I.L.M. Page 1184

[According to ITA interpretation, a domestic subsidy must be provided to a "specific enterprise or industry" to be countervailable. According to ITA, the Mexican programs and policies were not directed at the float glass industry]

II Standard of Review - I.L.M. Page 1185

[Deference of courts to an agency's statutory interpretation. The appellant (PPG) has failed to meet its burden of showing that ITA's interpretation is statutorily precluded]

III Requirement of Specificity - I.L.M. Page 1186

[PPG contends that ITA's specificity test exceeds the language of the statute, judicial definitions of "bounty or grant" and legislative intent]

A. [PPG argues that the "bounty or grant" language of the statute should be broadly interpreted. The court finds that ITA's "specificity" requirement is not precluded by the language of the statute and is not unreasonably construed]

B. [PPG argues that judicial precedent requires a broad interpretation. The court examines the cases cited by PPG and finds that they constitute weak authority for PPG's position]

C. [PPG argues that ITA's interpretation is contrary to Congress' intent. The court finds congressional purpose to be more complex than PPG's simplistic position]

D. [PPG argues that ITA's specificity test means that a subsidy will less likely be countervailable the more widespread its benefits. The court responds that such anomaly has been debated, but not resolved, in Congress]

E. [The court concludes that ITA's interpretation is reasonable and must be upheld]

IV [PPG argues that the specificity test is satisfied if recipients of the subsidy are simply "identifiable." The court upholds ITA's test that the subsidy is countervailable only if, in its application, it benefits only a specific enterprise or industry or group of enterprises or industries] - I.L.M. Page 1189

V [PPG argues that the Mexican programs and policies are countervailable under ITA's specificity test] - I.L.M. Page 1190

A. [Description of Mexico's Trust Fund for the Coverage of Exchange Risks (FICORA). The court upholds ITA's findings of fact]

B. [Mexico's] Natural Gas Pricing Policy [Description of the policy. The court uphold's ITA's findings of fact. The court also addresses and rejects PPG's argument, raised on appeal, that "energy-intensive" industries constitute a specific industry]

VI Conclusion - I.L.M. Page 1192

[The court affirms the CIT's decision (upholding ITA's determination)]

[Dissenting opinion delivered by Judge Michel] - I.L.M. Page 1192

[Asserting that: ITA's specificity test has been abrogated by settled law in a 6-year consistent line of CIT cases, starting with Cabot Corp. v. United States; Cabot requires that the effects of a benefit on the foreign enterprise or industry be compared with the effects on all other recipients of the same subsidy; ITA's determination contravenes the clear intent of Congress]

Journal of International Economic Law 13(3), 859–874
doi:10.1093/jiel/jgq043.

WTO SUBSIDIES DISCIPLINE DURING AND AFTER THE CRISIS

Gary N. Horlick and Peggy A. Clarke***

ABSTRACT

This article reviews the successes of the World Trade Organization (WTO) Agreement on Subsidies and Countervailing Measures (the strengthened discipline on export subsidies), and the failures (the lack of discipline on domestic subsidies) from the birth of the WTO in 1995 to the onset of the financial crisis in 2007–09. During the crisis, governments poured money into economically necessary or politically deserving industries. The prohibition on export subsidies held up fairly well during the crisis, but the prohibition on import-substitution subsidies was likely flouted by understandings that bail-outs of industrial companies would lead to use of local supply chains. Trillions of dollars were poured into service sectors, notably financial services and real estate, and there are no WTO rules for services subsidies, notwithstanding commitments to negotiate them in the General Agreement on Trade in Services. Most likely, if there had been any rules disciplining subsidies in the financial services sectors, they would have been ignored, as the disciplines on domestic subsidies for goods were often ignored during the crisis, and before it. The crisis threw into clearer relief the question of why governments agreed to rules in 1994 which they found too uncomfortable to obey, or to enforce against other governments. The Agreement on Subsidies and Countervailing Measures sets up rules which are not strict enough to eliminate the use of countervailing duties as protectionism, and disciplines on subsidies that are too loose to prevent politicians from over-subsidizing. The authors conclude with some thoughts on the future of subsidies disciplines within the WTO.

I. INTRODUCTION

The strengths and weaknesses of the World Trade Organization (WTO) Agreement on Subsidies and Countervailing Measures (SCM Agreement)[1]

* Attorney-at-Law, Law Offices of Gary N. Horlick, Washington, DC; the first Chair of the WTO Permanent Group of Experts. E-mail: gary.horlick@ghorlick.com
** Peggy A. Clarke is a partner, Blank Rome LLP, Washington, DC. E-mail: Clarke-P@BlankRome.com

[1] GATT Secretariat, *The Results of the Uruguay Round of Multilateral Trade Negotiations, the Legal Texts* (Geneva, 1994) 231.

were identifiable before the global financial crisis which erupted in 2007. The crisis highlighted both the strengths and the weaknesses of the SCM Agreement and WTO law, and perhaps paradoxically, will make it more difficult to fix its weaknesses. It also raised issues of whether it was in the interest of the global economy to restrict all manner of goods subsidies or whether, at certain times, certain types of subsidies may be trade enhancing rather than trade distorting.

The massive subsidies to the financial services industry raise a fundamental question about the notion of subsidies and subsidy discipline. One of the great triumphs of the SCM Agreement was the single definition of 'subsidy' hitherto lacking from the 1979 General Agreement on Tariffs and Trade (GATT) Subsidies Code. But politicians, left to their own devices, will tend to over-subsidize and to grant too much protection to domestic producers, through protective measures such as countervailing duties (CVDs). The SCM Agreement sets up rules which are not strict enough to eliminate the use of CVDs as protectionism, and disciplines on subsidies that are too loose to prevent politicians from over-subsidizing. The dynamics for subsidies to services may differ, but negotiators need to examine whether the same tension is likely to emerge.

The SCM Agreement covers trade in goods, and not services.[2] The General Agreement on Trade in Services (GATS), in Article XV, mandates the negotiation of disciplines on subsidies. Much work has been done on a draft agreement on services subsidies,[3] but the Members failed to complete it.[4] The significance of this omission is apparent from the calculation that at least $9.782 *trillion* of the $11.97 trillion in federal crisis relief in the USA alone was provided to services (as much as $7.537 trillion to financial services and $2.25 trillion to home building)[5]—not counting the very low

[2] As the WTO *EC – Bananas* case demonstrates, the same enterprise producing a single good can be providing both a good and a service. See WTO Appellate Body Report, *European Communities – Regime for Importation, Sale and Distribution of Bananas (EC – Bananas)*, WT/DS27/AB/R), adopted 25 September 1997.

[3] See, e.g. Report by the Chairperson of the Working Party on GATS Rules, S/WPGR/10, 30 June 2003 (providing a brief summary of the work done).

[4] The main areas of non-agreement were subsidy definition, modal applications and countervailing mechanisms—but far greater gaps were bridged in negotiating the SCM Agreement, so a more probable explanation is that either there was lack of political will to complete the deal and/or the lack of a 'round' to provide enough tradeoffs and momentum. See Pietro Poretti, *The Regulation of Subsidies within the General Agreement on Trade in Services of the WTO: Problems and Prospects* (Alphen aan den Rijn, Netherlands: Kluwer Law International, 2009). See also papers by Steve Charnovitz and by Panagiotis Delimatsis and Pierre Sauvé, in this issue at 743–761 and 837–857, respectively.

[5] Gary Hufbauer, Luca Rubini and Yee Wong, 'Swamped by Subsidies: Averting a US-EU Trade War after the Great Crisis', Policy Note, 24 July 2009. It should be noted that these numbers are disputed. Others have argued that much of the money included in the calculation by Hufbauer *et al.* would not be considered subsidies by the WTO. 'Do Bailouts For Banks And Detroit Mean Boeing vs. Airbus Should Be Suspended?', Inside U.S. Trade, 5 August 2009.

interest rates that the USA considers countervailable subsidies when allegedly maintained by China.

This raises the interesting question of whether the lack of WTO discipline on subsidies for services during the crisis was a problem or not. And that in turn raises the question of why one wants discipline on subsidies in the WTO.[6] The driving force seems to be a desire to let market forces reward the most efficient producer (of goods and services) without state intervention, although, as we shall see, there are other motives at work as well. We will return soon enough to issues of discipline on subsidies for services. But we will first review the SCM Agreement disciplines on subsidies for goods, the relevance of those disciplines during the crisis and the outlook. We do not discuss here whether the SCM Agreement rules in general are a reasonable approach to subsidies discipline. Sykes has written cogently on the subject.[7]

II. EXISTING SCM AGREEMENT

A. Export subsidies

The most successful WTO subsidy discipline has been the ban (for developed and most developing Members) on export subsidies (except for agriculture). This type of subsidy is considered to be so pernicious that it is prohibited without a complaining Member needing to show any adverse effects. While export subsidies may well be trade-distortive, the impetus for the successful prohibition may owe as much to the widespread use of export subsidies in the past, and to the consequent attraction of a 'seller's cartel' (since the benefit of the subsidy went mainly to foreign purchasers, an agreement by all Members to eliminate them made sense for each country).

This discipline seems to have held up fairly well in the crisis. None of the reported 'crisis measures'[8] seems to be an explicit export subsidy within the meaning of Article 3.1 of the SCM Agreement, although Organisation for Economic Co-operation and Development (OECD) countries as a whole reportedly increased export financing (which would be WTO-consistent) to

[6] The work on services subsidies is not modeled on the subsidies discipline for goods found in the SCM Agreement. Numerous Members have suggested that the definition of a subsidy and the scope of any disciplines provided must be different than that contained in the SCM Agreement with respect to subsidies for goods. They argue for an approach that expands the definition of a subsidy to include certain other forms of government intervention besides a financial contribution. See, e.g. Communication from Chile: The Subsidies Issue, S/WPGR/W/10, 2 April 1996.

[7] Alan O. Sykes, 'The Questionable Case for Subsidies Regulation: A Comparative Perspective', Stanford University School of Law, Law & Economics Research Paper Series, Paper No 380, http://papers.ssrn.com/sol3/papers.cfm?abstract_id=1444605 (visited 29 June 2010).

[8] For analysis and listings of the crisis measures, see Global Trade Alert, http://www.globaltradelert.org (visited 27 August 2010).

try to keep trade flowing. Even before the crisis, the prohibition seemed to be working well, with very few completely new export subsidies, and numerous successful WTO challenges to ones pre-existing the WTO.[9]

The two most obvious exceptions to the discipline had proven to be problems *before* the crisis:

(1) The WTO dispute resolution system has been erratic in detecting *de facto* prohibited export subsidies. In *Australia – Leather*, a loan not explicitly provided as a stimulus to exports was found to be a prohibited export subsidy by a panel because the sales needed to meet the terms of the subsidy eligibility would necessarily include exports,[10] while in *Canada – Aircraft* a government program was found *not* to be a prohibited export subsidy because it was not explicitly tied to exports even though the government knew or should have known that 99% of the final subsidized products would be exported.[11] Footnote 4 SCM to the Agreement notes that the mere fact of exportation does not mean that it was required. That footnote was included to take account of the lack of domestic markets for small countries such that any subsidies would go to production which was predominantly for export. But Canada is neither a small country nor an undiversified economy, so the Appellate Body ruling in *Canada – Aircraft* permits numerous *de facto* export subsidies to escape undisciplined. While such *de facto* considerations may be a feature in some of the crisis measures, they are not readily apparent in any of them, and, in any event, no Member has complained (although that is not the legal standard).[12]

(2) Item (k) of Annex I[13] of the SCM Agreement permits subsidized export credits if they are within the OECD arrangements on export

[9] See WTO Panel Report, *Australia – Subsidies Provided to Producers and Exporters of Automotive Leather (Australia – Leather)*, WT/DS126/R, adopted 16 June 1999; WTO Appellate Body Report, *Brazil – Export Financing Programme for Aircraft (Brazil – Aircraft)*, WT/DS46/AB/R, adopted 20 August 1999; WTO Appellate Body Report, *Canada – Measures Affecting the Export of Civilian Aircraft (Canada – Aircraft)*, WT/DS70/AB/R, adopted 20 August 1999; WTO Appellate Body Report, *USA – Tax Treatment for 'Foreign Sales Corporation' (US – FSC)*, WT/DS108/AB/R, adopted 20 March 2000; and WTO Appellate Body Report, *Canada – Certain Measures Affecting the Automotive Industry (Canada – Autos)*, WT/DS139, 142/AB/R, adopted 19 June 2000.

[10] *Australia – Leather*, above n 9, paras 9.63–9.69. It should be noted that neither party appealed this panel decision for whatever reason.

[11] WTO Appellate Body Report, *Canada – Aircraft – Recourse by Brazil to Article 21.5 of the DSU*, WT/DS70/AB/RW, adopted 4 August 2000, para 49.

[12] The conventional practice in Geneva that 'it must be alright if no one has complained' can be found nowhere in the WTO Agreement.

[13] There may be other flaws lurking in Annex I, which was incorporated from Annex A of the 1979 GATT Subsidy Codes without sufficient changes to prevent conflicts with the 1994 SCM Agreement.

credit financing.[14] The OECD arrangements are a clear example of sellers' cartels agreeing how much can be given away to their customers. The *Brazil – Aircraft* and *Canada – Aircraft* cases (in each of which retaliation has been authorized but not used), at least implicitly, extend item (k)'s Paragraph 2 grandfathering permission to subsidize to non-OECD WTO Members. While this has not been a feature of crisis measures so far, it may become more of a focus if export credit financing is used as a stimulus measure. For example, the USA recently proposed to increase the Export–Import Bank's credit available for small- and medium-sized businesses from the current $4 billion to $6 billion in the next year and to redirect $30 billion in Troubled Asset Relief Program (TARP) loans to small businesses as part of the Administration's export initiative.[15] More troubling is that, as interpreted, item (k) imposes disciplines on any Member that seeks to use export credits, on the basis of terms negotiated by only some of the WTO Members, and that those terms reflect a changing standard.[16] Proposals have been made in the Doha talks to eliminate or modify item (k), although the push behind those proposals (e.g. by Brazil and India) could wane if those countries are permitted to use the item (k) rules and economic circumstances make the same financing terms available to them.

A group of relatively poor developing Members is permitted to use explicit export subsidies in certain circumstances in accordance with Article 27.3 of the SCM Agreement; an exemption which has been extended several times.[17] This has the perverse effect of allowing developing countries to bid against each other in offering subsidies to investors and consumers in developed countries. These poor developing Members, however, are not large traders; therefore, the permission does not have a significant distorting effect on most trade.

[14] See 'The OECD Arrangement on Guidelines for Officially Supported Export Credits', http://www.oecd.org/officialdocuments/displaydocumentpdf/ (visited 29 June 2010).

[15] See Darrell A. Hughes, 'Obama Urges Export-Import Bank to Up Small-Firm Loans', *Wall Street Journal,* 4 February 2010.

[16] *Brazil – Aircraft,* above n 9, paras 7.24–7.33 (found that all countries must meet the OECD standard but that the standard at issue was whatever the OECD had decided at the time the credit was granted, not at the time the WTO was negotiated).

[17] In 2007, because of the continual extensions, the General Council adopted procedures for extensions subject to annual review. See Article 27.4 of the Agreement on Subsidies and Countervailing Measures Decision of 27 July 2007, WT/L/691, 31 July 2007. An annex to this decision lists the countries and specific programs covered by this decision.

B. Import-substitution subsidies

Import-substitution subsidies under Article 3.1(b) of the SCM Agreement had not been the subject of much discussion prior to the crisis.[18] The crisis measures taken in the automotive sector, however, have shone a spotlight on this problem. One leading subsidy practitioner, in an unpublished memorandum written on behalf of a client, claimed that a Member could give subsidies to a manufacturer contingent on producing automobiles within the Member's territory, without thereby running afoul of Article 3.1(b), because the grant would not be contingent on use of domestic inputs.

In *Canada – Autos* the Appellate Body read into Article 3.1(b) of the SCM Agreement a condemnation of *de facto* (as well as explicit, *de jure*) import-substitution subsidies, even though the text contains no such language.[19] (According to one of the drafters, the initial omission of *de facto* was indeed a mistake, but the decision not to correct it prior to signing was deliberate.)[20] The Appellate Body found that a program could violate the Article 3.1(b) prohibition if the value-added content was such that a company *would* need to use at least some domestic goods to meet the content requirement.[21] Some years later, in *US – Foreign Sales Corporation Tax*, Article 21.5 proceedings, the Appellate Body concluded that a government program which conditioned receipt of the benefits on use of domestic value added, even if the value added included services as well as goods, was prohibited under GATT 1994, Article III:4, as long as it created an incentive to use domestic over imported goods.[22]

[18] The *Indonesia – Auto* case arguably dealt with import-substitution subsidies, but the facts of the case were so unusual that the decision has not had much impact. (Indonesia conceded that the local content requirement for eligibility for the subsidy at issue would fall under Article 3.1(b) but argued successfully that Indonesia's status as a developing country meant that the program was not prohibited at that time.) See WTO Panel Report, *Indonesia – Certain Measures Affecting the Automobile Industry (Indonesia – Auto)*, WT/DS54, 55, 59, 64/R, adopted 23 July 1998. In addition, the *Canada – Autos* case also addressed import-substitution subsidies; however, the facts did not permit a full analysis of the issue (because the Appellate Body reversed a finding of the Panel that the law at issue did not involve an import-substitution subsidy and, in so doing, found that the Panel had not provided enough factual analysis to enable the Appellate Body to decide the issue). See *Canada – Autos*, above n 9. In the *US – Upland Cotton* case, the Appellate Body agreed with the Panel that because Step 2 payments were made only to consumers of domestic cotton, they constituted import-substitution subsidies prohibited under SCM Agreement, Article 3.1(b) and that the prohibition extended to products falling under the Agreement on Agriculture. See: WTO Appellate Body Report, *USA – Subsidies on Upland Cotton (US – Upland Cotton)*, WT/DS267/AB/R, adopted 21 March 2005.

[19] *Canada – Autos*, above n 9, para 143.

[20] Interview by Gary Horlick with one of the people most involved with the drafting.

[21] Ibid.

[22] WTO Appellate Body Report, *USA – Tax Treatment for 'Foreign Sales Corporations' – Recourse to Article 21.5 of the DSU by the European Communities' (US – FSC Art. 21.5)*, WT/DS108/AB/RW, adopted 29 January 2002, paras 220–22.

The spotlight on import-substitution was intensified in 2009 when President Sarkozy of France appeared to condition receipt of French government funds by French auto companies on their keeping auto plants in France open while closing them elsewhere.[23] The appearance of this conditional receipt, however, led to an outcry in the EU and potential scrutiny from the European Commission for consistency with state aid measures.[24] Similarly, in the negotiations leading up to both the US and Japanese cash-for-clunkers programs, efforts were made to limit the beneficiaries to domestically-produced cars, although both such efforts were generally defeated in the final programs.[25] In this context, it is worth noting that Article III:8 of GATT 1994 excludes national treatment and permits the payment of direct subsidies to domestic producers only. Such actions are not prohibited unless they require something (such as local content rules) which may violate the prohibition of import-substitution subsidies or rules on investment.[26] Thus, conditioning payments on a commitment to maintain local employment would not appear to be prohibited. A requirement to keep domestic production facilities open is more troubling; the larger the Member, the more likely that local physical inputs will be used, arguably triggering the prohibition of Article 3.1(b) of the SCM Agreement.

The use of overt import-substitution subsidies has been relatively limited in the economic crisis, with most taking the form of 'buy national' provisions in more general subsidies, which may or may not violate the import-substitution subsidy prohibitions.[27] Such provisions may be disciplined in other contexts.[28] Members that have joined the Government Procurement Agreement are constrained in the 'buy national' provisions they can enact. For example, the regulations implementing the American Recovery and Reinvestment Act specifically exempt from the 'Buy America' provisions

[23] See, e.g. 'Volvo Group Balks at Conditions Tied to French Aid to Renault Trucking Subsidiary', BNA Daily Report for Executives, 12 February 2009; 'Renault Agrees to Maintain Partial Production of Clio in France', 17 January 2010, http://www.France24.com (visited 23 April 2010).

[24] On EU disciplines see paper by Marsden and Kokkoris in this volume.

[25] See, e.g. 'Japan Changes Its Cash-For-Clunkers Program To Allow In U.S. Autos', Inside U.S. Trade, 19 January 2010; Press Release, 'Ambassador Bruton Urges Congress to Refrain from Discrimination in Car Scrappage Legislation', 22 April 2009, http://www.insidetrade.com (visited 23 April 2010).

[26] See SCM Agreement, Article 3.1(b) and Agreement on Trade-Related Investment Measures Annex, para 1(a).

[27] See, e.g. Global Trade Alert at http://www.globaltradealert.org (visited 27 August 2010).

[28] Even if measures do not violate SCM Agreement, Article 3.1(b), they may violate the national treatment requirements of GATT 1994, Article III:4 if they create a preference for the use of domestic goods over imported goods. See ibid, at paras 220–22.

the goods and services of countries with which the USA has relevant treaty obligations (such as members of the Government Procurement Agreement).[29] Nonetheless, even if not prohibited, such buy-national provisions could give rise to actionable subsidies. China, in its recent final CVD decision on *Grain-Oriented Electrical Steel from the USA* found that the 'Buy America' provision in various US laws requiring the use of US-produced iron and steel provided a countervailable subsidy because it enabled the US producers to charge the government above-market prices for the steel.[30]

C. Domestic subsidies

Most subsidies are domestic subsidies, i.e. measures that are neither contingent on exportation nor on the use of domestic over imported goods. The purpose of such domestic subsidies is to support production within a country either by supporting the production of the goods or by increasing the demand for such goods. Despite the thousands of pages listing subsidies reported by the Members collectively pursuant to Article 25.4 of the SCM Agreement, there have been very few cases addressing such subsidies, notably *US – Upland Cotton* (which implicates the Agreement on Agriculture). The most recent cases involving such domestic/production subsidies are the pending *US – Large Civil Aircraft* and *EC – Large Civil Aircraft* cases,[31] which will fill in a lot of the blanks on domestic production subsidies. Where domestic subsidies have been addressed in the context of disputes involving CVD proceedings, they have focused on the definitional aspects of subsidies such as the nature of financial contribution, entrustment and direction, the recipient of the benefit and the measure of benefits.[32]

Unlike export and import-substitution subsidies, harmful trade effects are not presumed by domestic subsidies and must be demonstrated by anyone challenging the existence of such actionable subsidies. Perhaps, this is because subsidies are widely recognized as a useful and popular tool of governments for distribution of money. Thus, there is little or no impetus to ban

29 *Requirements for Implementing Sections 1512, 1605, and 1606 of the American Recovery and Reinvestment Act of 2009 for Financial Assistance Awards – Interim Final Guidance,* 2 C.F.R. Part 176, 74 US Federal Register 18449ff, 23 April 2009.

30 Notice dated 12 April 2010, in Chinese at http://gpj.mofcom.gov.cn/aarticle/c/201004/20100406864469.html (visited 27 August 2010). The USA may challenge this in the WTO.

31 Request for Establishment of a Panel, *USA – Measures Affecting Trade in Large Civil Aircraft,* WT/DSC317, 8 December 2006; WTO Panel Report, *European Communities – Measures Affecting Trade in Large Civil Aircraft,* WT/DS316/R, 30 June 2010, appealed 21 July 2010.

32 For example, WTO Panel Report, *Mexico – Definitive Countervailing Measures on Olive Oil from the European Communities,* WT/DS341/R, adopted 21 October 2008; WTO Appellate Body Report, *Japan – Countervailing Duties on Dynamic Random Access Memories from Korea,* WT/DS336/AB/R, adopted 17 December 2007; WTO Appellate Body Report, *USA – Final Countervailing Duty Determination With Respect To Certain Softwood Lumber From Canada,* WT/DS257/AB/R, adopted 17 February 2004; WTO Appellate Body Report, *USA – Countervailing Measures Concerning Certain Products from the European Communities,* WT/DS212/AB/R, adopted 8 January 2003.

such subsidies or even to curtail their use.[33] Nevertheless, long-term use of such subsidies is likely to distort trade by preventing the closure of inefficient production facilities and leading to overcapacity. The SCM Agreement provides discipline by enabling action if trade harm can be demonstrated. That action may be multilateral in the context of a WTO challenge on the grounds that the subsidies are causing serious prejudice to another Member's interests or it may be unilateral through the imposition of CVDs (CVDs may also be imposed to address harm caused by export and import-substitution subsidies—but again, a showing of injury is required). Action has mostly been unilateral through the imposition of CVDs, with little evidence that these duties led to a withdrawal of domestic subsidies (logically, that would only occur if the exporter sold 100% of the subsidized production in the country imposing the CVD).

When the SCM Agreement first entered into force, it contained provisions reflecting Members' desires to provide different disciplines for different types of subsidies. Hence, Article 6.1 SCM of the Agreement defined certain types of subsidies for which serious prejudice was presumed, but unlike the prohibition on export and import-substitution subsidies, that presumption was rebuttable. They were:

- where the total *ad valorem* subsidization[34] exceeded 5% of the company's income;
- subsidies to cover operating losses sustained by an industry;
- subsidies to cover operating losses sustained by an enterprise, other than one-time, non-recurrent measures designed to provide time to develop long-term solutions and to avoid acute social problems; and
- direct forgiveness of debt.

The SCM Agreement also provided that three types of subsidies were not actionable, i.e. there was a non-rebuttable presumption that the subsidies led to no trade harm (or at least that the benefits of these actions outweighed any trade harm caused). Thus, as long as the subsidy met the criteria in Article 8, subsidies for research and development, regional development and to comply with environmental laws were not actionable. However, these provisions (both the rebuttable presumption of serious prejudice and the irrebuttable presumption of no harm) were controversial and were implemented on a trial basis for five years. Although no disputes arose under either provision, in the aftermath of the Seattle Ministerial, the provisions

[33] The EU has a highly developed internal discipline on subsidies, through Directorate General for Competition. The USA and most other nations have little or no discipline.

[34] These subsidies were also to be measured using a different standard than that applied in other contexts. Annex IV provides that the total ad valorem subsidization was to be measured as a cost to the government, rather than the benefit to the recipient standard used in other contexts under the SCM Agreement.

868 *Journal of International Economic Law (JIEL) 13(3)*

were allowed to lapse (if they had not lapsed, the Article 6.1 presumption might have had a great impact on agricultural trade—and Doha negotiations—with the lapse of the 'peace clause' in the Agreement on Agriculture).[35]

III. WHAT IS TO BE DONE?

We do not propose to fight the last war by suggesting disciplines on subsidies based on specific stimulus or bail-out packages. The next crisis will not mirror the past. Therefore, this section discusses possible subsidy disciplines for the general categories—subsidies on goods including export subsidies, import-substitution subsidies and domestic subsidies and subsidies on services—which we hope will advance subsidy discipline, whatever the future holds.

A. Export subsidies

As discussed above, export subsidies seem to be well disciplined. While there may be some discussion about when a *de facto* export subsidy occurs, in general, export subsidies are not widely used. The discipline appears to have held up so far during the crises and countries have rarely resorted to such subsidies. Therefore, perhaps no immediate changes to the export regime are required. Nevertheless, it would behoove Members to resolve the issues of item (k)—by extending its protections to all Members and ensuring that all Members have a say in the terms (or, perhaps, by deleting it).

B. Import subsidies

As discussed above, while the crisis has certainly led to national preferences to keep subsidies within their borders, there has been little use of explicit import-substitution subsidies. Years from now, it may prove that there was considerable use of *de facto* import-substitution, but so far peer pressure has prevented the most visible abuses. Because the extent of any such use is not now known, it is difficult to determine whether current levels of discipline are sufficient. Thus, more information is needed before deciding whether new or alternative disciplines should be adopted. One minor change would be to explicitly add *de facto* import-substitution to the SCM Agreement, Article 3 prohibition. Members may also wish to consider further disciplining the payment of subsidies to domestic producers to eliminate requirements

[35] The non-decision to allow Articles 6.1 and 8 to lapse through inertia was not well thought out. This outcome could have been avoided by making the lapse depend on 'reverse consensus' or something less than lapse based on one Member's objection.

that productive facilities be retained in one country at the expense of productive facilities in another.

C. Domestic subsidies

Perhaps not surprisingly, the most common type of measure taken to address the economic crisis was a domestic subsidy—although in many different forms, such as tax breaks, direct investment in failing companies, low-interest or no-interest loans, provisions of funds and incentives to purchasers to buy these items (e.g. cash-for-clunkers programs). Nevertheless, the use of such stimulus money was lopsided. Only the wealthier economies could afford to provide significant subsidies to their manufacturing sector (or to their services sector for that matter), thus the use of large domestic subsidies in this crisis was largely limited to the developed countries and a few of the emerging economies.

The domestic subsidy area, therefore, should be the focus of any reforms. Within the area of domestic subsidies, as discussed above, the Members in the SCM Agreement tried the experience of creating deep-amber (Article 6.1) and green-lighted (Article 8) subsidies. A return to this approach might work well, although the criteria and specific subsidies should be revised to reflect additional experiences.

As part of the ongoing Doha negotiations, the USA presented a proposal for new prohibited subsidies,[36] and then approximately one year later presented a revised proposal—which contained many changes largely reversing the initial proposal.[37] The US proposal's obvious attempt to avoid condemning those subsidies if they do not 'increase capacity' was no doubt spurred by the desire of the USA to insulate its 'emergency' loans to steel companies in the USA, which total several hundred million dollars.[38] We are aware of no

[36] Paper from the USA, 'Expanding the Prohibited "Red Light" Subsidy Category', TN/RL/GEN, 16 January 2006. The USA proposed to prohibit the Article 6.1 'dark-amber' subsidies and urged Members to expand the prohibitions still further to include other items, such as government equity investments in companies with poor financial prospects unable to attract commercial financing ('unequityworthy' in US countervailing duty parlance). The EU responded by indicating reluctance to address new issues through prohibition and that any new disciplines should focus on the actual trade effects of the measure, rather than presumed trade effects. Submission of the European Communities, 'Subsidies', TN/RL/GEN/135, 24 April 2006.

[37] Proposal from the USA, 'Expanding the Prohibited "Red Light" Subsidy Category Draft Text', TN/RL/GEN/146, 5 June 2007. This paper eliminated the prohibition on subsidies exceeding 5% *ad valorem* and when subsidies were made for 'prudential reasons pursuant to laws and regulations of general application, including the protection of investors, depositors, policy holders or persons to whom a fiduciary duty is owed by a financial service supplier, or to ensure the integrity and stability of the financial system.' This latter change appears remarkably prescient in light of the steps the USA took in late 2008 and throughout 2009.

[38] This concept that the effect on capacity is relevant contradicts the position long-taken by the US Department of Commerce in countervailing duty cases, wherein the Department countervails subsidies provided to close facilities and reduce capacity. See, e.g. *Carbon Steel Products from the United Kingdom*, 47 U.S. Federal Register 39384, 39392 (Department

other examples in the USA at the time of the proposal where there was a subsidy of the type that the USA proposed to prohibit, although there may be a few. In short, the USA proposed to maintain the ability of industrialized countries to subsidize 'sunset' industries, even if those companies are uncreditworthy, unequityworthy or running losses. Typically, the big subsidies in the USA are for companies building new plants, mostly provided at the state level, such as the competition that went on between Louisiana and Alabama to subsidize a new $3 billion steel mill. Because these are start-ups, none of them would have losses or appear uncreditworthy (with the obvious exceptions of the recent investments in General Motors and Chrysler, US governments do not make equity investments in manufacturing companies). Finally, the failure of the USA to propose a prohibition on subsidies greater than 5% (as exists in Article 6.1, SCM Agreement) may reflect the USA understanding that such a prohibition would hit the USA agricultural programs if the USA does not succeed in obtaining a 'peace clause' or other carve-out options for agriculture.

Subsidies, however, can be an effective tool of economic and fiscal policy in times of extreme economic stress. Economists also recognize that subsidies can be used to encourage behavior when the external costs of a desired behavior are so great as to discourage this behavior in the absence of such incentives. Therefore, any reform should also include a new group of green-lighted subsidies. We suggest that the following may make sense given the world's experience in recent years.

- R&D: Research and development is an area where some incentives could be useful because R&D can be so expensive that a company cannot expect to recover the costs. Therefore, companies invest less in R&D than is desirable. Thus, some form of carve-out for a limited level of R&D subsidy may be useful, but any such provision should be better drafted than the default language of Article 8 of the SCM Agreement, to try to avoid subsidizing research that would occur anyhow.
- Regional development: Many poorer developing countries experience extreme disparities in the costs of investment in different regions of the country and extreme variations in income and employment opportunities in those same areas. Therefore, some form of carve-out for regional development subsidies, perhaps limited to the developing country Members defined in Annex VII, would be likely to benefit trade flows.
- Natural disaster recovery: In recent years the world has experienced numerous natural disasters of such magnitude that recovery from

Commerce, 7 September 1982) (finding funds used for plant closures and redundancies still benefited company as a whole; impact on capacity was not relevant to subsidy analysis).

them requires extraordinary investment.[39] In crafting such a provision, the Members would need to find a method of determining which disasters are so large as to require such special treatment and when the recovery period had ended. Any such carve-out should be narrowly crafted (if possible) to permit subsidies to restore what was destroyed, rather than to expand capacity or modernize functioning but obsolete production facilities. Such recovery subsidies should also only be permitted for a limited period after a disaster (subsidies are notoriously difficult to end once provided, even if the original reason for the subsidy has ceased to apply).

- Environmental: The Article 8 provision on environmental subsidies was broad based and provided little discipline, covering as it did up to 20% of the cost of adapting to new environmental regulations.[40] However, as with R&D, environmental measures can have large externalities such that subsidies could be effective in encouraging environmental investment without distorting trade. The provision should not be the existing Article 8 provision. Any provision should not undermine the 'polluter pays' concept. If exceptions to polluter pays are to be permitted, the exceptions should be narrowly defined. Another possible area for agreement on environmental subsidies is where those subsidies arise from explicit action agreed upon by virtually all WTO Members—defined as representing more than 95% (or more, but less than 100%) of the world's trade[41]—such as a global climate change agreement.
- Small: In practical terms, small subsidies will not have much effect, so subsidies below a certain *de minimis* level (1, 2 or 3%?) could be ignored as not having much effect, or as being 'washed out' by other factors, such as currency fluctuations, while subsidies above that level should be disciplined much more than they are now. The vestiges of this idea are reflected in the now-defunct provisions of SCM Agreement, Article 6.1(a), providing for a 'presumption of serious prejudice' for subsidies in excess of 5% of value.[42]

[39] For example, the 2004 tsunami, Hurricane Katrina, and the recent earthquakes in Haiti and Chile.

[40] This provision was the result of a last-minute proposal by Mexico (drawn from a 1989 EC proposal). See Gary N. Horlick and Peggy A. Clarke, 'The 1994 WTO Subsidies Agreement', 17(4) World Competition 41 (1994), at 47 and n 34.

[41] We suggest an extreme definition of 'virtually all' because the actions should be universally agreed. However, we suggest that it requires less than 100% of trade because one extremely small country should not be able to control global environmental policy through the exercise of a veto.

[42] This should not be confused with the negligibility concept already found in SCM Agreement, Articles 11.9 and 27(b). A good argument can be made that imports below a certain level should not be the subject of CVD cases (0.5% of market share?), especially for developing countries. Some very low level of market share is so unlikely to cause injury—especially if split among many companies—that those companies should not have to pay the cost of defense of a case, nor be subject to duties. Therefore, a properly drafted 'negligibility' exception should

We do not propose a green-light category for subsidies in times of extreme financial crisis because we consider it unlikely that one could be sufficiently narrowly crafted (through temporal restrictions and/or a definition of what would be considered an adequate economic downturn) to avoid creating such a large loophole as to eliminate any effective discipline on domestic subsidies. Perhaps the solution for 'crisis subsidies' is a procedural one, using the SCM Agreement Committee or Permanent Group of Experts to approve time-limited, specific subsidy proposals on an emergency basis (i.e. quickly) during a crisis such as occurred in late 2008 and early 2009, with an EU-style prohibition on any subsidies not notified.

D. Subsidies to services

In an economic crisis created by a failure of liquidity in the financial sector, most major economies intervened with substantial money infusions into their banking and financial services sectors. Many economists considered that such intervention prevented the crisis from deepening still further into a widespread, long-term depression.[43] Thus, there may be a benefit to permitting intervention in financial services, at a minimum. However, such permission would have to be narrowly constrained or there would continue to be no discipline on subsidies to services. While the Members have been unable to agree to subsidy disciplines for services, some form of discipline should be concluded. Services continue to account for a growing portion of world trade, and subsidies can be as disruptive and distortive in the services sectors as they are in trade in goods. Any subsidy discipline, however, would have to be coordinated with the regulatory rules and have 'prudential' carve-outs.[44] Subsidies also need to be taken into account in constructing

be included. This is particularly the case for developing country exporters. Such a provision was included in the 'Dunkel' draft of the Agreement on the Implementation of Art. VI GATT (Anti-Dumping Agreement), but negotiators, pushed by the USA, Australia and the EU, rather strangely agreed on the bizarre provision found in Article 5.8 of the current Anti-Dumping Agreement that an exporter with less than 3% of *import share* is excluded *ex ante*—unless other countries with less than 3% of import share collectively have 7% of import share. This creates a very strong incentive to add as many small countries as possible to the case, thus forcing more and more small exporters to defend themselves. It also means that product markets with low import penetration, and thus arguably needing less protection, are more easily made a site for CVD cases, because 3% of the total imports will be low, while for markets with high import penetration, 3% of total imports will be quite high, and, thus, imports below the 3% will also be quite high.

43 See, e.g. IMF, World Economic Outlook, October 2009, at 1; 'Chapter 3: Market Interventions During the Financial Crisis: How Effective and How to Disengage?', in IMF, Global Financial Stability Report, October 2009.

44 This would be an example of the difficulty of untangling the 'real' amount of the 'net' subsidy from the 'gross' subsidy (although the US Department of Commerce tried to do so in CVD cases until it became politically unpopular in 1983). Bank 'bail-outs' are part of a package, which can include costly capital and other regulatory controls—and also rock-bottom interest rates, which can transfer money from savers to banks. See Sykes, above n 7, at 24.

new international financial regulations, e.g. derogations from regulations could well have the same effect as a subsidy.

As with subsidies on goods, it may be worth examining different types of subsidies to different services industries and determining if some are obviously harmful to trade and should be prohibited or if there is a class where harm can be presumed subject to rebuttal. It may also be possible to enable the use of certain types of subsidies in extreme economic situations, subject to time constraints and a need for prior notice so that other countries have the opportunity to argue either that the economic situation does not give rise to the exception on normal disciplines or that the type of subsidy proposed is unnecessarily trade restrictive.

Several Members have provided proposals that examine the nature of services and define subsidies differently from the way it is done with respect to goods, given the different nature of services and service commitments (and given experience with the definitions of the SCM Agreement). The proposals define government actions that may not involve a 'financial contribution' in the SCM Agreement sense as a subsidy.[45] They also suggest carve-outs for subsidies provided for certain policy goals as opposed to ones that afford an artificial competitive advantage.

We suggest that one area of focus for such carve-outs be services aimed at advancing the economic development of the least developed countries. For example, it may be that certain service sectors are critical to the development of an economic infrastructure such that their advancement would expand, rather than distort trade. Service sectors that come to mind include: logistics services, capital markets, and communication services. Nonetheless, any such carve-out must be carefully crafted to avoid discriminating against potential investors or otherwise creating distortions.

IV. CONCLUSION

While recent reactions to the global financial crisis raised some issues, in the main subsidy discipline held, although the long-term effects of the stimulus packages are still to be determined. Nevertheless, there are weaknesses to subsidy discipline, some highlighted by the crisis, others widely acknowledged prior to the crisis, which should be reduced or eliminated.

Most obviously, an effort should be made to repair the flaws, which have become apparent in the SCM Agreement disciplines on export subsidies (to make sure the discipline is not evaded by larger Members giving 'non-export subsidies' for production, 99% of which is known to be exported), import-substitution subsidies (such as subsidies to keep open those factories that will

[45] See, e.g. Communication from Chile: 'The Subsidies Issue', S/WPGR/W/10, 2 April 1996; Report by the Chairperson on the Working Party on GATS Rules, 'Negotiations on Subsidies', S/WPGR/10, 30 June 2003.

be likely to use local parts) and 'domestic subsidies' (where better calibration is needed of what disciplines should be applied). Beyond the text, a deeper reconsideration of the economics of subsidies disciplines (such as the questions raised by Sykes) and the political economic issues raised by the tension between the need for some—but different—disciplines on both subsidies and CVDs is called for.

PART III
Other Trade Issues

Part III. Other Trade Issues

The third group of papers reflects other challenges to the WTO that I have encountered in recent years. Almost certainly the most important is climate change. I have written very little on it, for fear of taking certain positions I (or future clients) might regret! The short article included here is my 2009 testimony to the US Senate Finance Committee. It was requested by the Senate staff and represents some common-sense thinking which was swept aside by the complicated politics of passing legislation in the US — which in any event was not passed. At bottom, climate change is an extreme challenge to global governance since each of the world's approximately seven billion inhabitants contributes in different amounts and ways to climate change, and each benefits (or suffers), again in different ways and amounts from climate change. It is not at all clear where or how to reconcile all those people's interests, and that is before taking into account people not yet born, who may be the most impacted.

Trade has many environmental benefits, as a way of both improving the efficiency of inputs, notably including energy, and also providing a means of (with help) accurately transmitting costs, including that of energy and emissions. An unusual coalition seeks to use trade barriers as a means to "advance" environmental goals, some as a disguised form of protection for uncompetitive industries, and others out of a sincere opposition to increased consumption (which is hardly a saleable proposition to poor and developing countries, or as a way to get votes for imposing environmental costs domestically). These efforts have to be opposed, while at the same time recognizing that a number of WTO rules will have to be modified in some way if climate change is an over-riding priority (such as permitting certain limited forms of subsidization to "kick start" renewable energy). Perhaps the best way to achieve this is an overall agreement on climate change, which can then be the subject of a WTO "waiver" to the extent necessary to comply with that agreement. This could also be done by amendment of the WTO, but that is more difficult within the WTO structure. Probably the worst solution is to let this be decided in dispute settlement cases. The WTO Appellate Body has so far shown itself unfortunately willing to defer to unilateral action by large, developed countries (see *US — Shrimp/Turtles*), and that may become only more complicated as China acquires similar market power (something the US should have given some thought to in the *Shrimp/Turtles* case).

Preferential trade agreements ("PTAs") are another problem for the WTO. While GATT Article XXIV:8 permits them within certain tight limitations, those limitations have been pretty much ignored since they were written, with the result that non-WTO trade may be more the norm than otherwise. As of this writing, only nine countries (the US, Canada, Australia, New Zealand, Japan, and a few others) pay WTO-level duties in the European Union, the world's largest market for customs purposes — and the EU is contemplating PTAs with Canada, Japan, the US and possibly others.

The most important limitation in Article XXIV is that "substantially all trade" be liberalized. The people drafting this were well aware of the numerous exceptions to the tariff-only rule in GATT, and required that "other restrictive regulations" also be removed. This has been completely ignored, and only very few regional trade agreements completely eliminate antidumping (the EU, Australia–New Zealand, Canada–Chile (purely as a demonstration project, since there has never been an antidumping case either way) and a few others). With my co-author, Angela Gobbi, we are, as far as I can tell, the only article to point out the need to eliminate antidumping in such agreements ("Mandatory Abolition of Anti-dumping, Countervailing Duties and Safeguards in Customs Unions and Free Trade Areas Constituted between WTO Members: Revisiting a Long-standing Discussion in Light of the Appellate Body's *Turkey–Textiles* Ruling"). The text is plain, and the intent perhaps even more important — the drafters would not have said that all tariffs must be eliminated if an unlimited quantity of antidumping duties can be imposed.

This is in many respects a subset — although the most important! — of the ongoing skirmishes between those who want standards to be used as import barriers for a variety of purposes, nefarious and otherwise, against those who seek to require a scientific basis for any such barriers (with the not-so-hidden goal of uniformity to improve commercial opportunities, lower costs and so on).

7

WTO Dispute Settlement from the Perspective of Developing Countries

Gary N. Horlick and Katherine Fennell

The law, in its majestic equality, forbids rich and poor alike to sleep under bridges, beg in the streets or steal bread.

Anatole France (1844–1924), *The Red Lily*, chap. 7 (1894)

I. INTRODUCTION

The balance between developed and developing countries in the international trade regime has been a matter of great concern since the inception of the World Trade Organization (WTO). As the WTO's foundational document, the Marrakech Agreement, states, "there is need for positive efforts designed to ensure that developing countries, and especially the least developed among them, secure a share in the growth in international trade commensurate with the needs of their economic development."[1] Mediating between the interests of developed and developing countries in the WTO has been a constant struggle, as highlighted most recently by the continued stalling of the Doha Round over issues such as agriculture and services.[2]

In light of these continued struggles, the question of whether the world trading system in its current form benefits or disadvantages developing countries has been the subject of considerable controversy. Historically, there has been much debate over whether free trade fosters economic development. In the 1960s and 1970s, numerous scholars advocated protectionist policies for developing countries on the basis of the belief that these countries were exploited in the world economy and that international trade only perpetuated developing countries' specialization in primary

[1] Marrakech Agreement, Preamble, available at: http://www.wto.org/english/docs_e/legal_e/04-wto_e.htm, accessed August 29, 2009.

[2] See, e.g., "EU and U.S. Try to Rekindle Trade Talks," *New York Times*, January 24, 2008.

This chapter is based in part on G. Horlick and N. Mizulin, "Developing Countries and WTO Dispute Settlement" (2005) 23 *Integration & Trade Journal* 125–133.

commodities and thereby stymied their economic development.[3] Many developing countries followed this advice during those decades and instituted high tariffs and import substitution models to encourage development. As these policies failed in many countries, however, countries increasingly began to move away from this model and embrace the benefits of trade. Although some scholars still espouse the view that high tariffs are better for economic development, most economists and trade practitioners today agree that trade liberalization in fact encourages economic growth, and they point to the results of trade liberalization policies in numerous developing countries over the past two decades to bolster this claim.[4]

Even assuming support for the benefits of trade liberalization for economic development, however, there is still a great deal of debate about the structure of the world trading system and of institutions such as the WTO. As Kent Jones noted, "the theoretical benefits of trade do not necessarily imply that WTO membership has always done an adequate or sufficient job of promoting economic development in poor countries."[5] Although development concerns have not been ignored in the WTO, as evidenced by the special and differential treatment given to developing countries, there are some scholars who believe that development concerns should assume an even higher profile in the WTO. One such scholar, Dani Rodrik, stated, "[t]he problem with current trade rules is not that they over-emphasize trade and growth at the expense of poverty reduction, but that they over-emphasize trade at the expense of poverty reduction *and* growth."[6] There are others who criticize the rules-based nature of the WTO.[7] Robert Howse, arguing that it is no longer possible to ignore the lack of a clear demarcation between what belongs inside the world trading system and what belongs outside, advocated dismantling some of the WTO structures and allowing for a "genuine transnational democratic deliberation" to restructure the trading system.[8]

The WTO Dispute Settlement Mechanism, one of the most significant developments in the WTO, is also the subject of debate with regard to the position of

[3] See D. Irwin, *Free Trade under Fire* (2nd ed., Princeton, NJ: Princeton University Press, 2005) 160. See also F. H. Cardoso and E. Faletto, *Dependencia y Desarrollo en America Latina: Ensayo de Interpretación Sociológica* (Mexico City: Siglo Veintiuno Editores, 1969); and R. Prebisch, *Change and Development – Latin America's Great Task: Report Submitted to the Inter-American Development Bank* (New York: Praeger, 1971).

[4] See K. Jones, *Who's Afraid of the WTO?* (New York: Oxford University Press, 2004), p. 147; Irwin (2005), supra note 3, p. 161 (noting that countries that have pursued trade liberalization have experienced greater economic development and have not been trapped into producing only raw materials).

[5] Jones (2004), supra note 4, p. 148.

[6] See D. Rodrik, "The Global Governance of Trade: As If Development Really Mattered," background paper to the United Nations Development Programme project on Trade and Sustainable Human Development (New York, October 2001), p. 6.

[7] See, e.g., R. Howse, "From Politics to Technocracy – and Back Again: The Fate of the Multilateral Trading Regime" (2002) 96 *American Journal of International Law* 94; D. Trubek and M. P. Cottrell, "Robert Hudec and the Theory of International Economic Law: The Law of Global Space," in C. Thomas and J. Trachtman (eds.), *Developing Countries in the WTO Legal System* (New York: Oxford University Press, 2009), pp. 143–146.

[8] Howse (2002), supra note 7, pp. 108–109, 113–117.

developing countries in the world trading system. Although those, like Howse, who take issue with the rules-based nature of the WTO, see the dispute settlement mechanism as one of the more rigid and potentially objectionable aspects of the system,[9] many scholars see the rules-based dispute settlement system as particularly beneficial for developing countries.[10] The binding nature of the dispute settlement mechanism allows developing countries to address WTO violations when they might not otherwise have the political or economic power to challenge developed countries, such as the United States and the European Union (EU).[11] Eduardo Perez Motta, chairman of the Mexican Federal Competition Commission and former ambassador of the Permanent Mission of Mexico to the WTO, asserted that "developing, and especially least developed countries are going to benefit more from a strong and solid dispute settlement mechanism."[12]

Whatever the theory, in practice developing countries face greater difficulties in bringing cases and enforcing rulings in the WTO dispute settlement system. Although in theory it would appear that the system offers developing countries equal opportunity, in practice there has been an imbalance in access to WTO dispute settlement. This chapter explores (a) the causes of this imbalance, (b) how recent developments in the world economy and shifts in the economic balance of power among nations might affect this imbalance, and (c) how this imbalance could be addressed.

II. CAUSES OF THE IMBALANCE

The imbalance in WTO dispute settlement has several causes. First, developing countries often lack the resources to participate in the litigation. Second, they may lack leverage to enforce the WTO rulings. Third, there are high indirect costs to bringing a WTO dispute that often act as a deterrent for developing countries.

Notably, the extent to which these causes affect a given developing country often depends on its size and its level of development. Much of the debate about the treatment of developing countries in the WTO fails to differentiate between middle-income and least developed countries. Particularly in the context of dispute settlement, the barriers to participation for developing countries have been disproportionately higher for the smallest, least developed countries. Although there is an imbalance in access more generally for developing countries, it is important to

[9] Ibid., 113.

[10] See J. Jackson, W. Davey, and A. Sykes, *Legal Problems of International Economic Relations: Cases, Materials and Text* (5th ed., St. Paul, MN: Thomson/West, 2008), pp. 336–337.

[11] See, e.g., Jones (2004), supra note 4, p. 150; Jackson, Davey, and Sykes (2008), supra note 10.

[12] Eduardo Perez Motta, chairman, Mexican Federal Competition Commission, former ambassador of the Permanent Mission of Mexico to the WTO, panel remarks at the American Society of International Law Centennial Regional Meeting: International Trade Under Rule of Law (March 23, 2006), in Occasional Papers, Dean Rusk Center, University of Georgia School of Law, Andre Barbric, ed., p. 47; see also Jones (2004), supra note 4, p. 150 ("the DSU gives all countries their day in court, a fair hearing of their case, and a decision by an independent panel of judges").

differentiate among the diverse developing countries and to recognize that there are certain so-called developing countries that have made greater use of WTO dispute settlementthan others.

Perhaps the most prominent group of developing countries – Brazil, Russia, India, and China, the so-called BRICs – present an interesting subset of larger, more economically potent developing countries that approach WTO dispute settlement in different ways.[13] Brazil, in many ways, is the exception to the tendency of developing countries to participate less in WTO dispute settlement; some would argue that Brazil in fact makes the greatest (and best) use of the WTO dispute settlement mechanism. India, although not as active as Brazil, has become an increasingly prominent player in the dispute settlement system. China, which only joined the WTO in 2001, has been reluctant to bring cases in WTO but in 2007–2010 filed several important cases against both the United States and the EU. Russia's interaction with the WTO in general has been the most hesitant, with accession talks still ongoing. The more active participation of these developing countries compared with others in the WTO dispute settlement system coincides with their higher economic power and the possibility of obtaining full benefits from their formal developing-country status under the WTO-covered agreements, regardless of their actual level of economic development, which is substantially higher than that of the rest of the developing world.[14]

In this section, we explore three main causes of the imbalance in access to the WTO dispute settlement: lack of resources, lack of leverage to enforce WTO rulings, and high indirect costs of bringing a dispute. In doing so, we differentiate between smaller, least developed countries and larger, more economically potent countries, using the BRICs as our primary examples for the latter.

A. *Lack of Resources*

Developing countries that consider bringing a WTO dispute face a disadvantage in terms of resources. The two largest developed WTO Members, the United States and the EU, by virtue of having the largest economies also tend to have the largest number of WTO disputes. Because both the United States and the EU can foresee that they will have a large and continuing number of WTO disputes, each is in a position to hire specialized lawyers in relatively large numbers on an ongoing

[13] Two Goldman Sachs economists coined the term "BRIC" in a 2003 paper. See D. Wilson and R. Purushotha, *Dreaming with the BRICs: The Path to 2050*, Goldman Sachs Global Economics Paper No. 99 (New York, 2003). Sometimes South Africa is included in this subset, and the group is referred to instead as the BRICS.

[14] For a further explanation on the different categories of developing countries, see A. Mitchell and J. Wallis, *Pacific Countries in the WTO: Accession and Accommodation, The Reality of WTO Accession* chap. 8; and P. Kleen and S. Page, *Special and Differential Treatment of Developing Countries in the World Trade Organization* (2005), Report of the Swedish Ministry of Foreign Affairs Global Development Studies 2, pp. 79–95.

basis. Depending on counting methodology, the United States has between twenty and thirty such lawyers and the EU nearly as many (albeit through more complex bureaucratic arrangements). In addition, both the United States and the EU can draw on a large number of other "in-house" WTO specialists.

By contrast, St. Lucia, which can reasonably foresee only one case every few years (in the event, *Bananas*), does not even have a mission in Geneva and could not reasonably hire as permanent staff a large core of WTO specialists. St. Lucia is not the only country in this position; as recently as 2007, approximately one-quarter of WTO Members did not have a WTO mission.[15] Even those that do have a mission often lack staff with training in international trade.[16] Not all developing countries, however, lack WTO missions with trade expertise. Brazil, by many accounts, is one of the most successful participants in the WTO dispute settlement system, and a large part of Brazil's success derives from the Brazilian government's organization with respect to international trade matters.[17] Brazil's Ministry of Foreign Affairs is professionalized and meritocratic, and it prioritizes international trade.[18] In addition to its mission in Geneva, Brazil has a specialized unit in Brasilia that specializes in dispute settlement and supports the Geneva mission.[19] This dedication of resources has facilitated much of Brazil's success.

Although the disparity in the resources that individual countries dedicate to WTO matters is a problem for the functioning of the WTO as a whole, it has a particularly large impact in dispute settlement. This is because the short deadlines in the dispute settlement mechanism – which are necessary to maintain confidence in the system and which, indeed, are being ignored to a point where the system is losing its credibility[20] – mean that doing the best work on a WTO case requires a high degree of dedication to that case. After the first submission is filed with the panel by the Complainant (which, at least in theory, has had unlimited time to prepare that submission, because the Complainant chooses when to start the case), the rhythm of work is far more intense than in normal court litigation or the predecessor GATT dispute settlement system. In one of the authors' experience with an early WTO dispute, we prepared drafts for a government based on the government's instructions, sent them off to Geneva around midnight for the government to revise, got back in the morning, and started working on our replies to the arguments that we *expected*

15 See K. Bohl, "Problems of Developing Country Access to the WTO Dispute Settlement" (2009) 9 *Chicago-Kent Journal of International & Comparative Law* 162 (citing N. Meagher, "Representing Developing Countries in WTO Dispute Settlement Proceedings," in G. Bermann and P. Mavroidis (eds.), *WTO Law and Developing Countries* (New York: Cambridge University Press, 2007), p. 219).

16 See Bohl (2009), supra note 15, p. 162.

17 G. Shaffer, M. R. Sanchez, and B. Rosenberg, "The Trials of Winning at the WTO: What Lies behind Brazil's Success" (2008) 41 *Cornell International Law Journal* 388.

18 Ibid., pp. 424–429.

19 Ibid.

20 WTO, *Negotiations on Improvements and Clarifications of the DSU*, Proposal by Mexico, WTO Document, TN/DS/W/23 (4 November 2002).

the other government to make in reply to the submission, which was filed later that day. This intense pace continues for most of the panel process with a few very short breaks at the end, and then repeats itself during the Appellate Body process.

Very few countries can dedicate staff more or less full time to that process. Most must rely on their relatively few WTO experts. The experts in Geneva are already responsible for numerous committee meetings a day as well as for dealing with the ministries back home on a wide range of issues. Their counterparts back home have to deal with ministers, other politicians, and the usual daily debris of public service. Thus, many WTO governments are forced to rely, for at least some litigated cases, on outside lawyers who can throw themselves into the project with the same dedication as U.S. or EU inside lawyers. In business terms, this is referred to as a "make or buy" decision – it is rational for the United States and the EU to have large staffs of inside lawyers, because of the expected large volume of cases, and it is equally logical for other countries to "outsource."

The first disparity this presents is that for the United States and the EU, virtually all the financial costs of participating in a WTO dispute are fixed costs – they are unrelated to the particular dispute, and thus the U.S. Trade Representative and the EU can decide to start a case, or decide to defend one rather than settle immediately, without having to consider the cost of lawyers. By contrast, cost is one of the first questions for many, if not most, WTO Members confronted with a WTO dispute (even the Advisory Center on WTO Law is not gratis when it comes to litigation). Hiring outside counsel for a WTO case costs at least USD 250,000 – and doubles if the United States or the EU is on the other side of the case (because neither has any cost beyond their inside lawyers' time, they both tend to throw up a lot of obstacles during litigation). Similarly, a small, poor country, faced with a claim of WTO inconsistency by the United States or the EU, asks itself, as one of several questions, where it will get the money to defend itself. Perhaps this is why smaller countries are more likely than the United States or the EU to settle cases as defendants during the initial consultations than are the United States and the EU, and why the United States and the EU are relatively successful at settling cases as plaintiffs during those consultations. As the representative of Antigua and Barbuda stated, "many small, developing countries had made . . . informal settlements that were beneficial to United States economic interests after being told their laws were in violation of WTO law."[21]

Developed countries, however, do not always have an advantage in terms of resources. This advantage disappears when the domestic industry of a developing country is strong and active enough in defending its interest before the WTO by hiring an external legal counsel. That makes domestic affected industry a major source

[21] WTO, *Statement by Sir Ronald Michael Sanders, Chief Foreign Affairs Representative of Antigua and Barbuda to the WTO Dispute Settlement Body* (June 24, 2003), WTO Document WT/DSB/M/151 (August 12, 2003).

of funding the WTO litigation. Among the prominent examples of such support are Ecuador's complaint in *Bananas*, Guatemala's defense in *Cement*, Antigua and Barbuda's representation in *Online Gambling*, as well as the case brought by Brazil against U.S. *Cotton Subsidies*.[22] Brazil, in particular, has been successful at utilizing industry financial support in bringing WTO disputes.[23] In fact, Brazil's successful use of public–private partnerships in WTO dispute settlement has at times put the United States (*Cotton Subsidies*) and the EU (*Sugar*) at a disadvantage, demonstrating that the involvement of domestic industry can have so great an impact as to reverse the imbalance in favor of developing countries.[24]

However, reliance by a government on industry's resources carries its own complications. The ability to bring cases in such a situation, or defend them well, could become more a function of local industries' particular interest in a case, rather than a national interest.[25] If the EU was fully dependent on its industries, it probably would have never brought the *Foreign Sales Corporations* complaint.[26] The case was started without industry pressure – indeed, many European companies' U.S. affiliates received Foreign Sales Corporation (FSC) treatment. Thus, although domestic industry funding may permit developing countries to bring WTO disputes in some cases, such funding will only be a viable option when the domestic industry and national interests are aligned.

B. *Lack of Leverage to Enforce WTO Rulings*

Another major constraint for smaller developed countries is the belief that they cannot retaliate against larger developed countries. Under the WTO rules, if a member does not voluntarily comply with a WTO ruling, the burden of enforcement falls on a complainant, which has a right to raise its tariffs or otherwise suspend WTO obligations against the products of a noncomplying member. There are several reasons for the belief that it is impossible for the developing countries to retaliate against large developed WTO Members such as the United States and the EU.

Economically, smaller countries calculate that if they raise tariffs against the imports from a developed country, it will raise costs in the developing country

[22] *European Communities – Regime for the Importation, Sale and Distribution of Bananas*, WT/DS27; *Guatemala – Anti-Dumping Investigation Regarding Imports of Portland Cement from Mexico*, WT/DS60; *Guatemala – Definitive Anti-dumping Measure regarding Grey Portland Cement from Mexico*, WT/DS156; *United States – Measures Affecting Cross-Border Supply of Gambling and Betting*, WT/DS285; *United States – Subsidies on Upland Cotton*, WT/DS267.

[23] See Shaffer et al. (2008), supra note 17, pp. 456–464.

[24] See *United States – Subsidies on Upland Cotton*, WT/DS267; *European Communities – Export Subsidies on Sugar*, WT/DS265.

[25] See, e.g., Shaffer et al. (2008), supra note 17, p. 464 ("The private sector is not always willing to fund a case that the Foreign Ministry believes Brazil should pursue or that it must defend as a respondent, particularly cases of a systemic nature for which the Ministry believes that it needs outside legal assistance.").

[26] *United States – Tax Treatment for "Foreign Sales Corporations,"* WT/DS108.

(and many argue that their imports tend to be either necessities such as food or medicine or fuel or inputs for local manufacturers). By contrast, a larger economy is less dependent on imports of any particular item and often produces a much wider range of the inputs. Politically, developing countries calculate that any foreseeable retaliation they could impose on the developed country will be a "pinprick" politically to the developed country, whereas WTO-authorized retaliation permits a developed country to impose politically impossible levels of retaliation on a developing country.

Additionally, on a more systemic level, developing countries understand the fragility of the world trading system and recognize that a rules-based system constrains the most powerful country more than it does the smaller countries. In consequence, some developing countries are willing to forgo retaliation, even if the largest country practices it, to maintain a system that most believe is favorable to them overall. Indeed, even the EU was noticeably more reluctant to impose WTO-authorized retaliatory measures against the United States than vice versa (the EU waited years to push forward its retaliation on the *FSC* case, but the United States "jumped the gun" in *Bananas* by three weeks).

That said, developing countries do have effective means of retaliation – most notably the ability to suspend their TRIPS obligation in cross-retaliation – that some countries, such as Ecuador, Antigua, and Brazil, have shown some interest in pursuing.[27] As Gabriel Slater noted, "[f]or developing countries, suspending United States and European IP [intellectual property] rights offers a powerful stick in their trade with developed countries."[28] The willingness to follow through on the retaliation may, however, differ for smaller, less developed countries and middle-income developing countries, such as the BRICs. Ecuador, in the *Bananas* case, received authorization from the WTO Dispute Settlement Body to suspend its TRIPS obligations in retaliation for violations. Ecuador did not actually suspend its TRIPS obligations, however; rather, it used the threat of such retaliation to help its position in negotiations with the EU and possibly to obtain EU support in its Club of Paris debt renegotiation.[29] Brazil also has threatened to cross-retaliate with the suspension of its TRIPS obligations in *United States – Subsidies on Upland Cotton*. Although it has not yet done so, Brazil's relatively stronger position and its lack of debt vulnerabilities may make it more likely that Brazil would find such retaliation to be in its strategic interest.

[27] See G. Slater, "The Suspension of Intellectual Property Obligations under TRIPS: A Proposal for Retaliating against Technology-Exporting Countries in the World Trade Organization," (2009) 97 *Georgetown Law Journal* 1368–1370; see also J. Reichmann, "Universal Minimum Standards of Intellectual Property Protection under the TRIPS Component of the WTO Agreement" (1995) 29 *International Lawyer* 345.

[28] Slater (2009), supra note 277, p. 1370.

[29] J. M. Smith, "Compliance Bargaining in the WTO: Ecuador and the Bananas Dispute," Conference on Developing Countries and the Trade Negotiation Process, UNCTAD (Geneva, November 6–7, 2003).

C. *High Indirect Costs*

Insufficient litigation resources and lack of leverage to enforce a WTO ruling are not the only reasons developing countries are less active in the context of the WTO dispute settlement. They, for example, do not explain why Egypt dropped out of the U.S.-led coalition against the EU's de facto Genetically Modified Organisms ban. In that case, Egypt would not have been the main complainant and could largely free ride on the U.S. arguments. Also, the U.S. retaliation alone would probably have been sufficient to induce compliance by the EU in the event of a victory at the WTO. Egypt nevertheless abstained from taking part in the complaint, even though this might have hurt prospects for an Egypt-U.S. free trade agreement.[30] The main reason seems to be that, under a cost-benefit analysis, initiating a dispute was not in Egypt's best interest. Egypt would have brought a WTO complaint if the benefits from pursuing it would have outweighed any losses in current or potential trade flows to the EU or development aid from the EU as a result of its decision to go to the WTO.

The key to understanding this analysis is that the initiation of a WTO dispute is considered to be a hostile act toward defendants. Members complained against normally "deplore," "deeply regret," or express "great dissatisfaction and concern" in connection with requests for the establishment of a panel. They can also respond to the initiation of a WTO case by either filing a counter-complaint or undertaking other unfriendly steps. Examples of such behavior are the EU filing a complaint against Australian quarantine regime as a tit-for-tat move following a complaint by Australia against EU protection of geographic indications[31] or Korea initiating a dispute against EU shipbuilding subsidies following the EU challenge to Korean shipbuilding subsidies.[32]

Although this approach to dispute settlement is not at all unique to trade relations between developed and developing countries, developed countries possess greater persuasive force as a function of their degree of economic development when dealing with developing countries. The result is that developing countries would think twice before bringing a WTO complaint against a developed country. For example, even though according to the president of the Mozambican Cotton Association, "the quality of life of millions of Mozambicans is being dramatically eroded by the low price of cotton," Mozambique did not participate in the WTO dispute against

30 "U.S. Interest in FTA Cools after Egypt Fails to Join GMO Complaint," *Inside U.S. Trade*, July 4, 2003; "U.S. Announces Panel on EU GMO Moratorium, as Grassley Warns Egypt," *Inside U.S. Trade*, June 20, 2003; "Egypt Tells EU It Will Not Be Co-complainant on U.S. GMO Case," *Inside U.S. Trade*, May 30, 2003.

31 "U.S., Australia Secure WTO Panel to Rule on EU Protection of Geographic Indications," *Daily Report for Executives* (BNA), October 3, 2003.

32 "South Korea Files Tit-for-Tat Complaint at WTO Against EU Shipbuilding Subsidies," *Daily Report for Executives* (BNA), September 4, 2003.

U.S. Cotton Subsidies.[33] One of the reasons may be that it was anxious to preserve untouched its benefits in trade with the United States, including such sensitive matters as sugar quotas, as well as other forms of development aid, the existence of which depends on the U.S. goodwill alone.[34]

The same rationale might explain why the four major victims of U.S. cotton subsidies – Benin, Burkina Faso, Mali, and Chad – were not complainants in the challenge to those subsidies (although Benin and Chad did take part as third parties). These countries may have worried that unnecessary hostility toward the United States might diminish their chances of success in the parallel-to-the-WTO-litigation Doha Round agricultural negotiations where those countries seek financial compensation to offset the income they are losing as a result of the U.S. cotton subsidies.[35] Although these negotiations have been stalled, recent Obama administration comments about moving the negotiations forward may continue to give affected countries a reason not to bring disputes against the United States.[36]

By the same token, if a WTO-inconsistent trade restriction against developing-country imports is so great that spoiling relations with a developed country is a worthwhile exercise, then a WTO case will be brought. In *Export Subsidies on Sugar*, Thailand reportedly was not deterred from launching a complaint against the EU when the latter warned that this might result in the reduction of Thai tuna imports under a Generalized System of Preferences (GSP) quota.[37] With the recent onset of the global financial crisis and the emergence of increasingly protectionist policies, it may become increasingly common that the losses from the trade restriction are so great as to justify the bringing of a dispute despite the political and economic risks.

III. THE IMPACT OF RECENT DEVELOPMENTS ON THE IMBALANCE

A. *Global Financial Crisis*

The fall of 2008 marked the onset of a global financial crisis that has affected nearly every country across the world. Already we have begun to see countries implement

[33] "The Cotton Sector in Mozambique: Challenges and Options after the WTO Conference in Cancun," transcript of a speech by João Ribas, president of the Mozambican Cotton Association, at Nairobi Conference "Business for Development – Challenges and options for Government and Business after the WTO Conference in Cancun" (March 30–31, 2004).

[34] For the proposition that small nations may fear that developed countries would retaliate by decreasing its development aid, see D. Collins, "Efficient Breach, Reliance and Contract Remedies at the WTO" (2009) 43 *Journal of World Trade* 228.

[35] WTO Negotiations on Agriculture, *Poverty Reduction: Sectoral Initiative in Favor of Cotton, Joint Proposal by Benin, Burkina Faso, Chad and Mali*, WTO Document, TN/AG/GEN/4, (16 May 2003).

[36] See "Obama and Trade: Low Expectations Exceeded," *The Economist*, April 30, 2009, available at: http://www.economist.com/world/unitedstates/displaystory.cfm?story_id=13578834.

[37] "Philippines Claims Victory over Europe Using WTO Mediations in Tuna Tariff Spat," *Daily Rep. for Executives* (BNA), June 10, 2003.

protectionist policies in reaction to the economic challenges their industries are facing.[38] Although this turn toward protectionist policies is problematic for international trade in general, it remains to be seen what impact it will have on the imbalance in access to WTO dispute settlement. At first glance, it would seem that developing countries, also suffering from the financial crisis, will be even more limited in the resources they can devote to bringing disputes in the WTO and thus that the imbalance will continue. However, there is another possible scenario: as developing countries' industries are forced to compete with developed countries' industries, which are receiving subsidies that developing-country governments cannot afford to offer, the developing countries may find bringing a WTO dispute to be the most cost-effective response. If bringing a dispute is less costly for developing-country governments than offering subsidies, then an unexpected consequence of the crisis may be that developing countries become more active participants in the WTO dispute settlement system.

Whether this will happen remains to be seen. It is also possible that developed countries, in response to the financial crisis, will bring more WTO disputes against developing countries in an effort to make their own industries more competitive and thereby relegate developing countries to a defendant role. In fact, both China[39] and the United States[40] have taken each other to the dispute settlement system to challenge measures affecting its industries during that period in order to improve industry-specific competitiveness. This set of disputes follows prior cases between countries from the Northern and Southern hemispheres, such as the *Bananas* case between Ecuador and Europe. In sum, the global financial crisis and the resulting protectionist policies are likely to have some impact on the WTO dispute settlement system and on how both developed and developing countries participate in the system.

B. *Climate Change*

The global financial crisis is not the only crisis facing the world economy; climate change has become an increasingly pressing issue, and there is growing political will to address this problem. However, most proposed measures (such as border barriers or massive subsidies) are likely to stretch WTO rules, thus creating a tension between trade law and the environment. In June 2009, the U.S. House of Representatives

[38] See World Trade Organization, *World Trade Report 2009: Trade Policy Commitments and Contingency Measures* (2009), available at: http://www.wto.org/english/res_e/publications_e/wtr09_e.htm; "The Nuts and Bolts Come Apart: As Global Demand Contracts, Trade Is Slumping and Protectionism Rising," *The Economist*, March 26, 2009, available at: http://www.economist.com/displayStory.cfm?story_id=13362027.

[39] *United States – Measures Affecting Imports of Certain Passenger Vehicles and Light Truck Tyres from China* (WT/DS399).

[40] *China – Measures Related to the Importation of Various Raw Materials* (WT/DS394).

passed the Waxman-Markey bill[41] (still not passed by the Senate) that would adopt a cap-and-trade program, which might contravene WTO rules if emission allowances are allocated discriminatorily or for free. The bill also includes the possibility of imposing border adjustment measures that could potentially violate any WTO rule governing border measures.[42] In case of any violation, any developed- or developing-country member of the WTO could challenge the bill at the dispute settlement level. In April 2009, the EU passed legislation imposing new sustainability requirements for biofuels and bioliquids[43] that has angered Malaysia, Indonesia, and Brazil, who have stated these new requirements are "unjustifiably complex" and threatened to "defend their rights at the WTO," as a last resort.[44] This tension is likely to spark WTO disputes, and the dispute settlement mechanism may serve as a primary means for mediating the conflicts that will arise out of climate change policies.

Climate change policies are certain to affect developing countries. They may also affect developing-country attitudes toward WTO dispute settlement. Depending on the magnitude of the impact of climate change policies on developing countries, the adoption of such policies may lead developing countries to initiate WTO complaints to protect their interests. Such complaints, should they be made, could pose a great challenge to the WTO dispute settlement system, and how the system handles these disputes will be critical to the future of the WTO. Although climate change issues may help to ameliorate the imbalance in access to the WTO dispute settlement by incentivizing developing countries to participate actively in the system, at the same time they may also put unsustainable strain on the system as a whole.

C. *Changes in the Economic Balance of Power*

Yet another recent development in the world economy, the rise of certain developing economies, such as the BRICs, will surely have, and has already had, a great effect on the profile and treatment of developing countries in the WTO, and more specifically in the WTO dispute settlement system. Brazil and South Africa, for example, have provided strong support for some developing countries' arguments in the debate over intellectual property rights and access to medicines.

Although the growing prominence of these countries has already contributed to the advancement of the development agenda in WTO negotiations, it may also help

[41] American Clean Energy and Security Act of 2009, available at: http://thomas.loc.gov/cgi-bin/query/z?c111:H.R.2454:.

[42] G. Hufbauer and J. Kim, *The World Trade Organization and Climate Change: Challenges and Options* (Peterson Institute for International Economics, September 2009), available at: http://www.iie.com/publications/interstitial.cfm?ResearchID=1301. See also B. Condon, "Climate Change and Unresolved Issues in WTO Law" (2009) 12(4) *Journal of International Economic Law* 895–926.

[43] Directive 2009/28/EC of 23 April 2009 on the promotion of the use of energy from renewable sources and amending and subsequently repealing Directives 2001/77/EC and 2003/30/EC.

[44] *EU's Sustainable Biofuels Push Angers Malaysia, Brazil*, available at: http://news.mongabay.com/2008/1107-biofuels.html, accessed May 31, 2010.

to correct the imbalance in access to the WTO dispute settlement system. Activity by developing countries with greater resources may benefit other developing countries when their interests align and thus give those countries with fewer resources indirect access to the system.

IV. WHAT IS TO BE DONE?

Although these new developments might help ameliorate the imbalance in access to the WTO dispute settlement system, there are also specific proposals that could help address the imbalance. Greg Shaffer, noting that developing countries are less likely than developed countries to be complainants under WTO than under the General Agreement on Tariffs and Trade and more likely to be defendants, identified a number of proposals, including monetary damages and attorneys' fees for developing countries, less costly procedures, and greater legal assistance.[45] These proposals, if adopted, may correct some of the imbalances described earlier in this chapter.

A. *Greater Legal Assistance and Attorneys' Fees*

Legal aid to developing countries may be provided in two forms – by providing developing countries with legal advice for free or at discounted rates or by giving successful developing-country complainants (or defendants) the opportunity to recover legal expenses from the losing side. The first scenario was implemented by the establishment of the Advisory Centre on WTO Law (ACWL), which functions as an independent international organization. In its first years in existence, the ACWL, whose services, although discounted, are not free, has been a remarkable success in terms of assistance to developing countries. There is every reason, therefore, to further support and expand activities of this organization, including by pushing the United States and the EU to become members of the ACWL. Additionally, because some least developed countries cannot afford even the sharply discounted rates of the ACWL, one might think about the creation of regional Advisory Centres on WTO Law, in particular an African Advisory Centre on WTO Law, whose services would be free for its members both for WTO dispute settlement and for legal support in the rounds of multilateral trade negotiations.

The second scenario, securing greater legal assistance through the reimbursement of legal costs, is complementary to the provision of affordable legal services. First, it would allow successful developing countries to get back their expenses, including those spent on the services of the Advisory Centre. Second, it would also allow developing countries to hire outside legal counsel in situations in which, for reasons of confidentiality or expertise, they prefer to do so. This is especially important when

45 G. Shaffer, *Defending Interests: Public–Private Partnerships in WTO Litigation* (Washington, DC: Brookings Institution Press, 2003).

a WTO case is a sequel to a WTO-inconsistent national trade remedies investigation. In such cases, a private law firm that represented the developing-country producers in the respective national investigation would have significant expertise and, more important, would be able to provide continuity between a national jurisdiction (where the real remedies are) and the WTO in terms of implementation of the WTO ruling in the jurisdiction concerned.

That said, the reimbursement of attorney's fees for the developing countries cannot be accepted without reservations. First, the experience of jurisdictions using the "costs follow the event" rule (such as in England) shows that not capping reimbursable expenses by some sort of reasonability standard can lead to abuse because there is no incentive for a meritorious complainant or defendant to oversee the efficiency of its lawyers. Second, if reimbursable costs are to be reasonable, a special costs arbitrator is needed to avoid a lengthy litigation on costs.

B. *Monetary Damages*

The lack of retaliation capacity with respect to a noncomplying developed member may be corrected by replacing the remedy of retaliation with other remedies such as compulsory compensation. In this context, the compensation may take the form of either a tariff reduction according to the choice of a developing-country plaintiff (as proposed by Joost Pauwelyn)[46] or monetary compensation for the damage caused by a WTO-inconsistent trade restriction.[47] Both remedies are familiar to the WTO membership. The option of compensation (although in a different form) is reflected in Article 22 of the WTO Dispute Settlement Understanding but has not been frequently used, probably because of its nonmandatory nature and the obligation to provide such compensation on a most-favored-nation basis. Monetary damages have been offered in practice (in *Broadcast Music* and *Upland Cotton*) and are being mentioned among the proposals in the ongoing DSU review.[48] It is important to mention that, by promising real relief to a complaining developing country, the remedy of compensation in either form significantly modifies the cost-benefit analysis of initiating a WTO dispute in a way that secures greater participation of developing countries in the WTO dispute settlement system.

[46] See J. Pauwelyn, "Enforcement and Countermeasures in the WTO: Rules Are Rules – Toward a More Collective Approach" (2000) 94 *American Journal of International Law* 337.

[47] For the argument for a monetary remedy, see Collins (2009), supra note 34, p. 228. However, the authors do not agree with Collins's assertions about efficient breach in the context of the WTO (which is quite different from a private commercial contract). See Collins (2009), supra note 34, p. 227n8 (citing to John H. Jackson, *Sovereignty, the WTO and Changing Fundamentals of International Law* (Cambridge: Cambridge University Press, 2006), p. 147).

[48] Dispute Settlement Body – Special Session – Text for the African Group Proposals on Dispute Settlement Understanding Negotiations – Communications from Kenya, WTO Document, TN/DS/W/42, January 24, 2001. It may be necessary for the damages to only be owed by developing countries (or to limit the amount they would owe).

C. *Less Costly Procedures*

Less costly procedures in the WTO dispute settlement system are necessary if the previously described proposals on reimbursement of attorneys' fees and/or monetary compensation are not adopted. Among procedures that can be adopted are obligatory use of mediation and the introduction of a small claims track with simplified procedures and a single panelist.[49] One could also think of penalizing defendants for complicating litigation by putting forward unmeritorious requests for preliminary rulings. The penalty may consist of deducting days of delay caused thereby from the reasonable period of time for compliance, or, if a proposal on reimbursement of attorneys' fees is adopted, of awarding additional costs. Furthermore, enforcing currently established deadlines for the Panel and Appellate Body hearings would reduce the financial burden on the parties to a WTO dispute. This, however, will require an increase in the budget of the WTO Secretariat.

V. CONCLUSION

Developing countries' access to WTO dispute settlement is an issue of great concern, and there is a need for positive efforts to ensure that developing countries are adequately represented when it comes to defending their interests in the WTO. Full-fledged participation of developing countries in the WTO dispute settlement system requires a change in the current rules so as to provide developing countries with the necessary resources and incentives for successful representation of their interests before the WTO Panels and Appellate Body. Greater legal assistance, viable remedies, and faster and streamlined procedures are key to providing that indeed "right perseveres over might."[50]

It is unclear what impact the uncertainty in the world economy will have on the issue of developing countries' access to WTO dispute settlement. The great challenges of today, like the global financial crisis and climate change, could inadvertently ameliorate some of the imbalances in the system or they could make these imbalances more acute. Should these imbalances persist, there may not be the political will to address these issues, given the gravity of the challenges facing the world economy. However, regardless of whether these issues receive attention in this time of crisis, developing countries' access to WTO dispute settlement is important to the health of the WTO as a whole and is deserving of attention in the short and long run.

49 B. Hoekman and P. Mavroidis, "Enforcing Multilateral Commitments: Dispute Settlement and Developing Countries," paper prepared for the WTO/World Bank Conference on Developing Countries in a Millennium Round, WTO Secretariat, Centre William Rappard (Geneva, September 20–21, 1999), available at: http://worldbank.org.

50 J. Lacarte-Muro and P. Gappah, "Developing Countries and the WTO Legal and Dispute Settlement System: A View from the Bench" (2000) 3 *Journal of International Economic Law* 395.

REFERENCES

American Clean Energy and Security Act of 2009, available at: http://thomas.loc.gov/cgi-bin/query/z?c111:H.R.2454:.

Bohl, Kristin, "Problems of Developing Country Access to the WTO Dispute Settlement" (2009) 9 *Chicago-Kent Journal of International & Comparative Law* 130.

Cardoso, Fernando Henrique, and Enzo Faletto, *Dependencia y Desarrollo en America Latina: Ensayo de Interpretación Sociológica* (Mexico City: Siglo Veintiuno Editores, 1969).

Collins, David, "Efficient Breach, Reliance and Contract Remedies at the WTO" (2009) 43 *Journal of World Trade*.

Condon, Bradley, "Climate Change and Unresolved Issues in WTO Law" (2009) 12(4) *Journal of International Economic Law*.

Directive 2009/28/EC of the European Parliament and of the Council of 23 April 2009 on the promotion of the use of energy from renewable sources and amending and subsequently repealing Directives 2001/77/EC and 2003/30/EC (June 5, 2009).

"Egypt Tells EU It Will Not Be Co-complainant on U.S. GMO Case," *Inside U.S. Trade*, May 30, 2003.

"EU and U.S. Try to Rekindle Trade Talks," *New York Times*, January 24, 2008.

Hoekman, Bernard M., and Petros C. Mavroidis, "Enforcing Multilateral Commitments: Dispute Settlement and Developing Countries," paper prepared for the WTO/World Bank Conference on Developing Countries in a Millennium Round, WTO Secretariat, Centre William Rappard, Geneva (September 20–21, 1999), available at: http://worldbank.org.

Horlick, Gary, and Nikolay Mizulin, "Developing Countries and WTO Dispute Settlement" (2005) 23 *Integration & Trade Journal*.

Howse, Robert, "From Politics to Technocracy – and Back Again: The Fate of the Multilateral Trading Regime" (2002) 96 *American Journal of International Law*.

Hufbauer, Gary, and Jisun Kim, "The World Trade Organization and Climate Change: Challenges and Options," *Peterson Institute for International Economics* (September 2009), Working Paper, available at: http://www.iie.com/publications/interstitial.cfm?ResearchID=1301.

Irwin, Douglas, *Free Trade under Fire* (2nd ed., Princeton, NJ: Princeton University Press, 2005).

Jackson, John, W. Davey, and A. Sykes, *Legal Problems of International Economic Relations: Cases, Materials and Text* (5th ed., St. Paul, MN: Thomson/West, 2008).

Jones, Kent, *Who's Afraid of the WTO?* (New York: Oxford University Press, 2004).

Kleen, Peter, and Sheila Page, *Special and Differential Treatment of Developing Countries in the World Trade Organization* (2005), Report of the Swedish Ministry of Foreign Affairs Global Development Studies.

Lacarte-Muro, Julio, and Petina Gappah, "Developing Countries and the WTO Legal and Dispute Settlement System: A View from the Bench," 3 *Journal of International Economic Law* (2000).

"Obama and Trade: Low Expectations Exceeded," *The Economist*, April 30, 2009, available at: http://www.economist.com/world/unitedstates/displaystory.cfm?story_id=13578834.

Pauwelyn, Joost, "Developing Countries and the WTO Legal and Dispute Settlement System: A View from the Bench" (2000) 3 *Journal of International Economic Law*.

"Philippines Claims Victory over Europe Using WTO Mediations in Tuna Tariff Spat," *Daily Rep. for Executives* (BNA), June 10, 2003.

Prebisch, Raul, *Change and Development – Latin America's Great Task: Report Submitted to the Inter-American Development Bank* (New York: Praeger, 1971).

Reichmann, Jerome, "Universal Minimum Standards of Intellectual Property Protection under the TRIPS Component of the WTO Agreement" (1995) 29 *International Lawyer*.

Ribas, João, President of the Mozambican Cotton Association, "The Cotton Sector in Mozambique: Challenges and Options after the WTO Conference in Cancun," transcript of a speech at Nairobi Conference "Business for Development – Challenges and options for Government and Business after the WTO Conference" in Cancun (March 30–31, 2004).

Rodrik, Dani, "The Global Governance of Trade: As If Development Really Mattered," background paper to the United Nations Development Programme project on Trade and Sustainable Human Development (New York, October 2001).

Shaffer, Gregory C., *Defending Interests: Public-Private Partnerships in WTO Litigation* (Washington, DC: Brookings Institution Press, 2003).

Shaffer Gregory C., M. R. Sanchez, and B. Rosenberg, "The Trials of Winning at the WTO: What Lies behind Brazil's Success" (2008) 41 *Cornell International Law Journal*.

Slater, Gabriel, "The Suspension of Intellectual Property Obligations under TRIPS: A Proposal for Retaliating against Technology-Exporting Countries in the World Trade Organization" (2009) 97 *Georgetown Law Journal*.

Smith, James McCall, "Compliance Bargaining in the WTO: Ecuador and the Bananas Dispute," Conference on Developing Countries and the Trade Negotiation Process, UNCTAD (Geneva, November 6–7, 2003).

"South Korea Files Tit-for-Tat Complaint at WTO against EU Shipbuilding Subsidies," *Daily Report for Executives* (BNA), September 4, 2003.

"The Nuts and Bolts Come Apart: As Global Demand Contracts, Trade Is Slumping and Protectionism Rising," *The Economist*, March 26, 2009, available at: http://www.economist.com/displayStory.cfm?story_id=13362027.

Trubek, David M., and M. Patrick Cottrell, "Robert Hudec and the Theory of International Economic Law: The Law of Global Space," in Chantal Thomas and Joel P. Trachtman (eds.), *Developing Countries in the WTO Legal System* (New York: Oxford University Press, 2009).

"U.S. Announces Panel on EU GMO Moratorium, as Grassley Warns Egypt," *Inside U.S. Trade*, June 20, 2003.

"U.S., Australia Secure WTO Panel to Rule on EU Protection of Geographic Indications," *Daily Report for Executives* (BNA), October 3, 2003.

"U.S. Interest in FTA Cools after Egypt Fails to Join GMO Complaint," *Inside U.S. Trade*, July 4, 2003.

Wilson, Dominic, and Roopa Purushotha, *Dreaming with the BRICs: The Path to 2050*, Goldman Sachs Global Economics Paper No. 99 (New York, 2003).

World Trade Organization, *General Agreement on Tariffs and Trade 1994*, LT/UR/A-1A/1/GATT/1 (January 1, 1995).

______, *Marrakesh Agreement Establishing the World Trade Organization*, LT/UR/A/2 (January 1, 1995).

______, Appellate Body Report, *European Communities – Regime for the Importation, Sale and Distribution of Bananas, Complaint by Ecuador*, WT/DS72/AB/R, adopted September 25, 1997, DSR 1997: II, 591.

______, Appellate Body Report, *Guatemala – Anti-Dumping Investigation Regarding Imports of Portland Cement from Mexico*, WT/DS60/AB/R, adopted November 25, 1998, DSR 1998:IX, 3767.

———, Appellate Body Report, *United States – Tax Treatment for "Foreign Sales Corporations,"* WT/DS108/AB/R, adopted March 20, 2000, DSR, 2000:III, 1619.

———, Panel Report, *Guatemala – Definitive Anti-dumping Measure regarding Grey Portland Cement from Mexico*, WT/DS156/R, adopted November 17, 2000, DSR 2000:XI, 5295.

———, *Dispute Settlement Body – Special Session – Text for the African Group Proposals on Dispute Settlement Understanding Negotiations – Communication from Kenya*, TN/DS/W/42 (January 24, 2001).

———, *Negotiations on Improvements and Clarifications of the DSU – Proposal by Mexico*, TN/DS/W/23 (November 4, 2002).

———, *Committee on Agriculture – Special Session – WTO Negotiations on Agriculture – Poverty Reduction: Sectoral Initiative in Favour of Cotton – Joint Proposal by Benin, Burkina Faso, Chad and Mali*, TN/AG/GEN/4 (May 16, 2003).

———, *Dispute Settlement Body – Minutes of Meeting Held in the Centre William Rappard on June 24, 2003*, WT/DSB/M/151 (August 12, 2003).

———, Appellate Body Report, *United States – Subsidies on Upland Cotton*, WT/DS267/AB/R, adopted March 21, 2005, DSR 2005:I, 3.

———, Appellate Body Report, *United States – Measures Affecting Cross-Border Supply of Gambling and Betting*, WT/DS285/AB/R, adopted April 20, 2005, DSR 2005:XII, 5663 (Corr.1 DSR 2006: XII, 5663 (Corr. DSR 2006: XII, 5475).

———, Appellate Body Report, *European Communities – Export Subsidies on Sugar*, WT/DS265/AB/R, WT/DS266/AB/R, WT/DS283/AB/R, adopted May 19, 2005, DSR 2005:XIII, 6365.

———, *World Trade Report 2009: Trade Policy Commitments and Contingency Measures* (2009), available at: http://www.wto.org/english/res_e/publications_e/wtr09_e.htm.

———, *China – Measures Related to the Importation of Various Raw Materials – Request for the Establishment of a Panel by the United States*, WT/DS394/4 (November 9, 2009).

———, United States – Measures Affecting Imports of Certain Passenger Vehicles and Light Truck Tyres from China – Request for the Establishment of a Panel by China, WT/DS399/2 (December 11, 2009).

Problems with the compliance structure of the WTO dispute resolution process

GARY N. HORLICK

The crown jewel of the Uruguay Round is the Dispute Settlement Understanding (DSU). The DSU, it is generally argued, brings quasi-juridical order to the General Agreement on Tariffs and Trade (GATT)[1] regime maintenance system. Several recent World Trade Organization (WTO) dispute settlement cases, however, have highlighted structural tensions within this dispute settlement system

I wish to thank Lisa Pearlman, of Harvard Law School, for her insights and assistance. Any errors are my responsibility.

1 I first heard the word GATT as a first-year law student in my contracts course, which may sound odd until you know that my contracts professor was Bob Hudec. I should begin by noting that Bob is the unacknowledged father of the most important single concept in the WTO Agreement on Subsidies and Countervailing Measures (SCM Agreement) – "specificity." One night in Poland in 1980, during the International Law Institute's Interface II Conference, the group took up the topic of the role of exchange rates in international trade and their interaction with theories of comparative advantage. This may sound like a fairly intense topic for conversation on a bus ride, but most other topics had been exhausted over a series of dinners during the previous days. One of the sessions was held, appropriately, in a meeting room at the aircraft factory, which was the assembly point for the famous Polish golf carts that became the source of the most ridiculed antidumping case ever. *Electric Golf Carts from Poland*, 40 Fed. Reg. 53383 (Treas. Nov. 18, 1975) (Antidumping Order), *revoked by Electric Golf Carts from Poland*, 45 Fed. Reg. 52780 (Dep't Comm. Aug. 8, 1990), and too many law review articles since to be cited. In theory (although rarely in practice, *see* Brink Lindsey, *The U.S. Antidumping Law – Rhetoric Versus Reality*, 34 J. WORLD TRADE 1–38 (Feb. 2000)), in an antidumping case, one compares the open market prices of comparable products in the exporting country and the importing country. At the time of the *Polish Golf Carts* case, however: (1) the US was the only country in the world where there was mass production of golf carts (or mass market for them), and (2) Poland was not a free market economy, and (3) Poland did not even have a golf course (except for a seven-hole diversion on the grounds of the British embassy), so (4) the US decided to calculate the true "fair value" of Polish golf carts and the amount of dumping by (5) calculating the precise cost of constructing those golf cars at the Polish golf-cart "factory" had the factory been in Spain. This methodology has since become imbedded in US law, resulting in completely unpredictable antidumping calculations, so that no non-market economy exporter can possibly know in advance if it is dumping. The methodology has been judged so successful as a trade barrier that its maintenance against China after China's WTO accession – in violation of the express language of the Ad Note to VI of GATT 1994 – became a higher priority for the US administration than further opening of the Chinese market to US exports. The underlying assumption of this methodology, of course, is that countries with equal GDP per capita (say, Germany and the United States) have equal costs – and thus will not trade with each other. *See* Gary N. Horlick & Shannon S. Shuman, *Nonmarket Economy Trade and U.S. Antidumping/Countervailing Duty Laws*, 18 INT'L. LAWYER 807–840 (Fall 1984). On this particular bus ride, Bob commented that it was important to distinguish between general changes in a national economy with floating exchange rates and distortions in favor of specific industries.

that have the potential to gradually undermine many of the substantive obligations contained in the WTO Agreements. The problems can be classed in three dovetailing categories: a lack of incentives for swift compliance, a lack of viable alternatives to trade sanctions, and a lack of consideration for the impact of the remedies on private actors. The first two are carrot and stick problems, and highlight the need for further streamlining of the DSU process – even beyond the recent proposals by some of the Members.[2] Effective reform will require the Members to rethink the timelines and ensure that governments which forestall compliance feel the true cost of the delay. The third, however, is a prospective problem, and cautions us against forgetting the vital need for flexibility in a supranational organization with such a diverse membership as the WTO. Not only must these problems be addressed, but the tensions between them reconciled before the DSU can fully underpin the WTO Agreements.

The first problem, the lack of incentives for swift compliance, can be seen by tracking the progress of a case along the existing DSU timeline. Assuming, charitably, that the losing Member finds out on the day the Appellate Body decision is released that it has been acting inconsistently with a WTO Agreement, it has already spent at least fifteen months in the state of inconsistency, but probably more since it would be unlikely for a Member to request consultations on the first day of existence of an inconsistent measure. Yet, even with all appeals exhausted, the only incentive to comply is enlightened (or diplomatic) self-interest, because the DSU allows a cost-free opportunity to delay compliance for several months.

A few months later, two related issues were rather forcefully brought to my attention while I was international trade counsel for the US Senate Finance Committee: US concerns about Canada's National Energy Program which attempted to set the price of oil for Canadian industry at 15 percent below the price in the United States, and EU complaints about low fixed natural gas prices in the United States. Fortunately, the two issues looked like ones that could be studied further. Unfortunately, the eventual study was severely cut back. *The Probable Impact on the U.S. Petrochemical Industry of the Expanding Petrochemical Industries in the Conventional-Energy-Rich Nations*, Inv. No. 332-137, United States International Trade Commission (April 1983).

Then, in 1982, a countervailing duty (CVD) petition was filed against imports of fresh asparagus from Mexico, alleging that the availability of cheap irrigation water – available to all crops – was a subsidy. The argument against cheap irrigation water was soon followed by CVD petitions claiming that everything from road building to Canadian provincial forest management practices to the racist apartheid system then in effect in South Africa was a subsidy. The "specificity" rule, enunciated in 1982 by the US Commerce Department, *see* Gary N. Horlick, *Introductory Note – United States: Court of Appeal for the Federal Circuit Opinion in* PPG Industries, Inc. v. United States, 30 I. L. M. 1179 (1991), and adopted in the WTO Agreement on Subsidies and Countervailing Measures, *see* Final Act Embodying the Results of the Uruguay Round of Multilateral Trade Negotiations, April 15, 1994, Agreement on Subsidies and Countervailing Duty Measures, Art. 2, was squarely based on Bob's reasoning that widely distributed government benefits do not cause a distortion within the economy and are not a subsidy, but government conferral of benefits limited in law or in fact to specific industries are countervailable subsidies if not otherwise exempted.

2 A proposal to begin the DSU reform process was initiated, and stalled, in conjunction with the December 1999 Seattle ministerial meeting. *See Proposed Amendment to the Dispute Settlement Understanding*, WTO doc. WT/MIN(99)/8 (Nov. 22, 1999). The proposed revisions would have established compliance panels, made up of the original panel or Appellate Body members, to deal with disputes as to the consistency of revised laws. It also clarified the retaliation authorization process.

The first step in the delay game is to seek an arbitration as to the length of the "reasonable period of time" for compliance. In practice, that can delay matters for two months after the Appellate Body Decision. In *European Communities – Measures Concerning Meat and Meat Products (Hormones) – Complaint by the United States* ("*Beef Hormones*"), the report of the Appellate Body was adopted on Feb. 19, 1998.[3] On April 16, the EU requested that the reasonable time for implementation of the recommendations be determined by arbitration pursuant to DSU Article 21.3(c).[4] In any arbitration, the losing Member has every incentive to ask for the longest possible "reasonable" period of time, and fifteen months is "normally" considered reasonable. This panel, whose report was circulated on May 29, 1998, set the period of implementation at fifteen months from the date of the adoption of reports.[5] At the end of the reasonable period of time, in May 1999, the EU had still not brought its beef import ban into compliance, and the United States requested authorization to suspend tariff concessions.[6] The losing Member can further stall retaliation for more months in arbitration over the amount of the retaliation. The EU did just this, and the matter was referred to arbitration pursuant to DSU Article 22.6.[7] The arbitrator finally ruled on the amount of the retaliation in July 1999.[8] The retaliatory tariffs authorized against the European Communities by the WTO in *Beef Hormones* did not finally come into effect until July 29, 1999.[9]

Furthermore, while an optimistic reading of the outcome in *European Communities – Regime for the Importation, Sale and Distribution of Bananas* ("*Bananas*") is that the retaliation can take effect while the losing Member works to bring its laws into compliance, *Australia – Subsidies Provided to Producers and Exporters of Automotive Leather* ("*Australian Leather*") suggests that a decision as to the adequacy of compliance (even without recourse to arbitration as to the amount of retaliation) can drag a proceeding out for another year. In *Australian Leather*, the DSB adopted the report of the

3 EC – *Measures Concerning Meat and Meat Products (Hormones), Report of the Appellate Body*, WTO docs. WT/DS26/AB/R, WT/DS48/AB/R (Jan. 16, 1998); EC – *Measures Concerning Meat and Meat Products (Hormones), Action by the DSB* (Feb. 19, 1998).

4 *European Communities – Measures Concerning Meat and Meat Products (Hormones), Surveillance of Implementation of Recommendations and Rulings, Request for Arbitration by the European Communities*, WTO doc. WT/DS26/14 (Apr. 16, 1998).

5 EC – *Measures Concerning Meat and Meat Products (Hormones) – Complaint by the United States, Arbitration under Art. 21.3 of the Understanding on Rules and Procedures in the Settlement of Disputes*, WTO doc. WT/DS26/15 (May 29, 1998).

6 *European Communities – Measures Concerning Meat and Meat Products (Hormones) – Complaint by the United States, Recourse by the United States to Art. 22.2 of the Dispute Settlement Understanding*, WTO doc. WT/DS28/19 (May 18, 1999).

7 *European Communities – Measures Concerning Meat and Meat Products (Hormones) – Complaint by the United States, Request for Arbitration under Art. 22.6 of the Dispute Settlement Understanding*, WTO doc. WT/DS26/20 (June 6, 1999).

8 *European Communities – Measures Concerning Meat and Meat Products (Hormones) – Complaint by the United States, Recourse to Arbitration by the European Communities Under Article 22.6 of the DSU, Decision by the Arbitrator*, WTO doc. WT/DS26/ARB (July 12, 1999).

9 *Implementation of WTO Recommendations Concerning EC-Measures Concerning Meat and Meat Products (Hormones)*, 64 Fed. Reg. 40,638–40,641 (pub. Jul. 27, 1999).

panel on June 16, 1999.[10] When Australia announced its compliance on September 17, 1999,[11] that prevented the implementation of retaliation while the US challenged the compliance, which it did on October 4, 1999.[12] The DSB recalled the original panel, and finally adopted its report on February 11, 2000, twenty days after the report had been circulated.[13] Had both parties not foresworn an appeal of the compliance ruling, the issue could have gone on for even more months.

Thus, it seems that each new modification (whether in good faith or bad) potentially extends the period of cost-free non-compliance. Indeed, the irresistibility of the temptation to delay in this manner is made clear by the US reversal of position: in *Bananas*, the US argued vociferously that Article 21.5 arbitration as to the reality of compliance could not delay Article 22.6 WTO-authorized trade retaliation for failure to comply. Yet as soon as the good faith of US compliance with the panel ruling on its antidumping rules was challenged, the US reversed course and insisted that retaliation be postponed for as long as the Article 21.5 arbitration – and presumably appeal of that arbitration – is ongoing.[14]

The time value of the money saved by stalling retaliation is reinforced by the absence, to date, of retroactive remedies in WTO practice.[15] Recently, however, the panel in *Australian Leather* recognized that unless the remedy for a one-time subsidy was retroactive, there would be no repayment and thus no withdrawal of a benefit disbursed before a panel recommendation to withdraw the subsidy. The governments involved in that dispute had disagreed over how to calculate the prospective portion of the subsidy, but firmly insisted that GATT/WTO custom and the DSU itself did not permit the levying of retroactive remedies. Both parties, however, had agreed in advance to waive an appeal, thus freeing the panel to declare itself not limited by the particular arguments of the parties, reject any distinction between retroactive and prospective (noting logically that once any part of a one-time grant must be repaid, the remedy has a retroactive effect), and order full repayment of the subsidy.[16]

10 *Australia – Subsidies Provided to Producers and Exporters of Automotive Leather, Report of the Panel*, WTO doc. WT/DS126/R (May 25, 1999) and *Action by the Dispute Settlement Body*, WTO doc. WT/DS125/5 (June 18, 1999).

11 *Australia – Subsidies Provided to Producers and Exporters of Automotive Leather, Status Report by Australia*, WTO doc. WT/DS126/7 (Sept. 2, 1999).

12 *Australia – Subsidies Provided to Producers and Exporters of Automotive Leather – Recourse by the United States to Art. 21.5 of the Dispute Settlement Understanding*, WTO doc. WT/DS126/8 (Oct. 4, 1999).

13 *Australia – Subsidies Provided to Producers and Exporters of Automotive Leather – Recourse to Art. 21.5 of the Dispute Settlement Understanding, Report of the Panel*, WTO doc. WT/DS126/RW (Jan. 21, 2000).

14 *WTO Panel to Review U.S. Compliance with Ruling on AD Rules*, INSIDE U.S. TRADE (April 28, 2000).

15 Note, however, that GATT panels have ordered retroactive remedies in AD/CVD cases: *New Zealand – Imports of Electrical Transformers from Finland*, BISD 32S/55-70 (Jul. 18, 1995); *United States – Countervailing Duties – Fresh, Chilled and Frozen Pork from Canada*, BISD 38S/30-47 (July 11, 1991); *Canadian Countervailing Duties on Grain Corn from the United States*, BISD 39S/411-436 (Mar. 26, 1992).

16 Ironically, it did so without requiring repayment with interest, effectively allowing an interest-free loan in the amount of the subsidy – a preferential loan contingent on export, which is itself a prohibited export subsidy.

The interpretation in *Australian Leather*, however, was linked to the language of the Agreement on Subsidies and Countervailing Measures (SCM Agreement). Thus, in situations where an inconsistent measure can be effectively withdrawn without retroactive effect, governments will likely continue to resist backwards reaching remedies. Each Member lives in a glass house, and is unlikely to request a remedy which could later be turned against it. Yet this logic of mutually assured destruction with respect to remedies, in which no Member will be the first to seek fully retroactive remedies, allows cynical or desperate governments to maintain unfair trade practices knowing that even after years of avoidance of effective WTO discipline, no retroactive remedy will be demanded. In the meantime, some domestic industry could well gain a cost-free (or at worst interest-free) competitive edge.

Where there is no retroactive remedy, it is difficult for a government to refuse to pursue the entire range of delay tactics when pressured by domestic interest groups with a stake in maintaining protection. Assuming a measure exists because someone had enough political clout to get it passed, that same someone will probably fight for its survival. In many cases, even if a government, and hence the domestic interest group, comes out a technical loser, it may already be a market winner because of the effects of its temporary cost-free unfair competitive advantage. In today's fast-paced market where product cycles are often only months long and brand loyalty develops in weeks, even a month or so of help can make a difference.

Not only are there no carrots or sticks incentivizing swift compliance, but there is no satisfactory remedial option. The DSU holds out the options of compensation or retaliation (limited to suspension of WTO concessions) – both are at best ineffective, and when effective, capable of undermining the logic of the entire system they are intended to enforce.

In theory, the temporary compensation envisioned by DSU Article 22.1 has an effective role to play as a carrot to speed along the compliance process. In practice, however, the WTO is generous enough about allowing a "reasonable" period for compliance that such temporary compensation will be rare indeed. If a Member truly intends to change an offending practice, it will have plenty of cost-free time to do so.

As a stick, however, it is extremely unlikely to be a "burr under the saddle" irritating enough to push the losing Member to compliance. Almost by definition, the compensation which the losing Member has chosen is presumably something less painful than compliance.[17] Compensation, granted, was intended by the WTO drafters as a compromise mechanism – to be used as a last resort to keep the full team on the field by allowing a Member to play with one arm tied behind its back, rather than ejecting it from the game, if the pain of compliance made it politically infeasible for that Member to immediately stop playing offside. The problem,

17 One could envision scenarios down the road where compensation – even as chosen by the loser – may actually be a desirable remedy for inconsistency with obsolete obligations.

however, is that the cost of compensation is often not levied on those who are keeping up the pressure to break the rules. That is, the Member's arm is punished when it is the foot that keeps fouling. Unless compliance truly makes the offending actors feel the cost of their inconsistency, it cannot be seen as an honest last resort alternative for democratic governments beset by unmovable domestic interest groups.

Finally, as a long-term solution, compensation arguably has the value of lowering some trade barriers, presuming that the winning party agrees to a level of "compensation" deeper than simply lowering duties from bound rates down to effective rates. Ultimately, however, there remains an ongoing state of suspension of WTO obligations (the inconsistency found by the panel) as between at least two Members, which if repeated a sufficient number of times could undermine the universality of the obligations.

Retaliation (higher trade barriers) is even more problematic as a remedy for WTO violations. Stated simply, the purpose of the WTO is not to impose 100 percent duties on importers of Roquefort cheese, or other innocent bystanders. To begin, retaliation, like compensation, is generally ineffective in terms of teaching specific interest groups the true cost of their protectionism because it is often imposed on sectors of the economy unrelated to those that benefit from the WTO inconsistency. The unconvincing record of retaliatory measures within the GATT/WTO demonstrates the ineffectiveness of retaliation as a stick. For example, the only GATT-authorized retaliation, by The Netherlands against the United States, was never in fact applied, and certainly had no influence on compliance.

The retaliatory measures imposed with at least implicit GATT acquiescence aptly illustrate the danger that retaliation, without carousel-like changes, can create a vested interest in the maintenance of those duties: at least one of the Chicken War tariffs placed on a variety of European products by the United States, the 25 percent duty on trucks, is still in effect (and on a most-favored nation basis at that). A further danger is that where retaliation fails to exact compliance, there exists, as with long-term compensation, a state of suspended obligation. Whereas compensation, however, leaves only the original inconsistency lingering on, retaliation raises new trade barriers, threatening the progress of liberalization and the integrity of the fundamental principles of free trade. While the retaliatory tariffs imposed by the United States in *Beef Hormones* have raised barriers that took a lot of work to lower, the European Union is no closer to bringing its beef import ban into conformity with the WTO Agreement.

Another problem with retaliation in the form of suspension of tariff concessions is that it raises the cost of the injured Member's purchases (even where those same goods could be supplied internally under tariff protections). Historically, the larger and stronger Members have been less likely to notice this effect, but it has made the retaliatory suspension of tariff concessions especially unattractive to the smaller and poorer countries authorized to retaliate against a Member on whom it relied for imports. The recent authorization of Ecuador to retaliate against the European Union by suspending certain intellectual property rights (and therefore paying less for certain forms of intellectual property) lowers, rather than raises Ecuador's costs – making retaliation a dangerously attractive option, rather than a last resort.

Although retaliatory tariffs may have been logical (if not perfectly so) in a GATT system based on the assumption that the predominant barriers would be tariffs, they are outdated in the WTO system, which essentially presumes the liberalization of most tariff barriers. Prohibitive tariffs are dinosaurs, but when revived as retaliatory measures and allowed to stampede through the existing structure they can be incredibly destructive.

While retaliatory tariffs may have been the only acceptable sticks in a world of formal national sovereignty boundaries, recent experiments suggest that as markets become global, notions of national sovereignty are on the whole becoming less rigid. For example, consider Canada's commitment in the North American Free Trade Agreement (NAFTA) side agreement on the environment which precludes retaliatory tariffs against Canadian exports, but allows for monetary enforcement assessments against the Canadian government to be enforceable in Canadian courts.[18] As jurisdiction becomes an increasingly fluid concept, it becomes possible to imagine new, more targeted approaches to achieving WTO compliance.

One intriguing proposal, by Joost Pauwelyn of the WTO Secretariat's Legal Affairs Division, is that the winning Member be allowed to choose the loser's trade compensation (subject to arbitration as to the amount), or that the loser pay monetary damages to the damaged foreign industry.[19] Other possibilities include limiting access by non-complying Members to the dispute resolution mechanism, or such "nuclear deterrents" as depriving the non-complying Member of its parking spaces at the WTO building! The key is to find remedies which lead to compliance and which also limit the incentives to delay. For example, while one cannot eliminate a parking space retroactive to the DSB adoption of the initial panel/AB report, one could extend the effectiveness of the "No parking" sign for the corresponding number of days. More seriously, in the case of monetary fines or damages, interest could run from some prior date. The possibility of interim relief should also be considered as a way to limit the amount of cost-free delay a Member can exploit.[20] While these will be considered radical thoughts by traditionalists, they barely begin to skim the surface of useful alternatives.

18 North American Agreement on Environmental Cooperation, Art. 34.5b and Annex 34. *See also* Canada–Chile Agreement on Environmental Cooperation, Art. 33.5b, Art. 35, and Annex 33 (creating a similar monetary enforcement assessment mechanism, enforceable in the courts of each jurisdiction).

19 Joost Pauwelyn, *Enforcement and Countermeasures in the WTO: Rules Are Rules – Toward a More Collective Approach*, 94 AM. J. INT'L L. 335, 346 (2000). Even Pauwelyn does not go so far as to advocate compensation (monetary or otherwise) for damage prior to or during the dispute settlement process.

20 *See* Georges A. Cavalier, *A Call for Interim Relief at the WTO Level: Dispute Settlement and International Trade Diplomacy*, 22(3) WORLD COMPETITION, 103–139 (1999).

Thus, the first two deficiencies, the incentives to delay compliance and the inadequacy of the remedies for noncompliance – the problems of inefficient carrots and sticks – militate in favor of increased procedural rigor. The lack of effective carrots and sticks is not, however, simply a drafter's error. It serves a very important purpose of accommodating governments under great pressure from constituents feeling the pain of compliance. The DSU states that compliance is its primary goal. Compensation is currently designed to appease injured Members when a violator cannot immediately comply with a DSU ruling. Compensation, however, should not just be thought of as working at the intergovernmental level, but also as a palliative at the private level, because uncompensated domestic constituencies – those injured by the violation and those injured by the remedy – can hamstring even the most committed free-trade governments. Thus, the attempt to fix compliance problems demands giving thought to ways to mitigate the effects of trade liberalization on private entities.

One effect of the current DSU procedure is the burden that the opportunity for cost-free delay has on individual entities injured by the underlying violation. The longer an inconsistent measure remains in place, the greater the disadvantage of non-benefiting private parties in the global marketplace. Furthermore, where governments will only demand prospective compliance, certain injuries due to unfair, even blatantly illegal, trade barriers will never be remedied.

Timely compliance, however, jostles private entities which previously benefited from the protectionist measure. Consider that even small, straightforward, "normal" WTO-legal tariffs are phased out over as much as eighteen years in some FTAs. Yet when a tariff is found to be illegal by the DSU, a country has on average fifteen months to remove it. From the perspective of private entities previously receiving protection, the period of cost-free delay is the only chance they have to adjust to the new market conditions. Only a fluid compliance mechanism can allow for this extra time, and the possibility of negotiating a compensatory lowering of alternative barriers to further extend the phase-out period, in order to give previously shielded domestic industries a chance to prepare themselves to compete in the liberalized market.[21]

The question of effective compliance is even more complicated when the removal of protection will destroy the affected domestic producer, delay or no. In *Australian Leather*, the government of Australia argued that retroactive repayment of the subsidy (and not even all of the economic benefit of the subsidy, at that) by the subsidized producer would put it (and its employees) out of business at once.[22] Could the WTO drafters have intended such a result? The consequences that attend the failure

21 *Japan – Taxes on Alcoholic Beverages, Arbitration under Art. 21.3(c) of the Dispute Settlement Understanding, Award of the Arbitrator*, WTO doc. WT/DS8/15 (Feb. 2, 1997); *Japan – Taxes on Alcoholic Beverages, Mutually Acceptable Solution on Modalities of Implementation*, WTO doc. WT/DS8/19 (Jan. 12, 1998).

22 While the government of Australia launched this argument on behalf of a private enterprise, the argument was also self-serving in that the ultimate cost of the repayment fell to the government itself, for the Australian government had initially extended a loan to the affected company in

of an industry may be too harsh for a society to bear. Furthermore, in the case of repayment of a subsidy as in *Australian Leather*, where the WTO has effectively reached directly into the pockets of a private entity, it will be all too tempting for private entities to save themselves by rejecting the authority of the supranational organization to make such demands. This puts national governments in a very awkward position, and quite possibly creates unintended private rights of actions as between government and its citizens. Such problems are more than cost-free delay and negotiated extensions can solve.

Compliance is not the only DSU action that affects private actors. Retaliation can have a similar impact on private entities, whether they are European exporters of Roquefort cheese or cashmere sweaters or American small businessmen specializing in the import of products from a specific country. Even some of the proposals mentioned above to replace retaliation (such as allowing the winning Member to choose the tariffs to be lowered as compensation) could have the same effect.

How, then, to reconcile the pressing need for streamlined, effective enforcement of DSU decisions with the realities of the effects of the transition on private entities? And is it necessary to think about these problems at the supranational level? In legal terms, the obligations under the WTO run between governments, not private enterprises. One could argue that such concerns about individuals ought to be addressed by domestic social welfare programs. Given, however, the ineffectiveness of some such programs combined with the moral and political imperative that the WTO respect individual concerns, some thought must be given in a new Round to ensure that WTO obligations are fulfilled without wreaking havoc on the private sector. This may be particularly important in poor and developing countries where the industries affected by violations and remedies are fragile or dependent on a few markets.[23]

One possibility would be to continue to formalize the enforcement process, but build compensatory assistance for private entities (in the form of time, money, or adjustment assistance) into the panel recommendations. WTO officials must be cautious about appearing as world governors legislating to a global citizenry, but they cannot remain blind to the reality that the effectiveness of the organization depends upon popular support. While effective sticks and carrots may seem to require that the DSU move in the opposite direction of effective consideration for private entities, it may in fact be that in many cases, attending to the effects of panel

order to cover the repayment of the subsidy. The panel, ironically, found the loan to be a part of the same transaction, nullifying the repayment and arguably suggesting that governments could not assume the burden of the repayment. In fact, however, the panel was quite careful not to rule broadly on the validity of such government loans, presumably recognizing that governments will have to find some way to ease the cost of repayment of subsidies if future decisions continue to require full repayment.

23 Bernard M. Hoekman & Petros C. Mavroidis, *Enforcing Multilateral Commitments: Dispute Settlement and Developing Countries*, WTO/World Bank Conference on Developing Countries in a Millennium Round (Sept. 20–21, 1999) at 30.

decisions on individuals will ease the pressure those injured individuals put on Member governments to resist compliance.[24] The tension between increasing juridical formality and increasing flexibility in the face of popular resistance may be resolved in practice, if the DSU considers compensation as part of, rather than an alternative to, compliance.

24 It has been argued that the DSU serves as a scapegoat, so that governments under excessive political pressure not to liberalize trade barriers can say to their constituents "the DSU made me do it." While this tactic may work for governments facing only superficial resistance, any deeply running popular sentiment could react with a vocal backlash against an "undemocratic supranational tyrant."

THE COMPLIANCE PROBLEMS OF THE WTO

Gary Horlick & Judith Coleman*

A. Forms of Non-Compliance

Every day, governments around the world comply with the WTO, and the GATT before it, tens of thousands of times, and probably even more often. WTO-limited ("bound") customs tariffs are charged at or below the agreed limits, valuation practices follow the WTO Customs Valuation Agreement, food crosses borders regulated in accordance with the SPS (Sanitary and Phytosanitary Measures) Agreement, and so on. On the rarer occasions when national governments decide, instead, not to comply, the WTO has proven to be a weak reed. This non-compliance has tended to take three forms (at least): (1) prior non-compliance, (2) delay, and (3) non-compliance, open and disguised.

1. Prior Non-Compliance

To judge just from the very limited sample offered by cases brought to WTO dispute settlement, virtually every major trading Member of the WTO has taken action knowing it was inconsistent with the WTO, apparently on the basis that at worst it would be challenged in the WTO dispute settlement process, and then dragged out in litigation for three to four years before having to comply with the rules to which it had agreed. This is done not just by the big players—the United States, the EU, Japan, Canada, Brazil, India—but also Argentina, Australia, Chile, China, Egypt, and so on (for the sake of politeness, individual cases are not named here, but a quick look at the list of requests for consultations will identify them for the reader). In effect, the WTO has been re-written by those Members to claim that none of the obligations applies for a three- to four-year period. And these are only the most blatant cases. The same phenomena are probably reflected in the very leisurely way in which WTO Members adapt to fairly definitive rulings by the Appellate Body in cases involving other Members. The most obvious example is the case of India against the EC on "zeroing," decided in India's favor by the Appellate Body in 2001.[1] The ruling was sufficiently clear to guide other Members. But very few complied (in the sense of adapting their own national systems) with any speed, and some have made it clear

---

* WilmerHale, Washington, D.C., and Yale Law School, New Haven, Connecticut. The views expressed here do not necessarily reflect the views of the entities with which the authors are associated. The authors thank the Legal Affairs Division of the WTO for its helpful comments. Any errors belong to the authors.

1. Appellate Body Report, *European Communities – Anti-Dumping Duties on Imports of Cotton-Type Bed Linen from India*, WT/DS141/AB/R (Mar. 1, 2001).

they will not comply until fully stretching out (for six years and counting) dispute resolution in additional cases brought directly against them. It will be interesting to observe over time whether empirical data confirms the suspicion that this could become discriminatory, as countries better able to afford the internal or external cost of defending themselves in WTO dispute resolution cases are in a better position to undertake this behavior than poorer countries.

2. Delay

Even assuming, charitably, that all WTO Members act in good faith to fulfill their obligations, and that they only discover they are in violation after an Appellate Body ruling, there are numerous cases where the post–Appellate Body process stretches on for years. Again, this is not just one or two Members—it is obvious that numerous governments are deciding to "game the system" and string out non-compliance for as long as possible. (And this ignores the numerous delays in litigation before the Appellate Body rulings—it is fascinating to hear lawyers for Members state openly that they are taking every delay they can.)

3. Non-Compliance, Open and Disguised

There is an increasing number of decisions where Members have openly decided not to comply and instead risk retaliation, starting with the 1998 *EC – Hormones* case[2] (where even full retaliation did not lead to compliance, and where the retaliation did not and could not compensate the exporters injured by the measure found to be WTO-inconsistent). Other non-compliance may not be so open. For example, the WTO website lists the case of *U.S. – Lead and Bismuth II*[3] as a success—the Appellate Body ruled and the defending country complied. It nowhere records that obtaining the compliance required a side payment to a competing company of many millions of dollars. Perhaps the losing Member would have eventually complied without the side payments, but the apparent lack of restrospectivity in the WTO Dispute Settlement Understanding (DSU) means that exporters would continue to pay duty deposits *after* the duties were found WTO-inconsistent without those duties being refunded—so the DSU seems to encourage non-transparent side payments.

---

2. Appellate Body Report, *European Communities – Measures Concerning Meat and Meat Products (Hormones)*, WT/DS26/AB/R, WT/DS48/AB/R (Jan. 16, 1998).

3. Appellate Body Report, *United States – Imposition of Countervailing Duties on Certain Hot-Rolled Lead and Bismuth Carbon Steel Products Originating in the United Kingdom*, WT/DS138/AB/R (May 10, 2000).

B. The Data

We have made a preliminary attempt to categorize how member countries have responded to WTO decisions, in the hope that people will be able to correct or amend these findings on the basis of better information that is perhaps not readily available to the public. We have attached our list, based on our quick survey.

Here are some quick statistics:

- Of the 98 final decisions since 1996, the panel or appellate body found violations in 85 cases (85.8%). That is to say, there was no violation found in 13 of the cases.

- Of those 85 cases where violations were found, the compliance period is still running on 6 of them, and the compliance status of 2 is unclear, leaving 77 cases for our analysis.

- Of those 77 cases, 53 (68.8%) ended in what we have (catchily) called **Apparent More-or-Less Full Compliance**, which includes compliance after threats of retaliation, compliance after decisions handed down by Article 21.5 panels, and especially long drawn-out compliance.

- In 19 cases (24.6%), the violating country has made gestures at compliance: **Partial Compliance** in 8 cases (where some but not all measures are revised), **Debatable Compliance** in 6 cases (where one country claims to have complied but other countries raise an eyebrow), **Sleazy Settlements** in 5 cases (of which 4 are related to the pending U.S.-Canada *Softwood Lumber* dispute).

- Six of the cases (6.1%) have resulted in **Unabashed Non-Compliance**. That non-compliance has been tolerated, however grudgingly, by the complainants—except in one case, *EC – Hormones*.

C. Why Worry?

A 6.1% rate of open non-compliance does not seem very bad. But because it is mostly cumulative (most of the cases do not disappear), that means an increasing stack of embarrassingly overt non-compliance. It is worth noting that Bob Hudec calculated that the GATT dispute settlement system "worked" 88% of the time, but it was the 12% of cases where GATT did not "work" that reduced the system's credibility enough to require the major changes in the Uruguay Round.

In that context, the 25% of less-than-full compliance, and the delays in reaching full compliance in other cases, suggests the need for DSU reforms such as some of those suggested by Mexico (repayment of illegally collected duties, disincentives for delay).

ANNEX:
WTO DECISIONS AND COMPLIANCE – 98 DECISIONS TOTAL

A. Compliance Not Needed (13)

U.S. – OCTG AD Measures
Korea – Commercial Vessels
U.S. – Corrosion Resistant Steel Sunset Review
EC – Pipe Fittings
U.S. – Textiles Rules of Origin
EC – Asbestos
U.S. – Certain EC Products
Korea – Government Procurement
U.S. – Section 301
EC – Computer Equipment
Japan – Film
Brazil – Dessicated Coconut
U.S. – Section 129

B. Apparent More-or-Less Full Compliance (53)

(includes eventual compliance, including agreements not obviously sleazy, and Article 21.5-induced compliance)

Japan – Laver Quotas
EC – DRAMS Countervailing Measures
EC – Trademarks / GIs
Canada – Wheat
Mexico – Telecoms
Japan – Apples
U.S. – Steel Safeguards
Argentina – Poultry AD Duties
Argentina – Peach Safeguards

U.S. – German Steel CVDs
EC – Sardines
Egypt – Rebar
U.S. – India Steel Plate
India – Autos
U.S. – Line Pipe Safeguards
U.S. – Cotton Yarn
Argentina – Floor Tiles AD Measures
U.S. – Export Restraints
U.S. – Lamb Safeguards
EC – Bed Linen
U.S. – Steel Plate from Korea
U.S. – Wheat Gluten
Korea – Beef
Guatemala – Cement
Canada – Patent Term
U.S. – DRAMS
Dominican Republic – Cigarettes
U.S. – 1916 Act
Canada – Automotive Industry
Canada – Pharmaceutical Patents
U.S. – FSC's
Argentina – Footwear Safeguards
Korea – Dairy Safeguards
Chile – Alcoholic Beverage
EC – Butter
Turkey – Textiles
India – QRs
U.S. – DRAMs AD
Japan – Agricultural Products
Korea – Alcoholic Beverages
Australia – Salmon
U.S. – Shrimp
India – Patents
Indonesia – Automobiles
EC – Poultry
Argentina – Textiles and Apparel
India – Patents
Canada – Periodicals
U.S. – Shirts and Blouses
U.S. – Cotton Underwear
Japan – Alcoholic Beverages
EC – Scallops
U.S. – Gasoline

C. Gestures at Compliance (19)

1. Debatable Compliance (currently questioned by another country) (6)

EC – Sugar Subsidies
U.S. – Cotton Subsidies
EC – Tariff Preferences
EC – Bananas
U.S. – OCTG Sunset Reviews
Chile – Agricultural Products

2. Partial / Piecemeal Compliance (8)

Argentina – Bovine Hides
U.S. – Byrd Amendment
U.S. – Section 110(5) of Copyright Act
Mexico – HFCS
Canada – Milk/Dairy
Australia – Leather
U.S. – CVDs on EC Products
U.S. – Hot Rolled Steel from Japan

3. Sleazy Settlements (5)

U.S. – Lumber (#236, 264, 277, 257)
U.S. – Lead Bars

D. Unabashed Non-Compliance (6)

1. Non-Compliance Apparently Tolerated by Other Countries (5)

U.S. – Havana Club
Thailand – Steel
Canada – Aircraft (#222, 70)
Brazil – Aircraft

2. Non-Compliance Not Tolerated (1)

EC – Hormones

E. To Be Determined (8)

1. Unclear (2)

EC – Chicken Classification
EC – Commercial Vessels

2. Compliance Period Still Running or Suspended (6)

Mexico – Soft Drinks
Mexico – Rice AD Measures
Korea – Paper AD Duties
U.S. – Gambling Services
U.S. – DRAMS CVD
U.S. – Zeroing

POLITICAL QUESTIONS IN INTERNATIONAL TRADE: JUDICIAL REVIEW OF SECTION 301?

Erwin P. Eichmann and Gary N. Horlick

Section 301 of the Trade Act of 1974 ("Section 301")[1] has become an increasingly potent and widely-used tool in the U.S. arsenal of trade policy measures. The past few years have seen a proliferation of Section 301 cases, affecting the trade of goods and services in Europe, Asia, and Latin America. Even so, in the debate over the Omnibus Trade and Competitiveness Act of 1988 ("Omnibus Trade Act"), Congress expressed impatience with the President's discretion in not undertaking more Section 301 retaliations.[2] But while much attention has focused on the politics and policy aspects of Section 301, little has been discussed of the legal issues underpinning it.

Section 301 provides the President with broad authority to take trade action against unfair foreign conduct. This fact, and experience under Section 301, have promoted the perception that Congress effectively abdicated its constitutional power over foreign commerce to the President. But Congress certainly did not grant the President unchecked powers over foreign trade. Quite the contrary, a closer examination of Section 301's statutory provisions reveals that Congress expressly limited the exercise of the President's authority to specific circumstances, particularly those which meet certain statutory definitions. Under Section 301, the President may grant relief only from "unfair" foreign trade practices. Since Congress has authorized action only to rectify these specific foreign trade practices, the President may be without authority if the foreign conduct falls outside of the statutory definitions. Because the President cannot undertake peacetime (i.e., nonemergency) trade action without Congressional authorization, the President would have to rely on other statutory grants of authority to impose any other action he may wish to take. This article will argue that U.S. courts may be able to review Executive Branch determinations of the "fairness" of foreign trade conduct as these de-

1. Trade Act of 1974, tit. III, § 301, Pub. L. No. 93-618 (current version at 19 U.S.C. § 2411 (1982)).

2. Bello & Holmer, *The Heart of the 1988 Trade Act: A Legislative History of the Amendments to Section 301*, 25 STAN. J. INT'L L. 1, 10 (1988).

terminations form the basis for Presidential authority under Section 301.

A major obstacle to judicial review of Section 301, though, is the political question doctrine. Under this label, courts will not adjudicate "political" issues: those which are nonjusticiable or would embarrass the President in the conduct of foreign relations. This article will analyze the justiciability of the unfairness definitions and conclude that while some of the criteria are easily justiciable, others may not be. However, even if some of the statutory criteria are nonjusticiable, a court may sever those questions that are nonjusticiable and continue its review. Secondly, the analysis will reveal that the need for finality of United States actions in foreign affairs causes the greatest political question difficulties, but does not undercut the entire basis of judicial reviewability.

Another obstacle to judicial review is the state secrets doctrine. Under this doctrine, courts will not intrude into certain areas of national defense. This article will argue that courts can follow Supreme Court precedent and use their discretion to separate state secrets from trade matters and adjudicate questions of unfair trade conduct.

Section 301 carefully limits the President's discretion in setting trade policy. Thus, the statutory criteria of Section 301 fall within that category of questions that courts will review. The first section of this article describes the limits of the President's authority under Section 301. The second and third sections demonstrate that while political question, jurisdictional, and state secrets issues provide some serious questions, incantation of "foreign affairs" alone is not enough to prevent judicial review.

I. The Necessity for Congressional Authorization of Executive Trade Action

The President does not have an unlimited, unbridled foreign affairs power.[3] While the President may have a certain "very delicate, plenary and exclusive power" in the field of international relations,[4] Congress has explicit constitutional powers to "regulate Commerce with

3. L. Henkin, Foreign Affairs and the Constitution, 64-65 (1972). As Justice Jackson wrote in his concurring opinion to Youngstown Sheet & Tube Co. v. Sawyer:

> The example of such unlimited executive power that must have most impressed the forefathers was the prerogative exercised by George III, and the description of its evils in the Declaration of Independence leads me to doubt that they were creating their new Executive in his image.

343 U.S. 579, 641 (1952) (*cited with approval in* Dames & Moore v. Regan, 453 U.S. 654, 662, (1981)).

4. United States v. Curtiss-Wright Export Corp., 299 U.S. 304, 319-320 (1936).

foreign Nations" and to "lay and collect Taxes, Duties, Imports and Excises."[5] Most commentators have interpreted this constitutional balance so as to limit the Presidential power over peacetime international trade to that available under an explicit or implicit grant from Congress.

The Supreme Court has examined the limits of Congressional and Executive powers in *Youngstown Sheet and Tube v. Sawyer.*[6] In that case, the Court invalidated President Truman's siezure of domestic steel mills, even though Truman claimed that the continued operation of the mills was necessary for the Korean War effort. Writing for the court, Justice Black found that "[t]he President's power, if any, to issue the order must stem from either an act of Congress or the Constitution itself."[7] Thus, under the reasoning of Black's majority opinion, the President can only undertake such trade retaliation as Congress or the Constitution has authorized.

Elaborating on Black's limitation of the President's powers, Justice Jackson, in an oft-quoted concurrence to *Youngstown*, identified three types of Presidential action. In the first category, as in the majority opinion, "[w]hen the President acts pursuant to an express or implied authorization of Congress, his authority is at its maximum, for it includes all that he possesses in his own right plus all that Congress can delegate."[8] Without Congressional authorization, Presidential action

5. U.S. CONST. art. I, § 8, cl. 1, 3.

6. 343 U.S. 579 (1952).

7. *Id.* at 585. The Court's rationale for overturning the President's order appears to overturn Justice Sutherland's dictum that gave the President an independent foreign relations power. *Curtiss-Wright, supra* note 4, at 319-20. Sutherland had based the President's foreign relations power on a transfer of sovereignty from the King of England to the President of the United States. Justice Black, by finding that the President's power may only come from Congress or the Constitution, implicitly overruled Sutherland's view of the President attaining power through the passage of sovereignty. However, Black never explicitly mentions or cites *Curtiss-Wright*, even though it had been decided only sixteen years earlier.

8. *Youngstown, supra* note 3, at 635. *See* Dames & Moore v. Regan, 453 U.S. 654, 670-89 (1981), where Justice Rehnquist minutely analyzed the Congressional intent behind the International Emergency Economic Powers Act ("IEEPA"), 50 U.S.C. § 1702 (Supp. V 1987), and the Hostages Act in upholding the President's settlement of the Iran hostage crisis. The Court evidently would rather find Congressional authorization for the President's foreign affairs powers than analyze a clash of authorizations.

See also Rehnquist and Stewart's comments during the oral argument of *Dames & Moore*. Rehnquist was concerned that an unlimited foreign affairs power would allow the President to negate provisions of the Bill of Rights. He asked, "What if the agreement provided that for one year no one should criticize the Ayatollah?" The attorney for Iran replied, "Then the United States would be obliged to attempt to accomplish that." Furthermore, as the Solicitor General's theory of Presidential power appeared to provide no limits, Justice Powell remarked, "[t]he President could have exchanged you [Solicitor General Rex Lee] for one of the hostages — you or me." N.Y. Times, June 25, 1981, at D3, col. 1, *quoted in* Nowak & Rotunda, *A Comment on the Creation and Resolution of a "Nonproblem:" Dames & Moore v. Regan, The Foreign Affairs Power, and The Role of the Court*, 29 UCLA L. REV. 1129, 1133 n.18 (1982).

enters Jackson's latter two categories. In Jackson's second category, "[w]hen the President acts in absence of either a congressional grant or denial of authority, he can only rely upon his own independent powers, but there is a zone of twilight in which he and Congress may have concurrent authority." In Jackson's third category, "[w]hen the President takes measures incompatible with the expressed or implied will of Congress, his power is at its lowest ebb, for then he can rely only upon his own constitutional powers minus any constitutional powers of Congress over the matter."[9]

Jackson's three-category balancing test is based on the same underlying principles as Black's absolutist answer—that the Constitution vests most federal powers in the Congress and that the President must find some constitutional underpinning for his exercise of power, even in foreign relations. Were the President to undertake trade retaliation in the absence of Section 301 or other grant, such trade action would have to rely on the President's inherent powers. Although the President has some inherent foreign affairs power over trade, the Constitution gives Congress explicit power over foreign trade, and a Court would have to stretch constitutional theory to uphold Presidential peacetime trade action without some Congressional authorization.[10] Indeed, if the President could always act without any Congressional authorization, then the President could effectively repeal any Congressional trade enactment!

Several court decisions have reviewed Congressional authorization for Presidential trade action. In *Dames & Moore v. Regan*, the Supreme Court analyzed Congressional authority for the President's settlement of the Iran hostage crisis,[11] and based the President's actions on Congressional acquiescence. Here, however, Congress has spoken loudly and frequently about U.S. trade policy and recently narrowed the President's discretion in using Section 301.[12] In *Yoshida International*,[13] the Customs Court examined Presidential power over

9. *Youngstown*, *supra* note 3, at 637.

10. *See* United States v. Guy W. Capps, Inc., 204 F.2d 655, 658 (4th Cir. 1953) (voiding an executive agreement between the United States and Canada on potato imports that contradicted a Congressional statute "because it was not authorized by Congress,"), *aff'd on other grounds*, 348 U.S. 296 (1954); *but see*, Consumer's Union of United States v. Kissinger, 506 F.2d 136, 143 (D.C. Cir. 1974) (upholding Presidential negotiation of steel import restraints because they "do not purport to be enforceable, either as contracts or as governmental actions with the force of law."), *cert. denied*, 421 U.S. 1004 (1975). While the President's actions in *Consumer's Union* were unenforceable, Presidential retaliation under Section 301 may include tariff increases and is enforceable.

11. *See Dames & Moore*, *supra* note 3.

12. Bello & Holmer, *supra* note 2, at 10-18.

13. Yoshida Int'l, Inc. v. United States, 378 F.Supp. 1155 (Cust. Ct. 1974), *rev'd* 526 F.2d 560 (C.C.P.A. 1975).

trade in interpreting section 255 of the Trade Expansion Act ("TEA"), the precursor to Section 301.[14] The Customs Court held that President Nixon had exceeded his authority in proclaiming a tariff surcharge because "the authority granted by statute to 'terminate, in whole or in part, any proclamation', does not include the power to determine and fix unilaterally a rate of duty which has not been previously legally established."[15] The Appeals Court agreed, noting that "no undelegated power to regulate *commerce*, or to set tariffs, inheres in the Presidency."[16] In another case, the Customs Court overturned a tariff rate quota which the President established after escape clause proceedings.[17] The President had rejected the Tariff Commission's recommendation on the matter, and the court held that, under the statute, the President could not devise his own remedy even if it accomplished the broad Congressional purpose. Thus, the President could only accept or reject the Commission's recommendation.

Yoshida, *National Silver* and *Dames & Moore* all contain the implicit notion that the President must meet the statutory criteria before he can invoke the powers delegated to him by Congress. In *Yoshida*, the court found that the TEA did not enable the President to implement a tariff surcharge; instead it relied on the President's authority during "any" period of national emergency as defined by the Trading With the Enemy Act.[18] In *Dames & Moore*, the Court found that an emergency existed under IEEPA, but that Congress' explicit delegation of authority was not broad enough for the President's actions; instead, the Court found an implicit delegation through Congressional acquiescence. Finally, in *National Silver*, the court overturned a Presidential trade action as outside the Congressional delegation.

Not all scholars agree with the interpretation that limits Presidential action to explicit constitutional or Congressional grants. Some would argue, based on *United States v. Curtiss-Wright Export Corp.*,[19] that the President has an independent foreign affairs power that allows him to take trade action outside his enumerated powers. However, *Curtiss-Wright* itself does not actually support that position. The sentence containing Justice Sutherland's famous dictum, that the Presi-

14. Trade Expansion Act of 1962, 19 U.S.C. § 1885(b) (1980).

15. *Yoshida*, *supra* note 13, at 1162.

16. United States v. Yoshida Int'l Inc., 526 F.2d 560, 572 (C.C.P.A. 1975) (reversing the Customs Court on other grounds) (emphasis in original).

17. National Silver Co. v. United States, 388 F.Supp. 1391 (Cust. Ct. 1975).

18. 50 U.S.C.A. app. § 5 (1982).

19. *Supra* note 4.

dent has a "very delicate, plenary and exclusive power" in foreign relations, also holds a significant qualifier—that this power "of course, like every other governmental power, must be exercised in subordination to the applicable provisions of the Constitution."[20] In context, Sutherland's enunciation of the President's foreign relations power may be no more than recognition of the President's particularized exclusive powers,[21] instead of an expansion of generalizable Executive powers. Indeed, one commentator has noted that the second half of Sutherland's sentence effectively cancels the broad reach of the first part because the reference to Constitutional provisions implies a limitation on Presidential powers through the Neccesary and Proper Clause.[22]

In addition, Sutherland's view of the alleged Presidential foreign affairs power may no longer be good law as it has been rejected by the Court and commentators alike. Sutherland based his view on a dubious interpretation of the transmission of sovereignty from England to the United States:

> As a result of the separation from Great Britain by the colonies acting as a unit, the powers of the external sovereignty passed from the Crown not to the colonies severally but to the colonies in their collective and corporate capacity as the United States of America . . . . It results that the investment of the Federal Government with the powers of external sovereignty did not depend upon the affirmative grants of the Constitution.[23]

First, this view is historically inaccurate. The Declaration of Independence, the Articles of Confederation, and contemporary writings all indicate that sovereignty was to reside in the people, acting legislatively through the individual states.[24] In contrast, the Constitution intended a federal government of limited powers,[25] such that the vestiges of sovereignty could not have passed undetected to the Presi-

20. *Id.* at 320.

21. For example, the Constitution grants the President exclusive power to act as the Commander-in-Chief of the armed forces. U.S. CONST. art. II.

22. *Transmittal of Executive Agreements to Congress, Hearings Before the Subcommittee on Foreign Relations, United States Senate*, 92 Cong., 1st Sess., 18 (1971) (statement of Ruhl Bartlett, then Professor at the Fletcher School of Law and Diplomacy, Tufts University) [hereinafter 1971 Hearings] The Necessary and Proper Clause grants to Congress the power "(t)o make all laws which shall be necessary and proper for carrying into execution the foregoing Powers, and all other Powers vested by this Constitution in the Government of the United States." U.S. CONST. art I.

23. *Curtiss-Wright*, *supra* note 4, at 316.

24. U.S. CONST. amend. X; ARTICLES OF CONFEDERATION art. II. ("Each state retains its sovereignty, freedom and independence, and every Power, Jurisdiction and Right, which is not in this Confederation expressly delegated to the United States in Congress assembled.").

25. McCullogh v. Maryland, 17 U.S. (4 Wheat.) 316, 421 (1819) ("the powers of government are limited, and that its limits are not to be transcended.").

dent.[26] Second, the Court has rejected this view repeatedly by declaring that the Constitution limits the powers of the federal government. Indeed, both *Youngstown* and *Dames and Moore* rely on constitutional grants of Presidential power; neither cite *Curtiss-Wright* for its view of extra-constitutional powers.[27] Thus, if the President is to have such an extra-constitutional foreign relations power, its basis must be found outside a literal recitation of *Curtiss-Wright*'s dictum.

In reviewing a Section 301 determination, a court must find the statutory criteria and decide on the scope of Presidential authority under it. A court could then examine the Presidential action to ascertain whether it meets the criteria both procedurally and substantively, and if the action does not, then it is beyond the President's Section 301 authority.

A. *Section 301 Must Have An "Intelligible Principle."*

Not every Congressional delegation to the President will withstand judicial review.[28]

> A constitutional delegation of powers requires that Congress enunciate a policy or objective or give reasons for seeking the aid of the President. In addition the act must specify when the powers conferred may be utilized by establishing a standard or 'intelligible principle' which is sufficient to make it clear when action is proper. . . . This means that Congress must tell the President what he can do by prescribing a standard which confines his discretion and which will guarantee that any authorized action he takes will tend to promote rather than flout the legislative purpose.[29]

The "intelligible principle" test of proper constitutional delegation has often arisen in the context of trade and tariff legislation. In the foreign affairs context, courts have often upheld broad delegations as proper.[30] On the other hand, in the international trade context, a

26. *See* 1971 Hearings, *supra* note 22, at 17-18.

27. *But see* Koh, *Why the President (Almost) Always Wins in Foreign Affairs: Lessons of the Iran-Contra Affair*, 97 YALE L. J. 1255, 1311 (1988) (arguing that "(c)oupled with *Chadha* [I.N.S. v. Chadha, 462 U.S. 919 (1983)], Justice Rehnquist's statutory interpretation in *Dames and Moore* radically undercuts *Youngstown*'s vision of a balanced national security process . . . . The decisions simultaneously strengthen the President vis-a-vis the judiciary by encouraging the courts to apply a special measure of deference to executive acts in foreign affairs, a requirement that Justice Jackson had soundly rejected in *Youngstown* itself.").

28. Field v. Clark, 143 U.S. 649, 692 (1891) ("That Congress cannot delegate legislative power to the President is a principle universally recognized as vital to the integrity and maintenance of the system of government ordained by the Constitution."); Schechter Poultry Corp. v. United States, 295 U.S. 495 (1935) ("The Congress is not permitted to abdicate or to transfer to others the essential legislative functions with which it is thus vested."), *quoted in* National Cable Television Ass'n v. United States, 415 U.S. 336 (1974).

29. Star-Kist Foods, Inc. v. United States, 275 F.2d 472, 480 (C.C.P.A. 1959).

30. *See Dames & Moore*, *supra* note 3, at 670 (upholding Presidential authority to regulate "any property in which any foreign country or a national thereof has any interest"); Amalga-

court may construe Congressional delegations more strictly since Congress has explicit authority to regulate commerce with foreign nations.[31] Nevertheless, in a possible judicial review of Section 301, a court would use the section's "intelligible principle" as a guidepost in determining whether Presidential action is properly authorized.

B. *Congress Has Delegated Broad, But Limited, Powers To Rectify Unfair Foreign Trade Practices Under Section 301.*

Although Congress drafted Section 301 with broad language, Congress did not authorize the President to undertake any trade retaliation at any time he pleases. Instead, the Presidential determination of an unfair trade practice and injury to United States commerce delimits the President's powers. While granting the President authority to suspend, withdraw or prevent the application of any trade concession or impose duties or other import restrictions on any product or service,[32] Congress limited when such remedies could be invoked. In particular, the United States Trade Representative ("USTR") must take mandatory action, "subject to the specific direction of the President," (a) to enforce rights under any trade agreement or (b) against any foreign act, policy or practice that (i) is inconsistent with or denies the benefits of any trade agreement or (ii) is unjustifiable and burdens or restricts United States commerce.[33] In addition, the USTR may take discretionary action, subject to Presidential discretion, if any foreign act, policy, or practice is unreasonable or discriminatory and burdens or restricts U.S. commerce.[34] If the foreign conduct does not meet this threshold test, then the USTR cannot make a positive determination,

mated Meat Cutters & Butcher Workmen of North America v. Connally, 337 F.Supp. 737 (D.D.C. 1971) (upholding the President's 1971 wage-price freeze as sufficiently following the statutory will of Congress).

31. Even under Justice Sutherland's expansive view of Presidential power in *Curtiss-Wright*, the President cannot act in trade matters without Congressional authorization. Sutherland's list of implicit Presidential powers only includes "the powers to declare and wage war, to conclude peace, to make treaties, [and] to maintain diplomatic relations with other sovereignties." *Curtiss-Wright, supra* note 4, at 318. *But see* Mast Ind., Inc. v. Regan, 596 F.Supp. 1567, 1575 (Ct. Int'l Trade 1984) (upholding a Congressional delegation of power over trade and finding that "[w]here Congress has given the President discretion in delegating authority in international trade, the courts have uniformly sustained action by the Executive Branch against a claim that it has exceeded the delegated authority."), *aff'd* 822 F.2d 1069 (Fed. Cir. 1987).

32. 19 U.S.C. § 2411(c) (Supp. V 1987).

33. S. 2613, 100th Cong., 2d Sess. § 301(a)(1) (1988). The USTR is not required to take action (1) if dispute resolution proceedings under the General Agreements on Tariff and Trade find no violation of U.S. trade rights, (2) if the foreign government is taking, has agreed to take, or it is impossible for it to take appropriate measures, (3) if the retaliation would have an excessive adverse impact on the U.S. economy, or (4) if the retaliation would cause serious harm to U.S. national security. *Id.* at § 301(a)(2).

34. *Id.* at § 301(b).

and the President has no authority to act.[35] Following a positive determination, the USTR must take action within 30 days, unless the President directs otherwise.[36] Furthermore, the legislative history shows that Congress intends the President to act upon positive USTR determinations.[37]

The statutory threshold test is crucial. If the petitioner does not meet it, no relief can be granted because the statutory precondition to Presidential authority has not been satisfied. Therefore, if the petitioner does not meet the test and the President does take action without another form of statutory authority, then the President enters the third Jacksonian category where "the President acts in contravention of the will of Congress, 'his power is at its lowest ebb,' and the Court can sustain his actions 'only by disabling the Congress from acting upon the subject.' "[38] Furthermore, if the petitioner meets the test, then Congress did intend that an investigation be initiated;[39] if the President does not investigate, then he would also be contravening the legislative intent.

Assuming that the political question doctrine does not bar judicial review of Section 301,[40] a court can review the merits of each petitioner's case to determine whether the foreign trade practice passes the threshold test. Even though Congress did not specify that Section 301 was intended to be subject to judicial review, the courts may legitimately infer such a requirement.[41] After all, Congress has enacted a statutory definition for an unfair trade practice under Section 301 and "under the Constitution, one of the judiciary's characteristic roles is to

35. *Id.* at § 304(a)(1).

36. *Id.* at § 305(a)(1). The USTR may delay action up to 180 days after a positive determination upon specific circumstances. *Id.* at § 305(a)(2).

37. "The [Senate Finance] Committee intends that the President, under the amended law, vigorously pursue appropriate action whenever necessary to enforce the rights of the United States under a trade agreement or to respond to other unfair foreign acts, policies, or practices determined by the USTR to be actionable under section 301." S. REP. NO. 71, 100th Cong., 1st Sess. 80 (1987). Nevertheless, the statutory language does permit the President to direct the USTR to take no action.

38. *Dames & Moore*, *supra* note 3, at 669 (quoting *Youngstown*, *supra* note 3, at 637-38).

39. S. REP. NO. 249, 96th Cong., lst. Sess. at 238 (1979) (the President's discretion "must be exercised in light of the need to vigorously insure fair and equitable conditions for U.S. commerce, and in cases including the enforcement of U.S. rights under the agreements negotiated in the MTN or where a petition has been filed requesting a response to an action inconsistent with such agreements, this discretion normally should be exercised by proceeding to investigate and to pursue valid claims in appropriate international fora when the petition properly presents issues covered by Section 301. . . .").

40. *See infra* section II.

41. California v. Yamaski, 442 U.S. 682, 693 (1979) (finding a right to a prerecoupment oral hearing under § 204(a) of the Social Securities Act, 42 U.S.C. § 404(a)(1), even though the statute does not so require).

interpret statutes, and [the judiciary] cannot shirk this responsibility merely because [its] decision may have political overtones."[42]

For example, the Supreme Court did not allow the political overtones of the Nicaraguan revolution to impinge on its adjudication of asylum statutes for Nicaraguan refugees.[43] There, the Court interpreted the "well-founded fear of persecution" standard under section 101(a)(42) of the Immigration and Nationality Act of 1952 to mean a subjective fear. Under the Court's view, refugees need not prove that it is more likely than not that they would be persecuted upon return to Nicaragua in order to be eligible for asylum. Indeed, the Court found no constitutional constraint against interpreting the statute, even though, as in Section 301, the Immigration and Nationality Act only creates categories of refugees from which the Attorney General may, at his discretion, grant asylum.[44] Thus, if the foreign trade practice does not pass the Section 301 test, then the President will have acted without Congressional authorization, and such action may not pass constitutional muster.[45]

II. Constitutional Bars to Judicial Review: Political Question and Prudential Considerations

Courts have traditionally abstained from reviewing cases involving foreign affairs on the grounds that they are "political questions."[46]

42. Japan Whaling Ass'n v. American Cetacean Soc'y, 478 U.S. 221, 230 (1986); *see also* Immigration and Naturalization Serv. v. Chadha, 462 U.S. 919, 943 (1983) ("Resolution of litigation challenging the constitutional authority of one of the three branches cannot be evaded by the courts because the issues have political implications. . ."). The legal and factual issues of foreign trade conduct and Presidential retaliation should satisfy the court's jurisdictional requirement of "cases and controversies." U.S. Const. art. III; *see* Buckley v. Valeo, 424 U.S. 1 (1976). The court can make such a review once the determination becomes final. *See infra* text accompanying notes 102-144.

43. Immigration and Naturalization Serv. v. Cardoza-Fonseca, 480 U.S. 421 (1987).

44. 8 U.S.C. § 1158(a) (1982).

45. Action without statutory authorization falls within Jackson's second category of concurrent authority where "congressional inertia, indifference or aquiescence may sometimes, at least as a practical matter, enable, if not invite, measures on independent presidential responsibility." *Youngstown*, *supra* note 3, at 637 (Jackson, J., concurring). For example, in *Dames & Moore*, the court found that the President had acted outside of his explicit authorization but upheld the action as constitutional in the face of Congressional acquiescence. *Supra* note 3, at 654. *See* W. Eskridge, Jr. & P. Frickey, Cases and Materials on Legislation: Statutes and the Creation of Public Policy 317-21 (1988).

Here, unlike the negotiation for hostage release at issue in *Dames & Moore*, Congress has not backed into acquiescence of Administration trade policy, judging from Congressional changes in Section 301 in 1988 which were subsequently vetoed. Since Congress has explicitly defined unfair trade conduct under Section 301 and recently reworked the definition to limit Presidental discretion, Presidential action outside the statutory guidelines would contravene the will of Congress and fall within Jackson's third category of presumably impermissible action. *See* Bello & Holmer, *supra* note 2, at 10-18.

46. *See e.g.*, Luther v. Borden, 48 U.S. (7 How.) 1 (1849); Marbury v. Madison, 5 U.S. (1

Nevertheless, "it is 'error to suppose that every case or controversy which touches foreign relations lies beyond judicial cognizance.' "[47] Although commentators generally agree that there is a constitutional basis to the political question doctrine,[48] they disagree as to its nature and scope.[49] Justice Brennan, writing for the U.S. Supreme Court, has described the doctrine as having "attributes which, in various settings, diverge, combine, appear, and disappear in seeming disorderliness."[50] Nonetheless, Brennan's six factor test has become the standard for political question analysis:[51]

> It is apparent that several formulations which vary slightly according to the settings in which the questions arise may describe a political question, although each has one or more elements which identify it as essentially a function of the separation of powers. Prominent on the surface of any case held to involve a political question is found [1] a textually demonstrable constitutional commitment of the issue to a coordinate political department; or [2] a lack of judicially discoverable and manageable standards for resolving it; or [3] the impossibility of deciding without an initial policy determination of a kind clearly for nonjudicial discretion; or [4] the impossibility of a court's undertaking independent resolution without expressing lack of the respect due coordinate branches of government; or [5] an unusual need for unquestioning adherence to a political decision already made; or [6] the potentiality of embarrassment from multifarious pronouncements by various departments

Cranch) 137, 170 (1803) (Marshall, C.J.) ("Questions, in their nature political . . . can never be made in this court").

47. *Japan Whaling Ass'n, supra* note 42, at 2866 (quoting Baker v. Carr, 369 U.S. 186, 211 (1962)); Ely, *Suppose Congress Wanted a War Powers Act That Worked*, 88 COLUM. L. REV. 1379, 1407 (1988) ("The 'political question doctrine' is a little like the Holy Roman Empire. It doesn't have much to do with whether the question is 'political' in any ordinary sense . . .").

Professor Ely notes that adjudication of "political cases" is entirely in line with the rather plain intent of the Constitution, which lists among the heads of federal judicial jurisdiction cases arising under treaties, cases affecting ambassadors and other public ministers and consuls, cases in admiralty or maritime jurisdiction, and cases to which the United States and/or foreign nations are parties—and indicates further that treaties shall be the supreme law of the land "and the Judges in every state shall be bound thereby." *Id.* at 1409 n.88.

48. *But see* Henkin, *Is There A "Political Question" Doctrine?*, 85 YALE L. J. 597 (1976). Professor Louis Henkin has argued that the leading cases on the political question doctrine should instead be understood as determinations that the President's decisions were within his authority, and that the holdings were justified on their merits. *Id.* at 612; Henkin, *Viet-Nam in the Courts of the United States: "Political Questions"*, 63 AM J. INT'L L. 284, 286 (1969) ("In regard to foreign affairs, I believe, the Supreme Court has never found a true 'political question,' "); *but see* Ramirez de Arellano v. Weinberger, 745 F.2d 1500, & 1514 n.50, 1515 (D.C. Cir. 1984) (en banc) (explicitly rejecting Henkin's assertions).

49. *See, e.g.*, Note, *The General 'Political Question' Doctrine and the Foreign Relations Power: The Parameters of the 'Political Question' Doctrine*, in T. FRANK & M. GLENNAN, FOREIGN RELATIONS AND NATIONAL SECURITY LAW 723 (1987).

50. Baker v. Carr, 369 U.S. 186, 210 (1962).

51. Champlin & Schwarz, *Political Question Doctrine and Allocation of the Foreign Affairs Power*, 13 HOFSTRA L. REV. 215, 220 (1985); Goldwater v. Carter, 444 U.S. 996, 998-99 (1979) (Powell, J., concurring).

on one question.[52]

The Constitution textually allocates international trade to the Congress in article 1, section 8.[53] Assuming *arguendo* that the Constitution does not allocate international trade entirely to either the legislature or executive, the five remaining factors of the test for Section 301 collapse to but two: justiciability (factors 2 and 3), and embarrassment (factors 4, 5 and 6).[54]

In *Ramirez de Arellano v. Weinberger*, the D.C. Circuit also used a three-step approach to identify nonjusticiable political questions and asked:

> (i) Does the issue involve resolution of questions committed by the text of the Constitution to a coordinate branch of Government? (ii) Would resolution of the question demand that a court move beyond areas of judicial expertise? (iii) Do prudential considerations counsel against judicial intervention?[55]

Writing for the court, Judge Wilkey found a justiciable controversy where a United States citizen alleged that United States government officials had unconstitutionally occupied and established a military training camp on his property in Honduras. The Court found that such a dispute over property would necessitate interpretation of the Constitution and of federal statutes, a quintessential task of the judiciary, and would not involve Executive embarrassment because the plaintiffs did not challenge U.S. foreign policy in Central America, only the Executive's taking of private property.[56] In a potential review of Section 301, judicial adjudication would likewise necessitate statutory interpretation involving a narrow injury to private property, not an assault on U.S. foreign policy.[57]

To determine whether Section 301 decisions are barred from review by the political question doctrine, this article will examine

52. Baker v. Carr, *supra* note 50, at 217.

53. U.S. CONST. art. I, § 8 (Congress shall 'regulate commerce with foreign nations'); *but see* Powell v. McCormack, 395 U.S. 486 (1969) (reducing the scope of the textual commitment prong).

54. In essence, factors two and three both go to the ability of the judiciary to resolve the question, and factors four, five and six consider the need for speed and finality in international relations and the possibility of embarrassment for both the courts and the executive if the courts were to overturn the President. *See Champlin & Schwarz, supra* note 51, at 221 (the *Baker* test collapses to two factors); *Goldwater, supra* note 51, at 999-1001 (reducing the test to three factors) (Powell, J., concurring).

55. *Ramirez, supra* note 48, at 1511 (quoting *Goldwater, supra* note 51, at 998), *vacated and rev'd on other grounds*, 471 U.S. 1113 (1985). *Ramirez* was vacated because changed circumstances effectively mooted the factual issues.

56. *Ramirez, supra* note 48, at 1511-14.

57. Moreover, courts have routinely adjudicated the existence or non-existence of hostilities—a quintessential "political question"—for the purpose of war risk clauses in insurance contracts. Ely, *supra* note 47, at 1408 n.87, 1409 (listing cases).

whether each factual determination underlying a Section 301 unfair trade practice is incapable of judicial resolution or would cause governmental embarrassment.

A. *Justiciability*

The justiciability factor analyzes whether a court can find "discoverable and manageable standards" with which to analyze the question;[58] if the court cannot, then the question is political. Section 301 grants the President authority to retaliate for violations of any trade agreement or foreign conduct which is unjustifiable, unreasonable, or discriminatory and burdens or restricts United States commerce.[59] Each of these tests is arguably justiciable.

1. *Violation of a Trade Agreement*

The President can act to "enforce the rights of the United States under any trade agreement" or to respond to foreign trade practices that are "inconsistent with the provisions of, or otherwise den[y] benefits to the United States under, any trade agreement."[60] The United States Trade Representative has interpreted "trade agreement" to include only the General Agreement on Tariffs and Trade ("GATT") and any of the GATT codes negotiated during the Tokyo Round.[61] The definition generally does not extend to treaties of friendship, commerce and navigation ("FCN") and agreements peripherally related to trade.[62]

58. *Baker*, *supra* note 50, at 217. For example, purely legal questions of statutory interpretation are justiciable, even if accompanied by significant political dimensions. Japan Whaling Ass'n. v. American Cetacean Soc'y., *supra* note 42, at 2866 (finding justiciable a challenge to the Secretary of Commerce's decision not to certify Japan for harvesting sperm whales in excess of International Whaling Commission quotas); Romer v. Carlucci, No. 86-1458, slip op. (8th Cir. May 18, 1988) (en banc) (finding justiciable the environmental impact statements filed by the Air Force in conjunction with the proposed deployment of MX missiles in Colorado and Nebraska).

In addition, once the Court accepts the issue for adjudication, it may have a duty to fashion manageable standards. "Thus manageability is certainly a consideration, but principally at the stage of devising principles and remedies as opposed to the stage of deciding whether to decide the issue at all." Ely, *supra* note 47, at 1408; *cf.* J. ELY, DEMOCRACY AND DISTRUST 124-25 (1980).

59. 19 U.S.C. § 2411(a)(1) (Supp. V 1987).

60. *Id.*

61. Bello and Holmer, *Section 301 of the Trade Act of 1974: Requirements, Procedures, and Developments*, 7 NW. J. INT'L L. & BUS. 633, 635 (1986) (for a list of GATT codes which fall under "trade agreement," see *id.*, at 634 n.4).

62. *Id.* The USTR chose the limited construction of "trade agreement" because § 303(a) of the 1974 Trade Act requires the Trade Representative to request "formal dispute settlement procedures" for violations of a "trade agreement." 19 U.S.C. § 2413(a) (Supp. V 1987). Since non-GATT agreements typically call for dispute resolution through the International Court of Justice, the USTR has consistently construed "trade agreements" narrowly in the belief that Congress did not intend § 303(a) to compel resolution in the World Court. Bello and Holmer, *supra* note 61, at 634 n.4.

Courts should have no problems of justiciability in analyzing violations of GATT.[63] In fact, U.S. courts have already interpreted provisions of GATT in various settings. In *Zenith Radio Corp. v. United States*,[64] the U.S. Supreme Court found the Treasury Department's interpretation of countervailing duty laws consistent with article VI(3) of the GATT. In *United States v. Star Industries, Inc.*[65], the Court of Customs and Patent Appeals found that the context and negotiating history of article XXVIII(3) required withdrawal of concessions to conform to the most-favored-nation principle. In *Sneaker Circus, Inc. v. Carter*[66], the U.S. District Court for the Southern District of New York found that, although GATT violations were nonactionable without statutory implementation, article XIX(1)(a) permitted the Orderly Marketing Arrangement negotiated by the President. Moreover, the Court of International Trade has formally introduced GATT into American trade jurisprudence. The Court held that Congressional statutes "should not be interpreted by means of a tenuous argument to yield a construction which would be in contravention of GATT."[67] Thus, the Court of International Trade now looks to the GATT to interpret trade provisions where Congress has not explicitly legislated. As the GATT is a legalistic treaty with an extensive negotiating history, and is amenable to standard rules of statutory construction, U.S. courts could easily find legal standards with which to discover violations of the GATT.

2. *Unjustifiable or Discriminatory Conduct*

Congress has defined foreign unjustifiability in Section 301 as "any act, policy or practice which is in violation of, or inconsistent with, the international legal rights of the United States."[68] Unjustifiability includes the denial of national or most-favored-nation ("MFN") treatment, the right to establish an enterprise abroad, protection of intellectual property rights,[69] or the breach of an agreement other than a trade agreement (such as an FCN treaty).[70] The definition of discriminatory action parallels that of unjustifiability and includes "any

63. *See Japan Whaling Ass'n*, *supra* note 42, at 2866 ("the courts have authority to construe treaties and executive agreements").

64. 437 U.S. 443, 458 (1978).

65. 462 F.2d 557, *cert. denied*, 409 U.S. 1076 (1972).

66. 457 F.Supp. 771, 795 (S.D.N.Y. 1978), *aff'd* 614 F.2d 1290 (1979).

67. U.S. Steel Corp. v. United States, 618 F. Supp. 496, 501-02 (Ct. Int'l Trade 1985), *appeal dismissed*, 792 F.2d 1101 (1986).

68. 19 U.S.C. § 2411(e)(4)(A) (Supp. V 1987).

69. *Id.*, at § 2411(e)(4)(B).

70. Bello & Holmer, *supra* note 61, at 640.

act, policy, or practice which denies national or most-favored-nation treatment to United States goods, services, or investment."[71]

MFN treatment in FCN treaties is not substantially different from MFN treatment in the GATT and should be justiciable by courts; their terms are as capable of judicial review as the GATT terms analyzed above.[72] For example, the Court of Customs and Patent Appeals analyzed the U.S.-Germany FCN treaty and voided a 50 percent tariff as inconsistent with the treaty.[73] Recent examples of unjustifiability findings involve the United States-Korea and United States-Japan FCN Treaties. In a Section 301 proceeding involving the Republic of Korea's domestic restrictions of foreign insurance companies, the President found unjustifiability in a violation of article VII of the FCN treaty.[74] Similarly, the President found the state-sponsored Japanese tobacco monopoly to be unjustifiable because of a violation of the United States-Japan FCN treaty.[75] To the extent that unjustifiability provisions concern the protection of intellectual property rights, courts already examine foreign treatment of intellectual property rights under section 337 of the 1930 Tariff Act,[76] and they should have little difficulty adjudicating slightly broader questions of those rights under Section 301.

Unjustifiable foreign trade practices may also theoretically include foreign conduct other than the denial of MFN treatment, and as the definition appears open-ended, the USTR could possibly fit any foreign conduct within the definition. Courts could consider overturning such a stretching of the definition in either of two ways. First, if the

71. 19 U.S.C. § 2411(e)(5) (Supp. V 1987).

72. General Agreement on Tariffs and Trade, opened for signature, Oct. 30, 1947, 61 Stat. 5, T.I.A.S. No. 1700, 27 U.N.T.S. 19, art. I (MFN treatment "with respect to customs duties and charges of any kind"), art. III (MFN treatment for internal taxes and regulations); *see also* Mentula v. State Land Bd., 244 Or. 229, 233, 417 P.2d 581 (1966) (adjudicating the MFN clause in the United States-Finland FCN treaty).

73. John T. Bill Co. v. United States, 104 F.2d 67 (C.C.P.A. 1939).

74. Memorandum of Aug. 14, 1986, for the United States Trade Representative, Determination Under Section 301 of the Trade Act of 1974, 51 Fed. Reg. 29,443 (1986). Article VII of the treaty provides that:

> Nationals and companies of either Party shall be accorded national treatment with respect to engaging in all types of commercial, industrial, financial and other activities for gain (business activities) within the territories of the other Party, whether directly or by agent or through the medium of any form of lawful juridical entity.

Nov. 28, 1956, 8 U.S.T. 2217, T.I.A.S. No. 3947; for a detailed treatment of the incident, see Bello & Holmer, *supra* note 61, at 640-41.

75. *See* Japan's Practice With Respect to the Manufacture, Importation and Sale of Tobacco Products, 50 Fed. Reg. 37,609 (USTR 1985) (initiation), based on United States-Japan Treaty of Friendship, Apr. 2, 1953, 4 U.S.T. 2063, T.I.A.S. No. 2863.

76. 19 U.S.C. § 1337 (Supp. V 1987). For a general analysis, see Walders, *Other Import Relief Laws* in THE TRADE AGREEMENTS ACT OF 1979—FOUR YEARS LATER 255 (H. Appelbaum & A. Victor eds. 1983).

foreign conduct falls just slightly outside an existing category, a court could find that Congress intended such conduct not to be a violation of Section 301. Second, a court could decide what are "the international legal rights of the United States"[77] and then decide whether the foreign conduct violated them.[78]

3. *Unreasonable Conduct*

Section 301 defines unreasonableness to mean "any act, policy, or practice which, while not necessarily in violation of or inconsistent with the international legal rights of the United States, is otherwise deemed to be unfair and inequitable;"[79] the statute explicitly makes reference to foreign action regarding market opportunities, opportunities for establishing an enterprise and intellectual property protection.[80] Since neither Congressional statute nor international agreement explicitly defines the boundaries of unreasonableness in foreign trade, courts may have difficulty in its adjudication because courts generally defer review on precisely these issues where delicate, non-legal choices of foreign relations must be made.[81]

The 1988 Omnibus Trade Act provides courts with an aid in defining unreasonableness. The Act defies unreasonable foreign actions to include the denial of various trade opportunities, foreign government export targeting and substandard labor safeguards.[82] Courts may find

77. 19 U.S.C. § 2411(e)(4)(A) (Supp. V 1987).

78. *See* The Paquete Habana, 175 U.S. 677, 700 (1900) ("International law is part of our law, and must be ascertained and administered by the courts of justice of appropriate jurisdiction, as often as questions of right depending upon it are duly presented for their determination."); *Ramirez de Arellano, supra* note 48, at 1540 ("When, however, the political branches have specified the controlling legal principles in a treaty with the foreign sovereign or when there are generally accepted tenets of international law concerning the foreign act, the danger of improper judicial interference with the Executive's responsibilities for foreign affairs is greatly reduced."); *but see* Garcia-Mir v. Meese, 788 F.2d. 1446, 1455 (11th Cir.), *cert. denied*, 479 U.S. 889 (1986) (Sustaining the President's authority "to disregard international law in service of domestic needs. . ."); Tel-Oren v. Libyan Arab Republic, 726 F.2d 774, 805 (D.C. Cir. 1984) (Bork, J., concurring).

79. 19 U.S.C. 2411(e)(3) (Supp. V 1987).

80. *Id.*

81. U.S. courts do not inquire into the termination of treaties, the recognition of foreign governments, the recognition of belligerency abroad, a person's status as a foreign government representative or the dates of duration of hostilities. *Baker, supra* note 50, at 212-13.

82. H.R. CONF. REP. NO. 596, 100th Cong., 2d Sess. 65 (1988). Section 301(d)(3)(b) of the Omnibus Trade and Competitiveness Act of 1988 defines unreasonable acts, policies or practices to include any combination which

(i) denies fair and equitable—
(I) opportunities for the establishment of an enterprise, (II) provision of adequate and effective protection of intellectual property rights, or (III) market opportunities . . .
(ii) constitutes export targeting, or
(iii) constitutes a persistent pattern of conduct that—
(I) denies workers the right of association, (II) denies workers the right to organize and bargain collectively, (III) permits any form of forced or compulsory labor, (IV) fails to

adequate guidance to adjudicate the Act's definitions by analogy from similar provisions in current antitrust, labor and intellectual property law. The Act, however, also exempts foreign countries which take "actions that demonstrate a significant and tangible overall advancement" in providing trade and for conduct which is "not inconsistent with the level of economic development of the foreign country."[83] These exemptions may be unjusticiable, particularly those for overall advancement in trade policy and consistency with economic development levels because they call for non-legal "political" choices.

In addition, several commentators have advanced guidelines for reasonableness under Section 301. One method would use the normative definition of reasonableness and decide whether foreign conduct is undertaken in bad faith, regardless of any justifications which may be posited.[84] Another method would weigh the economic distortion of comparative advantage against the legal exercise of jurisdiction to prescribe and find those practices reasonable which favor comparative advantage.[85] A court could fashion guidelines based on the definitions of reasonableness from commentators or from other areas of the law.

On the other hand, the courts could find the question justiciable and then defer to the President's findings in most circumstances:

> Both Supreme Court and Court of Customs and Patent Appeals precedent have established that the Executive's decisions in the sphere of international trade are reviewable only to determine [1] whether the President's action falls within his delegated authority, [2] whether the statutory language has been properly construed, and [3] whether the President's action conforms with the relevant procedural requirements. The President's findings of fact and the motivations for his action are not subject to review.[86]

Deference to the President's findings would not be applicable to all trade determinations. For certain unfair trade practices, Section 301 on its face requires mandatory action,[87] and the courts could review the President's actions against the statute. For discretionary actions, the courts can still review the President's actions for statutory compli-

---

provide a minimum age for the employment of children, or (V) fails to provide standards for minimum wages, hours of work, and occupational safety and health of workers.

83. *Id.* § 301(d)(3)(C).

84. Fisher & Steinhardt, *Section 301 of the Trade Act of 1974: Protection for U.S. Exporters of Goods, Services and Capital*, 14 L. & POL. INT'L BUS. 569, 598 (1982).

85. Hansen, *Defining Unreasonableness in International Trade: Section 301 of the Trade Act of 1974*, 96 YALE L.J. 1122, 1136-42 (1987) (offering the most perceptive insight into the statutory standards).

86. Florsheim Shoe Co. v. United States, 744 F.2d 787, 795 (Fed. Cir. 1984) (citations omitted) (construing the reviewability of section 504 withdrawal of duty-free treatment under the Generalized System of Preferences).

87. *See supra* text accompanying notes 32-37.

ance and due process claims under the Fifth Amendment.[88] After all, "[t]he Executive's power to conduct foreign relations free from the unwarranted supervision of the Judiciary cannot give the Executive carte blanche to trample the most fundamental liberty and property rights of this country's citizenry."[89]

Courts have reviewed some aspects of Presidential discretion in escape clause proceedings. In section 201 trade relief, the International Trade Commission ("ITC") determines whether increases in imports have seriously injured a domestic industry or threaten the industry with serious injury;[90] after receiving an affirmative finding from the ITC, the President may provide import relief.[91] Although the section grants no explicit judicial review, courts have reviewed section 201 relief to confirm that there was not "a clear misconstruction of the governing statute, a significant procedural violation, or action outside delegated authority."[92]

Courts have also reviewed Presidential authority for trade relief against unfair practices under section 337. Section 337 of the 1930 Tariff Act prohibits "[u]nfair methods of competition and unfair acts in the importation of articles into the United States" where the imports may destroy, substantially injure or prevent the establishment of

88. *See* Hampton v. Mow Sun Wong, 426 U.S. 88 (1976) (overturning the Civil Service Commission's citizenry requirement as an unconstitutional violation of the due process clause of the Fifth Amendment); Morgan v. United States, 304 U.S. 1, 14-15 (1938) (finding that the quasi-judicial character of administrative proceedings give rise to the "requirements of fair play").

USTR rule-making, though, is arguably not subject to the strictures of the Administrative Procedures Act (the "APA") and would not come under *Hampton* and *Morgan*. Section 553(a)(1) of the APA exempts from notice and comment certain rulemaking "to the extent that there is involved a military or foreign affairs function of the United States." 5 U.S.C. § 553(a)(1) (1982). International trade policy, including Section 301 proceedings, may fall under the exception. *See* Mast Ind., Inc. v. Regan, 596 F.Supp. 1567, 1580 (Ct. Int'l Trade 1984) (interim textile import regulations fall within the "foreign affairs" exception of the APA). However, the legislative history of the APA would not support a broad view of the "foreign affairs" exemption to include all aspects of Section 301. The House and Senate Reports to the APA specifically cautioned that:

> The phrase "foreign affairs functions" used here and in some other provisions of the bill, is not to be loosely interpreted to mean any function extending beyond the borders of the United States, but only those "affairs" which so affect relations with other governments that, for example, public rulemaking provisions would clearly provoke definitely undesirable international consequences.

Administrative Procedure Act: Legislative History, S. Doc. No. 248, 79th Cong., 2d Sess. 191, 199 (Senate Report), 257 (House Report) (1947). Moreover, the courts have continually construed section 553 exemptions from rulemaking procedures, including the "foreign affairs" exception, narrowly and granted them reluctantly. *See, e.g.*, Environmental Defense Fund v. Gorsuch, 713 F.2d 802, 816 (D.C. Cir. 1983).

89. *Ramirez*, *supra* note 48, at 1515.

90. 19 U.S.C. § 2251(b)(1) (1980).

91. 19 U.S.C. § 2252(a) (1980).

92. Maple Leaf Fish Co. v. United States, 762 F.2d 86, 89 (Fed. Cir. 1985) (upholding the President's actions).

an industry.[93] The ITC is given explicit authority to determine violations of this section[94] and has adjudicated claims of unfair imports involving patent claims, trademark infringements, false designations of goods, passing off goods, and misappropriation of trade secrets.[95] After an affirmative ITC determination, the President then has sixty days to reject the relief for "policy reasons" before it takes effect.[96] Courts have reviewed whether the ITC's definitions and standards of unfair imports are "reasonable in light of the language, policy, and legislative history of the statute" and whether the factual finding is supported by substantial evidence;[97] however, the courts have not reviewed the subsequent Presidential decision.[98]

Section 301 relief is bifurcated similarly to that of sections 201 and 337 and may also be reviewed. A court could examine whether the USTR's determination comports with the language, policy, and legislative history of the statute, whether the determination is supported by any (or substantial) evidence, and whether the determination exceeds the USTR's delegated authority. If the USTR determination meets these three tests, it would stand. The subsequent Presidential action, however, might be unreviewable.

Finally, even if a court finds the standard of "unreasonable" to be nonjusticiable and thus a political question, Section 301 as a whole would not necessarily be unreviewable. If "unreasonable" is severable from the other elements of Section 301, then a court cannot dismiss the entire challenge because of the presence of a political question. The doctrine "is one of 'political questions,' not one of 'political cases.' The courts cannot reject as 'no law suit' a bona fide controversy as to whether some action denominated 'political' exceeds constitutional authority."[99] Thus, each element of a Section 301 challenge must be nonjusticiable in order for the entire challenge to be labeled as a political question.

In sum, the courts could follow either of two alternatives for the justiciability of unreasonableness. First, they could declare unreasonableness to be unjusticiable, hence a political question, and retain re-

93. 19 U.S.C. § 1337(a) (1982).

94. *Id.* § 1337(c).

95. Kennedy, *Presidential Authority Under Section 337, Section 301, and the Escape Clause: The Case For Less Discretion*, 20 CORNELL INT'L L.J. 127, 131 (1987).

96. 19 U.S.C. § 1337(g)(2) (1982).

97. Corning Glass Works v. United States Int'l Trade Comm'n, 799 F.2d 1559, 1565 (Fed. Cir. 1986).

98. Duracell, Inc. v. United States Int'l Trade Comm'n, 778 F.2d 1578, 1581 (Fed. Cir. 1985).

99. *Baker*, *supra* note 50, at 217.

view for the other procedural and substantive aspects of Section 301 determinations. For example, a court could find unreasonableness to be a political question but retain review to determine whether the conduct burdens or restricts U.S. commerce. Second, the court could find unreasonableness to be justiciable and subject to review.

4. *Burden or Restriction on U.S. Commerce*

For unjustifiable, unreasonable, or discriminatory foreign conduct, the USTR must make a further injury determination that the conduct "burdens or restricts" United States commerce. This injury requirement can be demonstrated through increased imports into the United States, reduced availability of raw material imports into the United States, the displacement of United States export sales, in either the country engaged in an unfair trade practice or in a third-country market, or an inadequate protection of intellectual property rights.[100]

The "burdens or restricts" requirement is similar to the injury determination under antidumping and countervailing duty laws.[101] To impose antidumping duties and countervailing duties for GATT Subsidies Code signatories, the ITC must determine that the domestic industry is "materially injured" or "threatened with material injury" or its establishment is "materially retarded."[102] The ITC's findings are explicitly subject to judicial review and have encountered no political question problems.[103] If courts can find legal standards with which to review ITC decisions of material injury and threat to material injury, then they should be able to find legal standards with which to determine if a practice "burdens or restricts" U.S. commerce.

B. *Prudential and Jurisdictional Considerations*

Courts have refused to adjudicate political question issues because of article III constitutional problems or prudential issues. First, a court may only hear such challenges to Section 301 actions that involve an article III "case or controversy." Then, even after finding the challenge ripe for adjudication, a court may decline to hear it because of a need for the finality of political decisions in foreign affairs or because of potential embarrassment from "multifarious pronouncements by various departments on one question."[104] Indeed, once the Presi-

100. Bello & Holmer, *supra* note 61, at 644-45.

101. *See* Note, *ITC Injury Determinations in Countervailing Duty Investigations*, 15 L. & Pol. Int'l Bus. 987 (1983).

102. 19 U.S.C. §§ 1671(a)(2), 1673(2) (Supp. V 1987).

103. 19 U.S.C. § 1516a (Supp. V 1987).

104. *Baker, supra* note 50, at 217.

dent undertakes trade negotiations or retaliation against foreign conduct, he could be severely embarrassed by a judicial recall.

On the other hand, mere Presidential embarrassment has not been enough to keep the court out of political conflicts. President Truman did remove the National Guard from the steel mills during the Korean war, President Eisenhower complied with school desegregation orders with which he personally disagreed, and President Nixon made public the tape recordings which doomed his presidency.[105] Even in adjudicating the Iran Hostages Agreement, where the United States' credibility in the Middle East was on the line, the court did not dismiss the suit through an embarrassment rationale.[106] In fact, in one case, the court even cited to itself for the proposition that disobedience to the court's orders is unthinkable.[107]

This analysis of prudential considerations, though, is more complex. It is uncertain when a petitioner would challenge the Section 301 proceedings, if the challenge would be ripe at that point and whether finality problems would affect the decision of ripeness. Three distinct possibilities exist for the timing of actions challenging section 301: after a negative USTR determination, after a positive USTR determination, and after USTR action. Each of these scenarios may have embarrassment difficulties. Furthermore, there may be standing problems if a court were to find no "case or controversy" under any of the scenarios.

A court can review a final administrative action that "determines a 'right or obligation' so that 'legal consequences' will flow from it."[108] In addition, courts should not adjudicate premature, non-ripe cases so as to avoid "entangling themselves in abstract disagreements over administrative policies."[109] Assuming arguendo that a court would conduct judicial review of USTR determinations of foreign trade practices, the complaint could be brought immediately after USTR makes a determination.[110] If the USTR finds no unfairness in the foreign conduct, then the President will have taken no action and a court cannot embarrass the President through overturning a Presidential action. The concerns of finality and embarrassment would be moot for

105. Ely, *supra* note 47, at 1410 ("That the President will disobey an order of the Supreme Court seems less likely in 1988 than it might have 100 years ago.").

106. *Dames & Moore*, *supra* note 3, at 654.

107. Powell v. McCormack, *supra* note 53, at 549 n.86 (1969) ("The Court has noted that it is an 'inadmissable suggestion' that action might be taken in disregard of a judicial determination.") (citing McPherson v. Blacker, 146 U.S. 1, 24 (1982)).

108. Pennsylvania R.R. v. United States, 363 U.S. 202, 205 (1960).

109. Abbott Laboratories v. Gardner, 387 U.S. 136, 148 (1967).

110. Time limits for USTR determinations are found at 19 U.S.C. § 2414(a) (1980).

negative determinations. Furthermore, the petitioner who initiated the USTR investigation would have standing as she has been injured by the lack of relief.

Under the second scenario, a court could decide to accept the case before the USTR granted actual relief. Following a positive USTR determination, the USTR must implement the action it recommended within 30 days, unless the President directs otherwise.[111] Since the USTR need not grant any actual relief after the 30-day period, if the President so directs,[112] the reviewing court will not necessarily embarrass the Executive. Moreover, the USTR decision to take action provides enough injury to create a "case or controversy." First, since the USTR's formal decision to take action will lead to some form of retaliation, importers, and foreign businesses will be injured.[113] Second, even if the President decides not to take any current action, the decision itself affects the parties by pressuring the foreign government to reach a settlement.[114]

If the court accepts the suit immediately after the 30-day period, then the President may not yet have taken any trade action and embarrassment will not be an issue. The case, though, may remain in court for some length of time, potentially tying Presidential discretion during the review period. Although the President may not like having his hands tied by the courts, the length of law suits usually does not cause a court to deny legal or equitable relief.[115] If Congress truly intended the President to take action only under specified circumstances, without any check on the speediness of Presidential action, then delay in court should not trouble the judicial review. Moreover, Section 301 is not necessary to provide relief for true emergency situations; other trade acts, including IEEPA[116], provide explicit Presiden-

111. S. 2613, 100th Cong., 2d Sess. § 305(a) (1988). The USTR may delay the implementation of action for up to 180 days under specified circumstances. *Id.*

112. Bello and Holmer, *supra* note 61, at 652.

113. Railroad Reorganization Act Cases, 419 U.S. 102, 143 (1974) ("Where the inevitability of the operation of a statute against certain individuals is patent, it is irrelevant to the existence of a justiciable controversy that there be a time delay before the disputed provisions will come into effect. . . . 'One does not have to await the consummation of threatened injury to obtain preventive relief. If the injury is certainly impending that is enough.' " (quoting Pennsylvania v. West Virginia, 262 U.S. 553, 593 (1923) (citations omitted)).

114. Bello and Holmer, *supra* note 61, at 652.

115. *See, e.g.*, SSIH Equipment, S.A. v. International Trade Comm'n, 673 F.2d 1387, 1391 (C.C.P.A. 1982). The SSIH court held that under statutory construction of section 337 proceedings, "there is no fixed time limits on appeals from final determinations of the [International Trade] Commission." Congress, though, wanted speedier resolution of section 337 actions and instituted a 60-day cap. Trade Act of 1984 § 413, 19 U.S.C. § 1337(c) (West Supp. 1988). Moreover, if the need arose, the court could conduct an expedited review.

116. International Emergency Economic Powers Act, 50 U.S.C. §§ 1701-1706 (1982). For a description of practice under IEEPA, see Koh, *supra* note 27, at 1264-65 (arguing that recent

tial authority for fast trade relief.

The Omnibus Trade Act is persuasive authority toward finding ripeness after a positive USTR determination. First, the Act requires the President to take mandatory action for certain unfair trade practices.[117] Under the amendments to Section 301, the USTR "*shall* take action, . . . subject to the specific discretion, of the President regarding any such action, and *shall* take all other appropriate and feasible action within the powers of the President that the President may direct the Trade Representative to take" after a positive determination of any unfair trade practice which (i) violates, is inconsistent with, or denies benefit under any trade agreement, or (ii) is unjustifiable and burdens or restricts United States commerce.[118] If a positive USTR determination would lead to mandatory action, then such a determination would cause an actual injury and satisfy the jurisdictional requirement of ripeness.[119]

Furthermore, the Act's provision of mandatory retaliation, subject to Presidential disapproval, duplicates the procedure for section 337 relief, and courts have found section 337 determinations ripe for review. Under section 337, the President has sixty days to reject an affirmative ITC determination before it takes effect.[120] Courts have found section 337 determinations ripe after the President formally disapproves or the sixty-day period lapses.[121] If section 337 mandatory trade relief ripens once the President disapproves or fails to act, then Section 301 mandatory retaliation would also become ripe once the President disapproves or fails to act.

Second, the Act clarifies the distinctions between the standard for USTR determinations and the standard for Presidential determinations. If the USTR determination of unfairness is made on a different standard than the Presidential determination, then the courts could resolve disputes over the USTR determinations, even if the President

court decisions have transformed IEEPA into a sweeping delegation of authority); *see also* National Emergencies Act, 50 U.S.C. §§ 1601-1651 (1982).

117. "Subject to specified exceptions, action is mandatory." S. Rep. No. 71, 100th Cong., 1st Sess. 80 (1987).

118. S. 2613, 100th Cong., 2d Sess. § 1391 (1988) (emphasis added) The USTR, though, is not required to take mandatory action if (i) a GATT dispute resolution proceeding finds no violation of an international trade agreement with respect to the United States, (ii) USTR finds that the foreign country is, will, or cannot take satisfactory measures to provide the rights of the trade agreement or compensatory trade benefits, (iii) USTR action would have an adverse domestic economic impact in proportion to its benefits, or (iv) national security concerns militate against retaliation. *Id.*

119. *But see* Bello & Holmer, *supra* note 2, at 18 (arguing that the mandatory provisions of the 1988 Act still allow "ample discretion").

120. 19 U.S.C. § 1337(g)(2) (1982); *see also supra* text accompanying notes 94-98.

121. *Duracell, supra* note 98, at 1578.

might later have discretion to reject them.[122] As Congress explicitly allocated certain decisions to the USTR instead of the President, Congress intended the USTR to make independent decisions.[123] Moreover, by acting in a quasi-judicial role, not an Executive one, USTR proceedings must comply with due process standards.[124] In adopting a standard of review, the courts could conduct a de novo review of USTR determinations, or else could treat USTR as a quasi-administrative agency and apply administrative law doctrine to USTR determinations. Under either standard, USTR determinations would be reviewable.

The Federal Circuit has analyzed similar issues of standing in upholding an importer's challenge of a Customs Service classification under the Generalized System of Preferences ("GSP").[125] Florsheim, a shoe importer, had filed a petition with the USTR to create a separate category for water buffalo leather and asked for duty-free treatment of the leather pursuant to the GSP. The USTR denied the petition. Florsheim filed several protests with the Customs Service, and the Customs Service denied its petitions. Florsheim then brought suit pursuant to section 514 of the 1930 Tariff Act. Both the Court of International Trade and the Federal Circuit held that Florsheim had standing.

The Federal Circuit found two rationales for standing. First, the court held that an importer had standing under a Congressional statute.[126] The court, though, also examined the government's contention that "the existence of 28 U.S.C. § 2531 [the statute granting standing] does not obviate the fact that Section 504's zone of interests does not encompass importers such as Florsheim."[127] The court used a "zone of interests" standing analysis[128] and found that Congress had in-

122. *See* United States v. Nixon, 418 U.S. 683, 697 (1974) (finding justiciable a controversy between two officials of the Executive Branch, namely the President and the Special Prosecutor).

123. *See* S. REP. NO. 71, 100th Cong., 1st Sess. 80 (1987) (The determination whether foreign conduct is an unfair practice actionable under Section 301 "should be the province of the USTR, rather than the President, because it is a *technical* decision calling for the application of USTR's experience to the provisions of Section 301 and the particular practices at issue." (emphasis added)); *see also* Bello & Holmer, *supra* note 2, at 2-10.

124. *See Hampton*, *supra* note 88, at 88; *Morgan*, *supra* note 88, at 14-15. Sub-executive agencies must follow the rule of law, including due process, even where the President has full discretion.

125. *Florsheim*, *supra* note 86, at 787.

126. "A civil action contesting the denial of a protest, in whole or in part, under section 515 of the Tariff Act of 1930 may be commenced in the Court of International Trade by the person who filed the protest pursuant to section 514 of such Act." 28 U.S.C. § 2631(a) (Supp. V 1987).

127. *Florsheim*, *supra* note 86, at 790.

128. " 'Zone of interests' is a shorthand description of a test for standing, requiring that a complainant show that the interest it seeks to protect is 'arguably within the zone of interests to

tended importers to challenge Customs Service determinations so that the challenge fell within the requisite zone of interests.

The Court, though, did not question whether Congress may expand a court's jurisdiction if no "case or controversy" exists. Since Congress cannot create standing if no "case or controversy" exists,[129] a statutory definition of ripeness cannot expand a court's jurisdiction. The Federal Circuit's basis of standing on a Congressional statute is therefore irrelevant, and the holding must stand on the "zone of interests" analysis.[130] Since a potential review of Section 301 determinations is similar to a review of GSP classifications in that, in both cases, the President retains discretion to overturn the agency finding,[131] the Federal Circuit's *Florsheim* analysis would equally apply to questions of ripeness for Section 301 determinations.

In the third scenario, a court could reject the complaint as not ripe until USTR and the President actually grant trade relief.[132] In an analogous situation, several senators brought suit against President Carter's termination of a treaty with Taiwan. In that case, Justice Powell found that the controversy was not ripe because "a dispute between Congress and the President is not ready for judicial review unless and until each branch has taken action asserting its constitutional authority."[133] In a Section 301 action, the court could await Presidential action before undertaking judicial review. But, once the President has acted, the need for finality and lack of embarrassment would strongly suggest against judicial review.

Nevertheless, courts have overturned Presidential actions involving foreign affairs. For example, in *Guy Capps*, the Supreme Court voided an executive agreement between the United States and Canada on potato imports.[134] Moreover, if the courts could never overturn a Presidential action involving foreign affairs, then the President could

be protected or regulated by the statute of constitutional guarantee in question.' " *Id.* at 790 (citations to U.S. Supreme Court cases omitted).

129. *Buckley, supra* note 42, at 11 ("Congress may not, of course, require this court to render opinions in matters which are not 'cases or controversies.' ").

130. *See* Canadian Meat Council v. United States, 644 F.Supp. 1125 (Ct. Int'l Trade 1986) (upholding the statutory definition of standing for Department of Commerce final affirmative subsidy determinations under 19 U.S.C. § 1516a(a)(3) (Supp. V 1987)).

131. "The President may withdraw, suspend, or limit the application of the duty-free treatment accorded under section 501 [GSP treatment] with respect to any article or with respect to any country." 19 U.S.C. § 2464(a) (Supp. 1988).

132. *See Buckley, supra* note 42, at 13-14; *see also* Chicago & Southern Airlines, Inc. v. Waterman S.S. Co., 333 U.S. 103, 112-113 (1948) ("administrative orders are not reviewable unless and until they impose an obligation, deny a right or fix some legal relationship as a consummation of the administrative process.")

133. *Goldwater, supra* note 51, at 997 (Powell, J., concurring).

134. *Guy Capps, supra* note 10, at 655; *but see* Koh, *supra* note 27, at 1306-17.

always unilaterally form trade policy without either Congressional or judicial intervention.

To determine whether a question is ripe, a court could use standard principles of administrative law, particularly those applicable to other forms of trade relief. The ripeness doctrine in administrative law prevents courts from "entangling themselves in abstract disagreements over administrative policies" and "protect[s] the agencies from judicial interference until an administrative decision has been formalized and its effects felt in a concrete way by the challenging parties."[135]

In antidumping and countervailing duty proceedings, ripeness of judicial review is explicitly governed by statute. Petitioners can contest final affirmative and negative determinations, determinations of a duty suspension or an injurious effect, and determinations of classes of merchandise.[136] The Court of International Trade has upheld the legislature's choice of ripeness under article III of the U.S. Constitution[137] and has reviewed the determinations under the statutory scheme.[138] In section 337 unfair practice proceedings, Congress declared that ITC determinations become final after either a 60-day period or Presidential action;[139] courts have reviewed the ITC's determinations.[140] In escape clause proceedings, the President has 60 days after an ITC affirmative finding to determine what import relief he shall provide;[141] courts have reviewed escape clause proceedings.[142]

In Section 301 actions, a determination not to initiate an investigation or a negative USTR determination would be reviewable as final. For affirmative decisions, the USTR recommendation, followed within 30 days by a Presidential decision, could be an apt point to determine ripeness. As in section 201 review, the Presidential decision to take action will have already been made, and a court could determine whether the USTR and the President have exceeded their Congressional delegation.[143] In the third scenario, courts could review deci-

135. *Abbott Laboratories*, *supra* note 109, at 148-49 (1967); *see also* Golden v. Zwickler, 394 U.S. 103, 108 (1969) ("[T]he question in each case is whether the facts alleged, under all the circumstances, show that there is a substantial controversy, between parties having adverse legal interests, of sufficient immediacy and reality to warrant the issuance of a declaratory judgment.")

136. 19 U.S.C. § 1516(a)(1) (Supp. V 1987).

137. *Canadian Meat Council*, *supra* note 130, at 1125, 1128 (Ct. Int'l Trade 1986).

138. *See, e.g.*, Huffy Corp. v. United States, 604 F.Supp. 1250 (Ct. Int'l Trade 1985).

139. 19 U.S.C. § 1337(j) (Supp. V 1987).

140. *See, e.g.*, *Corning Glass*, *supra* note 97, at 1559; *Duracell*, *supra* note 98, at 1578.

141. 19 U.S.C. § 2252(b) (1980).

142. *See, e.g.*, *Maple Leaf Fish*, *supra* note 92, at 86.

143. Nonetheless, review of Executive decisions before actual relief may run afoul of the court's jurisdiction because the President may deem the court's opinion to be an advisory opinion and disregard it. *See* Hayburn's Case, 2 U.S. (2 Dall.) 409 (1792); *see also* *Waterman*, *supra* note

sions once the President takes action without necessarily embarrassing the United States. Finally, even if courts could not review Section 301 actions in some situations because of embarrassment problems, they could still review them in non-embarrassing contexts.[144] Embarrassment and ripeness do not seem to bar judicial review of Section 301 on "political question" grounds.

III. Judicial Review and the State Secrets Doctrine

Courts have declined to review some Presidential decisions because they involve national defense secrets into which the courts generally do not intrude. The lead Supreme Court decision which examined Presidential discretion in the foreign affairs context, *Chicago & Southern Air Lines, Inc. v. Waterman S.S. Corp.*, found that a major, if not the main, reason for denying review of Presidential discretion is the limited justiciability resulting from the need for secrecy of certain Executive information:

> The President, both as Commander-in-Chief and as the Nation's organ for foreign affairs, has available intelligence services whose reports neither are nor ought to be published to the world. It would be intolerable that courts, without the relevant information, should review and perhaps nullify actions of the Executive taken on information properly held secret.[145]

In *Waterman*, an airline company had protested the award of an international air route to another company. Under the statute then in effect, the Civil Aeronautics Board would recommend the proper distribution of foreign air routes to the President, and the President could approve, deny, transfer, amend, cancel or suspend the recommendation.[146] Although the statute granted judicial review for Board actions over domestic routes,[147] the court found that the Presidential discretion regarding the foreign routes was not reviewable, neither under the statute nor because of the need for secrecy.[148]

Although never reversed, the *Waterman* holding has been eroded through the evolution of the political question and state secrets doctrine. The political question doctrine, as formulated by Brennan four-

132, at 113-14 ("It has been the firm and unvarying practice of Constitutional Courts to render no judgments not binding and conclusive on the parties and none that are subject to later review by administrative action."). The need for binding opinions casts doubt over judicial review in section 201 and 337 cases. *See Maple Leaf Fish, supra* note 92, at 86 (review of section 201); *Duracell, supra* note 98, at 1578 (review of section 337).

144. *See supra* text accompanying note 99.

145. *Waterman, supra* note 132, at 111.

146. Civil Aeronautics Act, Ch. 9, 49 U.S.C. § 601 (repealed 1958).

147. *Id.* § 646 (repealed 1958).

148. *Waterman, supra* note 132.

teen years after *Waterman*, made no mention of the need for Executive secrets, but only referred to the need for Executive respect. Perhaps Brennan felt that Executive Privilege had no place in analyzing political questions because Executive Privilege gives rise to an autonomous body of law as part of the state secrets doctrine. Thus, if the Presidential discretion over foreign air routes is not a political question after *Baker v. Carr*, then the state secrets doctrine could prevent review of Presidential discretion. Moreover, since the state secrets doctrine has evolved considerably since *Waterman*, perhaps *Waterman* itself is no longer good law.[149]

The state secrets privilege protects the Executive from revealing certain information necessary to military, diplomatic, or intelligence activities. When national security and individual rights clash, courts must establish guidelines to distinguish between that information which the President could legally protect and that which must be surrendered.[150] Five years after *Waterman*, the Supreme Court established a three-part approach to determine issues of state secrets.[151] First, the privilege must be properly invoked: "[1] There must be a formal claim of privilege, [2] lodged by the head of the department which has control over the matter, [3] after actual personal consideration by that officer;" the underlying facts must then usually be submitted to the court in a sealed affidavit for *in camera* review.[152] Second, the court "must determine whether the circumstances are appropriate for the claim of privilege, and yet do so without forcing a disclosure of the very thing the privilege is designed to protect."[153] If the court decides to uphold the claim of privilege, the privilege is absolute and "even the most compelling necessity cannot overcome the claim of privilege."[154]

The state secrets privilege generally involves military affairs, not trade wars. For example, in *Reynolds*, the Court held that the official accident report of the crash of an Air Force B-29 bomber was privi-

149. L. TRIBE, AMERICAN CONSTITUTIONAL LAW 102 (2d ed. 1988) ("despite emphasis on judicially manageable standards, *Waterman* is something of a deviant case.").

150. *See, e.g.*, United States v. Nixon, 418 U.S. 683, 706 (1974) ("Absent a claim of need to protect military, diplomatic, or sensitive national security secrets, we find it difficult to accept the argument that even the very important interest in confidentiality of Presidential communications is significantly diminished by production of such material for *in camera* inspection with all the protection that a district court will be obliged to provide.").

151. United States v. Reynolds, 345 U.S. 1 (1953).

152. *Id.* at 7-8. The D.C. Circuit has found the privilege's invocation to necessitate "a decision of policy made at the highest level of the executive branch after consideration of the facts of the particular case." Halkin v. Helms, 690 F.2d 977, 996 (D.C. Cir. 1982).

153. *Reynolds*, *supra* note 151, at 8.

154. *Id.* at 11.

leged as a military secret.[155] In more recent cases, the D.C. Circuit ruled that Defense Department documents concerning sales of F-18 fighter aircraft to foreign governments were covered by the privilege,[156] and that CIA surveillance and interception of foreign communications during the Vietnam War were state secrets under the privilege.[157]

Even for military affairs, the state secrets privilege does not preclude all judicial review. The Supreme Court recently allowed judicial review of CIA hiring decisions.[158] Writing for the majority, Chief Justice Rehnquist reiterated that:

> [t]he District Court has the latitude to control any discovery process which may be instituted so as to balance respondent's need for access to proof which would support a colorable constitutional claim against the extraordinary needs of the CIA for confidentiality and the protection of its methods, sources, and mission.[159]

If the state secrets privilege does not prevent review of CIA hiring decisions, then trade decisions are arguably also reviewable.

Furthermore, the Court of International Trade, in adjudicating trade cases, has also not found the state secrets privilege to be absolute. In *Republic Steel Corp.*, the Court rejected *Waterman* for the context of international trade and declined to protect two cables from the Department of Commerce to the American Embassy in Bucharest, Romania which described conversations between the Ambassador of Romania to the United States and the Deputy Assistant Secretary for Import Administration of the U.S. Department of Commerce.[160] The Court distinguished international trade from military secrets or civil aviation by noting that

> [t]he privilege is being asserted here in the context of a comprehensive statutory scheme for the judicial review of these administrative acts. A conclusory assertion of privilege is not sufficient to deny plaintiffs access to material which is part of the record on which the contested decision is made.[161]

The Court of International Trade, though, has not released all

155. *Id.* at 1.

156. Northrop Corp. v. McDonnell Douglas Corp., 751 F.2d 395 (D.C. Cir. 1984).

157. *Halkin*, *supra* note 152, at 977.

158. Webster v. Doe, 56 U.S.L.W. 4568 (U.S. June 15, 1988).

159. *Id.* at 4571; *but see id.* at 4571 (O'Connor, J., dissenting) ("[t]he authority of the Director of Central Intelligence to control access to sensitive national security information by discharging employees deemed to be untrustworthy flows primarily from [the] Constitutional power of the President, and Congress may surely provide that the inferior federal courts are not used to infringe on the President's constitutional authority;" *id.* at 4574 (Scalia, J., dissenting) (national security concerns are beyond judicial review).

160. Republic Steel Corp. v. United States, 538 F.Supp. 422 (Ct. Int'l Trade 1982).

161. *Id.* at 423.

state documents related to trade. In *Star-Kist Foods*, the United States sought to supplement the administrative record in a countervailing duty determination with cables and internal memoranda from the USTR and the Departments of Commerce and State,[162] and moved for a protective order for the documents. The court agreed to the protective order and refused their release to petitioner's counsel. Although the Court found that it had the power to release the documents, it conducted an *in camera* review and found that the release "would pose a 'reasonable danger' to national security."[163]

The state secrets privilege should not be a complete bar to the adjudication of trade issues. A court should instead examine whether the documents sought in the Section 301 review contained state secrets. If they do, the court could disallow their use, and, as in *Star-Kist Foods*, the party seeking discovery would have to continue its action without that information. If the documents were not privileged as state secrets, then the court would allow their use. In short, the case-by-case analysis dictated by *Reynolds* would reach the result in *Waterman* for true problems of state secrets while permitting full review of non-sensitive Executive determinations.

IV. Conclusion

The Congressional delegation of Section 301 authority for import relief cannot have granted the President a blank check in international trade. Instead, Section 301 provides statutory relief under specified circumstances. Although courts may not review Presidential discretion, they can review certain aspects of Section 301 relief, and seeing that neither the "political question" nor state secrets doctrines present significant bars to judicial review, challenges to Section 301 proceedings are a distinct possibility.

162. Star-Kist Foods v. United States, 600 F.Supp 212 (Ct. Int'l Trade 1984).
163. *Id.* at 216.

Journal of World Trade **40(5)**: 909–944, 2006.

Mandatory Abolition of Anti-dumping, Countervailing Duties and Safeguards in Customs Unions and Free-Trade Areas Constituted Between World Trade Organization Members: Revisiting a Long-standing Discussion in Light of the Appellate Body's *Turkey–Textiles* Ruling

Angela T. Gobbi Estrella* and Gary N. Horlick**

I. Introduction

Article XXIV of the General Agreement on Tariffs and Trade (GATT) establishes an exception to GATT obligations (particularly to the obligation to provide all the parties to the Agreement with most-favored-nation treatment—MFN)[1] for customs unions and free-trade areas (FTAs) constituted between Members of the World Trade Organization—WTO.[2] The availability of this exception is conditioned to the meeting of certain requirements set forth in paragraphs 5–9 of Article XXIV regarding the level of trade liberalization that shall be maintained in the external trade of the parties to these arrangements, and accomplished in the internal trade between them.[3]

The level of internal trade liberalization required in a regional trade agreement (RTA),[4] for it to qualify as a customs union or a FTA is set forth in GATT Article XXIV:8(a)(i) and (b), and is virtually the same for both types of trade arrangements.[5]

* Counsel, Ministry of Finance, Brazilian Government. E-mail: <angela.estrella@fazenda.gov.br>. The views expressed here are those of the author in her personal capacity and do not necessarily coincide with those of the Brazilian Government.

** Wilmer Cutler Pickering Hale and Dorr LL.P., Washington, D.C. The views expressed here are not necessarily those of the firm, its lawyers or its clients.

1 The MFN obligation (that is, providing all the parties to the GATT with the same trade preferences) is set forth in GATT Article I, and is a cornerstone of the multilateral trading system.

2 GATT Article XXIV:5 states: "[T]he provisions of this Agreement shall not prevent, as between the territories of the contracting parties, the formation of a customs union or of a free-trade area or the adoption of an interim agreement necessary for the formation of a customs union or of a free-trade area ...".

3 Right after the sentence establishing that the provisions of the GATT shall not prevent the formation of a customs union or a FTA (see the text quoted at note 2 above), a second phrase in Article XXIV:5 adds "Provided that:" From there on are set forth the requirements that a preferential trade arrangement between WTO Members must meet to be allowed to benefit from the exception established in GATT Article XXIV. See John H. Jackson, *World Trade and the Law of the GATT: a Legal Analysis of the General Agreement on Tariffs and Trade* (Indianapolis: Bobbs-Merril, 1969).

4 The term "regional trade agreement—RTA" has been used to identify preferential trade arrangements in general, particularly those allegedly qualifying as customs unions or FTAs. See WTO, *Trade Topics, Regional Trade Agreements: Scope of RTAs*, at <http://www.wto.org/english/tratop_e/region_e/scope_rta_e.htm>.

5 GATT Article XXIV:8 establishes the definition of customs union and FTA, i.e., what kind of regional trade agreement (RTA) qualifies as a custom union or as a FTA for the purposes of the Agreement. In both cases, the definition encompasses the level of trade liberalization that shall be accomplished in the RTA internal trade, and, in the case of customs unions, also the level of harmonization that shall be accomplished in the duties and regulations applied by its members in the trade with third parties.

Subparagraph 8(a)(i) defines a customs union as the substitution of a single customs territory for two or more customs territories so that:

> ... duties and other restrictive regulations of commerce (except, where necessary, those permitted under Articles XI, XII, XIII, XIV, XV and XX) are eliminated with respect to substantially all the trade between the constituent territories of the union or at least with respect to substantially all the trade in products originating in such territories ...

Subparagraph (b) defines a FTA as a group of two or more customs territories in which

> .. the duties and other restrictive regulations of commerce (except, where necessary, those permitted under Articles XI, XII, XIII, XIV, XV and XX) are eliminated with respect to substantially all the trade between the constituent territories in products originating in such territories.

Thus, for an RTA to benefit from the exception authorized in Article XXIV, its level of internal trade liberalization must be such that duties and other restrictive regulations of commerce are eliminated with respect to substantially all the trade (SAT) between the parties to these arrangements. The trade restrictions permitted under Articles XI, XII, XIII, XIV, XV and XX of the GATT are expressly listed as excepted from this rule. The listing does not mention "trade remedies": Article VI, which regulates the imposition of anti-dumping and countervailing duties, or GATT Article XIX, which governs application of safeguards.

The absence of GATT Articles VI and XIX in the exceptions list in Article XXIV:8 has raised the question of whether this provision mandates or allows abolition of trade remedies within customs unions and FTAs since early reviews of RTAs under the GATT.[6] No consensus has ever been reached on the subject,[7] nor a definite

[6] See WTO Negotiating Group on Rules, *Compendium of Issues Related to Regional Trade Agreements—Background Note by the Secretariat (Revision)*, TN/RL/W/8/Rev.1 (1 August 2002), paras 73–75. Discussions often centred on safeguards, although the same issue applies to anti-dumping and countervailing duties. See Robert E. Hudec and James D. Southwick, "Regionalism and WTO Rules: Problems in the Fine Art of Discriminating Fairly", in Miguel Rodríguez Mendoza, Patrick Low and Barbara Kotschwar (eds), *Trade Rules in the Making: Challenges in Regional and Multilateral Negotiations* (Washington, D.C.: Organization of American States and Brookings Institution, 1999), pp. 47, 67–71:

> The issue of how to deal with safeguards in a RTA arose in several working party reviews of RTAs before the Uruguay Round. Members of the working parties objected to RTAs in which the members exempted each other from the application of safeguards. Parties to RTAs have defended exemption of their RTA partners from safeguards on the grounds that Article XIX is not in the list of exceptions to the "substantially all trade" rule, and therefore the "substantially all trade" rule permits or indeed requires RTA members to exclude each other from the application of safeguards restrictions.
>
> ...
>
> As with the absence of Article XIX, the absence of Article VI from the list of exceptions to the "substantially all trade" rule could be read to suggest that members of an RTA may not apply Article VI measures to each other. (Citations omitted).

[7] See WTO Panel Report, *Argentina—Safeguard Measures on Imports of Footwear (Argentina—Footwear)*, WT/DS121/R, adopted 12 January 2000, as modified by the Appellate Body, para. 8.96, where the Panel notes that

> Practice of the Contracting Parties to the GATT of 1947 and of WTO Members is inconclusive on the issue of imposition or maintenance of safeguard measures between the constituent territories of a customs union [or] of a free-trade area. It is a matter of fact that many agreements establishing free-trade areas or customs unions allow for the possibility to impose safeguard measures on intra-regional trade, while few regional integration agreements explicitly prohibit the imposition of intra-regional safeguard measures once the formation of such an integration area is completed.

See also WTO Negotiating Group on Rules, as note 6 above, paras 73–75.

clarification provided specifically on the matter by the multilateral trading system dispute settlement mechanism.[8] Nonetheless, a couple of Statements on Article XXIV:8 of the GATT in the WTO Appellate Body's *Turkey—Textiles* ruling,[9] which have passed mostly unnoticed so far, shed bright new light on the issue of application of trade remedies in customs unions and FTAs.[10]

---

[8] No ruling on the matter of application of trade remedies within customs unions and FTAs has ever been issued under the GATT, and the only two WTO Panel rulings on the issue were reversed and declared as having no legal effect by the Appellate Body. See WTO Negotiating Group on Rules, as note 6 above, paras 76–77. Contrast Mitsuo Matsushita, Thomas J. Schoenbaum and Petros C. Mavroidis, *World Trade Organization; Law, Practice, and Policy* (Oxford: Oxford University Press 2003), pp. 362–363, who state that the WTO Appellate Body rulings in the discriminatory safeguard cases "answer[ed] the question of whether the items figuring in the parenthesis of GATT Article XXIV:8 form an exhaustive list". (The discriminatory safeguard cases are a series of disputes brought to the WTO dispute settlement system where a WTO Member that was party to a RTA applied a safeguard measure, and excluded imports originating in their RTA partners from the scope of the safeguard. The discriminatory safeguard cases brought so far to the WTO dispute settlement system are: *Argentina—Footwear* (as note 7 above); *United States—Definitive Safeguard Measures on Imports of Wheat Gluten from the European Communities* (*US—Wheat Gluten*), WT/DS166, adopted 1 January 2001; *United States—Safeguard Measures on Imports of Fresh, Chilled or Frozen Lamb Meat from New Zealand and Australia* (*US—Lamb*), WT/DS177 and 178, adopted 16 May 2001; *United States—Definitive Safeguard Measures on Imports of Circular Welded Carbon Quality Line Pipe from Korea* (*US—Line Pipe*), WT/DS202, adopted 8 March 2002; and *United States—Definitive Safeguard Measures on Imports of Certain Steel Products* (*US—Steel Safeguards*), WT/DS248, adopted 10 December 2003). According to Matsushita, Schoenbaum and Mavroidis, "[o]n every occasion [in the discriminatory safeguard cases], the WTO adjudicating bodies held that parties to a PTA may impose safeguards against other parties to the PTA". See ibid., p. 363. This assertion overstates the discriminatory safeguard rulings. The Appellate Body decisions in those cases interpreted and applied the provisions in the Agreement on Safeguards, whose Article 2.2 expressly states that "Safeguard measures shall be *applied to a product being imported irrespective of its source*" (emphasis added). It was on the basis of this express commandment on MFN application of safeguards in the Agreement on Safeguards that the Appellate Body held that the safeguard measures at stake in the discriminatory safeguard cases had to (rather than might) be applied to products from all sources, including those imported from the defendants' RTA partners. See, e.g., Appellate Body Report, *Argentina—Footwear*, para. 112, where the Appellate Body stated: "Argentina was ... *required under Article 2.2* to apply [safeguard] measures to imports from all sources, including from other MERCOSUR member States" (emphasis added). A decision on the basis of the Agreement on Safeguards could not have led to a different result because that Agreement does not provide for any exception to the MFN rule established in its Article 2.2 on the grounds of participation in RTAs. Article XXIV of the GATT could arguably have provided a defense to justify the exclusion from RTA parties from the safeguard measure in violation of Article 2.2 of the Agreement on Safeguards if the requirements set forth in Article XXIV for the availability of such defense had been met. However, the Appellate Body never addressed the Article XXIV issue in the discriminatory safeguard cases, on the basis that that discussion would only become relevant if a certain requirement (that the Appellate Body understands the Agreement on Safeguards to set out) of parallelism between the scope of the injury determination and the scope of application of the safeguard measure had been met, which the Appellate Body did not find to occur in any of the discriminatory safeguard cases. See Appellate Body Report, *Argentina—Footwear*, paras 111–113, Appellate Body Report, *US—Wheat Gluten*, paras 93–99, Appellate Body Report, *US—Line Pipe*, paras 178–199, and Appellate Body Report, *US—Steel Safeguards*, paras 433–474. In *US—Lamb* the Panel declined to analyze the discriminatory safeguard issue on the grounds of judicial economy (see Panel Report, *US—Lamb*, para. 7.280), and the Appellate Body declined to review this decision on the basis that it had been only conditionally appealed, and the condition had not been met (see Appellate Body Report, *US—Lamb*, para. 196). For a further discussion on the relationship between parallelism and the discriminatory safeguard cases, and the use of the parallelism requirement as an issue avoidance technique to put aside the analysis of the controversial issues brought about in the assessment of the availability of a GATT Article XXIV defense, see Joost Pauwelyn, *The Puzzle of WTO Safeguards and Regional Trade Agreements*, 7 Journal of International Economic Law (2004), pp. 119–124.

[9] Appellate Body Report, *Turkey—Restrictions on Imports of Textile and Clothing Products* (*Turkey—Textiles*), WT/DS34/AB/R, adopted on 22 October 1999.

[10] The regional arrangement at stake in *Turkey—Textiles* was an alleged customs union between Turkey and the European Community (EC); hence, the Appellate Body ruled there on subparagraph 8(a)(i) of Article XXIV of the GATT, which sets forth the definitional requirements for a customs union, and did not address subparagraph 8(b), which establishes the definitional requirement for a FTA. Still, given that the wording of both provisions is virtually the same as regards the internal trade requirement, this article assumes that the guidance provided in the Appellate Body's *Turkey—Textiles* ruling informs the interpretation of Article XXIV:8 with regard to both customs unions and FTAs.

In *Turkey—Textiles*, the Appellate Body made its first (and only, as of the date this article was written) excursion into the controversial interpretative issues involving the provisions governing customs unions and FTAs in GATT Article XXIV, setting out of a framework for assessing the availability of a defense based on Article XXIV.[11] Within that ruling it also made noteworthy remarks which provide meaningful guidance on whether Article XXIV:8 shall be interpreted as mandating or allowing elimination of trade remedies in RTAs.

First, the Appellate Body resolved in *Turkey—Textiles* the long-lasting debate on the optional or mandatory nature of the list of exceptions in Article XXIV:8. This controversy centered on whether the exceptions listing provides for an option for parties to a RTA to maintain restrictions in their internal trade in certain fields, or rather establishes an obligation for those parties to maintain MFN treatment in the referred fields (i.e., maintaining the applicability of the trade restrictive measures in the listing also in the intra-RTA trade).[12] The Appellate Body did not discuss the issue in detail, but endorsed the first interpretation in its ruling, where it stated:

> "We note ... that the terms of subparagraph 8(a)(i) provide that members of a customs union *may* maintain, where necessary, in their internal trade, certain restrictive regulations of commerce that are otherwise permitted under Articles XI through XV and under Article XX of the GATT 1994."[13]

Second, the above statement on the exceptions list referred to the trade restrictions that may be maintained in a customs union's internal trade as "certain restrictive regulations of commerce that are otherwise permitted under Articles XI through XV and under Article XX".[14] This highlighting that it is permissible to maintain certain restrictions within a customs union, and the closed identification of such permissible restrictions with those governed by the provisions named in the exceptions list further suggests an exhaustive reading of the listing.[15]

Third, the Appellate Body identified both the permission to maintain the restrictions in the exceptions list, and the possibility to liberalize less than all the trade, and thus concluded that "some flexibility" is afforded by the terms of Article XXIV:8 to the constituent members of a customs union when liberalizing their internal trade.[16]

---

[11] See WTO Appellate Body Report, *Turkey—Textiles*, paras 58–59. See also WTO Analytical Index, para. 595, available at <http://www.wto.org/english/res_e/booksp_e/analytic_index_e/gatt1994_09_e.htm#articleXXIVD>.

[12] See Hudec and Southwick, as note 6 above, p. 64.

[13] See WTO Appellate Body Report, *Turkey—Textiles*, para. 48, (emphasis added).

[14] Id.

[15] This point has been made recently by Nicholas J.S. Lockhart and Andrew D. Mitchell. See Nicholas J.S. Lockhart and Andrew D. Mitchell, "Regional Trade Agreements under GATT 1994: An Exception and its Limits", in *Challenges and Prospects for the WTO* (London: Cameron May 2005), pp. 217, 239.

[16] See Appellate Body Report, *Turkey—Textiles*, para. 48 (italics added):

It is clear ... that "substantially all the trade" is not the same as "all" the trade, and also that "substantially all the trade" is something considerably more than merely "some" of the trade. We note also that the terms of subparagraph 8(a)(i) provide that members of a customs union may maintain, where necessary, in their internal trade, certain restrictive regulations of commerce that are otherwise permitted under Articles XI through XV and under Article XX of the GATT 1994. *Thus*, we agree ... that the terms of subparagraph 8(a)(i) offer "some flexibility" to the constituent members of a customs union when liberalizing their internal trade in accordance with this subparagraph.

This reasoning suggests that the Appellate Body understands the leeway left to RTA parties when liberalizing their internal trade to subsume in what can be encompassed within the boundaries of one of those two identified mechanisms of flexibility. Moreover, the Appellate Body expressly cautioned that the degree of flexibility allowed by Article XXIV:8 is limited by the requirement that "duties and other restrictive regulations of commerce" be "eliminated with respect to substantially all" internal trade.[17] This warning further suggests that the Appellate Body would regard trade liberalization either falling short from elimination of duties and other restrictive regulations of commerce or encompassing a part of the RTA trade corresponding to less than "substantially all" the trade as not meeting the internal trade requirement set forth in Article XXIV:8(a)(i) and (b).

The above statements lead to a construction of Article XXIV:8 of the GATT as mandating abolition of trade remedies as to the part of the trade within RTAs counting towards the fulfilment of the SAT threshold, and strongly indicate this to be the only way the text of that provision as currently written can be interpreted consistently with the Vienna Convention on the Law of the Treaties (VCLT).[18] The reasoning underlying this conclusion is developed in the following sections of this article, which revisit the controversies on the meaning of the relevant wording in Article XXIV:8 in light of the *Turkey—Textiles* statements and applying the VCLT rules on treaty interpretation.

II. Relevant Wording in Article XXIV:8 Interpreted Pursuant to the VCLT and in Light of the Appellate Body Statements in *Turkey—Textiles*

In the following sub-sections, this article revisits the discussions on the meaning of relevant wording in GATT Article XXIV:8 in the light of the Appellate Body statements in *Turkey—Textiles*. We first analyze the meaning of the expression "duties and other restrictive regulations of commerce" and discuss whether it encompasses trade remedies—an issue not comprehended within the Appellate Body *Turkey—Textiles* ruling, but key to proceeding any further on a discussion on applicability of trade remedies in RTAs on the basis of Article XXIV:8. The authors argue that trade remedies are not comprehended within the meaning of "duties" in Article XXIV:8, taking into account the text of the French and Spanish versions of the GATT, which indicate that the term "duties" in this provision refers to customs duties only. Nonetheless, the authors conclude that trade remedies are encompassed within the

[17] See WTO Appellate Body Report, *Turkey—Textiles*, para. 48: "Yet we caution that the degree of 'flexibility' that the subparagraph 8(a)(i) allows is limited by the requirement that 'duties and other restrictive regulations of commerce' be 'eliminated with respect to substantially all' internal trade."

[18] See Article 31(1) of the Vienna Convention on the Law of the Treaties (VCLT), 23 May 1969, which has been deemed to incorporate the customary rules of interpretation of public international law referred to in DSU Article 3.2. See Appellate Body Report, *Japan—Taxes on Alcoholic Beverages (Japan—Alcoholic Beverages)*, WT/DS8/AB/R, WT/DS10/R, WT/DS11/AB/R, adopted 1 November 1996, p. 10. See also Appellate Body Report, *United States—Standards for Reformulated and Conventional Gasoline*, WT/DS2/9, adopted 20 May 1996, p. 23: "[o]ne of the corollaries of the general rule of interpretation in the *Vienna Convention* is that interpretation must give *meaning* and *effect* to *all* the *terms* of the treaty" (emphasis added).

meaning of "other restrictive regulations of commerce" in Article XXIV:8. This conclusion relies on the wording on "other restrictive regulations of commerce" informed by the wording on "other regulations of commerce" in Article XXIV and in the Understanding on Application of Article XXIV of the GATT, as well as on an analysis of the scope of the provisions in the exceptions list in Article XXIV:8.

The second sub-section identifies the three distinct interpretations that have been defended for the meaning of the rule on elimination of duties and other restrictive regulations of commerce (ORRC) and the list of exceptions to this rule, and their implications for the issue of abolition of trade remedies in customs unions and FTAs. The assumptions underlying each of these interpretations are discussed in light of the text of Article XXIV:8 and the Appellate Body's discarding of the "must" interpretation of the exceptions list in *Turkey—Textiles*. The authors argue that only a "must" interpretation of the listing would provide support for constructing Article XXIV:8 as permitting non-application of trade remedies within customs unions and FTAs without leaving the whole exceptions list meaningless. Hence the authors conclude that the Appellate Body's discarding of the "must" interpretation in *Turkey—Textiles* confirms that the rule on elimination of duties and ORRC has to be interpreted as mandating abolition of trade remedies in customs unions and FTAs.

The third sub-section further discusses the meaning of the phrase "duties and other restrictive regulations of commerce . . . are eliminated with respect to substantially all the trade" in Article XXIV:8 of the GATT in the light of the Appellate Body's finding that this provision expresses a requirement that limits the flexibility afforded to the parties to customs unions when liberalizing their internal trade. The authors argue that the obligation to "eliminate" duties and other restrictive regulations of commerce must be understood as requiring parties to customs unions and FTAs to abolish these trade restrictions on the part of their trade counting towards the fulfillment of the "substantially all the trade" threshold. That is, the mere establishment of partial trade preferences, i.e., reduced duties or less restrictive regulations of commerce, or the simple non-application of duties and other restrictive regulations of commerce that are still in the books cannot be encompassed within the meaning of duties and restrictive regulations of commerce that "are eliminated" in Article XXIV:8. In other words, the phrase "duties and other restrictive regulations of commerce are eliminated with respect to SAT" means that no duty and no other restrictive regulation of commerce can be applicable in a part of the intra-RTA trade corresponding to substantially all the trade between the RTA parties. The authors find support for this understanding taking into account the ordinary meaning of the verb "eliminate", and contrasting the wording used in Article XXIV:8(a)(i) and (b) of the GATT with that used in Article XXIV:8(a)(ii), as well as that used in Article V of the GATS.

The fourth sub-section analyses the discussion on the exhaustive or illustrative character of the exceptions listing in Article XXIV:8, i.e., whether the parties to RTAs aiming at qualifying as customs unions or FTAs would be allowed to maintain trade restrictions in their internal trade beyond those mentioned in the listing. The authors argue that the list of exceptions in Article XXIV:8 must be understood as being exhaustive. We argue that a reading of the listing as merely illustrative does not find support in the text of Article XXIV:8, and would also leave the whole listing meaningless for allowing RTA parties to maintain whatever sort of trade restrictions they wish in their internal trade. We further argue that this interpretation is confirmed by the Appellate Body's statement on the exceptions list in *Turkey—Textiles*. We then examine the drafting history of Article XXIV:8 and discuss the argument that interpreting the exceptions listed in this provision as being exhaustive leads to a manifestly absurd result.[19] This argument is based on Article XXI of the GATT, which provides for an exception for security reasons that is the most broadly worded exception in the Agreement but is not included in the listing.[20] The authors review the drafting history of Article XXIV:8, which shows that there is a reasonable explanation for the non-inclusion of Article XXI in the exceptions listing, whereas there is no other reason, but a deliberate exclusion, for the provisions governing anti-dumping, countervailing duties and safeguards having been left out of the listing. Therefore, the authors conclude that the drafting history of Article XXIV:8 confirms the interpretation that the exceptions listing is exhaustive. Accordingly, the authors also conclude that Article XXIV:8, interpreted in accordance with the ordinary meaning to be attributed to its terms, in light of GATT's object and purpose, mandates the abolition of trade remedies in "substantially all the trade"[21] between the parties to customs unions and FTAs constituted between WTO Members.

The fifth sub-section seeks to determine whether the interpretation that Article XXIV:8 mandates the abolition of anti-dumping, countervailing duties and safeguards in substantially all the trade within customs unions and FTAs constituted between WTO Members is consistent with the context of GATT 1994, and the practice under the GATT and the WTO.[22] The authors argue that there are no decisions of the contracting parties on the matter of application of trade remedies in RTAs within the meaning of Article 1(b)(iv) of GATT 1994,[23] neither a consistent practice followed by the GATT contracting parties on Article XXIV:8 with regard to application of trade remedies in RTAs within the meaning of Article XVI:1 of the Agreement Establishing the World Trade Organization (WTO Agreement).[24] Yet, the authors recognize

---

[19] See VCLT, Articles 31and 32(b).

[20] See Report of the Sub-group of the Committee on the "European Economic Community" (EEC), L/778, adopted 29 November 1957, 6S/70, 94, para. 26, where the argument that the absence of Article XXI in the exceptions list in Article XXIV:8 demonstrates that the listing cannot be interpreted as being exhaustive was raised for the first time, within the examination of the consistency with Article XXIV of the EEC Treaty provisions for the association of overseas territories.

[21] That is, the part of the intra-customs unions or intra-FTAs trade counting towards the fulfillment of the "substantially all the trade" threshold.

[22] See VCLT, Article 31(1), (2), and (3)(b).

[23] Article 1(b)(iv) of GATT 1994 states that decisions of the contracting parties to GATT 1947 make part of GATT 1994 ("The General Agreement on Tariffs and Trade 1994 ('GATT 1994') shall consist of ... other decisions of the CONTRACTING PARTIES to GATT 1947;").

[24] Article XVI:1 of the WTO Agreement provides that "the WTO shall be guided by the decisions, procedures and customary practices followed by the CONTRACTING PARTIES to GATT 1947 and the bodies established in the framework of GATT 1947".

adopted Working Party Reports on customs unions and FTAs as decisions of the contracting parties within the meaning of Article XVI:1 of the WTO Agreement, and, as such, an important part of GATT (and WTO) *acquis* that shall be taken into account to interpret Article XXIV:8 with regard to application of trade remedies in RTAs.[25] Nonetheless, the authors note that there is only one Working Party Report where a RTA between GATT parties was declared to be fully compatible with Article XXIV,[26] and that report did not discuss or even note the issue of application of trade remedies to intra-RTA imports.[27] Therefore, the authors conclude that the working party report does not provide relevant guidance on the interpretation of Article XXIV:8 with regard to application of trade remedies in RTAs.

A. Meaning of "Duties and Other Restrictive Regulations of Commerce"

The examination of the controversies on the meaning of the wording in Article XXIV:8 that is relevant for the issue of application of trade remedies in RTAs begins with the discussion of whether the expression "duties and other restrictive regulations of commerce" in Article XXIV:8(a)(i) and (b) of the GATT (which describes the types of trade restrictions to be eliminated within a customs union or FTA)[28] encompasses anti-dumping, countervailing duties and safeguards. The absence of Articles VI and XIX in the exceptions list in Article XXIV:8 has given rise to the general question of whether trade remedies should be considered as "other restrictive regulations of commerce"—hence subject to the elimination rule—or not.[29] An answer in the negative would explain the absence of Articles VI and XIX in the exceptions listing on the basis that trade remedies are not comprehended within the trade restrictions whose elimination is required in Article XXIV:8. That is, if trade remedies are not encompassed within the meaning of "duties and other restrictive regulations of commerce" their elimination in RTAs is neither required, nor allowed. This article argues though that trade remedies, while not falling within the meaning of "duties", are comprehended within the meaning of "other restrictive regulations of commerce" (ORRC) in Article XXIV:8(a)(i) and (b).

An argument that the term "duties" in Article XXIV:8 encompasses trade remedies would be allowed based on the English version of the GATT, but does not find support

[25] See WTO Appellate Body Report, *Japan—Alcoholic Beverages*, at 15.

[26] See WTO Committee on Regional Trade Agreements, *Synopsis of "Systemic" Issues Related to Regional Trade Agreements—Note by the Secretariat*, WT/REG/W/37 (2 March 2000), para. 21. The RTA at stake in that case was an agreement notified as a customs union constituted between the Czech Republic and the Slovak Republic. See Working Party Report on the *Agreement Establishing the Czech Republic–Slovak Republic Customs Union*, L/7501, adopted 4 October 1994.

[27] See Working Party Report, on the *Agreement Establishing the Czech Republic-Slovak Republic Customs Union*, as note 26 above..

[28] See James H. Mathis, *Regional Trade Agreements and Domestic Regulation, what reach for "other restrictive regulations of commerce"?*, p. 5 (draft paper presented at the International Law Association British Branch 2005 Spring Conference—Regional Trade Agreements and the WTO Legal System). See also Lockhart and Mitchell, as note 15 above, p. 236.

[29] See WTO Negotiating Group on Rules, as note 6 above, para. 74.

in the French and Spanish versions of the Agreement. Anti-dumping and countervailing duties are described as "duties" in Article VI of the GATT, as well as in the Agreement on Implementation of Article VI of the GATT 1994 (Anti-dumping Agreement) and in the Agreement on Subsidies and Countervailing Measures, and safeguard measures can be applied under the form of duties.[30] Therefore, it would be arguable that anti-dumping duties and countervailing duties are species comprehended within the broader genus "duties" mentioned in Article XXIV:8. Yet, the French and the Spanish versions of Article XXIV:8 of the GATT use the terms "droits de douane" and "derechos de aduana", that is "customs duties", as the equivalent to the term "duties" used in the English version of the provision. The terms "droits *de douane*" and "derechos *de aduana*" obviously have a more specific meaning within which the terms "droits anti-dumping" or "derechos anti-dumping", and "droits compensateurs" or "derechos compensatorios" cannot be so easily encompassed.[31] Accordingly, given that all the versions of the Agreement are equally valid and have to be interpreted consistently, there is not support for the argument that "duties" in the English version of Article XXIV:8 comprehends trade remedies. In contrast, the argument that trade remedies are within the meaning of "other restrictive regulations of commerce" finds support in the text of Article XXIV:8(a)(i) and (b) of the GATT informed by the wording on "other regulations of commerce" in paragraphs 5(a), (b) and 8(a)(ii) and by the Understanding on the Interpretation of Article XXIV of the GATT (Understanding on Article XXIV).

The wording on "other regulations of commerce" (ORC) in paragraphs 5(a), (b) and 8(a)(ii) of Article XXIV coincides with that on "other restrictive regulations of commerce" in paragraphs 8(a)(i) and (b), with the striking difference of the term "restrictive", which qualifies the expression used in reference to the RTAs internal trade liberalization requirement. The coincident wording indicates that the measures referred to in Article XXIV:8(a)(i) and (b) are a subset of the regulations of commerce referred to in paragraphs 5(a), (b) and 8(a)(ii), distinguished by its restrictive nature, thus the meaning of ORC informs the meaning of ORRC. Hence the definition of ORC established in *Turkey—Textiles* (set out by the Panel and not rebutted by the Appellate Body) is relevant for defining ORRC. Referring to Article XXIV:5(a), the Panel stated there that

> the ordinary meaning of the terms "other regulations of commerce" could be understood to include *any regulation having an impact on trade* (such as measures in the fields covered by the WTO rules, e.g., sanitary and phytosanitary, customs valuation, anti-dumping, technical barriers to trade; as well as any other trade-related domestic regulation, e.g., environmental standards, export credit schemes).[32]

[30] See Lockhart and Mitchell, as note 15 above, pp. 237–238.

[31] The difference in the terms used in the English version ("duties") and the French version ("droits de douane"—customs duties) of Article XXIV:8 of the GATT was brought to light within a discussion on whether the requirement to eliminate "duties" in Article XXIV:8(a)(i) encompassed certain "revenue duties" allegedly having a fiscal and non-discriminatory purpose (rather than a protective one), which members of certain RTAs constituted between the EC and third parties applied on imports from parties to the RTA. See GATT doc L/3665, adopted on 29 May 1972, 19S/90, 94, para. 14. Of course, no conclusion was reached on the point. See ibid.

[32] See WTO Panel Report, *Turkey—Textiles*, para. 9.120, (emphasis added).

The *Turkey—Textiles* definition of ORC suggests the meaning of ORRC to encompass "any regulation of commerce having a restrictive impact on trade". That would comprehend either border measures, i.e., measures applied upon importation restricting the cross-border movement of goods, as market-place regulations applied to imported products that adversely affect them as compared with domestic products in the sense of GATT Article III.[33] However, the definition of ORC set out by the *Turkey—Textiles* Panel seems to be excessively broad in scope in contrast with the text of Article XXIV:5(a) informed by the text of paragraphs 5(b) and 8(a)(ii), as well in the Understanding on Article XXIV, and the same is arguable with regard to ORRC and the text of Article XXIV:8(a)(i) and (b).

The chapeau of paragraph 8(a) uses the word "customs", and paragraphs 5(a), 5(b) and 8(a)(ii) refer to regulations of commerce imposed (or applied) to "the trade" (as opposed to "the products" as in Article III of the GATT) of (or with) third parties. These terms suggests that the drafters intended the meaning of ORC to be of narrower scope, covering border measures only.[34] The requirement in the Understanding on Article XXIV that evaluation of ORC under Article XXIV:5(a) be made on the basis of "import statistics" for goods originating in third countries (with no reference to statistics on exports to third countries)[35] further indicates that ORC refers to border measures on imports only.[36] As to ORRC, the text of Article XXIV:8(a)(i) and (b) also refers to elimination of duties and ORRC with respect to "the trade" between the RTA parties, and the Understanding on Article XXIV refers to "elimination between the constituent territories of duties and other restrictive regulations of commerce".[37] This equally suggests that the scope of ORRC in Article XXIV:8(a)(i) and (b) is limited to regulations that restrict the cross-border movement of goods between the RTA parties.[38] Moreover, a definition of ORRC confined to restrictive border measures applicable on imports may be further confirmed by reference to the trade restrictions regulated in the provisions enumerated in the exceptions list in Article XXIV:8(a)(i) and (b).

All the provisions referred to in the exceptions list in Article XXIV:8(a)(i) and (b) regulate measures that, by definition, are ORRC that were exempted from the rule on elimination of duties and ORRC. Therefore, the meaning of ORRC in Article XXIV:8 can be inferred through an analysis of the listed provisions, that is, Articles XI, XII, XIII, XIV, XV and XX of the GATT.

In brief, the scope of the listed provisions is as follows:

---

33 See Lockhart and Mitchell, as note 15 above, pp. 236–237, who, though not taking into account the *Turkey—Textiles* Panel ruling, also state that ORRC are likely to include both border restrictions and market-place regulations adversely affecting imported goods within the meaning of the national treatment obligation.

34 See Lockhart and Mitchell, as note 15 above, p. 246.

35 See Understanding on the Interpretation of Article XXIV of the GATT 1994, para. 2.

36 See Lockhart and Mitchell, as note 15 above, p. 245.

37 See Understanding on the Interpretation of Article XXIV of the GATT 1994, preamble, fourth paragraph.

38 See Lockhart and Mitchell, as note 15 above, pp. 236–237, even though the authors later conclude that "ORRC are also likely to include marketplace regulations that adversely affect imported goods as compared with domestic goods".

[Article] XI	prohibits quotas and other restrictions on imports and exports other than duties and charges, except for certain import and export restrictions in the agricultural sector, such as those to support domestic supply management regimes.
[Article] XII	Permits import restrictions in the event of balance of payments emergencies.
[Article] XIII	Requires that in those areas where quotas are allowed (for instance, agriculture) quotas be applied on a nondiscriminatory basis.
[Article] XIV	Allows deviations from the nondiscriminatory application of quotas under Article XIII if necessary for balance of payment reasons.
[Article] XV	Allows deviations from GATT rules to comply with commitments to the International Monetary Fund.
[Article] XX	Allows qualified deviation from GATT rules for measures to protect health, safety, the environment, [and other public policy purposes].[39]

The above descriptions show that Articles XI, XII, XIII, XIV and XV basically regulate quantitative restrictions applicable at the border. Article XX, in contrast, has a much broader scope, which covers any kind of measures, applicable either at the border or internally, having any sort of restrictive effects on imports or adverse effects on imported products.[40] Notwithstanding, the presence of the broadly scoped Article XX in the exception's listing in Article XXIV:8(a)(i) and (b) does not necessarily imply that any kind of regulation having a restrictive effect on imports or an adverse effect on imported products would be encompassed within the meaning of ORRC. An interpretation more consistent with the wording in the other provisions in Article XXIV, and in the Understanding on Article XXIV would be that the presence of Article XX in the exceptions listing means that border restrictions justifiable under it are exempted from the rule on elimination of duties and ORRC, while market-place restrictions are outside the scope of that rule. Still, the presence of Article XX in the exceptions list is instructive on the meaning of ORRC for indicating that this expression is not limited to quantitative restrictions as an examination of Articles XI to XV alone could suggest, but encompasses any sort of restriction on imports. This is significant to clarify that trade remedies (which are normally applied through increased duties rather than through quantitative restrictions)[41] are also encompassed within the meaning of ORRC.

Trade remedies are border measures taking the form of increased duties or quantitative restrictions, whose very purpose is restricting imports of certain products. For this reason, they are undoubtedly encompassed within the meaning of "other restrictive regulations of commerce" in Article XXIV:8(a) and (b), irrespective of whether this expression is constructed broadly on the basis of the definition of ORC set

[39] See Hudec and Southwick, as note 6 above, p. 63.

[40] Once the requisites established in one of its paragraphs and in its chapeau are met, GATT Article XX may justify either restrictions on the cross-border movement of goods such as measures prohibiting the importation of certain goods to pursue environmental or health purposes, as market-place regulations providing less favorable treatment to imported products within the meaning of GATT Article III.

[41] Anti-dumping and countervailing duties are applied through increased duties. See Article VI:2 and 3 of the GATT, Article 9 of the Anti-dumping Agreement, and Article 19 of the Agreement on Subsidies and Countervailing Measures. Safeguard measures may be applied either through increased duties or through quantitative restrictions. See Article 5(1) of the Agreement on Safeguards.

out by the *Turkey—Textiles* Panel, or narrowly on the basis of the wording in Article XXIV and in the Understanding on Article XXIV.[42]

B. Interpretations proposed for the rule on elimination of duties and other restrictive regulations of commerce and the list of exceptions to this rule—the "may versus must" debate

The discussions between WTO Members on the meaning of the rule on elimination of duties and other restrictive regulations of commerce (ORRC) and the list of exceptions to this rule in Article XXIV:8(a)(i) and (b) of the GATT have centered in three distinct constructions of this provision, which lead to different conclusions on the issue of application of trade remedies in RTAs.[43] All those constructions build on the "may vs. must" debate on the nature of the list of exceptions to the rule on elimination of duties and ORRC in Article XXIV:8 of the GATT and make certain assumptions on the meaning of the relevant wording in that provision.

[42] An interesting discussion (without the scope of this article though) refers to whether a narrower definition of ORRC subsumed in border protectionist measures would permit an avenue for RTA parties to replace external restrictive measures for internal discriminatory measures such as discriminatory taxes levied upon RTA parties only, hence subverting the internal trade liberalization. See Mathis, as note 28 above, pp. 10–11. The correlate problem is that a broader definition of ORC, on the other hand, "would require customs unions members to externally harmonize all of the regulatory measures that can possibly affect trade[, which would be] far in excess of what a customs union could reasonably be understood to require." See James H. Mathis, *Regional Trade Agreements in the GATT/WTO* (The Hague: T.M.C. Asser Press, 2002), p. 252.

[43] There is some additional variation on the opinions defended by WTO Members on the issue of application of trade remedies in customs unions and FTAs. See *Committee on Regional Trade Agreements, Synopsis of "Systemic" Issues Related to Regional Trade Agreements—Note by the Secretariat*, as note 26 above, paras 56–58. See also Negotiating Group on Rules, as note 6 above, paras 73–75. This article focuses in the three referred interpretations because they seek support for their arguments on a construction of the meaning of the relevant wording in Article XXIV:8 alone. Notwithstanding, it is worth mentioning that an argument has been made that Article XXIV shall not be construed as either mandating nor allowing non-application of trade remedies within customs unions and FTAs. This argument does not rely on an assumption on the nature of the exceptions list, but rather on the view that "the invocation of Article XXIV d[oes] not mean that other Articles of the General Agreement should cease to apply". See the Reports of the Working Parties concerning the agreements between the European Communities and Austria, Iceland, Portugal, Sweden, and Switzerland and Liechtenstein, respectively, 20S/156, 169, 181, 194, 207 (and also in L/6379, p. 36), and L/7219, all adopted on 19 October 1973. This argument will not be further discussed within this article, but the authors note their understanding that the broadly worded phrasing in the chapeau of para. 5 of Article XXIV ("[n]othing in this agreement shall prevent the formation of a customs union or a free-trade area") makes clear that neither Article XIX nor any other provision in the GATT is *a priori* excluded from the scope of the regional trade exception. See Appellate Body Report, *Turkey—Textiles*, para. 45, where the Appellate Body stated: "[T]he chapeau makes it clear that Article XXIV may, under certain conditions, justify the adoption of a measure which is inconsistent with certain other GATT provisions, and may be invoked as a possible "defense" to a finding of inconsistency." The authors argue furthermore that GATT Article XXIV is not overruled by the prohibition on discriminatory safeguards set forth in Article 2.2 of the Agreement on Safeguards because there is no conflict between these rules within the meaning of the General Interpretative Note to Annex 1A of the Agreement Establishing the World Trade Organization (WTO Agreement). Article 1.1 of the Agreement on Safeguards clarifies that the safeguards provided for in the Agreement and those in GATT Article XIX are one and the same thing. See Panel Report, *US—Line Pipe*, para. 7.150. See also Appellate Body Report, *US—Lamb*, para. 69, where the Appellate Body reconciled the reference to "unforeseen developments" in Article XIX with the absence of this expression in the Agreement on Safeguards. For this reason, the exception in Article XXIV, which covers the safeguards regulated in GATT Article XIX, also encompasses the safeguards disciplined in the Agreement on Safeguards. See Appellate Body Report, *Turkey—Textiles*, para. 45, note 13, where the Appellate Body ruled that GATT Article XXIV may be invoked as a defense to a claim of inconsistency with the Agreement on Textiles and Clothing (ATC) because Article XXIV is incorporated in the ATC by Article 2.4 of the ATC, which provides that "[n]o new restrictions ... shall be introduced except under ... the provisions of this Agreement or relevant GATT 1994 provisions".

The debate on the mandatory or optional nature of the list of exceptions to the rule on elimination of duties and other restrictive regulations of commerce in Article XXIV:8 focuses on how the phrase "where necessary" in this provision shall be read.[44] The "may" interpretation reads that phrase as providing that a party to a customs union or FTA is allowed to apply the restrictions listed to imports from its RTA partners, when that party deems it necessary.[45] The "must" interpretation reads the same phrase as permitting a party to a customs union or FTA to apply the restrictions in the listing to the trade of its partners in the arrangement whenever that is necessary pursuant to the terms and principles of the listed provisions themselves.[46] Since most listed provisions set forth criteria prescribing that the measures they regulate shall apply on an MFN basis, the "must" interpretation implies that the measures regulated by the provisions in the listing must remain applicable in the intra-customs union or intra-FTA trade and must be imposed on RTA parties whenever imposed on third parties.[47]

One construction of Article XXIV:8 builds on the interpretation that the exceptions listing refers to measures that must be applied on an MFN basis to infer that other trade restrictions (those not listed, such as trade remedies) may (but do not have to) be applied to intra-customs union or intra-FTA imports. A second construction builds on the interpretation that the exceptions listing refers to trade restrictions that may be maintained in the intra-customs union and intra-FTA trade to infer that trade restrictions not listed (such as trade remedies) must be abolished within RTAs. A third view also builds on the interpretation that the exceptions listing refers to trade restrictions that may be maintained in the intra-RTA trade, but infers that non-listed restrictions (such as trade remedies) may be applied within the RTA to the extent that their application does not undermine the meeting of the "substantially all the trade" requirement. This section discusses these constructions and the implications of the Appellate Body's *Turkey—Textiles* ruling endorsing a "may" interpretation for the meaning of the exceptions listing in GATT Article XXIV for the issue of application of trade remedies within customs unions and FTAs.

1. Must *Apply Excepted Provisions to RTA Partners*—May *Eliminate Trade Remedies*

In several discussions reported under the GATT, RTA parties have relied on the "must" interpretation of the exceptions listing to argue that GATT Article XXIV allowed them to apply discriminatory safeguards (i.e., to exclude intra-customs union or intra-FTA imports from the scope of the safeguard). For instance, the Working Party Reports on the agreements between the European Communities (EC) and Austria, Iceland, Portugal, Sweden, and Switzerland and Liechtenstein all record a same statement by the representative of the EC, arguing that the omission of Article XIX

[44] See Hudec and Southwick, as note 6 above, p. 64.
[45] Id.
[46] Id.
[47] Id.

among the provisions mentioned in Article XXIV:8(b) implies that the EC is "free to exempt" its FTA partners from possible restrictions imposed under Article XIX.[48] Similar statements may be found in the records of various GATT Contracting Party meetings, such as the one made by the representative of Austria at the October 1991 GATT Council meeting, with respect to a safeguard which excluded imports originating in Austria's RTA partners in the European Free-Trade Association (EFTA) from the scope of the measure.[49] The representative of Austria argued there that "since Article XIX was not mentioned in the list in Article XXIV:8(b), measures taken thereunder *might* be not applied to other members of a free-trade area".[50]

Non-RTA parties are also reported to have relied on the "must" interpretation of the exceptions listing to challenge the discriminatory application of measures regulated by the provisions in the listing. During the examination of the Free-Trade Agreement between Canada and the United States a member of the Working Party argued that

> if a party to a free-trade agreement invoked *Article XX* to justify an export licensing scheme for short supply or conservation purposes, it *should apply* such measure in a *non-discriminatory manner* ... *Article XXIV:8(b) did not allow* parties to a free-trade agreement *to exempt* other parties from the measures taken *under the exceptions provided in that article*.[51]

Also, within the examination of the European Free-Trade Association (EFTA) and the Association between EFTA and Finland—Accession of Iceland, certain members of the Working Party expressed the view that "Article XXIV did not affect the obligations of contracting parties to apply *quota restrictions* in a *non-discriminatory manner*.[52]

The argument could be made that the "must–may" construction of the exceptions list and the elimination rule in GATT Article XXIV:8 finds support in an analysis of the nature of the measures regulated by the provisions in the listing.[53] The exceptions list refers to trade restrictions that are imposed to address global or external conditions (which are caused by imports from any source), and tend to apply across a range of products rather than as to particular products.[54] For this reason those measures, when applied, arguably must be imposed also to intra-RTA imports, either to be effective or to avoid undue harm to non-RTA parties.[55] However, all other types of trade restrictions (the ones not listed) may hypothetically be applied to address intra-RTA

---

[48] See, respectively, GATT docs L/3900, L/3902, L/3901, L/3899 and L/3898, all adopted on 19 October 1973, BISD 20S/145, 158, 171, 183 and 196. See also BISD 24S/73 (same views expressed in L/3901 repeated in 1977 Report).

[49] See GATT doc C/M/252, pp. 12–15, and GATT doc L/6899/Add.7/Suppl.1 (notification of import quota for cement of origin other than from EC or EFTA Member State).

[50] See ibid. (emphasis added).

[51] See *1991 Report of the Working Party on Free-Trade Agreement between Canada and the United States*, GATT doc L/6927, adopted 12 November 1991, BISD 38S/47, 61, para. 45 (emphasis added).

[52] See *Report of the Working Party on "European Free-Trade Association and Association between EFTA and Finland—Accession of Iceland*, GATT doc L/3441, adopted 29 September 1970, BISD 18S/174, 177, para. 10 (emphasis added).

[53] See Mathis, as note 42 above, pp. 245–246.

[54] Id.

[55] Id.

trade problems alone, therefore one can infer that these measures are always permitted between RTA parties.[56]

An arguable flaw in the above reasoning is that safeguards would also fall within the rubric of trade restrictions that are imposed to address conditions caused by imports from any source, and should therefore be imposed on a MFN basis to avoid that non-RTA parties end up bearing a disproportionate burden of the effect of the measure.[57] A more precise distinction between safeguards and the measures regulated by the listed provisions may be drawn on the basis of a broader framework which the last share, but within which safeguards do not fall. All provisions in the listing regulate measures that are enacted to address public policy concerns.[58] Safeguards, on the other hand, (as well as tariff duties, anti-dumping, countervailing duties, quantitative restrictions) are enacted to address commercial policy purposes, providing a domestic protection benefit to domestic producers.[59] It would be arguable that public policy measures, by their own nature, are simply not encompassed within the purposes of "substituting customs territories" or "liberalizing trade". Therefore, whenever a party to a RTA would have recourse to those measures, it would be required to do so in compliance with the MFN rule, i.e. applying the restrictions necessary to meet its public policy purposes also to its RTA partners. Yet, a distinction between measures addressing commercial policy purposes and measures addressing public policy purposes better supports the argument that safeguards (and the other trade remedies) must be eliminated in customs unions and FTAs, while the provisions in the listing may remain applicable, than the other way around.

Measures enacted to address public policy purposes arguably remain within the sovereign domain that parties to customs unions or FTAs would be less likely to give up to fulfill the requirement of "substitution of a single customs territory for two or more customs territories" or liberalization of the trade between "a group of two or more customs territories".[60] As a matter of logic, it would then be up to the parties to these arrangements to decide the grade of sovereign domain they would be willing to refrain from exercising. For this reason, the exceptions listing can be more reasonably construed as indicating areas where parties to customs unions and FTAs are allowed to maintain restrictions in the trade between them, than areas where they would be required to maintain MFN treatment. That being said, the authors stress that the most striking flaw they see in the "must–may" interpretation of GATT Article XXIV:8 does not reside on the nature of safeguard measures, but rather in the reading that interpretation makes of the rule on elimination of duties and ORRC.

To conclude that Article XXIV:8 permits (rather than mandates) non-application of trade remedies within RTAs, the "must–may" construction assumes that the rule on

[56] Id.
[57] Ibid. See also Hudec and Southwick, as note 6 above, p. 68.
[58] See Mathis, as note 42 above, pp. 246–247.
[59] Id.
[60] See ibid., pp. 245–247.

elimination of duties and ORRC with respect to SAT requires that trade restrictions not be applied (rather than applicable) to a portion of the intra-RTA trade correspondent to the SAT threshold.[61] This assumption (which is shared by the "may–may" interpretation, as noted in section II.B.3. below), is inconsistent with an interpretation of the text of Article XXIV:8 of the GATT as currently written pursuant to the VCLT. As it is further discussed in section II.C. below, to assume that the rule on elimination of duties and ORRC in Article XXIV:8(a)(i) and (b) merely requires non application of trade restrictions in a portion of the intra-RTA equal to SAT between them, the "must–may" (and also the "may–may") interpretation reads into the provision words that are not there, and reads out of the provision the words that are there.

In brief, the "must–may" (as well as the "may–may") interpretation reads the relevant wording in Article XXIV:8(a)(i) and (b) as if they provided that a customs union/FTA shall be understood to mean an area where "duties and other restrictive regulations of commerce ... are [not applied] with respect to substantially all the trade". Yet, the text in Article XXIV:8(a)(i) and (b) of the GATT reads "are eliminated", rather than "are not applied". For this reason, the authors argue that the "must–may" interpretation of the exceptions list and the rule on elimination of duties and ORRC is not allowed under the VCLT, and cannot support a construction of Article XXIV:8 of the GATT as permitting application of trade remedies within customs unions or FTAs.[62]

2. May *Apply Excepted Provisions to RTA Partners*—Must *Eliminate Trade Remedies*

The "may–must" construction for the exceptions list and the rule on elimination of duties and ORRC in GATT Article XXIV:8 was raised for the first time within the debates before the sub-group of the GATT Committee on the European Economic Community (EEC), which examined the consistency of the EEC Treaty provisions for the association of overseas territories with Article XXIV. Members of the sub-group relied on the "may" interpretation of the exceptions list to argue that the leeway Article

[61] Ibid., pp. 68–69, 238. This assumption (that the rule on elimination of duties and ORRC in Article XXIV:8 only requires that trade restrictions not be applied to an amount of the trade significant enough to jeopardize the meeting of the threshold that a part of the intra-RTA trade equivalent to SAT between them is not affected by trade restrictions) seems to underlie the following reply of the EC to an argument by Argentina that application of safeguards was prohibited within customs unions or FTAs:

> The European Communities contends that Article XXIV:8 of GATT does not prohibit the maintenance of the possibility to impose safeguard measures within customs unions or free-trade areas, either during the transitional period leading to their formation, or after their completion. The European Communities argues that safeguard measures are an exceptional emergency instrument of a temporary nature and *are limited to a specific product*, and that safeguard measures *do not as such affect the establishment and the nature of a customs union or a free-trade area*. Article XXIV of GATT *permits* the members of a customs union or free-trade area to *decide* whether, when applying a safeguard measure pursuant to Article XIX of GATT 1994 and the Agreement on Safeguards, to exempt other members of the customs union or free-trade area from the measure.

See Panel Report, *Argentina—Footwear*, para. 8.94 (emphasis added).

[62] The full reasoning underlying this conclusion is developed in section II.C. below.

XXIV:8 left to RTA parties in what regards the restrictions applicable in their internal trade is limited. They asserted there that

> ... paragraph 8(b) [of Article XXIV of the GATT], in derogation of the rule regarding the elimination of internal obstacles, made provision for certain restrictive trade regulations authorized under certain Articles of the General Agreement; the list of these did not, however, include Article XVIII, concerning governmental assistance to economic development. The application of the customs duties and of the restrictions instituted under Article XVIII did not therefore *benefit* from the exception for which provision was made in Article XXIV. The latter did not make provision for *allowing* one constituent territory of a FTA, in order to protect its industry, to levy import duties on imports from another constituent territory.[63]

In other words, according to this view RTA party is not allowed to apply duties on the basis of GATT Article XVIII to the trade of other constituent parties because this provision is not included among those for which the exceptions listing allows a derogation from the rule that RTA parties shall eliminate internal obstacles to the trade between them. The same reasoning would apply to all trade restrictions regulated by provisions not included in the listing, such as anti-dumping, countervailing duties and safeguards, regulated, respectively, in Articles VI and XIX of the GATT.[64]

As it is evident from the above quotation, the "may–must" interpretation relies, in the first place, on the assumption that the list of provisions excepted from the rule on elimination of duties and other restrictive regulations of commerce in GATT Article XXIV:8 is exhaustive, and that the trade restricted on the grounds of the provisions in the listing does not deduct from the part of the trade to be considered free of ORRC and counted in the meeting of the substantially all trade coverage requirement.[65] It draws, furthermore, on the understanding that the rule on elimination of duties and other restrictive regulations of commerce covers the application of trade restrictions as a possibility, rather than only as a fact.[66] That is, areas and products where trade restrictive measures remain applicable count against meeting the "substantially all the trade" threshold, even where those measures are not currently in place.[67] This particular aspect was underscored in a very enlightening way by a participant of the meeting of the WTO Negotiating Group on Rules held on 7 March 2005.[68] That participant is reported to have made the following remarks after having stated that a submission on definition for SAT that had been presented by another participant only proposed a partial definition for SAT, given that it did not deal with other directly or indirectly related issues:

---

[63] See *Report of the Sub-group of the Committee on the "European Economic Community"*, GATT doc L/778, adopted 29 November 1957, BISD 6S/70, 94, para. 16 (emphasis added).

[64] As discussed in section II.A. above, the authors purport that anti-dumping, countervailing duties and safeguards fall within the meaning of ORRC in GATT Article XXIV:8.

[65] See Mathis, as note 42 above, p 238. See also Lockhart and Mitchell, as note 15 above, pp. 241–242.

[66] Lockhart and Mitchell present a very clarifying explanation on this assumption. See Lockhart and Mitchell, as note 15 above, p. 238.

[67] Id.

[68] See Negotiating Group on Rules, *Summary Report of the Meeting Held on 7 March 2005—Note by the Secretariat*, TN/RL/M/24, 23 March 2005.

> [T]he concept of "other restrictive regulations of commerce" (ORRCs) and its exemption list were directly linked to SAT . . . [hence] the proponent [should] clarify whether ORRCs applied under Articles VI and XIX of the GATT 1994—i.e. anti-dumping, countervailing duties and safeguards—should also be addressed as part of the SAT clarification. The balance that existed in Article XXIV:8 should be maintained; therefore, a clarification of SAT should also encompass the extent to which such trade remedy measures could be applied in an RTA. *He noted his delegation's interpretation according to which trade remedy measures could not be applied to trade covered by free trade agreements or customs unions.*[69]

The "may–must" interpretation of the exceptions list and the rule on elimination of trade restrictions in GATT Article XXIV:8 was also invoked in the context of dispute settlement. In *Argentina—Footwear*, Argentina argued that it could not impose safeguard measures against imports from its RTA partners in the Southern Common Market (MERCOSUR) (an alleged customs union) because Article XXIV "prohibit[ed] it from doing so".[70] Argentina emphasized there that

> Article XIX of GATT is not listed in Article XXIV:8(a)(i) or (b) of GATT among the exceptions from the requirement to abolish all the duties and other restrictive regulations of commerce on substantially all trade between the constituent territories of a customs union or a free-trade area. Therefore, it [was], in Argentina's view, *incompatible with the purpose of Article XXIV:8 of GATT* to impose safeguard measures within the MERCOSUR customs union.[71]

The Panel rejected Argentina's argument that Article XXIV:8 prevented it from applying safeguard measures to its RTA partners' imports.[72] Though having earlier noted that "[p]ractice of the Contracting Parties to the GATT of 1947 and of WTO Members is inconclusive on the issue of the imposition or maintenance of safeguard measures between the constituent territories of a customs union or of a free-trade area",[73] the Panel ended up endorsing the "must–may" construction of Article XXIV:8.[74] The Panel also offered an "alternative" understanding that in case imposition of safeguards within customs unions were to be deemed prohibited, the

---

[69] Ibid., para. 14 (emphasis added).
[70] See WTO Panel Report, *Argentina—Footwear*, para. 8.93.
[71] See ibid. (emphasis added).
[72] See ibid., para. 8.101.
[73] See ibid., para. 8.96.
[74] See ibid., para. 8.97, where the Panel states:
Although the list of exceptions in Article XXIV:8 of GATT clearly does not include Article XIX, in our view, that paragraph itself does not necessarily prohibit the imposition of safeguard measures between the constituent territories of a customs union or free-trade area during their formation or after their completion. A frequently advanced justification for the maintenance or introduction of safeguards clauses within regional integration areas is the argument that the obligation of Article XXIV:8 to eliminate all duties and other restrictions of commerce applies only to "substantially all" but not necessarily to "all" trade between the constituent territories. It could be argued that for all practical purposes the application of safeguard measures to particular categories of like or directly competitive products is unlikely to affect a trade volume that could put the liberalization of "substantially all trade" between the constituent territories of a customs union into question. But the persuasiveness of this argument depends mainly on the extent to which safeguard measures are actually imposed. Thus we do not exclude the possibility that extensive use of safeguard measures within regional integration areas for prolonged periods could run counter to the requirement to liberalize "substantially all trade" within a regional integration area. In our view, the express omission of Article XIX of GATT from the lists of exceptions in Article XXIV:8 of GATT read in combination with the requirement to eliminate all duties or other restrictions of commerce on "substantially all trade" within a customs union, leaves both options open, i.e., abolition of the possibility to impose safeguard measure between the member States of a customs union as well as the maintenance thereof.

mechanism available for a customs union to implement that requirement would be the replacement of the application of safeguards by the customs union parties for the application of safeguards by the customs union as a single unit.[75] These findings of the *Argentina—Footwear* Panel on Article XXIV were later reversed by the Appellate Body on the basis that Argentina "did not argue before the Panel that Article XXIV of the GATT 1994 provided it with a defense to a finding of violation of a provision of GATT 1994", hence "[an] analysis of Article XXIV of the GATT 1994 was not relevant in th[e] case".[76]

Interestingly, in a later dispute under the MERCOSUR dispute settlement system, Argentina relied on the *Argentina—Footwear* Panel decision to reply to the argument made by Brazil that a safeguard Argentina had imposed on textile imports from Brazil was illegitimate because "imposition of safeguard measures has no place in a customs union.[77] Argentina made reference to the *Argentina—Footwear* Panel decision to argue that the application of safeguard measures within customs unions and FTAs was *allowed* by Article XXIV:8(a) and (b) of the GATT.[78] The *Productos Textiles* (Textile Products) MERCOSUR arbitration tribunal noted that the *Argentina—Footwear* Appellate Body Report did not prejudge the matter, and that the Panel Report had stated that the practice of GATT contracting parties and WTO Members was not conclusive on the issue.[79] The arbitration tribunal then stated that there was no need to further discuss that

[75] See WTO Panel Report, *Argentina—Footwear*, paras 8.99 and 8.102. In this "alternative" finding the Panel applied Footnote 1 to the Agreement on Safeguards, which is located right after the word "Member" in Article 2.1 of the Agreement. Article 2.1 provides:

> A Member[1] may apply a safeguard measure to a product only if that Member has determined, pursuant to the provisions set out below, that such product is being imported into its territory in such increased quantities, absolute or relative to domestic production, and under such conditions as to cause or threaten to cause serious injury to the domestic industry that produces like or directly competitive products.
>
> Footnote 1 states:
>
> A customs union may apply a safeguard measure as a single unit or on behalf of a Member State. When a customs union applies a safeguard measure as a single unit, all the requirements for the determination of serious injury or threat thereof under this Agreement shall be based on the conditions existing in the customs union as a whole. When a safeguard measure is applied on behalf of a member State, all the requirements for the determination of serious injury or threat thereof shall be based on the conditions existing in that Member State and the measure shall be limited to that Member State. Nothing in this Agreement prejudges the interpretation of the relationship between Article XIX and paragraph 8 of Article XXIV of GATT 1994.

It is noteworthy, however, that, by implying that *the means* by which customs union parties have to implement a prohibition on application of safeguards to their partners eventually established in Article XXIV is the application of the measure by the customs union as a single unit, instead of by its Member States, the *Argentina—Footwear* Panel prejudged the interpretation of the relationship between Article XIX and paragraph 8 of Article XXIV of GATT 1994. That is, the Panel did precisely what is forbidden by the last sentence in the Footnote 1 of the Agreement on Safeguards.

[76] See WTO Appellate Body Report, *Argentina—Footwear*, paras 109–110. The Appellate Body also reversed the Panel findings on Footnote 1 to the Agreement on Safeguards. In this regard, the Appellate Body first expressly stated that "[t]he ordinary meaning of the first sentence of footnote 1 [to Article 2.1 of the Agreement on Safeguards] appears to us to be that the footnote only applies when a customs union applies a safeguard measure 'as a single unit or on behalf of a member State'." See Appellate Body Report, *Argentina—Footwear*, para. 106. Then the Appellate Body noted that the safeguard at stake in that case had been applied by Argentina, on its own behalf (rather than by the MERCOSUR customs union on its own behalf or on Argentina's behalf), therefore the Footnote 1 did not apply to the measures challenged in that case. See ibid., para. 108.

[77] See Laudo del Tribunal Arbitral, *Argentina—Aplicación de Medidas de Salvaguardia sobre Productos Textiles (Res. 861/99) del Ministerio de Economia y Obras y Servicios Publicos* (*Laudo III—Productos Textiles—de Brasil a Argentina*) (3 March 2000), III, F, 3.

[78] Id.

[79] Id.

matter, given that the issue at stake in the case was rather if MERCOSUR law allowed the application of safeguards such as the challenged measure.[80]

Noteworthy, in a subsequent MERCOSUR case again brought by Brazil against Argentina, this time challenging anti-dumping duties imposed on imports of chicken, Brazil explicitly argued that

> legal scholars assert that anti-dumping measures are incompatible with RTAS, and pursuant Article XXIV:8(a)(i) of the GATT a customs union implies the elimination of duties and other restrictive regulations of commerce between its constituent territories. Anti-dumping measures in Article VI of the GATT are evidently trade restrictive and moreover are not mentioned within the exceptions to Article XXIV.[81]

The *Pollo* (Chicken) MERCOSUR tribunal ruled directly on the issue of whether GATT Article XXIV:8 prohibits application of trade remedies within customs unions and FTAs.[82] The *Pollo* MERCOSUR arbitration tribunal stated that Article XXIV:8 envisions the free movement of goods within a RTA, with no exception but those made explicitly in the text, and expressly stated that the measures regulated by GATT Articles VI and Article XIX are not permitted within RTAs because they are not explicitly provided for in the parenthetical language in Article XXIV:8.[83] Yet, this decision left unaddressed the main gap in the "may–must" construction of the exceptions list and the rule on elimination of duties and ORRC in GATT Article XXIV, which is the absence of Article XXI, the broadly worded exception for security reasons, in the supposedly exhaustive list of restrictions that could be maintained within a customs union or FTA.

The counter-argument that the absence of GATT Article XXI shows that the exceptions listing in Article XXIV:8 cannot be interpreted as being exhaustive was

[80] Id.

[81] See Laudo del Tribunal Arbitral, *Aplicación de Medidas Antidumping contra la exportación de pollos enteros, provenientes de Brasil, Resolución Nº 574/2000 del Ministerio de Economía de la República Argentina* (*Laudo IV—Pollos—de Brasil a Argentina*), 21 May 2001, I-C-1-15. In the original:

> medidas antidumping según la doctrina son incompatibles con esquemas de integración regional y según el artículo XXIV.8 (a) (i) del GATT 1947 una unión aduanera implica la eliminación de los aranceles y de otras reglamentaciones restrictivas del comercio entre los territorios que la componen. Las medidas antidumping del artículo VI del GATT son evidentemente restrictivas del comercio y además no son mencionadas entre las excepciones al artículo XXIV. ibid.

Argentina this time replied that anti-dumping measures were not ORRC within the meaning of Article XXIV:8, but rather "measures against unfair trade practices" ("Las medidas antidumping son acciones contra prácticas comerciales desleales y no constituyen 'reglamentaciones comerciales restrictivas')." ibid. I-C-2-64.

[82] See *Laudo IV—Pollos—de Brasil a Argentina*, II-E-3-245.

[83] In the original:

> [L]a libertad de circulación de bienes y la ausencia de restricciones es propio de la naturaleza de las áreas de libre comercio y las uniones aduaneras, como lo recoge la normativa de la OMC. El artículo XXIV del GATT 1994 dispone en su párrafo 8 (a i) y (b) que esos sistemas de integración se caracterizan por la eliminación de los derechos y de las regulaciones restrictivas del comercio. Mientras que el Entendimiento para la Interpretación del artículo XXIV dispone que las áreas de libre comercio y las uniones aduaneras, para ser compatibles con dicho artículo han de satisfacer, entre otras de sus disposiciones, el párrafo 8. Las excepciones admitidas por el artículo XXIV y que son señaladas expresamente -artículos XI, XII, XIII, XIV, XV y XX- no incluyen el artículo VI relativo al dumping. De conformidad con este criterio la experiencia comparada de procesos de integración muestra que en el comercio dentro del espacio integrado no se aplican los mecanismos antidumping sino regímenes de defensa de la competencia sometidos a una disciplina común y administrados por organismos comunes y no por autoridades nacionales.

See *Laudo IV—Pollos—de Brasil a Argentina*, II-E-3-245.

made by the EC at the debates before the sub-group of the Committee on the European Economic Community where the "may–must" construction of GATT Article XXIV:8 had been raised for the first time.[84] The EC argued there that a conclusion that the exceptions list is not exhaustive follows *a contrario* from the fact that the broadest worded exception in the GATT, the one for security reasons provided for in Article XXI, which the contracting parties' right to avail themselves of could not be disputed, is not included in the listing.[85] This argument has remained a shadow which the proponents of the "may–must" interpretation for the exceptions list and the rule on elimination of trade restrictions in Article XXIV:8 of the GATT in the field of trade remedies have had difficulties in overcoming. The Delegation of Australia, for instance, argued in a Communication to the WTO Committee on Regional Trade Agreements (CRTA) that

> A fully implemented customs union or free-trade area does not permit anything between free trade between the partners to the arrangement and MFN treatment for third countries. Taking again Article XIX as an example, a judgement would therefore have to be made whether, if there is no plan to eliminate safeguard action between the partners, the MFN rule would apply instead.[86]

The paper presented by the Australian Delegation adds that "[s]imilar observations could be made about Article VI and its application in a fully developed free-trade area or customs union".[87] These statements are preceded by a brief discussion on the provisions referred to in the exceptions list in GATT Article XXIV:8, and the absence of Article XIX.[88] The Australian paper seems however to be reluctant to explicitly endorse the "may–must" construction due to the difficulty in providing a reasonable explanation for the absence of GATT Article XXI in the listing. The paper notes in this regard that:

> Delegations have in the past pointed out that Article XXI is not listed. In their view, if resort to general exceptions is permitted, there could hardly be a reason why security exceptions should be out of bounds. But there has always been a recognition that this Article applies to matters quite different to those listed in Article XX, and that no WTO Member will give up its right to judge when its essential security interests are involved. It would therefore be more profitable to consider the relevance of the list in Article XXIV:8 to other GATT articles.[89]

Nonetheless, on the one hand, the text of Article XXIV:8 leaves no room for the list of exceptions to be interpreted as being merely illustrative, and, on the other hand, the provision's drafting history provides a reasonable explanation for Article XXI having been left out of the listing, hence overcoming the gap raised in this interpretation. The authors further discuss the exhaustive or illustrative character of the exception's listing in section II.B.3 and section II.D below.

---

[84] See *Report of the Sub-group of the Committee on the "European Economic Community"*, as note 63 above.
[85] See ibid., 6S/97, para. 26.
[86] See *Communication from Australia*, WT/REG/W/18, 17 November 1997, para. 22.
[87] See ibid., para. 23.
[88] See ibid., paras 15, 17–19.
[89] See *Communication from Australia*, as note 86 above, para. 16.

3. May *Apply Excepted Provisions to RTA Partners*—May *Eliminate Trade Remedies*

The "may–may" interpretation of the rule on elimination of duties and other restrictive regulations of commerce and the list of exceptions to this rule was initially relied upon by parties to RTAs under examination to rebut non-parties' arguments that GATT Article XXIV:8 requires RTA parties to apply the measures regulated by the provisions in the listing on a MFN basis. In the examination of the Free-Trade Agreement between Canada and the United States, one member of the Working Party argued that Article XXIV:8(b) did not allow parties to a free-trade agreement to exempt other parties from measures taken under the provisions enumerated in the exceptions list, in case certain export control measures which had been justified under Article XX of the GATT.[90] The member of the Working Party added that "[s]uch measures could not be considered 'other restrictive regulations of commerce' in terms of Article XXIV:8(b)".[91] The representative of Canada is reported to have replied that

> [U]nder Article XXIV:8(b) of the GATT, restrictions meeting the exceptions of Article XX *could be maintained* in a free-trade agreement. Export control measures were included in 'other restrictive regulations of commerce' in this article. ... *Article XXIV:8(b)* ... *did not preclude the parties* in a free-trade agreement *from undertaking elimination of restrictions vis-à-vis* the other party to the agreement.[92]

Also, in the light of earlier statements by certain members of working parties on RTAs that "Article XXIV did not affect the obligations of contracting parties to apply quota restrictions in a non-discriminatory manner",[93] representatives of the EEC and Finland "replied" in the discussions on the EC Agreements with Finland that,

> "*Article XXIV:8(b)*, specifically *mentioning Article XIII*, was *permissive* in this respect and covered certain *possibilities* in relation to the *maintenance of outward restrictive regulations of commerce* in certain circumstances, *while eliminating those between the parties to the Agreement*".[94]

Furthermore, within the debate on the consistency of the EEC Treaty provisions for the association of overseas territories with Article XXIV of the GATT, the EC relied on the "may–may" interpretation of the rule on elimination of duties and other restrictive regulations of commerce and the list of exceptions to this rule to argue that Article XXIV:8 of the GATT allows RTA parties to maintain restrictions in the trade between them, not limited to those referred to in the listing.[95]

---

[90] See *1991 Report*, as note 51 above.

[91] Id.

[92] See ibid. (emphasis added).

[93] See *Report of the Working Party on "European Free Trade Association and Association between EFTA and Finland—Accession of Iceland*, L/3441, as note 52 above.

[94] See *Report of the Working Party on "EC Agreement with Finland"*, L/4064, adopted 30 October 1974, BISD 21S/76, 80, para. 16 (emphasis added).

[95] See *Report of the Sub-group of the Committee on the "European Economic Community"*, as note 20 above. Noteworthy, the "may–may" interpretation of the exceptions list in Article GATT XXIV:8 defended by the EC before the Sub-group of the Committee on the European Economic Community is inconsistent with the "must–may" interpretation of the same provision later defended by the same EC before the above referred working parties on the agreements between the EC and Austria, Iceland, Portugal, Sweden, and Switzerland and Liechtenstein. See notes 43 and 48 above.

More recently, the "may–may" construction of Article XXIV:8 has also been at stake within dispute settlement procedures, more notably in *US—Line Pipe*, which is one of the discriminatory safeguard cases.[96] In *US—Line Pipe* Korea challenged a safeguard measure imposed by the United States which excluded imports originating in the US's RTA partners in the North American Free-Trade Agreement (NAFTA) (an alleged FTA) from the scope of the measure.[97] The United States invoked Article XXIV as a defense,[98] and argued that

> the *list of measures* that Article XXIV:8 specifically *authorizes* free-trade area parties *to maintain* against each other *does not* include *safeguard* measures applied under Article XIX, ... *therefore* ... *by implication*, *safeguard* measures *either may or must* be made *part of the general elimination of "restrictive regulations of commerce"* under any free-trade area.[99]

The United Stated further sustained the following interpretation for the relevant wording in GATT Article XXIV:8:

> Article XXIV *allows* FTA parties to *decide* whether to exclude each other from safeguard measures all of the time, some of the time, or not at all. Under Article XXIV:8, an FTA *must eliminate* restrictive regulations of commerce – like safeguard measures – *on substantially all trade* among the parties. Thus, the *package of trade liberalizing measures* that accompanies formation of an FTA *need not eliminate all duties and restrictive regulations of trade. If* FTA parties, while retaining some duties and restrictive regulations of commerce, *can still achieve the Article XXIV:8 threshold (covering "substantially all trade")*, they *may retain those regulations*. If the elimination of other restrictive regulations covers substantially all trade, the parties *may* also eliminate safeguard measures.[100]

The *US—Line Pipe* Panel implicitly endorsed the "may–may" construction of Article XXIV:8 that was argued by the United States. The Panel identified Article 802 of the NAFTA Agreement, which restricts the use, but does not abolish the possibility of application of Article XIX safeguards within the NAFTA,[101] as a mechanism "which provides for the elimination of safeguard measures between NAFTA members in certain circumstances.[102] Then, the Panel found that the non-application of a safeguard measure to intra-NAFTA imports on the grounds of Article 802 of the NAFTA Agreement "forms part of the elimination of 'duties and other restrictive regulations of commerce' " "which is the very raison d'être of any free-trade area".[103]

---

[96] See note 8 above.

[97] See WTO Panel Report, *US—Line Pipe*, para. 7.136.

[98] See ibid., para. 7.137.

[99] See ibid., para. 7.132 (emphasis added).

[100] See ibid., para. 4.260 (emphasis added).

[101] NAFTA Agreement Article 802 establishes that the NAFTA parties retain their rights and obligations on safeguards under GATT Article XIX, but shall exclude imports originating in the NAFTA partners from the scope of the measure unless: (a) imports from a party considered individually, account for a substantial share of total imports; and (b) imports from a party, considered individually, or, in exceptional circumstances, imports from NAFTA parties considered collectively contribute importantly to the serious injury or threat thereof, caused by imports.

[102] See WTO Panel Report, *US—Line Pipe*, para. 7.141, note 127.

[103] See ibid., para. 7.148. In so doing, the Panel agreed with the argument raised by the United States that "safeguard measures either may or must be made part of the general elimination of 'restrictive regulations of commerce' under any free-trade area". See WTO Panel Report, *US—Line Pipe*, para. 7.132.

As seen above, the "may–may" construction of GATT Article XXIV:8 draws on two assumptions to make the argument that the exceptions listing provides for the areas where RTA parties may apply restrictive measures to the intra-RTA trade, but the absence of a provision in the listing does not imply that the measures regulated by that provision cannot be applied within RTAs. One, shared with the "must–may" interpretation as discussed in section II.B.1. above, is that the rule on elimination of duties and ORRC in Article XXIV:8 requires only that trade restrictions not be applied in a portion of the intra-RTA equal to SAT. The other is that the exceptions list in Article XXIV:8 is not exhaustive. The authors disagree with both.

The assumption that the rule on elimination of duties and ORRC in Article XXIV:8 may be read as requiring the mere non-application of trade restrictions in a portion of the intra-RTA equal to SAT cannot prevail for the reasons already stated in section II.B.1. above and addressed in more detail in sub-section "D" below. The presumption of the non-exhaustive character of the exceptions list is inconsistent with an interpretation of the text of Article XXIV:8 of the GATT pursuant to the VCLT because it reads into that provision words that are not there: "except, where necessary [measures such as] those permitted under Articles XI, XII, XIII, XIV, XV and XX". Furthermore, an assumption on a non-exhaustive nature of the exceptions list within the context of the "may–may" interpretation renders the whole listing meaningless. This is so because the "may–may" interpretation asserts that all sorts of trade restrictions remain potentially applicable, and that the criterion to determine whether the application of a specific trade restriction is permissible or not is the part of the intra-RTA trade that is affected by the ensemble of the trade restrictions applied. The type of trade restriction applied is not relevant within this reasoning, given that what matters is the effect of the restriction on the trade between the RTA parties, therefore, an illustrative list of types of permitted trade restrictions would be fully unnecessary and redundant.[104]

4. *Resolution of the "May vs. Must" Dispute in* Turkey—Textiles

In *Turkey—Textiles* the Appellate Body resolved the long-lasting debate on the optional or mandatory nature of the list of exceptions in Article XXIV:8. When stating its framework for assessing the availability of a defense based on Article XXIV of the GATT, the Appellate Body ruled in *Turkey—Textiles* that

> Subparagraph 8(a)(i) of Article XXIV establishes the *standard* for the internal trade between constituent Members *in order to satisfy* the definition of a "customs union". It *requires* the constituent members of a customs union to eliminate "duties and other restrictive regulations of commerce" with respect to "substantially all the trade" between them.[105]

---

[104] An alternative approach that could arguably render a "may–may" construction meaningful would be to assume that the exceptions list is exhaustive and informs the trade restrictions that may be applied within RTAs without counting against the meeting of the SAT threshold.

[105] See WTO Appellate Body Report, *Turkey—Textiles*, para. 48 (emphasis added).

Furthermore, the Appellate Body noted, with regard to the exceptions list in the same provision, that

> "the terms of subparagraph 8(a)(i) provide that members of a customs union *may maintain*, where necessary, in their internal trade, certain restrictive regulations of commerce that are otherwise permitted under Articles XI through XV and under Article XX of the GATT 1994".[106]

The above quotations leave no doubt that the Appellate Body endorsed the "may" interpretation of the meaning of the exceptions listing.

5. *Conclusion*

The discussions reported above show that GATT Article XXIV:8 can be construed as permitting rather than mandating non-application of trade remedies within customs unions and FTAs on the basis of the "must–may" and the "may–may" interpretations of the meaning of the listing and the rule on elimination of duties and ORRC. The "may–must" interpretation, in contrast, leads to a construction of Article XXIV:8 as mandating non-application of trade remedies within customs unions and FTAs.

The Appellate Body's endorsement of the "may" interpretation on the nature of the exceptions list in Article XXIV:8 of the GATT discards the "must–may" construction for the meaning of the listing and the rule on elimination of duties and ORRC. That suggests either the "may–must" or the "may–may" constructions to be the appropriate reading. Yet, the "may–may" construction for both the meaning of the exceptions list and the rule on elimination of duties and ORRC is not permitted because it would leave the exceptions list meaningless as pointed out above. Hence, the Appellate Body's discarding of the "must" interpretation in *Turkey—Textiles* suggests that the rule on elimination of duties and ORRC has to be interpreted as mandating abolition of trade remedies in RTAs.

C. Meaning of the Phrase "Duties and Other Restrictive Regulations of Commerce ... Are Eliminated with Respect to Substantially All the Trade"

In *Turkey—Textiles* the Appellate Body made clear that Article XXIV:8 of the GATT sets forth the standard that must be met in the internal trade between the constituent members for a RTA to satisfy the definition of customs union or FTA under the GATT.[107] The Appellate Body noted that this standard requires RTA parties "to eliminate 'duties and other restrictive regulations of commerce' with respect to 'substantially all the trade between them' ".[108] It also noted that the terms of Article

[106] See ibid. (emphasis added).

[107] See WTO Appellate Body Report, *Turkey—Textiles*, para. 48. The statement in *Turkey—Textiles* referred only to customs unions, but applies to FTAs as well given that the wording on the internal trade requirement is virtually the same for both types of RTAs as already observed above under note 10.

[108] See WTO Appellate Body Report, *Turkey—Textiles*, para. 48.

XXIV:8 offer "some flexibility to the constituent members of a customs union when liberalizing their internal trade, upon having identified such "flexibility" in the possibilities of on the one hand, liberalizing "less than all" the trade, and on the other hand, maintaining the restrictions in the exceptions list within the RTA.[109] Finally, the Appellate Body further cautioned that the degree of flexibility that Article XXIV:8 allows is limited by the requirement that "duties and other restrictive regulations of commerce" be "eliminated with respect to substantially all" internal trade.[110] In light of these findings, this article now turns to the examination of the interpretative controversies on the meaning of the phrase "other restrictive regulations of commerce ... are eliminated with respect to substantially all the trade" with a view at the issue of application of trade remedies in customs unions and FTAs constituted between WTO Members.

The phrase "duties and other restrictive regulations of commerce are eliminated ... with respect to substantially all the trade" has been the subject of several proposed interpretations, many of which arguably pick and choose within the terms in its wording to build mosaics leading to targeted conclusions, with no regard to the text of Article XXIV:8 of the GATT. The authors, however, argue that pursuant to the rules of treaty interpretation prescribed in the VCLT, the only reading allowed for the phrase "are eliminated ... with respect to substantially all the trade" in Article XXIV:8 of the GATT is the one sustained by the "may–must" construction of the exceptions list and the rule on elimination of duties and ORRC. That is, the authors assert that the phrase "are eliminated ... with respect to substantially all the trade" in Article XXIV:8 establishes a standard for RTAs internal trade liberalization which is only met if the imposition of duties and ORRC,[111] in any degree, is eliminated as a possibility for a part of the internal trade corresponding to "substantially all the trade" [112] between the RTA parties.[113]

To begin with, we focus in the ordinary meaning of the expression "are eliminated". The ordinary meaning of the verb "to eliminate" is "to expel", "to exclude", "to remove", "to get rid of",[114] which is univocal with the meaning of the verbs "éliminer" ("exclure", "supprimer", "faire disparaître en supprimant l'existence")[115] and "eliminar"

[109] Id.

[110] Id.

[111] Except those referred to in the list of exceptions.

[112] This article does not discuss the extent of coverage required by the "substantially all the trade" threshold, nor whether its fulfillment shall be assessed in quantitative or qualitative terms. What the authors want to emphasize here is that the trade counted towards the fulfillment of the "substantially all" threshold must be that which is *a priori* freed from the possibility that trade restrictive measures of any sort apply between the constituent territories.

[113] The point made here is that, as it is further discussed below, trade restrictions that are not currently applied, but remain applicable do not fall within the meaning of restrictions that "are eliminated" in Article XXIV:8 of the GATT. Also, the ordinary meaning of the words "are eliminated" in Article XXIV:8 does not encompass less than full abolition of duties and ORRC (that is, merely reducing duties or adopting less restrictive regulations does not result in a situation where duties and restrictive regulations of commerce "are eliminated").

[114] See Compact Edition of the *Oxford English Dictionary* (Oxford: Clarendon Press, 1971), p. 845.

[115] See Paul Robert, *Dictionnaire Alphabetique et Analogique de la Langue Française* (Paris: Soc. du nouveau Littré, le Robert, 1973), p. 552.

("excluir")[116] used in the French[117] and in the Spanish[118] versions of Article XXIV:8 of the GATT. This confirms that for the internal trade requirement established in Article XXIV:8 of the GATT to be met, duties and ORRC must be abolished, and that the intra-RTA trade to which any type of duty or ORRC remains applicable cannot be counted towards the fulfillment of the SAT threshold even where no duty or ORRC is effectively imposed. Indeed, it is clear that an ORRC expelled, excluded, removed cannot remain applicable, and that if an ORRC is still applicable it cannot be said to be expelled, excluded, removed, or, ultimately, eliminated with respect to substantially all the trade between RTA parties. Accordingly, it becomes evident that the interpretation that elimination of ORRC may be assessed on the basis of a volume of trade threshold (where ORRC would be considered "eliminated" where the volume of intra-RTA trade not being affected by restrictive measures meets the SAT level), as asserted by the "must–may" and the "may–may" constructions, is inconsistent with the text of Article XXIV:8 of the GATT. Article XXIV:8 reads "duties and ORRC . . . are eliminated". Its drafters used a verb, "to eliminate", which has a meaning and, as already underscored in section II.B.1. above, cannot be read out—and replaced for the terms 'are not applied' as if Article XXIV:8 stated "duties and ORRC are *not applied* with respect to SAT"—even though that might be a more pleasant reading for RTA parties.

Second, the authors call attention to the precise wording adopted in Article XXIV:8(a)(ii) and (b) of the GATT. The relevant provision in Article XXIV:8 reads "duties and other restrictive regulations of commerce . . . are eliminated with respect to substantially all the trade". The authors note that some legal scholars have referred to the rule on elimination of duties and ORRC in Article XXIV:8 as requiring that "duties and ORRC be *substantially eliminated*",[119] as if this wording were interchangeable with the wording "duties and ORRC are eliminated with respect to substantially all the trade" effectively inscribed in Article XXIV:8 of the GATT.[120] Yet, the wording is different, since in the text in Article XXIV:8 the term "substantially" qualifies "all the trade", whereas in the other wording the term "substantially" qualifies "eliminated". These differences in wording must be ascribed some meaning pursuant to the VCLT, and this is even more relevant in this case because the phrase "all tariffs and other restrictive regulations of members as between the territories of the members

---

[116] See Real Academia Española, *Diccionario de la Lengua Española* (Madrid: Real Academia Española, 1953), p. 512.

[117] The French version of Article XXIV:8 of the GATT provides in the relevant part:

les droits de douane et les autres réglementations commerciales restrictives (à l'exception, dans la mesure où cela serait nécessaire, des restrictions autorisées aux termes des articles XI, XII, XIII, XIV, XV et XX) *sont éliminés* pour l'essentiel des échanges commerciaux entre les territoires constitutifs.

[118] The Spanish version of Article XXIV:8 of the GATT provides in the relevant part:

los derechos de aduana y las demás reglamentaciones comerciales restrictivas (excepto, en la medida en que sea necesario, las restricciones autorizadas en virtud de los artículos XI, XII, XIII, XIV, XV y XX) *sean eliminados* con respecto a lo esencial de los intercambios comerciales entre los territorios constitutivos.

[119] See, e.g., Jackson, as note 3, pp. 582–583: "A customs union is defined in Article XXIV, paragraph 8(a), to have the two characteristics listed in the original United States proposal: (a) trade restrictions between union members are '*substantially eliminated*' . . ." (emphasis added).

[120] Emphasis added.

are substantially eliminated", was the original phrasing of the internal trade requirement, and was replaced by the current phrasing in Article XXIV:8.[121] The authors affirm that the differences between the precise wording adopted in Article XXIV:8(a)(ii) and (b) and the previous phrasing of the RTA exception have a bearing in further confirming that Article XXIV:8 requires abolition of duties and ORRC in customs unions and FTAs. The *Turkey—Textiles* discussion on the meaning of "substantially the same regulations of commerce" in Article XXIV:8(a)(ii) is instructive on the point.

In *Turkey—Textiles* the Appellate Body discussed the meaning of the requirement in Article XXIV:8(a)(ii) that customs union members adopt "substantially the same regulations of commerce" by customs union members.[122] There, the Appellate Body ruled that customs union members may be deemed to adopt "substantially the same" regulations of commerce (i.e., most regulations of commerce would be the same), even when some regulations are different (in case, if some countries had quotas for textiles and others had not).[123] The above reasoning, however, is not extendable to the interpretation of the meaning of the requirement on elimination of duties and ORRC. The phrasing in Article XXIV:8(a)(i) and (b) does not permit the interpretation that RTA parties would be allowed to eliminate "less than all" duties and ORRC applicable to the part of the intra-RTA trade covered by the RTA trade liberalization program and meant to account for meeting the SAT requirement. Article XXIV:8(a)(ii) allows the interpretation made by the Appellate Body in *Turkey—Textiles* because it reads "substantially the same duties and ORC are applied". This wording is different from the one used in Article XXIV:8 subparagraphs (a)(i) and (b) of the GATT, which state "duties and ORRC ... are eliminated with respect in substantially all the trade".[124]

The Appellate Body noted in *Turkey—Textiles* that the term "substantially" in Article XXIV:8(a)(ii) qualifies the expression "the same regulations of commerce".[125] Hence, there was a textual basis for the Appellate Body's finding that some of the regulations of commerce applied by customs union members could be different, though most regulations of commerce shall be the same (i.e. substantially the same regulations of commerce are applied).[126] In contrast, as also noted by the Appellate Body in *Turkey—Textiles*, in Article XXIV:8 subparagraphs (a)(i) and (b), the term "substantially" qualifies the expression "all the trade",[127] not the verb "eliminate" (and by a deliberate change in wording by the drafters as highlighted above). Accordingly,

---

[121] See Article 33, Suggested Charter for an International Trade Organization of the United Nations, Department of State, September 1946.

[122] WTO Appellate Body Report, *Turkey—Textiles*, paras 48–63.

[123] Id.

[124] Compare also the wording of the RTA exception for trade in services in Article V:1(b) of the General Agreement on Trade in Services (GATS), which states the internal trade liberalization requirement in the following terms: "provides for the absence or elimination of substantially *all discrimination* ... among the parties, *in the sectors covered* ..." (emphasis added in footnote).

[125] See Appellate Body Report, *Turkey—Textiles*, para. 50.

[126] See ibid., para. 62.

[127] See ibid., para. 48.

with regard to the internal trade requirement it is in the amount of trade to be liberalized that, as noted by the Appellate Body in *Turkey—Textiles*, resides the "flexibility" offered by the terms of Article XXIV:8, not in the rule on elimination of duties and ORRC.[128] Therefore, there is no textual basis to affirm that the phrasing of XXIV:8 subparagraphs (a)(i) and (b) allows for grades in the elimination of duties and ORRC. Again, the provision does not read "duties and other restrictive regulations of commerce are substantially eliminated", but rather "duties and other restrictive regulations of commerce ... are eliminated with respect to substantially all the trade". The only interpretation consistent with this reading is that Article XXIV:8 requires the complete elimination of the possibility that duties and ORRC apply to the part of the RTA trade covered by the RTA trade liberalization program.[129]

Third, the authors take note of an additional element which further supports their conclusion on the inconsistency of constructing the rule on elimination of duties and ORRC in Article XXIV:8 as providing for an assessment of its fulfillment on the basis of how much trade is being affected by duties and ORRC at any given moment in time. If the assessment of the portion of trade affected by duties and ORRC were to be the criterion for determining whether the requirement on elimination of duties and ORRC had been met, then the meeting of the Article XXIV:8 internal trade requirement would vary according to the number and type of ORRC imposed within the RTA at any given moment. By implication, the RTA compliance with Article XXIV:8 would be also variable, hence uncertain.[130]

Finally, the authors recall the Appellate Body's statements on the rule on elimination of duties and ORRC, which confirm that this rule requires the complete elimination of the possibility that ORRC apply to the part of the RTA trade that is meant to be the SAT threshold. In *Turkey—Textiles* the Appellate Body implicitly recognized that the possibility to liberalize less than "all" the trade, together with the possibility to maintain the trade restrictions in the exceptions list in the RTA subsume all the flexibility that Article XXIV:8 affords RTA parties in what regards the internal trade requirement.[131] The remarks on the "substantially all the trade" threshold further highlight that this parameter provides for a leeway to RTA parties solely with regard to the part of the trade to be liberalized (which is defined as "not the same as 'all' the

[128] Id.

[129] Needless to say, the requirement of complete elimination of duties and ORRC applicable in the part of the intra-RTA trade covered by the trade liberalization regime cannot be fulfilled by applying reduced duties or ORRC, or by merely limiting the possibility that ORRC apply in the intra-RTA trade as, for instance, in the NAFTA safeguards regime. See note 101 above. In essence, where a NAFTA partner undertakes a safeguard action on a global basis (in accordance with GATT Article XIX), each NAFTA partner must be excluded from the action unless its exports account for a substantial share of total imports of the good and contribute importantly to the serious injury or threat thereof. See NAFTA, Chapter 8, Article 802, at 8–3. The Agreement provides that a NAFTA country normally will not be considered as being accountable for a substantial share of total imports, unless it falls among the top five suppliers of the good. See Leslie Alan Glick, *Understanding the North American Free Trade Agreement* (Deventer; Boston: Kluwer, 1993), p. 75.

[130] See Lockhart and Mitchell, as note 15 above, pp. 238–239.

[131] See note 16 above.

trade", but also "something considerably more than merely 'some' of the trade").[132] These remarks are followed by the warning that the degree of flexibility allowed by Article XXIV:8 "is limited by the requirement that 'duties and other restrictive regulations of commerce' be 'eliminated with respect to substantially all' internal trade".[133] This underscores that in the part of the trade meant to be deemed "liberalized" duties and ORRC must be eliminated, that is expelled, excluded, removed, gotten rid of. It follows that no trade restrictions can remain applicable for any part of the intra-RTA trade that is intended to comprise part of the SAT threshold.

D. Exhaustive or illustrative character of the exceptions listing

As already noted in section II.B. above, the discussion on the exhaustive or illustrative character of the exceptions listing in GATT Article XXIV:8 was part of the debates on the "must–may", "may–must" or "may–may" constructions of the exceptions list and the rule on elimination of duties and ORRC. This discussion gains particular relevance in light of the Appellate Body's endorsement of the interpretation that the exceptions list indicates the areas where RTA parties may deviate from the general rule prescribing elimination of duties and ORRC, and of its implied recognition that the listing and the possibility to liberalize less than all the trade subsume all the flexibility Article XXIV:8 affords RTA parties as regards the internal trade requirement. An illustrative listing would allow RTA parties to maintain other trade restrictions in their internal trade beyond those regulated by the provisions in the listing, whereas an exhaustive listing would imply that restrictions regulated by provisions not listed, such is the case of anti-dumping, countervailing duties, and safeguards, must be abolished in customs unions and FTAs.

The authors have argued in section II.B.3. above that the list of exceptions in Article XXIV:8 must be understood as being exhaustive. A reading of the listing as merely illustrative does not find support in the text of Article XXIV:8 for reading into that provision words that are not there ("except, where necessary [measures such as] those permitted under Articles XI, XII, XIII, XIV, XV and XX"). This reading would furthermore leave meaningless the listing[134] and the rule on elimination of duties and

---

[132] See WTO Appellate Body Report, *Turkey—Textiles*, para. 48. This becomes even more evident in the Spanish and French versions of the report, which read: " 'lo esencial de los intercambios comerciales' significa algo bastante más amplio que tan sólo *parte* de los intercambios comerciales" and " 'l'essentiel des échanges commerciaux' est quelque chose de beaucoup plus important que simplement une *certaine partie* des échanges."

[133] See effectively Appellate Body Report, *Turkey—Textiles*, para. 48, and note 17 above.

[134] See Mathis, as note 42 above, p. 61: "Indeed, if the listing of GATT Article restrictions provided in [GATT Article XXIV:8] would be understood to be non-exhaustive, then they also must be considered to be essentially redundant." Mathis also notes that the exhaustive character of the exceptions list is further confirmed by its legislative history. First, the provision originally encompassed only customs unions (CU), where there is "the substitution of a single custom territory for two or more customs territories", so that "substantially the same regulations of commerce are [to be] applied by all members". See ibid. In such a case, the application of safeguards was probably viewed as more likely to be made by the CU (at least after the transitional period), and no longer by the individual territories composing it, hence, the issue of intra-RTA safeguards would not arise. See ibid. The FTA exception was included later, and after hard debates regarding preferential trade arrangements, whose trade-distortional effects the most favoured nation (MFN) obligation was aimed at eliminating. The fact that FTAs

ORRC for allowing RTA parties to maintain whatever sort of trade restrictions they wish in their internal trade. The authors further noted their understanding that this interpretation is confirmed by the Appellate Body's statement on the exceptions list in *Turkey—Textiles*, where it referred to the trade restrictions that may be maintained in a customs union internal trade as "certain restrictive regulations of commerce that are otherwise permitted under Articles XI through XV and under Article XX".[135] As stated above, the Appellate Body's endorsement of the exhaustive character of the listing is suggested by the highlighting it made that certain restrictions may be maintained within a customs union, expressly referring to the provisions in the listing.[136]

In light of the above, it seems more relevant at this point to discuss the argument that interpreting the exceptions listing in GATT Article XXIV:8 as being exhaustive leads to a result that is "manifestly absurd or unreasonable" because GATT's broadest worded exception, Article XXI on measures for security reasons, is not included in the listing either.[137] At a first sight, it seems difficult to explain, based on textual interpretation only, the absence of a reference to Article XXI of the GATT, which is the broadest and more deferential exception, while narrower and less deferential exceptions (XI, XII, XIII, XIV, and even XX) are referred to in the exceptions list in Article XXIV. Yet, the singular wording in the chapeau of Article XXI of the GATT ("Nothing in this Agreement shall be construed ...") allows the argument to be made that Article XXI does not have to be mentioned in the exceptions list in Article XXIV:8 to remain applicable within RTAs. Given its peculiar reading, Article XXI informs the meaning of every other provision in the Agreement, pervasively limiting all commitments undertaken under the Agreement, including the RTA parties' commitment to liberalize their internal trade to benefit from the Article XXIV exception.

---

internal *cont.*
trade requirements mirror those of CUs, suggests that a high standard was established for FTAs to condition the MFN-regional exception only to those arrangements effectively aiming at and leading to a degree of internal trade liberalization as high as those of CUs. See ibid. It is worth recalling that restricting the leeway for RTAs was the prevalent aim then, especially on the part of the United States, which was not part of such arrangements and viewed itself as harmed by them. See ibid.

135 See WTO Appellate Body Report, *Turkey—Textiles*, para. 48. See also the introduction to section II of this article above.

136 See also on this matter Lockhart and Mitchell, as note 15 above, p. 239.

137 GATT Article XXI states:
Nothing in this Agreement shall be construed
(*a*) to require any contracting party to furnish any information the disclosure of which it considers contrary to its essential security interests; or
(*b*) to prevent any contracting party from taking any action which it considers necessary for the protection of its essential security interests
(i) relating to fissionable materials or the materials from which they are derived;
(ii) relating to the traffic in arms, ammunition and implements of war and to such traffic in other goods and materials as is carried on directly or indirectly for the purpose of supplying a military establishment;
(iii) taken in time of war or other emergency in international relations; or
(*c*) to prevent any contracting party from taking any action in pursuance of its obligations under the United

The VCLT provides that the interpreter may have recourse to legislative history for assistance in the clarification of the meaning of a provision when its textual interpretation "leaves the meaning ambiguous or obscure or" leads to a result that is "manifestly absurd or unreasonable".[138] Then, reviewing the drafting history of Article XXIV:8, the authors conclude that there is a reasonable explanation for the non-inclusion of Article XXI in the exceptions listing, which confirms the interpretation that the drafters understood that mentioning Article XXI in the listing was not necessary.

The drafting history of Article XXIV:8 shows that the non-inclusion of Article XXI in the exceptions list in Article XXIV:8 comes from the original structure of the International Trade Organization (ITO) Charter, which went through changes when GATT had to replace the non-created ITO. The original structure of the ITO Charter contained separately titled chapters, among them Chapter IV, dedicated to commercial policy, and Chapter IX, containing ITO general provisions, which applied to all the provisions contained in the other chapters.[139] The provision corresponding to the current Article XXIV was part of the original Chapter IV of the ITO Charter, dedicated to commercial policy (as were the general exceptions now under Article XX of the GATT, which were listed as "General Exceptions to Chapter IV").[140] The provision corresponding to current GATT Article XXI, however, was located under Chapter IX of the ITO Charter, and titled there as "General Exceptions".[141] Its preamble, which reads: "Nothing in this Charter shall be construed ..."[142] makes clear that the security exception provision applied to the whole ITO agreement. Therefore, it was not necessary and would have been redundant to have a specific reference to the security exception again in the provision that later became Article XXIV.[143] In contrast, it was necessary to make reference to the other restrictions permitted, which were inserted in the commercial policy chapter, under the title "General Exceptions to Chapter IV" together with the provision that later became Article XXIV.[144] This explains why when the corresponding provisions of the ITO Charter became Article XXIV of the GATT the security exception was omitted, maintaining the ITO Charter pattern. The drafters arguably understood that using the same wording ("Nothing in this Agreement shall be construed") was enough to make clear that the security exception applies to all provisions in the GATT, even though this may not stand out as evidently as it did in the ITO Charter structure with its separate chapters on Commercial Policy and General Exceptions.[145]

Nations Charter for the maintenance of international peace and security.

[138] See VCLT, Article 32(a) and (b).

[139] See Mathis, as note 42 above, pp. 62–63.

[140] Id.

[141] Id.

[142] Id.

[143] Id.

[144] Id.

[145] The GATT drafting history also raised another possible explanation for the absence of Article XXI in the exceptions list in Article XXIV:8. Mathis suggests that when the corresponding provisions of the ITO Charter became GATT Article XXIV, the security exception was probably inadvertently omitted in spite of the absence of

The above shows that the absence of Article XXI from the exceptions list in Article XXIV does have a reasonable explanation, and confirms the textual interpretation that the exceptions list in subparagraphs 8(a)(i) and (b) of Article XXIV is exhaustive. In contrast with the case of Article XXI, the absence of a reference to Articles XIX (safeguards) and to Article VI (anti-dumping and countervailing duties) in the exceptions list cannot be explained by the texts of these provisions or through negotiating history. Unlike the former version of Article XXI, the earlier versions of Articles XIX and VI were part of the same Chapter IV dedicated to commercial policy, together with the former version of Article XXIV. Therefore, as regards Articles XIX and VI of the GATT, one must conclude that they were *purposely* left out of the listing because the drafters did not want these trade restrictions to remain permissible in customs unions and FTAs. Therefore, this aspect of the drafting history of Article XXIV:8 also supports the conclusion that abolition of trade remedies is mandatory in customs unions and FTAs constituted between WTO Members.

E. PRACTICE ON CUSTOMS UNIONS AND FTAS UNDER THE GATT AND THE WTO

Pursuant to Articles 31(1), (2), and (3)(b) of the VCLT, the textual interpretation that Article XXIV:8 mandates the abolition of anti-dumping, countervailing duties and safeguards in substantially all the trade within customs unions and FTAs constituted between WTO Members has to be informed by the context of GATT 1994, and the practice under the GATT and the WTO. The context of GATT 1994 comprehends the provisions in Article XXIV, in the GATT 1947 and in the Understanding on Article XXIV, which have already been taken into account in the discussions raised in the previous sections, and may also encompass decisions of the contracting parties on the matter of application of trade remedies in RTAs within the meaning of Article 1(b)(iv) of GATT 1994. Practice under the GATT and the WTO may cover any practice followed by the GATT contracting parties on Article XXIV:8 with regard to application of trade remedies in RTAs which falls within the meaning of Article XVI:1 of the WTO Agreement, as well as equivalent practice by WTO Members. The authors also take into account adopted Working Party Reports on customs unions and FTAs, which are arguably decisions of the contracting parties within the meaning of Article XVI:1 of the WTO Agreement.

The context of GATT 1994 that is relevant for the discussion within this article does not go beyond the provisions in Article XXIV, in the GATT 1947 and in the Understanding on Article XXIV, already taken into account in the discussions raised in the previous sections. There are no decisions of the contracting parties within the meaning of Article 1(b)(iv) of GATT 1994 on the matter of application of trade remedies in RTAs. A decision of the contracting parties within the meaning of Article 1(b)(iv) of GATT 1994 is as "a formal legal text which represent[s] a legally binding determination in respect of the rights and/or obligations generally applicable to all contracting parties to GATT 1947".[146] In the case of RTA matters, however, none of the decisions adopted by GATT contracting parties on RTAs contains an express interpretation of Article XXIV:8 with regard to application of trade remedies within RTAs. On the contrary, there has been unwillingness by GATT contracting parties (and later WTO Members) to adopt decisions in respect of the rights and/or obligations generally applicable when the matter regards RTAs.[147]

There is also no practice followed by the GATT contracting parties on Article XXIV:8 with regard to application of trade remedies in RTAs within the meaning of Article XVI:1 of the Agreement Establishing the World Trade Organization (WTO Agreement). The enduring controversies between WTO Members on the same interpretative issues since the early examinations under the GATT to date[148] provide striking evidence of the absence of any subsequent practice in the application of Article XXIV:8 which establishes the agreement of the parties regarding its interpretation within the meaning of Article 31(3)(b) of the VCLT.[149]

Adopted GATT working party reports on customs unions and FTAs are arguably decisions of the contracting parties within the meaning of Article XVI:1 of the WTO Agreement because these reports were adopted by a joint decision of the contracting parties.[150] These adopted Working Party Reports shall therefore be taken into account in this analysis as an important part of GATT (and WTO) *acquis* whenever they provide relevant guidance on the issue of application of trade remedies within RTAs.[151] However, it is the authors' view that none of the Working Party Reports on RTAs adopted by the contracting parties has provided relevant guidance on the issue of application of trade remedies within customs unions or FTAs constituted between GATT Parties/WTO Members.

---

a General Exceptions chapter in the GATT. See Mathis, as note 42 above, pp. 62–63.

146 See WTO Panel Report, *United States—Tax Treatment for Foreign Sales Corporations* (*US—FSC*), WT/DS108/R, adopted 24 February 2000, as modified by the Appellate Body, para. 7.63.

147 See, e.g., *Background Note by the Secretariat, Systemic Issues Related to Other Regulations of Commerce*, WTO doc WT/REG/W/17 (31 October 1997), p. 3, which reports a draft decision on Article XXIV of the GATT which circulated among Uruguay Round negotiators on 24 September 1990, proposing to address the relationship between Articles XIX and XXIV so as to clarify that a safeguard imposed by a member of a customs union or FTA need not be applied to other members of the customs union or FTA. The report informs that the wording in that decision was rejected because "the language ... was found too permissive by delegations which held the view that Article XIX actions should not be applied to other members of the customs union and that the absence of any reference to Article XIX in paragraph 8 [of Article XXIV] supported this view." Ibid.

148 Compare WTO Committee on Regional Trade Agreements, as note 26 above, paras 56–58, WTO Negotiating Group on Rules, as note 6 above, paras 73–75, and *Report of the Sub-Group*, as note 63 above, 6S/70, 94, para. 16, and 6S/97, para. 26.

149 The interpretative controversies show the absence of a *concordant, common* and *consistent* sequence of acts or pronouncements establishing a discernable pattern implying the agreement of WTO Members regarding the interpretation of GATT Article XXIV:8. See WTO Appellate Body Report, *Japan—Alcoholic Beverages*, at 12 (emphasis added).

150 See WTO Appellate Body Report, *European Communities—Measures Affecting Importation of Certain Poultry Products* (*EC—Poultry*), WT/DS69, adopted 23 July 1998, para. 40, where the Appellate Body clarified that the "decisions, procedures and customary practices" referred to in Article XVI:1 of the WTO Agreement "include only those taken or followed by the CONTRACTING PARTIES to the GATT 1947 acting *jointly*."

151 See Appellate Body Report, *Japan—Alcoholic Beverages*, at 15, where the Appellate Body stated: "Adopted GATT Panel reports are an important part of the GATT *acquis*. They are often considered by subsequent panels. They create legitimate expectations among WTO Members, and, therefore, should be taken into account where they are relevant to any dispute."

The authors analyzed the few Working Party Reports where the members of the working party have made a statement approving the RTAs under examination.[152] Most these arrangements involved non-parties to the GATT, therefore their approval could only take place under GATT Article XXIV:10 (which allows for deviation from Article XXIV requirements),[153] even though reference to this provision was not expressly made in all the cases. That was the case of the Caribbean Free-Trade Area (CARIFTA) and its later formation, the Caribbean Community and Common Market (CARICOM). The CARIFTA Working Party Report stated that "[t]he Working Party agreed that the Agreement provided for the establishing of a free-trade area within the meaning of Article XXIV:8(b). The CARICOM Working Party Report stated that "[t]he Working Party generally agreed that the Caribbean Common Market constituted an interim agreement leading to the establishment of a customs union". Yet, as both arrangements involved non-parties to the GATT, they could not *qualify* as a FTA or a customs union under Article XXIV:8, which regulates customs unions and FTAs "as between the territories of *contracting parties*".[154] The only approved agreements involving GATT parties alone were the South Africa–Southern Rhodesia Customs Union Agreement and the Czech Republic–Slovak Republic Customs Union. The South Africa–Southern Rhodesia Customs Union Agreement was "granted the right to 'claim the benefits of ... Article XXIV' ", but was only provisionally accepted, and never fully recognized.[155] The Czech Republic–Slovak Republic Customs Union is recognized as the only Working Party Report where a RTA between GATT parties was declared to be fully compatible with Article XXIV of the GATT,[156] yet the report does not discuss or even note the issue of application of trade remedies to intra-RTA imports.[157]

The members of the Working Party Report on the Agreement Establishing the Czech Republic–Slovak Republic Customs Union did not raise any questions, nor made any comments on the issue of application of trade remedies within the Czech Republic–Slovak Republic Customs Union.[158] The absence of any note on the matter looks odd, since the issue is admittedly highly controversial, and the agreement

---

152 These are the reports of the working parties that examined the *Caribbean Community and Common Market (CARICOM)*, BISD 24S/68, para. 13, *Caribbean Free-Trade Area*, BISD 18S/129, para. 13, *Czech Republic–Slovak Republic Customs Union*, GATT doc L/7501, paras 13–18, *El Salvador–Nicaragua Free-Trade Area*, BISD II/30, *United Kingdom–Ireland Free Trade Area Agreement*, BISD 14S/122, 14S/23, *Participation of Nicaragua in the Central American Free-Trade Area*, GATT doc L/891, BISD 5S/29, and *South African–Southern Rhodesia Customs Union Agreement*, BISD II/176.

153 Article XXIV:10 allows the approval of "proposals that do not *fully comply* with the requirements of paragraphs 5 to 9 inclusive, provided that such proposals lead to the formation of a customs union or a free-trade area *in the sense of this Article*" (emphasis added). There is certainly a distinction between a proposal leading to the establishment of a customs union or FTA "in the sense" of Article XXIV and an agreement that meets the requirements in Article XXIV:8. The use of the expression "*fully meets*" in *Turkey—Textiles* suggests that the Appellate Body noted this difference. See WTO Appellate Body Report, *Turkey—Textiles*, para. 48

154 See GATT Article XXIV:5 (emphasis added).

155 See Jackson, as note 3 above, pp. 589–590.

156 See WTO Committee on Regional Trade Agreements, as note 26 above, para. 21. See also Working Party Report, as note 26 above.

157 See Working Party Report, as note 26 above.

158 Id.

arguably provides for the replacement of countervailing duties for State aids regulation (Article 19) and elimination of Article XIX safeguards within the customs unions (Article 22).[159] Furthermore, the agreement is unclear on whether a party to the agreement may apply anti-dumping duties to imports of goods originating in the customs unions, or is allowed to impose anti-dumping duties only to the trade of third parties with the other party to the customs unions (Article 13), and shall apply competition regulation to intra-customs union goods (Article 18).[160] In light of the foresaid, the authors conclude that the adopted Working Party Report on the Agreement Establishing the Czech Republic–Slovak Republic Customs Union does not provide relevant guidance on the interpretation of Article XXIV:8 with regard to application of trade remedies in RTAs, which could create legitimate expectations in the WTO parties.

III. Conclusion

This article concludes that abolition of the possibility of applying anti-dumping, countervailing duties and safeguards in the part of the intra-RTA trade counting towards the fulfillment of the "substantially all the trade" threshold is mandatory for a RTA between WTO Members to qualify as a customs union or a FTA under GATT Article XXIV:8 interpreted pursuant to the VCLT. Accordingly, the authors also conclude that RTAs between WTO Members that were notified as customs unions or FTAs but generally allow internal application of trade remedies are illegitimate departures from MFN that lack justification on the basis of Article XXIV. The authors purport that this interpretation is further confirmed by the Appellate Body's statements on Article XXIV of the GATT in *Turkey—Textiles*, and bears no inconsistency with the context of the GATT 1994 and its practice.

---

[159] See Agreement Establishing the Customs Union between the Czech Republic and the Slovak Republic, GATT doc L/7212, 30 April 1993.

[160] Id.

NAFTA Chapter 11B

A Private Right of Action to Enforce Market Access through Investments

Gary N. HORLICK* and Alicia L. MARTI**

INTRODUCTION

Businesses, especially globally oriented ones, increasingly view trade issues and investment issues as being integrally linked within the concept of "market access". Investment plans often require access to one or more imported components, and/or export opportunities for finished products; trade will often involve both local support and import of models and imports necessary to complement (or supplement) local production. Recent "trade" agreements are perceived as having more effective dispute resolution mechanisms than "investment" agreements. The oft-derided GATT dispute mechanism prior to 1994, for example, lead to binding decisions (and settlements "driven" by the litigation) 88 percent of the time,[1] while many investment disputes have dragged on for years and have been resolved based on direct negotiations not particularly dictated by the likelihood of success in the litigation.

The Convention on the Settlement of Investment Disputes between States and Nationals of Other States (ICSID)[2] was a major step forward in providing for investor-State arbitration. But its limitations (including of membership) have led to a continuing search for other means of dispute resolution in the investment field. The new WTO Dispute Settlement Understanding (DSU) applies to the investment rules contained within the WTO Agreement on Trade-Related Investment Measures,[3] but the limited scope of that Agreement renders the otherwise well-regarded DSU as inadequate in the

* O'Melveny & Myers, Washington, D.C. Counsel to one of the parties during the negotiation of the dispute resolution aspects of NAFTA.

** Duke University School of Law, Durham, North Carolina, U.S.A.

This article is based on a speech given by Mr Horlick at the Geneva Global Arbitration Forum, held on 19 September 1996. It is dedicated to Yong K. Kim (1970–1996), a 1995 graduate of Harvard Law School whose intellectual curiosity and creativity made this article possible. His good spirits and zest for life in the face of adversity made it an honour and a pleasure to work with him.

1 Robert E. Hudec, *Enforcing International Trade Law: The Evolution of the Modern GATT Legal System*, Butterworths, Salem, 1993, 286.

2 18 March 1965, 17 U.S.T. 1270.

3 Agreement on Trade-Related Investment Measures, Final Act Embodying the Results of the Uruguay Round of Multilateral Trade Negotiations, 15 April 1994, GATT Doc. MTN/FA, at 139, reprinted in *Message from the President of the United States Transmitting the Uruguay Round Trade Agreements, Texts of Agreements, Implementing Bill, Statement of Administrative Action and Required Supporting Statements*, H.R. Doc. No. 316, 103d Cong., 2d Sess., 1994, at 1448.

eyes of investors.[4] The multilateral investment agreement being negotiated within the Organisation for Economic Co-operation and Development (OECD)[5] will contain principles and a dispute settlement mechanism presumably more acceptable to developed countries and investors, but it would be limited initially to the OECD countries, as well as any others which choose to sign on.

Within this context, the investor state dispute settlement arbitration mechanism contained in Section B of Chapter 11 of NAFTA (Chapter 11B)—a binding agreement between a developing country and two developed countries—presents an interesting adventure in far-reaching arbitration of such disputes, going well beyond such traditional issues of expropriation and repatriation of profits to include such claims as advertising restrictions, pharmaceutical regulation and commercial contract disputes.

PROCEDURE

Chapter 11B provides that an investor of a party can submit to binding arbitration a claim that another party has breached an obligation under Section A of the Chapter, which covers national treatment, most-favoured-nation treatment, minimum standards of treatment, the imposition of performance requirements, senior management and board of directors requirements, expropriation and compensation, and transfers relating to investment; Article 1503(2), which covers State enterprises; or Article 1502(3)(a), which covers monopolies and State enterprises.[6] In order to have standing, the investor must have incurred loss or damage due to that breach.[7] An investor of a party can also bring a claim on behalf of an enterprise of another party which it owns or controls, alleging a breach of the above-described sections that has caused damage to the enterprise.[8] Any claim under Chapter 11B is barred, however, if not made within three years of when the investor first acquired, or should have acquired, knowledge of both the breach and the damage.[9]

Disputing parties are required to first attempt to settle any claims through consultation and negotiation, and if unsuccessful, an investor must notify a party of its intention to submit a claim to arbitration at least ninety days before submission.[10] The notification must list the provisions alleged to have been breached, the issues and factual basis for the claim, and the relief sought and amount of damages claimed.[11] After six

---

[4] Even if the WTO investment rules were modified to the desire of investors, the WTO dispute resolution mechanism would remain a State-to-State one, leaving investors subject to other possible priorities of the States which are meant to protect their interests.

[5] Kazushi Kawato, *MITI Chief Calls for Investment Liberalization World-Wide*, Asahi News Service, available on LEXIS/NEXIS, 15 July 1996.

[6] The North American Free Trade Agreement (NAFTA), 17 December 1992, Article 1116.1(a) and (b), 32 I.L.M. 1993, 605, at 642–643.

[7] Id.

[8] Article 1117.1, ibid., at 643.

[9] Articles 1116.2 and 1117.2, id.

[10] Articles 1118–1119, id.

[11] Id.

months have elapsed since the events giving rise to a claim, the claim can be submitted to arbitration under:

(a) the ICSID Convention, if the disputing party and the party of the investor are both parties to the convention;
(b) the Additional Facility Rules of ICSID, if either the party of the investor or the disputing party is a member; or
(c) the UNCITRAL Arbitration Rules.[12]

The applicable arbitration rules chosen will govern the arbitration except to the extent that they are modified by Chapter 11B.[13] One modification is the setting of the number of arbitrators at three.[14] One arbitrator is appointed by each of the disputing parties, and the third and presiding arbitrator is appointed by agreement of the disputing parties.[15] If they do not agree on a third arbitrator, the Secretary-General of ICSID will make the appointment from a roster of forty-five arbitrators selected by the parties by consensus, and with experience in international law and investment matters.[16] Nationality is not to be taken into consideration except that the arbitrator should not be a national of the disputing party or of the party of which the disputing investor is a national.[17] The panel may appoint experts, on its own initiative or at the request of a disputing party, to report to them on any scientific, environmental, health or safety related factual matters.[18]

The decision of the Tribunal is binding on the disputing parties in a particular case and each party shall provide for the enforcement of an award in its territory.[19] In the event that a party does not abide by or comply with the award, the party of the investor can request a panel under Article 2008 seeking a determination that the denying party's conduct is inconsistent with the obligations of NAFTA and a recommendation that the party abide by or comply with the arbitration award.[20] The party of the investor, in such a situation, can also seek enforcement under the ICSID Convention, the New York Convention or the Inter-American Convention, regardless of whether a Chapter 20 panel has been requested.[21]

SCOPE OF CHAPTER 11B

Chapter 11B offers a private right-of-action against States that are contracting

---

12 NAFTA Article 1120, id. Of the NAFTA parties, only the United States is a signatory of the ICSID Convention. *Treaties in Force*, Dep't of State Pub. 9433, June 1996, at 340. Therefore, another NAFTA party must become a signatory for that option to be available.

13 Article 1120(2), id.

14 Article 1123, ibid., at 644.

15 Id.

16 Article 1124, id. The roster has not yet been established.

17 Article 1124(3), id.

18 Article 1133, ibid., at 646. This is a provision more recently found in trade dispute resolution mechanisms, not investment dispute procedures. See *Understanding on Rules and Procedures Governing the Settlement of Disputes*, GATT Doc. MTN/FA, at 353, reprinted in *Message from the President of the United States, supra*, footnote 3, at 1654.

19 Article 1136(1) and (4), id. In the United States, the Treasury would pay any amend against sub-federal unit.

20 Article 1136(5), id.

21 Article 1136(6), id.

parties of NAFTA and has the potential to encompass a broad range of causes of action extending well beyond the traditional investor complaints of repatriation and expropriation issues. The potential breadth of its scope lies in Chapter 11B's broad definitions of both the entities who have standing to bring such cases and the type of conduct which can be addressed. The Chapter applies to measures adopted or maintained by a party relating to investors of another party, investments of investors of another party in the territory of the party and, with respect to performance requirements and environmental measures, all investments in the territory of the party.[22] The investor who has a right-of-action under Chapter 11B is not only a natural person or entity who is a national of one of the three NAFTA States, but also any company whose place of incorporation is in any one of the NAFTA States and has substantial activity.[23] Therefore, a subsidiary of a third-party State company located in a NAFTA State can have a cause-of-action against a NAFTA party—for example Mercedes-Benz Mexico, as an investor of a NAFTA party, can have a cause-of-action against the United States. Similarly, the subsidiary of a company located in a NAFTA State has a right-of-action against the State of its parent company. This definition of investor includes not only direct investment in manufacturing facilities (as in the example given above), but any form of investment, including equity securities, debt securities, or loans.[24] In addition, the investor need not have actually made an investment, but need only be seeking to invest.[25]

DEFINITIONS

An investor is defined by Chapter 11 as a party or State enterprise thereof, or a national or an enterprise of such party, or an investor of a non-party, that seeks to make, is making or has made an investment.[26] As discussed above, the definition therefore encompasses persons or entities who have not yet made an actual investment—the language "seeks to make" may significantly broaden the scope of those who have standing to bring such claims. Furthermore, the investment need not be in the party against whom the cause-of-action is brought, it can be in the territory of any NAFTA party.

Of equal significance is the wide range of causes-of-action which are available to an investor under Chapter 11B, which covers any violation of the obligations of Chapter 11A of NAFTA. These obligations to investors concern not only transfers and expropriation, but also national treatment, most-favoured-nation, minimum standards, performance requirements and citizenship requirements for senior management and board of directors.[27] However, affirmative prejudicial action by a government is

[22] Article 1101(1), ibid., at 639.
[23] Article 1139, ibid., at 648.
[24] Article 1139, ibid., at 647.
[25] Id.
[26] Id.
[27] Articles 1102, 1103, 1105, 1106, 1107, 1109 and 1110, ibid., at 639 to 641.

required—a measure must be adopted or maintained by a party in order to be actionable under 11B.[28] NAFTA parties are to accord the investors or investments both national treatment and most-favoured-nation treatment with respect to the "establishment, acquisition, expansion, management, conduct, operation, and sale or other disposition of investments." Terms such as the "conduct" and "operation" of investments could possibly be interpreted broadly enough to include the sale of goods, among other business practices that generally have fallen under more traditional trade dispute settlement mechanisms.

Furthermore, the definition of investment is very broad, including an enterprise, an equity security, a debt security, a loan, an interest in an enterprise that entitles the owner to share in income, profits, or assets on dissolution, real estate, tangible and intangible property, and interests arising from the commitment of capital or other resources to economic activity in the territory of a party.[29] It remains to be seen how broadly this definition will be interpreted—for example it would seem that if investment includes "an equity security", then a Mexican private individual as a minority shareholder of U.S. Company X could bring an action against Mexico for a practice that is allegedly in violation of the Chapter, even if Company X does not have any complaint with the practice at issue—which would be an extremely broad application. Of course the investor would have to show loss or damage individually—presumably a decline in the market price of the shares—in order to establish standing, but in any event, neither Company X nor Mexico would seem to have a way to stop an arbitration that they did not desire. An enterprise appears to need to consent to arbitration only if an investor is bringing a claim on its behalf against the party where the enterprise is located, and the investor directly or indirectly owns or controls it.[30] In such a case, both the enterprise and the investor must consent to the arbitration. Under this provision, a Mexican national who controls or owns a U.S. company can sue the United States under Chapter 11B, if the company consents. This might be unwise for the U.S. company, given its probable interest in maintaining good relations with its host government, however, the option remains.

Evidence within NAFTA Regarding the Scope of Chapter 11B

The text of Chapter 11 provides some guidance regarding the scope of Chapter 11B's provisions. The Chapter does not apply to measures adopted or maintained by a party which are covered by Chapter 14 on Financial Services.[31] The Chapter should not be construed in any way to prevent a party from providing services or performing functions such as law enforcement, correctional services, income security or insurance,

[28] Article 1101(1), ibid., at 639. Government inaction such as non-enforcement of a law or toleration of anti-competitive practices would probably not be covered. An affirmative statement of a policy of non-enforcement or inaction, such as within the various U.S. Department of Justice Antitrust Guidelines, would be more of a grey area.

[29] Article 1139, ibid., at 647.

[30] Articles 1117(1) and 1121(2), ibid., at 643.

[31] Article 1101(3), ibid., at 639.

social security or insurance, social welfare, public education, public training, or health and child care, in a manner that is not inconsistent with Chapter 11.[32]

Furthermore, Article 1113 provides that a party can deny the benefits of Chapter 11 to an investor of another party if investors of a non-party own or control the enterprise and the denying party:

(a) does not maintain diplomatic relations with the non-party; or
(b) adopts or maintains measures with respect to the non-party that prohibit transactions with the enterprise or that would be violated or circumvented if the benefits of this Chapter were accorded to the enterprise or to its investments.[33]

This provision would, for example, prohibit the wholly-owned Mexican subsidiary of a Cuban corporation from suing the United States. Chapter 11 also provides that a party can deny the benefits of Chapter 11 to the investor of another party that is an enterprise of such party, and to its investments, if investors of a non-party own or control the enterprise and the enterprise has no substantial business activities in the territory of the party under whose law it is constituted or organized.[34] This prevents non-NAFTA companies from creating "sham" subsidiaries simply to obtain the right to sue the government of a NAFTA party and to obtain access to an arbitral panel.

The Chapter does not make dispute settlement available, either under Chapter 11B or Chapter 20, to address decisions by a party restricting or prohibiting investments in its territory that are made pursuant to the National Security exceptions of Article 2102.[35] Review of decisions made and reviewed under the national investment acts of Mexico and Canada regarding acquisitions are similarly not subject to dispute settlement under Chapters 11B or 20.[36] The Agreement states that Chapter 11B should not be construed to prevent a party from adopting, maintaining or enforcing any measure which is otherwise consistent with the Chapter that it considers appropriate to ensure that investment activity is undertaken in its territory in a manner that is sensitive to environmental concerns.[37]

In its statement of purpose, Chapter 11B provides that the establishment of a dispute settlement mechanism specifically applicable to investment disputes does not prejudice the rights of the parties under Chapter 20.[38] Chapter 20 itself specifically excludes from its procedures only antidumping and countervailing duty matters which have their own dispute settlement mechanism provided in Chapter 19.[39] Finally, Chapter 11 allows an investor to pursue arbitration for money damages under Chapter 11B while simultaneously pursuing injunctive, declaratory or other extraordinary relief not involving the payment of damages before the party's own administrative tribunals

---

32 Article 1101(4), ibid., at 639.
33 Article 1113(1), ibid., at 642.
34 Article 1113(2), ibid., at 642.
35 Article 1138, ibid., at 647.
36 Article 1138.2, ibid., at 649.
37 Article 1114(1), ibid., at 642.
38 Article 1115, ibid., at 642.
39 Article 2004, ibid., at 694.

or courts.[40] All of this indicates that an investor could seek relief under Chapter 11B, in the form of money damages, while the investor's own State sought relief against the other State's practices under Chapter 20, in the form of the equivalent of an injunction, specific performance or other equitable remedy. Recognizing that Chapter 11B, making available only money damages, is not necessarily a complete remedy, the language of these provisions suggests as well that Chapter 11B is not an exclusive one.

LIMITATIONS OF CHAPTER 11B

Chapter 11B contains a number of provisions which have the potential to limit its apparently broad scope. In the event of an inconsistency between Chapter 11 and another Chapter of NAFTA, the other Chapter prevails to the extent of the inconsistency.[41] Review of the acquisition permission process of both Canada and Mexico is excluded from the Chapter 11B mechanism (as well as the Chapter 20 dispute settlement process).[42] An investor in a party cannot sue its own party under Chapter 11B, however, Chapter 11B does not prevent the foreign minority owner of a joint-venture from suing. For example, in a Sony Mexico–Sony U.S. joint-venture, Sony Mexico could sue the United States despite the fact that Sony U.S. has no rights against the United States under Chapter 11B. Parties are still allowed to prescribe "special formalities" in connection with investments from another party's investors, as long as they do not "materially impair" the protections of Chapter 11.[43]

When a disputing party asserts as a defence that the action alleged to be a breach falls within the scope of an exception found in Annexes I–IV, the Tribunal, on request of the disputing party, is required to request an interpretation from the Free Trade Commission.[44] The Commission must submit a response in writing within sixty days or the Tribunal will decide the issue.[45] The Commission decision is binding on the Tribunal.[46] This provision enables the parties, through their representatives in the Commission, to block an 11B action if it falls within the scope of sectors and matters covered by Annexes I through IV.[47] It is as yet undetermined whether the exclusion applies to the sectors indefinitely or only until they open up as per the Annex Schedules. It seems that the former is too restrictive a reading, and one that would have been more clearly expressed by simply excluding the sectors themselves from coverage rather than by reference to the Annexes. This would be a key issue in the current trucking stalemate.

---

[40] Article 1121, ibid., at 643.

[41] Article 1112.2, ibid., at 642.

[42] Article 1138, ibid., at 646; Annex 1138.2, ibid., at 649.

[43] Article 1111(1), ibid., at 642.

[44] Article 1132(1), ibid., at 645. The Free Trade Commission is comprised of cabinet level representatives of the parties, or their designees. Decisions are by consensus, except as the Commission may otherwise agree: Article 2001(1) and (4), ibid., at 693.

[45] Article 1132, ibid., at 645–646.

[46] Article 1132(2), ibid., at 646.

[47] Earlier drafts of NAFTA permitted the Commission (the three parties acting together) to block *any* Chapter 11B action.

RESERVATIONS AND EXCEPTIONS

Chapter 11B dispute resolution provides for a number of reservations and exceptions. The articles regarding national treatment (Article 1102), most-favoured-nation (Article 1103), performance requirements (Article 1106), and senior management and board of directors (Article 1107) do not apply to any non-conforming measure that existed and was maintained by a party at the federal level as set out by its Schedule in Annexes I or III.[48] Canada retained reservations under Annex I regarding:

- agricultural loans by the Farm Credit Corporation;
- review of acquisitions by non-Canadians;
- the sale of government-owned equity interests;
- residency requirements for directors and senior management of federally incorporated corporations;
- ownership of controlled land in Alberta;
- limitations on the percentage of non-resident ownership of certain corporations;
- performance requirements in the automotive sector; and
- the sectors of oil and gas, fishing, and transportation.

Mexico has reservations in the areas of:

- acquisition of land in the border and restricted zones;
- review of acquisitions of certain companies by non-Mexicans;
- citizenship percentages of co-operative production enterprises;
- micro-industry enterprises;
- ownership of land for agriculture, livestock and forestry purposes; and
- the industries of radio and television programming and broadcasting, construction, education, communications, films and cable television, petroleum, automobiles, mining, publishing, transportation, and some professional services.

The United States has Annex I reservations relating to:

- licensing for activities involving atomic energy and nuclear material;
- disclosure of information concerning pesticides;
- acquisition of certain mining rights;
- a variety of restrictions involving air and land transportation; and
- performance requirements for sewage treatment.

Chapter 11 also exempted non-conforming measures maintained by a State or province for two years after the entry into the NAFTA agreement, after which time each party was top set out within its Schedule to Annex I any existing measure maintained by a State or province.[49]

In Annex III, Mexico reserved the right to exclusively perform and refuse to allow investments in a number of activities. Mexico retained this right in the areas of

[48] Article 1108(1)(a)(i), *supra*, footnote 6, at 640.

[49] Article 1108(1)(a)(ii) and 1108(2), ibid., at 640–641. A very large number were notified. Those from the United States can be examined at the U.S. Trade Representative (USTR). The list in Annex I was intended to be exhaustive (i.e. any measure not notified in time would not benefit from the exception) but the parties reportedly have agreed to waive that limit.

petroleum, electricity, nuclear power and radioactive materials, satellite communications, telegraph and radiotelegraph services, postal services, railroads, issuance of currency, and the control, inspection and surveillance of maritime and inland ports, airports and heliports.[50] The Annex also provides that the initial sale of a State-owned asset or of an ownership interest in a State enterprise that performs one of these activities can be restricted to an enterprise with majority ownership by Mexican nationals.[51] After three years have passed since the initial sale, the obligations of national treatment in Article 1102 will apply.[52]

Articles 1102, 1103, 1106 and 1107 also do not apply to any measure that a party adopts with respect to sectors, subsectors or activities as set out in Annex II.[53] Canada has reserved in Annex II the right to:

- give aboriginal people preferences or rights as investors;
- adopt residency requirements for the ownership of oceanfront land by the investor of another party;
- place some restrictions on telecommunications transport networks and services;
- adopt any measure relating to the sale of government bonds and debt securities, and relating to investment in and provision of air and water transportation services.

Mexico can adopt measures relating to:

- the sale of bonds, treasury bills or other government-issued debt securities;
- the investment in or provision of telecommunications services related to air navigation; and
- the investment in telecommunications transport networks and services.

The United States reserves the right to adopt measures relating to:

- residency requirements for the ownership of oceanfront land;
- investment in telecommunications transport networks; and
- investment in maritime transportation.

However, no party may require another party's investor to sell an investment under any measure covered by this Annex.[54]

The most-favoured-nation treatment required by Article 1103 does not apply to treatment accorded by a party pursuant to agreements, or with respect to sectors, set out in its Schedule to Annex IV.[55] All of the parties take exceptions for matters involving aviation, fisheries, maritime matters and telecommunications transport networks and services.

National treatment and most-favoured-nation do not apply to any measure that is an exception to the obligations under Article 1703, which covers intellectual property.[56]

---

[50] Annex III, B, ibid., at 760.
[51] Annex III, C, id.
[52] Id.
[53] Article 1108(3), ibid., at 641.
[54] Article 1108(4), id.
[55] Article 1108(6), id.
[56] Article 1108(5), id.

National treatment, most-favoured-nation and senior management do not apply to government procurement or to subsidies or grants that a party or State enterprise might provide, including government supported loans, guarantees and insurance.[57] Some provisions of performance requirements do not apply to export promotions or foreign aid programmes, government procurement or import quantity requirements for preferential tariffs or quotas.[58] National treatment, most-favoured-nation, performance requirements and senior management and board of directors requirements do not apply to existing non-conforming measures maintained by local governments.[59]

Experience to Date

The most recent notice of claim to be given under Chapter 11B involved Signa SA de CV, a Mexican fine chemicals company which alleged that Canadian regulations governing the approval of generic pharmaceuticals make it difficult to obtain approval for the manufacture of an antibiotic for the Canadian market-place, injuring Signa's investment in Canada.[60] Signa claimed that the regulations violate Article 1105 which provides that a party must accord to investors of the other parties fair and equitable treatment and full protection and security in accordance with international law. Signa would have to show that it has suffered loss or damage[61] in order to establish that they have standing. This may be difficult considering that it is an upstream supplier and is essentially, or arguably, making the claim based on the facts that its related Canadian downstream customer, Apotex, is actually suffering the alleged loss (Signa could argue that it is suffering the loss by virtue of its investment link to Canada). This raises the additional issue that Signa is only one-third owned by the Canadian company, yet sought access to a NAFTA panel to address a dispute that on one level really involves the Canadian company and its government—a dispute possibly not envisioned as being subject to Chapter 11B. However, it is the broad definitions of the Chapter that might enable a company such as Signa to effectively seek redress for its Canadian affiliate based on a minority interest in a Mexican company. It also appears that Ethyl Corp., a U.S. company, will launch a Chapter 11B action against Canada for its ban on a fuel additive on health grounds.[62]

While there have been a number of other actions threatened under Chapter 11B, none of them have progressed to an arbitration (so that information about these cases is difficult to obtain). American tobacco companies threatened to bring Canada to a

[57] Article 1108(7), id.
[58] Article 1108(8), ibid., at 641.
[59] Article 1108(1)(a)(iii), ibid., at 640.
[60] *Examination of Bill C-28: Proceedings of the Standing Senate Committee on Legal and Constitutional Affairs*, Issue No. 15, at 15, Thirty-Fifth Parliament, 2d Session (Canada), Statement of James McIlroy, lawyer, (hereinafter Canadian Parliament Hearing), 1996.
[61] Article 1117(1), ibid., at 643.
[62] "Trade row looms over MMT", Toronto Globe and Mail, 10 September 1996. The attorney for MMT claims that the Helms-Burton sanctions imposed by the United States could be challenged under Chapter 11B by Mexican and Canadian companies, including those owned by nationals of third countries: *NAFTA Countries may Face Wave of Claims*, Financial Times, 13 September 1996.

Chapter 11B arbitration, challenging that its restriction on advertisements on cigarette packaging was expropriation of intellectual property (the restriction was tossed out by a Canadian court on other grounds). An American investor has notified Canada of its intention to submit a notice of intent to challenge, under Chapter 11B, a bill that would terminate its airport contracts, if passed, on the grounds that it violates the articles against expropriation (Article 1110) and requiring minimum standards of treatment (Article 1105).[63] A U.S. company threatened to sue a Mexican government-owned company in a contract dispute,[64] but did not proceed. Some interest was also expressed by a Quebec company with a claim against the United States. Finally, it was rumoured that a Canadian mining company threatened a Chapter 11B action to help spur a settlement of a complex controversy involving mining claims near a U.S. national park.

Mexican truckers could consider bringing a Chapter 11B action against the United States rather than waiting for the Mexican government to pursue a remedy under Chapter 20. Although the action would have fallen under the Annex I exceptions to national treatment, most-favoured-nation and performance requirements, according to Article 1108, that exception has run out.

A hypothetical case further illustrates the broad scope of potential applications of Chapter 11B. If Arlington County, Virginia was to deny a zoning variation to Goldstar U.S., while granting a similar one to Micron (or Sony U.S.), could Goldstar Mexico bring the U.S. to an arbitral panel under Chapter 11B? An important issue would be whether Goldstar Mexico had incurred loss or damage by reason of the denial. If Goldstar Mexico wanted to sue under Article 1116, as an investor, it would need to show that either its investment of capital in Mexico had suffered or that its interest in Goldstar U.S. had been damaged. Under Article 1117, Goldstar Mexico, if it owned or controlled Goldstar U.S., could sue the United States if Goldstar U.S. had incurred loss or damage by reason of the denial, as long as Goldstar U.S. consented to arbitration. Another significant issue would be whether the action by Arlington County could be excepted from Chapter 11B arbitration as a pre-existing non-conforming measure under Article 1108(a)(iii). The determination of this issue would depend on what the panel defines as "the measure" that had been adopted—the denial of the variance would not be a pre-existing non-conforming measure by local government, but if the prejudicial measure was defined as the ordinance pursuant to which the variance was defined, that would likely have existed when NAFTA was adopted.

Conclusion and Possible Problems in Attempting to Utilize Chapter 11B for Arbitrators and Investors

Arbitrators could very well be hesitant to open the flood gates by extending Chapter 11B arbitration to some of the kinds of disputes discussed here. They may

[63] Canadian Parliament Hearing, *supra*, footnote 60, at 15, 18.
[64] Id., at 15.

declare that without a clear expression of an intent on the part of the negotiators to extend Chapter 11B arbitration to traditional trade disputes, application of Chapter 11B will be limited to those topics traditionally covered under the term "foreign direct investment". Of course, the dispute mechanisms of Chapters 19 and 20 remain available avenues for the parties to address more traditional trade disputes, and extension of this access to NAFTA panels to private investors for the same types of disputes is unprecedented.

At the very least, an investor following the procedural requirements of the Chapter could get a panel established in order to decide whether the claim could be accepted—which is remarkable. Even if these types of claims are, in the end, rejected after arbitration because of restrictive interpretations of the Chapter, ambiguous intent of the negotiators, or lack of standing of an investor, the fact that an "investor" can force establishment of a panel (except where the three parties collectively block arbitration by invoking a number of possible Annex exceptions) and completion of the arbitration by itself can create some "leverage" in a dispute. Of course, foreign investors usually wish to avoid suing their host governments until all other avenues are explored, which may account for the scarce use of Chapter 11B. It remains to be seen whether investors will push the Chapter 11B dispute resolution mechanism to its limits—as yet it is an untapped source of extensive private investor rights, including guaranteed access to a NAFTA panel for a private party.

SOVEREIGNTY, TRADE, AND THE ENVIRONMENT – A U.S. PERSPECTIVE

Gary Horlick[*]

The topic of trade, the environment, and sovereignty raises some of the more passionate political debates going on within the United States and other countries, particularly in dealing with the world trading system. We are in a state of flux. This is a great time to be working in this field, since everything seems to be a case of first impressions. The boundaries are being rearranged, and a lot of the debates are white-hot.

As I prepared for this, I read a very apt summary of NAFTA by none other than Henry King, who pointed out in his conclusion the rather startling fact that, in Northeast Ohio, an area almost completely dependent on international trade in many respects, the Congressional representatives were against Fast Track. This scenario is repeated throughout the United States. Thirty of the fifty-two members of the House Agriculture Committee said they were against Fast Track. U.S. agriculture depends on exports; without exports it is in red ink. So this disjunction between economic reality and politics shows that Karl Marx indeed was wrong, but it also shows the current state of confusion we are in about the swirling interplay of issues such as trade, the environment, and sovereignty.

I am going to start with a deliberately simplistic way of looking at the world of international law and the environment, fairly conventional and somewhat over-generalized. You have environmental impacts within a country; local water pollution, for example. You have environmental impacts that cross borders, *Trail Smelter*[1] being, of course, the classic case for U.S. and Canadian lawyers. And you have environmental impacts in the global commons. Classically, this meant the high seas, and now it includes, as we all know, the atmosphere. One looks at the legal regimes, and to some extent the trade issues affecting those three spheres, and you see all three of those spheres being changed. You see legal rules that differ from the political pressures, and you see the categories being rearranged, NAFTA being an association of three sovereign countries.

---

* Gary Horlick is a Washington-based partner at the law firm of O'Melveny & Myers, L.L.P., specializing in international trade in goods and services. He is a graduate of Dartmouth College, Cambridge University, and Yale Law School.

[1] United States v. Canada, Arbitral Tribunal, Montreal, Apr. 16, 1938 and Mar. 11, 1941; U.N. REP. OF INT'L. ARBITRAL AWARDS 3 (1947) 1905.

Let us start with the most classically, supposedly non-international environmental impact – solely within the territory of a sovereign nation. I am ducking all the arguments about what sovereignty is because we have heard them all day today. But, certainly, you would think that something like local water pollution would be, at least in international legal terms, of no concern to anyone but the relevant government of the territory. This is no longer true.

We have two very hot issues, perhaps not under international law, but certainly in the politics of trade negotiations which are changing that view. The first, and it was very, very strong in NAFTA, is the view, whether legitimate or not, that by maintaining low environmental standards, or by lowering its existing environmental standards, a country will "steal investment" and steal jobs. This was certainly something that some U.S. environmental non-governmental organizations (NGOs) played to the hilt during the NAFTA debate. Environmental NGOs in the United States have had to learn how to play hard ball in domestic political battles, notably the Clean Air Act of 1990.[2] I would guess, to some extent, this concern for plant stealing and lower environmental standards was a tactical choice to line up support for labor unions. So, one can discount it as a tactic. One cannot discount the force of the political appeal. So here you have, hypothetically, Mexico lowering its environmental standards, something that is presumably its own concern under classic doctrines of international law, and being told, no, you cannot do that. There is language, though hardly hard law or crystal clear hard law language, in the investment chapter of NAFTA, that a Member should endeavor not to lower its environmental standards to attract investment. This is language that is repeated in at least some of the drafts of the Multilateral Agreement on Investment (MAI), at the insistence of the United States.

So that is something that is no one's business except Mexico's, but Mexico must agree to that under NAFTA, and now the United States is selling it to the rest of the world. As I mentioned, there is considerable controversy about whether this plant stealing actually happens much. But the political reality is perhaps stronger than the underlying economic reality. That is one side of the coin. You have groups, not even governments, but non-governmental organizations, self-styled in one country, telling a sovereign government what it can do with that sovereign government's environmental regulations. I thought the NAFTA debate itself got rather carried away on this, since, in effect, you had at least some NGOs saying that the United States, Canada, and Mexico should all have harmonized environmental standards. But they were not willing to give the Mexicans and Canadians votes

[2] Clean Air Act of 1990, 42 U.S.C. §§ 7401-7642 (1990).

on what those harmonized environmental standards would be. There is also something of a democracy deficit built into this debate as well.

The second aspect, the flip side, is represented by the recent WTO appellate body ruling in a case involving beef hormones.[3] U.S. exporters were trying to get the E.U. to comply with the result. But the nature of the debate, and I will stylize the case to avoid getting too tendentious, was essentially that the E.U. had no scientific evidence to support the ban on the use of certain natural hormones in beef.

So here you have a situation where a sovereign government, in this case the E.U., (let us assume there is no scientific support) acted inconsistently with the WTO. Prior to that, the E.U. argued that it could ban imports of beef that had been raised with these growth-promoting hormones if it also banned domestic production sales, which it did. It banned both. So, again, to stylize it a bit, you have a ban on something solely because of local political pressure for which there was no scientific evidence of danger. Yet, a WTO panel ruled that, under the WTO, this was inconsistent. This is not some accident, by the way. The sanitary and phytosanitary agreement within the WTO was negotiated very much with this specific dispute in mind.

So, the fact that the E.U. lost this dispute was not exactly a surprise, since the rules had been written to make sure it would lose. Indeed, you have since seen the E.U. propose that consumer concerns be considered a legitimate basis for regulation. Again, think about that in terms of a shift from what I would call the "classical doctrine" that a government basically can do whatever it wants. It can do that as long as that government bans domestic production as well as imports. We are now in this "brave new world," where the sovereign government cannot even make that decision if it does not have scientific support, as decided by an external supranational body. No wonder people all across Canada and the United States are worried about anonymous people in Geneva.

I would note that, while the E.U. spent ten years fighting off this imported beef when there was no scientific evidence of any harm, they did miss out on mad cow disease over the entire period. They also missed the point, that one does not encourage local beef consumption by bad-mouthing any beef, imported or domestic, without some scientific basis. You have never seen an ad by Coca-Cola saying that Pepsi is bad for you. It destroys the brand category. So within this first sphere, historically, the most sacrosanct in terms of sovereignty, we already see erosion, both legally and politically. No U.S. NGO believed that it was not allowed to push Mexico on Mexican environmental practices that had no cross-border effects.

---

[3] *E.C. - Measures Concerning Meat and Meat Products (Hormones)*, WT/DS48/AB/R (Jan. 16, 1998). The author is council to the U.S. exporters.

The next stage beyond that is what I would call "fairly indirect" cross-border effects. In my view it is probably the most controversial, and it is also one of the most emotional issues. A classic example is the current furor over leg-hold traps, not a ban on the traps in Europe, but a ban on the traps in Canada and the United States. Here you have an alleged cross-border effect, which is that high-income consumers in western Europe feel injured by Inuits in Northern Canada using leg-hold traps on animals. That is the cross-border effect, a psychological one. I am stating that very neutrally. I am not telling you it is good or bad. But it is a somewhat novel claim. In effect you have a claim that these people in Europe can tell Inuits how to do something they have been doing for years. This kind of environmental debate involving charismatic animals has not been a very pretty one. Typically, the debate has suffered from being played up in the press in a very one-sided way, and from there it just goes downhill.

The tuna/dolphin dispute had a lot to do with that.[4] If you actually read the tuna/dolphin opinion in the WTO, which had a lot of the same characteristics, you would see between the lines a very common characteristic of GATT panel opinions, which is a suspicion that the importing country was discriminating against foreigners. This was the case with the United States. If you actually go through the Dolphin Protection Consumer Information Act,[5] you will find that it does favor U.S. fishermen. Surprise. In fact, you will find many GATT panels where there is an underlying suspicion that a national law-making body will favor its own producers. I am sure you are all shocked. These are where the big controversies have been. We may be coming out of that in a more rational way, not in a legal sense, but because of public relations matters. I do not know how many of you followed the fight in CITES (Convention on International Trade in Endangered Species) last summer over elephant hunting and sales of ivory. It was the first time where you actually saw the public relations efforts more or less balanced. A group based in Harae called "Camp Fire" actually got to the media and put forward the view of the villagers, which was that they could make money having a controlled hunt of elephants. Since they had no control of the elephants, their fields were being trampled, and that had to be weighed against maintaining the species.

I cannot tell you which way is right or wrong. What I can say is this; it was the first time where the press reports were more or less balanced, and that led to some sort of compromise. I am addressing that carefully as a po-

[4] *See United States - Restrictions on Imports of Tuna*, 30 I.L.M. 1594, ¶¶ 5.26-5.27, 5.31-5.32 (1991); *United States - Restrictions on Imports of Tuna*, 33 I.L.M. 839, ¶¶ 5.26-5.27, 5.38-5.39 (1994).

[5] Dolphin Protection Consumer Information Act, 16 U.S.C.A. § 1385 (1998).

litical relations matter. One did not see much argument about whether classic principles of international law applied here. This was very much a question of who could get the public sympathy. So that area has been, and I think will continue to be, the most emotional. You can raise a lot of money if you are on the right side of the issue. You can get a lot of votes. It gets a lot of public sympathy. So, this indirect cross-border effect has probably already been the nastiest issue in public terms, and it probably will continue to be so.

The more classic cross-border effects go back to *Trail Smelter*, and these actually seem to be working out better within North America. One sees at least increasing attempts at cooperative work recognizing that there are cross-border effects. The last time I was in Toronto, someone reminded me that half the air pollution in that city came from the United States. The U.S./Canada Agreement on Air Quality[6] does show some attempt to work things out in a practical way. There are some things being done between the United States and Mexico in the same sense. One of the more interesting things, given the OECD principle that the polluter pays, is that the rules are not always followed. The best example is the Chernobyl cleanup. The E.U. is funding a lot of that project. The victim pays because the victim wants it cleaned up and wants to prevent it from happening again. The victim recognizes that the polluter cannot pay. You do not have people standing on principle there. You have someone figuring how to get the place cleaned up. I think that the legal side of that has not really had many implications for trade. It is odd because it is the most obvious cross-border effect. There have not been many trade fights about it. People are not using trade sanctions to try to force people into remedying cross-border pollution. It is unusual because that is where you would expect the most fights.

The third general area is the global commons. This is probably the most interesting because of the Kyoto Convention[7] and the likely follow-up. My personal view is that, politically, the global climate change movement will be a juggernaut. It is going to run over a lot of people. Once again, there are legal instruments for some of the global commons, but not for all. If you go through WTO opinions, you will see some that you might consider to be wishful thinking by panels. The party, typically the United States, that took unilateral action should have gone out and negotiated an international agreement. Usually, they tried and could not do it.

The WTO appellate body has certainly shown an enthusiasm for acting like an appellate body. They always change something, and they also criticize the panel. That area is where the most serious confrontation is likely to

---

6 Agreement on Air Quality, Mar. 13, 1991, Can.-U.S., 30 I.L.M. 676 (1991).

7 United Nations Framework Convention on Climate Change, Dec. 10, 1997, 37 I.L.M. 22 (1998).

occur. So far, despite much fussing about the relationship of the WTO to multilateral environment agreements (MEAs), there actually has not been any conflict. The most obvious example is the Montreal Protocol on chlorofluorocarbons (CFCs),[8] although there are provisions which are pretty obviously inconsistent and trade sanctions are permitted against non-members of the protocol, even though they are WTO members. That would violate the WTO, but none of those allegedly aggrieved people have ever bothered to challenge it.

That could change with the Kyoto Convention. That is why I think the most important item on the agenda right now is the so-far stagnant process of reaching some sort of accommodation between the WTO rules and the MEAs. I will not go through the entire debate, which has bored to tears everyone on the WTO's Committee on Trade and Environment for the last three years. There have been numerous proposals. Just to give you a very quick summary, one school of thought is that the WTO should create a set of *ex ante* standards, and any MEA that meets those standards is waived from the WTO rules. A second option would be a more conventional one-by-one waiver; as agreements come up, they should go through some sort of process and be waived.

The WTO rules are not set up for this. Getting waivers is an extremely difficult thing. Waivers, at least theoretically in the WTO, are supposed to be temporary, not permanent, although past history would not suggest that to be a firm rule. The Committee on Trade and Environment has been talking about this literally for three years and has gotten nowhere. If Kyoto is to work and become effective, then something will have to give there.

One x-factor for all us international lawyers is that, so far, the MEAs predated the signing of the WTO Agreement in 1994. Thus, you had considerable concern about the later-in-time rule from an MEA point of view. To the extent that there is a final agreement in Kyoto, binding on everyone – and we will get debates on that – it will be later in time. So the trade people can have heartburn about the later-in-time rule, rather than the MEA people. Speaking as an observer, I can only wish that both sides avoid heartburn by figuring out a common set of rules.

[8] Protocol on Substances that Deplete the Ozone Layer, Sept. 16, 1987, 26 I.L.M. 1541.

Chapter 25
The World Trading System at the Crossroad of Science and Politics
Gary N. Horlick
Partner, O'Melveny & Myers LLP

This thinkpiece will explore the "flash point" for the world trading system represented by recent controversies such as Shrimp/Turtle,[1] Beef Hormones,[2] and genetically modified organisms[3] ("GMO's").

The controversies can be placed in three (frequently overlapping) categories:

- The requirement of "sound science" as a basic for regulation
- The use of non-product related PPM's as a basis for trade control, and
- The use of the precautionary principle.

Arguably, all three categories are subsumed in the first, but the three categories are useful departure points for analysis.

1. "Sound Science"

The current controversy as of the time of writing [4] is the dispute in the WTO over the EU ban of imports of meat in which growth promoting hormones have been used.[5]

For purposes of this paper, the dispute may be stylized as follows:

- Assume that there is no scientific evidence that the use of the hormones in question causes any risk to humans consuming the beef. In the Beef Hormone case, three of the hormones used occur naturally in cattle. The remaining three are synthetic versions of the three naturally occurring ones. Of the six, the one identified by the EU as most dangerous is found in concentrations from ten times higher to hundreds of times higher in eggs, butter and broccoli.
- Assume that public opinion in the EU is firm against the the sale of meat on which the hormones have been used. Certain member states allow the use of some of the hormones, and this is permitted by the EU.

This situation poses directly the conflict between the WTO requirement of scientific evidence for import controls, and deference to consumer preference absent such scientific evidence. Within a single self-governing entity, this regulatory tension is resolved politically, and often by the use of

[1] United States – Import Prohibition of Certain Shrimp and Shrimp Products, WTO Doc. WT/DS58/AB/R (October 12, 1998).
[2] EC Measures Concerning Meat and Meat Products (Hormones), WTO Doc. WT/DS26/AB/R, WT/DS48/AB/R (January 16, 1998).
[3] In practice, there is much more controversy over GMO's in foods than in, e.g., medicines.
[4] June 1999
[5] The author is counsel to the U.S. cattle producers in this dispute.

a cost-benefit analysis not found in the WTO rules. The complication where international trade comes in is that one could well end up with markets segmented by different facially non-discriminatory choices expressed in each country. The WTO system is not structured (or robust enough ?) to determine which consumer preferences are acceptable and which are not, without some objective standard. The objective standard in the SPS Agreement is the requirement of the use of science as a basis.

In real life, the Beef Hormone case was considerably more complicated. The EU in 1995 convened a scientific conference which found no significant evidence of risk from hormones. In 1999, with two weeks to go before implementation of the panel and Appellate Body decision, the EU announced that all six of the hormones at issue (including the three naturally occurring ones) could well be dangerous in beef.[6] (Those announcements did not explain why the same hormones would not be dangerous in foods with far higher concentrations of the same hormones, such as milk, butter, eggs, broccoli, and squash).

The Beef Hormones case, as stylized above, is the extreme one, with no relevant scientific evidence at all in support of the ban. It is thus an easy one for the WTO system to condemn, and for conferences such as this one to discuss. Very few regulatory disputes are that clear, so one can expect future cases to interpret what is "enough science" in light of the Appellate Body report. The debate is not limited to WTO cases, however — the same issue is now being fought out in the Codex over the acceptability of non-scientific criteria as a basis for regulation of food safety (and this raises issues of the role of international standards such as Codex as a basis for a finding of WTO consistency).

One proposed solution has been labeling schemes. Many advocates of labeling in this context either ignore or are unaware of the well-established principles of consumer protection present in most countries' existing legal system. These principles can be summarized as requiring that consumer information (e.g., in a label or an advertisement) be truthful, verifiable, relevant, and non-deceptive to consumers. The WTO would presumably add a requirement that labeling requirements be non-discriminatory. The Beef Hormones cases illustrates the pitfalls of proposals to use labeling as a solution. First, given that the Appellate Body report on beef has been adopted, there is no basis in WTO law for imposing any labeling requirement on the imported beef (or the domestic beef, for that matter) since no scientific basis was found for any regulation. That said, a label requirement could be negotiated as part of a settlement, because the EU imposes a quota on imports of beef in the United States, so presumably U.S. exporters would be willing to accept a (WTO inconsistent) requirement of labeling in return for a quota increase large enough to offset any commercial damages (i.e., to buy them off — this is how many settlements of litigation work). That said, that would still leave EU-origin beef which has been treated with the same growth hormones unlabeled, thus creating the distinct possibility of consumer deception, and the residues in beef may be so small compared to other food products as to raise questions about the relevance of the factual statement that those hormones had been used.

[6] The EU may have been encouraged by reading paragraph 194 of the Appellate Body Report — one trusts incorrectly — to imply that one dissident scientist reviewing at least two sources could be a sufficient basis for a WTO-consistent import ban.

2. PPMs.

The Appellate Body in the Shrimp/Turtle case appears to have approved in principle the unilateral imposition of the trade barrier based on a non-product related PPM for the first time in a GATT/WTO case (although without any explicit discussion of the new precedent). Certainly the United States government has treated the Appellate Body as blessing the use of PPMs in the future, according to its statement at the High Level Meeting in Geneva in March 1999.[7] The Appellate Body decision raises many unanswered questions:

- Must there be a scientific basis for the unilateral decision (the Appellate Body decision notes the CITES listing but does not state that it was a required element)?
- Is there a rule of proportionality with respect to the nature of the import barrier?
- Is the reach of unilateral import barriers based on PPMs limited by some jurisdictional rule (e.g., some turtles of the same species swam in U.S. waters? birds migrating through the importing country's air space? air molecules passing through the importing country's air space, thus justifying regulation of forest practices in other countries?)?

The unilateral aspect of Shrimp/Turtle raises the same issues of market segmentation as does the "sound science" controversy. The attraction of avoiding unilateralism through multilateral environmental agreements (MEAs) is clear, but do MEAs raise more questions?

- What numerical membership in a MEA is necessary to bind non-members, or at least permit application to them of trade sanctions? Enough to be justifiable as "customary international law"?
- Can/should MEAs override WTO rules such as MFN among MEA parties ? What is the effect on the WTO?

PPMs are easier to deal with in a domestic context (e.g., by cost-benefit analysis or by a political decision), but less controversial, since the same goals can often be achieved within a domestic context by direct or indirect regulations. That said, it is worth noting that, at least for the United States, products made with domestic prison labor are legally less restricted (their sale is permitted, although with a patchwork of restrictions on sale or manufacture) than products made with foreign prison labor (the import of which are banned, as permitted by WTO).

3. "Precautionary Principle"

If the "precautionary principle" means "no risk" (i.e., a product that cannot be sold until it is conclusively proven — based on science, of course — to cause no risk), then very few countries, if any, apply it domestically (e.g., the EU does not ban the sale of GMO products — it has failed to approve new ones for a few years).[8]

[7] The PPM issue is not limited to the environment, or questions of science. Labor rights, animal rights, and government procurement rules and even tariffs all can involve controversies over how a product is made, rather than its physical characteristics. Mountain-climbing dairy cows are a classic example in tariff history, but the genre can be limited only by the imagination of creative legislators.

[8] The EU labeling requirements for GMOs raise the same questions as those discussed in part 1, above, concerning labeling.

A more likely set of controversies will arise from WTO member governments seeking to stretch Article 5.7 of the SPS Agreement as much as possible to justify import bans. The EU towards the end of the "compliance" "reasonable period of time" in Beef Hormones floated the possibility of issuing a new regulation under Article 5.7, within a month, but apparently did not pursue the possibility further. (It would have been interesting. The EU would have had to claim compliance under Article 21.5, to avert retaliation based on the already adopted Appellate Body report, and probably hesitated to expose a very hastily drafted regulation to that scrutiny.)

This issue is as much a domestic as international one, except to the extent that it is easier to impose one's preferences on foreigners than on one's own political system. Even domestically, a lot of refinement is still needed. For example, at least some of the groups seeking to ban GMO foods until there is conclusive evidence of "no risk" probably do not really mean it as a general principle (or else they would ban cheese made with unpasteurized milk, which carries a certain risk of exposure to tuberculosis). This suggests that domestic debates will help resolve some of the WTO issues.

In addition, it is not required that the WTO or other international bodies solve all these problems. An excellent study by George Berman for the Administrative Conference of the U.S. described how regulators in the U.S. and Europe working together informally could craft parallel sets of domestic rules that avoided trade-blocking inconsistencies.

CONCLUSION

The Seattle Round will see battles over these issues spread beyond the attempts to open the SPS and TBT Agreements. It is too early to guess the outcomes, and national elections in the U.S. and many other countries, and a new Commission in Brussels, may decide the outcomes more than factors which are visible now.

ARTICLE

Climate Change Legislation in the United States and the WTO

Gary Horlick*

The United States will very likely enact climate change legislation to reduce greenhouse gas (GHG) emissions in 2009 (or 2010 if the current financial crisis so dictates).[1] Senator McCain was one of the original sponsors, and President Obama joined as a sponsor early on. There is less Republican support in the Congress, but the strong Democratic majorities in both Houses will pick up enough Republican support to pass legislation. Neither members of Congress nor businesses, nor, apparently, voters will agree to anything called a 'tax' to restrain GHG emissions. Consequently, no matter how optimal a carbon or British thermal unit (BTU) tax might be from an economist's perspective, it is highly likely that a cap-and-trade system will be enacted, although the details – which are crucially important to businesses – will be greatly affected by the need to obtain the necessary majority.

While the US legislation will be important domestically – in many respects, it will be the most far-reaching industrial legislation since the original environmental legislation in 1970 – it may have greater significance internationally. The Bush Administration from 2001 to 2009 effectively blocked any international agreement imposing mandatory limits or reductions of GHG emissions. Whatever one thinks of the merits of such an agreement, the change in President – both candidates had expressed strong support for such an agreement – will effectively breach the dam, leading to a flood of initiatives and activity in the international arena, most obviously including the negotiation of a successor to the Kyoto agreement. The meeting in Pozuam in December 2008 foreshadows an agreement in late 2009 or 2010. Senior figures such as Senator John Kerry, the new Chairman of the US Senate Foreign Relations Committee, have rejected suggestions that the global economic crisis should postpone that date.

In addition to enthusiastic US participation (replacing prior US 'blocking'), there may well be an increase in domestic political reasons for major developing countries such as China and India to agree to mandatory measures. The negative effects of global warming, at least on agriculture, apparently would be far greater for India and China than, for example, the United States (which in fact, might benefit). By contrast, both China and India are often projected to show increasing desertification. This would both be very visible domestically, and also played up by local media. Thus, while a trade minister can sit in a multilateral trade negotiation and say 'no', and not pay a price domestically (because the beneficiaries of the tariff protection which he or she refused to dismantle are more visible and more vocal than consumers or the goods and services exporters who lose opportunities for greater market access), a prime minister or a president cannot afford the domestic fallout of being blamed for increased desertification, or deaths from flooding, and such blame would likely be apportioned by the local media, whether justified or not. The same might be true even in China, although the leadership there does not face popular elections. Consequently, it is likely that many world leaders cannot realistically face the prospect of the Kyoto agreement expiring in 2012 without being blamed domestically for letting it lapse without a successor agreement (and the US president seeking re-election that year would want a replacement, after promising in 2008 to 'do something' about climate change). So the stage seems set for domestic legislation, both in the United States and many other countries that have not yet followed the EU example, and an international agreement.

What kind of legislation and agreement? There seems a widespread agreement that, in many countries, a direct tax, especially on consumers, is not acceptable politically – voters may say they want something done about climate change, but many do not want to pay for it. A cap-and-trade permit system seems to be sufficiently indirect to accomplish the

Notes

* Gary N. Horlick, Washington, DC, <www.ghorlick.com>.

1 A survey of several hundred 'Washington Insiders' in the 13 Dec. 2008 issue of *National Journal* showed 91% of Democrats and 69% of Republicans rating the prospects for 'global warming legislation' as 'very' or 'somewhat' promising.

Global Trade and Customs Journal, Volume 4, Issue 4

same goal, and make money for financial intermediaries (which could even be environmental NGOs!) along the way.

A purely domestic cap-and-trade system – that is, one only applied to domestic production without impact on imports – would not seem to present obvious World Trade Organization (WTO) problems. But so far, at least in the EU and the United States, proposals for cap-and-trade systems are immediately met by 'competitiveness' concerns. 'Competitiveness' to date seems to refer mainly to the concerns of import-competing industries such as steel and cement. So far, at least in the US debate, few seem strongly focused on the competitiveness problems that would be faced by exporters from the United States – the country with one of the largest per-capita GHG emissions – facing cap-and-trade systems in their foreign markets. So the US legislation will almost certainly require permits from imports at some point, and that will raise issues under WTO.

Much of the debate to date in the United States about the trade aspects of climate change has revolved around whether the proposed cap-and-trade legislation is consistent with the WTO. The argument that the WTO legislation is consistent in the end relies on the claim that the WTO Appellate Body decision in the *United States – Import Prohibition of Certain Shrimp and Shrimp Products* (hereinafter '*Shrimp-Turtle*') permits a WTO Member to ban imports if it claims it wants to improve the environment, as long as that country goes through the motions of negotiating for the same length of time with each WTO Member. If that interpretation of the Appellate Body decision is correct, it permits the wholesale dismantling of trade liberalization by the United States and EU (because only big markets will have the market power to enforce their views,[2] using access to their markets as leverage). Europe, for example, could ban all imports involving animals whose welfare is not properly protected – even if the EU itself does not take care of such matters adequately (e.g., bullfighting, foie gras, and so forth). It does not seem to occur to many of the proponents of using cap-and-trade systems to limit imports from China, that China within a matter of a few years (and perhaps already) will be a big enough market to exert the same clout – although more likely on developed country exporter groups other than industries such as steel or cement, since they do not export as much to China (although their customers do).

A more charitable view of the Appellate Body decision in *Shrimp-Turtle* is that it is limited to the facts of that case – it only applies to Class 1 protected species under Convention on Trade in Endangered Species of Flora and Fauna (CITES) and can only be applied by countries where those animals go through the territorial waters of that country (although even that would give the United States and EU (and China!) enormous power to force their value preferences concerning endangered species on smaller WTO Members).

In short, if the Appellate Body decision in *Shrimp-Turtle* permits the United States to apply the import restrictions contemplated by the cap-and-trade legislation, it could well authorize any number of other process and production method (PPM)-based import bans – a position which the United States hitherto has mostly opposed.[3] That said, the US climate change legislation is almost certainly going to pass, so the real question is what to do about it (and the similar EU legislation, and similar legislation which is under consideration around the world).

The answer is not to seek an interpretation of *Shrimp-Turtle* that will justify cap-and-trade import restrictions, and many other PPMs. That would open the way for any number of other PPM-based restrictions, some of which sound quite desirable at first glance – such as bans or mandatory labels based on the use of child labour, or gender discrimination or any number of other workplace practices. However, the United States and EU should tread warily, since China could quite easily say that it will measure its pollution requirements based on the full life-cycle analysis of how products are made, including the size of workers' houses and their methods of transportation to their workplace – or, more simply, per capita GHG emissions. Instead, WTO Members and trade lawyers are going to have to find some way to accommodate whatever is negotiated internationally about climate change:

- One possibility would be to amend Article XX of the GATT 1994 to permit whatever approaches are taken in the future international agreement on climate change. This would require considerable care, and there is some reason for concern whether that level of care would be possible to maintain during the negotiation.
- A second approach would be to negotiate some sort of 'savings' clause in the successor to Kyoto, so that it could not be challenged under the WTO, at least by any party to the successor. This would open the possibility that it could be challenged by a WTO Member that is not a party to the

Notes

2 Anatole France, 'The law in its majesty forbids the rich and the poor alike to sleep under the bridges of Paris', *The Red Lily* (1894). But one finds very few rich people sleeping under the bridges of Paris!

3 The GATT and then the WTO rules did not permit discrimination among physically identical products based on how they were produced. That view was rather firmly held until the rather imprecise Appellate Body decision in *Shrimp-Turtle*.

successor to Kyoto. In practice, that seems rather remote – Korea when it was not a member of the Montreal Agreement to ban chlorofluorocarbons (CFCs) never challenged the trade provisions of that agreement in the WTO, although it could have, and any WTO Member challenging a climate change agreement would face considerable political problems since all the major countries would have been parties to this agreement. Nevertheless, it would be a terrible precedent for other agreements, and was a source of considerable disagreement when attempted in the negotiation of the Biosafety Protocol to the Convention on Biodiversity.[4]

- Perhaps the cleanest technique would be for WTO Members to agree to a waiver of WTO obligations for implementation of the negotiated successor agreement to Kyoto. That avoids the problems of the first two methods, but requires agreement by all WTO Members – including any which do not sign the successor to Kyoto. Perhaps this could be finessed by limiting the waiver to those agreeing to it.

- Some creative solution will have to be found because it is nearly certain that the United States will pass legislation, and highly likely that a successor to Kyoto with questionable trade provisions will be agreed before 2012.

Note

4 Sabrina Safrin, 'Treaties in Collision? The Biosafety Protocol and The World Trade Organization Agreements', *The American Journal of International Law* 96, no. 3 (Jul. 2002): 606-628.

17

Nonconclusions

Gary N. Horlick

A book on international trade law and development may strike some as brave, or even foolhardy, because there is no consensus on what "development" is, how to measure it, what causes it, or what law has to do with it. This book does not resolve those great questions but discusses in considerable detail issues that have arisen, and are likely to continue to arise, in the connection between international trade law, especially but not limited to the World Trade Organization (WTO),[1] and development.

Trade is not an end in itself but a means to improve human welfare (as is development). Since the end of World War II, the global economic system has produced a better than 50% improvement in life expectancy in developing countries and a better than 90% reduction in maternal and infant mortality; 80% of the world's population now has access to clean drinking water, and billions of people have been lifted out of poverty. The work is far from done – roughly 30% of the world's population is still poor, but for the first time, there is at least reason to believe that most of those can reach a better level of welfare than they have now.

The global economic system that provided these benefits is, of course, not a system at all. Governments have a lot to do with managing (and sometimes mismanaging) the process, both through formal international organizations such as the WTO, International Monetary Fund, World Bank, and regional organizations, but also through fluid informal mechanisms such as G-7/8/20/xx coordination at head of government and ministerial levels. The much-derided United Nations helped prevent the destructive wars that marked the first half of the twentieth century, as did careful

[1] The WTO follows and builds on the failed International Trade Organization (ITO) of the postwar arrangements and the successful-beyond-anyone's-dreams General Agreement on Tariffs and Trade (GATT). The ITO negotiators had devoted considerable time to development issues. Even the pruned-down GATT, with "only" twenty-three members (which included leading developing countries such as Brazil and India, as well as a majority of the WTO's existing 154 members, because it included, whether they wanted it or not, the colonies of the colonial powers such as Britain and France, who were original members) had some special provisions for developing countries and added more within a few years.

management (to date, at least) of the nuclear standoff between the United States and the Soviet Union/Russia. A united Western Europe provided the longest period of internal peace since at least 843 CE. Governments also learned how to live with the "invisible hand" of literally tens of millions of private enterprises that provided much of the economic growth and welfare improvements. Furthermore, universities and private nonprofit groups provided much of the research and dissemination to make possible the productivity improvements that took the world out of the Malthusian trap that had kept almost every person in the world living at bare subsistence levels until the nineteenth century. (For example, the growth of the world's food supply since World War II is a complex interaction of increasingly well-educated farmers, university research, and international consortia including governments, universities, and the Rockefeller and Ford Foundations.)

Trade policy, and international trade law rules, played a major role in this achievement.[2] This book discusses many of those aspects. Although clear conclusions are difficult, some of the following issues are worth considering.

1. The classical international trade rules – tariff bindings, unconditional most-favored-nation treatment, and national treatment – seem to have held up reasonably well for developing countries. South Korea is a good example. It was perhaps one of the poorest countries in the world in 1960. The postwar GATT system provided South Korea two sets of benefits:
   - South Korea, once it joined the GATT, had "bound" access to developed-country markets, which South Korean policy makers used as an important part of an export-led development policy.
   - Probably the main benefit of the GATT system for South Korea was the prosperity it helped create among developed countries, which helped create a market for South Korea. Interestingly, South Korea, as a medium-sized developing country, could build an industrial base by gaining relatively small shares of developed-country markets (despite much talk about South Korean automobile exports, South Korea's share of the U.S. automobile market (split among several producers) never reached 10%, even in the unusual

[2] Trade alone does not lead to development. However, trade from early times provided necessities (such as salt), luxuries (Mediterranean archeological sites include amber from the Baltic), and high-tech weapons (such as the obsidian from the upper west of the United States found in Mexican sites). Most important for purposes of this book, trade permits specialization of labor. The first "trade" was probably families, or perhaps clans, leaving goods on river banks for another clan or family to trade. If the other party did not reciprocate, the "game" was over. A key point this early is that trade – and indeed all "foreign relations" – was inherently ambiguous: trade provided the necessities/luxuries/weapons/better choice/more wealth than otherwise possible, but any contact with "The Other" was inherently dangerous. Family A could not take its goods across the territory of Family B to trade with Family C without the likelihood of being killed, but Family A could trade with Family B, which could trade with Family C. The Silk Road was a very long version of that transfer, with goods moving farther than people, although people were surprisingly safe – sovereigns along the route had worked out that it was more prosperous to allow trade than simply to seize the goods for themselves and kill the traders.

circumstances of 2009). As many have noted, North Korea eschewed this path – and remains poor.

The full benefits of international trade rules are only available to WTO Members. Thus, the process of accession to the WTO becomes relevant. As explained in this book by Andrew D. Mitchell and Joanne Wallis through the cases of Tonga, Vanuatu, and Samoa, the process of accession to the WTO is lengthy and demanding, and the way the principle of special and differential treatment operates in practice in this context, transforms that principle into pure rhetoric. As explained by Mitchell and Wallis, the process of accession to the WTO needs to be reformed to better meet the needs of developing countries, and these reforms should be combined by reforms to special and differential treatment. This is demonstrated by the unprecedented choice of Tonga and Vanuatu to suspend their WTO accession processes.

2. Special and differential treatment (SDT) is more ambiguous in its outcomes. Certainly developing countries (now Organization for Economic Cooperation and Development members!) such as South Korea, Japan, Mexico, and others were able to use SDT status to close "strategic" product markets, for better or worse. However, SDT turned out to be a double-edged sword. Innovative research by Edward Gresser about U.S. tariff policy shows convincingly (at least to me) that SDT in practice hampered developing-country exports to the United States. The "headline" from Gresser's research is that Bangladesh pays more tariffs on its exports to the United States than does France, even though France exports roughly ten times as much as Bangladesh (and the same is true for many other country pairs). As Gresser points out, the underlying phenomenon is that SDT meant the developed-country negotiators in GATT rounds did not spend much effort negotiating on items of interest to developing countries, because the developed-country negotiators knew that they would not achieve reciprocal tariff cuts from the developing countries. So tariff negotiations focused on trade between developed countries, and tariffs on developing-country exports remained high. Thus, U.S. tariffs on luxury silk clothing from France range from 0 to low single digits, whereas tariffs on less expensive cotton clothing from Bangladesh range from 17 to 30 percent. Similarly, U.S. tariffs on stainless steel knives and forks run around 15 percent, whereas the tariffs on sterling silver knives and forks from developed countries are zero or close to it.

3. Tariff preferences for developing countries: the Generalized System of Preferences (GSP) was originated by Raul Prebisch, a brilliant Argentinean who was secretary-general of United Nations Conference on Trade and Development in the early 1960s. Prebisch had been one of the original developers of formal import substitution schemes, as a path for developing countries out of monocultural dependence on commodity exports, in a period when commodity

> prices appeared continually to trend downward, while final consumption products' prices continually rose. By the early 1960s, it was clear to Prebisch that for even medium-sized, advanced developing countries such as Argentina, the size of the internal market was too small to permit the economies of scale necessary for cost-effective manufacturing. GSP was intended to provide the additional markets so that developing-country industries could reach the necessary economies of scale. At that point, a "virtuous circle" would permit the developing country in question to be "graduated" from the preferences for that specific product (and eventually from the entire system), thus permitting a different developing country to benefit from the tariff preference for that product.

The data discussed in this book seem to show what has been increasingly argued: that GSP initially helped several industries in several more advanced developing countries but that the countries most in need of help received the least. This view is elaborated here by Caf Dowlah through an analysis of the United States' GSP through the least developing countries' eyes, concluding that the scheme is not beneficial to the latter and that therefore some reforms should be made to address the development needs of those poor countries. GSP was also marred by the (perhaps inevitable) politicization of developed-country implementation. Numerous products were excluded, often those most suitable for developing countries (such as apparel). In the United States, Democrats led the charge to exclude as much as possible, including products (watches!) where the U.S. industry more or less disappeared within ten years.

The United States and European Union both continually added more and more policy/political conditions (intellectual property rights, expropriation, narcotics controls) with the WTO Appellate Body providing arguable cover for the proposition that the developed country is the one best suited to determine the development needs of the developing country (perhaps the Appellate Body will find a way to clarify that in some future case). Disputes over product eligibility are often decided following highly political campaigns in which the express needs of developed-country multinationals are often important – another (if unconsciously) colonial overtone. Even the procedures for renewing preferences (in the United States, often done retroactively after the tariff preferences have lapsed) can prevent reliance on the tariff preferences to build significant manufacturing facilities.

All of these problems have surfaced in greater or lesser form in other preference schemes, such as the European Union's Everything-but-Arms and Economic Partnership Agreement (EPA) programs; the U.S. Caribbean Basin Initiative (CBI), Andean Trade Promotion and Drug Eradication Act (ATPDEA), and Africa Growth and Opportunity Act (AGOA); and similar programs. The programs remain important commercially for some industries and for the countries where those industries are located, but overall, they have hardly delivered their initial promise (if ever that was possible – by the early 1970s, Prebisch was sufficiently disillusioned with GSP to suggest that the only salvation for Latin America was to negotiate the elimination of new military purchases, at a time when many of the regimes in power were military).

One positive result of the preference systems has been to provide an area in which the interests of multinational corporations and developing countries align closely.

One legal aspect of interest is the role of the Enabling Clause as a tool for development. The Enabling Clause was signed in 1979 and further adopted by WTO Members in 1995 without any modification that would reflect the principles of the new trade era. The result is certain inconsistencies between the text of the Enabling Clause and the development principles embraced by the WTO. Perhaps the text of the Enabling Clause should be amended to reflect these principles and therefore allow developed countries to also use the clause to negotiate tariff reduction or elimination with developing and least developed countries, in the context of regional trade agreements (RTAs). As of today, this opportunity is only given to developing and least developed countries among each other.

1. RTAs have had similarly mixed results for developing countries. On their face, many, if not most, of the North–South RTA negotiations are embarrassingly one-sided, with high-tariff, developing countries eliminating tariffs and low-tariff developed countries keeping their panoply of nontariff barriers, particularly in the trade remedy field. (And the negotiating tactics famously may be even more high-handed than the results.) As developed countries enter into more and more North–South RTAs, the benefits for any one developing country are inevitably diluted. Yong-Shik Lee elaborates on this issue in this book through an analysis of the economic and geopolitical impact of the U.S.-Korea free trade agreement – in case of approval by the U.S. Congress. Moshe Hirsch also analyzes the flaws in current North–South RTAs and proposes some legal mechanisms to enhance the benefits accruing to developing countries under these RTAs. South–South RTAs have less history. The most important one to date, Southern Cone Common Market (MERCOSUR), has managed to hold together despite many challenges and indeed offers the occasional lesson to the WTO (i.e., dispute settlement proceedings are limited to three months from the date of the establishment of the panel). The real question is the one originally posed by Prebisch – does a South–South arrangement such as MERCOSUR spur development more than any North–South arrangement would have?

   Regionalism and multilateralism both seek trade liberalization, although they use different methodologies. As discussed by Mitsuo Matsushita and Yong-Shik Lee in this book, the former option has become a significant alternative to the latter because of a stalled multilateral system. However, the proliferation of RTAs also poses a challenge to the multilateral system because RTAs do not generally adopt some important multilateral protections provided under the WTO, such as special and differential treatment. However, as Matsushita and Lee propose, regional rules could be coordinated through, for example, the WTO Trade Policy Review Body, in order not only to seek convergence and harmonization of trade rules but to also promote the interest of developing countries.

2. The WTO, in short, looks better and better for developing countries. In addition to formal equality, the rules offer a lot of "policy space" for developing countries (although at the cost of nearly as much space for developed countries – in a context in which the largest markets often set the rules, although it should be recalled that the second largest market, China, is a developing country, with other developing countries also growing in size). Large developing countries visibly throw their weight around just as much as large developed countries – and (small and) medium-sized developing countries such as South Africa, South Korea, Chile, Malaysia, New Zealand, and others probably have an impact in the WTO (often by sending skilled officials to Geneva) disproportionately greater than their population would suggest. As this book points out, many of these developing countries played leading roles in the GATT as well. As Faizel Ismail explains in this book, developing countries have been active in the GATT era, as well as in the Uruguay and the Doha Rounds. According to Ismail, the role of developing countries has significantly increased along the road, up to the point at which, in the current Doha Round, these countries are shaping not only the content and the outcome of the negotiations but also the architecture and trajectory of the multilateral trading system.
3. A much-debated topic is the role of developing countries in the WTO dispute settlement system. Developing countries have had a strong representation on the Appellate Body over the years, and because the European Union and the United States insist in being parties in almost every case, developing countries provide a frequent majority of panel members. Developing-country students are strongly represented in "feeder programs" that lead to employment within the WTO system, such as the University of Berne's World Trade Institute and law school programs such as Georgetown, Columbia, and Cambridge.

As more and more countries become involved in dispute settlement, the process becomes more routine, but also poses real challenges internally. The decisions in the cases brought against China on auto parts, intellectual property rights, and trading rights all pose interesting problems internally for the Chinese trade regime, whereas the decision of the Appellate Body in the *U.S.-Softwood Lumber* countervailing duty case on "specificity" significantly narrows the policy space for governments seeking to use the system as a development instrument. Large countries, such as the United States and the European Union, have a structural advantage in WTO dispute resolution by being able to keep a large number of specialized litigators on staff (thus turning the marginal cost of hiring counsel into a fixed cost). However, Brazil has one of the best track records in WTO dispute resolution and a very strong institutional structure combining a medium-sized, highly skilled internal staff with outside counsel retained as necessary and typically paid for by the affected Brazilian industry. Some of the decisions coming out of the dispute settlement system are strikingly neocolonial programs (such as the EU GSP case mentioned earlier or the U.S. *Shrimp-Turtle* case). The *Shrimp-Turtle* decision may reflect a weighting of environmental concerns large enough to permit unilateral action by a developed country against developing countries, but it may also reflect an underweighting of human rights concerns. (Should the Appellate Body have balanced the environmental concerns of a developed country's citizens with the human rights of the impoverished fishers in the developing-country parties?)

As described by Katherine Fennell and me in this book, there is an imbalance in the access to the WTO dispute settlement system that should be addressed to increase the possibility of developing countries pursuing development under the existing multilateral trade scheme. As explained by Tomer Broude in his chapter, the international community could also start conceiving certain international economic disputes that involve the interpretation and application of development issues, as part of a new group of disputes – international development disputes – to reflect the idea that every dispute settlement mechanism in the international economic law arena should bear the responsibility of pursuing the development of developing and least developed countries.

Once access is obtained to the WTO dispute settlement system, developing countries could lose cases in the WTO forum, but those losses are also lessons for the future.

1. The role of human rights and human rights agreements has been broached within the international trading system. Much of the impetus has come from attempts by developed countries to impose their labor standards on competitive industries in developing countries (even where the developed countries in question do not formally accept those standards as binding). This issue has been explored by Anthony E. Cassimatis in this book.
2. Perhaps it is inevitable that the GATT and the WTO, as agreements between sovereign entities, do not really get at the heart of economic development in developing countries (and even some areas and sectors of developed countries). Greater difficulties are often encountered in those countries and sectors, especially by workers and small businesses, than would be the case for big enterprises in developed countries. The term in Brazil is *cousto Brasileiro*, and there have even been attempts to measure it. International trade rules generally do not reflect an understanding of how difficult it is to export from

developing countries and how many challenges must be overcome. Just as the "microfinance" movement has attempted to deal with this issue in the credit area, perhaps international trade rules need a "microtrade" framework reflecting the size of the obstacles posed by paperwork, border security measures, and the documentation needed to qualify for preferences for developing countries where documentation is difficult. Even the concept of access to an international dispute resolution system could be rethought. Indeed, as discussed by Yong-Shik Lee in this book, the "microtrade" option constitutes a potential means to reduce or eliminate poverty in LDCs, if implemented correctly.

3. Intellectual property is another area of trade that could be used to pursue the development of the developing world. One way of doing it, as discussed by Bryan Mercurio in his chapter, is by developing countries maximizing the flexibilities found in the Agreement on Trade-Related Aspects of Intellectual Property Rights. This could attract scrutiny from interested actors but, according to Mercurio, it is the only option for countries seeking to prevent the protection of intellectual property rights from becoming a completely one-sided proposition that benefits developed countries at great cost to the developing world.

The purpose of this book has been to explore some of the existing imbalances between developed and developing countries in the international trade arena – not with the purpose of undermining international trade as such but to improve it as a tool for development. As explained by Yong-Shik Lee, Young-Ok Kim, and Hye Seong Mun in their chapter, international trade is a key element for materializing development in developing countries such as North Korea. In his chapter, Colin B. Picker calls for taking into account the special development needs of "economically heterogeneous states" in the international trade arena, so that development is obtained at every state level as opposed to only some of them. Furthermore, through the application of the specificity test to China's foreign investment policies, Xiaojie Lu considers in this book that the use of international trade law rules should also reflect an acceptable balance between legitimate development objectives adopted domestically and the possible trade-distorting effects at the international level of specific governmental measures.

Trade War or Growing Pains

Who's Who Legal Trade & Customs

Gary N. Horlick[1]

China's new trade policies spark furious debate among the 'Big Three' and holds important implications for the future, especially with regards to climate change and coming out of the global recession.

The recent controversy over China's "indigenous innovation" policy illustrates the challenges to US and EU trade policy involving investment, intellectual property, government procurement, and competition rules in China. It also illustrates the increased willingness of US, European and Japanese businesses with investments in China to raise these issues publicly because they are well-aware that they need to be successful in China to remain successful in the global market.

In 1986, when China began its negotiations to join the GATT (now WTO), no one in China or outside foresaw that China's economy would grow from a GDP of US$951 billion in 1986 to US$4.9 trillion in 2010 (calculated at the 2010 dollar rate). At that level, enough Chinese can afford the material possessions of modern civilization so that China in 2009 — already the world's largest market for mobile telephones, shampoo, and refrigerators — became the world's largest market for automobiles (and seems likely to remain so even after the US market recovers). Obviously, there is no guarantee that China will continue to grow as it has. All economies are subject to external price shocks, financial collapses, and dithering governments. But, notably, China's growth rate barely dipped during the 2008 to 2009 recession, so for planning purposes, businesses (and their lawyers) have to include a scenario of continued Chinese growth.

[1]Text reproduced with permission from Who's Who Legal (www.whoswholegal.com), December 2010.

As China's internal market grows, manufacturers with large market shares will achieve larger and larger economies of scale, making them more and more competitive against their rivals without access to a similarly large market. For any product where demand correlates roughly with number of people, China is or will be the largest market in the world, even though its economy measured by GDP is only one-quarter the size of the US. This is also true for services — China is or will be the largest market for X-rays and MRIs, for example, and Hong Kong in 2009 led the world in IPOs (initial public offerings).

Put most directly, in products where China is the biggest market, US, European and other countries' companies that are not number one, two or three in China may well become irrelevant even if they are successful in their home markets. In numerical terms, if the Chinese market for widgets is four times larger than the US market for widgets (perfectly plausible, as China's population is more than four times that of the US), and Chinese company A has 50 per cent of its own market and 25 per cent of the US market, and US company U has 50 per cent of its own market and 25 per cent of the Chinese market, Chinese company C will have 45 per cent of the combined markets, and US company U will have 30 per cent of the combined markets. In the many industries where economies of scale matter (for example, the ability to do more research and development, or to buy components more cheaply), that gap could be fatal. And if US company S had 25 per cent of the US market and 0 per cent in China, it will disappear as an independent company.

So what matters for US and EU trade law and policy and that of many other countries for the future is to ensure that their companies are competitive in the Chinese market. This analysis is not solely China-targeted, of course. It will be just as true for India if India continues to grow and also true for a US or EU company with 50 per cent of the Chinese (or Indian) market.

China's policymakers are well-aware of this impact of China's growth, and they are — logically enough — trying to use China's large internal market as a competitive advantage, especially as China is increasingly not the lowest-wage site for manufacturing (China's policymakers do not want its workers earning low wages). This is not necessarily bad news for non-Chinese economies. The "supply chain" has disaggregated production, so that it is plausible that a non-Chinese company, "manufacturing" and selling a large volume of product in China, could well generate a large number of jobs in the US. A 2007 study of the Apple iPod suggests that, of the US$299 retail price, more than US$130 (and the jobs that go with it) stayed in the US, while less than US$10 stayed in China, where the product was "manufactured". As suggested above, Apple would not be able to continue making iPods if it sells one million in the US and a Chinese competitor sells five million of a comparable product in China. The Chinese competitor would have enormous economies of scale and be able to out-compete Apple quite "fairly" worldwide, so Apple has to be able to sell large amounts in the Chinese market as well as the US market. But if it does, it will generate jobs and profits in the US more than in China.

None of this is really news, of course. Non-Chinese companies are well aware of China's use of its large internal market as leverage, and have pressured their governments to complain vigorously about China's "famous brands" subsidies (the subject of a WTO case), and the more recent "indigenous innovation" program. What is new is the growing consciousness of the need to re-think priorities in trade policy. The US and EU spent enormous amounts of their negotiating clout with China from 1999 to 2006 to limit imports from China into the US and EU of ladies' clothing. The textile quotas imposed by the US on other countries ended in 2005, so there are many other suppliers, and well under 4 per cent of all clothing sold at retail in the US is manufactured in the US, so there was no real possibility of growing a US industry making women's blouses. In the abstract, it may have made sense politically to protect that industry, but the effort may have been much better spent on ensuring US and the EU companies' access to the "government procurement" market in China, a market where possibly as much as 50 per cent of all purchases are by the government or state-owned enterprises. Of course, it is easier to close one's own borders than seek changes in the larger market, but that will only make it too easy to focus policy on the smaller of the two markets.

The obvious candidates for highest priority for future US and EU trade law and policy include (but are certainly not limited to):

- investment rules in China, to ensure that foreign companies have the same opportunities as Chinese ones (which, of course, implicates Western attempts to stop or limit Chinese investment in their countries);
- intellectual property rules to make sure that companies can sell their trademark, patented, or copyrighted products without facing competition from direct copies. It becomes extremely important in a global market to prevent production and sale of unauthorized copies of one's products. This could be copyrighted, trademarked or patented goods, or any

other type of intellectual property (and without ignoring the controversies about appropriate access to and protections for certain types of intellectual property products, such as medicines) and is the subject of ongoing WTO litigation between the US and China, so the topic is not new, but in this new context becomes even more important.

VAT rebates:

- China already uses differing VAT rebate rates for differing points in the supply chain to provide an incentive to locate perceived "value added" functions in China. So far, this has been limited to some fairly obvious industrial processes and products. What if other major markets start doing the same thing on the same products, leading to VAT "rebate wars", (but always within the total amount of the VAT, thus creating difficulties for a WTO challenge).

Standards:

- the EU and, to a lesser extent, US insistence on "policy space" to use unique standards often assumes that the EU and US are the largest markets. If China or India become the largest markets, do we want to continue to advocate the same relatively loose interpretation of WTO, SPS and TBT matters? This will be particularly true for climate-change issues, where the US and EU have relatively strict standards for factory emissions, and relatively quite high emissions per capita. Or do we prefer the approach advocated for TPP of greater binding use of internationally-agreed standards?
- subsidy rules, so that Chinese companies do not receive larger subsidies than their non-Chinese competitors (which may require some discipline in the West as well — the recent WTO panel reports on large commercial aircraft contain long lists of subsidies to industrial enterprises in the West, and they are not limited to aircraft producers);
- services rules, notably the WTO General Agreement on Trade and Services (GATS), must be substantially rethought and redrafted. The current GATS focuses on relatively narrow and separate categories and focuses on enterprises that are primarily services providers. But almost all "manufacturing" enterprises in developed and developing countries in practice are a bundle of "service" functions (from designers through production and shipping schedulers, and many others) rather than solely direct physical human manufacture (is tending or repairing a machine

a "service" function?). This mixed nature is recognized in the WTO "bananas case", but within a narrow services category of "wholesale distribution". There is a GATS language which permits a much broader interpretation, but so far the tendency has been to require that an activity fit within a specific relatively narrow service sector in which a commitment has been made. That approach does not recognize that an individual company may be performing a wide range of services (and manufacturing functions) along a very long supply chain. For example, manufacturing automobiles requires, among many other service functions, the operation of a test track. The current GATS does not recognize that reality.

- access to government procurement markets becomes exceedingly important, as the two largest future markets, China and India, have very large state and state-owned sectors. With perfect hindsight, some of the energy spent on other topics in, for example, the negotiations for China's accession to the WTO could better have been spent on government procurement.
- trade remedies (anti-dumping, countervailing duties, and safeguards), to date championed in negotiations by the US and the EU in alliance to protect their home markets, may look ill-advised if bigger markets decide to use them to keep out US and European imports from the US and Europe of final goods or, perhaps even more daunting in a supply chain world, key imported inputs, (thus, forcing transfer of manufacturing that might have stayed in the US or EU). China has an active trade remedy program of its own, with 16 anti-dumping (AD) cases (number five in the world) and three countervailing duties (CVD) cases (number three in the world) initiated in 2009. Little attention has been paid to the possibility that China is using these cases in a more tactical or strategic sense than other countries. For example, EU cases against imports of metal fasteners and of goods scanning systems from China were met not only with a sweeping WTO challenge to the results of the EU metal fasteners case, but also by parallel cases in China against imports of EU metal fasteners, X-ray scanners, in addition, China stopped soy bean imports from Argentina to protest AD cases there. Most strikingly, China initiated three CVD cases against US exports in 2009 and to date has issued a final ruling that the US "buy American" government purchasing preferences are a subsidy to US industry and a preliminary determination that US government subsidies to corn and soybeans subsidize US exports of poultry, and presumably, beef and pork (China does not complain about the allegedly subsidized US corn and soybean which it buys in

massive quantities), and China is poised to declare that the US auto bail-out was a subsidy to the Big Three.

This does not mean that the US and Europe have to abolish trade remedies, they are welcome to keep them as they are, if they are willing to pay the price.

This should not be viewed as a "trade war" with China, but rather as "growing pains" as the world adjusts to a player the size of the US and EU or larger, with US$2.5 trillion in reserves. The need for this adjustment is clear, both in terms of the current disputes and also in terms of management of future global issues, moving out of recession and into possible arrangements on climate change.

COLUMN—INTERNATIONAL TRADE

China and the Future of Trade Law

Gary Horlick*

In 1986, when China began its negotiations to join the General Agreement on Tariffs and Trade (GATT; now World Trade Organization (WTO)), no one in China or outside foresaw that China's economy would grow from a gross domestic product (GDP) of USD 951 billion in 1986 (in 2010 dollars) to USD 4.9 trillion in 2010. At that level, enough Chinese can afford the material possessions of modern civilization so that China in 2009—already the world's largest market for mobile telephones, shampoo, and refrigerators—became the world's largest market for automobiles (and seems likely to remain so even after the U.S. market recovers). Obviously, there is no guarantee that China will continue to grow as it has—all economies are subject to external price shocks, financial collapses, and/or dithering governments. However, notably, China's growth rate barely dipped during the 2008–2009 recession, so for planning purposes, businesses (and their lawyers) have to include a scenario of continued Chinese growth. That scenario will have implications far beyond trade policy—but what does that mean for international trade lawyers?

Most obviously, there will be more trade remedy cases (antidumping, countervailing duties, safeguards) against Chinese products in the EU, U.S., Brazil, Mexico, India, and almost everywhere. As China's internal market grows, manufacturers with large market shares there will achieve larger and larger economies of scale, making them more and more competitive against competitors without access to a similarly large market. For any product where demand correlates roughly with number of people, China is or will be the largest market in the world, even though its economy measured by GDP is only one-quarter the size of the U.S.

This is also true for services—China is or will be the largest market for X-rays/MRIs, for example. Of course, trade remedy laws only apply to goods, so other, more creative means would have to be used by competitors against Chinese service providers benefiting from the large home market.

It gets far less attention in the West, but China has an active trade remedy program of its own, with 16 anti-dumping (AD) cases (number 5 in the world) and 3 countervailing duty (CVD) cases (number 3 in the world) initiated in 2009. Even less attention has been paid to the possibility that China is using these cases in a more tactical or strategic sense than other countries.

For example, an EU case against imports of metal fasteners from China was met not only with a sweeping WTO challenge to the results of the EU case but also by a parallel case in China against imports of EU metal fasteners, and China stopped soybean imports from Argentina to protest AD cases there. Most strikingly, China initiated three CVD cases against U.S. exports in 2009 and to date has issued a final ruling that the U.S. Buy America government purchasing preferences are a subsidy to U.S. industry and a preliminary determination that U.S. government subsidies to corn and soybeans subsidize U.S. exports of poultry and, presumably, beef and pork (China does not complain about the allegedly subsidized U.S. corn and soybean, which it buys in massive quantities), and China is poised to declare that the U.S. auto bailout was a subsidy to the Big Three.

Both of these phenomena will continue to provide work for trade lawyers around the world out into the medium and long terms. However, by far the most important impact will be the long-term effect of China's growth, as it forces a complete reordering of U.S. and EU trade policy priorities. Put most directly, in products where China is the biggest market, U.S., European, and other countries' companies that are not number 1, 2, or 3 in China may well become irrelevant even if they are successful in their home markets. In numerical terms, if the Chinese market for widgets is four times larger than the U.S. market for widgets (perfectly plausible, as China's population is more than four times that of the U.S.), and Chinese Company A has 50% of its own market and 25% of the U.S. market, and U.S. Company U has 50% of its own market and 25% of the Chinese market, Chinese Company C will have 45% of the combined markets, and U.S. Company U will have 30% of the combined markets. In the many industries where economies of scale matter (e.g., the ability to do

Note

* Washington, D.C. E-mail: gary.horlick@ghorlick.com.

Global Trade and Customs Journal, Volume 5, Issue 10

more R&D, or to buy components more cheaply), that gap could be fatal. In addition, if U.S. Company S had 25% of the U.S. market and zero in China, it will disappear as an independent company. So what matters for the U.S. and EU trade policies, and that of many other countries, for the future is to ensure that their companies are competitive in the Chinese market (and the Indian market if India reaches Chinese levels of wealth, since India's population will soon pass that of China—this analysis is not China-targeted).

The obvious candidates for highest priority for future U.S. and EU trade policies include (but are certainly not limited to):

- Investment rules in China, to ensure that foreign companies have the same opportunities as Chinese ones (which of course complicates Western attempts to stop or limit Chinese investment in their countries).
- Government procurement, a large market in China.
- Intellectual property rules to make sure that companies can sell their trademark, patented, or copyrighted products without facing competition from direct copies.
- Standards can be an extremely effective market access barrier.
- Chinese trade remedy rules, to make sure products can be exported there as well as manufactured there.
- Subsidy rules, so that Chinese companies do not receive larger subsidies than their non-Chinese competitors (which may require some discipline in the West as well—the recent WTO panel reports on Large Commercial Aircraft contain long lists of subsidies to industrial enterprises in the West, and they are not limited to aircraft producers).

This is not necessarily bad news for non-Chinese economies. The "supply chain" has disaggregated production so that it is perfectly plausible that a non-Chinese company "manufacturing" and selling a large volume of product in China could well generate a large number of jobs in the U.S. A 2007 study of the Apple iPod suggests that, of the USD 299 retail price, more than USD 130 (and the jobs that go with it) stayed in the U.S., while less than USD 10 stayed in China, where the product was "manufactured." As suggested above, Apple would not be able to continue making iPods if it sells one million in the U.S. and a Chinese competitor sells 10 million of a comparable product in China. The Chinese competitor would have enormous economies of scale and be able to outcompete Apple quite "fairly" worldwide, so Apple has to be able to sell large amounts in the Chinese market as well as the U.S. market. However, if it does it will generate jobs and profits in the U.S. more than in China.

None of this is completely news, of course. Non-Chinese companies are well aware of the business exigencies of the future and have pressured their governments to complain vigorously about China's "famous brands" subsidies (the subject of a WTO case) and the more recent "indigenous innovation" program. What is new is the growing consciousness of the need to rethink the priorities in trade policy. The U.S. and EU have spent enormous amounts of their negotiating clout with China to limit imports from China into the U.S. and EU of ladies' clothing. The textile quotas imposed by the U.S. ended in 2005, so there are many other suppliers, and well under 4% of all clothing sold at retail in the U.S. is manufactured in the U.S. So there is no real possibility of growing a U.S. industry making women's blouses. In the abstract, it may make sense politically to protect that industry, but the effort may have been much better spent on ensuring U.S. and the EU companies' access to the "government procurement" market in China, a market where possibly as much as 50% of all purchases are by the government or state-owned enterprises. Of course, it is easier to close one's own borders than seek changes in the larger market—but that will only make it too easy to focus policy on the *smaller* of the two markets!